Handbook of
Social Comparison

Theory and Research

THE PLENUM SERIES IN SOCIAL/CLINICAL PSYCHOLOGY

Series Editor: C. R. Snyder

University of Kansas
Lawrence, Kansas

Current Volumes in the Series:

ADVANCED PERSONALITY
Edited by David F. Barone, Michel Hersen, and Vincent B. Van Hasselt

AGGRESSION
Biological, Developmental, and Social Perspectives
Edited by Seymour Feshbach and Jolanta Zagrodzka

AVERSIVE INTERPERSONAL BEHAVIORS
Edited by Robin M. Kowalski

COERCION AND AGGRESSIVE COMMUNITY TREATMENT
A New Frontier in Mental Health Law
Edited by Deborah L. Dennis and John Monahan

HANDBOOK OF SOCIAL COMPARISON
Theory and Research
Edited by Jerry Suls and Ladd Wheeler

HUMOR
The Psychology of Living Buoyantly
Herbert M. Lefcourt

THE IMPORTANCE OF PSYCHOLOGICAL TRAITS
A Cross-Cultural Study
John E. Williams, Robert C. Satterwhite, and José L. Saiz

PERSONAL CONTROL IN ACTION
Cognitive and Motivational Mechanisms
Edited by Miroslaw Kofta, Gifford Weary, and Grzegorz Sedek

PHYSICAL ILLNESS AND DEPRESSION IN OLDER ADULTS
A Handbook of Theory, Research, and Practice
Edited by Gail M. Williamson, David R. Shaffer, and Patricia A. Parmelee

THE REVISED NEO PERSONALITY INVENTORY
Clinical and Research Applications
Ralph L. Piedmont

SOCIAL COGNITIVE PSYCHOLOGY
History and Current Domains
David F. Barone, James E. Maddux, and C. R. Snyder

SOURCEBOOK OF SOCIAL SUPPORT AND PERSONALITY
Edited by Gregory R. Pierce, Brian Lakey, Irwin G. Sarason, and Barbara R. Sarason

---

A Continuation Order Plan is available for this series. A continuation order will bring delivery of each new volume immediately upon publication. Volumes are billed only upon actual shipment. For further information please contact the publisher.

Handbook of
Social Comparison
Theory and Research

Edited by

Jerry Suls
University of Iowa
Iowa City, Iowa

and

Ladd Wheeler
University of New South Wales
Sydney, Australia

Kluwer Academic / Plenum Publishers
New York   Boston   Dordrecht   London   Moscow

ISBN: 0-306-46341-5

©2000 Kluwer Academic / Plenum Publishers, New York
233 Spring Street, New York, N.Y. 10013

http://www.wkap.nl/

10 9 8 7 6 5 4 3 2 1

A C.I.P. record for this book is available from the Library of Congress

Printed in the United States of America

Contributors

Glenn Affleck, Department of Community Medicine, University of Connecticut Health Center, Farmington, Connecticut 06030

Mark D. Alicke, Department of Psychology, Ohio University, Athens, Ohio 45701-2979

Gudmundur B. Arnkelsson, Faculty of Social Sciences, University of Iceland, IS-101 Reykjavik, Iceland

Steven R. H. Beach, Department of Psychology, University of Georgia, Athens, Georgia 30602-3013

Oswald Buhrmann, Department of Psychology, University of Western Ontario, London, Ontario, Canada N6A 5C2

Bram P. Buunk, Department of Psychology, University of Groningen, NL-9712 TS, Groningen, The Netherlands

Rebecca L. Collins, RAND Corporation, Santa Monica, California 90407

David Dunning, Department of Psychology, Cornell University, Ithaca, New York 14853-7601

Robert Folger, A. B. Freeman School of Business, Tulane University, New Orleans, Louisiana 70118-5669

Donelson R. Forsyth, Department of Psychology, Virginia Commonwealth University, Richmond, Virginia 23284-2018

Frederick X. Gibbons, Department of Psychology, Iowa State University, Ames, Iowa 50011-3180

George R. Goethals, Department of Psychology, Williams College, Williamstown, Massachusetts 01267

Michael A. Hogg, School of Psychology, University of Queensland, Brisbane, Queensland 4072, Australia

Edward Eliyahu Kass, A. B. Freeman School of Business, Tulane University, New Orleans, Louisiana 70118-5669

William M. P. Klein, Department of Psychology, Colby College, Waterville, Maine 04901

Joachim Krueger, Department of Psychology, Brown University, Providence, Rhode Island 02912

James A. Kulik, Department of Psychology, University of California, San Diego, La Jolla, California 92093-0109

Heike I. M. Mahler, Department of Psychology, University of California, San Diego, La Jolla, California 92093-0109

Tara Eberhardt McKee, Department of Psychology, University of Connecticut, Storrs, Connecticut 06269-1020

René Martin, Department of Psychology, University of Iowa, Iowa City, Iowa 52242

Thomas Mussweiler, Universitaet Wuerzburg, Psychologie II, 97070 Wuerzburg, Germany

James M. Olson, Department of Psychology, University of Western Ontario, London, Ontario, Canada N6A 5C2

Allen Parducci, Department of Psychology, University of California at Los Angeles, Los Angeles, California 90024

Neal J. Roese, Department of Psychology, Simon Fraser University, Burnaby, British Columbia, Canada V5A 1S6

Richard H. Smith, Department of Psychology, University of Kentucky, Lexington, Kentucky 40506

William P. Smith, Department of Psychology, Vanderbilt University, Nashville, Tennessee 37240

Fritz Strack, Universitaet Wuerzburg, Psychologie II, 97070 Wuerzburg, Germany

Jerry Suls, Department of Psychology, University of Iowa, Iowa City, Iowa 52242

Abraham Tesser, Department of Psychology, University of Georgia, Athens, Georgia 30602-3013

Howard Tennen, Department of Community Medicine, University of Connecticut Health Center, Farmington, Connecticut 06030

Douglas H. Wedell, Department of Psychology, University of South Carolina, Columbia, South Carolina 29208

Ladd Wheeler, School of Psychology, University of New South Wales, Sydney 2052, Australia

Joanne V. Wood, Department of Psychology, University of Waterloo, Waterloo, Ontario, Canada N2L 3G1

Preface

"All knowledge may be reduced to comparison and contrast ..."

—I.F. Stone

One man: "How's your wife?"
Second man: "Compared to what?"

The juxtaposition of a statement of high seriousness with a (politically incorrect) old joke is intended to convey the breadth of issues for which comparison is relevant. Comparison of objects, events, and situations is integral to judgment. We cannot imagine everyday activity in the absence of this capability. Comparisons with other people have a similar role in social life because they comprise one of the building blocks of human conduct and experience. The self-concept, the formation of attitudes, group communication, attraction, and conformity—and this is only a partial list—seem contingent on social comparisons. This was appreciated in the early history of social psychology but reached a critical mass with the publication of two theoretical papers and a series of empirical studies by Leon Festinger in the early 1950s. Social comparison theory subsequently was fostered by Stanley Schachter through his research on affiliation and his teaching of a subsequent generation of psychologists. After four decades of research and theorizing, the subject is now more popular than ever. In light of its significance and the interest it has received, a major compendium describing research and theory in social comparison seems appropriate.

We cannot take full credit for this project. Our initial goal was modest. The idea for a volume began while we were having lunch at Elmo's Bar-B-Q at the conclusion of the Second Nags Head Social Comparison Conference. Both of us were struck by the strength of the presentations and thought that the work should be collected in one place. We left the lunch with plans to edit a short book featuring the work of conference attendees. However, when we submitted a prospectus to C. R. Snyder and Eliot Werner, general psychology editor at Plenum (now Kluwer Academic / Plenum Publishers), they suggested that something more comprehensive and ambitious might be more appropriate. As a result, we contacted additional comparison researchers to represent the broad range of classical and contemporary topics under the social comparison umbrella. We also wanted to cover some topics thought to be tangential but which share a family resemblance with social comparison. In this way, we hoped to insure that the study of social comparison would not become too inbred. Our aim was to provide a handbook that would describe both where the field has been and where it is likely to go next. Fortunately, a group of very able contributors agreed to participate.

The editors extend their appreciation to Rick Snyder and Eliot Werner for their fostering of this volume. Much thanks to Renny Martin, who was also at that BBQ lunch and encouraged us to begin this project and provided much needed advice and support along the way. We also appreciate the considerable efforts, patience, and good humor of our contributors. Special thanks are due to Frederick Gibbons and Bram Buunk who agreed to serve as commentators during the late stages of the book's development.

We dedicate this handbook to the memories of Leon Festinger (1919–1989) and Stanley Schachter (1922–1997) who gave social psychology many gifts.

Contents

PART III.   RELATED SOCIAL PHENOMENA

PART IV.   APPLICATIONS

PART V.   COMMENTARY

I

Introduction

1

A Selective History of Classic and Neo-Social Comparison Theory

JERRY SULS AND LADD WHEELER

In his brief history of the field from 1950 to the early 1980s, Wheeler (1991) observed that

> Social comparison theory has a most peculiar history. Pictorially, the history is like the tracks of a squirrel in my snow-covered backyard. The tracks zig and zag unpredictably and then disappear near an elm, to be next seen near a maple, or the tracks may be obscured by those of other squirrels, or rabbits. (p. 3)

In this chapter, we provide a historical context for the chapters in this handbook. Although we will cover some of the same ground as the previous brief history, we also provide an update of developments during the 1980s and 1990s. Perhaps with almost 20 additional years of research and theory, we will find that the tracks in the backyard no longer appear to be quite as haphazard. On the other hand, they may appear to be even more so, as a fundamental phenomenon—comparison with others—refuses to be contained by its previous constructions.

PRECURSORS AND FESTINGER'S CONTRIBUTION

Leon Festinger (1954a,b) was the first to use the term "social comparison" and the first to propose a systematic theory, but the general concept has been in circulation since we have had social philosophers and social scientists. While Platonists spoke of self-understanding stemming from comparison with absolute standards, Aristotle, notably in the *Nichomachean Ethics*, was concerned with comparisons between people. Indeed, comparisons can be seen to figure in such things as Bentham's utilitarian ethics, Rousseau's *Discourse on Social Inequality*, and Kant's *Critique of Moral Reasoning*. Karl Marx, the major architect of communism, showed that he was keenly aware of the power of social comparisons in his observation that,

JERRY SULS • Department of Psychology, University of Iowa, Iowa City, Iowa 52242.   LADD WHEELER • School of Psychology, University of New South Wales, Sydney, 2052 Australia.

Handbook of Social Comparison: Theory and Research, edited by Suls and Wheeler. Kluwer Academic/Plenum Publishers, New York, 2000.

A house may be large or small. As long as the surrounding houses are equally small, it satisfies all
social demands for a dwelling. But let a palace reside beside the little house, and it shrinks from a little
house to a hut. (quoted by Useem, 1975, p. 53)

However, a whole-hearted emphasis on the social origins of the self, and particularly comparisons with others and their role for subjective well-being, was first seen at the end of the last
century and blossomed in the last 100 years. This is evident in the writings of Cooley (1902),
James (1890), and Mead (1934). Commenting on the social comparative emphasis, Suls (1977)
observed that it may be more than coincidence that scientific views of the physical world also
took a relativistic turn during the same time period.

Early social psychological research provided evidence for the essential role of social
comparisons. Sherif's (1936) work on conformity with the autokinetic phenomenon, Newcomb's (1943) Bennington College project, Asch's (1956) studies of independence and dependence in response to a unanimous majority, and Hyman's (1942) reference group concept all
attest to the importance of comparisons with other people (Merton & Kitt, 1950). These efforts,
as well as two specific aspects of his early research background, appear to have influenced
Festinger's theorizing. His first publication, based on research done as an undergraduate, dealt
with social factors affecting level of aspiration (Hertzman & Festinger, 1940), as did his
Master's thesis, done at the University of Iowa Child Welfare Station under Kurt Lewin
(Festinger, 1942a,b). This research showed that subjects would lower their aspirations if they
found themselves above the group average and raise their aspirations if they scored below the
group average. Moreover, the status of the group made a difference. The undergraduate
participants raised their level of aspiration the most when they had scored below high school
students, and they lowered their level of aspiration the most when they had scored above
graduate students. The relevance of this research to social comparison theory is quite obvious.

The second major influence was the research on informal communication in small groups
that Festinger and his colleagues initiated at the Research Center for Group Dynamics,
founded by Lewin at MIT (relocating to the University of Michigan, following Lewin's death).
This research culminated in Festinger's theory of informal social communication (Festinger,
1950), a direct precursor of his theory of social comparison, which followed 4 years later. The
earlier theory posited that people in groups desire to attain uniformity of opinion either
because group consensus provides confidence in one's own opinion or because agreement was
needed to coordinate group goals. Several experiments on group communication and rejection
of opinion deviates provided confirmation for elements of the theory (Back, 1951; Festinger,
Schachter, & Back, 1950; Festinger & Thibaut, 1951; Kelley, 1951; Schachter, 1951; Thibaut,
1950).

In 1951, Festinger was awarded a grant from the Ford Foundation to summarize and
integrate empirical studies on social influence. During the same time, he also was invited to
give a paper at the second annual symposium on motivation held by the Department of
Psychology at the University of Nebraka. Both the symposium paper, published as part of an
edited volume (Festinger, 1954b), and the report, entitled "A theory of social comparison
processes," published in the journal *Human Relations* (Festinger, 1954a), along with some
related empirical papers, represented an extension and a change in emphasis from informal
communication theory. The power of the group over the individual was stressed in the earlier
paper. The new theory emphasized instead how individuals use groups to fulfill the informational need to evaluate their abilities and opinions. The major change, however, from the
earlier theory was the addition of abilities. In the new theory, people need to know not only that
their opinions are correct but also what their abilities allow them to do.

The *Human Relations* paper (Festinger 1954a) contained nine hypotheses, eight corol-

laries, and eight derivations, and is brutal reading. Let us instead cite from the Nebraska
Symposium paper (Festinger, 1954b):

> We started out by assuming the existence of a motivation to know that one's opinions are correct and to
> know precisely what one is and is not capable of doing. From this motivation, which is certainly non-
> social in character, we have made the following derivations about the conditions under which a social
> comparison process arises and about the nature of this social comparison process.
> 1. This social process arises when the evaluation of opinions or abilities is not feasible by testing
>   directly in the environment.
> 2. Under such circumstances persons evaluate their opinions and abilities by comparison with others.
> 3. This comparison leads to pressures toward uniformity.
> 4. There is a tendency to stop comparing oneself with others who are very divergent. This tendency
>   increases if others are perceived as different from oneself in relevant dimensions.
> 5. Factors such as importance, relevance, and attraction to a group which affect the strength of the
>   original motivation will affect the strength of the pressure towards uniformity. (p. 217)

It may not be clear from this brief summary why comparison should lead to pressures
toward uniformity. In the case of opinions, agreement with others who presumably also are
motivated to hold correct opinions makes us feel more confident in our own opinions. In the
case of abilities, observing those with similar abililties allows us to know what our own possibilities for action in the environment are; they are identical or very similar to those for these
other persons.

Inexplicably, the summary in the Nebraska Symposium article does not mention the
unidirectional drive upward for abilities, an important aspect of the *Human Relations* article
(Festinger 1954a) and subsequent developments in the study of comparison processes. The
unidirectional drive upward exists for abilities but not for opinions. Whereas complete opinion
agreement within the group will satisfy everyone, completely equal abilities within a group
will satisfy no one:

> The pressures cease acting on a person if he is just slightly better than the others. It is obvious that not
> everyone in a group can be slightly better than everyone else. The implication is that, with respect to the
> evaluation of abilities, a state of social quiescence is never reached. (Festinger, 1954a, p. 125)

The citations in the *Human Relations* article included several from the informal social
communication paper (as all predictions about opinions remained the same), as well as numerous level of aspiration articles. Other new evidence was Festinger, Gerard, Hymovitch, Kelley,
and Raven (1952) on the various manifestations of pressures to uniformity in opinions;
Festinger, Torrey, and Willerman (1954) on ability evaluation as a function of attraction to the
group and relative performance; Gerard (1953) on pressures to opinion uniformity as a
function of relevance for immediate action; and Hoffman, Festinger, and Lawrence (1954) on
task importance and comparability of the comparison target in ability evaluation.

AFTER FESTINGER GAVE UP THE THEORY FOR ADOPTION:
SCHACHTER AND THE SPECIAL SUPPLEMENT

Shortly after Festinger published his theory, he dropped it and went on to his theory of
cognitive dissonance. The theory continued to be of interest, however, because Schachter
extended it to emotional states. In his classic work, Schachter (1959) demonstrated that people
are more likely to affiliate when made fearful. In a series of experiments, Schachter demonstrated that the link between fear and affiliation was partly the result of comparison processes.
People affiliated in order to ascertain whether their emotional reaction was appropriate for the

circumstances (see Chapter 15, this volume, for a review and critique). Several researchers followed Schachter's lead, and there was a flurry of empirical papers on the role of comparison processes in affiliation. Schachter himself went on to research the social and cognitive determinants of emotional states (Schachter & Singer, 1962; Schachter & Wheeler, 1962). He demonstrated that unexplained arousal produces an ambiguous state that the individual needs to label. Other people's emotional states (via comparison) may provide such a label. Often the connection between Schachter's social–cognitive theory of emotion and social comparison is not mentioned, but it clearly was implicit. Further, because Schachter and his students were advancing an early version of self-perception processes (Bem, 1967), there was a link to attri-bution processes (Kelley, 1967). With the appreciation of Heider's (1958) implicit psychology and attribution theory (Jones & Davis, 1965), it was only a matter of time before explicit connections between attribution processes and comparison processes would follow.

The next development in the history of social comparison was the publication of a special supplemental volume of the *Journal of Experimental Social Psychology*, edited by Bibb Latané (1966). Most of the research represented in the issue was conducted by students at the University of Minnesota, who had been exposed to Schachter and his course on group dynamics.

Space considerations limit our discussion of the breadth of the contributions in the special issue, but it planted the seeds for subsequent developments. First, several experiments pro-vided additional support for the similarity hypothesis. For example, Gordon (1966) found that people who were uncertain about the correctness of their opinions choose to affiliate with others who held similar views. Radloff (1966) reported evidence suggesting that the absence of similar comparison others led to unstable and inaccurate evaluations. Darley and Aronson (1966) found evidence that the comparison motive was a more important determinant of the fear affiliation association than the fear reduction provided by the presence of other people. Latané, Eckman, and Joy (1966) showed that others are perceived to be more likable if they are present during a stressful situation, presumably because they satisfy the comparison motive.

Perhaps the most influential papers, however, were the ones using a new procedure that came to be known as the "rank-order paradigm." In this design, subjects completed a test under some cover story and then received their score and their rank among the other five or six co-participants who took the same test. Subsequently, subjects could choose to see the score of another participant: that comparison choice would indicate whether participants wanted to compare with someone better than themselves (an upward comparison) or worse than them-selves (a downward comparison) and whether participants wanted to compare with someone similar to themselves (an adjacent rank) or someone dissimilar (a nonadjacent rank). Wheeler (1962, 1966) devised this procedure to test the seemingly paradoxical prediction from social comparison theory that the more motivated a person is to do well, the more likely the person will make an upward comparison that will make more salient his inferiority to the comparison target. The social comparison theory prediction was supported, in that comparisons were more upward under (manipulated) higher levels of motivation than under lower levels. Supplemen-tary data suggested why this might be so. Those participants who believed that they were closer in rank to the person above them than to the person below were the most likely to compare upward. Wheeler speculated that, having assumed similarity upward, participants compared upward to confirm that the difference between their score and the one above them was small: that they were "almost as good as the very good ones" (Wheeler, 1966, p. 30). This identification with or assimilation to superior others has resurfaced in recent developments (see Chapter 9, this volume).

Thornton and Arrowood (1966) were the first to posit that two different motivations—

self-evaluation and self-enhancement—may operate in social comparison. These motives were proposed to explain their findings that subjects chose someone better than themselves in the rank order more frequently when a trait was described as a positive one than as a negative one. Self-evaluation is best addressed by comparing with someone who exemplifies the trait ("a positive instance"). However, self-enhancement is best addressed by asking, "How far am I from the best-off person?" presumably in order to identify with superior others. Combining these ideas, Thornton and Arrowood suggested that the choice of a better-off other for positive traits is optimal because the positive instance and best-off other are represented by the same point on the trait continuum. This is not the case for the negative trait. The distinction between self-evaluation and self-enhancement introduced by Thornton and Arrowood and also made by other authors in the supplement proved to be very influential in comparison theory's subsequent history.

The third influential experiment was conducted by Hakmiller (1962, 1966), who introduced the idea of downward social comparison. Through an elaborate cover story, some subjects received a higher score than expected on a supposed measure of "hostility toward one's parents." Half the subjects were given information suggesting that a high score represented a bad thing (high threat). The other subjects were led to believe that a high score represented something relatively positive (low threat). Subsequently, they were given the opportunity to see someone else's score in the rank ordering. Threatened subjects showed more interest in seeing the score of someone higher in hostility (i.e., presumably worse off) in the rank order. Hakmiller (1966) interpreted the results as support for the notion that self-esteem threat increases the self-enhancement motive and increases downward comparison. This work became a major inspiration for Wills' (1981) downward comparison theory. An important difference between the self-enhancement described by Thornton and Arrowood and that discussed by Hakmiller should be mentioned. The former thought self-enhancement was served by identifying with superior others, whereas the latter considered that self-enhancement came from comparing with persons of inferior status.

It should be noted that the rank order experiments extended the realm of social comparison from abilities, opinions, and emotions to personality traits, effectively saying that anything that can be compared is in the theory's realm. Second, they moved completely away from the previous typical dependent measure—manifestations of pressures to uniformity—and into the more direct measure of comparison selection.

THE FIRST BOOK ON SOCIAL COMPARISON

The 1966 *Journal of Experimental Social Psychology* Supplement 1 (Supplement 2 has yet to appear) did what its contributors hoped it would do: it stimulated research. The proof of this was the publication 11 years later of the first book devoted specifically to social comparison (Suls & Miller, 1977), an edited volume of theoretical essays, integrative reviews, and reports of research programs.

The flagship of the book was the chapter written by George ("Al") Goethals and John Darley (1977) who advanced an attributional reformulation of Festinger's theory. Because this approach is described in detail in other chapters (see Chapters 2, 3, and 6, this volume), only a brief description will be presented here. Festinger's (1954a) best-known statement about comparison selection was "Given a range of possible persons for comparison, someone close to one's own ability or opinion will be chosen for comparison" (p. 121, corollary IIIA). This states the critical "similarity hypothesis" of social comparison theory. In addition, later in the paper, Festinger wrote, "If persons who are very divergent from one's own opinion or ability are perceived as different from oneself on *attributes consistent with the divergence*, the tendency to narrow the range of comparability becomes stronger" (p. 133, hypothesis VIII, emphasis in original). Taken together, these statements had led Wheeler et al. (1969) to suggest that, "We do not merely seek out someone with an opinion similar to ours but rather seek out someone who ought to have, by virtue of similarity to us on attributes related to the opinion issue, a similar opinion" (p. 231). Goethals and Darley (1977) combined the corollary and hypothesis into the statement, "... given a range of possible persons for comparison, someone who should be close to one's own performance or opinion, given his standing on characteristics related to and predictive of performance or opinion, will be chosen for comparison" (p. 265).

In essence, the Goethals and Darley attributional approach to ability comparison proposed that people will compare with others who are similar on attributes related to and predictive of the attribute to be evaluated. Their reasoning was that if we compare to others more advantaged on related attributes, we are likely to perform less well than they, but this must be discounted in our attributions of ability because of the other's advantaged status (another plausible cause). The same holds if we compare to others who are disadvantaged on related attributes. Comparison with similar others on related attributes permits an unambiguous attribution to ability because we are matched on all other factors.

The attributional approach to opinion comparison departed from Festinger's in distinguishing between beliefs (i.e., potentially verifiable assertions about the true nature of an entity) and values (liking or disliking). Goethals and Darley (1977) proposed that similar others (on related attributes) were preferred to evaluate liking because dissimilar others are irrelevant. However, in the case of beliefs, they reasoned that people want to be sure the belief is entity based rather than a function of their own idiosyncratic biases (person caused). Since someone similar on related attributes may share one's own biases, he or she may not be useful, but agreement with someone dissimilar on related attributes implies that the judgment is entity caused. Hence, dissimilar others take on special status for belief comparison.

In their commentary to the Suls and Miller volume (1977), Wheeler and Zuckerman (1977) thought this was the strongest contribution to the book and used it as the device with which to integrate all of the other contributions. They urged that it be referred to as the "related attributes hypothesis" as a more descriptive and less confusing term than the "similarity hypothesis," and so it has been. Subsequent researchers also saw the value of the attributional reformulation, which remains influential.

Two other chapters in the volume also proved to be very important for subsequent research. Mettee and Smith (1977) ostensibly wrote about comparison and interpersonal attraction, but their chapter ranged widely. They made two main points. The first was that comparing with dissimilar others also can be highly informative. Their second point, culled from past literature, was their emphasis on the affective consequences of comparison. In contrast, Festinger (1954a,b) had been concerned with ability and opinion appraisals and subjective certainty. Mettee and Smith anticipated the era of "hot social cognitions." The third highly influential chapter was Brickman and Bulman's (1977), which proposed that people may be as motivated to avoid social comparison as to seek it. These authors described the potential interpersonal costs of social comparison. Comparisons between persons of unequal status can create bad feelings, with one person feeling resentful or envious and the other uncomfortable. Brickman and Bulman thought that even comparisons between equals could be problematic because no one would feel distinctive. Both the Mettee and Smith and

Brickman and Bulman chapters proved to be influential in directing attention to the hedonic consequences of comparisons.

In the interest of space and because they have not been as influential, we have not reviewed several of the other chapters in the Suls and Miller volume. However, we would suggest that graduate students looking for a dissertation topic may find many leads and intriguing suggestions that remain unexamined in the chapters on conformity (Allen & Wilder, 1977), group decision-making (Jellison & Arkin, 1977), justice (Austin, 1977), and modeling (Berger, 1977). Of the several edited books devoted to social comparison theory, it is generally recognized that the Suls and Miller volume to date has been the most important. Singer (1980) commented:

> "... the flavor of the book is much different from the 1966 collection. Social comparison is no longer on trial or even a hothouse flower. It is viewed as an established core of confirmed theory.... More experimental work has been done in basic social comparison two decades after its introduction than in the first decade. (pp. 171–172).

THE RISE OF DOWNWARD COMPARISON

Social comparison received an additional boost with the publication of an integrative theory paper on downward comparison by Tom Wills (1981). It undoubtedly caused a shift from concern about accurate self-evaluation to concerns about self-enhancement, which still has not abated.

Although Hakmiller's original rank-order paradigm study was the most obvious inspiration for Wills, the Brickman and Bulman and Mettee and Smith chapters in the 1977 Suls and Miller book also played a part. Wills posited one basic principle and several corollaries. His main hypothesis was that people can increase subjective well-being by comparing with someone less fortunate. He also contended that people who are low in self-esteem are more likely to make downward comparisons because of their greater need for self-enhancement. Wills also described several different ways in which downward comparisons can be made: through active derogation, by causing harm to others, or simply on a passive basis by taking advantage of opportunities to compare with people who are worse off. In the remainder of his article, Wills reviewed supportive evidence from the literature on fear affiliation, comparison choice, scapegoating, projection, and several other areas. The broad sweep of the paper was impressive and ushered in downward comparison as a basic, general principle for social psychology.

At roughly the same time that Wills' paper was in progress, Shelley Taylor and her student colleagues were investigating adjustment to threatening events, particularly breast cancer. Taylor and Levin (1976), in a review of the breast cancer literature, predicted that breast cancer patients would not know of many other patients but would be exposed to supercopers in the media, leading patients to perhaps feel worse about their own adjustment. The best-known study done partially to test this prediction was reported by Wood, Taylor, and Lichtman (1985). The investigators conducted a lengthy interview with each cancer patient covering a number of areas prior to asking questions about social comparison: they noticed that many respondents were voicing spontaneous comparisons throughout the interview. An analysis of the transcripts showed that a large majority of the comparisons were with patients who were less fortunate. Little evidence was marshaled for choices of similar or better-coping individuals. The historical conjunction between these data and Wills' theory was a fortuity with major impact. Wills had relied on already-published research, most of which had been produced for other purposes, and so there had not been a strong response to his paper prior to Wood et al. (1985). With the appearance of the breast cancer comparison data and references to Wills' paper, downward comparison theory took on the appearance of being able to predict comparison behavior.

In addition to providing dramatic evidence for downward comparison, the breast cancer research also emphasized an active, cognitive nature to social comparison. In particular, Wood and co-workers data suggested that availability of comparison choices did not dictate comparison choice. Often, participants invented comparison targets and seemed to manipulate the target or dimension to achieve the outcome they wanted: "At times, then, social comparison may not be particularly 'social' at all, in that one's comparisons may not necessarily involve actual comparisons with another real human being" (Wood et al., 1985, p. 1182).

The Wills (1981) and Wood et al. (1985) papers also had one other significant implication. By positing that downward comparisons can increase subjective well-being when people are under threat, the coping function of social comparison was identified. For example, Gibbons and Gerrard (Gibbons, 1986; Gibbons & Gerrard, 1989, 1991) reported how people use active and passive forms of downward comparison as coping strategies to help them deal with personal problems, such as eating disorders, smoking cessation, and depression. This became a major point of interest, inspiring numerous studies of downward comparison of populations experiencing stress, especially of a medical nature, for example, infertility patients (Tennen & Affleck, 1991) and rheumatoid arthritis patients (Blalock, DeVellis, & DeVellis, 1989). However, the chapter by Tennen, Eberhardt, and Affleck (Chapter 21, this volume) is extremely critical of this literature, asserting that there is scant evidence that downward comparisons function as coping strategies.

The focus on self-enhancement in downward comparison theory represented a significant departure from the classic theory, with its emphasis on accurate self-evaluation. The change in emphasis prompted Wheeler (1991) to refer to this new perspective as "neo-social comparison theory." Classic social comparison theory deals with the need to hold correct opinions and to have accurate appraisals of ability. Neo-social comparison theory deals with the positive affect or ego enhancement associated with being better off than others. An early example is the "Mr. Clean–Mr. Dirty study" (Morse & Gergen, 1970). The investigators found evidence that the self-esteem of subjects decreased after being exposed to a well-dresssed, very competent college student but increased after being exposed to a disheveled, disorganized student. This evidence implicated the social comparison process in self-concept. Because Ken Gergen was simultaneously reintroducing self-esteem and the self-concept to experimental social psychology, he made explicit links between comparison and the self that over time had considerable influence.

Wills' paper was published just as social psychologists were moving from attribution to social cognition and was well-established when researchers started to redirect their attention to motivated cognitions, such as ego protection and self-enhancement. A close examination of evidence for downward comparison indicates that most of strongest evidence comes from narrative or correlational methodologies with medical patients. The reasoning was that medical patients by definition are threatened. If they compare downward, that is evidence for the downward comparison theory prediction that threat leads to downward comparison. However, whenever threat is measured in these studies, it does not relate to comparison direction. Moreover, these studies rarely contain a nonpatient control group. Thus, it is not clear what conclusions can be drawn from much of this research. The experimental studies that Wills reviewed were conducted for different purposes. Aside from Hakmiller (1966), however, there is little experimental evidence demonstrating downward comparison under threat. Typically, the evidence shows avoidance of the highest most positive scores, which has been interpreted as evidence of defensive comparison (Smith & Insko, 1987). However, reluctance to compare with the most fortunate is not the same as seeking someone who is worse off. Students and researchers tended to blur the two patterns together because self-enhancement seems like a plausible explanation for both. Further, the results from narrative and correlational methodologies were exciting and seemed broadly consistent.

There were two other developments in the 1980s that contributed to interest in social comparison and its development. One was the self-evaluation maintenance model (SEM) proposed by Tesser (1988). This perspective posited that people have a basic motivation to maintain or enhance self-evaluation, which is achieved by two complementary processes: comparison and reflection. In this approach, comparison has some resemblance to Festinger's, but the aim in the SEM model is not to achieve cognitive clarity or reduce uncertainty, but to maintain a positive view of oneself. (The ties to Wills' theory therefore should be obvious.) Tesser reasoned that if people with whom we are psychologically "close" outperform us, this may reduce our self-evaluations (via comparison). However, in some cases, we can bask in the reflected glory of someone else; what Tesser referred to as the "reflection" process. Hence, another person's superior performance can threaten one's self-evaluation (via comparison) or enhance it (via reflection). According to the SEM model, whether reflection or comparison are dominant depends on the relevance of the performance dimension to the actor's self-definition and the psychological closeness with the other person. A considerable amount of evidence has been reported which support the SEM model. (See Chapter 7, this volume.)

As Tesser (1991) observed, "There simply is no analog to the reflection process in classical social comparison theory" (p. 118). Similarity to the other performer is also less critical in the SEM model than closeness (akin to Heider's unit or belongingness relationships). Although people who are close may share related attributes, the constructs are distinct. Finally, SEM is about performance and personal attributes; opinions have no explicit place in the model. However, despite the many differences in orientation, SEM has comparison elements; and with its emphasis on self-enhancement, it fits well with the downward comparison Zeitgeist.

A seemingly unrelated development in the 1980s also played a role. Although it was known for some time that people tend to assume that others share their opinions and attributes (Allport, 1924; Holmes, 1968), Ross, Greene, and House (1977) gave the phenomenon a new name—the "false consensus effect"—and a novel operationalization (Mullen et al., 1985). In a classic demonstration, Ross et al. showed that subjects who agreed to walk around campus wearing a sandwich board that said "Eat at Joe's" estimated that their own response was shared by a majority of their peers. This phenomenon reminds us of the quip: "When I want your opinion I'll give it you" (Lawrence Peter). These consensus estimates share elements with the "constructed, in-the-head" comparisons reported by the cancer patients described by Wood et al. (1985).

Only a few years later, evidence emerged for the "better than average effect," whereby people report that they possess more of positive attributes and less of negative attributes than other persons (Alicke, 1985; Taylor & Brown, 1988). In a related vein, Goethals, Messick, and Allison (1991) found evidence for a uniqueness bias, whereby people see their good attributes as rare (see also Suls & Wan, 1987). There might appear to be a clear contradiction between the false consensus effect and the better than average effect. But by "thinking one's abilities are unique and one's opinions are common" [the title of an article by Marks (1984)], one obtains a kind of ego bolstering. The main point, however, may be that these "constructive social comparisons," as Goethals et al. (1991) described them, provide an alternative to actual comparison (Suls, 1986). For some researchers, constructive comparisons also represent still another way that people may self-enhance (see Chapters 2, 14, and 16, this volume).

Recently, another type of constructive comparison has emerged as important. Gibbons and Gerrard (1995, 1997) have documented that people hold prototypes or images of social comparison targets that can have important effects on behavior. For example, teenagers have an image of the "typical adolescent heavy drinker." Those adolescents who tend to engage in much social comparison give the prototype more attention and compare themselves with it. Teenagers who hold a positive prototype of the drinker and see themselves as similar are more likely to engage in risky behavior. Of course, such prototypes may serve as instigators of behavior and also as ways to justify undesirable practices.

The developments just summarized portray the individual as moved mainly by self-enhancement or ego protection through a wide range of active and passive modes of actual or imagined comparison. By the end of the 1980s, motivated social comparison was a dominant interest whether it took the form of downward comparisons or constructed comparisons.

THE PENDULUM SWINGS

At the end of the 1980s, a summary statement of the field might have looked something like this: For accurate self-evaluation, people compare with similar others (on related attributes). For self-enhancement, usually prompted by threat, people compare with others who are worse off. The reader might notice that the statement about self-evaluation leaves out some critical details from the attributional formulation; for example, that belief and value-type opinions are assessed differently and that for abilities people may prefer to compare with others who are slightly better (a compromise between pressures toward uniformity and the unidirectional drive upward). These subtleties were passed over, however, because the empirical spotlight was on self-enhancement. The accurate appraisal of opinions and abilities was seen as relatively unproblematic, perhaps even effectively resolved. In fact, only a handful of experiments, however, tested the attributional perspective and some existing data were actually inconsistent. For example, in some experiments (Suls, Gaes, & Gastorf, 1979; Miller, 1982) people compared with others on attributes that were unrelated to performance. Perhaps the real reason for the relative lack of attention to self-evaluation was that most of the social psychological community assumed that people rarely wanted an accurate, veridical evaluation (see Trope, 1980, for an exception). Evidence of the focus on self-enhancement comes from the next compendium, edited by Suls and Wills (1991). Nine of its 15 chapters were devoted wholly or partly to the dynamics of self-enhancing comparisons, notably downward comparison.

By the end of the 1980s, there were indications that comparing with less fortunate others was not the only way to bolster self-esteem. First, evidence emerged that high- rather than low-self-esteem people were more likely to benefit from downward comparison, a finding inconsistent with one of Wills' corollaries (see Chapter 8, this volume). Debate ensued about whether this discrepancy was the result of a basic problem in the theory or the nature of the different methods (e.g., comparative rating scales vs. comparison choices) to test the hypothesis (Wills, 1991; Crocker, Thompson, McGraw, & Ingerman, 1987; Wood, 1996). Then came an influential paper published by Taylor and Lobel (1989) that argued that comparison processes can be served by different types of activity such as the desire for information about others and desire to affiliate with others. Rather than assume that these activities are interchangeable, the authors found suggestive evidence that cancer patients made comparisons with persons less fortunate (downward evaluations) but preferred information about and contact with more fortunate others (upward contacts). They proposed that the downward comparisons enhance one's self-perception, while upward contacts provide inspiration and information about how to improve. This approach argued that upward comparisons also can be effective for persons experiencing threat. Their observations fit nicely with Wood's (1989) proposal for a third motive for comparison: self-improvement.

A year later, an empirical paper by Buunk, Collins, Taylor, VanYperen, and Dakof (1990) complicated the picture still more. In the article, entitled "The Affective Consequences of Social Comparison: Either Direction Has Its Ups and Downs," Buunk et al. (1990) observed that there had been a general supposition that comparisons in a particular direction lead to a particular affective response, with downward comparisons creating positive affect and upward comparisons creating negative affect. [This was explicit in Brickman and Bulman (1977); Wills assumed positive affect resulting from downward comparison, but was mute about upward comparison.] Buunk et al. argued that comparison can produce positive or negative feelings independent of direction. In two studies, dispositional and situational variables seemed important. For example, cancer patients who were low in self-esteem and who perceived little control over symptoms were more likely to report negative consequences of downward comparison and less benefits of upward comparison. Patients high in self-esteem reported more benefits from both upward and downward comparison. One implication, consistent with Taylor and Lobel (1989), was that both upward and downward comparison can be self-enhancing. Furthermore, some people, by virtue of their predispositions, can better reap the benefits of social comparison. The broadest significance of the Buunk et al. (1990) and Taylor and Lobel's (1989) papers was to increase the recognition of the pervasiveness and importance of both upward and downward comparisons. The results of this broadband approach can be discerned in several of the chapters in this volume (see Chapters 10, 14, and 21).

Three other developments will also be described only briefly because they receive extensive treatment in this handbook. A paper by Rebecca Collins (1996) resurrected Wheeler's (1966) and Thornton and Arrowood's (1966) notion that people may compare upward because they identify or assimilate rather than contrast themselves with superior others. Whether assimilation or contrast occurs depends in part on the expected similarity with the comparison other. Collins elaborates on her "upward assimilation theory" in Chapter 9, this volume.

Another development was publication of an exhaustive review of social comparison methods (Wood, 1996) and the introduction of new methods to assess social comparisons in everyday life and in the laboratory. The dominant methods had been comparison selection and reaction effects (mainly in the psychological laboratory) and comparative ratings and narrative, open-ended responses. Narrative methods and retrospective questions about the direction of comparison and the reactions to it can be faulted, however, for their reliance on global recall, which is untrustworthy (Reis & Wheeler, 1991; Wood, 1996; Pietromonaco & Feldman-Barrett, 1997; Stone et al., 1998). What was lacking was *in situ* measurement. Wheeler and Miyake (1992) introduced the social comparison record, which asks respondents to keep a record of all of their comparisons as they occur. In addition, respondents indicate their mood before and after comparison and similarity to the comparison other (see Chapter 8, this volume). An important result was that respondents compared upward when in a negative mood and downward when in a positive mood, the opposite of what downward comparison theory would predict. Using palm tap computers and experience sampling, Tennen and Affleck (1997) (see also Chapter 21, this volume) initiated studies to assess the kinds of social comparisons that various patient samples make in everyday life. These new methods provide the opportunity to record naturally occurring comparisons and may provide better data about the effects of social information. Diary methods not only avoid retrospective biases, the effects of naive theories, and the artificial nature of the laboratory, they also provide the opportunity to assess comparisons that people seek and those that are forced on them. Some writers (Goethals, 1986; Suls, 1986) have suggested that understanding how people make selective use of comparison information presented in everyday social life but ignore other kinds is critical because we are inundated with such information. The new *in situ* methods may provide an answer to this question.

In addition to studying spontaneous social comparison, other investigators have developed new laboratory methods that provide more information than simply whether a superior, inferior, or similar other is preferred for comparison. For example, Wood (Wood, Giordano-Beech, Taylor, Michela, & Gaus, 1994; Chapter 11, this volume) has devised the "Test Selection Measure," which allows the researcher to assess the degree to which participants seek and avoid comparison information, compare on new comparison dimensions, and seek comparison on the same dimension. With the addition of new measures, researchers are obtaining a better understanding of how people use different comparison strategies for different comparison goals.

In 1997, a new collection of essays, *Health, Coping, and Well-Being: Perspectives from Social Comparison Theory*, appeared (Buunk & Gibbons, 1997). As the title indicates, the focus was on use of social comparison as a coping strategy, and its applied nature gives it a different flavor than previous collections. However, unlike the Suls and Wills volume (1991), with its emphasis on downward comparison, several chapters consider the benefits of upward comparison. There is extensive treatment of the role of constructive social comparisons (Gibbons & Gerrard, 1997), applications of the better than average effect to health threats (Klein & Weinstein, 1997), and detailed critiques of the evidence for upward and downward comparisons in adaptation to stress (Wood & Van der Zee, 1997; Tennen & Affleck, 1997). Although self-enhancement is still emphasized in the volume, two chapters—one on the role of comparison in medical referral (Suls, Martin, & Leventhal, 1997) and another on affiliation and coping (Kulik & Mahler, 1997)—focus on the self-evaluative motive. There is even a chapter (Diener & Fujita, 1997) that argues that comparisons are not important for subjective well-being; rather, global feelings of well-being are proposed to be mainly dispositional in nature and relatively immune from situational influences.

The 1990s also saw two other incipient developments. Wills and Suls (1991) have observed that "... the study of comparison processes has never made full contact with social judgment theory [Sherif & Hovland, 1961] and psychophysics, areas with which it shares similar interests" (p. 408). Kruglanski and Mayseless (1990) noted that research on comparison of objects in experimental psychology might fruitfully inform the social comparison area. Recent researchers have made increasing use and see more connections to the other areas of "relational judgment" in social cognition, cognitive psychology, psychophysics, and decision making. Some evidence for these trends can be seen in Chapter 8, this volume, on upward assimilation theory. Chapter 13, this volume, presents a provocative theory integrating the social cognition literature on assimilation and contrast and comparison theory. The explicit connections to psychophysical judgment are explored by Wedell and Parducci in Chapter 12, this volume. Olson, Buhrmann, and Roese consider the connections between social comparisons and counterfactual thinking in Chapter 18, this volume. Folger and Kass examine the role of comparisons and counterfactuals in determining fairness in Chapter 20, this volume. If social comparison research appeared too inbred for a time, this impression should have passed.

There also has been a recent renewal of interest in social comparison for accurate self-evaluation. In their proxy ability comparison theory, Wheeler, Martin, and Suls (1997) proposed that people frequently need to assess whether they should attempt some task they have not tried before ("can I do X?"). In many instances, there can be severe costs if one fails, and consequently people want as accurate a prediction as they can obtain before they decide to take the risk. Learning how a proxy (i.e., someone who has already attempted X) did can provide useful information, assuming that the proxy is an appropriate comparison other (see also Smith & Sachs, 1997). Building on the attributional perspective, the proxy model demonstrates how past performance similarity (on prior tasks involving the critical ability) and related attribute similarity both contribute to a proxy's informational utility. As such, the model provides a reconcilation between Festinger's emphasis on performance similarity and Goethals and Darley's emphasis on related attribute similarity (see Chapter 4, this volume). Another focus on accurate self-evaluation comes from Smith and Arnkelsson's (Chapter 3, this volume) extension of the attributional formulation. These authors showed how the stability or instability of related attributes influences the kind of inferential schemas that are used to generate self-evaluations via social comparison. Finally, opinion comparison has received renewed attention in the triadic comparison model, which builds on insights from the attributional perspective, the proxy ability theory, and research on projection processes (see Chapter 6, this volume).

CONCLUSION

The emphasis from the 1950s through the mid-1970s was on accurate self-evaluation through social comparison and on upward comparison. The 1980s saw a swing toward self-enhancement, mainly through downward comparison. In the 1990s, the pendulum swung back, but not completely. Contemporary researchers are examining the dynamics of both upward and downward comparison, and we hope that this is fairly reflected in the following chapters. The study of social comparison processes is much broader than Leon Festinger or Stan Schachter could have anticipated in the 1950s. Festinger told us on the occasion of the American Psychological Association 30th birthday party for the theory that he was concerned that the theory would no longer mean anything scientifically if it could be applied to everything. That is indeed a danger, but one that cannot be altogether avoided in a free scientific society. Moreover, if, as we believe, comparison of oneself with other people is a core aspect of human experience, it would be very premature to place limits. The best we can do is to stay alert for untestable statements, poor research, and uncritical acceptance of intuitively appealing ideas. The snow-covered backyard has more tracks than ever, and our eyes, then, must be sharper. Thanks for being here.

REFERENCES

Alicke, M. D. (1985). Global self-evaluation as determined by the desirability and controllability of trait adjectives. *Journal of Personality and Social Psychology, 49*, 1621–1630.

Allen, V. L., & Wilder, D. A. (1977). Social comparison, self-evaluation, and conformity to the group. In J. Suls & R. Miller (Eds.), *Social comparison processes: Theoretical and empirical perspectives* (pp. 187–208). Washington, DC: Hemisphere.

Allport, F. H. (1924). *Social psychology.* Cambridge, MA: Riverside Press.

Asch, S. (1956). Studies of independence and conformity: I. A minority of one against a unanimous majority. *Psychological Monographs, 70*(9), (whole No. 416).

Austin, W. (1977). Equity theory and social comparison processes. In J. Suls & R. Miller (Eds.), *Social comparison processes: Theoretical and empirical perspectives* (pp. 279–306). Washington, DC: Hemisphere.

Back, K. W. (1951). Influence through social communication. *Journal of Abnormal and Social Psychology, 46*, 9–23.

Bem, D. J. (1967). Self-perception theory: An alternative interpretation of cognitive dissonance phenomena. *Psychological Review, 74*, 181–200.

Berger, S. M. (1977). Social comparison, modeling, and perseverance. In J. Suls & R. Miller (Eds.), *Social comparison processes: Theoretical and empirical perspectives* (pp. 209–234). Washington, DC: Hemisphere.

Blalock, S., DeVellis, B., & DeVellis, R. (1989). Social comparison among individuals with rheumatoid arthritis. *Journal of Applied Social Psychology, 19*, 665–680.

Brickman, P., & Bulman, R. J. (1977). Pleasure and pain in social comparison. In J. Suls & R. Miller (Eds.), *Social comparison processes: Theoretical and empirical perspectives* (pp. 149–186). Washington, DC: Hemisphere.

Buunk, B., Collins, R., Taylor, S., VanYperen, N., & Dakof, G. (1990). The affective consequences of social comparison: Either direction has its ups and downs. *Journal of Personality and Social Psychology, 59*, 1238–1249.

Buunk, B., & F. X. Gibbons (Eds.). (1997). *Health, coping, and well-being: Perspectives from social comparison theory*. Mahwah, NJ: Lawrence Erlbaum.

Collins, R. L. (1996). For better or worse: The impact of upward social comparison on self-evaluations. *Psychological Bulletin, 119*, 1, 51–69.

Cooley, C. H. (1902). *Human nature and the social order*. New York: Scribner's.

Crocker, J., Thompson, L., McGraw, K., & Ingerman, C. (1987). Downward comparison prejudice and evaluations of others: Effects of self-esteem and threat. *Journal of Personality and Social Psychology, 52*, 907–916.

Darley, J. M., & Aronson, E. (1966). Self-evaluation vs. direct anxiety reduction as determinant of the fear-affiliation relationship. *Journal of Experimental Social Psychology, Supplement 1*, 66–79.

Diener, E., & Fujita, F. (1997). Social comparisons and subjective well-being. In B. Buunk & F. X. Gibbons (Eds.), *Health, coping, and well-being: Perspectives from social comparison theory* (pp. 329–358). Mahwah, NJ: Lawrence Erlbaum.

Festinger, L. (1942a). Wish, expectation, and group standards as factors influencing level of aspiration. *Journal of Abnormal and Social Psychology, 37*, 184–200.

Festinger, L. (1942b). A theoretical interpretation of shifts in level of aspiration. *Psychological Review, 49*, 235–250.

Festinger, L. (1950). Informal social communication. *Psychological Review, 57*, 271–282.

Festinger, L. (1954a). A theory of social comparison processes. *Human Relations, 7*, 117–140.

Festinger, L. (1954b). Motivation leading to social behavior. In M. R. Jones (Ed.), *Nebraska symposium on motivation* (Vol. 2, pp. 191–218). Lincoln: University of Nebraska Press.

Festinger, L., Gerard, H. B., Hymovich, B., Kelley, H. H., & Raven, B. (1952). The influence process in the presence of extreme deviates. *Human Relations, 5*, 327–346.

Festinger, L., Schachter, S., & Back, K. (1950). *Social pressures in informal groups*. New York: Harper & Brothers.

Festinger, L. , & Thibaut, J. (1951). Interpersonal communication in small groups. *Journal of Abnormal and Social Psychology, 46*, 92–99.

Festinger, L., Torrey, J., & Willerman, B. (1954). Self-evaluation as a function of attraction to the group. *Human Relations, 7*, 1161–1174.

Gerard, H. B. (1953). The effects of different dimensions of disagreement on the communication process in small groups. *Human Relations, 6*, 249–272.

Gibbons, F. X. (1986). Social comparison and depression: Company's effect on misery. *Journal of Personality and Social Psychology, 51*, 1–9.

Gibbons, F. X., & Gerrard, M. (1989). Effect of upward and downward comparison on mood states. *Journal of Social and Clinical Psychology, 8*, 14–31.

Gibbons, F. X., & Gerrard, M. (1991). Downward comparison and coping with threat. In J. Suls & T. A. Wills (Eds.), *Social comparison: Contemporary theory and research* (pp. 317–346). Hillsdale, NJ: Lawrence Erlbaum.

Gibbons, F. X., & Gerrard, M. (1995). Predicting young adults' health risk behavior. *Journal of Personality and Social Psychology, 69*, 505–517.

Gibbons, F. X., & Gerrard, M. (1997). Health images and their effects on health behavior. In B. Buunk & F. X. Gibbons (Eds.), *Health, coping, and well-being: Perspectives from social comparison theory* (pp. 63–94). Mahwah, NJ: Lawrence Erlbaum.

Goethals, G. R. (1986). Social comparison theory: Psychology from the lost and found. *Personality and Social Psychology Bulletin, 12*, 261–278.

17

Goethals, G. R., & Darley, J. (1977). Social comparison theory: An attributional approach. In J. Suls & R. L. Miller (Eds.), *Social comparison processes: Theoretical and empirical perspectives* (pp. 259–278). Washington, DC: Hemisphere.

Goethals, G. R., Messick, D., & Allison, S. T. (1991). The uniqueness bias: Studies of constructive social comparison. In J. Suls & T. A. Wills (Eds.), *Social comparison: Contemporary theory and research* (pp. 149–173). Hillsdale, NJ: Lawrence Erlbaum.

Gordon, B. F. (1966). Influence and social comparison as motives for affiliation. *Journal of Experimental Social Psychology*, Suppl. 1, 55–65.

Hakmiller, K. L. (1962) Social comparison processes under differential conditions of ego-threat. Doctoral dissertation, University of Minnesota, Minneapolis.

Hakmiller, K. (1966). Threat as a determinant of social comparison. *Journal of Experimental Social Psychology*, Suppl. 1, 32–39.

Heider, F. (1958). *The psychology of interpersonal relations*. New York: Wiley.

Hertzman, M., & Festinger, L. (1940). Shifts in explicit goals in a level of aspiration experiment. *Journal of Experimental Psychology*, 27, 439–452.

Hoffman, P. J., Festinger, L., & Lawrence, D. H. (1954). Tendencies toward group comparability in competitive bargaining. *Human Relations*, 7, 141–159.

Holmes, D. S. (1968). Dimensions of projection. *Psychological Bulletin*, 69, 248–268.

Hyman, H. (1942). The psychology of status. *Archives of Psychology*, No. 269.

James, W. (1890). *Principles of psychology* (Vol. 1). New York: Henry Holt.

Jellison, J., & Arkin, R. (1977). Social comparison of abilities: A self-presentation approach to decision-making in groups. In J. Suls & R. L. Miller (Eds.). *Social comparison processes: Theoretical and empirical perspectives* (pp. 235–258). Washington, DC: Hemisphere.

Jones, E. E., & Davis, K. E. (1965). From acts to dispositions: The attribution process in person perception. In L. Berkowitz (Ed.), *Advances in experimental social psychology* (Vol. 2, pp. 219–266). New York: Academic Press.

Jones, E. E., & Gerard, H. B. (1965). *Foundations of social psychology*. New York: John Wiley.

Jones, S., & Regan, D. (1974). Ability evaluation through social comparison. *Journal of Experimental Social Psychology*, 10, 133–146.

Katz, D., & Allport, F. H. (1928). *Student attitudes: A report of the Syracuse University research study*. Syracuse, NY: Craftsman Press.

Kelley, H. H. (1951). Communication in experimentally created hierarchies. *Human Relations*, 4, 39–56.

Kelley, H. L. (1967). Attribution theory in social psychology. In D. L. Levine (Ed.), *Nebraska symposium on motivation* (pp. 192–240). Lincoln: University of Nebraska Press.

Klein, W. M., & Weinstein, N. D. (1997). Social comparison and unrealistic optimism about personal risk. In B. Buunk & F. X. Gibbons (Eds.), *Health, coping, and well-being: Perspectives from social comparison theory* (pp. 25–62). Mahwah, NJ: Lawrence Erlbaum.

Kruglanski, A., & Mayseless, O. (1990). Classic and current social comparison research: Expanding the perspective. *Psychological Bulletin*, 108, 195–208.

Kulik, J. A., & Mahler, H. (1997). Social comparison, affiliation, and coping with acute medical threats. In B. Buunk & F. X. Gibbons (Eds.), *Health, coping, and well-being: Perspectives from social comparison theory* (pp. 227–262). Mahwah, NJ: Lawrence Erlbaum.

Latané, B. (Ed.) (1966). Studies in social comparison. *Journal of Experimental Social Psychology*, Suppl. 1.

Latané, B., Eckman, J., & Joy, V. (1966). Shared stress and interpersonal attraction. *Journal of Experimental Social Psychology*, Suppl. 1, 92–102.

Marks, G. (1984). Thinking one's abilities are unique and one's opinions are common. *Personality and Social Psychology Bulletin*, 10, 203–208.

Mead, G. H. (1934). *Mind, self, and society*. Chicago: University of Chicago Press.

Merton, R. K., & Kitt, A. (1950). Contributions to the theory of reference group behavior. In R. K. Merton & P. F. Lazarfield (Eds.), *Continuities in social research: Studies in the scope and method of "The American Soldier"* (pp. 40–105). Glencoe, IL: Free Press.

Mettee, D. R., & Smith, G. (1977). Social comparison and interpersonal attraction: The case for dissimilarity. In J. Suls & R. Miller (Eds.), *Social comparison processes: Theoretical and empirical perspectives* (pp. 69–102). Washington, DC: Hemisphere.

Miller, C. T. (1982). The role of performance-related similarity in social comparison of abilities: A test of the related attributes hypothesis. *Journal of Experimental Social Psychology*, 18, 513–523.

Morse, S., & Gergen, K. J. (1970). Social comparison, self-consistency, and the concept of self. *Journal of Personality and Social Psychology*, 16, 148–156.

Mullen, B., Atkins, J. L., Champion, D. S., Edwards, C., Hardy, D., Story, J. E., & Venderklok, M. (1985). The false consensus effect: A meta-analysis of 115 hypothesis tests. *Journal of Experimental Social Psychology, 21*, 262–283.

Newcomb, T. (1943). *Personality and social change: Attitude formation in the student community.* New York: Dryden Press.

Pietromonaco, P. R. & Feldman-Barrett, L. (1997). Working models of attachment and daily social interactions. *Journal of Personality and Social Psychology, 73*, 1409–1423.

Radloff, R. (1966) Social comparison and ability evaluation. *Journal of Experimental Social Psychology*, Suppl. 1, 6–26.

Reis, H. T., & Wheeler, L. (1991). Studying social interaction with the Rochester Interaction Record. In M. P. Zanna (Ed.), *Advances in experimental social psychology* (Vol. 24, pp. 270–312). San Diego, CA: Academic Press.

Ross, L., Greene, D., & House, P. (1977). The "false consensus effect": An egocentric bias in social perception and attribution processes. *Journal of Experimental Social Psychology, 58*, 119–128.

Schachter, S. (1951). Deviation, rejection, and communication. *Journal of Abnormal and Social Psychology, 46*, 190–207.

Schachter, S. (1959). *The psychology of affiliation.* Stanford, CA: Stanford University Press.

Schachter, S., & Singer, J. E., (1962). Cognitive, social, and physiological determinants of emotional state. *Psychological Review, 69*, 370–399.

Schachter, S., & Wheeler, L. (1962). Epinephrine, chlorpromazine, and amusement. *Journal of Abnormal and Social Psychology, 65*, 121–128.

Sherif, M. (1936). *The psychology of social norms.* New York: Harper.

Sherif, M., & Hovland, C. (1961). *Social judgment.* New Haven: Yale University Press.

Singer, J. E. (1980). Social comparison: The process of self-evaluation. In L. Festinger (Ed.), *Retrospections on social psychology* (pp. 158–179). New York: Oxford University Press.

Smith, R., & Insko, C. (1987). Social comparison choice during ability evaluation: The effects of comparison publicity, performance feedback, and self-esteem. *Personality and Social Psychology Bulletin, 13*, 111–122.

Smith, W. P., & Sachs, P. (1997). Social comparison and task prediction: Ability similarity and the use of a proxy. *British Journal of Social Psychology, 36*, 587–602.

Stone, A. A., Schwartz, J. E., Neale, J. M. Shiffman, S., Marco, C. A., Hickcox, M., Paty, J., Porter, L. S., & Cruise, L. J. (1998). A comparison of coping assessed by ecological momentary assessment and retrospective recall. *Journal of Personality and Social Psychology, 74*, 6, 1670–1680.

Suls, J. (1977). Social comparison theory and research: An overview from 1954. In J. Suls & R. Miller (Eds.), *Social comparison processes: Theoretical and empirical perspectives* (pp. 1–19). Washington, DC: Hemisphere.

Suls, J. (1986). Notes on the occasion of social comparison theory's thirtieth birthday. *Personality and Social Psychology Bulletin, 12*, 289–296.

Suls, J., Gaes, G., & Gastorf, J. (1979). Evaluating a sex-related ability: Comparison with same-, opposite-, and combined sex norms. *Journal of Research in Personality, 13*, 294–303.

Suls, J., Martin, R., Leventhal, H. (1997). Social comparison, lay referral, and the decision to seek medical care. In B. Buunk & F. X. Gibbons (Eds.), *Health and coping: Perspectives from social comparison theory.* (pp. 195–226). Mahwah NJ: Lawrence Erlbaum.

Suls, J., & Miller, R. L. (Eds.). (1977). *Social comparison processes: Theoretical and empirical perspectives.* Washington, DC: Hemisphere.

Suls, J., & Wan, C. K. (1987). In search of the false-uniqueness phenomenon: Fear and estimates of social consensus. *Journal of Personality and Social Psychology, 52*, 211–217.

Suls, J., & Wills, T. A. (Eds.). (1991). *Social comparison: Contemporary theory and research.* Hillsdale, NJ: Lawrence Erlbaum.

Taylor, S., & Brown, J. (1988). Illusion and well-being: A social-psychology perspective on mental health. *Psychological Bulletin, 103*, 193–210.

Taylor, S., & Levin, S. (1976). *The psychological impact of breast cancer: A review of theory and research.* San Francisco, CA: West Coast Cancer Foundation.

Taylor, S., & Lobel, M. (1989). Social comparison activity under threat: Downward evaluation and upward contacts. *Psychological Review, 96*, 569-575.

Tennen, H., & Affleck, G. (1991). Social comparison and coping with major medical problems. In J. Suls & T. A. Wills (Eds.). *Social comparison: Contemporary theory and research* (pp. 369–394). Hillsdale, NJ: Lawrence Erlbaum.

Tennen, H., & Affleck, G. (1997). Social comparison as a coping process: A critical review and application to chronic pain disorders. In B. Buunk & F. X. Gibbons (Eds.), *Health, coping, and well-being: Perspectives from social comparison theory* (pp. 263–298). Mahwah, NJ: Lawrence Erlbaum.

Tesser, A. (1988). Toward a self-evaluation maintenance model of social behavior. In L. Berkowitz (Ed.), *Advances in experimental social psychology* (Vol. 21, pp. 181–227). New York: Academic Press.

Tesser, A. (1991). Emotion in social comparison and reflection processes. In J. Suls & T. A. Wills (Eds.), *Social comparison: Contemporary theory and research* (pp. 117–148). Hillsdale, NJ: Lawrence Erlbaum.

Thibaut, J. (1950). An experimental study of the cohesiveness of underprivileged groups. *Human Relations, 3,* 251–278.

Thornton, D., & Arrowood, A. J. (1966). Self-evaluation, self-enhancement, and the locus of social comparison. *Journal of Experimental Social Psychology*, Suppl. 1, 40–48.

Trope, Y. (1980). Self-assessment, self-enhancement, and task preference. *Journal of Experimental Social Psychology, 16,* 116–129.

Useem, M. (1975). *Protest movements in America*. New York: Bobbs-Merill.

Wheeler, L. (1962) Desire: A determinant of self-evaluation through social comparison. Doctoral dissertation, University of Minnesota, Minneapolis.

Wheeler, L. (1966). Motivation as a determinant of upward comparison. *Journal of Experimental Social Psychology*, Suppl. 1, 27–31.

Wheeler, L. (1991). A brief history of social comparison theory. In J. Suls & T. A. Wills (Eds.), *Social comparison: Contemporary theory and research* (pp. 3–21). Hillsdale, NJ: Lawrence Erlbaum.

Wheeler, L., Martin, R., & Suls, J. (1997). The proxy social comparison model for self-assessment of ability. *Personality and Social Psychology Review, 1,* 54–61

Wheeler, L., & Miyake, K. (1992). Social comparison in everyday life. *Journal of Personality and Social Psychology, 62,* 760–773.

Wheeler, L., Shaver, K. G., Jones, R. A., Goethals, G. R., Cooper, J., Robinson, J. E., Gruder, C. L., & Butzine, K. W. (1969). Factors determining choice of a comparison other. *Journal of Experimental Social Psychology, 5,* 219–232.

Wheeler, L., & Zuckerman, M. (1977). Commentary. In J. Suls & R. L. Miller (Eds.), *Social comparison processes: Theoretical and empirical perspectives* (pp. 335–367). Washington, DC: Hemisphere.

Wills, T. A. (1981). Downward comparison principles in social psychology. *Psychological Bulletin, 90,* 245–271.

Wills, T. A. (1991). Similarity and self-esteem in social comparison. In J. Suls & T. A. Wills (Eds.), *Social comparison: Contemporary theory and research* (pp. 51–78). Hillsdale, NJ: Lawrence Erlbaum.

Wills, T. A., & Suls, J. (1991). Commentary: Neo-social comparison theory and beyond. In J. Suls & T. A. Wills (Eds.), *Social comparison: Contemporary theory and research* (pp. 395–412). Hillsdale, NJ: Lawrence Erlbaum.

Wood, J. (1989). Theory and research concerning social comparisons of personal attributes. *Psychological Bulletin, 106,* 231–248.

Wood, J. V. (1996). What is social comparison and how should we study it? *Personality and Social Psychology Bulletin, 22,* 520–537.

Wood, J. V., Giordano-Beech, M., Taylor, M. K., Michela, J. L., & Gaus, V. (1994). Strategies of social comparison among people with low self-esteem: Self-protection and self-enhancement. *Journal of Personality and Social Psychology, 67,* 713–731.

Wood, J. V., Taylor, S., & Lichtman, R. (1985). Social comparison in adjustment to breast cancer. *Journal of Personality and Social Psychology, 49,* 1169–1183.

Wood, J. V., & Van der Zee, K. (1997). Social comparisons among cancer patients: Under what conditions are comparisons upward and downward. In B. Buunk & F. X. Gibbons (Eds.), *Health, coping, and well-being: Perspectives from social comparison theory* (pp. 299–328). Mahwah, NJ: Lawrence Erlbaum.

II

Foundations of Social Comparison

2

Interpreting and Inventing Social Reality

Attributional and Constructive Elements in Social Comparison

GEORGE R. GOETHALS AND WILLIAM M. P. KLEIN

Clearly, Leon Festinger hit upon an important subject when he formulated social comparison theory nearly 50 years ago. The ways that people view their opinions, their abilities, and their life situations vary according to the standing of other people. Recently, during the National Basketball Association lockout, star New York Knicks center Patrick Ewing said that current NBA salaries were "about survival, about being able to feed our families" (*Newsweek*, January 4, 1999, p. 108). Ewing's salary was $18.5 million per year. That is probably enough to eat on. However, the amount of money made by owners is Ewing's standard of comparison. Similarly, in resigning Bernie Williams, the New York Yankees baseball team paid the star outfielder $87.5 million for 7 years, so that Williams would not feel underpaid in comparison to first baseman Mo Vaughn, who signed with the California Angels for $80 million for 6 years. Why would Williams only feel happy if his salary compared well to Vaughn's?

William James's (1892) classic discussion of what we now call level of aspiration explains "So we have the paradox of a man shamed to death because he is only the second pugilist or second oarsman in the world.... Yonder puny fellow, however, whom every one can beat, suffers no chagrin about it...." (pp. 186–187). People's satisfaction with themselves and their lot depends on a range of social comparisons with others whom they perceive to provide relevant comparison points. While most of us might feel that Bernie Williams should be happy with a salary roughly 100 times our own, that is not the way he thinks about it. The ways people do think about comparing with others are endlessly fascinating. In this chapter we want to discuss one particularly interesting facet of social comparison: the balance between the careful logic and rationale that people sometimes bring to social comparison versus the seemingly irrational and biased thinking that just as often affects the way they to compare to others.

GEORGE R. GOETHALS • Department of Psychology, Williams College, Williamstown, Massachusetts 01267.
WILLIAM M. P. KLEIN • Department of Psychology, Colby College, Waterville, Maine 04901.

Handbook of Social Comparison: Theory and Research, edited by Suls and Wheeler. Kluwer Academic/Plenum Publishers, New York, 2000.

We will begin by discussing the way social comparison has been integrated into highly rational models of attribution processes that became central to social psychology in the 1970s. This integration imagined a social comparer who was generally thoughtful, logical, and rational. Next we will consider the way models of a much lazier, self-protective and self-enhancing social thinker suggested a less logical but no less clever social comparer who constructed a view of his standing in relation to others that supported a self-satisfied appraisal of important personal characteristics. Not surprisingly, we think that social comparison is characterized by both rational and irrational thinking. Our challenge is to understand both kinds of thinking, the conditions that elicit each one, and how people actually move between them.

ATTRIBUTION AND SOCIAL COMPARISON

The view of the social comparer as rational goes back to the opening of Leon Festinger's original statement of social comparison in 1954. Festinger stated as hypothesis I, "there exists, in the human organism, a drive to evaluate his opinions and his abilities" (p. 117). This statement set the tone for the original understandings of social comparison theory. It imagined a person who really wanted to know how good his abilities were and whether his opinions were actually correct.

Festinger argued that people needed to accurately assess their abilities and opinions in order to make smart choices about dealing with the world. He noted that "the holding of incorrect opinions and/or inaccurate appraisals of one's abilities can be punishing or even fatal in many situations" (1954, p. 117). A strong link to attribution theory is apparent. Festinger's view of the rational comparer is consistent with Fritz Heider's (1944) early formulation of attribution theory that viewed people as needing to order and predict their environment so that they can act effectively in it. Thus both social comparison theory and attribution theory, in their early formulations, stressed the rational actor trying to think carefully and objectively and to act adaptively in a complex world. In the introduction to their early book on attribution processes, Jones et al. (1972) stressed that attribution theory shared social comparison theory's concern with "the factors motivating the individual to obtain causally relevant information" (p. x).

The link between social comparison and attribution is especially clear when we note Festinger's (1954) statement that "abilities are of course manifested only through performance which is assumed to depend upon the particular ability" (p. 118). Thus in evaluating an ability one must make inferences about the links between performances and abilities. Doing so requires careful attributional analysis. Does our superior performance compared to another reflect a higher level of ability or more experience with that kind of performance? Though not quite so obvious, attributional analysis is also involved in evaluating opinions. Goethals and Darley (1977) note that like performances, "opinions are also multidetermined, by the person's beliefs about reality, his basic values, his more specific likes and dislikes, and his immediate needs and interests" (p. 261). To the extent that opinion comparison involves evaluating one's underlying judgment or system of values, attributional analysis is important. Does another person's disagreeing opinion about impeaching President Clinton reflect different moral values or different beliefs about the role Monica Lewinsky played in initiating their relationship?

Attribution Principles and the Related Attributes Hypothesis

The role of attributional processes in social comparison is perhaps most clear in Festinger's original statements regarding the preference for comparing with similar others, the so-called "similarity hypothesis." Festinger's (1954) hypothesis III states that "The tendency to compare oneself with some other specific person decreases as the difference between his opinion or ability and one's own increases" (p. 120). The closely related corollary IIIA states that "given a range of possible persons for comparison, someone close to one's own ability or opinion will be chosen for comparison" (p. 121). The meaning of these statements has been a matter of debate for some time (cf. Goethals & Darley, 1977; Wheeler et al., 1969). In fact, a later statement in Festinger's original theory, hypothesis VIII, helps clarify them. Hypothesis VIII states "If persons who are very divergent from one's own opinion or ability are perceived as different from oneself on *attributes consistent with the divergence*, the tendency to narrow the range of comparability becomes stronger" (1954, p. 133, emphasis in original). That is, one is more likely to compare with people who are similar to oneself on attributes related to the performance or opinion in question.

Goethals and Darley (1977) combined these statements about similarity into a statement that Wheeler and Zuckerman (1977) called the "related attributes hypothesis": "given a range of possible persons for comparison, someone who should be close to one's own performance or opinion, given his standing on characteristics related to and predictive of performance or opinion, will be chosen for comparison" (Goethals & Darley, 1977, p. 265). That is, people will prefer comparing with others who are similar on attributes that are related to their opinion or performance level.

Let us first consider how this principle works in the domain of ability comparison. Take, for example, an individual evaluating his or her tennis-playing ability. He or she might compare with others who are about the same age, who have the same degree of recent practice and comparable equipment, and who are the same sex. The rationale for this approach to comparison is found in two key principles of attribution theory stated by Harold Kelley (1972). The first is the *discounting principle*: "the role of a given cause in producing an effect is discounted if other plausible causes are also present" (p. 8). If I beat my younger sister in tennis, it might be because I have more tennis-playing ability. However, the fact that she has never picked up a tennis racket might explain her poor performance better than my superior ability. The engaged social comparer wants to control and thereby rule out the role of nonability factors in explaining any performance difference. If standing on the nonability factors is equal, then any performance difference is attributable to ability.

The closely related *augmentation principle* is also relevant. It states that "if for a given effect, both a plausible inhibitory cause and a plausible facilitative cause are present, the role of the facilitative cause in producing the effect will be judged greater than if it alone were present as a plausible cause for the effect" (Kelley, 1972, p. 12). For example, if our little sister were to beat us in tennis despite having played the game only once, we would be highly impressed with her tennis-playing ability. Her lack of experience would be seen as an inhibitory cause and her tennis-playing ability a facilitative cause. The role of the facilitative cause—ability—would be judged greater than if it alone were present, that is, if she had not been inexperienced. In this way the discounting principle and the augmentation principle can be seen as two sides of the same coin. When the more experienced player wins, her experience is a plausible cause for winning and her ability is discounted. We would have been more certain of her ability if she had less experience. When the less experienced player wins, her lack of experience is not a plausible cause for her winning. Rather, it is viewed as an inhibitory cause. Therefore, the facilitative cause—ability—is seen as greater than it would have been if she had more experience.

While these attribution principles are somewhat difficult to state, people seem to have a ready understanding of them. This is shown in many experiments. While people do not always discount, they clearly do in many situations. For example, in Berglas and Jones's (1978) well-known study of self-handicapping, subjects seem to realize that a poor performance can be attributed to an external handicap rather than to low ability, if an obvious performance handicap is indeed in play. Likewise, we are impressed when an actor seems to overcome a handicap and succeed in spite of it.

These attribution principles underlie the "related attributes hypothesis" explaining social comparison choice. Again, in evaluating our tennis-playing ability, if the people we compare with are less advantaged in their standing on related attributes, such as recent practice, physical condition, or life experience, then our superior performance is less diagnostic of ability. Ability is discounted as a likely cause of our doing better. On the other hand, if we perform better than advantaged comparison persons, for example, those with more practice, then augmentation comes into effect and we might infer that our performance is caused by a very high level of ability. And the reverse reasoning applies when our performance is inferior. If the other person is disadvantaged on related attributes, we augment the inference that low ability is a cause of our poor performance. If the other is advantaged, discounting applies, and we must discount our own low ability as an explanation for failure.

What do these considerations imply about comparison choice? Simply put, we can always learn something by comparing performances with someone who is similar on related attributes. If we compare with someone who is dissimilar, that is, more advantaged or disadvantaged, there is some chance of learning a great deal, but typically the outcome—doing better than someone who is less advantaged and worse than someone who is more advantaged—is ambiguous. If we are truly interested in evaluating our abilities as Festinger suggests, we should compare our performances with others who are similar on related attributes.

Can the same analysis be applied to the comparison of opinions? Goethals and Darley (1977) argued that it could be. However, a key distinction needs to be made between beliefs (potentially verifiable statements about the true nature of an entity) versus attitudes (people's liking or disliking for a broad range of entities, including people, ideas, policies, activities, foods, and objects) (Bem, 1970). In addition, we need to consider the third of Kelley's key attribution principles: the *covariation principle* (Kelley, 1967, 1972). The covariation principle states that an effect will be attributed to the causes that are present when the effect is present and absent when the effect is absent. In the case of beliefs, two plausible causes are the entity about which the belief is held and the person holding the belief. For example, consider a voter who believes that a politician is lying. It might be that the voter has accurately penetrated the politician's persona and that her opinion is an accurate reflection of the politician's dishonesty. Or, it may be that she is biased in her view of the politician. Kelley specified three variables that should be considered in making either an entity attribution (the lying politician caused this belief) or a person attribution (the voter's bias caused this belief). These three variables are distinctiveness, consistency, and consensus. Responses, including beliefs about entities, co-vary with the entity and thus are attributed to the entity if a person's responses to them are distinctive, consistent, and consensual. In the case of the voter believing that the politician is lying, her response will be attributed to the entity, that is, seen as correct, if the voter judges this politican as lying but not all politicians as lying (her response is distinctive), if she believes he is lying every time she hears his voice (her response is consistent), and if other people think he is a liar (her response is consensual). The key dimension for the social comparison of opinions is consensus. In general, we can more confidently attribute our response to the entity we are judging if other people agree with our appraisal. If others disagree, we are more likely to suspect that our belief is person caused and reflects some kind of bias.

But social comparison is more than just considering agreement or disagreement. Just as in the case of ability comparison we consider standing on related attributes to interpret performance differences, for belief comparison we think people's beliefs are affected by their personal attributes. A range of personal characteristics might be considered related attributes. People might think that beliefs are affected by a person's values, interests, needs, or experience. We know, for example, that people expect that others who are similar in the way they think about people to make the same interpersonal judgments (Goethals, 1972). What does this imply about the significance of agreement or disagreement? If a similar person agrees with us, perhaps their agreement reflects the fact that they share the same bias as we do, not that both of us are correct. The potentially biasing personal characteristic is a plausible cause for both of our opinions, and so true discernment must be discounted. In Kelley's (1972) terms, it might be that both our own opinion and the other's are person caused. However, if someone who was dissimilar on related attributes agrees, it is far less likely that he or she shares the same personal bias. Their agreement provides a correction for our own bias, a comforting triangulation of our judgment, even though they could be equally wrong for a different reason. These considerations combine to suggest that we should be more certain of our beliefs if dissimilar people agree than if similar people agree, and that we should show interest in comparing with dissimilar people when beliefs are at issue. Studies by Crano and his colleagues support this argument (Gorenflo & Crano, 1989; Crano & Hannula-Bral, 1994). At the same time, disagreement from similar others is likely to be more influential than disagreement from dissimilar others. When dissimilar others disagree, it is likely that we will view their opinions rather than our own as biased. Dismissal on the basis of bias is more difficult for people who are similar.

A different set of concerns arises in comparisons for attitudes, that is, judgments involving evaluative assessments of entities. Here people are not concerned with the true objective qualities of an entity but whether they like it or should or would like it. There is a general expectation that similar others will agree and dissimilar others disagree. In fact, agreement from dissimilar others might produce troubling dissonance rather than reassuring triangulation (Berscheid, 1966; Goethals, 1972). Our prediction is that people will be more influenced by similar others in the case of attitudes or subjective judgments, and that there will be more interest in comparing with similar others in the case of attitudes than in the case of beliefs (Goethals & Nelson, 1973; Gorenflo & Crano, 1989).

The discussion above illustrates how a social comparer might think about comparing with people who are similar or dissimilar on related attributes in order to accurately evaluate their ability or opinion. There are a number of studies that show that people do compare with people who are similar on related attributes (Gastorf & Suls, 1978; Miller, 1982; Wheeler & Koestner, 1984; Wheeler, Koestner, & Driver, 1982) and sometimes show interest in the opinions of dissimilar others (Goethals, 1972; Goethals, Darley, & Kriss, 1978; Goethals & Zanna, 1979; Gorenflo & Crano, 1989; Reckman & Goethals, 1973). These studies reveal a rational side to social comparison that takes advantage of the fundamental principles of attribution formulated by Kelley (1972). From the outset, however, social comparison was recognized as being far from a disinterested process. We will turn now to discuss how concerns other than the motivation to objectively evaluate opinions and abilities figure into the social comparison process. We will do this first within the attributional framework for social comparison spelled out by Goethals and Darley, and then within a more general "social construction" approach.

Self-Validation and Social Comparison

Festinger's (1954) original statement of social comparison theory considered concerns other than self-evaluation somewhat more than is generally acknowledged. For example, Festinger talked about derogation and hostility as possible consequences of cessation of comparison, especially in the realm of opinion comparison. Also, Festinger discussed the importance of society segmenting itself into smaller groups of similar people to allow for self-evaluation but also to protect self-esteem. Here he noted that by associating primarily with similar others, members of lower-status groups can "relatively ignore the differences and compare themselves with their own group" (1954, p. 136). However, the most important principle touching on considerations besides self-evaluation was Festinger's important hypothesis IV, the "unidirectional drive upward in the case of abilities" (Festinger, 1954, p. 124). People want their abilities to be good. They want to do more than discover how good they are. In fact, it is not much of a stretch to infer from the statement that "incorrect opinions and/or inaccurate appraisals of one's abilities can be punishing or even fatal" to think that people would have a strong preference for information that suggests that their opinions are correct and their abilities are good. Would these preferences for self-validational comparison information, as contrasted with self-evaluational comparison information, creep into the social comparison process in some way? Would they affect how we seek comparison information, how we choose it, or even how we interpret it? That is, would concerns with self-validation perturb an essentially rational, disinterested social comparison process? We will consider both abilities and opinions.

Self-Validation and Ability Comparison

How might the desire to have a very high level of ability and the desire to perceive oneself as having a high level affect the way we seek and interpret social comparison information? First, people should be more likely to compare with others who are disadvantaged on attributes related to performance relative to people who are advantaged. Disadvantaged others are likely to perform less well than ourselves. Although the inferior performance of a disadvantaged other may be discountable in line with Kelley's attribution principle of discounting, the fact that one's performance is better may possibly be attributable to superior ability. There is ambiguity, but the superior performance is likely to be self-validating. This is especially so if the person is able to perceive the other's standing on related attributes in a self-serving way. People's standings on related attributes may be difficult to assess and therefore easy to perceive in comforting ways. For example, one can overestimate the other's degree of recent practice, early training and education, and the quality of his or her equipment, or perhaps his or her motivation to perform well. All these nonability related attributes could have contributed to the other's performance level. The more favorably one perceives them, the more one can take pride in one's superior performance.

In addition, the person can bolster the significance of besting a disadvantaged other by doing cognitive work on one's own standing on related attributes. For example, one won the tennis match in spite of being dead tired, having a sore back, and not having played in months. Or, one studied less than one's roommate and still beat him by a point on the exam.

In short, one can think about other people's standing on related attributes strategically. One can use information about their standing to pick comparison person's and then fudge that information to make the most of the comparison outcome.

Self-Validation and Opinion Comparison

In ability comparison, one wants one's performance level to be better than other people's. In opinion comparison, one wants one's stated opinions to be the same as others. Since similar others are more likely to agree, one should turn to them first. However, in the case of beliefs, agreement from similar others might be discountable if they are matched on related attributes and therefore likely to share similar biases. Still, the person wanting to believe that he is correct could likely work more easily with agreement from a similar person than disagreement from a dissimilar person to convince himself that he is correct. One way would be to convince oneself that the agreeing others are actually more different from oneself than it first appears, and that the agreeing consensus is actually quite broad and heterogeneous. In the case of attitudes, one might not be so concerned about viewing agreeing others as somewhat different. In this case, it seems that similar others are both the best way to evaluate one's opinions and the most likely to support them.

Perceptions of the Magnitude and Diversity of Social Support

As discussed in Goethals and Darley (1977), the considerations above lead to two specific predictions. First, "the individual concerned with validating an opinion is interested in discovering that his opinions are the same as those of others" (p. 276). That is, when people want to believe that their opinions are correct, they want to believe that others agree with them. That agreement provides validation for their opinions. Perhaps as a result of the wish to believe that others agree, they simply adopt the belief that they do so. Second, people "would like to view as broad and varied whatever consensus there is supporting" their belief (p. 277). This allows them not to discount the entity as a cause for their opinion, since no shared bias provides a plausible alternative explanation. That is, they would like to discover or imagine the supporting consensus for their opinion as quite diverse and heterogeneous, especially in comparison to the group that disagrees with them. Perhaps as a result of that wish they simply adopt the belief that many different kinds of people share their beliefs, and that those who disagree are narrow and heterogeneous.

What evidence is there that people do believe that consensus is high for their opinions and that it is broad? Two major bodies of evidence have emerged that strongly support these predictions from the attributional analysis of social comparison. While they grow out of other research traditions and have generated considerable controversy as to their best explanations, the findings themselves have been very clear. First, people do overestimate the extent to which others agree with them. Just why this is so is not clear (see Chapter 16, this volume). Second, people do overestimate the extent to which agreeing others are diverse, while they perceive those who disagree and more generally people who are in out-groups as homogeneous. The second of these findings ties quite closely to the attributional approach to social comparison we are considering here. We will discuss it now. We will return to the first finding—that people overestimate consensus—in a later portion of the chapter.

In-Group Heterogeneity Effects

Taking a position that is shared by many others may be comforting. However, if those others are particularly similar, such a situation creates attributional difficulties because the presence of consensus may be seen as deriving from one or more common personal charac- teristics held by this opinion group. Feminists who believe that lying under oath about an adulterous affair constitutes sufficient grounds for impeachment from political office might not want to believe their view is a "feminist" view, but rather a more general view held by many types of individuals. Otherwise, their opinion may be perceived by themselves and others as person caused, following Kelley's (1967) covariation logic. Indeed, speakers who take positions allied with their personal beliefs and affiliations are viewed as less credible (Crowley & Hoyer, 1994; Koeske & Crano, 1968).

One may reason, then, that individuals holding a given opinion will judge the diversity of others holding a similar opinion to be greater than the diversity of those who hold the opposite opinion. Goethals, Allison, and Frost (1979) tested this prediction in three studies. Undergraduates reported their opinions about sexism, about the performance of then-President Jimmy Carter, and about divestment from holdings in South Africa, and then estimated the percentage of their peers who shared these views and those who did not. Moreover, participants indicated how diverse these two groups were (using both implicit and explicit measures). As expected, participants on one side of any given topic estimated the percentage of others holding this view to be higher than did participants holding the opposite view, providing another demonstration of people's tendency to see many others as agreeing with them. Importantly, participants also rated their opinion group as relatively more diverse. For example, in the first study, supporters of the women's movement estimated that approximately 19 different types of people (among 28 types including artistic, athletic, and religious) also endorsed the women's movement. However, those not supporting the movement estimated that approximately 14 types did so. The findings were unrelated to the absolute size of the opinion group; they were true for majorities and minorities alike, illustrating that perceptions of diverse support are not the property of large or small groups.

Additional supportive evidence that people perceive greater diversity among consensual others may be found in the literature on stereotyping. Members of groups generally view their own groups (in-groups) as more variable than members of other groups (out-groups), a tendency referred to as the "out-group homogeneity effect." This tendency has been demonstrated across many different groups using many disparate measures, though judgments are usually about a group's intelligence or likeability (Linville & Fischer, 1998) rather than its opinions. A variety of information-processing explanations has been offered for the out-group homogeneity effect, including less familiarity with the out-group, reduced exposure to exemplars than prototypes in the out-group, and enhanced need to make differentiations among members of one's in-group (for review, see Linville & Fischer, 1998).

Information-processing explanations do not tell the whole story. For example, Brewer (1993) argues that the effect also may arise from a motivation to attain self-identity and differentiation from others. Indeed, some studies are difficult to interpret from an information-processing perspective, such as one by Perdue (1983) which showed that when participants had their picture randomly placed on a pile of other people's pictures, they divided the pile into a larger number of categories than they did other piles. In our view, one of several motives that may be present when judging the variability of in-groups and out-groups is to see one's own opinions as mirroring a diverse consensus [although it is important to note that in-group heterogeneity is weaker than out-group homogeneity (Mullen & Hu, 1989)].

The argument that people see consensual others as diverse in order to sidestep a person-based attribution about their opinion leads to another prediction: That individuals will perceive their expressions of an attitude to be unrelated to any enduring personality attributes. Although this idea has not been tested directly, it is consistent with recent findings by Linville, Fischer, and Yoon (1996). These authors found that people perceive stronger relations (i.e., greater covariance) among the attributes of out-groups than of in-groups (dubbed the "out-group covariation effect"). In other words, if I know that an out-group possesses a certain shared attribute, I will be more confident in inferring that this group possesses other related attributes than I would if attempting to make a similar judgment about my own group. For example, suppose it is my perception that members of group X are against pumping a federal budget surplus into Medicare, but that I support the Medicare plan. I might infer that members of group X are also selfish, ultra-conservative, and against equal rights for gays and disabled individuals. Yet I may be less likely to infer covariation between my support for the Medicare plan and these other dimensions. Similarly, people may be less willing to infer covariation between attitudes and personality attributes among a consensual in-group than they would for an out-group.

We do not wish to argue that people will perceive greater diversity among others who share their opinion under all circumstances. In some cases, person-based attributions for one's personal attitudes may be considered desirable. A physician who maintains that a given medical practice is efficacious will feel more confident in the validity of his or her attitude if a select sample—other physicians—holds this attitude than if the attitude is also held by a number of other groups who do not possess the educational acumen to make a credible judgment. It is likely that the physician's patients will feel this way as well. Researchers already have highlighted several conditions that may promote perceptions of in-group homogeneity, such as when making variability judgments on dimensions that are central to group membership (Simon, 1992).

CONSTRUCTIVE SOCIAL COMPARISON

Thus far we have discussed the work that has grown out of the attributional approach to social comparison processes discussed by Goethals and Darley in 1977. That approach highlights the fact that comparers think in terms of their similarity to others on attributes related to their performances and opinions. They choose to compare with other people on the basis of that similarity, and they assess the meaning of relative performance levels and degree of opinion concordance in terms of that same similarity. While social comparison is often concerned with truly evaluating personal characteristics, sometimes self-serving motives come into play and lead people to think about similarity on related attributes in biased ways. Thus, for example, people tend to perceive people in their own groups as more diverse than those who belong to other groups, who in turn are perceived as relatively homogeneous.

The attributional approach emphasizes the seeking and interpretation, sometimes biased and sometimes not, of information about specific other people's performance levels and opinions. However, in recent years social comparison theorists have emphasized the possibility that self-evaluation through social comparison can actually take place without any real social comparison information. Rather than dealing with actual comparison data, people might simply imagine or make up information about what others are like; about how they might perform and what they might think. Instead of dealing with the real thing, people just might construct social data about others' thoughts and actions. For example, we can devise predictions about how jurors are going to decide a case; construct beliefs about how people feel about a political issue, a piece of music, or a new car; or make up assessments about how many of them can sail a boat or play bridge as well as we can. Suls (1986) referred to this kind of thinking as producing self-generated social comparison information that might preempt reality-based comparison data. He noted that in many instances "in-the-head" comparison data might be used rather than actual information. Similarly, Goethals (1986) discussed the ways people fabricate and ignore social reality. When people are interested in reassuring self-validation rather than truly evaluating their opinions and abilities, they might both ignore social comparison information that is available and make up information that is not. In the same vein, Orive (Orive, 1988; Gerard & Orive, 1987) discussed "implicit comparison" based on self-generated information about other people's opinions. Taylor, Buunk, and Aspinwall (1990) noted that "people have the cognitive capacity to manufacture" comparison persons. Finally, Wood (1989) suggested that "social comparison often may be a process of *construction*," again meaning that comparison data can be fabricated.

This cluster of ideas suggests that in addition to comparison based on real information, there is an entire world of *constructive* social comparison based on people's thoughts about others, thoughts that may have anywhere from an imperfect relation to social reality to no relation at all. Let us explicitly distinguish constructive from realistic social comparison and then more fully discuss the origins of the idea of constructive social comparison. Goethals, Messick, and Allison (1991) defined realistic social comparison as "self-appraisal based on using and analyzing actual information about social reality." In contrast, constructive social comparison was defined as "self-appraisal based on 'in-the-head' social comparison based on guess, conjecture, or rationalization" about social reality that is often believed (Goethals et al., 1991, p. 154).

Related to the distinction between realistic and constructive social comparison is the distinction between objective or disinterested versus biased and self-serving social comparison. Goethals et al. (1991) noted that constructive social comparison is often self-serving and that it is "typically engaged when people want to devise esteem-maintaining views of social reality" (p. 155). Realistic social comparison, in contrast, was suggested to occur when people want objective self-appraisal. While the correlation between constructive and self-serving social comparison might be high, it should be acknowledged that it is not perfect. There may be times when people want an objective evaluation of their opinions or abilities but engage in constructive comparison to formulate that evaluation. For example, a young man might want to know whether his singing ability is good enough to perform during an "open-mike" night at a local pub. He might think about how he compares with other people, not because he wants to devise a self-serving construction of his singing ability—after all, he really does not want to make a fool of himself—but because he does not have the real comparison data he needs or it would be too costly to get it. In this case, we have an example of unbiased constructive comparison. There also may be times when people engage in realistic social comparison, using real data, in an attempt to bolster their self-image. Perhaps our aspiring rock star would enter a contest with the hope that he would perform relatively well and make the most flattering interpretation he could of his relative performance.

There might be a strong correlation between a motive for self-validation, rather than self-evaluation, and the use of constructive, rather than realistic, social comparison because it is often easier to construct a positive view of oneself without much real data. But the correlation might be imperfect for a number of reasons. First, if realistic comparison produced flattering data, then the resulting positive self-construction would be all the more meaningful. So people might be tempted to put their egos on the line in real comparison in an attempt to gain lots of positive data. Also, people might want a realistic self-evaluation, but find it easier to do in-the-head comparisons rather than in-the-field ones.

We think it is worth discussing how the notion of constructive comparison fits with Festinger's early thinking about social comparison and also fits with extensions of social comparison theory that have appeared in the decades following the original formulation.

Origins of Constructive Social Comparison

It is notable that Festinger's 1954 presentation of social comparison theory gave no hint that he believed comparison processes were in any way biased. However, within 2 years Festinger first proposed the highly influential theory of cognitive dissonance, a theory that was based on his insights about people constructing self-justifying beliefs about reality (Festinger, Riecken, & Schachter, 1956). At the time dissonance theory developed, Festinger and his colleagues had been studying rumor transmission. He was still concerned with issues of interpersonal communication, issues that had concerned him for some years, as is evident in his 1950 theory of informal social communication and in his theory of social comparison processes (Festinger, 1950, 1954). Festinger puzzled as to why people in India who lived near but outside areas that had been devastated by earthquakes were spreading rumors about further disasters that might affect them. Why should they spread fear-arousing rumors? His insight was that the rumors were not actually fear arousing. People were already frightened. Rather, the rumors were fear justifying (Festinger, 1975). People were scared, but there was nothing really to be scared about. By making up rumors, they justified their fear. This insight led Festinger to propose the general idea that people have to have cognitions to fit their feelings, and then to the idea that they had to have cognitions to justify their behavior, and finally to the general idea that there is discomfort, or dissonance, when thoughts do not fit. In that case, there is pressure to "make them fit" (Festinger, 1975).

Thus the theory of cognitive dissonance quite explicitly generates the idea that people will engage in "fabricating and ignoring social reality" (Goethals, 1986). The rumor studies Festinger reviewed (e.g., Prasad, 1950) show that people will fabricate cognitions to justify their fears. And Festinger (Festinger, 1957; Festinger et al., 1956) also suggested that people will forget dissonant cognitions or try to deny them. For example, Festinger (1957) noted that people will "set up quick defensive processes" to prevent dissonant cognitions "from ever becoming firmly established" (p. 137).

In short, while Festinger's 1954 theory of social comparison processes does not contain the roots of the notion of constructive social comparison, had it been published 2 years after rather than 2 years before the first treatment of dissonance theory, it might have looked very different. It almost surely would have suggested the inventive ways that people fabricate or ignore social reality.

Extensions of Social Comparison Theory and Constructive Social Comparison

While developments associated with the theory of cognitive dissonance clearly informed the idea of constructive social comparison, subsequent work on social comparison theory also contributed to this perspective. One important new idea already has been mentioned: the idea of self-validation. This notion was discussed by several authors in the 1966 *Journal of Experimental Social Psychology* supplement issue on social comparison, including Hakmiller, Latané, Singer, and Wheeler. Subsequently, it was elaborated in some detail in Wills' important 1981 paper on downward comparison. A second key idea is the notion of pleasure and pain in social comparison discussed by Brickman and Bulman (1977) in the breakthrough volume entitled *Social Comparison Processes: Theoretical and Empirical Perspectives* edited by Suls and Miller. Brickman and Bulman wrote that people often avoid comparison information, if they can. Sometimes it is better simply to imagine how one compares rather than engage in the real thing. Linked to the idea of pleasure and pain in social comparison is the idea that comparison is often forced. We cannot always control whether we compare or with whom we compare (Allen & Wilder, 1977; Mettee & Smith, 1977; Miller, 1983). Together these ideas suggest that we care about the implications of social comparison and we avoid unpleasant comparison if we can. But in the absence of real comparison we find it tempting to construct a social reality in which we are a star player.

In the pages that follow we will discuss briefly several lines of research that illustrate constructive social comparison at work: research on false consensus effects, the uniqueness bias, constructive changes in the self-concept based on information about others, and constructive social comparison related to complementary conceptions of self and others.

False Consensus

The knowledge or perception that one or two other people share our preferences, even if those individuals are similar, is unlikely to inspire in us a sense of normative "correctness." One hopes to know where *most* similar others stand, a goal that may derive from an intuitive understanding of the unreliability of small samples (Nisbett, Krantz, Jepson, & Kunda, 1983). In some cases, consensus information is readily available. American readers of *Newsweek* and *Time* can learn on a regular basis what percentage of their fellow citizens (sometimes citizens of their same age, race, and sex) support the President, endorse the death penalty, and patronize fast-food establishments. In most cases, however, consensus information is not available, allowing for the goal of self-validation to construct estimates of consensus in a biased manner.

The classic work by Ross, Greene, and House (1977) illustrates the tendency for people to perceive relatively more consensus for their actions, preferences, and beliefs than other people perceive. In their most well-known study, participants who agreed to wear an unattractive, cumbersome sign advertising a local restaurant were found to give higher estimates (than those who refused) of the number of their peers who would do the same. Dozens of studies have illustrated this phenomenon across many domains. In a recent study, for instance, female college students who were sexually active estimated higher levels of peer sexual activity than did students who were not sexually active (Whitley, 1998).

Despite (or perhaps because of) the elegant simplicity of such findings and the methodology behind them, it has been difficult to achieve a firm understanding of the false consensus effect. (The controversial nature of false consensus is beyond the scope of this chapter, and the reader is referred to Chapter 16, this volume, for a more detailed treatment.) One early review of the literature (Marks & Miller, 1987) offered several antecedents of false consensus, and concluded that while no one might be considered necessary and sufficient, combinations of antecedents may occur in different situations. More recent analyses (e.g., Krueger, 1998; Dawes & Mulford, 1996) debate the propriety of calling this tendency a bias. These authors argue that higher estimates of consensus among individuals endorsing an item may simply reflect a dispassionate (though egocentric) attempt at induction from a sample of one (namely one's own standing on a dimension). Interestingly, this interpretation turns social comparison on its head in that it addresses the manner in which people make judgments of others based on self-knowledge, or what Felson (1993) aptly describes as "reverse social comparison." Dunning and colleagues (Chapter 17, this volume; Beauregard & Dunning, 1998) have argued that many social perception activities (including social comparison) ultimately derive from a motive to assess oneself favorably. Finally, it is also possible that people are aware of the influence of others on their own self-appraisals (as a consequence of social comparison, perhaps), and thus infer logically that others share their beliefs, preferences, and behaviors.

False or not, the false consensus effect is a highly robust finding, as shown in a metaanalysis of 115 tests (Mullen et al., 1985). We know much less, however, about how the motive to perceive consensus interacts with other motives. For example, we also are motivated to simplify and predict the world, and one consequence of this motive is that we attribute others' behaviors to their dispositions (Jones, 1990). The motive to perceive consensus and the motive to maintain predictability can conflict with each other if other people behave in a manner that violates the attitude we share with them. Suppose that I believe capital punishment is a deterrent, and that I perceive wide consensus regarding this opinion. I then read that many people castigated the state of Texas for executing a woman on death row who had become a born-again Christian. I may conclude that these individuals behaved hypocritically, which maintains my perception of consensus. However, I cannot make a dispositional attribution for their behavior (given that I do not believe their behavior corresponds with their attitude), which in turn reduces my ability to predict their later behavior. Future research might consider how people cope with the conflicting motives in such situations.

Pluralistic Ignorance

Another example of constructive social comparison derives from an interesting disparity in the literature. Research on the false consensus effect suggests that we may see relatively more consensus for our opinions, thereby assuring ourselves of the "accuracy" of our opinions through social comparison. Thus, the motivation to assess consensus for one's opinions is met with a complementary motivation to see consensus where it may not exist. However, another line of work presents what seems to be a different picture. In a variety of situations, people perceive *less* than the actual consensus for their attitudes, often leading to unusual consequences. For example, research on bystander intervention shows that individuals underestimate consensus regarding the belief that a given situation requires intervention (Latané & Darley, 1970). Similarly, college students often overestimate the percentage of their peers who engage in binge drinking and believe their peers are more comfortable with alcohol norms on campus than they really are (e.g., Prentice & Miller, 1993). As many professors have witnessed, students also overestimate the extent to which their peers comprehend material presented in class lectures, inferring that others' lack of interruption reflects genuine understanding of what is being presented. Fearing a violation of the norm, students respond to these perceptions by drinking more alcohol at parties and asking fewer questions in class. The explanation usually given for this phenomenon, called pluralistic ignorance, is that people infer that others have different motives or attitudes underlying identical behaviors (Katz & Allport, 1931; Miller & McFarland, 1987; Schanck, 1932).

Why is it that people perceive low consensus in these situations, contrary to the research on false consensus? This disparity may have something to do with the consequences of holding inaccurate beliefs. In many situations, holding an incorrect belief about others' attitudes can make us look foolish. As a result, we may fear inaccurate perceptions of consensus, and this fear may boomerang into overly conservative consensus estimates. It also is the case that when we infer others' attitudes from their behavior, we are biased toward dispositional causes (Jones, 1990). Thus, when we see bystanders failing to act, we assume that they do not perceive the situation as an emergency, and when students see others drinking heavily, they assume this drinking to reflect dispositional interest in such a pattern of drinking (rather than a calculated response to peer pressure). The correspondence bias here may be exacerbated by the power of vivid information; in the case of alcohol, binge drinkers and their behaviors are more salient and more memorable than are moderate drinkers and their behaviors. At parties where there are many binge drinkers creating many disruptions, students who have concerns about alcohol abuse may be *especially* likely to infer that their concerns are not consensual. What is happening here is that vivid behavior is *decreasing* perceptions of consensus, because others' behavior is believed to reflect underlying attitudes that are different than those of the perceiver: I am drinking a lot of alcohol to fit in (despite having some reservations about doing so), and they are drinking a lot because that is how much they intrinsically and unhesitatingly want to drink.

In short, our fear of inaccurately estimating consensus (which can lead to embarrassment) and our tendency to miss the situational demands influencing others' behaviors may lead us to see less consensus for our attitudes than we should. At present, no studies have systematically addressed variables that may determine whether one engages in false consensus or participates in pluralistic ignorance, so there are likely other reasons to explain this disparity.

False Uniqueness

While there may often be a desire to see consensus as broad, so that one can feel that one's opinions are correct, or more generally that one's decisions and actions are an appropriate response to the objective environment, there may be times when people want to underestimate consensus. Such underestimation of consensus has been referred to as "false uniqueness" (Goethals, 1986).

The source of the desire to underestimate consensus is linked to social comparison theory in an important article by Marks (1984) entitled "Thinking One's Abilities Are Unique and One's Opinions Are Common." Recall Festinger's hypothesis of a "unidirectional drive upward for ability." People want their abilities to be good. While for opinions they may want others to agree, for abilities they want their own performances to be superior. For that reason they may tend to think that few other people could perform at the same level that they perform. They may underestimate consensus when asked to judge how many people could accomplish what they have accomplished. Marks' (1984) study and work by Campbell (1986) support this idea.

However, the "unidirectional drive upward" may exist for personal attributes other than ability. People want their abilities to be at a high level for two reasons. First, it is highly adaptive to have abilities and be able to perform well. Second, having abilities brings social approval and status. High ability levels are socially desirable. But there are other personal characteristics that have high social desirability. We value cooperation, honesty, bravery, kindness, fairness, and morality. Should not we expect people to underestimate consensus for behaviors that reflect such desirable qualities? Should they not want to see these qualities, as well as their abilities, as unique?

Research reported by Goethals (1986) shows that people do underestimate consensus for a range of desirable behaviors. In one study behaviors were presented hypothetically, such as whether one would help an elderly couple stranded in the rain with a flat tire. Subjects who said that they would stop to help actually underestimated the number of their peers who would do the same. In several other studies, subjects were asked to estimate consensus for actual desirable behaviors, such as the percent of their peers who would volunteer to give blood in a Red Cross blood drive or play cooperatively in a Prisoner's Dilemma game. In these studies, subjects who performed these desirable behaviors themselves underestimated consensus.

In sum, while the false consensus effect is quite robust—people who perform certain actions or hold certain opinions give higher estimates of the percent of their peers who do these things than do people who think or act differently—this does not mean that people always overestimate consensus. Underestimations, or false uniqueness effects, are as robust as false consensus. Over- or underestimation is quite easily predicted by the social desirability of the behavior (Mullen & Goethals, 1990). To paraphrase Marks (1984), people see their good behaviors as unique and their bad behaviors as common. When it really is not clear whether their behavior is good or bad, they overestimate as well. Perhaps such overestimation convinces people that their opinions or behavior are highly consensual and therefore socially desirable. It is only when the social desirability is clear that people underestimate consensus.

The Uniqueness Bias: On Being Better than Average

The other side of the coin of people's tendencies to underestimate consensus for desirable action is to overestimate consensus for undesirable actions. The latter tendency is shown strongly in the studies reported by Goethals (1986). This finding is entirely consistent with the idea that people want to feel that their actions are appropriate. Even if those behaviors are not particularly admirable, they are performed widely and in that sense may be "not so bad." These two tendencies—to underestimate desirable behaviors and overestimate undesirable behaviors—combine to lead the population as a whole to seriously underestimate the percent of people willing and able to perform socially desirable behaviors. Goethals et al. (1991) reported a number of studies that showed that people's estimates of the percentage of their peers who would or could perform a range of socially desirable behaviors was considerably lower than the actual percent who indicated that they would or could perform the behavior. For example, in one study 80% of high school juniors said, yes, they could solve a hard problem. However, the average estimate these students gave of the percent of their peers who could solve a hard problem was 38%. In another study, 51% of college students said that they would leave the larger of two pieces of pizza for their friend rather than eat it themselves. However, the average estimate these students gave of the percent of their peers who would leave the larger piece is 35% (Goethals, 1986). The overall peer estimate obscures the false consensus effect that exists in many of these data. For example, in the pizza example, the people who say they would leave the larger piece estimate that 38% of their peers would leave the larger piece. However, the students who said they would not leave the larger piece estimated that 31% would leave the larger piece. The difference showing that those who would leave the larger piece give a higher estimate of that behavior than those who would not leave the larger piece is the classic false consensus effect. But, as suggested above, this effect does not mean that people consistently overestimate the percent of others who would act as they do. The people who would leave the larger piece actually underestimate the actual percent of people who would act as they do. In contrast, the people who would not leave the larger piece do overestimate the percent who would act as they do. In this way, both groups underestimate the proportion of people who would perform the socially desirable action, leaving the larger piece. The group that does the socially desirable action thinks that that action is rare. The group that does the undesirable action thinks that that action is common. As stated above, we think concerns with comparing favorably with others drive both the overestimate by those who would perform the undesirable action and the underestimate by those who would perform the desirable action.

Research on the uniqueness bias, the tendency for groups as a whole to underestimate the frequency of socially desirable behavior, shows that the magnitude of the bias varies with a number of important variables. One important variable is the specificity of the behavior in question (Goethals et al., 1991). The more specific and the more easily measured the behavior, the less the uniqueness bias. For example, when subjects are asked whether they could do well in a course outside their major, the uniqueness bias is stronger than when they are asked if they could get an A− in a 300-level English course. Another important variable is the domain of behavior. Four domains have been studied systematically: behaviors involving intelligence, creativity, athleticism, and morality. The uniqueness bias is strongest in the moral domain, less strong in the athletic domain, and weak or absent in the intellectual domain. People seem to feel that they are better than others, but not necessarily smarter; or, as the boxer Muhammad Ali once quipped, revealing both the general importance of social comparison and the limits even he had on perceiving himself as superior, "I only said I was the greatest, not the smartest" (Ali, 1975, p. 129).

Another important factor is gender (Goethals et al., 1991). Men generally show stronger uniqueness biases than women, although the reverse tends be true for moral items. Also, while the magnitude of an individual's tendency to perceive themselves as better than average is positively correlated with self-esteem and negatively correlated with depression, the sexes differ on the details. For example, women have a positive correlation between their self-esteem and their report of how many socially desirable behaviors they would or could do. However, there also is a positive correlation for women between their self-esteem and their estimates of consensus for desirable behaviors. For men, the latter correlation is negative. They have higher self-esteem when they think that their peers could or would perform socially desirable behaviors less often.

Constructing the Self in Social Comparison

The research on false uniqueness and false consensus reviewed above demonstrates the remarkable facility with which people can construct social reality in such a way as to validate their own standing on a dimension (see also Chapter 17, this volume). However, the focus in this research is exclusively on how people construct distorted beliefs about other individuals, usually their peers. Doing so, of course, makes the arguable assumption that perceptions of self-standing are largely fixed and that we construct consensus information with knowledge of this standing in mind. Notice that this assumption deviates significantly from Festinger's original explication of the motive behind social comparison, which was to use information about others in order to arrive at judgments about self-standing.

We know, of course, that self-standing on a variety of dimensions is highly malleable. People alter their attitudes in order to achieve consistency with their behaviors, as shown again and again by dissonance researchers. Ross (1989) has demonstrated that people reconstruct beliefs about their past standing on a dimension in ways that confirm their theories about self-change. For example, people theorize that their skills improve over time, leading such individuals to derogate their past performance below a threshold that objective measures would consider appropriate (Conway & Ross, 1984). Even subtle manipulations can alter perceptions of self-standing. For example, individuals may consider their risk of having a health problem to be higher when asked to list three risk factors than when asked to list eight, presumably due to reliance on an ease of recall heuristic (Rothman & Schwarz, 1998).

It seems reasonable to expect that, in attempts to achieve favorable social comparisons, the construction of social reality may focus on the self. This may be particularly true when the ability to construct beliefs about social consensus is constrained. In a test of this idea, Klein and Kunda (1993) presented college students with consensus information indicating how often their same-sex peers engaged in potentially problematic behaviors such as eating greasy food and getting anxious. In pilot studies, the authors had found standard false uniqueness effects: participants believed that they engaged in these behaviors less often than their peers. However, the experimental manipulation challenged these exaggerated beliefs. Now that construction of others was more difficult, participants responded by reconstructing the self: they revised estimates of how often they engaged in the behaviors in what seemed to be an attempt to preserve their belief in superiority.

Moreover, when another group of participants was given fabricated consensus information suggesting that their peers engaged in the behaviors even less than in the above condition, participants revised their self-estimates still more. In two follow-up studies, Klein (1996) found that participants may even engage in memory distortion of their prior beliefs so as not to appear as if reconstruction has occurred. They also might begin to alter their perceptions of the importance of these behaviors so that being superior is no longer considered essential. Rothman, Klein, and Weinstein (1996) found that people also may reduce their estimates of personal risk upon hearing actuarial information about the risk faced by people in their age group.

Self-reconstruction may occur in domains other than risk. In two studies (Klein & Goethals, 1999, unpublished manuscript), participants learned how many of their peers endorsed a variety of athletic (e.g., "could catch ten frisbees in a row"), creative (e.g., "could learn how to paint with watercolors"), intellectual (e.g., "could complete 80% of the New York Times Sunday crossword puzzle"), and moral behaviors (e.g., "would give up one's seat on a crowded bus for a pregnant woman"). In response to this consensus information, participants endorsed more of the items than a no-information control group. Participants were especially likely to endorse more of the items that appeared early in the questionnaire (independent of domain), suggesting a strategic attempt to restore perceptions of superiority quickly. Also, participants even endorsed items that were considered high in difficulty and low in controllability, showing again the ease with which self-reconstruction might occur in the response to challenging social comparison information. These studies show that the construction of social reality can occur on both ends of a social comparison.

Constructing the Self versus Constructing Others

We now have reviewed evidence to suggest that people not only construct illusory and self-serving perceptions of other people (Goethals et al., 1991), but also of themselves (Klein & Goethals, 1999, unpublished manuscript; Klein & Kunda, 1993). No research up until now, however, has addressed the tension between constructing the self and constructing social reality. In many cases, such a tension may not exist because one piece of information is clear and highly accessible, making distortions of the other source necessary if one is to achieve a desirable comparison. For example, if Jack earns $40,000, he will find it easier to construct distorted perceptions of how much other employees make than he will to convince himself that he earns more (or less) than $40,000. Alternatively, if Jack learns that the average tennis player in his ability class double faults only 10% of the time, Jack may attempt to convince himself that he double faults no more often than that. In both cases, one source of information is unambiguous and the other is carefully manipulated to sustain a favorable comparison with others. At other times, however, we have in our possession information about ourselves and others that is ambiguous, and thus potentially modifiable in a self-serving manner. In such cases, how do we go about achieving a desirable comparison? In general, is the tendency to construct others more or less powerful than the tendency to construct the self?

Festinger's (1954) notion was that people engage in social comparison because they are uncertain of their own standing, and thus need to obtain (presumably unambiguous) information about other people in order to reduce this ambiguity. If we integrate Festinger's notion with the more recent observation that people engage in constructive social comparison in order to make favorable self-evaluations, we are left with the prediction that people might achieve the *most* comforting social comparisons when possessing ambiguous information about the self and unambiguous information about comparison others.

Klein (unpublished manuscript) tested this prediction in three studies. In the first study, participants were asked to circle as many spelling errors as they could in ten different passages (which had been edited to include a large number of such errors). Participants were then told the percentage of total errors they ostensibly had been able to detect in each passage. Some participants were given scores that were tightly clustered around 70%, making it easy for them to determine that their average score across the ten trials was in fact 70%. Another condition received scores whose mean was still 70% but which varied greatly (i.e., the standard deviation of the scores was much higher), making it more difficult to determine mean performance across the trials. Participants also received fabricated scores based on the performance of 38 fictional other participants on each of the ten trials. Again, in one condition the scores were clustered around 70%, and in another they were not. The dependent variable was how well participants believed they had performed on the spelling task relative to how the other 38 participants were said to have been in the study.

As predicted, participants made the most favorable comparative self-evaluations when their own scores varied greatly (i.e., high self-ambiguity) and the average person's scores were closely clustered around the mean (i.e., low other ambiguity). Moreover, the more positive ratings in this condition seemed to result from inflated estimates of one's own performance (i.e., constructions of self) rather than deflated estimates of the average person's performance (i.e., constructions of others). A second study replicated these findings and also showed that people show more positive affect in the high self-ambiguity/low other ambiguity condition. In fact, it was shown that affect mediates the influence of informational ambiguity on self-evaluations. Finally, a third study suggested that, all other things being equal, people who have ambiguous information about self-standing and unambiguous information about others' standing on a dimension will consider that dimension relatively more important to their self-definition.

Although more research needs to be conducted on this question, these studies begin to tell an interesting story. Evidently, when people enter social comparisons with the a priori goal of appearing superior, they prefer to have some flexibility in their self-judgments while knowing where others stand. In general, it is probably easier to create new beliefs about the self, given the wealth of information available (and the equally impressive list of strategies such as self-affirmation and self-deception that can be called on to enhance attention to positive information about the self). Moreover, in an attempt to be rational and dispassionate in their judgments (cf. Kunda, 1990), people may prefer not to create distorted perceptions of others given that such perceptions may be harder to defend. More research on the tension between self-construction and other construction is clearly needed.

CONCLUSION

In this chapter we have outlined a range of attributional and constructive processes in social comparison. Our consideration of attributional processes makes use of central principles of attribution theory to predict how people might make social comparison choices and interpret information derived from social comparison. Special attention is given to the notion that people think about the meaning of comparisons with others who are similar on related attributes. Their thoughts affect both social comparison choice and the way they interpret the results of comparison. Our consideration of constructive social comparison makes clear that there are a variety of ways that people invent social reality to help in the process of self-evaluation. Constructive processes can be especially useful when people are interested in self-validation. Such constructive processes can affect they way we think about ourselves as well as the way we think about others. There is a dynamic relationship between views of the self and views of others. In the future more thought needs to be given to movement from realistic to constructive comparison. How are they combined? How does the switching operate, taking us from one kind to the other? Consider a scene that probably occurs frequently in coffee lounges and copy rooms. A small number of employees share information about their most recent salary increases and speculate on the average increase awarded to all employees in the company. In this case, each of these individuals possesses realistic social comparison information (the specific salaries of others in their proximity) and also may engage in constructive social comparison by estimating the average increase to be lower (or the same as) their own. Which source of information will be more prominent in determining a given employee's behavioral and affective reactions to his or her latest salary increase? Little research considers the interplay of realistic and constructive social comparison, yet answers to questions like these would lead to a better understanding of social comparison. We need to understand that both types of comparison are prevalent. There is probably a fluid interplay of both. We hope future work will address their relationship.

ACKNOWLEDGMENT

Preparation of this chapter was supported by a Colby College Social Science grant (#01-2290) to William M. P. Klein.

REFERENCES

Allen, V. L., & Wilder, D. A. (1977). Social comparison, self-evaluation, and conformity to the group. In J. M. Suls & R. L. Miller (Eds.), *Social comparison processes: Theoretical and empirical perspectives* (pp. 187–200). Washington, DC: Hemisphere.

Ali, M. (1975). *The greatest: My own story.* New York: Random House.

Beauregard, K. S., & Dunning, D. A. (1998). Turning up the contrast: Self-enhancement motives prompt egocentric contrast effects in social judgments. *Journal of Personality and Social Psychology, 74,* 606–621.

Bem, D. J. (1970). *Beliefs, attitudes, and human affairs.* Pacific Grove, CA: Brooks/Cole.

Berglas, S., & Jones, E. E. (1978). Drug choice as a self-handicapping strategy in response to noncontingent success. *Journal of Personality and Social Psychology, 36,* 405–417.

Berscheid, E. (1966). Opinion change and communicator-communicatee similarity and dissimilarity. *Journal of Personality and Social Psychology, 4,* 670–680.

Brewer, M. B. (1993). Social identity, distinctiveness, and in-group homogeneity. *Social Cognition, 11,* 150–164.

Brickman, P., & Bulman, R. J. (1977). Pleasure and pain in social comparison. In J. M. Suls & R. L. Miller (Eds.), *Social comparison processes: Theoretical and empirical perspectives* (pp. 149–186). Washington, DC: Hemisphere.

Campbell, J. D. (1986) Similarity and uniqueness: The effects of attribute type, relevance, and individual differences in self-esteem and depression. *Journal of Personality and Social Psychology, 50,* 281–294.

Conway, M., & Ross, M. (1984). Getting what you want by revising what you had. *Journal of Personality and Social Psychology, 47,* 738–748.

Crano, W. D., & Hannula-Bral, K. A. (1994). Context/categorization model of social influence: Minority and majority influence in the formation of a novel response norm. *Journal of Experimental Social Psychology, 30,* 247–276.

Crowley, A. E., & Hoyer, W. D. (1994). An integrative framework for understanding two-sided persuasion. *Journal of Consumer Research, 20,* 561–574.

Dawes, R. M., & Mulford, M. (1996). The false consensus effect and overconfidence: Flaws in judgment or flaws in how we study judgment? *Organizational Behavior and Human Decision Processes, 65,* 201–211.

Felson, R. B. (1993). The (somewhat) social self: How others affect self-appraisals. In J. Suls (Ed.), *Psychological perspectives on the self: The self in social perspective* (Vol. 4, pp. 1–26). Hillsdale, NJ: Lawrence Erlbaum.

Festinger, L. (1950). Informal social communication. *Psychological Review, 57,* 271–282.

Festinger, L. (1954). A theory of social comparison processes. *Human Relations, 7,* 117–140.

Festinger, L. (1957). *A theory of cognitive dissonance.* Stanford, CA: Stanford University Press.

Festinger, L. (1975). An interview with Leon Festinger, Charles Harris (Ed.). [Audio tape]. Scranton, PA: Harper & Row Media Program (Distributor).

Festinger, L., Riecken, H., & Schachter, S. (1956). *When prophecy fails.* Minneapolis: University of Minnesota Press.

Gastorf, J. W., & Suls, J. (1978). Performance evaluation via social comparison: Performance similarity versus related-attribute similarity. *Social Psychology, 41,* 297–305.

Gerard, H. B., & Orive, R. (1987) The dynamics of opinion formation. In L. Berkowitz (Ed.), *Advances in experimental social psychology* (Vol. 20, pp. 171–202). San Diego, CA: Academic Press.

Goethals, G. R. (1972). Consensus and modality in the attribution process: The role of similarity and information. *Journal of Personality and Social Psychology, 21,* 84–92.

Goethals, G. R. (1986). Fabricating and ignoring social reality: Self-serving estimates of consensus. In J. M. Olson, C. P. Hermann, & M. P. Zanna (Eds.), *Relative deprivation and social comparison.* The Ontario Symposium (Vol. 4. pp. 135–157). Hillsdale, NJ: Lawrence Erlbaum.

Goethals, G. R., Allison, S. J., & Frost, M. (1979). Perceptions of the magnitude and diversity of social support. *Journal of Experimental Social Psychology, 15,* 570–581.

Goethals, G. R., & Darley, J. (1977). Social Comparison theory: An attributional approach. In J. M. Suls & R. L. Miller (Eds.), *Social comparison processes: Theoretical and empirical perspectives* (pp. 259–278). Washington, DC: Hemisphere.

Goethals, G. R., Darley, J. M., & Kriss, M. (1978). The impact of opinion agreement as a function of the grounds for agreement. *Representative Research in Social Psychology, 15,* 105–113.

Goethals, G. R., Messick, D. M., Allison, S. T. (1991). The uniqueness bias: Studies of constructive social comparison. In J. M. Suls & T. A. Wills (Eds.), *Social comparison, contemporary theory and research* (pp. 149–173). Hillsdale, NJ: Lawrence Erlbaum.

Goethals, G. R., & Nelson, R. E. (1973). Similarity in the influence process: The belief-value distinction. *Journal of Personality and Social Psychology, 25,* 117–122.

Goethals, G. R., & Zanna, M. P. (1979). The role of social comparison in choice shifts. *Journal of Personality and Social Psychology, 37,* 1469–1476.

Gorenflo, D. W., & Crano, W. D. (1989). Judgmental subjectivity/objectivity and locus of choice in social comparison. *Journal of Personality and Social Psychology, 57,* 605–614.

Hakmiller, K. L. (1966). Threat as a determinant of downward comparison. *Journal of Experimental Social Psychology, 2*(Suppl. 1), 32–39.

Heider, F. (1944). Social perception and phenomenal causality. *Psychological Review, 51,* 358–374.

James, W. (1892). *Principles of psychology* (Vol. 1). New York: Henry Holt.

Jones, E. E. (1990). *Interpersonal perception.* New York: W. H. Freeman.

Jones, E. E., Kanouse, D., Kelley, H. H., Nisbett, R. E., Valins, S., and Weiner, B. (Eds.) (1972). *Attribution: Perceiving the causes of behavior.* New York: General Learning Press.

Katz, D., & Allport, F. H. (1931). *Student attitudes: A report of the Syracuse University research study.* Syracuse, NY: Craftsman Press.

Kelley, H. H. (1967). Attribution theory in social psychology. In D. Levine (Ed.), *Nebraska symposium on motivation* (Vol. 15, pp. 192–240). Lincoln: University of Nebraska Press.

Kelley, H. H. (1972). Attribution in social interaction. In E. E. Jones, D. Kanouse, H. H. Kelley, R. E. Nisbett, S. Valins, & B. Weiner (Eds.), *Attribution: Perceiving the causes of behavior* (pp. 1–26). New York: General Learning Press.

Klein, W. M. (1996). Maintaining self-serving social comparisons: Attenuating the perceived significance of risk-increasing behaviors. *Journal of Social and Clinical Psychology, 15,* 120–142.

Klein, W. M., & Kunda, Z. (1993). Maintaining self-serving social comparisons: Biased reconstruction of one's past behaviors. *Personality and Social Psychology Bulletin, 19,* 732–739.

Klein, W. M. P. (1999). Self-evaluation, self-definition, and constructive social comparison: Effects of ambiguous and unambiguous information about self and others. Unpublished manuscript.

Klein, W. M. P., & Goethals, G. R. (1999). Social reality and self-construction: A case of "bounded irrationality?" Unpublished manuscript.

Koeske, G. F., & Crano, W. D. (1968). The effect of congruous and incongruous source-statement combinations upon the judged credibility of a communication. *Journal of Experimental Social Psychology, 4,* 384–399.

Krueger, J. (1998). On the perception of social consensus. In M. Zanna (Ed.), *Advances in experimental social psychology* (Vol. 30, pp. 164–240). New York: Academic Press.

Kunda, Z. (1990). The case for motivated reasoning. *Psychological Bulletin, 108,* 480–498.

Latané, B. (1966). Studies in social comparison—Introduction and overview. *Journal of Experimental Social Psychology, 2*(Suppl. 1), 1–5.

Latané, B., & Darley, J. M. (1970). *The unresponsive bystander: Why doesn't he help?* New York: Appleton-Century-Crofts.

Linville, P. W., & Fischer, G. W. (1998). Group variability and covariation: Effects on intergroup judgment and behavior. In C. Sedikides, J. Schopler, & C. A. Insko (Eds.), *Intergroup cognition and intergroup behavior* (pp. 123–150). Mahwah, NJ: Lawrence Erlbaum.

Linville, P. W., Fischer, G. W., & Yoon, C. (1996). Perceived covariation among the features of in-group and out-group members: An outgroup covariation effect. *Journal of Personality and Social Psychology, 70,* 421–436.

Marks, G. (1984). Thinking one's abilities are unique and one's opinions are common. *Personality and Social Psychology Bulletin, 10,* 203–208.

Marks, G., & Miller, N. (1987). Ten years of research on the false-consensus effect: An empirical and theoretical review. *Psychological Bulletin, 102,* 72–90.

Mettee, D. R., & Smith, G. (1977). Social comparison and interpersonal attraction: The case for dissimilarity. In J. M. Suls & R. L. Miller (Eds.), *Social comparison process: Theoretical and empirical perspectives* (pp. 69–101). Washington, DC: Hemisphere.

Miller, D. T. (1982). The role of performance-related similarity in social comparison of abilities: A test of the related attributes hypothesis. *Journal of Experimental Social Psychology, 18,* 513–523.

Miller, D. T. (1983). Presentation given at the Ontario Symposium on Relative Deprivation and Social Comparison. London: Ontario.

Miller, D. T., & McFarland, C. (1987). Pluralistic ignorance: When similarity is interpreted as dissimilarity. *Journal of Personality and Social Psychology, 53,* 298–305.

Mullen, B., Atkins, J. L., Champion, D. S., Edwards, C., Hardy, D., Story, J. E., & Venderklok, M. (1985). The false consensus effect: A meta-analysis of 115 hypothesis tests. *Journal of Experimental Social Psychology, 21,* 262–283.

Mullen, B., & Goethals, G. R. (1990). Social projection actual consensus, and valence. *British Journal of Social Psychology, 29,* 279–282.

Mullen, B., & Hu, L. (1989). Perceptions of ingroup and outgroup variability: A meta-analytic integration. *Basic and Applied Social Psychology, 10,* 233–252.

Nisbett, R. E., Krantz, D. H., Jepson, C., & Kunda, Z. (1983). The use of statistical heuristics in everyday inductive reasoning. *Psychological Review, 90,* 339–363.

Orive, R. (1988). Social projection and social comparison of opinions. *Journal of Personality and Social Psychology, 54,* 953–964.

Perdue, C. (1983). Perceived ingroup heterogeneity and evaluative complexity: Evidence for a bias in information acquisition. Unpublished doctoral dissertation, Princeton University, Princeton, NJ.

Prasad, J. (1950). A comparative study of rumours and reports in earthquakes. *British Journal of Psychology, 41,* 129–144.

Prentice, D. A., & Miller, D. T. (1993). Pluralistic ignorance and alcohol use on campus: Some consequences of misperceiving the social norm. *Journal of Personality and Social Psychology, 64,* 243–256.

Reckman, R. F., & Goethals, G. R. (1973). Deviancy and group orientation as determinants of group composition preferences. *Sociometry, 36,* 419–423.

Ross, L., Greene, D., & House, P. (1977). The "false consensus effect": An egocentric bias in social perception and attribution processes. *Journal of Experimental Social Psychology, 13,* 279–301.

Ross, M. (1989). Relation of implicit theories to the construction of personal histories. *Psychological Review, 96,* 341–357.

Rothman, A. J., Klein, W. M., & Weinstein, N. D. (1996). Absolute and relative biases in estimations of personal risk. *Journal of Applied Social Psychology, 26,* 1213–1236.

Rothman, A. J., & Schwarz, N. (1998). Constructing perceptions of vulnerability: Personal relevance and the use of experiential information in health judgments. *Personality and Social Psychology Bulletin, 24,* 1053–1064.

Schanck, R. L. (1932). A study of community and its group institutions conceived of as behavior of individuals. *Psychological Monographs, 43,* 1–133.

Simon, B. (1992). Intragroup differentiation in terms of in-group and out-group attributes. *European Journal of Social Psychology, 22,* 407–413.

Singer, J. E. (1966). Social comparison—Progress and issues. *Journal of Experimental Social Psychology, 2*(Suppl. 1), 103–110.

Suls, J. (1986). Notes on the occasion of social comparison theory's thirtieth birthday. *Personality and Social Psychology Bulletin, 12*, 289–296.

Taylor, S. E., Buunk, B. P., & Aspinwall, L. G. (1990). Social comparison, stress, and coping. *Personality and Social Psychology Bulletin, 16*, 74–89.

Wheeler, L. (1966). Motivation as a determinant of upward comparison. *Journal of Experimental Social Psychology, 2*(Suppl. 1), 27–31.

Wheeler, L., & Koestner, R. (1984). Performance evaluation: On choosing to know the related attributes of others when we know their performance. *Journal of Experimental Social Psychology, 20*, 263–271.

Wheeler, L., Koestner, R., & Driver, R. E. (1982). Related attributes in the choice of comparison others. *Journal of Experimental Social Psychology, 18*, 489–500.

Wheeler, L., Shaver, K. G., Jones, R. A., Goethals, G. R., Cooper, J., Robinson, J. E., Gruder, C. L., & Butzine, K. W. (1969). Factors determining choice of a comparison other. *Journal of Experimental Social Psychology, 5*, 219–232.

Wheeler, L., & Zuckerman, M. (1977). Commentary. In J. Suls & R. Miller (Eds.), *Social comparison processes* (pp. 335–357). Washington, DC: Hemisphere.

Whitley, B. (1998). False consensus on sexual behavior among college women: Comparison of four theoretical explanations. *Journal of Sex Research, 35*, 206–214.

Wills, T. A. (1981). Downward comparison principles in social psychology. *Psychological Bulletin, 90*, 245–271.

Wood, J. V. (1989). Theory and research concerning social comparisons of personal attributes. *Psychological Bulletin, 106*, 231–248.

3

Stability of Related Attributes and the Inference of Ability through Social Comparison

WILLIAM P. SMITH AND GUDMUNDUR B. ARNKELSSON

INTRODUCTION AND OVERVIEW

Festinger (1954) pointed out that a valid assessment of one's opinions and an accurate appraisal of one's ability is of great functional significance. Yet, a direct test of one's opinion or ability is often not feasible. Hence, Festinger proposed that much of what passes as valid knowledge in those realms has a social basis.

Festinger drew his logic from work on opinions and conformity, which demonstrated consensual validation and pressures toward uniformity (Festinger, 1950). He argued that subjective validity of opinion stemmed from the agreement of others, if no objective test was feasible. When uncertain, people would validate their opinions by seeking others with similar opinions. Festinger extended this logic to peoples' appraisals of their own abilities. He proposed that subjectively valid self-assessments of ability often come from social comparison rather than by engaging in tasks relevant for the ability.

The theory of social comparison processes (Festinger, 1954) has been invoked to explain a wide range of phenomena, ranging from self-assessment of emotions (e.g., Schachter, 1959; Schachter & Singer, 1962) to the goodness of wages (e.g., Levine & Moreland, 1987; Major & Testa, 1989). We shall be concerned with social comparison in the self-appraisal of ability. Of special interest are the consequences of social comparison as opposed to the strategies people use in acquiring social comparison information. The latter heretofore has been a major emphasis in social comparison research (Wood, 1989). Although we are interested in the appraisal of ability, we believe that similar processes underlie knowledge in other domains. Ability in particular can be viewed as a subset of personal dispositions (Wood, 1989). We

WILLIAM P. SMITH • Department of Psychology, Vanderbilt University, Nashville, Tennessee 37240.
GUDMUNDUR B. ARNKELSSON • Faculty of Social Sciences, University of Iceland, IS-101 Reykjavik, Iceland.

Handbook of Social Comparison: Theory and Research, edited by Suls and Wheeler. Kluwer Academic / Plenum Publishers, New York, 2000.

believe, however, that the domain of ability appraisal has a richness of meaning that researchers in social comparison have neglected.

We recognize two meanings of ability, which the social comparison literature typically does not treat separately. Ordinary day-to-day language includes those two conceptions and we argue that they lead to differences in the inference of ability. The more common meaning of ability is one of a typical level of motivated performance. A less common conception is that of a potential to benefit from training or maturation, sometimes called aptitude. We suggest that people use this latter conception only under special circumstances in ordinary life.

We also differentiate three referents of ability. Ability can be absolute with respect to a task or some class of tasks. It also can be relative with respect to either an individual or individuals or relative to a group of people. We suggest that processes of ability inference differ across different meanings and across different referents of ability.

A major focus of our discussion is on how people think about characteristics thought to influence performance level, characteristics such as practice at a task, and education (usually called performance-related attributes) in making inferences about their ability. In particular, we propose that the perceived temporal stability influences how a comparer uses a performance-related attribute in inferring ability.

Finally, we differentiate among three inferential schemata used in the appraisal of ability: a causal schema, the multiple sufficient causes schema (Kelley, 1971), and two noncausal logical schemata—a cue consistency schema and a transitivity schema. We propose that the particular schema used by a comparer in ability appraisal will depend on the ability conception he or she accesses, the stability he or she sees in any known performance related attributes, and the salient referent for the ability appraisal.

THE FESTINGER THEORY

Despite numerous problems and ambiguities, the Festinger (1954) theory has largely dominated the kinds of issues examined in the social comparison of abilities. Hence, it seems worthwhile to examine briefly those issues in the context of the original theory.

Festinger (1954) posited a drive in people to obtain subjectively valid appraisals of their opinions and of their abilities. He went on to argue for the functional significance of subjectively (and objectively) valid knowledge of the environment and one's capacities. Few contemporary social psychologists would accept a drive argument for the motivation for social comparison. Indeed, most would agree that epistemic processes are instigated for numerous reasons, only one of which is the desire for a valid picture of self or environment (Kruglanski, 1989; Smith, 1994). Nonetheless, people sometimes seek valid self-assessment. We believe it is sought when the truth about one's own ability has some adaptive significance, that is, when possession of such an appraisal is functional (Sedikides & Strube, 1995; but see Brown & Dutton, 1995, for a different view).

Specifically, we assume that valid appraisals of self or environment are sought when some decision involving the welfare of the appraiser is imminent and maximizing welfare requires valid appraisal (e.g., Jones & Regan, 1974; Harkness, DeBono, & Borgida, 1986; Wheeler, Martin & Suls, 1997). In short, there must be some "fear of invalidity" (Kruglanski, 1989) for valid appraisals to be sought. With this proviso, we assume with Festinger (1954) that uncertainty about the validity of a self-appraisal of ability motivates attempts to reduce that uncertainty. These efforts will be manifest in the seeking of social comparison when more direct routes to a subjectively valid judgment are not feasible.

The similarity hypotheses are the primary hypotheses of the Festinger theory (Latané, 1966). They state that people seek to compare with others whose abilities are similar to their own (hypothesis III, and corollary IIIA) and that in the absence of similar others, people will be uncertain in their self-appraisal of ability (corollary IIIB). Two hypotheses concern the seeking of comparison information, and much of the early work on the social comparison of abilities focused on those hypotheses (Wheeler, 1991; Wood, 1989).

As Latané (1966) points out, the two similarity hypotheses as stated are not necessarily causally related. Nevertheless, the underlying motivation for comparison is to reduce uncertainty, and comparison with similar others reduces that uncertainty. Hence, the preference for similar others is rooted in the experience of reduced uncertainty when comparing with similar rather than dissimilar others.

In retrospect, the almost exclusive focus of early research on selection of a comparison person seems odd. The fact that people seek some particular kind of information, for example, performances of similar others, need not reflect on judgmental consequences of the information or even the motivation for seeking it (Taylor, Neter, & Wayment, 1995). Yet, despite the stress on the consequences for ability judgment and the certainty of those judgments, relatively little research has addressed those consequences.

We are not concerned with the selection of comparison others, but rather with the process of ability inference after the individual has received information via social comparison. In effect, we consider cases of forced social comparison (see Goethals, 1986; Suls, 1986; Wood, 1989). However, such cases are pervasive in social life, for example, losing a tennis game to a friend or being accepted to medical school when acquaintances are known to have been rejected. Furthermore, the process of inference should be the same whether the individual seeks the information or receives it by circumstance. We further assume that the level of uncertainty following social comparison reflects the usefulness of the information, given similar levels of uncertainty to begin with. Of course, a confident inference does not translate by necessity to a valid appraisal of ability. Hence, a rational and logical process does not ensure an objectively valid appraisal of ability. Many factors, such as prior beliefs and stereotypes about social categories, can and do affect ability appraisal. Hence, the appraisal can simultaneously be rational and grievously wrong.

WHAT IS ABILITY?

We take a functional approach to the analysis of the ability concept in everyday life. With Heider (1944, 1958), we believe the functional significance of ability appraisal to be the predictability of behavior. Thus, the function of ability inferences is to predict one's fate vis-à-vis some class of tasks or some type of social context. Hence, we argue that perceivers view ability as a stable personal disposition that enables prediction and decision making.

We suggest that the ordinary use of the term "ability" in everyday language refers to the typical level of motivated performance. It follows from the essence of ability, as a stable personal disposition, that what one assesses now will be present at some future time of interest. If I seek someone with skills at multivariate analysis, I am asking who might offer good advice or a good course on such analysis today, tomorrow, and next year. Likewise, when I appraise my ability, I seek knowledge from my current performance that predicts future performance. Most of our subsequent discussion assumes such a meaning of ability.

Another use of the term ability is also quite common, though we would argue less so than ability as the typical level of motivated performance. This is the conception of ability as a potential for developing a different (usually higher) level of stable performance in the future. This conception corresponds to the words "aptitude" and "talent," that is, the potential for benefiting from training or maturation.

To contrast the two conceptions, let us consider a young woman with some particular level of competence at photography. Knowing her level of ability may help her decide whom to approach for help and what projects to attempt. Should she, for instance, join the amateur photography club or just take pictures for her own and her family's enjoyment? She may be interested in the more distant future, however, a future that will include decisions about courses and vocations. In this case, the issue is not how much skill she has presently but whether she has the potential for improving her present typical performance level. This may involve assessing the speed of acquisition for the skill or assessing the impact of possible changes in ability-related attributes such as long-term training, experience, or maturation.

On occasion, people use this second meaning of ability in a defensive, retrospective way, exemplified by the statement, "I could have been a great soccer player had I kept at it when I was a kid." This clearly has no predictive function but may well serve to create good feelings about self. Self-handicapping phenomena (Jones & Berglas, 1978) involve a more immediate defensive function. Thus, a person who values a high ability level in a given area but fears he or she may not possess it will undermine his or her performance. He or she, for instance, may resort to substance abuse to permit the self-serving belief that the performance does not reflect his or her underlying capacity. Again, this does not truly serve a predictive function for the individual. While such defensive uses of the ability concept are undoubtedly important (e.g., Brown & Dutton, 1995), our concern is with social comparison under conditions that encourage efforts to make a realistic prediction about future performances.

It is important to note that these distinctions are not explicit in the literature on social comparison of abilities. Festinger (1954) refers only to abilities, and later investigators have typically not addressed the issue. However, Darley and Goethals (1980) did make reference to "inherent" ability, which appears to be similar to the concept of aptitude, the second meaning we discuss.

REFERENTS OF ABILITY

The Festinger (1954) theory not only failed to state just what ability meant, it also was silent on the topic of the referent of ability appraisal. Yet, it is apparent that the particular referent of an ability appraisal will vary significantly, depending on the prediction goal of the appraiser. For instance, a novice runner contemplating the Boston marathon alternatively may desire to know her ability vis-à-vis (1) the task requirements of the run, (2) some specific runners, or (3) some population or group of interest.

The runner might want to know whether she can complete the 26 miles of the marathon, in order to decide whether to take the time and cost of entering the race. Here the referent is simply the task outcome itself. To borrow from Festinger's (1954) own example, one may simply wish to know whether he or she can jump over the brook successfully. If our runner is one of a group of companions traveling to the marathon, she may be interested in how able she is relative to one or more of her companions. This might be important, for example, in choosing an appropriate running partner. Here the referent of ability appraisal is an individual or individuals. Third, our runner may want to know her ability relative to all entrants to the marathon or some subset, such as women between 26 and 30. Here the referent is normative, in the sense that the appraiser wants to know how her ability compares with the average member of some population or reference group. More generally, she may desire to know her rank within a population or a group. We consider only the more restricted case, since such extensive distributional information is typically unavailable.

Ability as Typical Level of Task Outcomes

Let us consider the goal of predicting one's stable level of performance on a set of tasks in an ability domain, that is, appraising one's ability with reference to the typical outcomes one can expect from tasks in the ability domain. Can I in fact do my own income tax on my personal computer? How quickly can I run 5 miles on the campus track? While these particular questions are trivial, questions about what outcomes one can expect from a task can be of life-and-death significance: Can I swim to the sandbar and back? Can I drive my injured child to the hospital or should I wait for an ambulance? The answers to such questions not only are of significance with respect to specific tasks but they play a role in the individual's sense of self-efficacy. These are not inherently socially comparative appraisals of ability, since they refer only to the individual's own outcomes from a task. Nonetheless, information about others' task performances can be helpful in evaluating this aspect of ability, and social comparison plays an important role in how such information is used (Jones & Regan, 1974; Smith, 1984; Smith & Sachs, 1997; Wheeler et al., 1997). We shall elaborate on these issues later in our chapter.

Standing on Ability Relative to Specific Others

Clearly, knowledge of one's competence relative to another's is important in many aspects of life, from finding one's place in a working group to choosing a teacher or guide. For instance, knowing one's ability within the hierarchy of a work group is of considerable importance. It affects how the group divides work responsibilities, whose opinions get significant weight, and how both intangible rewards such as esteem and concrete rewards are awarded. In other words, knowing one's competence relative to that of other specific individuals is functionally significant in its own right, regardless of its implications for where one's ability lies in the distribution of some social category of interest.

An accountant may wish to know her command of various computer programs relative to other accountants in general, especially those with whom she competes on the job market. However, if she is to work as part of a team doing accounts for a large business, she also wants to know how she compares with specific others in her work group. The relevance of social comparison for this type of ability appraisal is obvious.

Work in expectation states theory underscores the importance of this type of ability appraisal. This theory in sociology addresses the issue of how judged relative competence affects patterns of influence and esteem in work groups (Berger, Conner, & Fisek, 1974; Berger, Wagner, & Zelditch, 1985). The bulk of research associated with the theory has demonstrated that information about the relative competencies of work group members significantly affects the influence hierarchy of the group (Berger et al., 1985). While this research does not typically assess relative competence judgments (it assumes them as intervening variables), research that has done so supports this assumption (Driskell & Mullen, 1990).

Ability Relative to a Reference Group

Most experimental studies leave the referent of social comparison undefined. Implicitly they may assess ability vis-à-vis some significant population. Commonly, participants rate their abilities on an adjective dimension. They may use an adjective rating scale (Gastorf & Suls, 1978; Radloff, 1966; Wilson, 1973), indicate "how good" (Klein, 1997) or "high"

(Alicke, LoSchiavo, Zerbst, & Zhang, 1997) they are on some ability, or how "smart," "intelligent," or "simple-minded" they may be (Brown & Dutton, 1995; Lockwood & Kunda, 1997). Intuitively, adjective measures seem to engage a comparison relative to some standard. A population or a comparison group is a prominent source of such standards. Exceeding the standard results in satisfaction with ability and performance, which may be what adjective measures are primarily assessing.

A group norm as the ultimate referent of social comparison of abilities may come naturally to a person seeking to assess his or her ability. This is consistent with the notion that social identity is an important part of our self-definition (Tajfel & Turner, 1979; Turner, Hogg, Oakes, Reicher, & Wetherell, 1987; Turner & Oakes, 1997). Hence, we gain identity partly through membership in various societal groups differentiated in terms of power, status, common expectations, and fate. Common origin or ancestry, education, occupational status, gender, and other socially important factors may loosely define these groups. The importance of such membership groups for our self-identity may result in a prevailing interest in assessing ability relative to the ability distribution within such reference groups.

Results of selection studies accentuated the prominence of social reference groups as referents for ability assessment. Generally they indicate a prevailing preference for similar others whether or not the similarity is on factors related to performance on a task (Wood, 1989). Interestingly, one finds this blind preference for similar others on such socially defining attributes as gender (Feldman & Ruble, 1981; Miller, 1984; Suls, Gaes, & Gastorf, 1979; Suls, Gastorf, & Lawhon, 1978; Zanna, Goethals & Hill, 1975) and class in school (Suls et al., 1978; Zanna et al., 1975) but not for the more neutral attribute of more or less practice (Wheeler, Koestner, & Driver, 1982). This suggests that the socially defining nature of the attribute is crucial rather than the similarity as such. Indeed, Miller (1984) offers some suggestive evidence in this regard. She showed that interest in comparing with a same-sex other was more likely for people for whom gender was an important feature of their identity than for those who found it of little importance.

Social comparison relative to a group average or distribution also may have a more direct functional value. It can be crucial for me to know my standing relative to the population, especially when I have to compete for some scarce resources. To the extent that only a selected few can reach some goal or reap the benefits from some actions, it becomes essential to know my chances of succeeding relative to other people. Hence, standing within some population must be crucial for the budding artist, the young athlete, as well as the student preparing for graduate school or sending out resumes. Some of this information has been institutionalized through the use of standardized tests like the GRE and SAT to assess academic achievement and potential. Other information, such as likely success as a businessperson, one can only gain by social comparison or through possibly bitter experience.

Choosing a Referent

In our example of the novice runner, all three referents—task outcomes, individual other, and reference group average—seem plausible. We also presume that simultaneous concern with more than one referent must be common. However, it seems obvious that they can and undoubtedly do occur singly and independently. Furthermore, it seems clear that the information required to answer a question about ability with one referent may not offer much enlightenment with respect to the other two.

Ability vis-à-vis some member of a group, for instance, does not provide any explicit information as to my standing relative to the group as a whole. While I may have some presumptions about the other, ideally I would need to know how his or her ability ranks within the group. Thus, knowing that I can typically run faster than a friend does not say much about my ability relative to the average male runner of our age. In fact, both my friend and I may be above, at, or below average in running speed. Similarly, knowing my standing relative to a group average may not predict my ability relative to some specific member; again, that particular member may be nonaverage.

A similar argument holds for task outcomes. Success or some specific outcome on a task does not inform me by itself about my ability relative to some specific individual or a group. This inference requires information on how the others did on the task. Knowing that I can run 26 miles in a stretch does not in itself allow me to infer my ability relative to a friend or the average male runner of my age.

We will address these issues in some detail later in the chapter. Our current intent is simply to delineate the different referents of ability appraisal, in preparation for a discussion of the role of social comparison in inferring ability with respect to each.

Most studies and theoretical statements have not differentiated between different referents of social comparison and experimental studies do not typically specify them. Hence, it is rarely possible to know what comparison is of interest to participants in any particular study: comparison relative to a given individual, a given or assumed population or group, or relative to the requirements of the task at hand. Further, measures that fail to specify a referent can result in uninterpretable findings. For example, if a subject completes correctly, say, three items on an intellectual task while a confederate manages seven correct items, what will an undifferentiated rating of ability refer to? Are participants assessing their three correct items out of the maximum of ten, their three items compared to the confederate's seven, or how good their ability is relative to some unspecified (but possibly implicit) group average? A few recent studies have avoided this ambiguity by obtaining self-appraisals specifically referenced to either a group or another individual (Alicke, Klotz, Breitenbecher, Yurak, & Vredenburg, 1995; Kulik & Gump, 1997).

INFERENCE OF ABILITY VIA SOCIAL COMPARISON

The original Festinger (1954) theory did not address explicitly how people infer ability from social comparison information. Indeed, it simply stated that people would be more certain in their appraisals when comparing with similar others rather than others different from them in ability. As noted earlier, Festinger did not define ability but stated that the subject matter of social comparison of abilities must be task performances, since ability is not observable. Hence, comparison with others of similar ability was translated by researchers to similarity in performance level, as was manifest in early studies of comparison preference (e.g., Wheeler, 1966). Relatively little research, especially early in the development of social comparison as a research area, actually addressed the issue of ability inference. Instead, most studies were concerned with the selection hypotheses, that is, with preferences for comparison, cast in terms of the similarity versus dissimilarity of performances.

Festinger (1954) cited the level of aspiration literature, including a study conducted specifically within the context of the theory (Dreyer, 1954), as evidence for the stated consequences of social comparison. The fundamental meaning of level of aspiration is the performance level a person expects in the future (Lewin, Dembo, Festinger & Sears, 1944). This is analogous to what we describe as ability, that is, task outcomes one can reliably obtain. Interestingly, the theory rarely refers to task outcomes relative to those obtained by others, that is, relative ability. Hence, it is far from clear that the latter was the referent of the Festinger theory, although most scholars interpreted it as such.

In their restatement of social comparison theory, Goethals and Darley (1977) directly addressed the issue of ability inference via social comparison. They were explicitly concerned with how people infer an ability difference between themselves and another or others. They were not clear, however, on the particular referent they were addressing. They pointed to the curious feature of the similarity hypotheses: that if I knew that another was similar in ability, I had already accomplished the primary aim of the comparison. Drawing on Kelley's (1971) concept of causal schemata, they assumed that people would bring some knowledge of the potentially multiple factors that may influence performance to the comparison situation. Rather than ability or performance, those factors, called performance-related attributes, would be the focus of interest in similarity.

The Role of Performance-Related Attributes

The Goethals and Darley Formulation. We gain information about ability from consistent differences in performances between self and the other. Schwartz and Smith (1976) demonstrated this for ability relative to another individual, but the same should be the case when comparing with the performance typical for a group of people. We also have beliefs about the influence of various performance-related factors, as Goethals and Darley (1977) pointed out. Those include brief practice, fatigue, acute illness, the effects of drugs and alcohol on performance, as well as educational status and occupational experience, and for some comparers, ethnic background and sex.

Goethals and Darley (1977) argued that in order to make inferences about one's ability relative to that of others, one has to be able to attribute performance differences to ability differences, rather than to other performance-related attributes. They proposed that with more than one plausible cause of performance, the comparer uses a multiple sufficient causes schema (Kelley, 1971) for interpreting the performance effect. If the causes are all facilitative or inhibitory, any of the causes can account for the effect (or lack of it). Hence, the perceiver discounts any given cause and is uncertain as to which cause he should attribute the effect.

Thus, if the perceiver is attempting to determine whether a performance difference is due to ability, and other causes of performance difference are present, he or she will discount ability as the cause and be uncertain of his ability. Let us consider a tennis player who loses badly to an unfamiliar opponent who subsequently states that she just returned from tennis camp. The defeated player can entertain the view that the defeat may be due either to the other's temporary advantage at tennis or to her own inferior ability at tennis. Hence, she will be highly uncertain as to the correct inference.

However, if the perceiver and the comparison other are similar on all performance-related attributes, he or she can attribute the performance difference to difference in ability. If both players have just returned from tennis camp, they will probably attribute any performance difference unequivocally to an ability difference. Hence, the Goethals and Darley (1977) theory predicts a preference for others who are similar to self on performance-related attributes. It also predicts greater certainty about ability differences when others are similar on such attributes than when they differ in such a way that it would account for the performance difference.

The multiple sufficient causes schema also results in very strong attributions to ability— augmentation—when the differences on performance-related attributes are incongruent with performance differences. If our tennis player defeats an opponent who has just returned from tennis camp and she has not, her attribution of the performance difference to her own superior ability will be very confident indeed. Such turns of events are undoubtedly rare in everyday life, though far from unheard of.

The focus of research coming out of the reformulation of the theory was on comparison preferences. As we noted, most of this research did indeed demonstrate that people preferred comparison with others who were similar to them, especially with respect to such categories as sex and class in school. Studies also have used other types of attributes, for instance, personal attributes such as beauty (Miller, 1982) and amount of practice at a task (Wheeler et al., 1982). In most cases, people did indeed prefer to see comparison information from others similar to them in social category or personal attribute. Yet, as Wood (1989) has noted, such a preference only rarely has been restricted to attributes related to performance (see Miller, 1982, 1984; Wheeler et al., 1982, for exceptions); in other words, comparisons are often made on dimensions that have no obvious relationship to performance.

Few studies have addressed the impact of performance-related attributes on ability inference. Both Gastorf and Suls (1978) and Wilson (1973) examined the effects of variations in performance-related attributes (participant and comparison other similar or dissimilar) on evaluative ratings of performance (Radloff, 1966). However, neither study examined ability inference per se.

Gilbert, Giesler, and Morris (1995) used a somewhat different paradigm in which student participants were asked to rate their own ability and that of the average student on rating scales after having compared performances with another student. They found that participants (when not distracted) discounted ability difference as a cause of performance difference when the other had received explicit training on the task but the participant had not (experiment 1). They also found (experiment 2) that participants who performed better than someone with a more difficult task or worse than another with an easier task discounted ability as a cause of the performance difference. In contrast, when the participant and the comparison other had tasks of the same difficulty level, participants inferred ability differences from performance differences. No certainty measure was included in this research.

Finally, Kulik and Gump (1997) presented findings from three experiments examining participants' ratings of their performances relative to students like themselves. They found that participants tended to see their performance standing (note that this was not an ability rating) as higher the higher their performance had been relative to the other person. But more importantly for the multiple sufficient causes formulation, self-ratings of standing tended to be higher the higher the other's standing on a performance-related attribute (a kind of physical endurance variable).

While the findings from this body of research on ability inference are suggestive, they are less than conclusive, especially since most of them do not address the issue of ability inference in any direct fashion.

The Role of Stable versus Unstable Attributes.   It is true that some performance-related factors, such as brief practice, fatigue, acute illness, and drug and alcohol consumption, imply nothing about the stable pattern of performance, that is, ability. They imply nothing about ability because they are unstable factors that compete at that moment with ability as causes of performance. Since they are independent of ability, the comparer will attempt to control for them, as Goethals and Darley (1977) pointed out. Hence, people will use a multiple sufficient causes schema in making inferences about ability when such factors are recognized in the comparison setting.

We suggest that there are other performance-related attributes recognized by the comparer as indicative of ability itself. These are attributes considered stable by the comparer. That is, factors that the comparer views as performance related but not easily altered by the comparer or circumstances; for instance, long-term training and experience, educational status, sex, and ethnic background. Along with performance differences, people often regard them as informative of ability.

While findings directly related to this point are rare, research on stereotypes related to social categories is of relevance. Thus, studies show that ethnic stereotypes contain references to ability (Karlins, Coffman, & Walters, 1969). For instance, Katz and Braly (1933) found that white Princeton students of that era endorsed a stereotype of African Americans that included "musical" and "stupid" in over one fifth of the cases. In contrast, they endorsed "intelligent" over one quarter of the time for their own group and for Jews. To be sure, these are very general "abilities" or "competencies"; they may constitute glorification of one's own group and derogation of the out-group. Yet, the inclusion of musical and intelligent for generally disliked groups seems oddly out of character for a simple pattern of derogation. Sex as a category also carries with it, at least in American society, a stereotype containing a number of characteristics relevant to competence (e.g., Broverman, Vogel, Broverman, Clarkson, & Rosenkranz, 1972.)

More generally, expectation states theory has addressed the issue of social categorization and attributions of competence, as a function of numerous status characteristics, including educational attainment, military rank, ethnicity, and sex (Driskell & Mullen, 1990). As noted earlier, the general theory assumes that esteem and influence in work groups is driven by judgments of relative competence, expressed as expectancies for performance at a relevant task (Ridgeway & Walker, 1994). These expectancies are associated with the status characteristics of the group members (Berger, Fisek, Norman, & Zelditch, 1977). Status characteristics can be relatively specific, such as level of training in computer networking, or diffuse, such as ethnicity, gender, or general educational attainment. In each case, different placements on a status characteristic will result in different expectancies for task performances.

Unfortunately, most data addressing the status characteristics hypothesis have studied the linkage between status and influence without examining the presumed intervening step involving competence judgments (Driskell & Mullen, 1990). Nonetheless, there is some evidence that salient status characteristics influence performance expectancies and that performance expectancies, in turn, affect task-related behavior such as efforts to influence others and willingness to accept influence from others [see, for example, Wood and Karten (1986) for the case of sex as a diffuse status characteristic]. That status characteristics have their impact on influence patterns in groups through their effects on performance expectancies is clear from the fact that in status characteristics research, which has measured such expectancies, the status characteristics (diffuse or specific) have only a trivial effect on behavior in the task group when expectancies are partialled out (Driskell & Mullen, 1990).

In short, there is good reason to believe that people treat some performance-related attributes as cues to the possession of ability rather than as nonability factors that might influence performance (thereby obscuring ability). It is obviously important to distinguish between the two kinds of performance-related attributes: those treated as cues to ability and those treated as nonability performance-related attributes. It is also important to understand how these two kinds of performance-related attributes are treated in the inference of ability in a social comparison context.

We believe that the difference between these two types of factors consists in their temporal stability. The inference of ability involves finding a relatively constant internal cause of performance. This must be the essence of a dispositional cause; that relatively constant features of the person are inseparable from the disposition itself. A student's height is associated with her skill at basketball, in fact both a component and an indicator of her skill. Surely, it is odd to state that a short player is more able than her teammates "but for her height." Likewise, a carpenter is skilled partly due to his or her training and experience; it seems peculiar to say, "I am as skilled as he, but for his superior training." In contrast, ephemeral experiences, such as brief practice, contribute transiently to performance. As they are unstable in their effects, they cannot be part of a stable disposition.

A functional argument will lead to the same conclusion. If a person I compare with has more education and performs better than I at one point in time (t_1), I can expect that performance advantage to appear again at a later time (t_2). If the function of ability inference is to predict the future, people should use stable personal features as indicators of ability, since doing so permits prediction. The converse is true if the person with whom I compare at time t_1 has simply practiced more the day before, for instance, throwing baskets with her friends. The difference between us at t_1 (e.g., today) in the number of successful baskets is not a good predictor of performance at t_2 (i.e., tomorrow). I may simply practice today, while she does other things, thereby equalizing the unstable attribute. Hence, it is functional for the comparer to eliminate unstable but not stable performance-related attributes or factors when inferring relative ability.

A preference for similar others on performance-related attributes seems eminently reasonable with respect to unstable attributes. They contaminate the effects of ability on performance, since they are unlikely to remain effective with respect to performance over time. However, efforts to eliminate the influence of stable attributes would seem to be maladaptive, since these are informative about ability rather than being confounding factors. The question remains: How do people make ability inferences in the presence of cues to stable attributes, attributes that are informative about ability?

The Cue Consistency Schema.   We propose a simple consistency schema: When confronted with cues to ability, the consistency of the cues determines the certainty of the inference. In the comparative situation, there are generally two cues to relative ability: performance and standing on stable performance-related attributes, both relative to the other person.

For example, a person may believe that women have more empathic ability than do men. If she discerns the underlying aim of a dinner invitation while her husband does not, then she should be highly confident that her empathic ability is greater than his. Her performance (sensing the underlying motive) and gender are consistent cues to her superior ability. If instead a female friend showed this failure of empathy, she would be less confident of her own superior ability. The lower confidence stems from less consistency than in the former case; notice that this is in spite of similarity on the performance-related attribute.

Our argument is conceptual, but findings from research on expectations states theory do offer indirect empirical support. Most of the studies look at relative influence in work groups with relative status as the independent variable. As noted, in this research competence judgments are generally assumed as intervening variables [see, for example, Pugh and Wahrman (1983) and Wagner, Ford, and Ford (1986) for findings from sex as a diffuse status characteristic]. Of interest to us is how people combine the related attribute (e.g., sex) and the performance information in making inferences about ability. There is some research examining attributions of performance to ability in the context of information about social category information [see Deaux (1984) and Foschi (1992) for sex as a category; Foschi and Takagi (1991) for ethnicity]. However, this research typically focuses on how social category information about a performer influences the judged quality of a performance (e.g., Goldberg, 1968), or the extent to which a successful performance is attributed to ability versus nonability factors such as luck (e.g., Deaux & Emswiller, 1974). Our concern is with the impact of social category information on judgments of ability differences in the context of performance comparison, not judgments of quality of performance or partitions of causality.

Some research in the context of expectation states theory in fact has addressed questions of the inference of relative ability, but without consistent findings (Foschi & Takagi, 1991; Wallston & O'Leary, 1981). However, Foschi (Foschi, 1992; Foschi & Takagi, 1991) has pointed to numerous methodological problems in this research, including such matters as salience of social category and the problem of multiple category membership. This makes a definitive statement about how people combine social category and relative performance information very difficult.

However, both Foddy (Foddy & Smithson, 1989) and Foschi (1989) have proposed what they call a "double-standard" approach to attributions about ability, an approach very close to what we are suggesting. Both propose different standards for inferring ability depending on standing on some status characteristic relevant to the task. A given performance will more likely lead to an inference of high ability when it belongs to the person with the more valued status characteristic than when it belongs to a person with a less valued characteristic. Hence, a low-status person is subjected to a stricter standard than is a high-status person, even when they are both equally successful. Thus, the performance of the former is less likely to be attributed to ability (Foschi, 1989). Foschi has argued that the limited data appropriate for testing the double-standard hypothesis with respect to both gender (Foschi, 1992) and ethnicity (Foschi & Takagi, 1991) support this position.

One study (Foschi, Lai, & Sigerson, 1994) that does not suffer from the limitations of most in the area did show support for the double-standard hypothesis. In this study, men and women made competence judgments of two job candidates: a man and a woman. While this is not a comparison of self with other but between two others, this should not affect the underlying logic (though it certainly would affect self-enhancement and self-esteem maintenance motives). They found that when males had some performance advantage, men made more extreme ratings of competence for the man relative to the woman than they did when the woman was the better performer. If we can infer confidence from extremity of ratings, this seems to offer partial support for the cue consistency position.

Kulik and Gump (1997) report another study consistent with this view, but again not directly addressing the issue of confidence in judgment. They were concerned with other issues, including the inference of population standing from performance comparison with a single other party. Nevertheless, they found that participants tended to rate a comparison other's status as an additive function of his standing on a more or less stable performance-related attribute and his performance relative to their own. Thus, a higher-status other who performed better than the participant received a higher rating of "advantage" at the task than a higher status other who performed the same or worse.

In a more direct examination of this issue, Arnkelsson and Smith (2000) conducted several experiments to examine the impact of stable and unstable attributes on the inference of ability relative to another individual. In each of these experiments, participants judged their standing relative to another person with respect to an unfamiliar ability ("complex information processing"). The task in each experiment involved selecting and manipulating relevant information from an array of distracters (finding numbers to sum, or letters that formed meaningful words). In two of the experiments, participants received comparative performance information from an individual (or several individuals) whose standing on what we assumed would be a stable attribute (occupation in one experiment, educational status in another) was known to them. In addition, in each case, before they received comparative performance information, participants learned that standing on the attribute was related to performance, that is, higher standing on the attribute was typically associated with higher performance.

The results were in accord with the cue consistency schema. While participants inferred an ability difference corresponding to the performance difference, confidence in relative ability judgment and the extremity of the judgment itself were a function of the consistency between standing on the stable attribute and relative performance. When college students performed below a skilled professional (an air traffic controller) or a better-educated person (a graduate student), they were more confident of inferior ability than when they performed below another college student or a high school student. The pattern was similar but weaker for equal and superior performance. To the extent that relative performance implied the same ability difference as standing on the stable performance-related attribute, relative ability judgments were confident. Conversely, to the extent that standing on the attribute and relative performance had conflicting implications for ability, ability judgments were tentative.

In a third experiment, the performance-related attribute was one we assumed participants would treat as unstable: brief practice on the task. The pattern of ability judgments was dramatically different from that obtained when stable attributes were involved and congruent with the multiple sufficient causes schema, as suggested by Goethals and Darley (1977). Confidence in relative ability judgment was greatest when standing on the attribute would predict a different relative performance (e.g., when participants performed better than someone did with more practice than they had), implying an augmentation effect. Judgments were weakest when standing on practice would predict the relative performance obtained, implying a discounting effect (though this effect was marginal).

Figure 1 shows the confidence index plotted against consistency of attribute standing and relative performance for each of two experiments with comparable design, one using a stable attribute (education) and one using an unstable attribute (brief practice). It can be seen that the impact of relative standing on the performance-related attribute clearly depended on the attribute, and we contend that it is the relative stability of the two attributes that accounts for this difference.

We also asked participants to estimate their ability and performance relative to the comparison person before they had performed and received any scores. Their performance estimates reflected the information we had given them about related attribute standing: The higher their standing, the better they expected to do relative to the other. However, only when

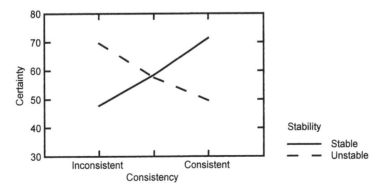

Figure 1. The effect of cue consistency and attribute stability on certainty of ability inference.

the performance-related attribute was stable did they estimate their relative ability in accord with standing on the attribute (education). In other words, participants clearly regarded information about standing on a stable attribute, but not on an unstable attribute, as informative of ability.

The Referent of Ability Inference and the Role of Attribute Stability

Our discussion of the cue consistency schema, particularly the work from expectation states theory and from the Arnkelsson and Smith (2000) experiment, has focused on cases where the referent of ability inference was clearly ability relative to another individual or individuals. However, it is not obvious that the same processes of ability inference need characterize efforts to estimate one's ability relative to some reference group. We now turn to the question of how related attributes affect inferences about ability relative to a reference group.

Inferring Ability Relative to a Reference Group.   In an ideal case, to determine one's ability relative to a reference group, one would compare with some aggregate index of the group's ability level, an average perhaps. Note that this will be true whether or not membership in the group is performance related: If the question is where one's ability falls within some group, then the obvious first choice for comparison is that very same group. Indeed, Suls and Tesch (1978) demonstrated that when receiving scores on class examinations (where one could assume that the class is the relevant reference group), students preferred information about the class average to any other comparison information (e.g., highest score, number worse than self, etc.). One's performance relative to the group's (e.g., the group average) defines one's ability within the group. Thus, neither the choice of the comparison group nor the confidence in the resulting ability inference has anything to do with controlling for nonability causes of performance. A simple comparison with a reference group is directly informative of one's standing within that same group.

In a more typical case, the only comparison available might be to a group different from the reference group. If a woman wants to know about her ability relative to other women, what should she make of a performance superior to the average for men? In itself, the information about men is uninformative. However, any knowledge she has about the average performance difference between the two groups changes the picture considerably. If the average performance is the same for men and women, then she can obviously compare with either group. If men are on average superior to women, performance superior or similar to the male average has clear implications for ability vis-à-vis women, while inferior performance does not. If men are inferior, superior performance is ambiguous if she wants to know her standing within her own gender. Let us assume the ability refers to leadership, and the woman comparing believes (falsely or correctly) that men are generally better at leading others than are women. It seems obvious that the woman would conclude that her performance—superior to the average for men—must indicate that she is also superior to women. If on the other hand she had performed worse than the average for men, it is less clear what conclusion she would draw.

This mimics the pattern of inference that Goethals and Darley (1977) proposed as the consequence of using the multiple sufficient causes schema. Doing better than someone whose standing on a performance-related attribute is higher than your own leads to augmentation—a judgment that your ability is clearly higher than that of the comparison other. Doing worse permits no confident inference, owing to discounting. In our example, gender is a performance-related attribute, that is, when average performance (i.e., ability) is different for the two genders.

It is important to note that the above judgments involve no causal reasoning at all and therefore the multiple-causes schema does not apply. Reliance on a simple transitivity schema of logic, that if $A > B$, and $B > C$, then $A > C$, is all that is required. By transitivity, if your performance is above a group assumed to be better than your own group, you also must be better than the average for your own group. The same rule applies if your performance is inferior to the average of a group thought to be inferior in ability to your own reference group. That such a schema plays a role in social cognition has been demonstrated (e.g., DeSoto, 1960). Doing worse than the average of a superior group or better than an inferior group in contrast does not permit the application of the transitivity rule. If transitivity is the only salient schema, an uncertain ability inference vis-à-vis one's own group should result. Parenthetically we note that it makes no difference for the basic inference whether the superiority or inferiority of the other group is real or imaginary. The same inferential process applies, although the objective accuracy of the conclusion will vary.

It also is important to recognize the possible application of the cue consistency schema in the cases under discussion. Performing above the average of a group superior to your own does imply a conflict of cues. Prior belief (e.g., stereotype) indicates one should be inferior to a group thought to be superior to one's own, but relative performance information suggests otherwise. However, these conflicting cues apply directly only to the question of where one's ability lies relative to the comparison group, not relative to one's own group. The discovery that one performs above the level of a presumed superior group adds new information reinforcing the notion that one may be superior to one's own reference group. The same analysis applies to cases of doing worse than a group thought to be inferior to one's own. Likewise, when performance fits expectation, that is, doing worse than a superior group or better than an inferior group, this might be seen as cue consistency. We must stress again, however, that we are concerned here with the question of where one stands relative to one's own group, not relative to the comparison group.

The transitivity logic applies whether or not the attribute characterizing the comparison group is stable or unstable. To take an extreme example, let us consider a high school student with a swimming performance that is worse than the average of a team from another high school. Let us further assume that the team of the other school had suffered food poisoning on the way to the swim meet (unstable attribute). Then he or she can conclude that her or his ability is worse than that of his or her own (unpoisoned) team. The same conclusion is forced also for a stable attribute, that is, if the comparison was with a middle school team (stable attribute).

It is useful to contrast cases where we have access to a group average versus an individual member of a group. A comparison with a single other individual is uninformative of performance vis-à-vis the group, unless we know his or her status within the group. Indeed, there is always the possibility that the other is deviant within his or her own group, that is, the middle school swimmer could be a prodigy. When comparing with the average of the group itself, of course the question of representativeness of the comparison other does not arise.

If the comparer assumes that the other is representative of a group average, the inference of standing relative to a reference group is much the same as comparing with the group itself. It is possible of course that the comparer assumes himself or herself to be representative of his or her own group. Then the other must be deviant and the comparison offers no information on the comparer's standing within his or her own group. This should be true to the extent that the comparer brings to the comparison a relatively confident expectancy regarding his or her own standing within the group.

Which assumption will characterize the comparer in any given situation must depend in part on how much prior information the comparer has about his or her standing in the group. Existing empirical evidence, drawn from cases where we would expect prior information to be lacking, is inconsistent. Kulik and Gump (1997) have found that people use the comparison other to discover where they stand in their own group. Those who performed better than a single advantaged other judged themselves more able relative to their own group than did those who performed worse than the other. Those who outperformed the advantaged other appear to have assumed that the other was representative of the advantaged group (and that they themselves were deviant from their own group, that is, superior to the average of their own group). Unfortunately, other empirical research contradicts this. Alicke et al. (1997) examined comparisons with others who did not differ from the comparer on performance-related attributes. They found that comparers attributed deviance to others who performed differently from themselves, apparently in efforts to self-enhance. Participants assumed that better-performing others were geniuses and even that worse-performing others were above average. Participants thereby preserved a view of themselves as above average in their own group.

Ability as Indexed by Task Outcomes: Stability of Attributes and the Proxy Effect.

Appraising one's ability with respect to the task outcomes one can expect is again essentially a matter of generalizing from known performance outcomes—in this case, specific task outcomes—to unknown outcomes in the future. If I have some task experience, I can generalize from my present level of performance to future performances, as work on aspiration level indicates (Lewin et al., 1944). If I do not have any experience, level of aspiration research as well as recent research and theory in social comparison suggests that the performances of others will often substitute for one's own experience. This is the "proxy" effect, that is, I use the performance of a similar other to predict my own performance on the task (Jones & Regan, 1974; Smith & Sachs, 1997; Wheeler et al., 1997).

Identifying a person who is similar to oneself in ability can help in predicting one's own fate on novel tasks in the ability domain. Due to similar ability, one can use his or her performance as a proxy for one's own performances. Smith and Sachs (1997) demonstrated this proxy effect experimentally. Participants first performed on a task tapping an unfamiliar ability, and then predicted how well they would do at a new task drawing on the same ability. They received the overall performance outcome of another person, described as a student from an area college, on the novel task before they made their prediction. Some of the participants had seen comparative performance information from themselves and the other person on the first task, while others had not. The former had found their performances to be superior, the same, or inferior to the other, and hence, had some basis for judging their ability relative to him or her.

All participants appeared to use information about others' performances on the novel task. Both those who had not compared and those who had and found the other to be of similar ability (inferred from performance on the first task) predicted that they would do about the same as the other on the novel task. Their strength of belief was different though, with those with performance similar to the other on the first task being more confident than were those with no prior performance comparison information. Those seeing the performances of another with superior or inferior ability predicted performance levels below and above, respectively, the other on the second task, with only moderate confidence. Smith and Sachs (1997) argued that participants used the other person's outcome on the novel task as a proxy for their own and found this most useful when comparison on the first task established the other as similar in ability. In short, participants made confident inferences about their own ability (defined by obtainable task outcomes in the future) from knowledge about the task outcomes of another of similar ability on that same task.

The basic problem for someone attempting to predict his or her outcomes from an unfamiliar task is that of identifying a proxy who has similar ability. We have noted that both performance comparison and standing on stable performance-related attributes provide information about ability. Hence, we would expect both types of information to contribute to the confidence with which information from a proxy is used. The sophomore math student trying to determine how much time her math homework requires will make a confident estimate if she can discover how long it takes her roommate to solve a subset of the problems. But knowing how long the teaching assistant takes or how long her father the country musician takes is unlikely to be as useful. The Smith and Sachs (1997) study did not address the role of performance-related attribute information for the proxy effect. However, this is a promising issue to study empirically within the emerging area of the proxy effect, as the work by Martin (Chapter 4, this volume) attests.

We agree with Wheeler et al. (1997) that having performance comparison information from a previous task should provide greater confidence than simply knowledge of performance-related attributes. The comparer will recognize the considerable variability within any social category (some middle-aged hikers are in better shape than others). When there is information about both stable attribute standing and relative performance, often we would expect the cue consistency schema to operate in the inference of relative ability. The middle-aged hiker will be less confident if he finds a 20-year-old hiking at his speed on an earlier hike than if the other is his own age. Of course, with sufficient performance comparison information (and/or attribute information of doubtful validity), related attribute influence will be overwhelmed, since performance is the ultimate criterion for ability (see Chapter 4, this volume).

Turning to unstable performance-related attributes, the picture would appear to be more complex. The issue in predicting one's future performance is not only similarity in ability (judged via the multiple sufficient causes schema) but also similarity on the unstable attribute at the time of performance on the novel task. Even with ability similar to the proxy's, if the proxy were fresh when she took up the task and the comparer fatigued, predictions will be shaky. Even a proxy of similar age and fitness may be of little use, if the proxy did the hike early in the morning after a good night's sleep while our hiker is making the third hike of the day.

Differences on stable related attributes would appear to undermine the usefulness of performance information from the other on the target task, at least to some extent. One cannot expect to do as well as a superior other, whether that superiority is manifest via actual performance comparison [which the Smith and Sachs (1997) experiment demonstrated] or through standing on stable performance-related attributes. Yet different others convey some useful information: They restrict the range of plausible outcomes for oneself, narrowing the set of likely outcomes (Smith & Sachs, 1997; Wheeler et al., 1997). I will not expect to perform as well as another of superior ability, but just where in the range below his or her task outcomes my own will fall is not confidently discernible. Likewise, I do not expect to do as poorly as someone of lower ability, but how much better I will do is unclear.

We should note that this discussion centers on cases where people seek to determine, more or less precisely, which of a set of possible task outcomes one might obtain from an unfamiliar task. For example, it applies to the undergraduate student wondering whether her grades will be higher if she chooses to major in physics or psychology: this is a question of what grades one will get in physics and in psychology. However, there are many instances when we simply want to know whether we can reach or exceed some criterion task outcome:

"Can I swim the lake?" as opposed to, "How long will it take me to swim the lake?" In such cases, as Wheeler et al. (1997) have noted, one can use the performance outcomes of *both* inferior and similar others to make a confident prediction. If someone equally *or* less able than me can do it, so can I. Information from others who are superior on a stable attribute, however, are not a good basis for predicting one's own fate.

WHAT DETERMINES THE STABILITY OF AN ATTRIBUTE?

We have based attribute stability on a comparer's belief as to whether the attribute is likely to change over a brief period. Thus brief practice, fatigue, and minor illness are all factors that affect performance and change over a short time span; as a consequence, the comparer will typically treat them as unstable attributes. Other attributes, such as educational level, occupational preparation, experience, and gender, change only over longer time spans, if at all; these attributes are typically treated as stable. Indeed, we would argue that some notion of "change within a reasonable time" is likely the default definition of instability of performance-related characteristics. Thus, brief practice changes within a short time; similarly, waiting for a brief period is all it takes for fatigue to change; perhaps a slightly longer wait is required for an upper respiratory infection. In contrast, a sex change is theoretically possible but beyond the realm of possibility for most of us. Changes in education and occupational experience are within the realm of possibility but require so much time and cost that they typically meet the requirement of "stable."

Nevertheless, there certainly are instances where people are concerned with appraising their ability over long time perspectives. The period may be lengthy enough for what may normally be considered a stable attribute (such as education) to change between the time of comparison and the time of interest with respect to relative ability. Understanding how such attributes are treated in the inference of ability is of considerable importance.

We argue that naive perceivers view ability as a stable personal disposition. We further argue that stable performance-related attributes of a person cannot be separated from ability itself. In fact, ability is itself a stable attribute related to performance, distinguishable from other stable attributes such as sex and so forth only by being unobservable. However, it would be clearly incorrect to claim that stable performance-related attributes are immutable: one can obtain education, occupational experience, and so on. This clearly implies the question: Are performance-related attributes that typically are seen as stable sometimes treated as unstable in the process of ability inference, and if so, under what circumstances?

It is worthwhile returning to a functional analysis of the ability concept as used in everyday life. With Heider (1944, 1958), we argue that the functional significance of the inference of stable personal dispositions lies in the consequent predictability of behavior: that of others, or one's own. In other words, the function of inferences about one's own ability is to permit one to predict one's fate when faced by a certain class of tasks in the future. The question is: "Will my performance level relative to the comparison other be the same at the time of interest to me in the future?" The answer will only be a confident "yes" if I can assume that my standing and that of the other are likely to be the same at that future time.

The focus of the comparer's interest in prediction can be at a somewhat distant time in the future, a time when an attribute ordinarily considered stable might have changed. Hence, we might expect him or her to treat the stable attribute as unstable in making inferences about this future ability. The 8-year-old basketball player who is regularly beaten by his 12-year-old brother when they shoot baskets in their driveway might readily admit that his brother is better at basketball (after all, his brother is taller). However, he might be considering some years into the future, when he hopes his increased height will permit him to win those competitions. In such a case, we would suggest that the question of who has more ability becomes more uncertain, despite the consistency between relative performances and an attribute—age or height—normally considered to be stable. In other words, the attribute that the comparer normally considers stable operates as an unstable attribute owing to the time perspective of the comparer. Hence, the superior concurrent performance of the older boy may not lead the younger to conclude that his ability is in fact lower, or at least he will have little confidence in that conclusion.

Yet, we would not expect the normally stable attribute to be treated in quite the same way as a truly transient feature of self, that is, unstable attributes such as brief practice or its absence, fatigue, and so forth. After all, the comparer is expecting to incorporate the attribute as a stable part of self: The young basketball player will become taller. Since stable attributes are cues to ability, a person who expects to attain an attribute expects to attain the ability level that it signals. The young player expects to reach the ability level of his brother. Indeed, this appears to be a case of appraising ability in the second sense we have discussed—as potential or aptitude, rather than typical level of motivated performance.

This raises the interesting possibility that the 8-year-old may treat the success of his brother on the team as a proxy for his own outcome in the future, as indicating his aptitude. Hence, in this case the proxy is not someone currently proven similar to self, but someone representing the possible self of the more distant future (Markus & Nurius, 1986; see also Lockwood & Kunda, 1997). If the comparer expects to develop the attribute level exemplified by the comparison other, then the other is an appropriate proxy for that future. The model proposed by Major, Testa, and Bylsma (1991) incorporates a similar process, though that model emphasizes control as well as stability of the ability and is not concerned primarily with ability inference itself. Collins's (1996) proposal that comparisons with "objectively" better others are often treated as comparisons with a similar other through a process of construal also points to a phenomenon similar to what we propose here.

CONCLUSIONS

The questions of just what people hope to learn and what they conclude from social comparison seem very important both in their own right and in terms of understanding what types of comparison information are sought. In this chapter, we have proposed that in order to answer these questions it is necessary to understand the nature of the ability concept people attempt to appraise, its referent, and the ways in which they conceive of related attributes. We hope that this approach will further understanding of social comparison and will inspire new research.

ACKNOWLEDGMENTS

We thank the Vanderbilt University Research Council, the Department of Psychology of Vanderbilt University, and the Faculty of Social Sciences of the University of Iceland for providing financial and facility support. We also express our sincere gratitude to Jerry Suls and Ladd Wheeler for their encouragement and support, as well as their helpful criticisms.

REFERENCES

Alicke, M. D., Klotz, M. L., Breitenbecher, D. L., Yurak, T. J., & Vredenberg, D. S. (1995). Personal contact, individuation, and the better-than-average effect. *Journal of Personality and Social Psychology, 68*, 804–825.

Alicke, M. D., LoSchiavo, F. M., Zerbst, J., & Zhang, S. (1997). The person who outperforms me is a genius: Maintaining perceived competence in upward social comparison. *Journal of Personality and Social Psychology, 73*, 781–789.

Arnkelsson, G. B., & Smith, W. P. (2000). The impact of stable and unstable attributes on ability asessment in social comparison. *Personality and Social Psychology Bulletin*, in press.

Berger, J., Conner, T. L., & Fisek, M. H. (1974). *Expectation states theory: A theoretical research program.* Cambridge, MA: Winthrop.

Berger, J., Fisek, M. H., Norman, R. Z., & Zelditch, M. (1977). *Status characteristics in social interaction: An expectation states approach.* New York: Elsevier.

Berger, J., Wagner, D. G., & Zelditch, M. (1985). Expectation states theory: Review and assessment. In J. Berger & M. Zelditch (Eds.), *Status, rewards, and influence* (pp. 1–72). San Francisco: Jossey-Bass.

Broverman, I. K., Vogel, S. R., Broverman, D. M., Clarkson, F. E., & Rosenkrantz, P. S. (1972). Sex-role stereotypes: A current appraisal. *Journal of Social Issues, 28*, 59–78.

Brown, J. D., & Dutton, K. A. (1995). Truth and consequences: The costs and benefits of accurate self-knowledge. *Personality and Social Psychology Bulletin, 21*, 1288–1296.

Collins, R. L. (1996). For better or worse: The impact of upward social comparison on self-evaluation. *Psychological Bulletin, 119*, 51–69.

Darley, J. M., & Goethals, G. R. (1980). People's analyses of the causes of ability-linked performances. In L. Berkowitz (Ed.), *Advances in experimental social psychology* (Vol. 13, pp. 1–37). New York: Academic Press.

Deaux, K. (1984). From individual differences to social categories: Analysis of a decade's research on gender. *American Psychologist, 39*, 105–116.

Deaux, K., & Emswiller, T. (1974). Explanations for successful performance on sex-linked tasks: What is skill for the male is luck for the female. *Journal of Personality and Social Psychology, 29*, 80–85.

DeSoto, C. B. (1960). Learning a social structure. *Journal of Abnormal and Social Psychology, 60*, 417–421.

Dreyer, A. (1954). Aspiration behavior as influenced by expectation and group comparison. *Human Relations, 7*, 175–190.

Driskell, J. E., & Mullen, B. (1990). Status, expectations, and behavior: A meta-analytic review and test of the theory. *Personality and Social Psychology Bulletin, 16*, 541–553.

Feldman, N. S., & Ruble, D. N. (1981). Social comparison strategies: Dimensions offered and options taken. *Personality and Social Psychology Bulletin, 7*, 11–16.

Festinger, L. (1950). Informal social communication. *Psychological Review, 57*, 271–282.

Festinger, L. (1954). A theory of social comparison processes. *Human Relations, 7*, 117–140.

Foddy, M., & Smithson, M. (1989). Fuzzy sets and double standards: Modeling the process of ability inference. In J. Berger, M. Zelditch, & B. Anderson (Eds.), *Sociological theories in progress* (pp. 73–99). Newbury Park, CA: Sage.

Foschi, M. (1989). Status characteristics, standards, and attributions. In J. Berger, M. Zelditch, & B. Anderson (Eds.), *Sociological theories in progress* (pp. 58–72). Newbury Park, CA: Sage.

Foschi, M. (1992). Gender and double standards for competence. In C. L. Ridgeway (Ed.), *Gender, interaction and inequality* (pp. 181–207). New York: Springer-Verlag.

Foschi, M., Lai, L., & Sigerson, K. (1994). Gender and double standards in the assessment of job applicants. *Social Psychology Quarterly, 57*, 326–339.

Foschi, M., & Takagi, J. (1991). Ethnicity, task outcome, and attributions: A theoretical review and assessment. *Advances in Group Processes, 8*, 177–203.

Gastorf, J. W., & Suls, J. (1978). Performance evaluation via social comparison: Performance similarity versus related attribute similarity. *Social Psychology, 41*, 297–305.

Gilbert, D. T., Giesler, R. B., & Morris, K. A. (1995). When comparisons arise. *Journal of Personality and Social Psychology, 69*, 227–236.

Goethals, G. R. (1986). Social comparison theory: Psychology from the lost and found. *Personality and Social Psychology Bulletin, 12*, 261–278.

Goethals, G. R., & Darley, J. M. (1977). Social comparison theory: An attributional approach. In J. M. Suls & R. L. Miller (Eds.), *Social comparison processes: Theoretical and empirical perspectives* (pp. 259–278). London: Hemisphere.

Goldberg, P. (1968). Are women prejudiced against women? *Transaction, 5*, 28–30.

Harkness, A. R., DeBono, K. G., & Borgida, E. (1986). Personal involvement and strategies for making contingency judgments: A stake in the dating game makes a difference. *Journal of Personality and Social Psychology, 49,* 22–32.

Heider, F. (1944). Social perception and phenomenal causality. *Psychological Review, 51,* 358–374.

Heider, F. (1958). *The psychology of interpersonal relations.* New York: Wiley.

Jones, E. E., & Berglas, S. (1978). Control of attributions about the self through self-handicapping strategies: The appeal of alcohol and the role of underachievement. *Personality and Social Psychology Bulletin, 4,* 200–206.

Jones, S. C., & Regan, D. T. (1974). Ability evaluation through social comparison. *Journal of Experimental Social Psychology, 10,* 133–146.

Karlins, M., Coffman, T. L., & Walters, G. (1969). On the fading of social stereotypes: Studies in three generations of college students. *Journal of Personality and Social Psychology, 13,* 1–16.

Katz, D., & Braly, K. (1933). Racial stereotypes of one hundred college students. *Journal of Abnormal and Social Psychology, 28,* 280–290.

Kelley, H. H. (1971). *Attribution in social interaction.* Morristown, NJ: General Learning Press.

Klein, W. M. (1997). Objective standards are not enough: Affective, self-evaluative, and behavioral responses to social comparison information. *Journal of Personality and Social Psychology, 72,* 763–774.

Kruglanski, A. W. (1989). *Lay epistemics and human knowledge.* New York: Plenum Press.

Kulik, J. A., & Gump, B. B. (1997). Affective reactions to social comparison: The effects of relative performance and related attributes information about another person. *Personality and Social Psychology Bulletin, 23,* 452–468.

Latané, B. (1966). Studies in social comparison: Introduction and overview. *Journal of Experimental Social Psychology,* Suppl. 1, 1–5.

Levine, J. M., & Moreland, R. L. (1987). Social compariosn and outcome evaluation in group contexts. In J. C. Masters & W. P. Smith (Eds.), *Social comparison, social justice, and relative deprivation: Theoretical, empirical, and policy perspectives* (pp. 105–127). Hillsdale, NJ: Lawrence Erlbaum.

Lewin, K., Dembo, T., Festinger, L., & Sears, P. S. (1944). Level of aspiration. In J. M. Hunt (Ed.), *Personality and the behavior disorders* (Vol. 1, pp. 333–378). New York: Ronald.

Lockwood, P., & Kunda, Z. (1997). Superstars and me: Predicting the impact of role models on the self. *Journal of Personality and Social Psychology, 73,* 91–103.

Major, B., & Testa, M. (1989). Social comparison processes and judgments of entitlement and satisfaction. *Journal of Experimental Social Psychology, 25,* 101–120

Major, B., Testa, M., & Bylsma, W. H. (1991). Responses to upward and downward social comparisons: The impact of esteem-relevance and perceived control. In J. Suls & T. A. Wills (Eds.), *Social comparison: Contemporary theory and research* (pp. 237–260). Hillsdale, NJ: Lawrence Erlbaum.

Markus, H., & Nurius, P. (1986). Possible selves. *American Psychologist, 41,* 954–969.

Miller, C. T. (1982). The role of performance-related similarity in social comparison of abilities: A test of the related attributes hypothesis. *Journal of Experimental Social Psychology, 18,* 513–523.

Miller, C. T. (1984). Self-schemas, gender, and social comparison: A clarification of the related attributes hypothesis. *Journal of Personality and Social Psychology, 46,* 1222–1229.

Pugh, M. D., & Wahrman, R. (1983). Neutralizing sexism in mixed-sex groups: Do women have to be better than men? *American Journal of Sociology, 88,* 746–762.

Radloff, R. (1966). Social comparison and ability evaluation. *Journal of Experimental Social Psychology,* Suppl. 1, 6–26.

Ridgeway C. L., & Walker, H. A. (1994). Status structures. In K. Cook, G. A. Fine, & J. S. House (Eds.), *Social psychology: Sociological perspectives* (pp. 281–310). New York: Addison-Wesley.

Schachter, S. (1959). *The psychology of affiliation: Experimental studies of the sources of gregariousness.* Stanford, CA: Stanford University Press.

Schachter, S., & Singer, J. E. (1962). Cognitive, social and physiological determinants of emotional state. *Psychological Review, 69,* 379–399.

Schwartz, J. M., & Smith, W. P. (1976). Social comparison and the inference of ability difference. *Journal of Personality and Social Psychology, 34,* 1268–1275.

Sedikides, C., & Strube, M. J. (1995). The multiply motivated self. *Personality and Social Psychology Bulletin, 21,* 1330–1335.

Smith, E. R. (1994). Social cognition contributions to attribution theory. In P. G. Devine, D. L. Hamilton, & T. M. Ostrom (Eds.), *Social cognition: Impact on social psychology* (pp. 77–108). San Diego, CA: Academic Press.

Smith, W. (1984). Judgmental goals in the social comparison of ability. *Representative Research in Social Psychology, 14,* 36–51.

Smith, W. P., & Sachs, P. (1997). Social comparison and task prediction: Ability similarity and the use of a proxy. *British Journal of Social Psychology, 36,* 587–602.

Suls, J. (1986). Notes on the occasion of social comparison theory's thirtieth birthday. *Personality and Social Psychology Bulletin, 12,* 289–296.

Suls, J., Gaes, G., & Gastorf, J. (1979). Evaluating a sex-related ability: Comparison with same-, opposite-, and combined-sex norms. *Journal of Research in Personality, 13,* 294–304.

Suls, J., Gastorf, J., & Lawhon, J. (1978). Social comparison choices for evaluating a sex- and age-related ability. *Personality and Social Psychology Bulletin, 4,* 102–105.

Suls, J. M., & Tesch, F. (1978). Students' preferences for information about their test performance: A social comparison study. *Journal of Applied Social Psychology, 8,* 189–197.

Tajfel, H., & Turner, J. (1979). An integrative theory of intergroup conflict. In W. G. Austin & S. Worchel (Eds.), *The social psychology of intergroup relations* (pp. 33–47). Monterey, CA: Brooks-Cole.

Taylor, S. E., Neter, E., & Wayment, H. A. (1995). Self-evaluation processes. *Personality and Social Psychology Bulletin, 21,* 1278–1287.

Turner, J. C., Hogg, M. A., Oakes, P. J., Reicher, S. D., & Wetherell, M. S. (1987). *Rediscovering the social group: A self-categorization theory.* Oxford, England: Blackwell Publishers.

Turner, J. C., & Oakes, P. J. (1997). The socially structured mind. In. C McGarty & S. A. Haslan (Eds.), *The message of social psychology: Perspectives on mind in society* (pp. 355–373). Oxford, England: Blackwell Publishers.

Wagner, D. G., Ford, R. S., & Ford, T. W. (1986). Can gender inequalities be reduced? *American Sociological Review, 51,* 47–61.

Wallston, B. S., & O'Leary, V. E. (1981). Sex makes a difference: Differential perceptions of women and men. *Review of Personality and Social Psychology, 2,* 9–42.

Wheeler, L. (1966). Motivation as a determinant of upward comparison. *Journal of Experimental Social Psychology,* Suppl. 1, 27–31.

Wheeler, L. (1991). A brief history of social comparison theory. In J. Suls & T. A. Wills (Eds.), *Social comparison: Contemporary theory and research* (pp. 3–22). Hillsdale, NJ: Lawrence Erlbaum.

Wheeler, L., Koestner, R., & Driver, R. E. (1982). Related attributes in the choice of comparison others: It's there, but it isn't all there is. *Journal of Experimental Social Psychology, 18,* 489–500.

Wheeler, L., Martin, R., & Suls, J. (1997). The proxy model of social comparison for self-assessment of ability. *Personality and Social Psychology Review, 1,* 54–61.

Wilson, S. R. (1973). Ability evaluation and self-evaluation as types of social comparison. *Sociometry, 36,* 600–607.

Wood, J. V. (1989). Theory and research concerning social comparisons of personal attributes. *Psychological Bulletin, 106,* 231–248.

Wood, W., & Karten, S. J. (1986). Sex differences in interaction style as a product of perceived sex differences in competence. *Journal of Personality and Social Psychology, 50,* 341–347.

Zanna, M. P., Goethals, G. R., & Hill, J. F. (1975). Evaluating a sex related ability: Social comparison with similar others and standard setters. *Journal of Experimental Social Psychology, 11,* 86–93.

4

"Can I Do *X*?"

Using the Proxy Comparison Model to Predict Performance

RENÉ MARTIN

The holding of … inaccurate appraisals of one's abilities can be
punishing or even fatal in many situations

—Festinger (1954a, p. 117).

INTRODUCTION

Self-evaluative processes can speak to a variety of motivations. However, as Festinger
(1954a,b) observed, one major goal of self-evaluation is the accurate assessment of ability. The
proxy model (Wheeler, Martin, & Suls, 1997) prescribes how social comparison information
can be used to address the evaluative question, "Can I do *X*?" Specifically, the model pertains
to situations where an individual confronts a novel task of some consequence. The undertaking
of such a task would be effortful and failure costly. Thus, the individual attempts to formulate
as accurate a performance prediction as possible, before committing to the task itself. Social
comparison may facilitate prediction accuracy. A comparison other who already has completed the novel task may, under certain conditions, function as a substitute, or *proxy*, for the
self in anticipating one's own performance. However, as specified by the proxy model, not all
comparison others are equally informative. The applicability of a given comparison target will
depend on similarity to self and the alignment of variables such as effort and related attributes.

An example will be useful in explicating the key points of the proxy model. Imagine that
you are tempted to climb Longs Peak during a Colorado vacation. Being from Iowa flatland,
you have no past experience with similar tasks and are uncertain whether the hike is a
reasonable goal. Fellow campers tell you that the Longs Peak climb is quite popular, both

RENÉ MARTIN • Department of Psychology, University of Iowa, Iowa City, Iowa 52242.

Handbook of Social Comparison: Theory and Research, edited by Suls and Wheeler. Kluwer Academic / Plenum
Publishers, New York, 2000.

because it is the highest point (14,255 feet) in Rocky Mountain National Park and because it can be scaled without technical equipment. Despite its popularity, the ascent is challenging and potentially dangerous. Only 30% of hikers who attempt the climb actually succeed (Malitz, 1993) and at least 43 people have died on the slopes of Longs Peak from hypothermia and fall-related injuries (Dannen & Dannen, 1994). Further, the climb cannot be attempted at a leisurely pace, because the high risk of afternoon lightening strikes makes it necessary for climbers to be off the summit before noon (Malitz, 1993). It is clear that before lacing up your hiking boots, you will want to carefully consider whether you are likely to succeed in your attempt to reach the summit. In the language of the proxy model, the evaluative question is "Can I do X?" (i.e., "Can I climb Longs Peak?").

The spirit of this example is consistent with Festinger, who pointed out that "it is not enough for the individual to have vague and inexact ideas concerning his possibilities for action in his environment. It seems to be quite important for persons to know quite precisely what their abilities are, what they can and cannot do" (1954b, pp. 193–194). Festinger astutely observed that reality testing can be risky in the natural environment and that there "is the frequent desire to evaluate the ability *before* engaging in the action which would test it" (1954b, p. 195, emphasis in the original). Festinger (1954a,b) indicated that we prefer to use objective standards of evaluation whenever possible. However, there is no obvious objective standard that will help you accurately predict whether you can climb Longs Peak. You might obtain a trail guide from one of the ranger stations in Rocky Mountain National Park. These short books do provide objective information, such as the fact that the Longs Peak trail is 8 miles long, with an altitude gain of 4855 feet (Malitz, 1993). Trail guides also document the potential risks, such as hypothermia and lightening strikes (Dannen & Dannen, 1994; Malitz, 1993). These facts might be enough to persuade the timid at heart (me!) from attempting the climb, regardless of ability level. However, for more adventurous souls, facts about the trail will not provide a definitive answer to the question, "Can I climb Longs Peak?" Because not all abilities can be directly tested, Festinger (1954a,b) proposed that we sometimes resort to comparisons with other persons in lieu of objective standards. The vacationers, backpackers, campers, and rock climbers that crowd Rocky Mountain National Park provide one with a plethora of opportunities for social comparison. However, not all comparisons will yield an accurate prediction of one's ability to climb Longs Peak.

FESTINGER'S SIMILARITY HYPOTHESIS AND PERFORMANCE OUTCOMES

In what came to be known as the similarity hypothesis, Festinger (1954a) proposed that "given a range of possible persons for comparison, someone close to one's own ability or opinion will be chosen for comparison" (p. 121, corollary IIIA). This suggested that a similar comparison other would be most informative in attempting to evaluate one's abilities. The meaning of similarity has been a point of controversy among social comparison theorists and researchers, however. Similarity initially was operationalized in terms of performance outcomes (Wheeler, 1966; Thornton & Arrowood, 1966). That is, a similar other would be someone who performed at your level. From this perspective, if you successfully reached the top of Longs Peak, you then would seek to compare yourself to another successful climber. However, given your concerns regarding whether you should even attempt the climb at all and the potentially catastrophic consequences of failure, delaying comparison until the performance outcome (i.e., whether or not the summit is scaled) is available seems unwise and uninformative. Such a comparison would fail to answer the critical question, "Can I do *X*?"

GOETHALS AND DARLEY'S ATTRIBUTIONAL REFORMULATION

In their attributional reformulation of Festinger's theory, Goethals and Darley (1977) redefined similarity in terms of related attributes, rather than performance outcomes. Related attributes are stable or transient characteristics (see Chapter 3, this volume) that contribute to or predict performance, such as height, age, or fatigue. Goethals and Darley used related attributes to demonstrate how attributional principles operate in social comparisons. According to their perspective, I would not deprecate my hiking abilities if I, at age 40, climbed Longs Peak more slowly than someone who was 20 years my junior. It would not be reasonable for me to expect to climb as briskly as that young adult. In other words, because of the discounting principle (Kelley, 1967), her advantaged related attribute status would lead me to discount the relevance of the comparison. In contrast, if I kept pace up the Longs Peak trail with a climber 20 years younger, I probably would form a positive evaluation of my climbing abilities. That fact that I managed to hold my own, despite being disadvantaged on related attributes, would augment my self-evaluation. Thus, the Goethals and Darley reformulation helps place one's abilities in context, relative to others who are similar, advantaged, or disadvantaged on related attributes. Their approach also has affective implications. A person might feel good if he outperforms someone with superior related attributes or bad if she does not perform as well as someone with similar related attributes. However, these comparisons will not provide an answer to the "Can I do *X*?" question. Knowing that one has performed better or worse than a comparison other with similar related attributes assumes that the performance outcome already has been determined; it is not information that can be used in formulating a performance prediction for a novel task.

COMPARISON MOTIVES

A number of social comparison studies have emphasized the affective consequences of comparing with others more or less fortunate than the self (Morse & Gergen, 1970; Brown, Novick, Lord, & Richards, 1992; Tesser & Campbell, 1982). Downward comparisons are thought to enhance well-being through the comforting realization that things could be worse (Wills, 1981; Wood, Taylor, & Lichtman, 1985). Upward comparisons can be inspirational and facilitate efforts toward self-improvement (Buunk, Collins, Taylor, VanYperen, & Dakof, 1990; Major, Testa, & Bylsma, 1991; Taylor & Lobel, 1989). Alternatively, upward comparisons might represent identification with a superior other (Collins, 1996; Wheeler, 1966). Although there are clear adaptive consequences of construing social comparison information favorably, it would be maladaptive to engage in self-enhancement or affect regulation when predicting performance on a novel, risky task. For example, you might feel inspired to emulate some skilled climber. Or, you might derive satisfaction from the fact that you have the opportunity to enjoy the mountains while your poor colleagues are laboring away back at the office. Whatever positive affect is derived from such comparisons quickly will be ameliorated if you overestimate your capabilities, leaving you stranded on an icy, lightening-swept slope.

Social comparisons motivated by self-enhancement speak to the question of how one might feel good about the self, but these comparison will not address the accurate assessment of ability, or "Can I do X?"

USING THE PROXY MODEL FOR PERFORMANCE PREDICTION

Unlike previous approaches, the proxy model (Wheeler et al., 1997) is unique in its utility for performance prediction. According to the proxy model, a comparison other, or proxy, will be most serviceable when both self and proxy have undertaken some familiar, relevant task (task 1) and proxy has gone on to complete the novel task under evaluation (task 2). If self and proxy performed similarly on task 1, then proxy's task 2 performance might (depending upon certain conditions described below) provide an appropriate basis for self's task 2 performance prediction. However, if self and proxy performed dissimilarly on task 1, the utility of proxy's task 2 outcome for self's performance prediction may be compromised.

Returning to our example, imagine that proxy already climbed Longs Peak successfully. Does proxy's success imply that you too can reach the summit? The informational utility of proxy's performance depends on your history with proxy. Suppose you know that you and proxy both run 10 miles every day. In mapping this example onto the proxy model, the 10-mile run represents task 1. Task 1 is familiar to both you and proxy. Task 1 also is relevant to climbing Longs Peak. The ability to run long distances is likely to be positively correlated with the ability to scale a steep mountain trail. The Longs Peak climb is novel to you (but not to proxy), and it represents task 2.

In this example, proxy and you performed similarly on task 1. That is, you both ran 10 miles. Given this similarity, the fact that proxy successfully climbed Longs Peak *may* suggest that you too can climb the mountain, depending on the configuration of other important variables to be discussed below. But imagine instead that you and proxy had dissimilar task 1 performances. Perhaps proxy runs 20 miles daily, whereas you only run 10. Now information about proxy's Longs Peak climb does not lead to a clear inference regarding your own likely performance. The fact that proxy runs farther than you every day suggests that she might be in better physical condition than you. Thus, if you attempt the Longs Peak climb, you might fail. Then again, you might not. Perhaps if the climb did not tax proxy's abilities too greatly, you might succeed. In other words, proxy's informational utility is compromised if you do not share a history of similar performance on a relevant task (task 1).

The Importance of Knowing Proxy's Maximum Effort

Let us return to the scenario where you and proxy performed similarly on task 1 (i.e., you both ran 10 miles). Even when self and proxy share a similar task 1 performance, some proxies will be more informative than others. If proxy is to be used in formulating an accurate performance prediction, it is important know whether proxy's effort on task 1 represented his or her *maximum possible effort*. Imagine that you head up the trail, based on the information that both you and proxy can run 10 miles and that proxy successfully climbed Longs Peak. Perhaps proxy runs only 10 miles daily because of a hectic schedule, but she actually is capable of running 20 miles. In this case, proxy's task 1 performance was not an accurate reflection of her maximal ability. It may be that the Longs Peak trail requires a "20-mile run capacity," rather than the "10-mile run capacity" that you possess. Consequently, you have placed yourself at considerable risk on the mountainside.

How might you determine whether proxy's task 1 performance was a reasonable reflection of her maximum ability? You would have access to this information if you had observed proxy on several occasions or even competed with her. If past experience told you that proxy was spent after a 10-mile run, that she could not possibly knock off another mile or 3, then you would be confident that her task 1 effort was maximal. Thus, if you knew that you and proxy performed similarly on task 1 and that proxy's performance represented her best effort, then you could reasonably expect to perform at proxy's level on task 2. So, if proxy succeeded in scaling Longs Peak, you would predict your own success. However, if proxy failed, you would conclude that the climb is too risky for you as well. Note that at this stage of the proxy model, proxy's applicability, or relevance, is a function of task 1 performance similarity and maximal effort. In this scenario, related attribute information is unnecessary in formulating an accurate task 2 prediction.

Given that you are far from home in a national park, odds are that the most informative proxy—that comparison other who performed similarly on task 1 and for whom a history of shared experience allows a confident assessment of maximal effort—will not be available. Instead, you probably will have to make do with relative strangers, perhaps an acquaintance from a neighboring campsite or someone you met at the ranger station. Under these conditions, when proxy tells you that she too runs 10 miles daily, you will be unsure whether this reflects her maximum. Fortunately, ambiguous information regarding task 1 maximal effort does not render this comparison other completely irrelevant. Information regarding related attributes can be used to extrapolate whether proxy's task 1 performance probably represented maximum effort. If self and proxy are similar on related attributes, then proxy's task 2 performance probably provides a reasonable basis for prediction, even when task 1 maximum effort is ambiguous.

The Role of Proxy's Related Attribute Standing

For example, imagine you and proxy both run 10 miles daily (task 1 performance similarity) and that proxy previously climbed Longs Peak. However, you are unsure whether proxy's task 1 performance was an accurate reflection of proxy's maximum ability. This should make you cautious about using proxy's Longs Peak success as a basis for your own actions. However, if you and proxy share similar related attributes—for example, you both are 40 years old and from flatland regions—you will be inclined to predict that you can match proxy's task 2 performance. In other words, the model uses related attribute similarity as a substitute for clear information regarding maximal effort.

What if proxy's task 1 maximum is uncertain and proxy is dissimilar on related attributes? Imagine that proxy is 15 years younger and accustomed to high altitudes. In this case, proxy's advantaged related attribute status makes it difficult to infer that the 10-mile daily run is a sound index of proxy's maximum ability. In general terms, you might expect to do more poorly than this advantaged proxy on task 2. Similarly, if you found a proxy whose related attribute standing was disadvantaged (e.g., 15 years older), you might generally expect to outperform that comparison other. However, these performance predictions are imprecise and poorly suited to a consequential undertaking, such as the Longs Peak climb.

Summary

The proxy model is consistent with Festinger's original formulation of social comparison theory in two essential ways. First, Festinger (1954a,b) emphasized accuracy and prediction in his discussions of self-evaluation. For example, consider the following passage:

... let us imagine a high school student who wants to know whether his intellectual ability is such as to enable him to go through college. He also cannot adequately evaluate his ability in the real world. Clearly, going to college and seeking what happens would give him an evaluation of his ability for that purpose, but it is not possible to "reality test" his ability before going to college. (Festinger, 1954b, p. 195)

Festinger's emphasis on accuracy in predicting future performance is captured in the fundamental question of the proxy model: "Can I do X?"

Second, as in Festinger's approach, the proxy model proposes that performance similarity can provide the basis of accurate self-evaluation. However, the model extends Festinger's conceptualization by specifying that information about maximum effort is an important determinant of whether performance similarity represents useful information. Previous social comparison theory and research have not considered the importance of the comparison other's maximum effort and its implications for performance prediction.

As in Goethals and Darley (1977), related attributes play a prominent role in the proxy model. However, the model differs from Goethals and Darley's attributional reformulation in two ways. First, the two approaches address different evaluative questions. If the proxy model asks "Can I do X," Goethals and Darley asked "How good am I, relative to others?" Second, the proxy model specifies that related attributes are especially informative when the comparison other's maximum capacity is ambiguous. When maximum effort is clearly known, the proxy model proposes that related attributes actually are irrelevant in formulating accurate performance predictions.

Classic social comparison theory has emphasized similarity and similarity clearly plays an important role in the proxy model as well. Specifically, task 1 performance similarity and related attribute similarity are figured into the prediction equation. It would be a mistake, however, to assume that the proxy model is about similarity per se. True, the model does propose that a proxy who performed similarly on task 1 will provide a basis for accurate performance prediction (given unambiguous information about maximum effort). However, the model also specifies that a similar comparison other is not useful if that person's maximum effort was ambiguous. Further, the model suggests that dissimilar others (e.g., those with superior or inferior related attributes) sometimes can provide a general sense, albeit imprecise, of how one is likely to fare. Thus, as detailed below, the proxy model addresses the applicability of various comparison others, rather than endowing the similar comparison other with special significance (Higgins, 1996; Mussweiler & Strack, in press; Stapel & Winkielman, 1998).

EMPIRICAL TESTS OF THE PROXY MODEL

The first step toward empirical testing of the proxy model was the development of a feasible laboratory paradigm that incorporated performance of an initial task and prediction regarding a second, novel task. Once developed, this procedure was used, with minor variations, in a series of studies. The general paradigm is detailed below.

The Hand Dynamometer Paradigm

Consistent with the proxy model, participants were asked to predict their performance on a novel task (task 2). Participants had access to two sources of information in formulating their performance predictions: prior personal performance on a discrete, but relevant task (task 1) and social comparison information from a proxy who allegedly had completed both tasks 1 and 2. For several initial tests of the proxy model, both tasks relied on hand strength. Task 1 involved squeezing a handgrip, such as those used by athletes to exercise and strengthen the hand muscles. Participants were required to squeeze the grip as many times as possible during a 30-second period. Task 2 required participants to grip a hand dynamometer as hard as possible on three separate trials. The hand dynamometer uses a hydraulic gauge to measure grip strength in kilograms/force.

All participants took part in individual sessions with a same-sex experimenter. Participants began by completing task 1. The experimenter provided each participant with his or her task 1 score (i.e., the number of handgrip squeezes/30 seconds) verbally and in writing. During a brief rest period, the experimenter left the room to prepare bogus social comparison information. The experimenter then returned and introduced task 2 by briefly displaying and describing the hand dynamometer. Each participant was told that the researchers were interested in how accurately people could formulate performance predictions and that he would be asked to predict his own hand dynamometer performance in kilograms/force.

Before proceeding, some participants received social comparison information regarding a proxy. Different characteristics of the proxy (e.g., task 1 similarity, task 1 maximum effort, related attribute similarity) were manipulated depending on the purpose of each experiment. In some experiments, the incentive for prediction accuracy also was manipulated.

Participants who received information regarding a proxy were told that it sometimes was useful in predicting one's own performance to consider how someone else had fared on the same tasks. Specifically, participants were provided with information regarding the proxy's sex (which always matched that of the participant), task 1 performance, effort, and task 2 performance. In some experimental variations, participants also received related attribute information regarding the proxy. The proxy's task 2 performance was presented in terms of grip strength in kilograms/force for each trial and the average kilograms/force exerted. Information regarding the proxy's task 2 performance always was based on gender and age-specific grip strength norms (Mathiowetz, Federman, & Wiemer, 1986). Thus, all male participants learned that the proxy's average task 2 performance was 46 kilograms/force, whereas all female participants learned that the proxy's task 2 score was 30 kilograms/force.

After a thorough review of the proxy information, participants were asked to predict their task 2 performance in kilograms/force. Prior to analyzing participants' predictions, a prediction difference score (PDS) was calculated by subtracting the proxy's average task 2 performance from each participant's performance prediction. This procedure allowed us to standardize participants' predictions, given that male and female participants received different, gender-normed information regarding the proxy's task 2 performance. The PDS also provided a useful representation of how participants expected to perform relative to the proxy. When participants anticipated a task 2 performance similar to that attained by the proxy, the PDS was near zero. In contrast, participants who expected to perform worse than the proxy had a negative PDS, whereas participants who thought they would outperform the proxy had a positive PDS. The PDS provided the dependent variable for each of the experiments.

How Does Information Regarding Task 1 Outcome Influence Performance Predictions?

The purpose of the initial pilot experiment was to determine the effects of task 1 performance similarity when the proxy's maximum effort was known. Recall that the proxy model proposes that a person can expect to match a proxy's task 2 performance if self and proxy performed similarly on task 1 and if it is known that the proxy exerted maximal effort on task 1. Undergraduate psychology students participated.

The general hand dynanometer protocol was used. Information regarding the proxy's task 1 performance was manipulated and participants were randomly assigned to one of three task 1 performance similarity conditions. In the *similar* condition, the proxy's task 1 score was within one squeeze (above or below) of the participant's score. In the *superior* and *inferior* conditions, the proxy's task 1 score was five greater or five less than the participant's score, respectively. For all participants, the social comparison information conveyed that the proxy had exerted maximal effort on task 1. Specifically, handwritten comments from the experimenter indicated that the proxy had appeared to try as hard as possible during task 1. The PDS, calculated from participants' task 2 performance predictions, provided the experiment's dependent variable. In order to encourage participants to attempt to be as accurate as possible in formulating their task 2 performance predictions, participants were told that the person who formulated the most accurate prediction over the course of the study would receive a $10 prize.

The proxy model suggested three hypotheses. First, in the similar condition, participants should expect to perform at about the same level as the proxy (i.e., PDS near zero). Although information regarding a proxy whose task 1 performance was dissimilar would offer little specific information for a highly consequential task such as climbing Longs Peak, we expected participants to use the proxy's dissimilar task 1 performance in a heuristic manner. Specifically, participants in the superior condition should predict a performance inferior to that attained by the proxy (i.e., negative PDS). Finally, participants in the inferior condition should predict that they would outperform the proxy (i.e., positive PDS).

The pattern of PDS cell means generally was consistent with the hypotheses. Participants in the *superior* condition expected to underperform the proxy (mean = -3.20, SD = 2.95), whereas participants in the *inferior* condition predicted that they would perform above the proxy's level (mean = 3.05, SD = 5.19). Participants in the similar condition fell in the middle (mean = -2.00, SD = 5.75); these participants expected to do better than those participants exposed to a superior proxy, but not as well as those participants who had learned about an inferior proxy, overall $F(2,57) = 9.62$, $P < .001$. Post-hoc comparisons revealed that the performance predictions formulated by the participants in the inferior condition were significantly higher than those observed in both the similar and superior conditions. However, in this pilot sample, no significant difference was found between the superior and similar cells.

This pattern of results emerged more strongly in a follow-up study with a second, larger sample. Information regarding the proxy's task 1 performance again was manipulated as in the pilot experiment. Participants again predicted that they would perform at the proxy's level in the similar condition. Performance expectations were significantly diminished when participants had learned of a proxy with a superior task 1 outcome and significantly larger when the proxy's task 1 score had been lower than that attained by the participant.

In an effort to mirror the tangible consequences that often accompany ability evaluation in the real world, incentive also was manipulated in the follow-up study. Some participants were told that they could receive a monetary prize for formulating a highly accurate performance prediction. It was thought that the incentive manipulation might prompt those participants to be especially rational in evaluating the social comparison information. However, all participants appeared to process the information carefully and rationally, regardless of whether an incentive was provided. This may reflect the fact that the academic laboratory environment often encourages undergraduate participants to pursue the "correct" answer in cognitive tasks (Orne, 1962). In addition, participants' rational behavior, even in nonincentive conditions, suggests that experience may teach us the importance of routinely devoting careful attention and precision to ability self-evaluation.

How Does Information about Ambiguous Task 1 Effort Influence Performance Predictions?

In the first pilot experiment, all participants were led to believe that the proxy's task 1 performance represented maximum effort. In the second pilot experiment, we considered how participants would use information regarding related attributes when the effort exerted by the proxy on task 1 was ambiguous.

The hand dynamometer protocol again was used, with the following modifications. In all conditions, participants learned that the proxy's task 1 performance was similar to their own (within one squeeze). All participants also learned that the proxy's task 1 maximum performance capacity was ambiguous. On the bogus performance record, the experimenter had recorded that she or he was not confident that the proxy had exerted maximum effort on task 1. This conclusion was supported by the following handwritten comment:

> Participant had a severe cold and indicated that he (or she) wasn't feeling well. Said took two decongestant pills about 30 minutes before appointment. Rescheduled to return to lab in 1 week to complete task 2. I was concerned that task 1 performance might not accurately reflect participant's ability. Illness might reduce performance. However, decongestants increase arousal and might actually enhance performance.

Prior to task 1, each participant's hand width was measured in centimeters and it was explained that hand width is positively correlated with grip strength. Hand width provided the basis for related attribute comparisons in this experiment. Participants were randomly assigned to one of three related attribute conditions. In the *similar* related attribute condition, participants learned that the proxy's hand width was within 1 cm of their own. In the *superior* related attribute condition, the proxy's hand width was 5 cm greater than the participant's width. Participants in the *inferior* related attribute condition were told that the proxy's hand width was 5 cm smaller than their own. We expected participants to use information regarding related attributes in formulating their task 2 performance predictions. Specifically, we expected PDS to be near zero in the similar condition, negative in the superior condition, and positive in the inferior condition.

Once again, participants' predictions were consistent with the hypotheses. The mean PDS in the similar related attribute condition was near zero (mean = 0.25, SD = 2.99), indicating that those participants expected their task 2 performances to be equivalent to that of the proxy. Participants in the superior related attribute condition expected to perform below the proxy's level (mean = -1.75, SD = 3.91), whereas participants in the inferior condition predicted that they would outperform the proxy (mean = 3.89, SD = 6.83), overall $F(3,74) = 4.61$, $P < .01$. Post hoc comparisons indicted that predictions in the inferior condition were significantly lower than those in the superior related attribute condition. Significant differences among performance predictions emerged more clearly in a replication using a larger sample. Incentive for prediction accuracy again had no effects in the replication study.

Are Performance Predictions Influenced by Irrelevant Related Attribute Information?

So far, we have seen that when a proxy's maximum effort is known, participants use information regarding that proxy's task 1 performance in a systematic fashion in formulating personal task 2 performance predictions. We also observed that performance predictions are influenced by related attribute information when the proxy's maximum task 1 effort is ambiguous. However, what happens when participants are presented with related attribute information, even though the proxy exerted maximal effort on task 1? The proxy model proposes that related attribute information is irrelevant under such conditions and should be disregarded. Alternatively, some studies (Miller, 1982; Miller, Turnbull, & McFarland, 1988; Suls, Gaes, & Gastorf, 1979) have shown that people sometimes use related attribute information, even when those attributes are known to be uncorrelated with the evaluative dimension.

We initially used the basic dynanometer paradigm to test the effects of irrelevant related attribute information. Information regarding the proxy's task 1 effort was manipulated. Half the participants were told that the proxy appeared to have tried as hard as possible on task 1, whereas the remaining participants learned that the proxy's task 1 effort was ambiguous due to illness and decongestant use. Related attribute information was manipulated as in previous studies, with participants learning about a proxy whose hand width was similar, larger, or smaller than their own. A marginally significant interaction was observed between effort and related attribute information. Post hoc comparisons indicated that when the proxy's task 1 effort was ambiguous, participants used the proxy's related attribute standing in formulating their performance predictions. The cell means were similar to those previously observed. Participants expected to perform at the level of a proxy with similar related attributes. Performance predictions were significantly lower and significantly higher when participants learned about a proxy with superior and inferior related attributes, respectively. A very different pattern of performance predictions was found, however, when it was clear that the proxy had exerted maximum effort on task 1. In these conditions, participants consistently predicted that they would perform at the proxy's level, regardless of the proxy's related attributes. In other words, participants disregarded related attribute information when the proxy's task 1 maximum effort was known.

This very interesting outcome was replicated using a new sample and a new paradigm. The hand dynanometer studies all had tapped physical strength. The new protocol instead utilized an intellectual task. For task 1, participants were asked to attempt to solve a series of difficult paper-and-pencil spatial relations problems. Participants then predicted how long it would take them to correctly assemble a three-dimensional tetrahedron puzzle. Information regarding maximum effort was manipulated as before, yielding two levels (maximum known vs. maximum ambiguous). In order to provide related attribute information, participants responded to a questionnaire regarding how often they engaged in a variety of daily tasks requiring spatial expertise. Participants then were assigned to one of the related attribute conditions (proxy similar, superior, or inferior).

A significant two-way interaction was found between effort and related attribute information. As in the previous study, participants used the related attribute information in formulating their performance predictions only when the proxy's task 1 effort had been ambiguous. When they were told that the proxy had exerted maximal effort on task 1, they disregarded the related attribute information and predicted that they would perform at the proxy's level. To conclude, participants behaved as if related attribute information only was applicable to their predictions under certain conditions.

OTHER EMPIRICAL EVIDENCE

Other research also has yielded findings generally consistent with the proxy model. For example, in a study that helped inspire the development of the proxy model, Jones and Regan (1974) created a laboratory situation in which participants expected to take two separate tests assessing their "cognitive flexibility." After completing the initial test, participants were asked to select a personally appropriate level of difficulty for the second test. Participants' selections were associated with tangible consequences, with a cash prize going to those who made correct selections. Prior to making their choices, participants could choose to speak to one of several comparison others. All comparison others previously had completed the first test. The comparison others' initial test scores were manipulated to be either similar or dissimilar to the participants' scores. In addition, some comparison others already had completed the second test, whereas others had not. Participants tended to select a comparison other whose initial test score was similar to their own and who already had experienced the second test.

Similar to the findings reported here, Smith and Sachs (1997) found that performance predictions varied as a function of receiving information about a proxy who was similar, superior, or inferior to the self. Notably, Smith and Sachs observed that participants were most confident that their performance predictions were accurate when they had received information regarding a similar proxy. This work represents an important precursor to the proxy model, and in fact, Smith and Sachs introduced the term "proxy" to the social comparison literature. The proxy model extends beyond Smith and Sachs' perspective, however, by addressing the selective application of related attribute information as a function of information regarding the proxy's task 1 effort.

Two of Kulik and associates' studies of affiliation under threat are relevant to the proxy model. Kulik, Mahler, and Earnest (1994) randomly assigned participants awaiting a cold pressor task to wait with a partner who either had or had not already undergone the painful procedure. Experienced partners provided an opportunity for participants to seek information, or cognitive clarity, about the upcoming task. Those participants waiting with an experienced comparison other capitalized on the opportunity to gain information by asking questions about both the procedure itself and the partner's evaluation of the experience.

Kulik, Mahler, and Moore (1996) studied social comparison processes among hospitalized patients awaiting open heart bypass surgery. Preoperative patients were randomly assigned either to roommates who had previously undergone cardiac surgery or roommates with noncardiac diagnoses. Similar to subjects awaiting the cold pressor task (Kulik et al., 1994), preoperative patients who were housed with a postoperative roommate actively sought information regarding the surgical procedure. Compared to participants with noncardiac roommates, patients with postoperative roommates ambulated more quickly following surgery, had shorter hospital stays, and reported lower levels of anxiety. Both studies (Kulik et al., 1994, 1996) suggest that exposure to an experienced proxy provides important informational opportunities to gain information and reduce anxiety.

SUMMARY AND CONCLUSIONS

The evidence reviewed generally supported the proxy model and suggested several conclusions. First, as long as the proxy's maximum effort was known, similarity on task 1 performance outcomes provided a sufficient basis for subsequent performance prediction. This outcome is interesting because performance similarity was emphasized in early social comparison research. Similarity on performance outcomes later was discounted as redundant information. For example, Goethals and Darley (1977) observed that "there is the somewhat baffling paradox that presumably the comparison is made in order to find out what the other's opinion or score is, yet prior knowledge of the similarity of his score or opinion is assumed as the basis for comparison" (p. 265). However, our data indicate that performance similarity can be quite useful under certain conditions, that is, when future outcome predictions are based on comparisons of past performance.

We also found that related attribute similarity was useful in formulating performance predictions when the proxy's maximum effort was ambiguous. Although more specific in its operationalization, this finding is largely consistent with Goethals and Darley's (1977) attributional approach. Thus, the proxy model accommodates both the field's early emphasis on performance outcome similarity and its later focus on related attribute similarity. Notably, however, the proxy model goes beyond both Festinger (1954a,b) and Goethals and Darley (1977) in its theorizing. The proxy model is unique in its consideration of information regarding maximum effort and the selective application of related attribute information.

Perhaps our most interesting finding was that participants disregarded related attribute information when the proxy was known to have performed at maximal capacity on task 1. This outcome was quite rational at a prescriptive level. Returning to our Longs Peak example, if you know that your proxy could not possibly have run farther than 10 miles, and that you yourself can run 10 miles, then it is logical to conclude that you will match the proxy's task 2 performance, regardless of the fact that she happens to be 10 years younger than yourself (i.e., advantaged on related attributes). The empirical findings indicate that we can be quite logical and precise in evaluating our abilities, at least under conditions of sufficient motivation and cognitive capacity. Thus, the proxy model represents a reconciliation between Festinger's original conception, which seemed to emphasize performance similarity and later approaches, which emphasized related attribute similarity.

Although our similar comparison others exerted predictable effects on performance predictions, information about dissimilarity also was systematically used. Specifically, participants tended to expect to outperform the inferior proxies and to underperform superior proxies. Dissimilar others probably lack the predictive precision provided by a similar other. For example, comparison with a similar proxy might allow you to predict that you can match her performance by hiking 8 miles. In contrast, comparison with an inferior proxy would suggest that you could hike farther than her 8-mile performance. However, you would be left with uncertainty regarding exactly how far you could hike. Nonetheless, when confronted with information regarding a dissimilar proxy, we attempt to use that information. This response has obvious adaptive value, since few real-world situations are likely to provide the perfectly matched comparison other. It seems likely that potential comparison others fall on a continuum of relevance for any given situation. Some potential proxies clearly do not apply and consequently are ignored. Other potential proxies are more or less useful, depending on their status on variables such as maximal effort and related attributes. For these comparison others, we harvest whatever information can be applied to our personal evaluative question.

This chapter began with a quote from one of Festinger's 1954 papers in which he described how flawed ability appraisals could yield "punishing or even fatal" (Festinger, 1954b, p. 117) consequences. Forty-five years of social comparison research has taught us that comparisons can serve a host of motivations, including self-enhancement and self-improvement. However, Festinger's emphasis on comparison for the purpose of predicting what one can do often has been overlooked, if not entirely lost. Wheeler et al. (1997) provided a systematic explication of how a proxy can provide the sort of test Festinger (1954b) described. Thus, in my view, the proxy model brings social comparison theorizing and research full circle, back to Festinger's original emphasis on answering the question, "Can I do X?"

ACKNOWLEDGMENTS

This research was supported, in part, by grant SBR-9631808 from the National Science Foundation. Portions of these studies were presented at the Nags Head Conference on social comparison, May 1997, and the Nags Head Conference on the self, June 1998. The author thanks Natalie K. Adams and H. Lockett Stewart for their contributions to data collection and analyses and Walter Martin for his assistance in manuscript preparation.

REFERENCES

Brown, J. D., Novick, N. J., Lord, K. A., & Richards, J. M. (1992). When Gulliver travels: Social context, psychological closeness, and self-appraisals. *Journal of Personality and Social Psychology, 62*, 717–727.

Buunk, B. P., Collins, R. L., Taylor, S. E., VanYperen, N. W., & Dakof, G. A. (1990). The affective consequences of social comparison: Either direction has its ups and downs. *Journal of Personality and Social Psychology, 59*, 1238–1249.

Collins, R. L. (1996). For better or worse: The impact of upward social comparisons on self-evaluations. *Psychological Bulletin, 119*, 51–69.

Dannen, K., & Dannen, D. (1994). *Hiking in Rocky Mountain National Park*. Old Saybrook, CT: Pequot Press.

Festinger, L. (1954a). A theory of social comparison processes. *Human Relations, 7*, 117–140.

Festinger, L. (1954b). Motivation leading to social behavior. In M. R. Jones (Ed.), *Nebraska symposium on motivation* (Vol. 2, pp. 191–218). Lincoln: University of Nebraska Press.

Goethals, G. R., & Darley, J. M. (1977). Social comparison theory: An attributional approach. In J. Suls & R. L. Miller (Eds.), *Social comparison processes: Theoretical and empirical perspectives* (pp. 259–278). Washington, DC: Hemisphere.

Higgins, E. T. (1996). Knowledge activation: Accessibility, applicability, and salience. In E. T. Higgins & A. W. Kruglanski (Eds.), *Social psychology: Handbook of basic principles* (pp. 133–168). New York: Guilford Press.

Jones, S. C., & Regan, D. (1974). Ability evaluation through social comparison. *Journal of Experimental Social Psychology, 10*, 133–146.

Kelley, H. H. (1967). Attribution theory in social psychology. In D. Levine (Ed.), *Nebraska symposium on motivation* (Vol. 15, pp. 192–238). Lincoln: University of Nebraska Press.

Kulik, J. A., Mahler, H. I. M., & Earnest, A. (1994). Social comparison and affiliation under threat: Going beyond the affiliate-choice paradigm. *Journal of Personality and Social Psychology, 66*, 301–309.

Kulik, J. A., Mahler, H. I. M., & Moore, P. J. (1996). Social comparison and affiliation under threat: Effects on recovery from major surgery. *Journal of Personality and Social Psychology, 71*, 967–979.

Major, B., Testa, M., & Bylsma, W. H. (1991). Responses to upward and downward social comparison: The impact of esteem—Relevance and perceived control. In J. Suls & T. Wills (Eds.), *Social comparison: Contemporary theory and research* (pp. 237–260). Hillsdale, NJ: Lawrence Erlbaum.

Malitz, J. (1993). *Rocky Mountain National Park: Dayhiker's guide*. Boulder, CO: Johnson Books.

Mathiowetz, V., Federman, S., & Wiemer, D. (1986). Grip and pinch strength: Norms for 6- to 19-year-olds. *The American Journal of Occupational Therapy, 40*, 705–711.

Miller, C. T. (1982). The role of performance-related similarity in social comparison of abilities: A test of the related attributes hypothesis. *Journal of Experimental Social Psychology, 18*, 513–523.

Miller, D. T., Turnbull, W., & McFarland, C. (1988). Particularistic and universalistic evaluation in the social comparison process. *Journal of Personality and Social Psychology, 55*, 908–917.

Morse, S., & Gergen, K. J. (1970). Social comparison, self-consistency, and the concept of self. *Journal of Personality and Social Psychology, 16*, 148–156.

Mussweiler, T., & Strack, F. (In press). Comparing is believing: A selective accessibility model of judgmental anchoring. In W. Stroebe & M. Hewstone (Eds.), *European review of social psychology* (Vol. 10). Chichester, England: Wiley.

Orne, M. T. (1962). On the social psychology of the psychological experiment: With particular reference to demand characteristics and their implications. *American Psychologist, 17*, 776–783.

Smith, W. P., & Sachs, P. R. (1997). Social comparison and task prediction: Ability similarity and the use of a proxy. *British Journal of Social Psychology, 36*, 587–602.

Stapel, D. A., & Winkielman, P. (1998). Assimilation and contrast as a function of context-target similarity, distinctness, and dimensional relevance. *Personality and Social Psychology Bulletin, 24*, 634–646.

Suls, J., Gaes, G., & Gastorf, J. W. (1979). Evaluating a sex-related ability: Comparison with same-, opposite-, and combined sex norms. *Journal of Research in Personality, 13*, 294–304.

Taylor, S. E., & Lobel, M. (1989). Social comparison activity under threat: Downward evaluation and upward contacts. *Psychological Review, 96*, 569–575.

Tesser, A., & Campbell, J. (1982). Self-evaluation maintenance and the perception of friends and strangers. *Journal of Personality, 50*, 261–279.

Thornton, D., & Arrowood, A. J. (1966). Self-evaluation, self-enhancement, and the locus of social comparison. *Journal of Experimental Social Psychology, 2*(Suppl. 1), 40–48.

Wheeler, L. (1966). Motivation as a determinant of upward comparison. *Journal of Experimental Social Psychology, 2*(Suppl. 1), 27–31.

Wheeler, L., Martin, R., & Suls, J. (1997). The proxy model of social comparison for self-assessment of ability. *Personality and Social Psychology Review, 1*, 54–61.

Wills, T. A. (1981). Downward comparison principles in social psychology. *Psychological Bulletin, 90*, 245–271.

Wood, J. V., Taylor, S. E., & Lichtman, R. R. (1985). Social comparison in adjustment to breast cancer. *Journal of Personality and Social Psychology, 49*, 1169–1183.

5

Social Comparison and Influence in Groups

DONELSON R. FORSYTH

Kathi Hudson worried that members of Operation Rescue, a pro-life group, were engaged in illegal activities that would limit women's rights. So she infiltrated the group to spy on their procedures and activities. Two years later she abandoned her pro-choice attitudes and became a born-again Christian. Tobias Schneebaum (1969), a painter from New York City, encountered a tribe called the Akaramas when visiting Peru. For 6 months he lived with them, adopting their customs so completely that he joined them in attacks on neighboring tribes and cannibalistic rituals. David Moore joined a new-age group interested in personal development, religion, and space travel. He gradually adopted the group's standards as his own, to the point that he believed that a passing comet was actually a spacecraft sent to collect his consciousness. He and 38 other members of the group (Heaven's Gate) tried to board the ship by committing suicide.

Although people generally believe that their actions reflect only their personal desires and inclinations, the empirical evidence suggests otherwise. Newcomb (1943), after examining students' attitudes over a 4-year period, concluded their attitudes changed to match those of their classmates at college. Asch (1955) confirmed that individuals change their judgments to match the opinions, judgments, or actions of the people around them. Milgram's (1963) studies of obedience offer suggestive evidence of the limits—or absence of limits—of social influence pressure. Moscovici (1994) found that a group member who steadfastly defends a contrarian view can change the opinions of other group members. Latané and his colleagues discovered that as group members interact over time their attitudes change in predictable ways, for people generally shift to agree with the majority unless they are spatially separated from others (Latané & L'Herrou, 1996). In all these studies individuals' beliefs and self-appraisals were shaped and reshaped by the groups to which they belonged.

But what is the source of the group's power over its members? Do groups intimidate their members? Threaten them? Offer them irresistible rewards? This chapter assumes that the

DONELSON R. FORSYTH • Department of Psychology, Virginia Commonwealth University, Richmond, Virginia 23284-2018.

Handbook of Social Comparison: Theory and Research, edited by Suls and Wheeler. Kluwer Academic/Plenum Publishers, New York, 2000.

influence of a group on its members is subtle rather than intrusive, for it is rooted in the principle of comparison: Individuals evaluate the accuracy of their beliefs and gauge the quality of their personal attributes by comparing themselves to other individuals. The pro-choice advocate who interacts with people who are utterly opposed to abortion cannot forget that everyone in the group thinks the beliefs she holds are not just wrong but immoral. The explorer who lives with a tribe that has no taboo against cannibalism performs such rituals without considering how the members of other societies might judge him. Cult members believe that the leader's plans are reasonable ones, even though they seem outlandish to non-members. In such instances group members change, not because they are pressured directly by others, but because they implicitly formulate and revise their opinions and beliefs and identify their strengths, assets, weaknesses, and liabilities by comparing themselves to specific individuals in their group, to a generalized conception of the average group member, or to members of other groups.

This chapter is a reminder of social comparison theory's foundations in group processes rather than an extension of social comparison to groups. Social comparison research and theory, by tradition, stress individualistic, psychological purposes of comparison, such as satisfying basic drives, defining and enhancing the self, and alleviating distress or anxiety; but Festinger (1954) used the theory to explain shifts in members' opinions, elevated motivation and competition among members, opinion debates, and the rejection of dissenters in groups (Allen & Wilder, 1977; Goethals & Darley, 1987; Singer, 1981; Turner, 1991; Wheeler, 1991). This chapter revisits the theory's roots in groups before sampling some of the roles played by comparisonlike mechanisms in contemporary accounts of group dynamics.

EARLY STUDIES OF COMPARISON IN GROUPS

People are influenced in substantial ways by other people. This assumption, although the cornerstone of social psychology, flies in the face of much of Western thought. Do people depend on others or are they self-reliant? Are they autonomous individualists or enmeshed in complex networks of relationships? Are they group centered or relatively independent? Early studies, such as Sherif's 1936 (1966) experimental study of norms, Newcomb's 1943 "Bennington Study," and Hyman's 1942 (1980) analysis of reference groups, not only provided evidence of the people's social nature and the consequences of this interdependence, but also suggested that much of this interdependence is rooted in social comparison processes.

Norms as Comparison Standards

The theoretical impact of a study is not always related to its external validity. Some of the most important studies in this field, despite using volunteer subjects working on inconsequential tasks in laboratory settings, have nonetheless substantially influenced subsequent theory and research by reliably producing important social events in controlled settings, by breaking down and identifying the components of complex social processes, or by confirming or disconfirming some previously untested assumption of a theory or model (Mook, 1983).

Sherif's 1936 study of norms is one such study, for even though he studied groups working in artificial circumstances he verified one of social psychology's fundamental assumptions: "when external surroundings lack stable, orderly reference points, the individuals caught in the ensuing experience of uncertainty mutually contribute to each other a mode of orderliness to establish their own orderly pattern" (1966, pp. xii–xiii). Sherif, following a tradition established by Durkheim (1897/1966), Sumner (1906), Cooley (1909), Moore (1921), Thrasher (1927), and Shaw (1930), argued that "rules, customs, values, and other sorts of norms" develop, inevitably, whenever people "come together in a situation that lasts for any considerable time" (1966, p. 3). If a group of people find themselves in an unstructured, ambiguous situation where they have no reference point to define their expectations, perceptions, or activities, they spontaneously seek out information from others in the group. Sherif did not think that the group members grudgingly conform to the judgments of others, but rather they use the information contained in other's responses to revise their own opinions and beliefs.

Sherif decided that the autokinetic effect provided an ideal opportunity to study this normative process. This effect occurs when individuals seated in a totally darkened room mistakenly believe that a fixed pinpoint of light is moving. Sherif found that over the course of 100 judgment trials most people establish their own idiosyncratic average estimates, which usually varied from 1 to 10 inches. But when he asked dyads and triads to make judgments, their personal estimates blended with those of other group members until a consensus was reached. In most cases the group's final appraisals reflected an averaging of individual's judgments, such that members who initially believed that the dot was moving relatively large distances (8 to 10 inches) revised their estimates downward, and those judges who reported little or no movement when alone "saw" slightly more movement when making judgments in groups.

Sherif's work verified the operation of social comparison processes under controlled conditions. Although his theoretical framework maintained that the influence he observed was caused by the development of distance norms in the groups he studied, these normative processes were sustained by comparative processes. Individuals were not just acquiescing to the group's decisions, but instead were spontaneously revising their estimates so as to reduce the discrepancy between themselves and others:

> Each compares his judgments with the others, consciously or unconsciously seeking interpersonal support in establishing secure boundaries and reference points where none existed before. This process is one of mutual seeking and mutual support, and not a question of succumbing to or resisting suggestions. (Sherif, 1966, p. xii)

Sherif also documented the relative stability of the changes created by comparison-induced influence. When he dismantled the groups and put participants back in the room by themselves, their judgments followed the pattern established by the group rather than the pattern they displayed as individuals. This carryover effect convinced Sherif that he had documented the development of a norm rather than a momentary shift in judgment resulting from group pressure. Subsequent researchers verified this internalization process by putting a confederate in each three-member group. The confederate deflected the group's consensus upward by consistently overestimating the distance moved before he was replaced with a new, naive subject. The remaining group members still relied on the exaggerated norm, however, and so this newest addition to the group gradually adapted to the higher standard. The researchers continued to replace group members with new subjects, but new members continued to shift their estimates in the direction of the group norm. This arbitrary group norm disappeared eventually, but in most cases the more reasonable norm did not develop until group membership had changed five or six times (Jacobs & Campbell, 1961; MacNeil & Sherif, 1976; Pollis, Montgomery, & Smith, 1975).

Sherif (1966) also noted, but could not completely explain, his subjects' lack of insight into the influence process. A few individuals recognized that they were amending their judgments to take into account the others' judgments, but most were not aware that they were influenced or that the group was converging on a single distance norm: "the majority of the subjects reported not only that their minds were made up as to the judgment they were going to give before the others spoke, but that they were not influenced by the others in the group" (1966, p. 108). He likened this insensitivity to other perceptual illusions, in which individuals are certain that the evidence of their senses is accurate, even when they are repeatedly mistaken in their perceptions.

Normative Pressure in Groups: The Bennington Study

When Sherif was documenting the emergence of consensus in small groups of strangers, Newcomb was studying shifts in college students' political attitudes at Bennington College. Newcomb was intrigued by the dramatic shifts in public opinions in the 1930s when many Americans changed to endorse more liberal, progressive political opinions symbolized by the New Deal. Newcomb believed that these opinion shifts must be tied to changes in the opinions of the groups to which individuals belonged, and he sought to document these influence processes in the women at Bennington College. Newcomb, as a member of the faculty, could not help but recognize the impressive change in students' opinions during the course of their studies. Most came from politically conservative New England families who endorsed Alfred M. Landon, the Republican candidate, rather than Franklin D. Roosevelt, a Democrat, in the 1936 presidential election. Most of the first-year students at Bennington shared the attitudes of their families, for 62% preferred the Landon to Roosevelt. The juniors and seniors, however, were much less conservative in their political beliefs, with only 15% endorsing the Republican candidate (Newcomb, 1943). In explanation, Newcomb suggested that the students' unwittingly changed their beliefs to match the college community's standards. Even though they came from families with conservative attitudes, the college community supported mainly liberal attitudes, and Newcomb hypothesized that many Bennington women shifted their attitudes in response to this peer group pressure.

Newcomb, like Sherif, based his explanation on one fundamental assumption: Individuals evaluate their attitudes by comparing themselves to other members of their group. He gathered indirect evidence of this comparison process by asking students to describe their own political opinions as well as estimate the political beliefs of first-year students, juniors–seniors, and faculty at the college. His measures of political beliefs revealed that 34% of the first-year students were politically conservative, but this percentage was 20% and 10% for the juniors–seniors and faculty, respectively. The women also were relatively accurate when estimating the opinions of these groups, particularly when they were evaluating their own groups. Seniors estimated that 61%, 30%, and 21% of the first-year students, juniors–seniors, and faculty were conservative, thereby overestimating conservatism by 27%, 10%, and 11%. First-year students' same estimates were 52%, 43%, and 39%, thereby overestimating conservatism by 18%, 23%, and 29%. Thus, the first-year students tended to overestimate the conservatism of the seniors and the seniors underestimated first-year students' liberalism.

But why did the relatively conservative first-year students adopt the liberal attitudes of another group of students (the seniors)? Newcomb found evidence that the first-year students tended to accept the seniors as their "frame of reference" rather than their own class. He asked each student to indicate if, on a series of items, their opinion matched the opinion of their classmates. Overall, the women showed an "amazing tendency to assume that their own attitude responses correspond to those of the majority of their classmates" (Newcomb, 1943, p. 49). This tendency was much greater for seniors, however. They felt their opinions were shared by the majority of their classmates (fellow seniors) 76% of the time. First-year students, in contrast, only felt that they agreed with other first-year students for 52% of the items. These same students also felt that their attitudes corresponded to seniors' attitudes 64% of the time. Seniors, in contrast, were much more likely to feel that their opinions were different from those expressed by the first-year students.

Newcomb felt that the opinion shifts that he documented occurred because liberal individuals had more influence on opinions than conservative members. This greater influence was due, in part, to the dominant values of the college, where the faculty were known for their liberal, and even radical, viewpoints. The more popular students tended to be the more liberal students, and those who shifted to become more liberal themselves tended to be (1) "both capable and desirous of cordial relations with the fellow community members" (1943, p. 149), (2) more frequently chosen by others as friendly, and (3) a more cohesive subgroup than the conservative students. Individuals who did not become more liberal tended to express negative attitudes toward the college community or they were very family oriented. Newcomb and his colleagues later summarized these findings by stressing the "*informational environment* of the community and the *status structure* embedded in that environment" (Alwin, Cohen, & Newcomb, 1991, p. 52, italics in original).

Reference Groups as Comparative Baselines

Newcomb did not use the term "reference group" in his 1943 analysis, but his findings are consistent with the idea that people use groups or social aggregates as standards or frames of reference when evaluating their abilities, attitudes, or beliefs (Hyman, 1960). Any group can function as a reference group, including those that are actually statistical aggregations of noninteracting individuals, imaginary groups, or even groups that deny the individual membership (Singer, 1981). When students first enrolled at Bennington their family was their reference group, so their attitudes matched their families' attitudes. The longer students remained at Bennington, however, the more their attitudes changed to match the attitudes of their new reference group, the rest of the college population.

Roper (1940) first introduced the idea of a reference group by suggesting that individuals' perceptions of their own status depends on where they stand in relationship to other people. For example, a man who earns $40,000 may feel very affluent if he lives in a community where most people earn only $20,000, but this same individual will feel relatively impoverished if living in an exclusive, high-dollar suburb. Hyman (1942/1980), however, is generally credited with launching the systematic study of reference groups. At about the same time that Newcomb was completing his analysis of the Bennington findings, Hyman was exploring some of the psychological and sociological factors that determine people's evaluations of their status in society. He based his analysis on Lewin's (1935) general discussion of the impact of social groups on individual's judgments and perceptions. Lewin maintained that the group, like the ground in a figure–ground relationship, influences members' perceptions and judgments but remains relatively unnoticed. Because people belong to many groups, their perceptions vary as their membership in these groups become more or less salient.

Hyman applied Lewin's analysis to people's estimates of their social standing, or status. Status, Hyman noted, is a relational attribute, for it can only be defined by comparing one's accomplishments to other's accomplishments. When Hyman asked his respondents if they ever thought about the standing relative to others, over 80% of his respondents reported that they thought about their relative superiority in at least one of the following domains: economic, intellectual, social, physical appearance, cultural, athletic, prestige, character, political, sexual, religious, self-esteem, and general achievements. Hyman suspected that many of the remaining subjects also thought about their status but were not willing to admit it.

Hyman asked his respondents to identify the individuals and groups they used as reference points in determining their status evaluations in these various domains. He discovered that whereas some individuals compared themselves to actual groups, such as friends, neighbors, work groups, and their families, others used general social categories such as race, occupation, or socioeconomic class. Some individuals used a single reference group across all the domains. For example, one woman who worked as a nurse evaluated her economic, intellectual, and social standing by estimating where she stood relative to other women who were nurses. Most people, however, used multiple reference groups, particularly when shifting from one domain to another. Some individuals also identified subgroups within a larger reference group, like one individual who evaluated his intellectual achievements relative to all academic people, but to social scientists in particular.

In 1950, Merton and Kitt (1950) used the concept of reference groups to reexamine Stouffer and associates' studies of the adjustment of soldiers to military life summarized in *The American Soldier* (Stouffer et al., 1949a; Stouffer, Suchman, DeVinney, Star, & Williams, 1949b). They noted that, in many cases, the men defined their attitudes about the military, combat, and themselves by gathering information from the squads to which they were assigned. New recruits, for example, often described themselves as "ready for battle," whereas few veterans reported any enthusiasm about combat. But when new recruits were transferred into established combat squads, they quickly lost their fervor. The men's attitudes and satisfactions also were shaped by comparison groups that they did not belong to, yet used as the basis for defining the relative quality of their current situation; what Merton and Kitt called nonmembership reference groups. Anticipating the distinction between upward and downward social comparison, the researchers discovered that soldiers who suffered the most—those who had fewer promotions, who experienced racial discrimination, those assigned overseas, and those serving in the front lines of battle—were not necessarily the most dissatisfied. Rather, those individuals who felt their privations were greater than others were more likely to respond negatively to their military service. For example, a married man "comparing himself with his unmarried associates in the Army" felt dissatisfied, but not so much as a married man "comparing himself with his married civilian friends" (Stouffer et al., 1949b, p. 125). Similarly, African-American soldiers often responded more positively to army life than Anglo-American soldiers, because "Relative to most Negro civilians whom he saw in southern towns, the Negro soldier had a position of comparative wealth and dignity" (Stouffer et al., 1949b, p. 563). Merton and Kitt concluded that if individuals compare themselves to a group that is outperforming their group, they will experience dissatisfaction, but should they compare themselves to a group facing even greater hardship, then they will report more satisfaction with their own circumstances.

Studies of reference groups foreshadowed contemporary interest in such processes as social identity, upward and downward social comparison, referent power, and social categorization and stimulated applications to "problems of mental illness, formal organization, marketing and public relations, mass communications, acculturation, political behavior, consumer behavior, labor relations, and juvenile delinquency, as well as to opinion formation" (Hyman & Singer, 1968, p. 7). Singer (1981) offers a comprehensive overview of this work.

Conformity in Small Groups

Other investigators continued to refine the concept of reference groups, but social psychological researchers were more influenced by Kelley's 1952 paper, "Two Functions of Reference Groups." In that paper Kelley drew a distinction between the normative function of reference groups and the comparative function of such groups, and suggested that prior re-searchers had not always distinguished between these two functions. Newcomb's Bennington study (1943), for example, illustrated the normative function of a reference group. This highly cohesive, isolated group developed a relatively well-accepted set of social standards, which many members of the community accepted as their own. It functioned as a positive reference group for most members, for they were motivated to assimilate the values of the group to secure their acceptance by the group. In some cases, though, a group may function as a negative reference group. Individuals may adopt standards that conflict with those of the group to ensure their differentiation from that group.

Hyman's (1942/1980) original studies of reference groups, in contrast, focused on their comparative functions. Hyman discovered that people did not derive their values from their reference groups, but instead used them as baselines to inform their appraisals of their prosperity. Kelley (1952, p. 412) writes, "A group functions as a comparison reference group for an individual to the extent that the behavior, attitudes, circumstances, or other characteristics of its members represent standards or comparison points which he uses in making judgments and evaluations." Deutsch and Gerard (1955), Thibaut and Strickland (1956), and Jones and Gerard (1967) offer similar distinctions, and Shibutani (1955) suggests a tripartite division: normative groups (groups whose norms and outlooks are accepted by the individual), comparative groups (groups that serve as reference points for comparisons and contrasts, particularly about personal qualities), and aspired groups (groups the individual wishes to join or maintain his membership in). Shibutani suggested that the term "reference group" should apply only to comparative groups.

This distinction explains the two types of reactions Asch (1952, 1955) observed in his studies of conformity. Asch, in his pioneering work on conformity in small, temporary groups, arranged for a single naive subject to make simple judgments about the lengths of lines in the presence of his trained confederates who deliberately made mistakes on 12 of the 18 trials. Asch's subjects frequently conformed, even though the task was very simple and the pressures to agree with others were relatively minimal. Yet, on further review, Asch discovered that the groups influenced members both by providing them with a standard judgment that was accepted by all other members and by providing subjects with information about the correctness of their original line choices. Thus, some of Asch's subjects conformed because of informational influence: They thought they were mistaken in their personal judgment and decided the group was correct. Others, though, were responding to normative pressures: they merely went along with the majority, even though they thought the majority was making a mistake.

Deutsch and Gerard (1955) confirmed and extended Kelley's distinction in their study of normative social influence and informational social influence. They defined normative influence as "an influence to conform with the positive expectations of another," with positive expectations described as "expectations whose fulfillment by another leads to or reinforces positive rather than negative feelings, and whose nonfulfillment leads to the opposite, to alienation rather than solidarity" (p. 629). Informational social influence, like Kelley's comparative function, occurs when individuals "accept information obtained from another as *evidence* about reality" (Deutsch & Gerard, 1955, p. 629, italics in original).

Deutsch and Gerard (1955) contrasted these two forms of influence in an Asch-type conformity situation where naive subjects made judgments about the length of lines in the presence of confederates who made deliberate and obvious errors. They sought to separate informational influence from normative influence across a series of experimental variations. In one condition both sources of influence were high, for like the Asch paradigm subjects made their judgments when seated face-to-face with others. In a second condition subjects were sequestered in booths and the choices they made were communicated to others mechanically rather than orally. In other conditions subjects recorded their judgments on a sheet of paper that only they would see (self-commitment), on a sheet of paper that they had to sign (public commitment), or on a "magic pad" (a pad that was erased by lifting up the plastic covering) that was erased after each trial (magic pad self-commitment). They suggested that these commitment conditions would create a second form of normative influence, in which members would feel compelled to be "true to themselves" by not expressing opinions that they personally did not believe. As they predicted, the number of errors was greatest in the face-to-face groups, since informational and normative pressures were high. Conformity dropped when subjects were in small booths that protected their anonymity. Findings from the commitment conditions moreover suggested that commitment to one's choices reduces conformity, particularly for unambiguous problems. From Deutsch and Gerard (1955, p. 634):

> in the Magic Pad variation the normative influences to conform to one's own judgment had to be sustained by the S himself. Normative influences from the S's self (to be, in a sense, true to himself) were undoubtedly also operating in the noncommitment variation. What the Magic Pad did was to prevent the S from distorting his recollection of his independent judgment after being exposed to the judgments of the others. ... The behavior of writing one's judgment down on the Magic Pad makes the original decision less tentative and less subject to change.

The distinction between normative and informational influence continues to be a central theme in studies of social influence, but like all dichotomies the division between groups as sources of information and groups as sources of normative pressure is too simplistic (Forsyth, 1999; Raven, 1992). Turner (1991, p. 147), for example, argues that "informational influence is socially mediated and normative" and "that norms about preferences and values are informative about appropriate, correct beliefs." He suggests that the distinction is actually referring to the source of change: in "others," in the case of normative influence, or in the "self," in the case of informational influence. Forsyth (1999) also focuses on the source of the change when drawing a distinction between informational, normative, and interpersonal influence. Informational influence produces change through persuasion and other cognitive operations, normative information produces change by making salient relevant situational and personal norms, and interpersonal influence works by creating social pressures, such as threats, promises, withholding of reinforcers, and so on. French and Raven (1959) expand this list to six bases of influence: reward, punishment, legitimate, referent, expert, and informational. These various conceptualizations, despite their differences, agree that influence includes both cognitive, informational, and psychological elements *and* interpersonal, normative, interpersonal elements.

Social Communication and Comparison in Groups

Researchers and theorists, up until Festinger's 1954 publication of his theory of social comparison, examined comparative processes in groups, but they did not focus exclusively on comparison per se. Sherif (1966), for example, maintained that norms result from a comparative process that diminishes once the norm is set in place; as group members compare themselves to others a social standard emerges, which individuals then use as a reference point. Newcomb (1943) explored the consequences of this comparative process by finding that new group members will change their attitudes to match the majority's outlook in his Bennington Study, but he did not discuss comparison processes. Similarly, Hyman (1942/1980) addressed comparison processes directly in his analysis of reference groups, but he focused on how people select targets for comparison rather than the interpersonal consequences of that comparison process. Even though these early researchers did not actually use the term "social comparison," the processes that they studied fundamentally depended on the individuals' perceptions of the skills, abilities, and attitudes of the people around them.

In 1954, Festinger's pulled together these various theoretical threads and empirical findings in his theory of social comparison. In that theory he argued that individuals have a fundamental need for accuracy and cognitive clarity, which they satisfy by seeking out information about the accuracy of their opinions and the adequacy of their abilities by comparing themselves to others. The theory (eventually) sired various programs of research into self-evaluation and self-enhancement processes, but as Allen and Wilder (1977) note, it also served to summarize Festinger's early work into the complex dynamics that occur when members of small groups share information about their personal opinions and attitudes. These studies, which provide a backdrop to the 1954 theory, are reviewed briefly below.

The Westgate Study.   Festinger developed social comparison theory in the heyday of group dynamics, long before the self, attributions, heuristics, and other cognitive mechanisms captured researchers' attention. As Cartwright (1979) writes in his historical analysis of the field, social psychology after World War II was very much a group-focused social psychology, with major advances in studies of group cohesiveness, leadership, productivity, conformity, and social-comparison-like processes. Much of this group-oriented emphasis resulted from Lewin's influence on the developing discipline, for he assumed that individuals cannot be understood apart from the small face-to-face groups to which they belong. Indeed, Lewin's Research Center for Group Dynamics, which he founded at MIT, was the site of Festinger, Schachter, and Back's 1950 study of Westgate and Westgate West (Festinger, 1980).

Festinger, Schachter, and Back (1950, p. 7) were convinced that "groups have power over their members. They exert influence on their attitudes, on their behavior, and even on the kinds of activities in which their members engage." But what is the source of this influence? To answer this question they surveyed the residents of Westgate and Westgate West, two housing developments filled, at random, with students and their families. These two projects offered Festinger and colleagues (1950) an excellent opportunity to not only study group formation, but also the "relatively subtle influences which are exerted during the normal communication process among members of a group" (p. 7).

The Westgate studies confirmed Festinger's suspicions about the role propinquity plays in determining the formation of relationships among members. Residents reported the closest relationships with those who they encountered frequently during the course of the day, due to the close proximity of their mailboxes or residences. But Festinger et al. (1950) also discovered that the group members' attitudes closely paralleled these spontaneously emerging inter-personal networks, such that "within each of these small face-to-face groups, group standards" developed that defined members' opinions on various attitudinal issues. Moreover, "each group exerted strong influences on its members to conform to its standards," and the effectiveness of the group in swaying its members "depended to a major extent on how cohesive the small social group was" (Festinger et al., 1950, p. 11). Festinger believed that some of this influence resulted from residents' conformity to the group's attitudinal norms— normative influence—but much of the influence was also rooted in social comparison:

> The hypothesis may be advanced that the "social reality" upon which an opinion or attitude rests for its justification is the degree to which the individual perceives that this opinion or attitude is shared by others. An opinion or attitude that is not reinforced by others of the same opinion will become unstable generally. There are not usually compelling facts which can unequivocally settle the question of which attitude is wrong and which is right in connection with social opinions and attitudes as there are in the

case of what might be called "facts." If a person driving a car down a street is told by his companion that the street ends in a dead end, this piece of information may be easily checked against physical "reality." ... The situation with regard to social opinions and attitudes is quite different, however. Here there is no such "physical reality" against which to check. (Festinger et al., 1950, pp. 168–169)

Festinger discovered that residents, during their daily interaction, discussed attitudinal issues and thereby gained information about the consensus of opinion within their groups and the relative uniqueness of their attitudes. Individuals who expressed deviant attitudes tended to be individuals who, due to isolation from others, could not engage in this comparative process or misinterpreted the distribution of attitudes within their groups. But those closely connected by friendship or membership in a clique shared "a common fund of information about a variety of matters.... they will know and they will not know many of the same things" (p. 167).

Communication Pressures in Small Groups.   Festinger and his colleagues explored some of the implications of the Westgate and Westgate West findings in a series of laboratory studies and dissertation projects (Back, 1951; Festinger, Gerard, Hymovitch, Kelley, & Raven, 1952; Festinger & Thibaut, 1951; Festinger, Torrey, & Willerman, 1954; Gerard, 1953; Hoffman, Festinger, & Lawrence, 1954; Schachter, 1951). These projects tested Festinger's (1950) "informal social communication" theory, which argued that people in groups—particularly cohesive groups—will gradually drift toward uniformity of opinion over time. His theory suggests that when individuals find that they disagree with their group, they can (1) communicate with one another until the discrepancy is resolved; (2) change their opinion to match the views expressed by the majority of the members; or (3) minimize the group's relevance as a reference point by leaving the group, rejecting disagreeing group members or avoiding information that suggests members disagree. Which of these reactions will occur depends on the cohesiveness of the group, the nature of the attitudinal issue under discussion, and the goals of the group.

All these studies assume group members engage in social comparison, but they focus more on the interpersonal dynamics that this comparative process stimulates. Festinger and Thibaut (1951), for example, studied the impact of persuasive messages on people who disagreed with the majority of the group members. They carefully measured the persuasive messages members of small groups sent to each other, after manipulating the stress on the group to reach consensus, members' knowledge of the issues the group was discussing, and their perceptions of the group's diversity. Festinger and Thibaut reasoned that these three variables should act in concert to increase communication with people who hold extreme opinions. When the group members felt compelled to reach agreement, then they would be more likely to locate and influence people who held opposing views. Members also would feel more confident in influencing others when they were secure in their beliefs, so they also should give rather than accept influence. Members of heterogeneous groups also would be more likely to recognize the need to communicate their opinions to others, and so would likely communicate at a higher rate. (Festinger and Thibaut, however, manipulated diversity by telling some groups that the members varied considerably in terms of their expertise. Hence, this manipulation also may have influenced communication patterns by convincing members of the supposed heterogeneous groups that others would be more accepting of influence, since they were less capable.) These predictions were all confirmed, but Festinger and Thibaut also noted that these pressures usually resulted in the outliers changing at a higher rate; but if they did not change, then they were rejected by the group members. Festinger et al. (1952) extended these results by discovering that people who have beliefs and opinions that differ to a great extent from others withdraw from the group before the group has an opportunity to reject them.

Schachter (1951) studied the intensity of communication efforts with a disagreeing group member in his dissertation. He planted three kinds of confederates in a number of all-male discussion groups. The "deviant" always disagreed with the majority. The "slider" disagreed initially, but conformed over the course of the discussion. The "mode" consistently agreed with the majority. Schachter also manipulated the groups' cohesiveness, and asked groups to discuss a topic that was either relevant or irrelevant to group's stated purposed. He discovered that the group members initially communicated with the mode, deviant, and slider at equal rates, but once they became aware of the deviant and slider's disagreement, communication centered on these two. When the slider capitulated to the group's consensus, then the interaction shifted to the deviant alone. This concentrated communication lasted until the end of the session in all but one type of group: cohesive groups working on an issue that was relevant to the group goals in which members developed a negative attitude toward the deviant. In such groups communication with the deviant dropped precipitously, evidence that group had reached consensus by excluding him (Berkowitz, 1971; Levine, 1980).

COMPARISON IN GROUPS: CONTEMPORARY APPLICATIONS

Even though early social psychologists did not explicitly used the term "social comparison," they nonetheless frequently investigated processes that were fundamentally driven by comparisonlike processes. Festinger and colleagues recognized the impact of comparison processes on groups, and they carried out an impressive series of studies of the postcomparison group processes framed around the question: Once members discover that other people hold differing opinions, when do they try to persuade them, when do they change themselves, and when do they reject dissenters? Festinger stressed group processes to such an extent in his work that he was chosen to author the groups chapter for the *Annual Review of Psychology* in 1955.

Given this historical context, it is not surprising that many group researchers and theorists, when they encounter an anomalous finding or perplexing bit of group behavior, offer explanations that refer to the principle of comparison. Few directly test the theory's assumptions in their studies, but their theoretical conceptualizations rely on it so much that, to paraphrase Arrowood (1978), social comparison theory is everyone's second favorite explanation of group processes. Here we consider but a sample of the theoretical analyses that rely in part on social comparison to explain group-level processes.

Group Formation

Schachter (1959), in his classic analysis of affiliation, took Festinger's (1950, 1954) theories of social communication and comparison one step farther by suggesting that individuals, when in need of information, will seek out others so that they can determine whether their views are "correct," "valid," and "proper" (Festinger, 1950, p. 272). He tested this idea by leading his subjects to think that they were going to receive a series of electric shocks. He discovered that 63% of the women who were told the shocks would be very painful (high-anxiety condition) preferred to await their turn with other people, but that only 33% of those told the shocks would be hardly noticeable chose to wait with others (low-anxiety condition). Schachter maintained that these differences in affiliation reflected participant's need for information and the satiation of that need through social comparison processes, and he summarized his findings with the phrase "misery loves company" (see Chapter 15, this volume).

Contemporary analyses continue to stress the informational value of joining with others in groups, but add additional functions served by groups, such as esteem, social support, identity, the opportunity to influence others, and self-exploration (Deaux, Reid, Mizrahi, & Cotting, 1999; Helgeson & Michelson, 1995; Wright & Forsyth, 1997). Many of these alternative functions are sustained, in part, by social comparison processes. Social identity theory, for example, stresses the value of achieving a collective identity based on categorizing oneself as a group member. These categorization and identification processes that are posited by the theory, however, assume that members compare themselves to the prototypical group member and compare their own group to other groups (Turner, Hogg, Oakes, Reicher, & Wetherell, 1987; see Chapter 19, this volume).

Studies of downward and upward comparison also confirm the self-esteem building and threatening consequences of comparisons with groups and group members whose performance, adjustment, skills, abilities, or aptitudes are relatively superior or inferior. When group members compare themselves to members who are experiencing even more severe hardships or are failing to cope well with their problems, members' sense of victimization decreases and their self-esteem increases (Gibbons & Gerrard, 1989; Wood, Taylor, & Lichtman, 1985). When they compare themselves to people who are coping effectively with their problems, this upward social comparison helps members identify ways to improve their own situation and promotes their feelings of hope (Buunk, 1995; Snyder, Cheavens, & Sympson, 1997). But upward comparison can also undermine self-esteem. Wheeler and Miyake (1992), for example, asked students to keep track of the people they compared themselves to over a 2-week period; they found that students reported feeling depressed and discouraged when they associated with superior people. Taylor, Falke, Shoptaw, and Lichtman (1986) suggest that self-help groups, or support groups, that include people who are coping extraordinarily well with their illness can make other members feel as though their coping efforts are inadequate.

Because these negative consequences of upward comparison appear to be greatest when comparisons involve attributes or skills that are central to individuals self-definitions (Lockwood & Kunda, 1997), individuals may deliberately avoid joining groups that include people who outperform them in spheres they consider to be personally important. Extending Tesser, Campbell, and their associates's self-evaluation maintenance (SEM) model to groups suggests that ideal groupmates perform worse on tasks that other members think are important but very well on tasks that other members do not think are important. Such associates provide members with targets for downward social comparison, and by drawing attention to their association with them, members bask in the glory of their accomplishments in areas that do not interest them (Tesser, 1988, 1991; Tesser & Campbell, 1983; Tesser, Campbell, & Smith, 1984). Indeed, Winkel and Renssen (1998) report that individuals may not understand the comparison needs of the fellow group members, and so too frequently provide them with upward social comparison information ("The same thing happened to Ed, but he's doing fine now") rather than downward social comparison information ("You are doing so much better than Ed").

Social Influence and Social Comparison

As early theorists like Asch (1955) and Kelley (1952) noted, people sometimes conform, not because they are pressured by others or because they are loathe to deviate from the group's norms, but because they discover new information about a situation by observing others' responses. When individuals face ambiguous situations or see others acting in unexpected ways, they undertake a systematic analysis of their position to determine whether it requires revision. If this review reveals additional information relevant to their opinions, then they revise those opinions, not because they buckle under social pressure but because the data gathered from social sources provide them with a new interpretation (Allen & Wilder, 1977).

Majority Influence and Social Comparison.   Mackie (1987) investigated the cognitive foundations of conformity in groups by leading her subjects to believe that they were part of a small minority that disagreed with the majority on such matters as foreign policy and juvenile justice. After her subjects listened to members of both the minority and the majority argue their positions, Mackie asked them to record their thoughts and reactions. These thoughts, when analyzed, revealed that the subjects recalled more thoughts that were consistent with the arguments offered by those who disagreed with them, particularly when they were members of the minority. Mackie also found that people who processes the majority's message more extensively also changed their opinions more than those who did not process the message (De Dreu & De Vries, 1996; Trost, Maass, & Kenrick, 1992).

Allen and Wilder (1980) argued that exposure to others' positions, in addition to stimulating thoughtful analysis of available evidence, also can cause group members to reinterpret, or cognitively restructure, key aspects of the issue (Allen & Wilder, 1980; Tindale, Smith, Thomas, Filkins, & Sheffey, 1996; Wood, Pool, Leck, & Purvis, 1996). They documented this restructuring by asking subjects to define the meaning of certain phrases in a series of statements. Each statement was accompanied by information about the opinions of a previous group of participants, and subjects' interpretations of the phrases were influenced by this information about opinions. If, for example, the subjects were shown the item, "I would never go out of my way to help another person," and then they learned that a four-person group had unanimously agreed with the statement, subjects interpreted the phrase "go out of my way" to mean "risk my life" rather than "be inconvenienced" (Allen & Wilder, 1980, p. 1118). In such situations people who spend more time thinking about the issues are the ones who conform more (Campbell, Tesser, & Fairey, 1986).

Social comparison also generates conformity by capitalizing on group members' willingness to use heuristics when they process information gathered in social situations. Although Festinger (1954) assumed that social comparison serves the need for accurate information about the correctness of one's opinions when cognitive resources are limited or the motivation to do the cognitive work necessary to weigh the information available is minimal, people use heuristics to generate decisions efficiently and rapidly (Baker & Petty, 1994; Peterson & Nemeth, 1996; Wood et al., 1996). When individuals are in groups and social comparison processes convince members that most of the group members are in agreement, then such heuristics as "majority rules" will prompt them to accept the majority's viewpoint (Chen, Schechter, & Chaiken, 1996). As a result, when people are asked why they changed their opinions in conformity situations, they rarely admit that others influenced them, for these changes were driven by hard-to-access heuristic thought rather than systematic thought (Buehler & Griffin, 1994; Griffin & Buehler, 1993).

Minority Influence and Social Comparison.   Researchers, in the years since Festinger and colleagues (1950) demonstrated that groups tend to become more attitudinally homogeneous over time, have sought to explain why some groups change to agree with the minority's position. This work was stimulated in large part by Moscovici's (1994) studies of the impact of a consistent minority on a majority. Moscovici argued that minorities influence majorities by creating "cognitive conflicts" that challenge the status quo of the group by calling for a reevaluation of issues at hand. Such a minority undermines the majority's certainty and forces the group to seek out new social comparison information. When a minority is present, groups take longer to reach their conclusions and they are more likely to consider multiple perspectives when drawing conclusions (Peterson & Nemeth, 1996).

Nemeth and Wachtler (1983) examined minority influence by having people work a series of puzzles alone, in groups, or in groups with a consistent minority. When people worked alone, their solutions were not very creative, and when they worked in a group, they usually just picked the solution favored by the majority. But when a minority of two confederates argued for a nonobvious solution, the group's solution was more creative. The group did not necessarily accept the minority's proposal, but the minority did stimulate reevaluation of the original answer. Other research suggests that minorities are the most influential when they adopt a consistent behavioral style and offer compelling arguments and the majority is uncertain of the correctness of its position (Witte, 1994). Minorities become less influential when the other members of the group redefine the boundaries of the group so that the minority is thought to be a member of the out-group (Alvaro & Crano, 1997). All these factors influence the impact of minorities by changing their value as sources of social comparison. Just as the individual who hears that eight other people favor position X is likely to reconsider her decision to favor Y, exposure to two individuals who consistently and enthusiastically argue that Z is the correct choice stimulates cognitive reevaluation of the available information. If the minority's viewpoint is a reasonably one, the group may shift to adopt it; but if the majority continue to favor an alternative, then the communication pressures that Festinger (1955) identified will likely be brought to bear on the dissenters.

This comparison process may lead to immediate change, but as Moscovici (1994) argues in many cases the impact of the minority on the majority emerges only over time. His dual-process model of minority influence argues that individuals who are part of the group's majority rarely review the arguments that support their position. But when they discover, through social comparison, that someone in the group disagrees with them, they must devote more cognitive resources to their position. This review may not lead to change immediately, but it may cause members to change their positions at a later time or on a related task (Moscovici, Lage, & Naffrechoux, 1969).

Collective Information Processing

Festinger's (1950) early studies of communication in groups argued that such communication is functional, for it creates channels through which information flows among members. Similarly, recent studies of groups making decisions suggest that groups, when faced with a problem in need of solution, use discussion as a vehicle for gathering social comparison information. Indeed, many procedures used by groups to control discussion—rules of discussion (such as Robert's Rules of Order), voting, round-robin presentations like the nominal group technique, secret ballots, and straw polls—deliberately augment or suppress the collection of social comparison information (Hinsz, Tindale, & Vollrath, 1997; Kerr, MacCoun, & Kramer, 1996).

Jury Decisions. Juries, by design, free members from comparison pressures. They meet for a limited period of time in a highly formal setting and members are cautioned not to engage in any discussion of the case before they begin deliberations. Indeed, as Hastie, Penrod, and Pennington (1983) note, many juries move toward their final verdict cautiously. These evidence-driven juries deliberate by first reviewing the evidence available, and only then try to create a coherent story that accounts for the questioned events.

Hastie and colleagues, however, also identified a second type of jury: one that engages in social comparison as the first stage of deliberation. They call such juries verdict driven, for members "advocate only one verdict at a time," and they cite evidence to support their preferred interpretation. The deliberation also tends to contain "many statements of verdict preferences and frequent pollings" (1983, p. 163).

This striving for social comparison information speeds up the deliberation process, for verdict-driven juries needed only 63% of the time an evidence jury uses to make its decision (Hastie et al., 1983). The discussion in such juries also tends to be less rigorous and fails to a degree to tie the evidence presented during the trial to the legal specifications of the charges. The two types of juries, though, do not differ consistently in the verdicts they favor.

Oversampling Shared Information. Stasser and colleagues have discovered that groups' reliance on social comparison to reach agreement on decisions has one negative consequence: groups spend too much of their discussion time examining shared information—details two or more of the group members know in common—rather than unshared information (Stasser, 1992; Stasser, Taylor, & Hanna, 1989; Wittenbaum & Stasser, 1996). This bias, although not always calamitous, can cause the group to make an incorrect decision if the full disclosure of all information would yield the correct solution, whereas the disclosure of only shared information yields an incorrect decision.

This tendency to oversample shared information reflects, in part, the dual functions of social comparison identified by Kelley (1952). As a means of acquiring data, discussions help individuals process the information they need to make good decisions. But as a form of normative influence, discussions give members the chance to influence each others' opinions on the issue. Discussing unshared information may be informationally useful, but discussing shared information helps the group reach consensus on the matter. Indeed, group members who anticipate a group discussion implicitly focus on information that they know others possess, instead of concentrating on information that only they possess (Wittenbaum, Stasser, & Merry, 1996); and they discuss shared information first and only later get to unshared information (Larson, Foster-Fishman, & Keys, 1994).

Consensus Estimation and Pluralistic Ignorance. Just as oversampling shared information can lead group members to make errors, too little social comparison can cause group members to misinterpret the amount of consensus present in their groups. Janis (1982), in his insightful analysis of groupthink, argues that many disastrous decisions are caused by group members' assumption of consensus when consensus does not, in fact, exist. In his case studies of groups that made disastrous decisions he repeatedly discovered that the members seemed to agree so completely that they only went through the motions of debate. Members' retrospective accounts usually revealed that many of the group's members had grave doubts about the decisions being made, but they short-circuited social comparison processes by not expressing their misgivings during the meetings. In such settings Janis (1982, p. 39) believes group members play up "areas of convergence in their thinking, at the expense of fully exploring divergences that might disrupt the apparent unity of the group."

Miller and McFarland (1991, p. 287) review empirical studies of the conceptually similar process known as pluralistic ignorance: "a state characterized by the belief that one's private thoughts, feelings, and behavior are different from those of others, even though one's public behavior is identical." They trace this concept back to Allport (Katz & Allport, 1928), who used the term to explain instances in which a substantial proportion of a group privately disagrees with a group decision, practice, or standard, yet the unpopular element remains firmly entrenched in the group. Latané and Darley (1970) use this concept to explain why bystanders sometimes mistakenly interpret an emergency as a nonemergency. Although the individual witness feels that something is wrong, he or she misinterprets the nonreaction of others as evidence that no help in fact is required. This misinterpretation could be corrected if individuals share their interpretation of the situation rather than only relying on others behavior as evidence of the nature of the problem.

Attitude Polarization and Comparison. Researchers in the 1960s, after intensive analysis of the tendency for groups to make riskier decisions than individuals, concluded that the so-called risky-shift was part of a larger, more general process. When people discuss issues in groups, they tend to make more extreme decisions than would be suggested by the average of their individual judgments. Discussion, rather than subduing and moderating, polarizes: Judgments made after group discussion are more extreme in the same direction as the average of individual judgments made prior to discussion (Myers & Lamm, 1976).

Researchers initially argued that this polarization process occurs because people in groups feel less responsible for their decisions and are overly influenced by risk-prone leaders. In time, however, they recognized that the shift is likely a comparative processes (Isenberg, 1986). When people make decisions individually, they have no way to determine whether they are risk averse or risk takers. But when group members make choices together, they use others as an index of their risk-taking tendencies (Goethals & Zanna, 1979; Myers, 1978). Polarization occurs because group members, through discussion, discover the group's norm, or average, degree of risk, and they stake claim to a position that exceeds that norm in whatever direction the majority of the members endorse (usually risk). As Brown (1974, p. 469) explains, "To be virtuous ... is to be different from the mean—in the right direction and to the right degree." Polarization may also occur because the presence of more risky (or more cautious) individuals "releases" the individual group member from normative constraints in the group, so that they feel free to express more extreme opinions (Pruitt, 1971). Social comparison theory also explains why just knowing the positions of the other people in the groups, and not the reasons behind these opinions, is sometimes sufficient to produce polarization (Blascovich, Ginsburg, & Howe, 1975).

An alternative explanation of group polarization—persuasive arguments theory (Vinokur & Burnstein, 1974, 1978)—focuses on informational influence rather than interpersonal and normative influence. This theory assumes that individuals base their decisions on the number and persuasiveness of the arguments that they have for and against each position. If, for example, a group generates more arguments favoring a risky choice than a cautious choice during discussions, then the group will polarize. And groups can, in most cases, generate more arguments that support the position endorsed by the majority of the group or the position that is most consistent with dominant social values, in part because members may be more willing to express arguments that are consistent with social norms. In all likelihood, then, polarization processes are sustained by comparison processes that not only provide members with additional cognitive information, but also help them determine whether their views are "correct," "valid," and "proper" (Festinger, 1950, p. 272).

Social Loafing and Comparison

Ringelmann (1913), a French agricultural engineer, was the first researcher to document the loss of productivity in groups working on collective tasks. Even though groups generally outperform individuals, they rarely reach their full potential. Inadequate coordination of effort explains part of this productivity loss, but much of the loss is caused by social loafing: People do not work quite so hard in groups. This loss of motivation is sustained, in part, by members' tendency to compare their contributions. Group members may want to do their share to help the group reach its goals, but they do not want to do more than their share. So they compare their contributions to those of others, and reduce their effort so that it matches the average rate. Loafing increases when this comparative process convinces group members that their co-workers are holding back. Hence, groups loaf less when they are confident that others are also working hard, when individual contributions are known, and when a standard can be used to evaluate performance (see Karau & Williams, 1993).

The same productivity-limiting processes explain the relatively poor performance of brainstorming groups, for social comparison processes conspire to lower standards for perfor-mance when generating ideas. Although undercontributors are challenged to reach the pace established by others, overcontributors tend to reduce their contributions to match the group's mediocre standards. This *social matching effect* tends to lower performance levels overall, but it can be minimized by increasing feelings of competition among members (Brown & Paulus, 1996; Paulus & Dzindolet, 1993; Seta, Seta, & Donaldson, 1991). Social matching also undermines productivity in groups working via computers (Paulus, Larey, Putman, Leggett, & Roland, 1996). Researchers controlled how much information was exchanged among participants with three types of displays. Some subjects saw only their own ideas, others gained access to all the group's ideas at the end of the session, and still others were shown a continuously updated list of ideas generated by the group members. Group members who could monitor others' idea production in real time—they could see each new idea as it was posted rather than waiting for a summary at the session's end—displayed social matching. Their rate of idea generation decreased during the course of the session to match the produc-tion rates of the other group members (Roy, Gauvin, & Limayem, 1996)

Studies of Normative Influence

Social comparison—of the more normative than informational variety—also influences the transmission of religious, economic, moral, political, and interpersonal beliefs in groups. Conceptually extending Newcomb's (1943) Bennington Study, Crandall (1988) found that eating disorders, such as excessive dieting, binging, and purging, are supported by group norms. The college women he studied who did not purge began to purge when they joined a sorority in which the most popular members purge. And which women were the most popular in these groups? Those women who purged at the rate established by the group's norms.

Fisher (Fisher, 1988; Fisher & Fisher, 1993) also links healthy and unhealthy behavioral tendencies to comparison-based processes. Even though people recognize the consequences of unprotected sex, they rarely take steps that will reduce their vulnerability to AIDS and other sexually transmitted diseases. Indeed, people often claim that the threat of AIDS has made them more cautious when it comes to sex, but self-reports of change do not always correspond to behavioral changes. Fisher, in explaining this gap between health attitudes and healthy behaviors, notes that social norms do not support preventive behaviors. Norms of many college campuses are either silent on the issue of condom use or openly antagonistic. Norms may even encourage some risk-increasing behaviors by sanctioning casual relationships and promoting the value of risk. Some social groups may embrace a risky practice to such a degree that the individual risks ostracism by breaking the norm.

Prentice and Miller (1993) describe a related cycle of normative influence in their study of alcohol abuse on a college campus. Most of the students who participated in their study endorsed a personal norm against overindulgence, but they believed that their campus's norms encouraged heavy alcohol consumption. The men responded to this normative influence by gradually internalizing the misperceived norm. They began to drink more the longer they stayed at the school. The women, in contrast, responded by distancing themselves from their university and its norms about drinking (Prentice & Miller, 1993).

Normative influence also can be used to promote healthy, prosocial behaviors. Fisher (1988), for example, has developed an extensive educational program designed to change people's perceptions of norms related to sexual conducted. Similarly, Cialdini and colleagues have used normative social influence to increase pro-environment actions (Cialdini, Kallgren, & Reno, 1991; Cialdini, Reno, & Kallgren, 1990). In their field studies of littering they distinguish between *descriptive norms* and *injunctive norms*. Descriptive norms promote informational influence, for they define what most people would do, feel, or think in a particular situation. Injunctive norms, in contrast, promote normative influence by including an evaluative component. "Most people don't litter" is a descriptive norm, whereas "Harming the environment is wrong" is injunctive. Cialdini contrasted these two forms of influence in a field study of subjects getting into their cars. Subjects encountered a confederate either in the lot where their car was parked or on the path leading to the parking lot. In the descriptive norm condition the confederate dropped a bag of trash into a garbage can. In the injunctive norm condition the confederate picked up a piece of litter and disposed of it in the garbage can. In the control condition the confederate merely walked by the subject. When subjects reached their car, they found a handbill under their windshield wipers. Descriptive norms were nearly as influential as injunctive norms, but their impact wore off rapidly. If the encounter between the subject and the confederate occurred in the parking lot only 17% of the subjects in the descriptive norm condition littered. This percentage jumped to 36%, however, if the confederate's litter-conscious actions had occurred on the path leading to the lot. In contrast, the injunctive norm became more powerful over time. No one who saw the confederate pick up litter on the path leading to the lot littered (Reno, Cialdini, & Kallgren, 1993, study 3).

This distinction between descriptive and injunctive norms is consistent with Festinger's (1950) original insights. As he noted, social comparison lets people determine whether their conclusions are accurate ("correct"), whether their perceptions are veridical ("valid"), and whether their actions are moral ("proper"). Additional research is needed to determine the role that comparison processes play in determining moral thought, judgment, and action, for as Miller and Prentice (1996, p. 799) note, "there is nothing either good or bad but comparison makes it so."

Social Comparison as Group Process

Social comparison theory argues that people, by comparing themselves to others, can satisfy a profusion of personal motives (Helgeson & Michelson, 1995). They can, as Festinger (1954) originally noted, erase their self-uncertainties by comparing their beliefs and abilities to others. People also can raise their self-esteem by comparing themselves to worse-off others (Wills, 1991), buoy up their hopes through comparison with high achievers (Major, Testa, & Bylsma, 1991), and reassure themselves by comparing themselves to people who are not worried (Affleck & Tennen, 1991). They can even confirm their sense of uniqueness by discovering their views are relatively unique ones (Goethals, Messick, & Allison, 1991) or downplay their idiosyncrasies by recognizing they are shared by many others (Gross & Miller, 1997).

But social comparison theory is as much a theory about group dynamics as it is a theory about individual's perceptions of their opinions and abilities. The theory springs from studies of small, interacting groups, for Festinger used the principle of comparison to explain why groups tend to be homogeneous with respect to attitudes and values. It remains a central tenet in studies of reference groups' power to sway the attitudes of their members. The principle of comparison also has informed researchers' and theorists' analyses of group formation, affiliation, social identity, majority influence, minority influence, group discussion, polarization, social loafing, brainstorming, and the transmission of beliefs and values from groups to individuals. Indeed, this chapter, by only sampling the ways that researchers and theorists have used the concept of comparison to explain the behavior of individuals in group contexts, underestimates the impact of the concept. Given its importance as an explanatory concept, perhaps the theory should be elevated from number 2 to number 1: from "everyone's second favorite" theory of group processes to "everyone's favorite theory."

REFERENCES

Affleck, G., & Tennen, H. (1991). Social comparison and coping with major medical problems. In J. Suls & T. A. Wills (Eds.), *Social comparison: Contemporary theory and research* (pp. 369–394). Hillsdale, NJ: Lawrence Erlbaum.

Allen, V. L., & Wilder, D. A. (1977). Social comparison, self-evaluation, and conformity to the group. In J. M. Suls & R. L. Miller (Eds.), *Social comparison processes* (pp. 187–208). Washington, DC: Hemisphere.

Allen, V. L., & Wilder, D. A. (1980). Impact of group consensus and social support on stimulus meaning: Mediation of conformity by cognitive restructuring. *Journal of Personality and Social Psychology, 39*, 1116–1124.

Alvaro, E. M., & Crano, W. D. (1997). Indirect minority influence: Evidence for leniency in source evaluation and counterargumentation. *Journal of Personality and Social Psychology, 72*, 949–964.

Alwin, D. F., Cohen, R. J., & Newcomb, T. M. (1991). *Political attitudes over the life span: The Bennington women after fifty years*. Madison: University of Wisconsin Press.

Arrowood, A. J. (1978). Social comparison theory: Revived from neglect. *Contemporary Psychology, 23*, 490–491.

Asch, S. E. (1952). *Social psychology*. Englewood Cliffs, NJ: Prentice Hall.

Asch, S. E. (1955). Opinions and social pressures. *Scientific American, 193*(5), 31–35.

Back, K. W. (1951). Influence through social communication. *Journal of Abnormal and Social Psychology, 46*, 9–23.

Baker, S. M., & Petty, R. E. (1994). Majority and minority influence: Source-position imbalance as a determinant of message scrutiny. *Journal of Personality and Social Psychology, 67*, 5–19.

Berkowitz, L. (1971). Reporting an experiment: A case study in leveling, sharpening, and assimilation. *Journal of Experimental Social Psychology, 7*, 237–243.

Blascovich, J., Ginsburg, G. P., & Veach, T. L. (1975). A pluralistic explanation of choice shifts on the risk dimension. *Journal of Personality and Social Psychology, 31*, 422–429.

Brown, R. (1974). Further comment on the risky shift. *American Psychologist, 29*, 468–470.

Brown, V., & Paulus, P. B. (1996). A simple dynamic model of social factors in group brainstorming. *Small Group Research, 27*, 91–114.

Buehler, R., & Griffin, D. (1994). Change-of-meaning effects in conformity and dissent: Observing construal processes over time. *Journal of Personality and Social Psychology, 67*, 984–996.

Buunk, B. P. (1995). Comparison direction and comparison dimension among disabled individuals: Toward a refined conceptualization of social comparison under stress. *Personality and Social Psychology Bulletin, 21*, 316–330.

Campbell, J. D., Tesser, A., & Fairey, P. J. (1986). Conformity and attention to the stimulus: Some temporal and contextual dynamics. *Journal of Personality and Social Psychology, 51*, 315–324.

Cartwright, D. (1979). Contemporary social psychology in historical perspective. *Social Psychology Quarterly, 42*, 82–93.

Chen, S., Schechter, D., & Chaiken, S. (1996). Getting at the truth or getting along: Accuracy- versus impression-motivated heuristic and systematic processing. *Journal of Personality and Social Psychology, 71*, 262–275.

Cialdini, R. B., Kallgren, C. A., & Reno, R. R. (1991). A focus theory of normative conduct: A theoretical refinement and reevaluation of the role of norms in human behavior. *Advances in Experimental Social Psychology, 24*, 201–234.

Cialdini, R. B., Reno, R. R., & Kallgren, C. A. (1990). A focus theory of normative conduct: Recycling the concept of norms to reduce littering in public places. *Journal of Personality and Social Psychology, 58*, 1015–1026.

Cooley, C. H. (1909). *Social organization*. New York: Scribner.

Crandall, C. S. (1988). Social contagion of binge eating. *Journal of Personality and Social Psychology, 55*, 588–598.
De Dreu, C. K. W., & De Vries, N. K. (1996). Differential processing and attitude change following majority versus minority arguments. *British Journal of Social Psychology, 35*, 77–90.
Deaux, K., Reid, A., Mizrahi, K., & Cotting, D. (1999). Connect the person to the social: The functions of social identification. In T. R. Tyler, R. M. Kramer, & O. P. John (Eds.), *The psychology of the social self* (pp. 91–113). Mahwah, NJ: Lawrence Erlbaum.
Deutsch, M., & Gerard, H. B. (1955). A study of normative and informational social influences upon individual judgment. *Journal of Abnormal and Social Psychology, 51*, 629–636.
Durkheim, É. (1897/1966). *Suicide*. New York: Free Press.
Festinger, L. (1950). Informal social communication. *Psychological Review, 57*, 271–282.
Festinger, L. (1954). A theory of social comparison processes. *Human Relations, 7*, 117–140.
Festinger, L. (1955). Social psychology and group processes. *Annual Review of Psychology, 6*, 187–216.
Festinger, L. (1980). Looking backward. In L. Festinger (Ed.), *Retrospections on social psychology* (pp. 236–254). New York: Oxford University Press.
Festinger, L., Gerard, H. B., Hymovitch, B., Kelley, H. H., & Raven, B. H. (1952). The influence process in the presence of extreme deviates. *Human Relations, 5*, 327–346.
Festinger, L., Schachter, S., & Back, K. (1950). *Social pressures in informal groups*. New York: Harper.
Festinger, L., & Thibaut, J. (1951). Interpersonal communication in small groups. *Journal of Abnormal and Social Psychology, 46*, 92–99.
Festinger, L., Torrey, J., & Willerman, B. (1954). Self-evaluation as a function of attraction to the group. *Human Relations, 7*, 161–174.
Fisher, J. D. (1988). Possible effects of reference group-based social influence on AIDS-risk behavior and AIDS-prevention. *American Psychologist, 43*, 914–920.
Fisher, W. A., & Fisher, J. D. (1993). A general social psychological model for changing AIDS risk behavior. In J. B. Pryor & G. D. Reeder (Eds.), *The social psychology of HIV infection* (pp. 127–153). Hillsdale, NJ: Lawrence Erlbaum.
Forsyth, D. R. (1999). *Group dynamics* (3rd ed.). Belmont, CA: Wadsworth.
French, J. R. P., Jr., & Raven, B. (1959). The bases of social power. In D. Cartwright (Ed.), *Studies in social power* (pp. 150–167). Ann Arbor, MI: Institute for Social Research.
Gerard, H. B. (1953). The effect of different dimensions of disagreement on the communication process in small groups. *Human Relations, 6*, 249–271.
Gibbons, F. X., & Gerrard, M. (1989). Effects of upward and downward social comparison on mood states. *Journal of Social and Clinical Psychology, 8*, 14–31.
Goethals, G. R., & Darley, J. M. (1987). Social comparison theory: Self-evaluation and group life. In B. Mullen & G. R. Goethals (Eds.), *Theories of group behavior* (pp. 21–47). New York: Springer-Verlag.
Goethals, G. R., Messick, D. M., & Allison, S. T. (1991). The uniqueness bias: Studies of constructive social comparison. In J. Suls & T. A. Wills (Eds.), *Social comparison: Contemporary theory and research* (pp. 149–176). Hillsdale, NJ: Lawrence Erlbaum.
Goethals, G. R., & Zanna, M. P. (1979). The role of social comparison in choice shifts. *Journal of Personality and Social Psychology, 37*, 1469–1476.
Griffin, D., & Buehler, R. (1993). Role of construal processes in conformity and dissent. *Journal of Personality and Social Psychology, 65*, 657–669.
Gross, S. R., & Miller, N. (1997). The "golden section" and bias in perceptions of social consensus. *Personality and Social Psychology Review, 1*, 241–271.
Hastie, R., Penrod, S. D., & Pennington, N. (1983). *Inside the jury*. Cambridge, MA: Harvard University Press.
Helgeson, V. S., & Michelson, K. D. (1995). Motives for social comparison. *Personality and Social Psychology Bulletin, 21*, 1200–1209.
Hinsz, V. B., Tindale, R. S., & Vollrath, D. A. (1997). The emerging conceptualization of groups as information processors. *Psychological Bulletin, 121*, 43–64.
Hoffman, P. J., Festinger, L., & Lawrence, D. H. (1954). Tendencies toward group comparability in competitive bargaining. *Human Relations, 7*, 141–159.
Hyman, H. H. (1960). Reflections on reference groups. *Public Opinion Quarterly, 24*, 383–396.
Hyman, H. H. (1980). The psychology of status. *Archives of Psychology, 38*(269). (Originally published in 1942).
Hyman, H. H., & Singer, E. (1968). Introduction. In H. H. Hyman & E. Singer (Eds.), *Readings in reference group theory and research* (pp. 3–21). New York: Free Press.
Isenberg, D. J. (1986). Group polarization: A critical review and meta-analysis. *Journal of Personality and Social Psychology, 50*, 1141–1151.

Jacobs, R. C., & Campbell, D. T. (1961). The perpetuation of an arbitrary tradition through several generations of a laboratory microculture. *Journal of Abnormal and Social Psychology, 62,* 649–658.

Janis, I. L. (1982). *Groupthink: Psychological studies of policy decisions and fiascos* (2nd ed.). Boston: Houghton Mifflin.

Jones, E. E., & Gerard, H. B. (1967). *Foundations of social psychology.* New York: Wiley.

Karau, S. J., & Williams, K. D. (1993). Social loafing: A meta-analytic review and theoretical integration. *Journal of Personality and Social Psychology, 65,* 681–706.

Katz, D., & Allport, F. H. (1928). *Student attitudes: A report of the Syracuse University research study.* Syracuse, NY: Craftsman Press.

Kelley, H. H. (1952). Two functions of reference groups. In G. E. Swanson, T. M. Newcomb, & E. L. Hartley (Eds.), *Readings in social psychology* (2nd ed., pp. 410–414). New York: Holt.

Kerr, N. L., MacCoun, R. J., & Kramer, G. P. (1996). Bias in judgment: Comparing individuals and groups. *Psychological Review, 103,* 687–719.

Larson, J. R., Foster-Fishman, P. G., & Keys, C. B. (1994). The discussion of shared and unshared information in decision-making groups. *Journal of Personality and Social Psychology, 67,* 446–461.

Latané, B., & Darley, J. M. (1970). *The unresponsive bystander: Why doesn't he help?* New York: Appleton-Century-Crofts.

Latané, B., & L'Herrou, T. (1996). Social clustering in the Conformity Game: Dynamic social impact in electronic groups. *Journal of Personality and Social Psychology, 70,* 1218–1230.

Levine, J. M. (1980). Reaction to opinion deviance in small groups. In P. B. Paulus (Ed.), *Psychology of group influence* (pp. 375–429). Hillsdale, NJ: Lawrence Erlbaum.

Lewin, K. (1935). Psycho-sociological problems of a minority group. *Character and Personality, 3,* 175–187.

Lockwood, P., & Kunda, Z. (1997). Superstars and me: Predicting the impact of role models on the self. *Journal of Personality and Social Psychology, 73,* 91–103.

Mackie, D. (1987). Systematic and nonsystematic processing of majority and minority persuasive communications. *Journal of Personality and Social Psychology, 53,* 41–52.

MacNeil, M. K., & Sherif, M. (1976). Norm change over subject generations as a function of arbitrariness of prescribed norms. *Journal of Personality and Social Psychology, 34,* 762–773.

Major, B., Testa, M., & Bylsma, W. H. (1991). Responses to upward and downward social comparisons: The impact of esteem-relevance and perceived control. In J. Suls & T. A. Wills (Eds.), *Social comparison: Contemporary theory and research* (pp. 237–260). Hillsdale, NJ: Lawrence Erlbaum.

Merton, R. K., & Kitt, A. S. (1950). Contributions to the theory of reference group behavior. In R. K. Merton & P. F. Lazarfeld (Eds.), *Continuities in social research: Studies in the scope and method of "The American Soldier"* (pp. 40–105). Glencoe, IL: Free Press.

Milgram, S. (1963). Behavioral study of obedience. *Journal of Abnormal and Social Psychology, 67,* 371–378.

Miller, D. T., & McFarland, C. (1991). When social comparison goes awry: The case of pluralistic ignorance. In J. Suls & T. A. Wills (Eds.), *Social comparison: Contemporary theory and research* (pp. 287–313). Hillsdale, NJ: Lawrence Erlbaum.

Miller, D. T., & Prentice, D. A. (1996). The construction of social norms and standards. In E. T. Higgins & A. W. Kruglanski (Eds.), *Social psychology: Handbook of basic principles* (pp. 799–829). New York: Guilford Press.

Mook, D. G. (1983). In defense of external invalidity. *American Psychologist, 38,* 379–387.

Moore, H. T. (1921). The comparative influence of majority and expert opinion. *American Journal of Psychology, 32,* 16–20.

Moscovici, S. (1994). Three concepts: Minority, conflict, and behavioral styles. In S. Moscovici, A. Mucchi-Faina, & A. Maass (Eds.), *Minority influence* (pp. 233–251). Chicago: Nelson-Hall.

Moscovici, S., Lage, E., & Naffrechoux, M. (1969). Influence of a consistent minority on the responses of a majority in a color perception task. *Sociometry, 12,* 365–380.

Myers, D. G. (1978). The polarizing effects of social comparison. *Journal of Experimental Social Psychology, 14,* 554–563.

Myers, D. G., & Lamm, H. (1976). The group polarization phenomenon. *Psychological Bulletin, 83,* 602–627.

Nemeth, C. J., & Wachtler, J. (1983). Creative problem solving as a result of majority vs. minority influence. *European Journal of Social Psychology, 13,* 45–55.

Newcomb, T. M. (1943). *Personality and social change.* New York: Dryden Press.

Paulus, P. B., & Dzindolet, M. T. (1993). Social influence processes in group brainstorm. *Journal of Personality and Social Psychology, 64,* 575–586.

Paulus, P. B., Larey, T. S., Putman, V. L., Leggett, K. L., & Roland, E. J. (1996). Social influence processes in computer brainstorming. *Basic and Applied Social Psychology, 18,* 3–14.

Peterson, R. S., & Nemeth, C. J. (1996). Focus versus flexibility: Majority and minority influence can both improve performance. *Journal of Personality and Social Psychology, 22,* 14–23.

Pollis, N. P., Montgomery, R. L., & Smith, T. G. (1975). Autokinetic paradigms: A reply to Alexander, Zucker, and Brody. *Sociometry, 38,* 358–373.

Prentice, D. A., & Miller, D. T. (1993). Pluralistic ignorance and alcohol use on campus: Some consequences of misperceiving a social norm. *Journal of Personality and Social Psychology, 64,* 243–254.

Pruitt, D. G. (1971). Choice shifts in group discussion: An introductory review. *Journal of Personality and Social Psychology, 20,* 339–360.

Raven, B. H. (1992). A power/interaction model of interpersonal influence: French and Raven thirty years later. *Journal of Social Behavior and Personality, 7,* 217–244.

Reno, R. R., Cialdini, R. B., & Kallgren, C. A. (1993). The transsituational influence of social norms. *Journal of Personality and Social Psychology, 64,* 104–112.

Ringelmann, M. (1913). Research on animate sources of power: The work of man. *Annales de l'Institut National Agronomique,* 2nd series (XII), 1–40.

Roper, E. (1940). Classifying respondents by social status. *Public Opinion Quarterly, 4,* 270–272.

Roy, M. C., Gauvin, S., & Limayem, M. (1996). Electronic group brainstorming: The role of feedback and productivity. *Small Group Research, 27,* 214–247.

Schachter, S. (1951). Deviation, rejection, and communication. *Journal of Abnormal and Social Psychology, 46,* 190–207.

Schachter, S. (1959). *The psychology of affiliation.* Stanford, CA: Stanford University Press.

Schneebaum, T. (1969). *Keep the river on your right.* New York: Grove Press.

Seta, J. J., Seta, C. E., & Donaldson, S. (1991). The impact of comparison processes on coactors' frustration and willingness to expend effort. *Personality and Social Psychology Bulletin, 17,* 560–568.

Shaw, C. (1930). *The jack-roller.* Chicago: University of Chicago Press.

Sherif, M. (1966). *The psychology of social norms.* New York: Harper & Row. (Originally published in 1936)

Shibutani, T. (1955). Reference groups as perspectives. *American Journal of Sociology, 60,* 562–569.

Singer, E. (1981). Reference groups and social evaluations. In M. Rosenberg & R. H. Turner (Eds.), *Social psychology: Sociological perspectives* (pp. 66–93). New York: Basic Books.

Snyder, C. R., Cheavens, J., & Sympson, S. C. (1997). Hope: An individual motive for social commerce. *Group Dynamics, 1,* 107–118.

Stasser, G. (1992). Pooling of unshared information during group discussions. In S. Worchel, W. Wood, & J. A. Simpson (Eds.), *Group process and productivity* (pp. 48–67). Newbury Park, CA: Sage.

Stasser, G., Taylor, L. A., & Hanna, C. (1989). Information sampling in structured and unstructured discussions of three- and six-person groups. *Journal of Personality and Social Psychology, 57,* 67–78.

Stouffer, S. A., Lumsdaine, A. A., Lumsdaine, M. H., Williams, R. M., Jr., Smith, M B., Janis, I. L., Star, S. A., & Cottrell, L. S., Jr. (1949a). *The American soldier: Combat and its aftermath* (Vol. 2). Princeton, NJ: Princeton University Press.

Stouffer, S. A., Suchman, E. A., DeVinney, L. C., Star, S. A., & Williams, R. M., Jr. (1949b). *The American soldier: Adjustment during army life* (Vol. 1). Princeton, NJ: Princeton University Press.

Sumner, W. G. (1906). *Folkways.* New York: Ginn.

Taylor, S. E., Falke, R. L., Shoptaw, S. J., & Lichtman, R. R. (1986). Social support, support groups, and the cancer patient. *Journal of Consulting and Clinical Psychology, 54,* 608–615.

Tesser, A. (1988). Toward a self-evaluation maintenance model of social behavior. *Advances in Experimental Social Psychology, 21,* 181–227.

Tesser, A. (1991). Emotion in social comparison and reflection processes. In J. Suls & T. A. Wills (Eds.), *Social comparison: Contemporary theory and research* (pp. 117–148). Hillsdale, NJ: Lawrence Erlbaum.

Tesser, A., & Campbell, J. (1983). Self-definition and self-evaluation maintenance. In J. Suls & A G. Greenwald (Eds.), *Psychological perspectives on the self* (Vol. 2, pp. 1–31). Hillsdale, NJ: Lawrence Erlbaum.

Tesser, A., Campbell, J., & Smith, M. (1984). Friendship choice and performance: Self-evaluation maintenance in children. *Journal of Personality and Social Psychology, 46,* 561–574.

Thibaut, J. W., & Strickland, L. H. (1956). Psychological set and social conformity. *Journal of Personality, 25,* 115–129.

Thrasher, F. M. (1927). *The gang.* Chicago: University of Chicago Press.

Tindale, R. S., Smith, C. M., Thomas, L. S., Filkins, J., & Sheffey, S. (1996). Shared representations and asymmetric social influence processes in small groups. In E. H. White & J. H. Davis (Eds.), *Understanding group behavior: Consensual action by small groups* (Vol. 1, pp. 81–104). Hillsdale, NJ: Lawrence Erlbaum.

Trost, M. R., Maass, A., & Kenrick, D. T. (1992). Minority influence: Personal relevance biases cognitive processes and reverses private acceptance. *Journal of Experimental Social Psychology, 28,* 234–254.

Turner, J. C. (1991). *Social influence*. Pacific Grove, CA: Brooks/Cole.

Turner, J. C., Hogg, M. A., Oakes, P. J., Reicher, S. D., & Wetherell, M. S. (1987). *Rediscovering the social group: A self-categorization theory*. New York: Blackwell.

Vinokur, A., & Burnstein, E. (1974). The effects of partially shared persuasive arguments on group-induced shifts: A group-problem-solving approach. *Journal of Personality and Social Psychology, 29*, 305–315.

Vinokur, A., & Burnstein, E. (1978). Depolarization of attitudes in groups. *Journal of Personality and Social Psychology, 36*, 872–885.

Wheeler, L. (1991). A brief history of social comparison theory. In J. Suls & T. A. Wills (Eds.), *Social comparison: Contemporary theory and research* (pp. 3–21). Hillsdale, NJ: Lawrence Erlbaum.

Wheeler, L., & Miyake, K. (1992). Social comparison in everyday life. *Journal of Personality and Social Psychology, 62*, 760–773.

Wills, T. A. (1991). Social comparison process in coping and health. In C. R. Snyder & D. R. Forsyth (Eds.), *Handbook of social and clinical psychology: The health perspective* (pp. 376–394). New York: Pergamon Press.

Winkel, F. W., & Renssen, M. R. (1998). A pessimistic outlook on victims and an "upward bias" in social comparison expectations of victim support workers regarding their clients: Uncovering a potential threat to the quality of victim-supportive interactions. *International Review of Victimology, 5*, 203–220.

Witte, E. H. (1994). Minority influences and innovations: The search for an integrated explanation of psychological and sociological models. In S. Moscovici, A. Mucchi-Faina, & A. Maass (Eds.), *Minority Influence* (pp. 67 93). Chicago: Nelson-Hall.

Wittenbaum, G. M., & Stasser, G. (1996). Management of information in small groups. In J. L. Nye & A. M. Brower (Eds.), *What's social about social cognition? Research on socially shared cognitions in small groups* (pp. 3–28). Thousand Oaks, CA: Sage.

Wittenbaum, G. M., Stasser, G., & Merry, C. J. (1996). Tacit coordination in anticipation of small group task completion. *Journal of Experimental Social Psychology, 32*, 129–152.

Wood, J. V., Taylor, S. E., & Lichtman, R. R. (1985). Social comparison in adjustment to breast cancer. *Journal of Personality and Social Psychology, 49*, 1169–1183.

Wood, W., Pool, G. J., Leck, K., & Purvis, D. (1996). Self-definition, defensive processing, and influence: The normative impact of majority and minority groups. *Journal of Personality and Social Psychology, 71*, 1181–1193.

Wright, S. S., & Forsyth, D. R. (1997) Group membership and collective identity: Consequences for self-esteem. *Journal of Social and Clinical Psychology, 16*, 43–56.

6

Opinion Comparison

The Role of the Corroborator, Expert, and Proxy in Social Influence

JERRY SULS

> ... of course, that's just my opinion. I could be wrong.
>
> —Dennis Miller, comedian

The power of opinions to inspire individual and collective action is well-documented in history, such as the tulip mania of Europe in the 1400s, the Salem witch trials of the 1600s, and the genocide practiced in contemporary Bosnia. But just as dramatic as the power of opinion is the speed with which opinions about values and beliefs change. For example, not too long ago, most of Eastern Europe was dominated by communist governments and a wall separated East and West Berlin. Important events illustrate both the power of opinions and their quixotic nature, but the same observations can be made about seemingly mundane things, such as hairstyles, manners, and taste in cuisine. These features of opinions can be attributed in part to the fact that they are formed through a process of comparison with others. This was demonstrated by the results of several important programs of research beginning in the 1930s and continuing into the 1950s. These include Sherif's (1936) experimental studies of social influence, Newcomb's (1943) field study of the changing attitudes of students at Bennington College, Asch's (1956) conformity experiments, and Merton and Kitt's (1950) use of the reference group concept to account for the morale of the American soldier during World War II.

Festinger (1954a,b) was the first, however, to provide a systematic psychological theory of social comparison. His initial research on the effects of communication on opinion change in groups culminated in his theory of informal social communication (Festinger, 1950) and served as the backbone of social comparison theory, which was published 4 years later. In a brief history of this area of study, Wheeler (1991) noted that comparison theory subsumed informal communication theory, with the major difference being that comparison theory

JERRY SULS • Department of Psychology, University of Iowa, Iowa City, Iowa 52242.

Handbook of Social Comparison: Theory and Research, edited by Suls and Wheeler. Kluwer Academic/Plenum Publishers, New York, 2000.

included abilities as well as opinions. However, despite the origins of social comparison theory in the opinion domain, in the last two decades, the lion's share of researchers' attention has been devoted to comparison of abilities and other personal attributes (Wood, 1989; Suls & Wills, 1991). Social comparison theory may be "everybody's second favorite theory," as Arrowood (1978) observed, and ability comparison appears to be everybody's favorite topic within the theory, indicated by the scarce attention paid to opinions. This is a surprising circumstance in light of the role opinions played in the theory's original development and the reputed role of comparison in a wide range of social phenomena, such as conformity, persuasion, and group decision making. In this chapter, I briefly survey prior theories of opinion comparison models and describe some of their shortcomings. Then I introduce the triadic theory, which by positing that there are three distinct kinds of opinion comparison seeks to overcome some of the limitations of past approaches.

FESTINGER'S THEORY

As reviewed in more detail elsewhere in this volume (see Chapter 1), Festinger (1954) proposed that people have a drive to know whether their opinions are correct. He thought that accuracy was important because incorrect beliefs could lead to unpleasant consequences. "Testing" the opinion against objective reality or objective standards is most desirable. But Festinger recognized that objective standards are not always available. Therefore, in the absence of objective standards, people compare with others to evaluate the validity of their opinions. Others who were similar were proposed to be the most preferred comparison selection because they would allow the most precise evaluation of the opinion. It was also proposed that comparisons with similar others were assumed to lead to consensus or agreement concerning the opinion in question, leading to a sense of subjective validity. Festinger further hypothesized that, if there were discrepancies in opinion about an issue among group members, this divergence would create pressures to reduce the divergence. This meant that the individual would either attempt to persuade others or would change his or her views to obtain group uniformity. Festinger (1954a,b) reviewed original evidence and studies from the group dynamics tradition, which provided empirical support for these propositions. However, Festinger soon turned his attention to cognitive dissonance theory, and it was left to others to extend the comparison work.

Experiments on opinion comparison were published by Gordon and Hakmiller in the special *Journal of Experimental Social Psychology* supplement (Latané, 1966), "Studies on Social Comparison Processes." Gordon (1966) found that desire to affiliate for social comparison purposes increased as opinion discrepancy with others decreased. Hakmiller (1966) reported that interest in comparison increased more when the group has been shown to be correct than when it had been incorrect. Although evidence for the similarity hypothesis was reported, it was not uniformly consistent (Kruglanski & Mayseless, 1990). Moreover, several important criticisms of the similarity hypothesis were lodged. One was that people frequently seek out novelty and difference, and such experiences can provide self-knowledge just as comparison with similars can (Deutsch & Krauss, 1965). Another criticism was that opinion agreement need not imply correctness. Nissen (1954) observed that some people conceitedly believe opinion divergence as evidence of being correct. But perhaps the most important criticism concerned the ambiguity surrounding the notion of similarity. Festinger was vague about what comparison dimensions were important for people to be similar on. Certainly, the dimension of similarity could not be the (opinion) dimension about which the person was uncertain, because then the person already would have had to conduct an implicit comparison (Jellison & Arkin, 1977; Jones & Regan, 1974) to know the other was similar. This circular reasoning, the ambiguity of the similarity concept, and reservations about the special utility ascribed to similarity created problems for researchers. As a consequence, empirical interest in opinion comparison was inactive for a time.

THE ATTRIBUTIONAL REFORMULATION

Goethals and Darley's (1977) attributional reformulation of comparison theory clarified thinking about the role of similarity (see Chapter 2, this volume). They took their inspiration from one of Festinger's (1954a) statements from the original theory: "If persons who are very different on attributes consistent with the divergence [in opinion], the tendency to narrow the range of comparability becomes stronger" (p. 133) (see also Wheeler et al., 1969). This statement implies that we prefer to compare with others who are similar on attributes related to and predictive of the opinion to be evaluated. Related attributes might be other opinions and/or other characteristics of the person. These background attributes were proposed to be the basis of comparison, and thus, resolved the circularity described earlier.

Goethals and Darley also recognized that the role of similarity in related attributes for opinion comparison depended on what type of opinion was at issue. Following Jones and Gerard's (1967) distinction, Goethals and Darley (1977) observed that there are two kinds of opinions: values and beliefs. A person making a value judgment is asking, "Is this right or appropriate for me? Will I like it?" Beliefs, however, refer to potentially verifiable assertions about the true nature of an entity. For belief-type opinions, the person is asking "Is X true or correct?" X might be "Line A is equal in length to line B," "Grasshoppers are highly nutritious," "Listening to too much rock music at loud volumes can damage one's hearing," and so forth. Attributional considerations become important once one considers the belief–value distinction, as I will describe below.

According to attribution theory (Kelley, 1967), in trying to evaluate the correctness of a belief, the perceiver tries to establish whether the belief is entity caused, that is, actually reflects the compelling features of the entity itself, or is person caused, based on idiosyncratic or biasing characteristics of the judge or perceiver. Goethals and Darley (1977) reasoned that persons who are similar on related attributes may share the same biasing characteristics so agreeing with them does not assure correctness. According to the attributional principle of discounting, the individual may discount agreement with others to the extent that they share one's perspective. On the other hand, if one finds agreement from someone who is dissimilar on related attributes, then it is more likely that the person is seeing things as they really are. In other words, support from others with different perspectives (i.e., related attributes) provides a kind of "triangulation effect," in the same way a surveyer gets a better fix on a target by viewing it from different perspectives (see Fig. 1).

Goethals and Darley (1977) proposed that value comparison operates differently than belief comparison because the former has no truth per se; the question is whether one likes or dislikes the entity. Deciding whether one likes a particular movie, jazz group, or politician may be best answered by comparing with a person who is similar on related attributes with respect to the cinema, music, or political persuasion (see Fig. 2).

In sum, the attributional reframing of social comparison theory posited that persons similar on related attributes are preferred and bolster confidence for value judgments. In contrast, persons who are dissimilar on related attributes (because they share a different

Goethals and Darley: Belief Comparison

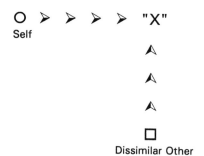

Figure 1. Value comparison in the attributional approach.

perspective and therefore provide a way to correct one's idiosyncratic biases) are preferred and bolster confidence regarding beliefs. Not only did the attributional approach clarify the similarity construct, but it also acknowledged that similar others are not always preferred. In the case of beliefs, dissimilar others were posited to be of greater utility.

There is some empirical support for these propositions. In one experiment (Goethals & Nelson, 1973), disguised as a study of "college admissions procedures," students evaluated two applicants either in terms of their academic superiority (belief) or liking (value). After making their initial judgments, subjects learned that someone with a similar orientation about judging people or someone with a dissimilar orientation agreed about the applicants. Confidence in the value condition was increased the most when a similar other agreed. In contrast, and consistent with the triangulation notion, confidence in the belief was increased more when a dissimilar other agreed (see also Goethals, 1972; Goethals, Darley, & Kriss, 1978).

With regard to comparison selection, Reckman and Goethals (1973) tested whether persons choose dissimilar others for a belief-type opinion, but choose similar others for a value. Participants preferred a more similar discussion group member in the congeniality condition (i.e., value condition) than in the predict academic plans condition (i.e., belief); however, although statistically significant, a strong preference for dissimilar others in the belief evaluation was not exhibited. Better evidence for selection of dissimilar others in the belief domain was reported by Gorenflo and Crano (1989) who had students play the role of college admissions officers and review an applicant's credentials for likelihood of success in college.

Goethals and Darley: Value Comparison

Figure 2. Belief comparison in the attributional approach.

GERARD AND ORIVE'S THEORY OF OPINION FORMATION

In contrast to Festinger and the attributional approach, which emphasized explicit social comparisons, Gerard and Orive (1987) proposed that much of opinion comparison occurs at an implicit level and is self-generated. People project their views onto others, especially those who are similar: the classic false consensus effect (Allport, 1924; Ross, Green, & House, 1977; Mullen et al., 1985). Gerard and Orive argued that projection short-circuits the need for actual comparisons with others (see also Suls, 1986; Goethals, Messick, & Allison, 1991). People who are similar on related attributes are assumed to agree because of projection (see Chapter 16, this volume). Consequently, according to Gerard and Orive (1987), learning that a similar other agrees with us should not bolster confidence, because agreement is assumed. However, if one learns that a similar other disagrees, confidence should decrease because of the loss of assumed consensus. Dissimilar others were posited to have no impact because they are irrelevant.

In an experimental study involving a mock jury case, Orive (1988) found evidence that agreement with similar others was implicitly assumed and provided no increment in confidence. Disagreement with similar others lowered confidence as predicted. However, inconsistent with their perspective, when a dissimilar other agreed, subject's confidence increased, a result more consistent with the triangulation notion described by Goethals and Darley.

Unlike Goethals and Darley, Gerard and Orive make no distinction between value and belief judgment. (The only difference between value and belief comparison, according to Gerard and Orive, is that the range of background similarity is narrower in its informational utility for value-laden opinions. This proposal, however, has not received any direct empirical attention.) Some evidence, as mentioned earlier (Goethals, 1972; Goethals & Nelson, 1973) indicated that the two classes of judgment *are* subject to divergent comparison processes, contrary to the implicit projection model.

LIMITATIONS OF PAST THEORIES

Both the attributional approach and Gerard and Orive's projection model represent significant extensions of Festinger's formulation. Further, both have received some empirical support. However, despite their strengths, these approachs remain incomplete for three reasons. The first has to do with the utility of dissimilarity; the second with the assumption that the same sources of information are both preferred and have the strongest effects on resulting opinions; and finally, these prior approaches overlook a third type of opinion judgment.

Recall that one premise of the attributional formulation for belief comparison is that dissimilarity per se provides a kind of triangulation. In fact, all kinds of dissimilarity are treated as if they were comparable. Intuitively, all types of dissimilarity should not be equally informative. Consider the case where an individual wants to establish the correctness of a belief. The attributional framework contends that agreement from any dissimilar others, by virtue of their seeing things from a different vantage point, would provide valuable triangulation. However, two potential referents may both be dissimilar from the individual, but one may be dissimilar because of more knowledge or experience than oneself, while the other may be dissimilar because of having less knowledge or experience. To evaluate the validity of a belief, the former is *more advantaged on related attributes* and should be preferred to someone less advantaged (or less "expert").

Another weakness of the attributional perspective concerns the blurring of two different kinds of value judgments. Goethals and Darley focused on personal preferences, the "Do I like X?" question, which involves sorting out my feelings about an experience. However, their analysis obscures this question with a different one. This blurring can be illustrated with one of their examples involving a hypothethical person who is going on summer vacation and is trying to decide what book to take for pleasurable reading. Goethals and Darley consider this to be a value-type opinion, one concerned with liking or disliking. Note, however, their example actually involves the question "Will I like X?"; that is, the prediction of one's likely reaction to a future event. This is quite different from asking, after finishing the book, "Did I find it to be an enjoyable experience?" Below, I describe the somewhat different comparison dynamics for answering these two distinct questions.

The third limitation of past approaches is that the comparison choice most preferred also is assumed to be the most influential. For example, it is hypothesized that people prefer to compare *and* obtain greater confidence regarding beliefs after learning that a dissimilar other agrees. In contrast, the triadic model posits that people do not necessarily seek out the information that logically should be of greatest utility. However, if people happen to learn that a dissimilar other agrees, this information might be very influential.

THE TRIADIC MODEL OF OPINION COMPARISON

The triadic model builds on the attributional elements advanced by Goethals and Darley (1977) and the projection notions of Gerard and Orive (1987). The model also expands on elements concerning comparison and the logical structure of attitudes outlined by Jones and Gerard (1967) in their classic social psychology text. Unlike the Goethals and Darley formulation, the triadic model posits that there are three types of opinion comparison rather than two. The present model also disagrees with Gerard and Orive's hypothesis that projection always serves as a substitute for comparison and their contention that belief and value comparison follow the same dynamic.

To preview the triadic approach, the three types of opinion comparison can be conceptualized in terms of three basic questions: Preference assessment or "Do I like X," belief assessment, whereby the individual is trying to evaluate the correctness of an assertion, which is potentially verifiable, that is, "Is X true," and preference prediction, or "Will I like X?" The following sections describe the processes for the three legs of the model.

Preference Assessment

Comparing for preference assessment concerns whether a judgment or opinion is appropriate for oneself. In this category of judgment, the person is gauging the personal appropriateness of his or her reaction to an object or situation. "Do I like foreign films with subtitles, industrial rock, or abstract expressionism?" are preference assessment questions or personal likes and dislikes. Preference assessment actually includes several related questions: "Do I like X," "Should I like X," "Am I comfortable about liking X," and "What does liking X mean for me?" All are concerned with whether one's reaction is personally appropriate.

A question that instantly arises is why people need to compare with others to assess their personal preferences. Do they not already know how they feel? Zajonc (1980) has demonstrated that often "preferences need no inferences"; people make affective preferences rapidly, often without any conscious processing. If one knows what one likes, why should there be uncertainty prompting the need for social comparison?

The answer, I think, is that precisely *because* many preferences are automatic and non-conscious, people may be surprised by some of their likes and dislikes. Seeking consensus through comparison may satisfy this epistemic need. Self-perception processes also seem relevant in this regard. Bem (1972) demonstrated that people often do not know how they feel about things, whether it is brown bread or attitudes about peg turning. Seeking comparison information can reduce this uncertainty.

A classic example of preference assessment is found in Schachter's (1959) experiments on fear and affiliation. Schachter argued that people expecting to receive painful electric shocks preferred to wait with others also awaiting the shock to gauge whether they were having the appropriate reaction, in this case, level of fear, in response to the situation; that is, "Should I be this scared?" (see also Darley & Aronson, 1966). Emotional comparison is one variant of preference assessment (see Chapter 15, this volume, for a different perspective).

The critical element in value assessment is what the stimulus means for the self, whereas in belief assessment (considered next), one wants to establish the truth about some external proposition or entity. The triadic model concurs with Goethals and Darley's (1977) treatment of values.

> ... when the issue is one of value ... the person's interest is in discovering what is affectively positive or negative for him. Here we should welcome the support of a "co-oriented peer" (Jones & Gerard, 1967), a person who has the same basic interests and perspectives. (Goethals & Nelson, 1973, p. 118)

Hence, the attributional approach, depicted in Fig. 2, represents the dynamics of preference assessment. In the triadic model, these similar comparison others as referred to as "corroborators."

Up to this point, comparison for preference assessment has been treated exclusively as a form of informational influence because other people serve as reference points to assess the correctness or appropriateness of one's opinions (Kelley, 1952). There is, however, an equally important *normative* function played in value comparison. In many cases, people are not necessarily evaluating their own responses, but trying to define what opinion is "proper and awarded acceptance and approval (by one's membership group)" (Kelley, 1952, p. 213). Establishing whether "one should like X or appear to like X" are important considerations for obtaining the approval (or escaping the disapproval) of group members. The opinions and preferences of co-oriented peers, that is, similar others, often define the norms of these groups. Of course, in many cases, both normative and informational functions are served simultaneously. But, in other instances, the person may have no uncertainty about his or her feelings but *is* uncertain about how members of an important group members feel (Schachter, 1951). These members' approval or disapproval may be critical for joining or remaining in the group. In short, preference assessment may be motivated by normative as much as informational pressures. The classic Westgate housing study demonstrated this (Festinger, Schachter, & Back, 1950). Crandall's (1988) study of women who showed increases in bulimic behavior as a function of joining college sororities where excessive dieting, binging, and purging were the norm also provides a good example of such normative social comparison pressures.

Based on the above reasoning, the following hypothesis can be made: *Comparisons with similar others should be preferred and have the strongest effects on preference assessment; dissimilar others should be irrelevant to one's personal preferences and have little if any impact.* Under typical circumstances, selection and effects should operate comparably. However, when certain kinds of normative considerations are salient, the process may shift somewhat. For example, we probably do not go out of our way to learn whether a negative reference group shares our personal preferences. However, if through happenstance we learn that a group with which we wish to "disidentify" shares our personal preferences, then we may exhibit a boomerang effect and "disown" our prior preferences. Hence, for normative reasons, a dissimilar group's values may not always be irrelevant and in fact may prompt the individual to adopt very divergent views. The corollary, then, is that *people probably rarely seek out the preferences of dissimilar groups; but if they learn of agreement with a negative reference groups, they may exhibit reactance and adopt an opposing preference.*

Evidence that individuals are most influenced by others who are similar on related attributes for preference-type judgments was demonstrated in the Goethals and Nelson (1973) experiment. In a recent experiment testing the comparison preference hypothesis, Suls, Martin, and Wheeler (in press) asked college students, who were led to believe that they were participating in a study of "college admissions procedures," to form impressions of liking for two college applicants. Subsequently, they were given the opportunity to learn the opinion of four potential comparison others: a same-age, same-sex student with a similar personality, a same-age, same-sex student with a dissimilar personality (information about personality scores was a credible cover story because most research participants had completed a series of personality measures weeks before), a student who was a couple of years older who worked in the college registrar's office, or a high school graduate person who was a couple of years older and worked in a local convenience mart. Thus, the possible comparisons ranged from someone who was very generically similar in background (i.e, similar personality), someone who was very generically dissimilar (i.e., dissimilar personality), dissimilar but advantaged (a senior with more academic experience), and dissimilar but disadvantaged (older, but with less education). (The reason for all of these options will be clearer when we describe belief assessment, the second kind of opinion comparison.) Consistent with the hypothesis, for evaluation of liking (i.e., preference assessment), participants indicated greatest interest in the opinion of the student whose personality was similar to theirs. Experimental evidence for the hypothesis concerning the effects of a negative reference group is scarce, although there are numerous anecdotes about people changing their opinions when they learn a negative reference group happens to hold the same opinion as themselves.

Belief Assessment

In assessing truth or correctness, Goethals and Darley posited that triangulation with a person (or persons) holding a different perspective (i.e., dissimilar related attributes) can correct for any misperceptions resulting from one's own idiosyncratic biases. As mentioned earlier, however, people are rarely just different in perspective, but different in specific and valenced ways. Some related attributes pertain to levels of experience or knowledge that make the individual more or less useful for establishing truth value. Hence, people should prefer to assess their beliefs by comparing with others who are more advantaged or "expert" with regard to to the domain under evaluation. Conversely, comparisons should not be preferred with others who are dissimilar by virtue of them being less knowledgeable or disadvantaged with respect to the domain under consideration. These assertions are compatible with Jones and Gerard's (1967) suggestion that beliefs can be more influenced by experts.

The preceding argument suggests that not all dissimilar others should be preferred for triangulation and leads to a different hypothesis than Goethals and Darley's: *Only dissimilar-advantaged persons should be preferred to check one's belief-type opinions and should bolster confidence significantly if they agree. Dissimilar-disadvantaged others should be non-preferred and should have minimal impact on belief confidence if one learns their opinion through happenstance.* Comparison of Figs. 1 and 3 illustrates the difference between the classic attributional formulation and the triadic model.

Belief Assessment

Figure 3. Belief assessment in the triadic approach.

Recognizing that related attribute similarity in the belief domain is a continuum from "more" to "same" to "less" expertise acknowledges that beliefs have ability-like characteristics. Just as there are related attributes that contribute to better or worse performance in the ability domain, so, too, certain attributes and experiences make some people better judges of the "facts." The proposition is also consistent with social identity researchers (Turner, 1991) who argue that some attributes associated with in-group membership are perceived in more positive (i.e., advantaged) terms, and thereby confer greater "expertise" about the facts.

The hypothesis that "experts" are preferred for belief comparison could simply be seen as an acknowledgment of Festinger's basic premise that objective sources of information are preferred. There is certainly a sense in which experts represent a kind of "physical or objective" standard. However, the triadic model hypothesizes that even a "little bit" of expertise (advantage on related attributes) makes a comparison other a more meaningful source of information than is someone who is merely "different" or someone who is similar in standing. Thus, sources who would scarcely be considered arbiters of "objective reality" still have an advantage.

Evidence supporting the hypothesis regarding belief comparison was found in the "college admissions preference experiment" (Suls et al., in press) described earlier. While some students made value (liking) judgments, a second group was provided the same information about two past college applicants but was asked to predict which applicant had the more academically superior record 3 years after admission; in other words, these subjects were asked to make a belief judgment. The same comparison options were offered: someone described as having a similar personality to the participant's, someone dissimilar in personality, a senior with experience working in the registrar's office, and the high school graduate who worked in a convenience mart. The last two options were created to represent a dissimilar-advantaged other and a dissimilar-disadvantaged other, respectively. Results indicated that participants preferred comparing with the student who had experience in the registrar's office, that is, the person with more "expertise." It is worth noting that although working in a college registrar's office might provide somewhat more knowledge about the ingredients for academic success, there is no sense that the student aide is highly "expert" in the way a professor or academic counselor is about the likelihood of a student's academic success. Presumably, if a certified expert had been offered as a source of information, he or she would have been most preferred. Other studies conducted in our laboratory support this hypothesis. In addition to supporting the "expert" hypothesis, the results of the college admissions preference experiment have bearing on Goethals and Darley's triangulation hypothesis. Contrary to their hypothesis, the student who was dissimilar in personality was relatively unpreferred as a source of information and occasioned even less interest than the student with a similar personality. (The generically dissimilar other was rated, however, more highly than the "less advantaged" high school graduate.) The findings of the college admissions preference experiment offer little support that people prefer just any kind of triangulation for belief judgment.

Persons with more advantaged standing are, by definition, dissimilar; but for "experts" to be influential, they also may need to hold certain basic underlying values in common with those who rely on them. This argument is consistent with the self-categorization theory of social influence (Turner, 1991) where the expert–leader is the individual who best represents the values of the group (see also Hains, Hogg, & Duck, 1997):

> One takes advice from a medical doctor, for example, because he or she has been socially designated as an acceptable representative of modern, scientitic medicine, an institution defined by social values one shares (such as the belief in science and its normative procedures). (Turner, 1991, p. 165)

The necessity for an expert to share certain fundamental values to be considered knowledgeable is compelling if we consider that a physician with prestigious credentials, who performs or recommends abortions, is probably not considered a credible source of any kind of medical information by someone who holds strong "anti-choice" values.

The importance of shared values held by the expert also can be found in more mundane contexts. For example, recently a friend wanted to have a pool constructed in his backyard and consulted with some experts. My friend wanted a complex pond with fish and plants and everything ecologically balanced. One expert was a minimalist, suggesting a pond with only rocks in it and kept clear with chemicals. His idea was that this would require little work (his value), while a complex pond would require constant maintenance and adjustment (my friend's value). My friend did not take the expert's advice because they were "in different ballparks." The expert was used to having a great deal of land to take care of, where a complicated pool could become a problem, but my friend just had a little plot. In this example, the expert, despite all his greater knowledge and experience, was not relevant because his minimalist values differed from my friend's.

Based on the preceding reasoning, the triadic model hypothesizes that dissimilar-advantaged others are preferred and selected for belief comparison judgment. However, *in addition to possessing more knowledge, the "more expert" other also must share basic values connected with the particular belief question under consideration.* Hence, there is a sense that the most useful comparison other for belief judgments is a "similar expert."

Evidence for the similar expert hypothesis can be found in the sociological literature on diffusion of innovation (Rogers, 1983). In a classic study, Ryan and Gross (1943) examined patterns of communication and influence concerning the diffusion of hybrid corn in Iowa in the 1920s and 1930s. The researchers documented that although the hybrid corn was highly effective, the average farmer moved slowly from awareness of the innovation to adoption. Interviews revealed that when farmer made the change, it resulted not from communication with salesmen or representatives of the agricultural extension, that is, persons who were presumably highly expert, but from communications with neighbors who were early adopters. These innovators tended to have larger farms, higher incomes, more years of formal education, and were more cosmopolitan as measured by the number of trips they took to the largest city in the state. Although salesman and representatives of the agricultural extension service had more expertise, the adoption of the new seed occurred through communication with somewhat more knowledgeable persons who also shared fundamental background with the late adopters; in others words, a similar expert. Other research in the diffusion of innovation tradition reports similar patterns regarding opinion leaders (see Rogers, 1983).

A third aspect of belief comparison in the triadic model concerns how expert the comparison other needs to be. A literal rendering of the model would suggest that comparing with others who possess superior knowledge should be most preferred; however, there are good reasons why someone too expert might not be sought. First, for some belief questions, truly expert sources may be unavailable. In addition, there may be social costs associated with comparing directly with a certified expert. In their essay on the costs of social comparison, Brickman and Bulman (1977) described how explicit comparisons between parties of unequal status can make the inferior other feel embarassed and the superior other anxious about the envy and resentment produced by his or her superior status. Seeking out someone else who is somewhat more knowledgeable but not vastly superior represents a compromise that may reduce awkwardness of such social encounters.[1] For these reasons, people may prefer to compare with someone who is more expert but not too divergent from self. This prediction is reminiscent of Festinger's prediction that people prefer to compare with others who are only *somewhat better* in ability, a compromise choice between the so-called "undirectional drive upward," whereby people want to do better and better, and the similarity hypothesis. Although Festinger meant this prediction to apply only to abilities, as we have suggested, beliefs have ability-like characteristics (see also Jones & Gerard, 1967).

The costs of interacting with a highly expert source may have been partly responsible for the greater impact of early adopting neighbors, who were only somewhat more knowledge-able, in the Ryan and Gross (1943) study. Similarly, the perceived interpersonal costs of comparing with highly expert others may account for why people often initially seek out medical advice from laypeople who have somewhat more medical knowledge rather seek assistance directly from medical professionals (Suls, Martin, & Leventhal, 1997). In light of these considerations, I hypothesize that *people probably rarely seek out greatly superior experts, and then only when they can shield themselves from the social costs of actual interaction. On the other hand, if they happen to learn that a learned expert concurs with them, then this should confer considerable confidence in judgment.*

A Special Case. A major difference between the triadic model and Goethals and Darley's is that the former proposes that a dissimilar-advantaged other should be most preferred and influential for belief judgments, while the latter assumes that triangulation should obtain with any dissimilar other. The triadic model, however, seems to be contradicted by Goethals and Nelson's finding that an agreement from a generically dissimilar other bolstered confidence. Actually, I suggest that in social life in the vast majority of cases people probably perceive dissimilar others to be better–worse or advantaged–disadvantaged in related attributes. One reason for this speculation is the research (Tajfel, 1981) with the minimal groups paradigm demonstrating that people assigned to arbitrary groups tend to perceive members of the out-group in negative ("disadvantaged") terms, even in the absence of real differences.

There are cases, however, where the Goethals and Darley scenario probably does occur. One can imagine two individuals who are dissimilar by virtue of having different but comparable amounts of knowledge. For example, in deciding whether there will be an

---

[1] Another reason is that, as the expert knowledge increases, so does the probability that there may be basic disagreement about basic values underlying the belief in question.

imminent economic depression (a belief), one person may have extensive knowledge about the national economy, while the other person may have extensive knowledge about the international economy. They are different on related attributes, but neither is more advantaged than the other. In this case, learning that one agrees with the other may provide belief bolstering via triangulation. Hence, triangulation with generically dissimilar others probably does occur in social life, but the scenario envisioned by the triadic model seems more common.

Although the "special case" seems operative with regard to the consequences of learning someone else's opinion, the triadic model is skeptical about Goethals and Darley's (1977) contention that people *actively* seek out others with a different perspective (unless, again, they have somewhat greater knowledge). Their empirical proposition has received only limited support. One reason is that people generally use a positive test strategy, that is, seek hypothesis-consistent information (Wason, 1960; Klayman & Ha, 1987; Kunda, 1989). Because *disagreement* with a dissimilar other is implicitly assumed (Gerard & Orive, 1987), only under exceptional circumstances do people seek out a dissimilar other's view. This may help to explain why, even though confidence was bolstered more by a dissimilar other in the belief condition in the Goethals and Nelson (1973) experiment, afterward subjects actually reported being more influenced by the similar other in both the belief and value conditions. Routine use of a positive test strategy may discourage people from actively seeking out or appreciating the opinions of dissimilar others even when it could have great utility.

Preference Prediction

The third form of opinion evaluation concerns future behavior: one's likely reaction to an anticipated situation, "Will I like X?" Such predictions are important because they figure in our decisions about desirable courses of action and the likely consequences of our choices. The comparison dynamics in this case follow a similar form to that advanced in the proxy model of ability comparison (Wheeler, Martin, & Suls, 1997). In that model, the evaluative question is "Can I do X?"

A brief description of the proxy ability model may help provide a context for the comparison dynamic underlying value prediction. The proxy model posits that predictions concerning whether self can do "X" are made by comparing with someone who has already attempted "X," that is, a proxy. But not everyone who has attempted X is a good proxy. The model proposes that a comparison other's success–failure at X is applicable to the self depending on similarity to self and alignment of other variables such as effort and related attributes (see Chapter 4, this volume).

The ability scenario has a parallel in the preference prediction domain. Suppose I am trying to decide whether to see a particular movie that has recently opened. I want to know whether "I will enjoy it" (see Fig. 4). I know someone who already has seen the film and also that they liked it. To what extent can I rely on their reaction to predict my own? If proxy and I tend to agree in our likes and dislikes about past movies ("Y") we have both seen, then I can predict with some certainty that I too will enjoy the new film. If proxy did not enjoy the new film, I can predict with some certainty that I will not enjoy it. But now imagine instead a potential proxy whose pattern of likes and dislikes vis-à-vis my past film preferences is very inconsistent. Under such circumstances, this proxy's reaction to the new film is a poor prognosticator of my response. *Thus, the triadic model predicts people will assume that their affective reaction to a new stimulus will match proxy's reaction if they share a consistent set of prior preferences regarding stimuli of the same category.*

An important element in the model is that that proxy and self need *not* consistently agree

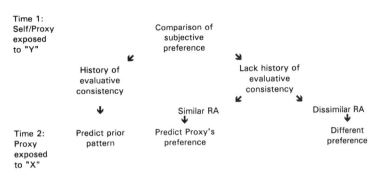

Figure 4. Preference prediction in the triadic approach.

about previous stimuli, but only that there is consistency in the area of agreement–disagreement. Thus, if proxy enjoyed the new film but in the past proxy and I disagreed about virtually all other films, I may conclude that I would not enjoy the film. However, if proxy and I showed a very inconsistent pattern of agreement and disagreement about films, then proxy would be a poor source of information about my likely response. The relevance to Heider (1958) and Newcomb's (1961) balance principle should be apparent.

Just as in the proxy ability model, *related attribute information can substitute for prior experience, so knowledge about similarity on related attributes can serve as a substitute if information about prior preferences is absent.* For example, I am more likely to use someone else's opinion about the new film if he or she is similar in age, education, intellectual, and artistic background, lacking any information about their previous likes and dislikes. In contrast, the response of someone dissimilar on related attributes would not be considered relevant to predicting my future reaction. However, just as a consistent history of disagreement about past films may lead me to infer that proxy's dislike of a new film signals that I might like it, so too, related attribute dissimilarity and knowing that proxy disliked a film might signal that I would like it. This effect is reminiscent of Aronson and Cope's (1968) "My enemy's enemy is my friend" effect.

The preceding reasoning suggests that a consistent history of disagreement or consistent differences in related attributes should lead individuals to anticipate having a diametrically opposite response to proxy's. Consequently, even consistent patterns of disagreement can be informative. However, again, because people tend to use positive case strategies (Wason, 1960), they may not actively seek out someone with whom they consistently disagree in their preferences. But if one learns by happenstance that they, for example, liked the new film, the inference is that the person would not enjoy it.

Some of these hypotheses were tested in a study (Suls et al., in press) purportedly about "reading preference and comprehension." Participants read and rated some brief literary passages and were then led to expect that they would be reading a much longer excerpt. The experimenter explained that people comprehend more when they enjoy what they are reading, so the participants would have some choice of the longer passage. To keep them "blind" for experimental purposes, the participants were told that they could see the long passage enjoyed by one of three previous participants (i.e., a proxy). Three possible proxies were described: someone who made ratings of the first five passages that were very similar to those of the subject, another who made very dissimilar ratings, and an expert (a college literature professor). Subjects preferred to learn which longer passage the proxy with a similar history of likes enjoyed. In a parallel set of conditions, subjects could learn which longer passage someone similar on related attributes (major, career aim, amount of time devoted to leisure reading), dissimilar on related attributes, or the literature professor (the expert) enjoyed. Subjects who were given these choices were most interested in learning the passage that the person who was similar in related attributes enjoyed. These results confirm that comparison others with a similar history of preferences *or* similar in related attributes are perceived to most informative about one's own future affective responses. Interestingly, the literary expert was not preferred, which is sensible, since subjects were deciding which passage they would most likely enjoy, not necessarily which passage was a literary classic.

One aspect of these results might appear to conflict with the model and needs some clarification. According to the triadic approach, information about dissimilar others can also be informative (if they exhibit a consistent history), but dissimilar others were not preferred in the reading preference and comprehension experiment. The likely reason is that subjects were led to believe that they would learn through their choice which longer passage the other enjoyed but nothing about the other alternatives. So, if a subject chose a dissimilar other's preference, the subject could expect to only learn what they would dislike, not what they would like. Under such circumstances, the similar other in prior history or related attributes provides greater informational utility.

In another study that removed this source of ambiguity, we examined whether people would use information from someone with a dissimilar pattern of past preferences. Subjects made a short list of the films they most enjoyed and films they most disliked. A week later they were presented with a list supposedly completed by another student. Some subjects received a list that suggested a very similar set of preferences with a majority of shared "likes" and "dislikes." Other subjects received a list that suggested that the other had diametrically opposite taste in films. A final group received lists that suggested no consistent pattern of agreement or disagreement. Then, all subjects were told that the person whose list they examined had just seen a new film that opened in local theaters and enjoyed it very much. Subjects were asked whether they thought they would attend and whether they would enjoy the new movie. Results showed that participants who shared past movie preferences with the "other student" were more likely to think that they would attend the film and probably would enjoy it. Those participants who disagreed completely with the other student thought they they were unlikely to attend the new film, and if they did go, would probably not enjoy it. Hence, even though their past experiences were completely opposite, subjects concluded something. Only in the condition where the pattern of agreement–disagreement was random did subjects exhibit uncertainty about whether they would go to the film and whether they would enjoy it. These results support the importance of a consistent affective history rather than similarity per se with regard to preference prediction.

Social Comparison of Complex Opinions

Some opinions do not fall neatly into the belief–value categories (Goethals et al., 1978), but represent a mixture of fact and value. For example, in the recent impeachment hearings of President Clinton, one aspect of the debate involved whether it would be "good" for the country that he leave office prior to the end of his term. This question hinged on issues of value, that is, how one feels personally about the President's behavior, and belief, that is, what would actually happen if he left office prematurely. Although the impeachment question was an especially complex issue (as indicated by the considerable public debate), everyday social life is ripe with complex opinions that represent a combination of belief and value elements. What pattern does the comparison process take in these cases?

Discussion of the structure of complex opinions may be informed by Jones and Gerard (1967) and Bem's (1970) conceptualization of an atttitude as the implication of combining a belief with a relevant value (see also Abelson & Rosenberg, 1958). For example, the attitude "fluoride is bad," is, according to Jones and Gerard, the conclusion of a syllogism, which has "poison is bad"—a value, as a major premise; and "fluoride is a poison"—a belief, as a minor premise.

The truth of the syllogistic attitude conclusion depends on the appropriateness of the value aspect and the truth of the belief. The fluoride syllogism is straightforward, but other attitude syllogisms may be much more complex. A culminating attitude may be the conclusion of a value and belief premise, each of which are conclusions of other syllogisms. All opinions share this structure, although for some opinions the value part of the syllogism is so universal that it is rarely considered and remains implicit, "Poison is bad" would be one such example (of course, even here there are exceptions; witness the Hemlock Society). Many of the cultural truisms researched by McGuire (1964) in his work on the inoculation theory of resistance to persuasion have this nature. One reason that the underlying similarity in values that credible experts have may not be recognized is because many of these values are so fundamental. Another reason is that people may assume via projection, that experts share their values (Gerard & Orive, 1987).

However, there are complex opinions in which value and belief constituents are more debatable, such as in the impeachment example described above. Adopting the reasoning outlined earlier, agreement about the attitudinal conclusion with a person who shares one's values and agreement with another person who is more expert should bolster confidence regarding complex opinions. Consequently, people may evaluate their more complex opinions by following both the belief and value routes, that is, the views of both similar and more expert (dissimilar) others.

A less complicated strategy is to compare with someone who is both similar in values but more expert (dissimilar). As described earlier, this already is operative in the pure belief scenario but becomes more salient for complex opinions. At first thought it would seem that comparing with two different people, the expert and the corroborator, provides more precise evaluation because of the strength in numbers. But it may be more efficient comparing with someone who combines similar values with more knowledge, that is, if such is available.[2] Since similar experts will not always be readily available, people will sometimes have to suffice with separate comparisons—one with a co-oriented peer and the other with an expert.

SUMMARY AND CONCLUSIONS

In this chapter, I have described a theory of opinion comparison that builds on the attributional and projection elements of previous approaches. The triadic social comparison

---

[2]Actually, seeking out a "value" comparison other and a "belief" other could present ambiguity. Someone with superior information might have dissimilar values that could make one question whether one really wants to hold the opinion afterall. Someone with similar values might possess inadequate information, also rendering the attitudinal conclusion less tenable. Of course, if one finds agreement with both, these concerns will probably be minimal. However, if one is trying to decide whose opinion to sample, there is less ambiguity in finding an expert who shares one's values. Furthermore, one can be assured that the attitude represents the conclusion of the same belief and value premises. Sampling opinions from different people does not assure they are using the same premises to draw logical inferences.

model is unique, however, in its identification of three distinct types of opinion questions that commonly arise in social life and in delineating the ability-like aspects of belief judgments that may render more expert sources as important sources of social influence. The three questions, "Do I like X," "Is X true," and "Will I like X" set in motion different judgment processes culminating in the preference for and differential effects of corroborators, experts, or proxies. Considerable evidence already available supports the plausibility of the theory. Perhaps, given its plausibility and accessibility to test, the triadic model may inspire opinions to be "everybody's favorite" comparison domain.

ACKNOWLEDGMENTS

The author wishes to acknowledge the helpful comments of Renny Martin and Ladd Wheeler. The writing of this chapter was supported partly by a grant from the National Science Foundation.

REFERENCES

Abelson, R. P., & Rosenberg, M. J. (1958). Symbolic psycho-logic: A model of attitudinal cognition. *Behavioral Science, 3*, 1–13.

Allport, F. H. (1924). *Social psychology*. Cambridge, MA: Riverside Press.

Aronson, E., & Cope, V. (1968). My enemy's enemy is my friend. *Journal of Personality and Social Psychology, 8*, 8–12.

Arrowood, A. J. (1978). Social comparison theory: Revived from neglect. *Contemporary Psychology, 23*, 490–491.

Asch, S. (1956). Studies of independence and conformity: I. A minority of one against a unanimous majority. *Psychological Monographs, 70*, No. 9, (No. 416).

Bem, D. J. (1970). *Beliefs, attitudes, and human affairs*. Belmont, CA: Brooks/Cole.

Bem. D. J. (1972). Self-perception theory. In L. Berkowitz (Ed.), *Advances in experimental social psychology* (Vol. 6, pp. 2–62). New York: Academic Press.

Brickman, P., & Bulman, R. J. (1977). Pleasure and pain in social comparison. In J. Suls & R. Miller (Eds.), *Social comparison processes: Theoretical and empirical perspectives* (pp. 149–186). Washington, DC: Hemisphere.

Crandall, C. S. (1988). Social contagion of binge eating. *Journal of Personality and Social Psychology, 55*, 588–598.

Darley, J. M., & Aronson, E. (1966). Self-evaluation vs. direct anxiety reduction as determinant of the fear-affiliation relationship. *Journal of Experimental Social Psychology*, Suppl. 1, 66–79.

Deutsch, M., & Krauss, R. M. (1965). *Theories in social psychology*. New York: Basic Books.

Festinger, L. (1950). Informal social communication. *Psychological Review, 57*, 271–282.

Festinger, L. (1954a). A theory of social comparison processes. *Human Relations, 1*, 117–140.

Festinger, L. (1954b). Motivation leading to social behavior. In M. R. Jones (Ed.), *Nebraska symposium on motivation* (Vol. 2, pp. 191–218). Lincoln: University of Nebraska Press.

Festinger, L., Schachter, S., & Back, K. (1950). *Social pressures in informal groups*. New York: Harper and Brothers.

Gerard, H., & Orive, R. (1987). The dynamics of opinion formation. In L. Berkowitz (Ed.), *Advances in experimental social psychology* (Vol. 20, pp. 171–202). New York: Academic Press.

Goethals, G. R. (1972). Consensus and modality in the attribution process: The role of similarity and information. *Journal of Personality and Social Psychology, 21*, 84–94.

Goethals, G. R., & Darley, J. (1977). Social comparison theory: An attributional approach. In J. Suls & R. L. Miller (Eds.) *Social comparison processes: Theoretical and empirical perspectives* (pp. 259–278). Washington, DC: Hemisphere.

Goethals, G. R., Darley, J., & Kris, M. (1978). The impact of opinion agreement as a function of the grounds for agreement. *Representative Research in Social Psychology, 9*, 30–42.

Goethals, G. R., Messick, D., & Allison, S. T. (1991). The uniqueness bias: Studies of constructive social comparison. In J. Suls & T. A. Wills (Eds.), *Social comparison: Contemporary theory and research* (pp. 149–173). Hillsdale, NJ: Lawrence Erlbaum.

Goethals, G. R., & Nelson, R. E. (1973). Similarity in the influence process: The belief-value distinction. *Journal of Personality and Social Psychology, 25*, 117–122.

Gordon, B. F. (1966). Influence and social comparison as motives for affiliation. *Journal of Experimental Social Psychology*, Suppl. 1, 55–65.

Gorenflo, D. W., & Crano, W. D. (1989). Judgmental subjectivity/objectivity and locus of choice in social comparison. *Journal of Personality and Social Psychology*, *57*, 605–614.

Hains, S. C., Hogg, M. A., & Duck, J. M. (1997). Self-categorization and leadership: Effects of prototypicality and leader stereotypicality. *Personality and Social Psychology Bulletin*, *23*, 1087–1199.

Hakmiller, K. (1966). Need for self-evaluation, perceived similarity, and comparison choice. *Journal of Experimental Social Psychology*, Suppl. 1, 45–54.

Heider, F. (1958). *The psychology of interpersonal relations*. New York: Wiley.

Jellison, J., & Arkin, R. (1977). Social comparison of abilities: A self-presentation approach to decision-making in groups. In J. Suls & R. L. Miller (Eds.), *Social comparison processes: Theoretical and empirical perspectives* (pp. 235–258). Washington, DC: Hemisphere.

Jones, E. E., & Gerard, H. B. (1967). *Foundations of social psychology*. New York: John Wiley.

Jones, S., & Regan, D. (1974). Ability evaluation through social comparison. *Journal of Experimental Social Psychology*, *10*, 133–146.

Kelley, H. L. (1952). Two functions of reference groups. In T. M. Newcomb & E. L. Hartley (Eds.), *Readings in social psychology* (rev. ed., pp. 210–214). New York: Holt, Rinehart, and Winston.

Kelley, H. L. (1967). Attribution theory in social psychology. In D. L. Levine (Ed.), *Nebraska symposium on motivation* (pp. 192–241). Lincoln: University of Nebraska Press.

Klayman, J., & Ha, Y. (1987). Confirmation, disconfirmation, and information in hypothesis testing. *Psychological Review*, *94*, 211–228.

Kruglanski, A., & Mayseless, O. (1990). Classic and current social comparison research: Expanding the perspective. *Psychological Bulletin*, *108*, 195–208.

Kunda, Z. (1989). The case for motivated reasoning. *Psychological Bulletin*, *108*, 480–498.

Latané, B. (Ed.). (1966). Studies in social comparison. *Journal of Experimental Social Psychology*, Suppl. 1.

McGuire, W. (1964). Inducing resistance to persuasion: Some contemporary approaches. In L. Berkowitz (Ed.), *Advances in experimental social psychology* (Vol. 1, pp. 191–229). New York: Academic Press.

Merton, R. K., & Kitt, A. (1950). Contributions to the theory of reference group behavior. In R. K. Merton & P. F. Lazarfield (Eds.), *Continuities in social research: Studies in the scope and method of "The American Soldier"* (pp. 40–105). Glencoe, IL: Free Press.

Mullen, B., Atkins, J. L., Champion, D. S., Edwards, C., Hardy, D., Story, J. E., & Venderklok, M. (1985). The false consensus effect: A meta-analysis of 115 hypothesis tests. *Journal of Experimental Social Psychology*, *21*, 262–283.

Newcomb, T. (1943). *Personality and social change: Attitude formation in the student community*. New York: Dryden Press.

Newcomb, T. (1961). *The acquaintance process*. New York: Holt, Rinehart, and Winston.

Nissen, H. W. (1954). Comments on Professor Festinger's paper. In M. R. Jones (Ed.), *Nebraska symposium on motivation* (Vol. 2, pp. 219–223). Lincoln: University of Nebraska Press.

Orive, R. (1988). Social projection and social comparison of opinions. *Journal of Personality and Social Psychology*, *54*, 953–964.

Reckman, R. F., & Goethals, G. R. (1973). Deviancy and group-orientation as determinants of group composition preferences. *Sociometry*, *36*, 419–423.

Rogers, E. M. (1983). *Diffusion of innovations*. New York: Free Press.

Ross, L., Greene, D., & House, P. (1977). The "false consensus effect": An egocentric bias in social perception and attribution processes. *Journal of Experimental Social Psychology*, *58*, 119–128.

Ryan, B., & Gross, N. C. (1943). The diffusion of seed corn in two Iowa communities. *Rural Sociology*, *8*, 15–24.

Schachter, S. (1951). Deviation, rejection, and communication. *Journal of Abnormal and Social Psychology*, *46*, 190–207.

Schachter, S. (1959). *The psychology of affiliation*. Stanford, CA: Stanford University Press.

Sherif, M. (1936). *The psychology of social norms*. New York: Harper.

Suls, J. (1986). Notes on the occasion of social comparison theory's thirtieth birthday. *Personality and Social Psychlogy Bulletin*, *12*, 289–296.

Suls, J., Martin, R., & Leventhal, H. (1997). Social comparison, lay referral, and the decision to seek medical care. In B. Buunk & F. Gibbons (Eds.), *Health and coping: Perspectives from social comparison theory* (pp. 195–226). Mahwah NJ: Lawrence Erlbaum.

Suls, J., Martin, R., & Wheeler, L. (in press). Three types of opinion comparison: The triadic model. *Personality and Social Psychology Review*, *4*.

Suls, J., & Wills, T. A. (Eds.). (1991). *Social comparison: Contemporary theory and research*. Hillsdale, NJ: Lawrence Erlbaum.

Tajfel, H. (1981). *Human groups and social categories: Studies in social psychology*. London: Cambridge University Press.

Turner, J. C. (1991). *Social influence*. Pacific Grove, CA: Brooks/Cole.

Wason, P. C. (1960). On the failure to eliminate hypotheses in a conceptual task. *Quarterly Journal of Experimental Psychology, 12*, 129–140.

Wheeler, L. (1991). A brief history of social comparison theory. In J. Suls & T. A. Wills (Eds.), *Social comparison: Contemporary theory and research* (pp. 3–21). Hillsdale, NJ: Lawrence Erlbaum.

Wheeler, L., Martin, R., & Suls, J. (1997). The proxy social comparison model for self-assessment of ability. *Personality and Social Psychology Review, 1*, 54–61

Wheeler, L., Shaver, K. G., Jones, R. A., Goethals, G. R., Cooper, J., Robinson, J. E., Gruder, C. L., & Butzine, K. W. (1969). Factors determining choice of a comparison other. *Journal of Experimental Social Psychology, 5*, 219–232.

Wood, J. (1989). Theory and research concerning social comparisons of personal attributes. *Psychological Bulletin, 106*, 231–248.

Zajonc, R. B. (1980). Feeling and thinking: Preferences need no inferences. *American Psychologist, 35*, 151–175.

7

Self-Evaluation Maintenance and Evolution

Some Speculative Notes

STEVEN R. H. BEACH AND ABRAHAM TESSER

One model that has helped to guide research in which social comparison is central is the self-evaluation maintenance (SEM) model. In this chapter we attempt to place the model in evolutionary context. To do this we review the SEM model and some of its basic predictions. We then review some recent speculations regarding the origins of self-evaluative feelings. We also add our own speculation about a social performance ecology that may have emerged late in human evolutionary history and could plausibly have led to a sharpening of the comparison and reflection processes that are at the heart of the SEM model. The goal of this exercise is to explore the heuristic potential of placing models of social comparison in an evolutionary framework. Accordingly, we conclude by examining the intellectual gains that follow from asking whether SEM processes represent a specific adaptation to cooperative group living.

WHY PLACE THE SEM MODEL IN EVOLUTIONARY CONTEXT?

As we shall see below, the SEM model describes two basic processes relating the dimensions of performance: closeness and relevance. Investigations designed to explore the implications of SEM processes have examined individual behavior and emotion (Tesser, 1988) and marriage (Beach & Tesser, 1993; Beach et al., 1996). What has been lacking, however, is an adequate account of why. Why do people behave in ways consistent with the model? What is the function that this intricate, interrelated set of processes is meant to serve? The theory of natural selection is an important framework within which such questions can be addressed. Along with others (e.g., Tooby & Cosmides, 1992), we expect that asking why will carry with it a number of benefits. We potentially may come to a new understanding of the basic SEM

STEVEN R. H. BEACH AND ABRAHAM TESSER • Department of Psychology, University of Georgia, Athens, Georgia 30602-3013.

Handbook of Social Comparison: Theory and Research, edited by Suls and Wheeler. Kluwer Academic/Plenum Publishers, New York, 2000.

parameters. In addition, we have the opportunity to consider explicitly the hypothesis that SEM processes are adaptive, or were adaptive in the evolutionary environment of adaptedness (EEA). For humans, the EEA is commonly taken to be the Pleistocene. If SEM processes are an adaptation and not simply a spandrel, or nonfunctional by-product of other functional aspects of mind, better understanding the function of SEM processes may provide new insights into human interaction and human nature (see Buss, Haselton, Shackelford, Bleske, & Wakefield, 1998; Gould & Lewontin, 1979). At a minimum, by introducing new issues and perspectives, an evolutionary account is likely to prove fruitful in suggesting hypotheses and new directions for research on social comparison (Cosmides & Tooby, 1992).

A REVIEW OF THE SEM MODEL

Reviews of the SEM model and its extension are readily available elsewhere (e.g., Beach & Tesser, 1995; Tesser, 1988), so we will not go into much detail here. However, a brief overview follows in order to set the stage for our discussion of the possible adaptive advantage provided by SEM mechanisms.

A key assumption of the SEM model is that persons are motivated to maintain positive feelings about the self. However, work by Swann (e.g., 1990) and others reminds us that persons are also motivated by predictability and control. Indeed, there is some evidence that persons choose other people and situations that verify their view of self even when that view of self is negative. However, when a view of self is verified, if that aspect of self is negative, then one's emotional response to that feedback tends to be negative (Shrauger, 1975). Likewise, negative feedback from a close other may increase one's level of depression even though it is verifying (Katz & Beach, 1997). Moreover, when individuals are made "cognitively busy" so that their ability to process information is impaired, they tend to prefer positive feedback regardless of accuracy (Swann, Hixon, Stein-Seroussi, & Gilbert, 1990). Thus, situations that agree with one's negative self-view produce a kind of cognitive–emotional cross fire: An increase in cognitive control–predictability but at some emotional cost (Swann, Griffin, Predmore & Gaines, 1987).

In sum, our key assumption that individuals are motivated to maintain positive feelings about the self remains viable. There is some evidence of acceptance of self-confirming negative feedback. However, in general, persons tend to have a positive emotional response to and be drawn to favorable self feedback, whereas they have a negative emotional response to negative self feedback. They are therefore likely to engage a variety of mechanisms to protect a positive self-evaluation from negative feedback, while being constrained to some extent by a need for accuracy, consistency, and control. Underscoring the positivity bias among humans, Gilbert (1992) proposed that humans may have evolved a tendency err on the side of overestimating their own abilities, because this is associated with greater willingness to display unique talents and so to be recognized and appreciated by others. We shall argue that any such evolutionary pressures also would provide a selective advantage to mechanisms that lead the individual to define and develop unique talents (which could then be displayed). Thus, we suspect the motivation to maintain positive feelings about the self may have evolved to serve a social purpose and may be somewhat more powerful on average than the motivation to be accurate. In order to lay the groundwork for our discussion of the evolution of mechanisms that maintain positive feelings about the self, we briefly discuss social comparison in general and SEM dynamics as described by the original and extended SEM models.

SOCIAL COMPARISON AND SELF-EVALUATION

Central to the SEM model is the notion that our self feelings are often the result of learning about the performance of others, particularly the performance of those who are psychologically close to us. The good performance of people with whom we have nothing in common and with whom we have little association or connection has little impact on our self feelings one way or the other. On the other hand, the good performance of our friends or relatives can affect us greatly. Sometimes we rejoice and take great pride in their accomplishments. We brag by telling others, "My cousin is the first violinist in the New York symphony"; or, "My girlfriend made law review in her first year of law school." Sometimes, however, the accomplishments of those close to us make us feel inferior and threaten our self-evaluation. It is as if their accomplishments make our own failures or mediocrity salient.

The accomplishments of persons close to us can bolster our self feelings (by basking in their reflected glory) or threaten our self feelings (by comparison). The reflection process and the comparison process are the two basic processes the SEM model is designed to describe. Accordingly, the model is designed to describe the conditions that push us toward the reflection process or toward the comparison process. A preliminary step in this direction may be taken by performing a *Gedanken* (thought) experiment. Suppose playing the violin well is very important to Amadeus. He has studied violin all his life and is trying to find an orchestra for which he can play. So far, he is having little luck. Now imagine how Amadeus would feel if he learned that his cousin was awarded the coveted first chair in the violin section of the New York Philharmonic orchestra. Is he likely to bask in reflected glory or suffer by comparison? For the purposes of the *Gedanken* experiment, contrast your intuition about Amadeus with your predictions for the following situation. Ever since he could remember, Clarence's ambition has been to be a great lawyer. He has no personal ambition to play the violin. He has always thought of his cousin as the "violinist" in the family. Imagine that Clarence learned his cousin was awarded the coveted first chair in the violin section of the New York Philharmonic. Is Clarence likely to bask in reflected glory or suffer by comparison? Our intuition is that Amadeus is likely to suffer by comparison and that Clarence is likely to bask in reflected glory.

The SEM model captures that intuition. The SEM model suggests that the more important or relevant a performance dimension is to one's self identity, the greater the tendency to suffer by comparison to a close other's outstanding performance; the less relevant the performance dimension to one's self identity, the greater the tendency to engage in reflection.

To summarize, one's self-evaluation can be raised by another's good performance (the reflection process) or lowered by another's good performance (the comparison process). The effects on self are more pronounced with psychologically close others than with psychologically distant others. The importance of the comparison process (relative to the reflection process) is a direct function of the relevance of the performance domain to one's self.

SOME SEM DYNAMICS

We have sketched out how, according to the SEM model, another's performance affects one's self-evaluation. Our key assumption, that people are motivated to protect positive self-evaluation (at least within reasonable limits), when combined with the sketch of how another's performance affects self-evaluation provides the information needed to predict self-evaluation maintenance behavior.

Suppose our premed hero, Sigmund, learns that he made a B+ on the test. The only other person from Sigmund's dormitory in this biology class, Pasteur, made an A+. This should be threatening to Sigmund: Pasteur outperformed him; Pasteur is psychologically close (same dormitory); and biology is high in relevance to Sigmund who is studying to be a doctor. What can Sigmund do to reduce this threat and maintain a positive self-evaluation? He can change the performance differential either by working harder himself or by preventing Pasteur from doing well, for example, hide the assignments, put the wrong cells on Pasteur's microscope. He can reduce his psychological connection to Pasteur, for example, change dorms, avoid the same classes. Or, he can convince himself that this performance domain is not self-relevant, for example, biology is not highly relevant to the kind of medicine in which he is most interested. We briefly review a study to illustrate evidence for each of the three basic responses to self-evaluation threat.

Performance

In one of the first studies completed to explore the SEM and model, Tesser and Smith (1980) asked participants to report with a friend. On arrival they found that they would be participating with another pair of friends. The task consisted of a "password game." Three participants passed in clues (that were graded in difficulty) to the experimenter who "randomly" selected one clue to give to the fourth person who was trying to figure out passwords. Each participant was given a turn to figure out passwords. Relevance to self was manipulated: Some groups were led to believe that the task measured attributes that were important to them (high relevance); other groups were told that no systematic relationship between performance on the task and important attributes has been found (low relevance). The experimenter arranged things so that one participant from each friendship pair performed poorly on the task. The subsequent clue-giving behavior of the poor performer was measured. Would he give more difficult clues to his friend or to the stranger?

The SEM model suggests that on a self-relevant task, one will suffer by comparison to a better-performing other, particularly a close other. Therefore, one should be more motivated to prevent the success of a close other than a stranger. Indeed, when the task was high in personal relevance, participants gave more difficult clues to their friend than to the stranger. On the other hand, when relevance is low, one might bask in the reflected glory of a close other's better performance. As predicted, when relevance was low, participants gave easier clues to their friend than to the stranger.

Relevance

Tesser and Paulhus (1983) had pairs of participants individually seated before microcomputers that presented them with a novel cognitive–perceptual task. Psychological closeness of participant pairs was manipulated by telling some that they were scheduled together because they had so much in common; others were told that they were scheduled together because they had so little in common. Performance also was experimentally manipulated. Half the participants were led to believe that they had higher cognitive–perceptual scores than the other participant and half were led to believe that they had poorer scores. It is not surprising that those told that they had done better than the other said and behaved as if the ability was personally more important to them than those told they did less well. What is particularly interesting is the confirmation of the SEM prediction that this effect would be stronger in the close other condition.

Closeness

One of our favorite experiments examining closeness literally measured how physically close experimental participants sat to one another (Pleban & Tesser, 1981). Participants participated with a stranger in a kind of "college bowl" competition. A preliminary questionnaire gave the experimenter the information he needed to assign participants to a topic of high or low personal relevance. The other participant was really an experimental confederate who had memorized all the answers before the experiment even began. Thus, on the basis of random assignment he outperformed some participants and allowed himself to be outperformed by others. After the competition the confederate went into a second room to fill out some questionnaires. The participant soon followed. How close would he sit to the confederate? The SEM model predicted the outcome. When the topic was high in relevance, the more decisively the participant was outperformed by the confederate the less close he sat to him; when the relevance of the topic was low, the more decisively the participant was outperformed by the confederate the closer he sat to him.

The Extension of the SEM Model

As is suggested in the selective review above, the original SEM model for interactions involving strangers, acquaintances, and friends has been well supported (e.g., Tesser, Millar, & Moore, 1988; Tesser, 1988). However, the SEM model was limited in its ability to predict affective reactions to performance situations with close others. In particular, the model made little allowance for someone's investment in the relationship with the other, and no attempt was made to take into account empathic responses to possible partner outcomes. If SEM processes represent common reactions to performance situations, one might expect that partners in committed relationships would anticipate and attend to such potential reactions in their partner. Partners in committed romantic relationships such as marriage show a communal orientation, leading them to keep track of and to respond sympathetically to each other's needs (Clark, 1984; Clark, Mills, & Powell, 1986) and to distinguish less between benefits to the self and benefits to the partner (Aron, Aron, Tudor, & Nelson, 1991). Accordingly, the model was extended to propose that partners in committed relationships would respond sympathetically to their partner's SEM outcomes, as well as directly to their own outcomes (Beach & Tesser, 1993; Clark & Bennett, 1992; Pilkington, Tesser, & Stephens, 1991; see also Brickman & Bulman, 1977; Campbell, 1980).

To illustrate the issues involved, it may be helpful to conduct another *Gedanken* experiment. Consider Bill and his wife Jollie, who are on a skiing vacation. Bill is a pretty good skier, but he knows that Jollie is working to sharpen her skiing skills so that she can enter an upcoming skiing competition. Skiing is very important for Jollie, but her skiing is a little bit off this trip. Bill ends up with better times and performances down the slope all day. Imagine Bill's reaction if he anticipates that Jollie will be feeling badly about her poor relative performance. For the purposes of the *Gedanken* experiment, contrast this with the situation in which Jollie is not very interested in competitive skiing and Bill anticipates no negative response to outperforming Jollie. The extended model predicts that a spouse's emotional benefit from positive comparison (or reflection) may be offset by perceiving that the partner is suffering negative comparison (or failing to benefit from positive reflection). Alternatively, if the partner is basking in reflected glory, the individual's reaction to positive comparison might be enhanced. The extended SEM model therefore suggests the potential for a diminished positive response to outperforming the partner and a diminished negative response to being outperformed by the romantic partner in the area of high self-relevance to both partners.

In an initial study of affective reactions predicted by the original and extended models, Mendolia, Beach, and Tesser (1996) examined 53 young, mostly childless, recently married couples recruited in and around a college campus. Spouses were contacted by phone and asked to recall each of eight situations. The situations involved activities important to the respondent (or not), or important to the spouse (or not), and on which the respondent outperformed their spouse (or not). Husbands and wives were asked to indicate their degree of overall positive (e.g., active, elated, enthusiastic) affect and overall negative (e.g., distressed, nervous, hostile) affect. As predicted by the SEM model, a Performance × Self-relevance interaction was found. Respondents reported more pleasant affect when they outperformed their partner, particularly when the area was important to the self. In addition, Performance × Spouse Relevance interaction predicted by the extended SEM model was found. Respondents reported more pleasant affect when they outperformed their partner, but less so if the area was important to their partner. Accordingly, results supported predictions of both the original and extended SEM models.

A series of studies reported by Beach et al. (1998) also examined the affective impact of performance comparisons in romantic relationships. In study 1 of this series, the affective signature of SEM processes was detected among romantically involved dating partners. The interaction of Self-relevance × Performance was present for both men and women, and indicated that being outperformed by a romantic partner in some types of situations (areas high in Self-relevance), was relatively less pleasant than being outperformed in others (areas low in Self-relevance). There was little support for the extended SEM model among all dating partners. However, a median split on couple satisfaction revealed the predicted performance by partner relevance effect among the more satisfied couples. Perhaps the extended model is more descriptive of committed couples. Indeed, when a sample of married persons was examined, support for the extended model was obtained. In particular, for both husbands and wives, there was a significant effect of Partner Relevance × Performance on pleasantness of affective reactions. The interaction indicated that it was more pleasant to be outperformed by the partner in an area of high rather than low Partner Relevance but more pleasant to outperform the partner in an area low rather than high in Partner Relevance. Consistent with the extension of the SEM model, as couples become more interdependent and communal in orientation, they appear to become more motivated or more adept at extending empathy and sympathy toward the partner.

The results reviewed above suggest the possibility that SEM processes are sufficiently well intuited by spouses that partners in committed relationships could make adjustments in perceived partner relevance to avoid the discomfort of anticipating the other's probable negative reaction. Following up on this possibility, we found that partners appeared to minimize the number of situations in which the self outperformed the partner in areas perceived to be high in relevance to the partner (or vice versa) (study 2: Beach et al., 1998). Likewise, we found that spouses engaged in apparent self-deception to minimize the perception of negative comparison for the partner (study 3: Beach et al., 1996). Thus, perceived relevance to the partner appears to influence behavior in a variety of ways and the effect is consistent with concern about negative effects of social comparison for the partner. Increasingly, this line of research has led to the conclusion that SEM processes and an "awareness" of potential SEM processes in partners is deeply embedded in the structure of close relationships. Indeed, it seems so deeply embedded that it begs the question why. Why do people engage in SEM adjustments? Why do they show the pattern of adjustments and affective reactions predicted by the SEM model and its extension?

ON THE EVOLUTIONARY ANTECEDENTS OF SEM

The SEM model assumes that individuals are motivated to maintain a positive self-evaluation. It further assumes that the "performances" of close others impacts one's self-evaluation. The particular impact, positive or negative, depends on how relevant the other's performance is to one's own self-definition. These are very specific situations and they trigger a very specific array of responses, that is, changes in closeness, performance, and relevance. Why this particular configuration? Are the responses we reviewed in the sections above simply a result of learning arbitrary cultural rules or do these responses reflect some deeper, evolutionary adaptation to social life?

Given our current resources and knowledge it is not possible to answer this question with certainty. We suggest that the behaviors associated with the SEM model are rooted in specific evolutionary adaptations to social life. Below we focus on self-esteem in general and various aspects of the SEM model in particular and speculate on their evolutionary antecedents. We hope that the case we make is plausible and that this exercise is scientifically useful.

SELF-EVALUATION IS AN ADAPTATION TO SOCIAL LIFE

Scientific research on self-esteem has a relatively long and active past (Wylie, 1974, 1979). Self-esteem has been related to adjustment, depression, prejudice, and achievement. Given its importance it may be surprising to learn that empirical, experimental research on the origins of self-esteem are relatively recent. However, questions about the origins of self-esteem have begun to be addressed with greater frequency in recent years (Barkow, 1980; Buss, 1988; Gilbert, 1992; MacDonald, 1988). In particular, our discussion of the nature of self-evaluation draws heavily on recent theorizing and research by Leary and Downs (1995).

As noted above, the evidence that people are motivated to maintain a positive self-esteem is voluminous, strong, and relatively consistent (but see Swann, 1990). Why is there a need for a positive view of self? From what is it derived? A number of answers have been suggested. For example, changes in self-esteem tend to be associated with changes in affect (Tesser & Collins, 1988; Tesser, Millar, & Moore, 1988). A boost to self-esteem is associated with positive affect and a threat to self-esteem is associated with negative affect. Chronic levels of self-esteem tend to be inversely related to affective states such as depression and anxiety (Taylor & Brown, 1988). Perhaps the motive for positive self-esteem is simply derived from preferences for positive affective states. A problem with this approach is that it does not explain why good feelings tend to be associated with positive evaluations of the self by others.

Another suggestion is that people develop a motive for high self-esteem because high self-esteem helps with goal achievement. Indeed, self-esteem is associated with achievement; people high in self-confidence, for example, self-efficacy (Bandura, 1977), tend to perform better and persist longer at various tasks. However, high self-esteem also can have negative consequences for achievement. Persons high in self-esteem may take on tasks that are too difficult; they may persevere at impossible tasks (McFarlin, Baumeister, & Blascovich, 1984).

Some explanations have a decidedly evolutionary cast. Barkow's (1980) notion that self-esteem is an indicator of dominance in a group is explicitly derived from evolutionary psychology (see also Buss, 1988). Prehomonid groups had dominance hierarchies. Individuals higher in the dominance hierarchy had greater access to mates, food, and all the other amenities of social life. With the development of cognitive abilities, on the evolutionary track toward *Homo sapiens* came the ability to keep track of one's place in the hierarchy and the motivational mechanism—self-esteem—for moving toward dominance. In this view, self-esteem is associated with deference given by others. It evolved as a mechanism to maintain or achieve dominance.

In Gilbert's (1992) theorizing, the motive to dominate through threat or aggression is phylogenetically old but has been partially supplanted by a motive to control others' attention through attractiveness. In the context of a social system characterized by greater investment in offspring, alliances, and sharing, social attention holding potential [(SAHP) i.e., attractiveness] should come to be more important for survival and reproductive success than resource-holding potential [(RHP) i.e., strength and aggressive potential]. This argument suggests an evolutionary context in which the desire to gain recognition from others, to make a contribution to the group, or to have one's talents valued by others in the group could become a target of evolutionary pressure and could enhance inclusive fitness. Indeed, Gilbert (1992) suggests that perceived success in gaining SAHP may more closely map onto self-esteem than does perceived success in gaining dominance through aggression.

Another perspective derived from evolutionary thinking is terror management theory. Pyszczynski, Greenberg, and Solomon (1997) suggest that with the emergence of self-consciousness comes terror associated with the awareness of death. Being a spart of one's culture reduces that terror because the culture lives on or because it promises an afterlife. Self-esteem may have evolved as an affective indicator of the extent to which the individual is meeting cultural standards. It is high when the individual believes he is meeting such standards and it is low when he is not.

There have been many successful tests of terror management theory. Since the terror of death is the presumed linchpin, it follows that concerns with cultural standards will be particularly pronounced when death is made salient. This prediction has been confirmed in a large number of studies using a variety of measures. For example, people asked to think about death evaluate cultural heroes more positively and cultural transgressors more negatively than people not asked to think about death (Greenberg et al., 1990). People who think about death also show greater attraction to persons who share their religious beliefs than people who do not think about death (Greenberg, Simon, Pyszczynski, Solomon, & Chatel, 1992). The theory may seem implausible when first encountered but the corpus of experimental tests is persuasive. Still, self-esteem also appears to be sensitive to a number of conditions not associated with the threat of death. Thus, terror management theory is not comprehensive.

The position that we find most persuasive is that self-esteem evolved as a sociometer (Leary & Downs, 1995). In a very broad-ranging review of the literature, Baumeister and Leary (1995) have made a case for the importance of social belonging and the pain of being excluded from important groups. Their analysis is similar in important respects to Gilbert's (1992). Both would argue that as *Homo sapiens* were engaging in the late Pleistocene, group life was crucial to survival. Maintenance of social bonds were important not only for mating but for defense, the acquisition of food, shelter, and so forth. One might suppose that only those who were able to maintain relationships and not be excluded from social groups survived. Given the importance of maintaining group membership, some genetically driven mechanism should have evolved to avoid social exclusion (but see Maryanski & Turner, 1992). According to Leary and Downs (1995) self-esteem is such a mechanism. It functions "… as a sociometer that (1) monitors the social environment for cues indicating disapproval, rejection, or exclusion and (2) alerts the individual via negative affective reactions when such cues are detected" (Leary & Downs, 1995, p. 129).

It is impossible to test directly notions regarding the specific evolutionary path and difficult to test the "innateness" of the need to belong. However, a review of the literature and several new studies are consistent with the sociometer idea. For example, Leary, Tambor,

Terdal, and Downs (1995) presented subjects with different behaviors (study 1) and asked them to rate the extent to which others would reject them if they engaged in the behavior. Later, subjects rated the extent to which they would experience esteem deflating-emotions, for example, shame, dejection, worthlessness, if they engaged in the behavior. They found a substantial positive correlation between these two sets of ratings. In a second study, subjects reported on personal events that had a positive or negative impact on their self-feelings. They then rated their self-feelings and the extent to which each of the situations involved social exclusion. Again, the correlation between these variables was significant. In a third and fourth study subjects were randomly assigned to be either accepted or rejected by a group or another person. Rejected subjects showed greater negative self-feelings. These studies clearly suggest that behaviors or situations associated with exclusion are also associated with decrements in self-esteem.

EVOLUTION AND SEM

The sociometer notion and the equation of perceived SAHP with self-esteem both resonate well with the SEM model. The bedrock assumption of the SEM model is that people wish to maintain self-esteem and that self-esteem is often the result of social forces. Leary and Downs (1995) "... assert that people are motivated to behave in ways that maintain self-esteem because behaviors that maintain self-esteem tend to be ones that decrease the likelihood that they will be ignored, avoided, or rejected by the other people" (p. 129). We accent this view as a starting point, but we believe that it does not go far enough.

Leary and Downs suggest that self-esteem is rooted in concerns with being excluded by others. Certainly however, we are not equally concerned with being excluded by all people and all groups. The SEM model helps us to understand this. It suggests that the social consequences to self-esteem are amplified in the context of psychologically close others rather than distant others. Recall, psychological closeness refers to the extent to which people see themselves connected in some way to the other, that is, what Heider (1958) calls "unit relatedness," or, more recently, what group perception researchers (e.g., Campbell, 1958; Hamilton, Sherman, & Lickel, 1998) call "entitativity." Thus, we suggest that self-esteem as a sociometer is more sensitive to social exclusion among close than among distant others.

Leary and Downs [along with William James (1950), some time ago, and Jennifer Crocker (unpublished data, 1998), more recently] recognize that the self-esteem of different people are sensitive to feedback in different domains: "People can follow many routes to social acceptance. Only when people have staked their connections to others on certain aspects of themselves should their self-esteem be affected by events that reflect on those aspects" (Leary & Downs, 1995, p. 137). However, Leary and Downs do not specify how certain aspects of the self become important to connections with others.

The SEM model also recognizes the idea of different domains of self-esteem. The SEM construct of relevance refers to the extent to which doing well in some particular domain is important to the self. Moreover, the SEM model goes further in attempting to understand the social ecology that leads a person to "stake his all" (James, 1950) on one particular domain rather than another. Below we will argue that not only is self-esteem an adaptation to group living but that the selection of personally relevant domains of self-esteem also emerges, at least partly, from adaptations to group living.

One might argue that the general sociometer as described by Leary and Downs is the only evolutionary adaptation and that the qualifications associated with the SEM model are "add-ons." If, however, the sociometer and the SEM add-ons are separate (independent) mechanisms they should function additively. However, in study after study we find that the variables of closeness, relevance, and feedback (performance) consistently interact in affecting one another and in affecting self-feelings. Rather than acting as separate, general mechanisms, they appear to be an integrative answer to some complex social questions.

In sum, self-esteem may be a very specific adaptation to group life. It appears to be especially sensitive to social exclusion. However, that sensitivity is highly contingent on the closeness of others and the distribution of domains of self-esteem or relevance in the group. As we shall argue below, SEM mechanisms appear to exhibit the characteristics that raise the possibility of special design (Williams, 1966). That is, it appears that SEM mechanisms may solve an evolutionary problem confronted by *Homo sapiens* at a key point in their evolution.

THE EVOLUTIONARY BACKGROUND: SOME IMPORTANT CHARACTERISTICS OF EARLY HUMAN SOCIAL ORGANIZATION

As a first step toward thinking about the potentially adaptive nature of SEM mechanisms, it may be useful to think about characteristics of the early human social environment. In particular, we focus on those aspects of social life that were relatively constant and so could more plausibly influence evolutionary outcomes over long periods of time.

It is not known at what point SEM mechanisms were developed. However, at present there is little evidence to suggest that they preceded other complex social adaptations. For example, at some point humans developed language and the corresponding capacity to symbolize situations in a complex manner (Sedikides & Skowronski, 1997). This clearly could influence social organization and the contingencies associated with group life. In particular, this adaptation presumably allowed individuals to think of the self as an object, to create mental representations of in-group–out-group distinctions, and to represent one's value to the in-group. Likewise, humans have specialized abilities to recognize particular faces and so track individual identity over time. It appears as well that some of the mechanisms for face recognition are specific to this task, suggesting that face recognition per se has been the target of selection pressure. Such an adaptation is critical for the formation of special patterns of affiliation and to allow for more complex status and friendship hierarchies. At some point in their evolution, humans begin to engage in the sharing and exchange of surplus resources. As resources became more plentiful, there was greater opportunity to benefit from group membership (Cosmides & Tooby, 1992). Because such exchange behavior is universal across human cultures (e.g., Cashdan, 1989), and some of our primate relatives also engage in forms of this behavior (e.g., chimpanzees, macaques, and baboons) (see de Wall & Lutrell, 1988), it seems possible that this was a relatively early adaptation to group life. Similarly, the strong affiliative tendencies shown among humans (Baumeister & Leary, 1995) and strong evidence of long-term associations for mutual benefit that include nonkin may have long evolutionary histories.

Likewise, human societies are characterized by recognition of status, group membership, exchange, and pricing in the coordination of their interactions (Fiske, 1992; Fiske & Haslam, 1997). Of these, the market pricing strategy appears to be a relative uniquely human adaptation. Market pricing is one of the four patterns of coordinating interaction widely available among humans (Fiske, 1998). It is characterized by attention to socially meaningful ratios of value, such that people are aware of the differing value of various resources or contributions. In turn, these differing values can translate into different levels of status or exchange in social contexts. Use of market pricing is consistent with the further development of specialization, as it provides an additional incentive to focus on the production of something rare, which therefore may have substantially enhanced value instead of several things that each have substantially less value. For example, if making a specialized contribution could result in a 100-fold increase in recognition and resources, there would be considerable advantage to successfully specialize. Conversely, in the absence of a valuation mechanism in which one thing could be viewed as equivalent to several items of lesser value, there would be little incentive to specialize.

As is implicit in this overview, we assume that for much of human evolutionary history, probably preceding the emergence of *Homo sapiens* as a distinct species, the social environment has been characterized by complexity, cooperation, social exchange, and coalition building. As *Homo sapiens* began to emerge as a distinct species, however, there appears to have been a distinct shift toward greater within-group specialization. As we shall elaborate below, this shift may have required the corresponding adaptations of market pricing and SEM mechanisms.

The long history of group living for human beings should have exerted strong selective pressure for individual characteristics that facilitated survival in social groups (e.g., Wilson & Sober, 1994). That is, if group living among humans has particular recurrent patterns of danger and opportunity, over time this structure should come to be represented in the design of human beings (Cosmides & Tooby, 1992). In addition, because of the strong survival and reproductive benefits of status and social attractiveness (e.g., Ellis, 1992; Gilbert, 1992), humans who were able to enhance their status within their primary social group should have been overrepresented in subsequent generations. Once again, this underscores the possibility that individuals who could more easily solve the recurrent adaptive problem of coordination of effort may have had a selective advantage (Caporael, 1997).

A salient characteristic of human groups is the tendency to develop specialized castes or roles. Indeed, the tendency for human beings to specialize may have begun early in human history. Specialization may have been useful for humans because it allowed them to take advantage of group life. One might imagine as well that as tool use emerged among humans, this should have facilitated the drive toward specialization. That is, with increasingly powerful and complex tools to manipulate the environment (e.g., fire, weapons, clothing, food preparation devices), the need for greater specialization may have increased as well.

If the emergence of specialized tool use is believed to confer selective advantage, it must be noted that it also brings with it obvious problems of social coordination. A mechanism that increased specialization in the absence of some additional mechanism for reducing overlap in specialization could lead to disaster rather than abundance for the group. If too many individuals selected the same specialization, the individuals who specialized could find selection pressures working against them rather than in their favor. Accordingly, the fact of human specialization suggests the possibility of a mechanism to guide specialization so that it is adaptive for the individual given the distribution of specialization of his or her social group. The capacity to consider market pricing (Fiske, 1992) in transactions introduces the possibility of further refining specialization to be responsive to pricing considerations.

Because specialization per se may not guarantee that the social environment will reward one's skills, on particular specialization should be the target of consistent selective pressure over time. Rather, in light of market pricing, it is specialization targeted at the opportunities (i.e., scarcity) existing within one's primary social group at a given time that confers selective advantage. Accordingly, a mechanism emerging in such an environment should be targeted at identifying opportunities (i.e., underpopulated specializations) and directing the individual to take advantage of available opportunities.

In an environment characterized by market pricing and surplus, being able to produce benefits or resources of relatively greater social value as defined by one's primary group should confer additional adaptive advantage by potentially increasing one's social status and attractiveness and so one's survival and reproductive opportunities. A mechanism adapted to a social environment characterized by market pricing should consistently put the individual in a position to deliver highly valued resources in demand by the group. Such a mechanism should be sensitive to competition in areas of possible specialization and to one's own special capabilities and weaknesses relative to others in one's primary social group. If so, the well-adapted mechanism would lead the individual to distinguish between valued areas in which there were many potentially superior competitors and areas in which there were few or no superior competitors. In addition, the well-adapted mechanism should lead the individual to specialize in an area in which the potential competition is unlikely to outperform the self and lead the individual to specialize in an area that is both available, valued by others in the group, and whose mastery will confer survival and reproductive advantages for the self.

One way for such a mechanism to work would be to influence the individual to find him- or herself losing interest in the crowded areas in which the self is outperformed, and gaining interest in the more open areas in which the self is outperforming others. By doing so, the individual would effectively cede some areas to others in the social group while staking a claim in some of the remaining potential areas of specialization. As we have argued elsewhere (Beach et al., 1996; 1998), this is precisely the effect of a well-functioning SEM mechanism.

SEM processes orient the individual toward socially valued dimensions and help maintain attention on nuances in performance along these dimensions. Being outperformed leads to changes in behavior or self-construal associated with *negative comparison*. These processes appear well designed to render the individual either better on the original dimension (through increased effort), or alternatively, more likely to invest him- or herself in other socially valued activities (through decreased relevance). As the self is reconfigured to make more central (or relevant) those dimensions that are associated with good relative performance, a self is created that is more focused on those socially valued areas in which a unique, or salient, valued contribution can be made. Conversely, as the self makes less central (or relevant) those areas on which the self is routinely outperformed, *reflection processes* ensure that one is more likely to respond positively to close others who perform well. As a result, the self is gradually molded to find ways to make a unique or salient contribution to the larger group while simultaneously being molded to support the efforts of others to make contributions in other important ways.

Along with a mechanism for focusing one's attention and ceding some areas to others, also needed is a mechanism that orients the individual to the outstanding behavior of others and encourages the self to facilitate relationships that allow for the exchange of resources with such persons. Particularly important would be a mechanism that oriented the self toward positive, cooperative relationships with those who provide resources that are complementary to the self. Reflection also serves this function by facilitating feelings of closeness with others that are complementary to the self with regard to their areas of expertise.

POSITIVE FEEDBACK LOOPS, EXPLOSIVE HUMAN EVOLUTION, AND THE MECHANISMS OF SPECIALIZATION AND NICHE BUILDING

As a digression, it is also interesting to note that the mechanisms of pricing and specialization provide a social context in which SEM mechanisms may be selected for, but also may combine with SEM to create a changed social environment with even more complex demands. As niche building became better represented among early humans, it also must have led to a changing social environment. The more the social environment became characterized by cooperation and sharing, the greater the opportunity for specialization. The greater the selective advantage of targeted specialization the greater the selective advantage in favor of a niche-building mechanism and the resulting advantage to belonging to an affiliative network. Thus, the SEM mechanism may have become part of an evolutionary positive feedback loop, leading to increasing selection pressure until the trait became uniformly represented throughout the species. This leads to the expectation that SEM processes will be found across societies. Also of interest, the evolutionary hypothesis raises but does not answer the question of whether there should be stages of development characterized by greater activity of some SEM mechanisms. For example, if specialization was a particularly salient problem in young adulthood, there might be some greater propensity for openness regarding identity and a greater willingness, on average, to change self-relevance in response to feedback during this stage of development.

PLACING KEY EXAMPLES OF THE SEM MODEL
INTO EVOLUTIONARY CONTEXT

A key assumption of the SEM model is that persons are motivated to maintain some level of positivity regarding the self. Why? As with Leary's sociometer hypothesis, such a characteristic should be selected for because it represents a way of keeping individuals focused on group membership and helps orient them to threats to group membership. In its broader form, such a mechanism is probably phylogenetically older than *Homo sapiens* and reflects an early adaptation to the selective power of the social environment. The SEM model, however, goes further in suggesting that performance by close others rather than strangers is most important in threatening self-evaluation and so prompting changes and adjustments in the self-view. Why? Selection for attention to the performance of close others is an excellent adaptation to pricing and so maximizing one's potential to benefit from the group context. Adjusting the self in response to the performance of distant or irrelevant others would seem unlikely to improve one's fit with the group and so have minimal impact on reproduction and survival.

Likewise the SEM model posits that individuals may bask in the glory of the outstanding performance of close others. Why? Such a characteristic would seem ideal for ensuring that the self is drawn to others who are producing valuable products and resources. As a result, one should be placed in better position to share, form coalitions, or engage in social exchange that will enhance personal survival and reproduction. Accordingly, one of the consequences of the reflection process is increased group cohesion. The individual is drawn to others who perform well, creating a positive environment for him- or herself and at the same time advancing group goals.

As noted in the overview of the model, sometimes the response to the threat of being outperformed is to sabotage the performance of another, and this is more likely with a close other than with a distant other. Why? If the function of SEM mechanisms is to maximize one's own ability to provide valued resources to the group, it is important for the individual to defend a viable niche within the group if possible. In particular, if a potential competitor for one's niche can be shunted toward some other niche, one may transform the potential competitor into a potential reflection opportunity. On average, particularly when one has an established position, it often may be more cost-effective for the self to discourage potential competitors than to change one's own area of specialization, even if the group might be better served by the competitor. Only when another, better niche is clearly available; or when repeated outperformance by the competitor appears inevitable, should a change in relevance regarding an established area of specialization result. Interestingly, this suggests some social circumstances in which reduction in relevance should be quite rare as well as conditions that might facilitate change in relevance.

Sometimes the adjustment to the threat of being outperformed is to change closeness to the other. Why? If another threatens one's place in the primary social unit and there is no alternative available niche, one's relevance to the group and so one's survival and reproductive opportunities are in jeopardy. Thus, decreasing closeness to the competitor may sometimes be a message to discourage the activity of the potential competitor. Or, antipathy may function as the precursor to taking action against the other and so reducing the threat to one's position in the group. However, should one lose to the competitor and lose one's place in the group, decreased closeness may serve as a precursor to breaking away from the group and finding a new group with which to affiliate. In either case, it often should be more adaptive to reduce closeness to the competitor who threatens one's position within the group than to remain close and find one's status within the group lowered.

DOES GROUNDING IN EVOLUTIONARY THEORY CHANGE SEM THEORY?

One of the goals of placing the SEM model in an evolutionary context is that it highlights certain aspects of the model and may lead to previously unanticipated predictions. Likewise, combining SEM theory with propositions derived from evolutionary psychology may yield new predictions from the SEM model or suggest additional implications for social functioning and social development. Some such implications are already apparent in the forgoing analyses. For example, juxtaposing SEM mechanisms with human attention to pricing highlights the potential importance of value considerations in determining SEM adjustments, an area that has not previously been considered within this framework. However, there are other potential implications that may deserve attention as well. Each parameter of the SEM model is highlighted and perhaps changed by placing the model in evolutionary context. Due to space limitations we briefly sketch rather than exhaustively examine some of these implications.

Self-Relevance

In evolutionary context self-relevance is the parameter most subject to change. It is change in self-relevance that directs or redirects the individual's activities over time. Performance and closeness may be influenced by events, but in the context of small-group life, performance and closeness appear more consistently as inputs into the SEM system, whereas self-relevance appears more consistently as an output. In addition, change in self-relevance appears particularly useful as a guide for behavior among young or low-status individuals who are attempting to develop a niche in their social group. If so, one might anticipate that the parameters in the SEM model would show differential flexibility in response to challenge, and this differential flexibility might change, depending on important aspects of the situation and important characteristics of the individual. In particular, it should be easier to find changes in the self-relevance of a performance dimension if one provides both feedback that one has performed poorly in one area along with feedback that one has performed well in another area. Similarly, it should be easier to change self-relevance to the extent that the area is less directly tied to an individual's specialization or the way they see themselves gaining status from others. Finally, it may be easier to change relevance among adolescents than among adults in mid-life.

Performance

Likewise, in evolutionary context the SEM model may be viewed as serving the function of identifying and helping to create relatively unique spheres of competence or performance niches in the context of the primary reference group. That is, a well-functioning SEM mechanism should enable the individual to find socially valued dimensions on which the self can perform better than close others. This highlights both the importance of the extent to which others in the social group hold a dimension in high esteem, and the importance of a primary social group as the ultimate source of definitions of closeness. Accordingly, one might predict that the effect of perceived attitudes of significant others about a particular performance dimension might influence the degree to which individuals change self-relevance or closeness in response to performance feedback. In addition, one might expect greater changes if the connection between the performance dimension and certain highly valued areas of personal specialization were highlighted.

Closeness

With regard to the definition of closeness, an evolutionary perspective highlights that unit relatedness is merely a proxy for seeing oneself as being in some type of group relationship with another. The natural groups from an evolutionary perspective are rather small such as dyads (2), family–work groups (5), deme (band) (30), and macrodeme (300) (see Caporael, 1997). Taking such core configurations as a starting point suggests the possibility that SEM mechanisms might function in slightly different ways at each level of groupness. In addition, these considerations suggest that regardless of the number of potential others in the environment there may be a strong tendency for SEM parameters to respond as if the relevant comparisons were within one of the natural groups. For example, it may be that comparison with other individuals occurs when the focus is at the dyad level (group of two), family or work group level (a group of about five persons) or the group level of deme (a group of about 30 persons). In such natural groups the problem of coordinating one's own specialization with those of others in the group may have been most acute. However, at the level of macrodeme (i.e., groups of 300 or more) comparisons may tend to occur between deme's or work groups. That is, there may be a disinclination to compare the self to others in groups that exceed 300, and perhaps even in groups that exceed 30. Rather, after a certain group size is exceeded, comparisons may tend to focus on the relative performance of one's group relative to other groups. Here, however, there may be less room for SEM processes and more room for primitive dominance processes. Accordingly, it is possible that the smooth functioning of SEM mechanisms may be impaired when groups exceed a certain size.

CONCLUSION

Incipient SEM processes add survival value to group living and to specialization within the group. As human society becomes increasingly complex and greater specialization is possible, there is increasing selection pressure in favor of well-functioning SEM mechanisms.

As increasing specialization drives further expansion of human cognitive capacity, the group environment and individual survival within the group environment come increasingly to depend on something like the SEM model to guide adaptation to the social group and help with normative social transitions throughout the life span. In brief, over human evolutionary history there has emerged a complex social environment in which there is considerable payoff for having specialized skills and abilities that are needed and valued by one's social group. The complex social environment and the survival and reproductive benefits attendant on finding a way to contribute to the welfare of the group may have created increasingly intense selective pressure as humans evolved. Indeed, SEM processes may have solved an adaptive problem of cooperative living, and in combination with cognitive, language, and tool-using capabilities may help explain certain unique aspects of human behavior.

REFERENCES

Aron, A., Aron, E. N., Tudor, M., & Nelson, G. (1991). Close relationships as including other in the self. *Journal of Personality and Social Psychology, 60,* 241–253.

Bandura, A. (1977). Self-efficacy: Toward a unifying theory of behavioral change. *Psychological Review, 84,* 191–215.

Barkow, J. (1980). Prestige and self-esteem: A biosocial interpretation. In D. R. Omark, F. F. Strayer, & D. G. Freedman (Eds.), *Dominance relations* (pp. 319–332). New York: Garland.

Baumeister, R. F., Smart, L., & Boden, J. M. (1996). Relation of threatened egotism to violence and aggression: The dark side of high self-esteem. *Psychological Review, 103,* 5–33.

Beach, S. R. H., & Tesser, A. (1993). Decision making power and marital satisfaction: A self-evaluation maintenance perspective. *Journal of Social and Clinical Psychology, 12,* 471–494.

Beach, S. R. H., & Tesser, A. (1995). Self-esteem and the extended self-evaluation maintenance model: The self in social context. In M. Kernis (Ed.), *Efficacy, agency, and self-esteem* (pp. 145–170). New York: Plenum Press.

Beach, S. R. H., Tesser, A., Fincham, F. D., Jones, D. J., Johnson, D., & Whitaker, D. J. (1998). Pleasure and pain in doing well, together: An investigation of performance related affect in close relationships. *Journal of Personality and Social Psychology, 74,* 923–938.

Beach, S. R. H., Tesser, A., Mendolia, M., Anderson, P., Crelia, R., Whitaker, D. G., & Fincham, F. D. (1996). Self-evaluation maintenance in marriage: Toward a performance ecology of the marital relationship. *Journal of Family Psychology, 10,* 379–396.

Brickman, P., & Bulman, R. J. (1977). Pleasure and pain in social comparison. In J. M. Suls & R. L. Miller (Eds.), *Social comparison processes: Theoretical and empirical perspectives* (pp. 149–189). Washington, DC: Hemisphere.

Buss, D. M. (1988). *Personality: Evolutionary heritage and human distinctiveness.* Hillsdale, NJ: Lawrence Erlbaum.

Buss, D. M., Haselton, M. G., Shackelford, T. K., Bleske, A. L., & Wakefield, J. C. (1998). Adaptations, expectations and Spandrels. *American Psychologist, 53,* 533–548.

Campbell, D. T. (1958). Common fate, similarity, and other indices of the status of persons as aggregates. *Behavioral Science, 3,* 14–25.

Campbell, J. (1980). Complementarity and attraction: A reconceptualization in terms of dyadic behavior. *Representative Research in Social Psychology, 11,* 74–95.

Caporael, L. R. (1997). The evolution of truly social cognition: The core configurations model. *Personality and Social Psychology Review, 1,* 276–298.

Cashdan, E. (1989). Hunters and gatherers: Economic behavior in bands. In S. Planttner (Ed.), *Economic anthropology* (pp. 21–48). Stanford, CA: Stanford University Press.

Clark, M. S. (1984). Record keeping in two types of relationships. *Journal of Personality and Social Psychology, 47,* 549–557.

Clark, M. S., & Bennett, M. E. (1992). Research on relationships: Implications for mental health. In D. N. Ruble, P. R. Costanzo, & M. E. Oliveri (Eds.), *The social psychology of mental health* (pp. 166–198). New York: Guilford.

Clark, M. S., Mills, J., & Powell, M. C. (1986). Keeping track of needs in communal and exchange relationships. *Journal of Personality and Social Psychology, 51,* 333–338.

Cosmides, L., & Tooby, J. (1992). Cognitive adaptations for social exchange. In J. H. Barkow, L. Cosmides, & J. Tooby (Eds.), *The adapted mind* (pp. 163–228). Oxford: Oxford University Press.

de Waal, F. M. B., & Lutrell, L. M. (1988). Mechanisms of social reciprocity in three primate species: Symmetrical relationship characteristics or cognition? *Ethology and Sociobiology, 9,* 101–118.

Ellis, B. J. (1992). The evolution of sexual attraction: Evaluative mechanisms in women. In J. H. Barkow, L. Cosmides, & J. Tooby (Eds.), *The adapted mind* (pp. 267–288). Oxford: Oxford University Press.

Fiske, A. P. (1992). The four elementary forms of sociality: Framework for a unified theory of social relations. *Psychological Review, 99,* 689–723.

Fiske, A. P. (1998). Human sociality. *International Journal for the Study of Personal Relationships Bulletin, 14,* 4–9.

Fiske, A. P., & Haslam, N. (1997). The structure of social substitutions: A test of the relational models theory. *European Journal of Social Psychology, 27,* 725–729.

Gilbert, P. (1992). *Depression: The evolution of powerlessness.* New York: Guilford.

Gould, S. J., & Lewontin, R. C. (1979). The spandrels of San Marco and the Panglossian program: A critique of the adaptationist programme. *Proceedings for the Royal Society of London, 250,* 281–288.

Greenberg, J., Pyszczynski, T., Solomon, S., Rosenblatt, A., Veeder, M., Kirkland, S., & Lyon, S. (1990). Evidence for terror management theory II: The effects of mortality salience on reactions to those who threaten or bulster the cultural worldview. *Journal of Personality and Social Psychology, 58,* 308–318.

Greenberg, J., Simon, L., Pyszczynski, T., Solomon, S., & Chatel, D. (1992). Terror management and tolerance: Does mortality salience always intensify negative reactions to others who threaten one's world view? *Journal of Personality and Social Psychology, 63,* 212–220.

Hamilton, D., Sherman, S. J., & Lickel, B. (1998). Perceiving social groups: The importance of the entitativity continuum. In C. Sedikides & C. Insko (Eds.), *Intergroup cognition and intergroup behavior* (pp. 47–74). Mahwah, NJ: Lawrence Erlbaum.

Heider, F. (1958). *The psychology of interpersonal relations.* New York: Wiley.

James, W. (1950). *The principles of psychology.* Chicago: Encyclopaedia Britannica. (Original work published in 1890)

Katz, J., & Beach, S. R. H. (1997). Self-verification and depression in romantic relationships. *Journal of Marriage and the Family, 59,* 903–914.

Leary, M. R., & Downs, D. L. (1995). Interpersonal functions of the self-esteem motive: The self-esteem system as a sociometer. In M. Kernis (Ed.), *Efficacy, agency, and self-esteem* (pp. 123–144). New York: Plenum Press.

Leary, M. R., Tambor, E. S., Terdal, S. K., & Downs, D. L. (1995). Self-esteem as an interpersonal monitor: The sociometer hypothesis. *Journal of Personality and Social Psychology, 68,* 518–530.

MacDonald, K. B. (1988). *Social and personality development: An evolutionary synthesis.* New York: Plenum Press.

Maryanski, A., & Turner, J. H. (1992). *The social cage: Human nature and the evolution of society.* Stanford, CA: Stanford University Press.

McFarlin, D. B., Baumeister, R. F., & Blascovich, J. (1984). On knowing when to quit: Task failure, self-esteem, advice and non-productive persistence. *Journal of Personality, 52,* 138–155.

Mendolia, M., Beach, S. R. H., & Tesser, A. (1996). The relationship between marital interaction behaviors and affective reactions to one's own and one's spouse's self evaluation needs. *Personal Relationships, 3,* 279–292.

Pilkington, C. J., Tesser, A., & Stephens, D. (1991). Complementarity in romantic relationships: A self-evaluation maintenance perspective. *Journal of Social and Personal Relationships, 8,* 481–504.

Pleban, R., & Tesser, A. (1981). The effects of relevance and quality of another's performance on interpersonal closeness. *Social Psychology Quarterly, 44,* 278–285.

Pyszczynski, T., Greenberg, J., & Solomon, S. (1997). Why do we need what we need? A terror management perspective on the roots of human motivation. *Psychological Inquiry, 8,* 1–20.

Sedikides, S., & Skowronski, J. (1997). The symbolic self in evolutionary context. *Personality and Social Psychology Review, 1,* 80–102.

Shrauger, J. S. (1975). Responses to evaluation as a function of initial self-perceptions. *Psychological Bulletin, 82,* 581–596.

Swann, W. B. (1990). To be adored or to be known? The interplay of self-enhancement and self verification. In E. T. Higgins & R. M. Sorrentino (Eds.), *Handbook of motivation and cognition* (Vol. 2, pp. 408–448). New York: Guilford Press.

Swann, W. B., Griffin, J. J., Predmore, S. C., & Gaines, B. (1987). The cognitive affective crossfire: When self-consistency confronts self-enhancement. *Journal of Personality and Social Psychology, 52,* 881–889.

Swann, W. B., Hixon, J. G., Stein-Seroussi, A., & Gilbert, D. T. (1990). The fleeting gleam of praise: Cognitive processes underlying behavioral reactions to self-relevant feedback. *Journal of Personality and Social Psychology, 59,* 17–26.

Taylor, S. E., & Brown, J. D. (1988). Illusion and well being: A social psychological perspective on mental health. *Psychological Bulletin, 103*, 193–355.

Tesser, A. (1988). Toward a self-evaluation maintenance model of social behavior. In L. Berkowitz (Ed.), *Advances in experimental social psychology* (Vol. 21, pp. 181–227). New York: Academic Press.

Tesser, A., & Collins, J. (1988). Emotion in social reflection and comparison situations: Intuitive, systematic, and exploratory approaches. *Journal of Personality and Social Psychology, 55*, 695–709.

Tesser, A., Millar, M., & Moore, J. (1988). Some affective consequences of social comparison and reflection processes: The pain and pleasure of being close. *Journal of Personality and Social Psychology, 54*, 49–61.

Tesser, A., & Paulhus, D. (1983). The definition of self: Private and public self-evaluation maintenance strategies. *Journal of Personality and Social Psychology, 44*, 672–682.

Tesser, A., & Smith, J. (1980). Some effects of friendship and task relevance on helping: You don't always help the one you like. *Journal of Experimental Social Psychology, 16*, 582–590.

Tooby, J., & Cosmides, L. (1992). The psychological foundation of culture. In J. H. Barkow, L. Cosmides, & J. Tooby (Eds.), *The adapted mind* (pp. 19–136). Oxford: Oxford University Press.

Williams, G. C. (1996). *Adaptation and natural selection: A critique of some current evolutionary thought.* Princeton: Princeton University Press.

Wilson, D. S., & Sober, E. (1994). Reintroducing group selection to the human behavioral sciences. *Behavioral and Brain Sciences, 17*, 585–654.

Wylie, R. C. (1974). *The self-concept* (Rev. ed., Vol. 1). Lincoln: University of Nebraska Press.

Wylie, R. C. (1979). *The self-concept* (Rev. ed., Vol. 2). Lincoln: University of Nebraska Press.

8

Individual Differences in Social Comparison

LADD WHEELER

The study of individual differences in social comparison is a fairly recent phenomenon, created largely by the downward comparison theory prediction (Wills, 1981, 1991) that low self-esteem individuals will choose to make downward comparisons as a self-enhancement strategy. Prior to that theory (and to a large extent afterward), social comparison researchers have been more concerned with situational influences on comparison behavior than with the influence of individual differences. Opposed to downward comparison theory is Beck's (1967, 1976) cognitive model of depression, which argues that depressives have a "systematic bias against the self" that is reflected in and maintained by their upward comparisons. A later self-worth contingency model of depression (Kuiper & Olinger, 1986; Swallow & Kuiper, 1988) argued that the self-worth of depressives is contingent on positive performance evaluations and the resulting approval of others. Thus, depressives are particularly sensitive to social comparison. Perceived threats to self-worth activate dysfunctional social comparison processes, such as failing to discount the superior performance of others advantaged on related attributes (see Chapters 2 and 3, this volume), and hence make an inordinate number of unfavorable comparisons leading to negative self-evaluations. In short, the cognitive depression models argue that dysphoric individuals should engage in dysfunctional social comparison, particularly when threatened. Downward comparison theory, on the other hand, predicts that low self-esteem or dysphoric individuals should try to make (functional) downward comparisons for self-enhancement, particularly when threatened. These are the most articulated theoretical positions and account for most of the research, but several recent studies have investigated individual difference variables other than self-esteem and dysphoria, and I think that these attempts may ultimately be quite fruitful.

My strategy in this chapter is to present the research in some detail so that readers have the opportunity to develop their own hypotheses about why results differ from study to study. Furthermore, each section will deal with a particular method or question. I will include in this review only those studies that I feel actually measure social comparison (rather than some

LADD WHEELER • School of Psychology, University of New South Wales, Sydney 2052, Australia.

Handbook of Social Comparison: Theory and Research, edited by Suls and Wheeler. Kluwer Academic/Plenum Publishers, New York, 2000.

other behavior), and measure it in ways that I think are adequate. For example, I will not include studies in which the measure of social comparison is retrospective, for example, "How often do you realize that you are better off than most other people?" Some will disagree with this decision, because comparison often has been measured in this manner, but I think that responses to such a question are more likely to reflect one's theory about what one has done or ought to have done than to reflect actual comparisons (see Reis & Gable, 2000; Reis & Wheeler, 1991, for a discussion of problems with retrospective accounts). Recent evidence from other researchers also has shown a divergence between retrospective and contemporaneous accounts (Pietromonaco & Feldman-Barrett, 1997; Stone et al., 1998). Nor will I include studies in which participants are asked to make a comparative rating, for example, "Is your proficiency at cunnilingus better or worse than average," unless there is independent evidence that social information has been used in making the rating. As Alicke, Klotz, Breitenbecher, Yurak, and Vredenburg (1995) pointed out, people may just apply the simple heuristic that they are better than average on everything (see Chapter 14, this volume). Finally, I will exclude role-playing studies, for example, "Whom would you want to compare with if you were in such-and-such a situation?" Like retrospective accounts, they may say more about one's theories about behavior than about one's behavior. For an excellent discussion of methods used in studying social comparison, see Wood (1996).

THE SOCIAL COMPARISON RECORD

The social comparison record (SCR) technique, first used by Wheeler and Miyake (1992) is an example of event-contingent self-recording (Wheeler & Reis, 1991). The participant is asked to record every social comparison made over an extended period, usually 10 to 14 days. The participant records the dimension of comparison (e.g., academic, physical appearance), the relationship to the comparison target (e.g., close friend, stranger), similarity to the target or the dimension (e.g., much better, much worse), and affect just before and just after the comparison. Other questions about the comparison can be added to the SCR, as long as participants are requested to record every comparison as soon as they are aware of it. The advantages of this contemporaneous or on-line method are that investigators do not have to trust participants' memory, the comparisons are those that take place in everyday life, and the relatively large number of comparisons by each person permits reliable estimates.

Wheeler and Miyake (1992) found that high self-esteem participants made more downward comparisons (which in general produced an increase in positive affect). In addition, high self-esteem participants responded with less negative (more positive) affect to lateral and upward comparisons.

Miyake (1993) found that low self-esteem participants made more upward comparisons. This is consistent with, if not exactly the same as, the Wheeler and Miyake (1992) results. In both cases, high self-esteem participants made comparisons that were more downward than those of low self-esteem participants. Replicating Wheeler and Miyake (1992), Miyake (1993) found that high self-esteem participants responded with more positive (less negative) affect to upward comparisons. Miyake also measured the stability of self-esteem by obtaining the standard deviation of numerous measures of self-esteem over the course of the study (see Kernis, Grannemann, & Mathis, 1991; Kernis, Grannemann, & Barclay, 1989; 1992). Unstable self-esteem participants made more upward comparisons, and this effect was independent of low-self-esteem participants making more upward comparisons. Interestingly, the more unstable the self-esteem, the greater the variability in comparison direction, as one might expect, but unfortunately there is no way to know the direction of causation. Finally, those with unstable self-esteem responded with more positive affect to lateral comparisons. With both their self-esteem and their comparison direction fluctuating, finding a similar comparison target was possibly a relief.

Giordano and Wood (1998) replicated the finding of Wheeler and Miyake (1992) that high self-esteem respondents made more downward comparisons than did low self-esteem respondents and responded with less negative affect to upward comparisons. In a companion paper, Wood, Michela, and Giordano (in press) distinguished between those comparisons respondents felt were voluntary versus those that were involuntary and concluded that the results just described were more true for involuntary than for voluntary comparisons. The authors suggested that low and high self-esteem people may be equally likely to want to make downward comparisons, but high self-esteem people are more likely to encounter targets they regard as inferior to themselves.

Olson and Evans (1999) related the big five NEO Personality Inventory-Revised (NEO PI-R) (Costa & McCrae, 1992) to the frequency of comparisons and affective reactions to them. Extraversion, sometimes referred to as "surgency" (facets = warmth, gregariousness, assertiveness, activity, excitement-seeking, positive emotions) predicted a greater frequency of comparisons that were more downward, whereas openness to experience (facets = fantasy, aesthetics, feelings, actions, ideas, values) and agreeableness (facets = trust, straightforwardness, altruism compliance, modesty, tender-mindedness) predicted a greater frequency to comparisons that were more upward. Contrary to prediction, neuroticism was not related to direction of comparison.

In general, positive affect decreased after upward comparisons, as in all of the studies using the SCR, but this was particularly pronounced among those high in "agreeableness," and was attenuated among those high in "openness." In general, positive affect increased after downward comparisons, again, as in all SCR studies, and this was particularly pronounced among those high in neuroticism (facets = anxiety, angry hostility, depression, self-consciousness, impulsiveness, vulnerability).

Locke and Nekich (in press) compared participants high in agentic traits (dominant, competitive, ambitious) with those high in communal traits (warm, tender, sympathetic), as measured by the Bem Sex Role Inventory (Bem, 1974) and the Personal Attributes Questionnaire (Spence, Helmreich, & Stapp, 1974). Agency was related to making downward comparisons, avoiding upward comparisons, and feeling confident. Communion did not predict direction of comparison but was related to stronger feelings of connectedness. Self-esteem also was measured and produced the same results as agency: High self-esteem participants made more downward comparison, fewer upward comparisons, and felt more confident as a result of the comparisons. In addition, high self-esteem participants felt happier and more connected than did those with low self-esteem.

The results of these studies are fairly consistent. Downward comparisons are more likely to be made by those high in self-esteem, high on agentic traits, and high on extraversion; those, in short, who are confident, dominant, active, and who experience positive emotions. Upward comparisons are more likely to be made by those low in self-esteem, those with unstable self-esteem, low agentics, and those high on agreeableness and openness to experience. The results of the latter two traits, investigated only by Olson and Evans (1999), require some explanation. People high on agreeableness tend to be modest, endorsing items that state that they would rather praise others than themselves, and that they are no better than others, no matter what their (the others) condition. Individuals low on agreeableness are skeptical of others, see themselves as superior to most people, and compete with others rather than cooperate. Thus it is not surprising that those who are low would make comparisons that were more downward than those high on agreeableness. What is surprising to me is that high agreeables were particularly likely to indicate reduced positive affect after upward comparisons, when in fact an upward comparison would be quite consistent with their humility. However, this was an unexpected effect of only marginal significance and awaits replication.

Olson and Evans predicted and found that those high on openness to experience would compare more upwardly and would respond with less decrement in positive affect to these upward comparisons. The reasoning was that individuals high on openness to experience presumably really want to know about people superior to them and perhaps how they got to be that way, leading them to make comparisons that are more upward. For participants high on openness to experience, the affective responses should not be as negative as for those who are low; if one wants to find out about superior people and how they got that way, an upward comparison will not have such a damaging effect on mood. The interesting thing about this is that none of the items measuring openness refer to curiosity about other people. Rather, the facets measure involvement in fantasy, aesthetic concerns, the experience of strong feelings, the seeking of variety in action, the enjoyment of ideas, and a view of values as relative. Either these facets generalize to curiosity about how other people are successful or there is some other explanation for the results.

The other two traits that predicted affective responses to comparison in the SCR studies were self-esteem and neuroticism. In three studies, high self-esteem individuals responded with less negative affect to upward comparisons than did low self-esteem individuals. This is what most theorists would predict; high self-esteem provides some protection against threatening comparisons. The only trait that predicted responses to downward comparison is neuroticism. While the affective response to downward comparison was generally positive, it was even more so for those high on neuroticism. Probably neurotics, with their lower self-esteem and greater dysphoria, have a stronger need for information that someone else is even worse off. Moreover, neuroticism is characterized by emotional liability. Note, however, that they did not make more downward comparisons than did low neurotics. They benefit from downward comparisons but do not (or cannot) find them more than do low neurotics.

EXPERIMENTAL STUDIES:
AMOUNT OF COMPARISON INFORMATION SOUGHT

Pinkley, Laprelle, Pyszczynski, and Greenberg (1988) manipulated success–failure on a test of social sensitivity and then measured the amount of comparison dysphorics and non-dysphorics requested when they anticipated that the comparison scores would be either high or low. Nondepressed failure participants requested more information when they expected the scores to be low than when they expected them to be high, presumably to confirm through consensus that the reason for their failure was external rather than internal; when nondepressed participants had succeeded, they showed no such bias. Depressed participants exhibited an entirely different pattern. After failure, depressed participants showed no difference in information seeking as a function of information expectancy. After success, however, they sought more information when they expected the scores to be low than when they expected them to be high. In short, although depressed participants did not try to convince themselves that the reason for their failure was external, they did attempt to convince themselves that the reason for their success was internal.

Swallow and Kuiper (1992) allowed dysphorics and nondysphorics the opportunity to compare freely with previous participants following actual performance on a task. Thus, those with high task performance received predominantly favorable comparison information and those with low task performance received largely unfavorable information. At the beginning of the comparison period, however, participants had no idea how well they had done, and so their status as having done well or poorly was only gradually revealed as they made comparisons. Dysphorics and nondysphorics did not differ on the number of comparisons made following high task performance, but dysphorics made many more comparisons than nondysphorics following low task performance. Apparently, as nondysphorics with low task performance begin to receive unfavorable comparison information, they simply stopped comparing; dysphorics showed no such inhibition.

Wood, Giordano-Beech, Taylor, Michela, and Gaus (1994) devised a clever new measure of social comparison (see Chapter 11, this volume). Participants select which of a number of tests of various abilities they will take and which tests another person will take. By selecting the same tests for the self and the other person to take, they show evidence of comparing with that person. In two experiments, low self-esteem participants who had been given a success manipulation vis-à-vis another person choose to subsequently compare with that person on more tests (unrelated to the success dimension) than did similar participants who had failed (or, in study 2, those who had received no feedback). This was not true of high self-esteem participants, who either showed no difference between success and failure conditions (study 1) or who compared more after failure or no feedback (study 2). The results were interpreted as showing that low self-esteem individuals self-enhance through social comparison when it appears safe to do so, and that high self-esteem individuals use social comparison to compensate for failure. Some additional evidence for compensation by high self-esteem people was provided by Wood, Giordano-Beech, and Ducharme (1999), but because only high self-esteem participants were used in that research, I will say no more about it here.

Roney and Sorrentino (1995) tested participants on the Alport and Vernon (1931) Values Survey (measuring theoretical, aesthetic, political, social, religious, and economic values for individuals), presented participants' scores to them, and then allowed them to see scores of as many other people as they wished on any of the values. Uncertainty-Oriented participants chose to see more scores than did Certainty-Oriented participants, regardless of whether they believed the scores were from similar others (students) or dissimilar others (community sample). Uncertainty Orientation, a composite of a projective measure of need to reduce uncertainty (nUncertainty) (Sorrentino, Hanna, & Roney, 1992) and the acquiescence-free authoritarianism measure (Cherry & Byrne, 1977) reflects differences in the desire to find out about oneself and about one's environment. Uncertainty-Oriented participants handle uncertainty by seeking out information and engaging in activity that will resolve uncertainty. Certainty-Oriented participants, on the other hand, develop a self-regulatory style that circumvents uncertainty confrontation. However, this is not always the case (Sorrentino, Hodson, & Huber, in press), and more use of the Uncertainty Orientation measure in social comparison research is encouraged.

The studies in this section dealing with self-esteem and dysphoria are consistent with one another. Nondysphoric individuals who have failed compare more with others whom they expect to have low scores in order to obtain consensus that the failure had an external cause (Pinkley et al., 1988), and they stop comparing with those who have done better than themselves (Swallow & Kuiper, 1992). High self-esteem individuals attempt to compensate for their failure by comparing with their competitor on dimensions other than the dimension of failure (Wood et al., 1994). In short, high self-worth people use social comparison, after failure or low performance in particular, to maintain high self-regard.

Dysphoric individuals who have succeeded compare more with others whom they expect to have low scores in order to demonstrate that their success had an internal cause (Pinkley et al., 1988), and those with low self-esteem respond to success by comparing with their competitor on additional dimensions (Wood et al., 1994). Thus low self-worth people do try to enhance their self-regard when they have been successful. When dysphorics have performed poorly, however, they do not avoid upward comparisons as nondysphorics do (Swallow & Kuiper, 1992).

EXPERIMENTAL STUDIES: TARGET SELECTION

Wilson and Benner (1971) attempted to use a modification of the rank order paradigm to determine whether self-esteem influenced comparison choice, but the results varied with certainty–uncertainty, public–private, and sex of the participant. I have no idea what to make of these results.

Using the rank order paradigm, Friend and Gilbert (1973) compared participants high and low on Fear of Negative Evaluation (Watson & Friend, 1969), who were either threatened or not by an unexpectedly low score on a test of social intelligence. Fear of Negative Evaluation items measure concerns about being evaluated negatively, rather than expectations that one will be evaluated negatively; it is a measure of social anxiety rather than of self-esteem or depression. On an initial version of the test of social intelligence, participants were told that they had an average score and were ranked fourth in the group of seven. They then took a second version of the test, which was supposed to be a more precise and accurate measure of the trait and in the threat condition received a much lower score than on the first test. In the no-threat condition, they received a much higher score on the second and more accurate test. They were not told what their rank was on the second test. The dependent variable was their choice of which other score to see in the group of seven, based on the rank order achieved on the initial test. Between 73 and 89% of the participants made an upward comparison except in the condition in which participants high in Fear of Negative Evaluation were also threatened by an unexpectedly low score; only 38% of these participants made an upward comparison.

Again using the rank order paradigm, Smith and Insko (1987) placed participants at rank 5 in a group of seven on a test of "social intelligence." The dependent variable was the choice to see the score of the person at rank 1, because the authors believed that to be the most diagnostic choice. Anything that reduced choices of the top score was seen to be "in some way motivated by defensive, self-esteem-related concerns" (p. 112). The three independent variables were self-esteem, score magnitude (either 270 or 710 on a scale with an implied range of 200–800), and whether the comparison would be public (meeting and talking with the comparison target) or private (examining the target's score and test materials). There were main effects for each variable and no interactions. Choice of the top score was less frequent for low self-esteem participants, for those with a low score, and for those in the public condition. What is important for this chapter is that low self-esteem participants made fewer choices of the top score and according to Smith and Insko, therefore, were motivated by defensive concerns.

Although it is true that choice of the highest score was more frequent among high self-esteem participants (63%) than among low self-esteem participants (44%), choice of one of the two highest scores was the same for high self-esteem (71%) and low self-esteem (72%) participants. In other words, low self-esteem participants simply dropped down to rank 2 for their comparison choices, still well above their own rank 5 position. If the low self-esteem participants were really motivated by defensive concerns, they could have done much better than that. For example, they could have made downward comparison of ranks 6 or 7, as shown by Friend and Gilbert (1973), but only one low self-esteem participant did that (this study is often cited incorrectly as showing downward comparison, but this is no fault of Smith and Insko, who made no such claim). Another difficulty with the defensive comparison explanation is that there was no interaction between performance and self-esteem. One would expect low self-esteem individuals who scored low to have stronger defensive comparison needs than those who scored high. The key to understanding these results may be the fact that low self-esteem participants initially expected to score lower on the test of social intelligence than did high self-esteem participants (Smith & Insko, 1987, p. 116–117). Thus the top score would be more relevant (and similar) for the high self-esteem participants than for the lows. Collins (1996, p. 66) made a similar point.

Gibbons (1986, study 1) manipulated mood by having depressed and nondepressed college students write about a significant positive (or negative) event in their recent lives. Then participants chose to read similar statements by other students from a list of several categories based on the type of affect displayed in the statement, from 1 (very negative) to 7 (very positive). Depressed participants who had written about a negative event in their lives expressed more negative affect than the other groups and chose less positive statements (mean = 3.8) to read than those in the other three groups (means = 5.6–6.0). It should be noted that the depressed participants were very depressed indeed, with a Beck Depression Inventory score of greater than 21, so there is no evidence that the depressed–negative event participants chose to compare with others they believed to be actually worse off than themselves. They may have perceived their comparison targets to be similar to themselves, or even better off. This is another study that should not be cited as evidence for downward comparison (but often is).

Swallow and Kuiper (1993) tested participants on digit recall, described as tapping one component of intelligence. Without being given feedback about their performance, participants then chose a quartile (based on performance of previous subjects) from which comparison scores would be drawn. Among subjects with high task performance, there was no difference between dysphorics and nondysphorics: both groups preferred to be exposed to scores they expected to be slightly higher than their own. Among participants with low task performance, however, nondysphorics wanted to see scores they expected to be below their own, while dysphorics wanted to see scores similar to their own. The authors concluded that dysphorics are less likely than nondysphorics to use self-protective social comparison strategies following failure.

In a second study, Swallow and Kuiper (1993) allowed participants to request additional information about each comparison target (gender, age, number of years in university, major, etc.). The authors reasoned that if one has performed poorly and therefore is receiving predominantly unfavorable comparison information, one way to protect self-esteem would be to attribute a variety of advantaging characteristics to the target, allowing superior performances to be discounted (Goethals & Darley, 1977). Thus *not* requesting information would be an indication of ego enhancement following low task performance. If one knows nothing about the characteristics of superior performers, one is free to attribute advantaging characteristics without reality intruding. As predicted, nondysphorics requested considerably less information about comparison targets following low task performance than following high task performance, while dysphorics showed a slight reversal of this pattern. Thus, nondysphorics were more likely than dysphorics to use comparison opportunities to bolster or to defend their self-esteem.

It is difficult to reconcile four papers that have four different results, and I merely summarize the inconsistent evidence. Friend and Gilbert (1973) found that, after failure only, high Fear of Negative Evaluation participants made downward comparisons. Smith and Insko (1987) found that, regardless of performance, low self-esteem participants compared less upward than high self-esteem participants, but both groups made upward comparisons. Swallow and Kuiper (1993) found that, after low performance only, nondysphorics compared more downward than dysphorics. Gibbons (1986) found that depressed individuals in a negative mood compared more downward than the other groups (but not necessarily downward relative to themselves).

EXPERIMENTAL STUDIES: TARGET SELECTION
AS SHOWN BY REACTIONS TO MIXED INFORMATION

Ahrens (1991) argued that in real life people are exposed to a wide range of information that they must combine; it is in this combinatorial process that dysphorics will selectively attend to information supporting a negative view of the self. Dysphoric and nondysphoric participants were given information that a previous participant had scored worse on a spatial abilities test, that a previous participant had scored better on the test, or that one previous participant had scored worse and another had scored better (mixed comparison). Subsequently, participants' self-evaluation was measured by asking them to estimate how many of the next 99 participants would do worse than they had done on the test, how many would do better, and what the median score would be. As predicted, dysphoria did not influence self-evaluations in either the favorable or unfavorable comparison condition. In the mixed condition, however, nondysphorics evaluated themselves the same as in the favorable comparison condition, whereas dysphorics evaluated themselves the same as in the unfavorable comparison condition. When combining information, dysphorics attended to that which supported a negative view of the self, but nondysphorics attended to positive information.

In a conceptually similar study, McFarland and Miller (1994) compared participants with negative orientations (depressives and pessimists) to those with positive orientations. In study 1, feedback was given based on either a large sample of 1000 or a small sample of 10. It was predicted that the orientation groups would differ more on assessment of their ability when feedback was based on a large sample than on a small sample, because negatively oriented participants would focus on the number of people better than themselves, whereas positively oriented participants would focus on the number of people worse than themselves. A large sample would provide more people who were better and more people who were worse than would a small sample. This prediction was confirmed when participants had been given relatively negative feedback. In study 2, when feedback was given, attention was focused on the number of people who did better or the number of people who did worse. Mood was negatively affected for the positively oriented participants when attention was focused on the number of people who did better (an unaccustomed focus for them) and mood was positively affected for the negatively oriented participants when attention was focused on the number of people who did worse (again, an unaccustomed focus).

These studies are consistent in showing that when individuals are faced with comparison information that can be interpreted as placing them in either a good light or a bad light, depressives–pessimists will focus on that portion of the information that places them in a bad light, whereas nondepressives–optimists will do the opposite. Such as conclusion is consistent with the results from the studies reviewed earlier obtained with the SCR.

REACTIONS TO COMPARISON INFORMATION

Most of the research reviewed here was done to test the prediction of downward comparison theory (Wills, 1981) that threatened and/or low self-esteem individuals will compare downward in order to improve their subjective well-being. This theoretical statement should be broken down into two statements. (1) Threatened and/or low self-esteem people will choose to compare downward more than nonthreatened/high self-esteem individuals. (2) Threatened/low self-esteem people will benefit more from downward comparisons than will nonthreatened/high self-esteem people. It is quite possible that one of these statements could be correct and the other not.

With regard to the first statement, about comparison selections, evidence reviewed earlier in this chapter certainly does not support downward comparison theory. Research with the SCR shows that high self-esteem individuals are more likely to make downward comparisons, and the experimental studies by Ahrens (1991) and McFarland and Miller (1994) support that conclusion. The research reviewed on information seeking indicated that dysphorics do not self-protect after poor performance as nondysphorics do. Finally, the evidence reviewed in the section on experimental studies of target selection allowed no conclusions to be drawn. An unbiased observer would conclude that the theory is incorrect about choice of comparison direction.

Nevertheless, it is possible that the second prediction of downward comparison theory—that low self-esteem people will benefit the most from downward comparison—is true. Providing an adequate test, however, is incredibly tricky. In the typical study to be described below, the experimenter imposes a threat manipulation on low and high self-esteem individuals, measures mood, provides them with comparison information, and measures mood again. The dependent variable is mood improvement, the cause of which is attributed to the comparison information. The problem is that negative mood may become less negative for reasons other than the nature of the comparison information. There have been numerous studies of spontaneous mood recovery or remission (e.g., Berkowitz & Troccoli, 1990; Clark & Isen, 1982; Erber & Erber, 1994; Forgas & Ciarrochi, 1999; Sedikides, 1994). Furthermore, after a threat manipulation, low self-esteem/dysphorics are typically affected more than are high self-esteem/nondysphorics, making it even more likely that spontaneous recovery from negative moods will occur for the former group. The rubber band of mood has been stretched more for the low self-esteem/dysphorics. What this implies is that experiments should contain a no-comparison control condition, which would permit the conclusion that mood change is due to the comparison information rather than to spontaneous remission of the negative mood. Some authors attempt to deal with the problem by referring to an analysis of covariance controlling for precomparison mood. However, there is no indication that the major and critical assumption of the analysis of covariance—equal regression coefficients (slopes) in the two groups—has been examined. An upward comparison condition sometimes has been used as a control, but it is far less desirable than a no-comparison control because the upward comparison information might in itself contribute to a negative mood. This could mask any remission of negative mood.

An example of the missing control group problem is one of the first downward comparison studies (Gibbons, 1986, study 2), in which depressed and nondepressed participants were exposed to a story about a unhappy event that had happened to another student (an accident harming a child, which the student felt guilty about and responsible for). The mood of the depressed participants, initially quite negative, became significantly more positive after reading the story, whereas the mood of nondepressed participants did not change. There was no control group (that read no story or that read a positive story). All we can conclude from the experiment is that the group with the most negative initial mood improved their mood over the course of the experiment, either because of spontaneous mood recovery or because of downward comparison information.

Wenzlaff and Prohaska (1989), in a more complete study, exposed depressed and non-depressed participants to a recent negative or positive event in another student's life, for which the student was either responsible or not. The hypothesis was that depressed participants would show more positive mood change after hearing another's misfortune only if the other person was perceived as a victim of circumstances. On the other hand, if the other person was perceived as responsible for the negative event, it might make a depressed person feel worse by activating his or her own self-blaming tendencies. As hypothesized, depressed participants showed mood improvement only when exposed to a blameless unhappy target. Their moods became more negative when exposed to a story about a positive event for which the target was responsible, but not when exposed to a merely fortunate other (such as a lottery winner). Nondepressed participants, on the other hand, had the worse moods after hearing about the blameless unhappy target (probably out of sympathy).

In Gibbons and Gerard (1989), participants wrote about problems they were having adjusting to college; they then read one of three statements allegedly written by another student in the support group. In the Upward Comparison (UC) condition, the author had only minor problems and was adjusting well. In the Downward Comparison (DC) condition, the author had few problems but still was not adjusting well. In the Severe Problem (SP) condition, the author had severe problems but had coped with the problems and was adjusting well. Prior to reading the statements, low self-esteem participants were in a more negative mood than high self-esteem participants, thought they were coping less well, and thought they were having more difficulty adjusting. Both self-esteem groups improved mood in the SP condition. Low self-esteem mood improved in the DC condition but was unchanged in the UC condition. In contrast, mood of the high self-esteem participants was unchanged in the DC condition and improved in the UC condition.

Gibbons and McCoy (1991) reported that low self-esteem participants who had been given threatening feedback improved mood more than high self-esteem participants as a result of hearing about a student having trouble adjusting to college. These experiments did not contain a no-comparison control or an upward comparison condition, and thus we cannot conclude that downward comparison was responsible for mood change.

Reis, Gerrard, and Gibbons (1993) found that female low self-esteem effective contracep-tors (oral contraceptives or condoms at least 90% of the time) exposed to ineffective contra-ceptors (downward comparison) increased self-esteem more than when exposed to effective contraceptors (lateral comparison), but high self-esteem respondents showed no difference. The low self-esteem participants' increase in self-esteem was not accompanied by an improve-ment in mood, and Reis et al. argued that "... downward comparison does facilitate mood improvement among people who are depressed as well as those with low self-esteem, but only in the presence of some kind of threat" (1993, p. 13). It is puzzling to me why threat would be necessary for mood improvement but not for a self-esteem increase. The authors offered some speculations but not evidence.

Aspinwall and Taylor (1993) exposed high and low self-esteem participants to a positive or negative mood induction (by having them recall a relationship event in their lives) and provided them with an upward or downward comparison with another student adjusting to college. Self-esteem made a difference when participants were in a negative mood and given a downward comparison: low self-esteem participants increased positive mood, and high self-esteem participants did not.

The authors noted that the absence of a no-comparison control group was a problem, because the low self-esteem participants in a negative mood might have felt better simply because of attenuation of the negative mood rather than because of downward comparison (low self-esteem participants' initial mood was well below that of the high self-esteem participants). Accordingly, study 2 compared the responses of high and low self-esteem participants to one of three kinds of comparison information (upward, downward, and no comparison). The comparison information was in the form of a statement from a former student who had done very well or poorly. In addition, participants were blocked on the basis of a median split on an index of academic threat, based on whether the student has experienced some sort of academic setback recently, as well as the severity of the threat and the amount of personal distress it had caused. There was no mood manipulation.

The affect results from study 1 did not replicate at all, and the authors implicated procedural differences between the two studies as the cause for this. Two measures, however, did produce differences roughly similar to the mood effects in study 1: expectations for future success in adjusting to college and current adjustment relative to the average college student. Both measures showed that low self-esteem participants who were under academic threat benefited the most from downward comparison relative to no comparison or upward comparison. High self-esteem participants, threatened or not, were unaffected by comparison direction. The authors concluded that the benefits of downward comparison apply more narrowly than predicted by downward comparison theory (Wills, 1981, 1991): that downward comparison is good only for those who have low self-esteem *and* are threatened.

Lyubomirsky and Ross (1997) compared participants in the top and bottom quartiles on a happiness scale and manipulated whether peer performance on an anagrams test was faster or slower than the participant's performance. Unhappy participants responded with negative mood to being outperformed and with positive mood to outperforming the peer. Happy participants, on the other hand, were not bothered by being outperformed but did respond with positive mood when they outperformed the peer. Controlling statistically for self-esteem and for optimism did not change the pattern of results. In study 2, participants used hand puppets to teach children about conflict resolution. They were then given positive or negative feedback by an expert about their performance. Half the participants in each of these feedback conditions received no further information, and thus were no-comparison control groups. For the remaining half, the positive feedback group was given information that a peer had done even better (upward comparison), and the negative feedback group was given information that a peer had done even worse (downward comparison). Consistent with study 1, upward comparison had no effect on happy participants but decreased the mood of unhappy participants. Also consistent with study 1, downward comparison increased the mood of both groups. Taken together, the studies provide clear evidence that happy participants are more able to deal with being outperformed than are unhappy participants. The conditions most similar to other studies discussed in this section were the negative feedback (threat) conditions of study 2, in which downward comparisons were provided. Happy and unhappy participants responded equally positively to this comparison information.

To summarize, five articles had sufficient conditions to allow us to draw some conclusions. Wenzlaff and Prohaska (1989) found that depressed participants more than the non-depressed increased positive mood after exposure to a downward target who was not responsible for his misfortunes, but not if the person was responsible. Gibbons and Gerard (1989) found that threatened low self-esteem participants more than high self-esteem participants improved mood after downward comparison but not after upward comparisons. Reis et al. (1993) found that low self-esteem participants increased more in self-esteem following a downward comparison than did high self-esteem participants. Aspinwall and Taylor (1993) found that threatened low self-esteem participants showed more mood improvement to downward comparison than high self-esteem participants, and in a second study that threatened low self-esteem participants showed higher expectations for future success and higher current adjustment following downward comparison. Lyubomirsky and Ross (1997) demonstrated that happy and unhappy participants respond equally positively to downward comparison, but that happy participants are less negatively affected by upward comparison.

Four of the five articles are roughly in accord with the downward comparison theory prediction that low self-esteem/depressive individuals will respond with more positive affect to downward comparisons than will individuals with higher self-regard. The study (Lyubomirsky & Ross, 1997) that did not show this simply found no difference. Moreover, this study used happiness as the individual difference variable, and it may differ in important ways from self-esteem and depression (indeed, the authors claim so). Finally, Lyubomirsky and Ross (1997) used task performance to create upward and downward comparison, whereas the other studies used life events/situations. The four supportive articles leave many questions unanswered, the role of threat being perhaps the most perplexing.

We have seen earlier that low self-regard individuals do not select downward comparisons, and we have seen that when faced with mixed comparison information, they focus on the upward information rather than the downward information. Thus, the validity of downward comparison theory predictions about individual differences appears to be limited to situations in which individuals are exposed only to downward comparison information.

STUDIES OF INDIVIDUALS WITH CANCER

This research is discussed separately, because it has not used threat–failure manipulations, and thus is not really comparable to most of the research done with healthy participants. In addition, without participants who are not cancer patients, it is difficult to discuss it with the other research. It is nevertheless good and interesting research.

Van der Zee, Buunk, and Sanderman (1998) exposed cancer patients to a bogus interview with another patient who was doing better than participants (upward condition) or worse (downward condition). Overall, participants responded with more positive affect to upward than to downward comparisons. Neuroticism interacted with comparison direction such that high neurotics expressed less positive affect than low neurotics after upward comparisons but not after downward comparisons. These data were supplemented by questions measuring the degree of identification with the comparison target, showing that for downward comparison neuroticism was positively related to identification, whereas for upward comparison neuroticism was negatively related to identification. In summary, neurotics were less able to identify with an upward comparison target, and thus to assimilate to that target, which attenuated their positive affective reactions to upward comparison.

Van der Zee, Oldersma, Buunk, and Bos (1998) allowed cancer patients to select and read as many interviews with other patients as they wished, with the interviews clearly labeled as being with others who were doing better than the respondents or doing worse. Individual difference variables were neuroticism (Eysenck & Eysenck, 1991) and social comparison orientation as measured by the Iowa–Netherlands Comparison Orientation Measure (Gibbons

& Buunk, 1999). In general, the respondents selected more upward comparisons than downward comparisons and spent more time reading the upward comparisons. Both those high on neuroticism and on the INCOM selected more interviews to read, regardless of direction. This result is consistent with the research of Olson and Evans (1999) using the SCR; they also found that neuroticism was unrelated to direction of comparison.

In general, participants responded with more positive affect and less negative affect to upward comparisons than to downward comparisons, as also found by Van der Zee et al. (1998). This difference (at least for positive affect) was more pronounced for those high on neuroticism than for those who were low. High and low neurotics experienced the same amount of positive affect during upward comparisons, but high neurotics experienced less during downward comparisons. Thus, in this study, neurotics were less able to benefit affectively from downward comparison, whereas in the Van der Zee, Buunk, and Sanderman (1998) study, they were less able to benefit affectively from upward comparisons. It is possible that this is due to methodological differences between the two studies. In the Van der Zee, Oldersma, Buunk, and Bos (1998) study, participants selected as many comparisons as they wished, but in the Van der Zee, Buunk, and Sanderman (1998) study, they were given a single comparison.

The INCOM did not relate to affect and comparison direction. It did, however, interact with neuroticism in predicting overall negative affect regardless of comparison direction. Neuroticism predicted negative affect among those also high on the INCOM, but not among those who were low.

NEW MEASURES OF SOCIAL COMPARISON TENDENCIES

The INCOM (Gibbons & Buunk, 1999) has 11 items and 2 factors: "ability" and "opinions" (but the authors caution against using the factors separately). Examples of items are: "If I want to find out how well I have done something, I compare what I have done with how others have done," and "I often try to find out what others think who face similar problems as I face." Six of the items include the word "compare." The INCOM correlates moderately with scales of other orientation such as Attention to Social Comparison Information (ATSCI) (Lennox & Wolfe, 1984), Public Self-consciousness, and Swap and Rubin's (1983) Interpersonal Orientation Scale. There are smaller positive correlations with negative affectivity (depression, self-esteem, anxiety) and with neuroticism.

To establish criterion-related validity, experimental participants were told they had scored above average on the Wilder Proximal Parts Test (e.g., vocabulary, emotional maturity). On three measures, INCOM predicted the amount of comparison sought. Oldersma, Buunk, and de Dreu (1997) found that relationship-distressed persons who were high on the INCOM reported the largest increase in relationship satisfaction following downward comparisons. Buunk et al. (1998) found that downward comparison produced the most negative affect among health care workers who were high in professional burnout and high on the INCOM. Other supporting data sets are described in Gibbons and Buunk (1999), and a number of studies using the scale are in process. The INCOM should be an important and exciting addition to social comparison research.

A Dispositional Envy Scale (DES) has been proposed by Smith, Parrott, Diener, Hoyle, and Kim (1999). This eight-item scale correlates positively with depression and neuroticism and negatively with self-esteem and social desirability. The DES predicted participants' envy reported during random moments over the course of 2 weeks, during daily assessments over 4 weeks, and with respect to general tendencies to feel envy across multiple domains of social comparison. It predicted even when effects of the other scales with which it correlates were removed.

In an experimental study, participants watched a videotaped interview with another student who was average or with another student who was clearly superior to the student (upward comparison). Those high on the DES responded with greater envy and jealously to the upward comparison than did those low on the scale. The authors suggest that the DES could be useful in determining when people will assimilate to upward comparisons and when they will contrast themselves (see Chapter 9, this volume). Again, I look forward to wider use of this scale.

CONCLUSIONS

I will deal first with selection of comparison targets, then with reactions to comparison information. The term "selection" is used broadly to refer to the comparisons people make; it is not meant to necessarily imply a conscious choice any more than does smiling on a sunny day.

Selection

Research with the SCR (Giordano, Wood, & Michela, in press; Wood, Michela, & Giordano, in press; Locke & Nekich, in press; Miyake, 1993; Olson & Evans, 1999; Wheeler & Miyake, 1992) is an attempt to discover what comparisons people make and how they feel about them in everyday life, where multiple comparison opportunities are always present. A consistent result of this research is that high self-esteem is related to downward comparison. In addition, those high on agentic traits—dominant, competitive, ambitious—compare downward. Consistent with this, extraverts—high on assertiveness and positive emotions—compare downward. It is clear that downward comparisons are not being made by hurt or threatened people attempting to reduce their distress, but rather by confident, high self-worth people. The characterization of people who make upward comparisons is not as clear at this point. Those with unstable self-esteem compare upward, as do those high on the "big five" dimensions of agreeableness and openness to experience. There are reasonable explanations for these results, but the results need to be replicated.

Laboratory studies on the amount of information sought consistently have shown that high self-worth people (nondysphorics–high self-esteem) more than those of lower self-worth use social comparison to maintain high self-regard, particularly after failure or low performance. They compare more with others they expect to also have low performance (Pinkley et al., 1988), stop comparing with those who have done better (Swallow & Kuiper, 1992), and compare with their competitors on dimensions other than the dimension of failure (Wood et al., 1994). Low self-worth people are more likely to self-enhance after success than after failure (Pinkley et al., 1988; Wood et al., 1994) and they do not avoid upward comparisons after poor performance as high self-worth people do.

Experimental studies of target selection have produced totally inconsistent results (Friend & Gilbert, 1973; Gibbons, 1986; Smith & Insko, 1987; Swallow & Kuiper, 1993). The studies of reactions to mixed information as evidence of target selection are consistent, however (Athens, 1991; McFarland & Miller, 1994), in showing that depressives–pessimists focus on that portion of mixed information that shows them to be inferior, whereas nondepressives–optimists "select" that portion that shows them to be superior.

Reaction

A consistent result from the SCR research is that high self-esteem individuals respond less negatively to upward comparisons than do those of low self-esteem. The same is true for those high in openness to experience. It is not yet clear how much of this is due to stronger defenses against unfavorable information and how much is due to upward assimilation (see Chapter 9, this volume). Only neuroticism has predicted responses to downward comparison, with high neurotics responding more favorably. It should be noted that there is little relationship between selection and reaction in the SCR research. High self-esteem people make more downward comparisons, but they do not benefit more from them. Neurotics do not make more downward comparisons, but they do benefit more from them. Comparisons are not driven by their consequences, although there has been a tendency in the social comparison literature to assert that if downward comparisons are particularly rewarding to threatened people, it must be true that threatened people will make more downward comparisons. In a different social comparison context, Latané (1966) noted that the fact that similar comparisons make for better self-evaluations does not imply that people who want to self-evaluate will make similar comparisons: "... it is not legitimate to infer desire to do something from the desirability of its outcome" (p. 1).

Laboratory studies of reactions almost always have lacked a no-comparison control group, making their interpretation ambiguous; to have enough material to write about, I have had to accept upward comparison conditions as less than perfect controls. Four studies are reasonably consistent with one another (Aspinwall & Taylor, 1993; Gibbons & Gerard, 1989; Reis et al., 1993; Wenzlaff & Prohaska, 1989) in showing that low self-esteem or dysphoric individuals, particularly when threatened, are the most likely to benefit in some way from downward comparison information. This is consistent with the SCR research of Olson and Evans (1999) who found that high neurotics were most likely to benefit from downward comparison. The role of threat remains a murky issue. Aspinwall and Taylor (1993) found and stressed that both low self-esteem and threat were necessary conditions for benefiting from downward comparison, but Wenzlaff and Prohaska's (1989) participants were not threatened. Reis et al. (1993) agreed that both threat and low self-esteem are necessary for mood changes, but not for changes in self-esteem. Gibbons and Gerard's (1989) participants were threatened only by writing about any problems they might have had, which would have been threatening only for some people.

The threat issue aside, these studies are the only support I have found for the individual difference prediction of downward comparison theory (Wills, 1981). Certainly the evidence reviewed above does not show that low self-regard people, threatened or not, are more likely to make downward comparisons or to in other ways use social comparison to reduce their distress. In fact, the evidence goes the other way. But when presented with downward comparison information without any competing information, they appear to respond to it more favorably than high self-regard people do. Unfortunately for these people, I doubt that this happens very often in real life. Quite strongly, the evidence reviewed here is more consistent with the cognitive model of depression than with downward comparison theory. Non-dysphorics and those with high self-esteem are most likely to use social comparison in ways that are self-enhancing. It is easy, though, when reviewing such a mass of complicated literature to allow one's biases too free a rein, and I recommend another and excellent review of much the same literature by Wood and Lockwood (1999).

What of the future? I would like to see a broader set of individual difference variables than the ubiquitous self-esteem and dysphoria, and several have been suggested above. More attention should be paid to the design of experiments: Control groups are good things, and editors should be more stringent about requiring them. I would like to see greater use of naturalistic methods such as the social comparison record, but not to the exclusion of experiments. The new scales described above, the Comparison Orientation Measure and the Dispositional Envy Scale, should become increasingly useful as data are accumulated. I would particularly like to see less concern with who makes downward comparisons and more concern with who makes and is energized by upward comparisons, simply because upward comparisons seem more likely to make exciting things happen.

REFERENCES

Ahrens, A. H. (1991). Dysphoria and social comparison: Combining information regarding others' performances. *Journal of Social and Clinical Psychology, 10,* 190–205.

Alicke, M. D., Klotz, M. L., Breitenbecher, D. L., Yurak, T. J., & Vredenburg, D. S. (1995). Personal contact, individuation, and the better-than-average effect. *Journal of Personality and Social Psychology, 68,* 804–825.

Allport, G. W., & Vernon, P. E. (1931). *A study of values.* Cambridge, MA: Houghton-Mifflin.

Aspinwall, L. G., & Taylor, S. E. (1993). Effects of social comparison direction, threat, and self-esteem on affect, self-evaluation, and expected success. *Journal of Personality and Social Psychology, 64,* 708–722.

Beck, A. T. (1967). *Depression: Clinical, experimental, and theoretical aspects.* New York: Harper & Row.

Beck, A. T. (1976). *Cognitive therapy and the emotional disorders.* New York: International Universities Press.

Bem, S. L. (1974). The measurement of psychological androgyny. *Journal of Counseling and Clinical Psychology, 42,* 155–162.

Berkowitz, L., & Troccoli, B. T. (1990). Feelings, direction of attention, and expressed evaluations of others. *Cognition and Emotion, 4,* 305–325.

Buunk, B. P., Ybema, L. F., Van der Zee, K., Ipenburg, M. L., Schaufeli, W. B., & Gibbons, F. X. (1998). Affect generated by social comparisons as related to professional burnout and to individual differences in social comparison orientation. Manuscript submitted for publication.

Cherry, F., & Byrne, D. (1977). Authoritarianism. In T. Blass (Ed.), *Personality variables in social behavior* (pp. 109–133). Hillsdale, NJ: Lawrence Erlbaum.

Clark, M. S., & Isen, A. M. (1982). Towards understanding the relationship between feeling states and social behavior. In A. H. Hastorf & A. M. Isen (Eds.), *Cognitive social psychology* (pp. 73–108). New York: Elsevier-North Holland.

Collins, R. L. (1996). For better or worse: The impact of upward social comparison on self-evaluations. *Psychological Bulletin, 119,* 51–69.

Costa, P. T., & McCrae, R. (1992). *Revised NEO Personality Inventory (NEO PI-R) and NEO Five-Factor Inventory (NEO-FEI): Professional manual.* Odessa, FL: Psychological Assessment Resources.

Erber, R., & Erber, M. W. (1994). Beyond mood and social judgment: Mood incongruent recall and mood regulation. *European Journal of Social Psychology, 24,* 79–88.

Eysenck, H. J., & Eysenck, S. B. G. (1991). *Manual of the Eysenck Personality Scales (EPS Adult).* London: Hodder & Stoughton.

Friend, R., & Gilbert, J. (1973). Threat and fear of negative evaluation as determinants of locus of social comparison. *Journal of Personality, 41,* 328–340.

Forgas, J. P., & Ciarrochi, J. V. (1999). From sad to happy: Self-esteem and mood-congruent and incongruent thoughts over time. Manuscript under review.

Gibbons, F. X. (1986). Social comparison and depression: Company's effect on misery. *Journal of Personality and Social Psychology, 51,* 140–148.

Gibbons, F. X., & Buunk, B. P. (1999). Individual differences in social comparison: The development of a scale of social comparison orientation. *Journal of Personality and Social Psychology, 76,* 129–142.

Gibbons, F. X., & Gerard, M. (1989). Effects of upward and downward social comparison on mood states. *Journal of Clinical and Social Psychology, 8,* 14–31.

Gibbons, F. X., & McCoy, S. B. (1991). Self-esteem, similarity, and reactions to active versus passive downward comparison. *Journal of Personality and Social Psychology, 60,* 414–424.

Giordano, C., Wood, J. V., & Michela, J. L. (In press). Depressive personality styles, dysphoria, and social comparison in everyday life. *Journal of Personality and Social Psychology.*

Goethals, G., & Darley, J. (1977). Social comparison theory: An attributional approach. In J. M. Suls & R. L. Miller (Eds.), *Social comparison processes: Theoretical and empirical perspectives* (pp. 259–278). Washington, DC: Hemisphere.

Kernis, M. H., Grannemann, B. D., & Barclay, L. C. (1989). Stability and level of self-esteem as predictors of anger arousal and hostility. *Journal of Personality and Social Psychology, 56,* 1013–1022.

Kernis, M. H., Grannemann, B. D., & Barclay, L. C. (1992). Further examination of stability of self-esteem: Correlates, self-ratings of stability, and the roles of stability and level of self-esteem in excuse-making. *Journal of Personality, 60,* 621–644.

Kernis, M. H., Grannemann, B. D., & Mathis, L. D. (1991). Stability of self-esteem as a moderator of the relation between level of self-esteem and depression. *Journal of Personality and Social Psychology, 61,* 80–84.

Kuiper, N. A., & Olinger, L. J. (1986). Dysfunctional attitudes and a self-worth contingency model of depression. In P. C. Kendall (Ed.), *Advances in cognitive–behavioral research and therapy* (Vol. 5, pp. 115–142). New York: Academic Press.

Latané, B. (1966). Studies in social comparison—Introduction and overview. In B. Latane (Ed.), *Studies in Social Comparison* (pp. 1–5). *Journal of Experimental Social Psychology, 2*(Suppl. 1), 1–115.

Lennox, R. D., & Wolfe, R. N. (1984). Revision of the self-monitoring scale. *Journal of Personality and Social Psychology, 46,* 1349–1369.

Locke, K. D., & Nekich, J. C. (In press). Agency and communion in naturalistic social comparison *Personality and Social Psychology Bulletin.*

Lyubomirsky, S., & Ross, L. (1997). Hedonic consequences of social comparison: A contrast of happy and unhappy people. *Journal of Personality and Social Psychology, 73,* 1141–1157.

McFarland, C., & Miller, D. T. (1994). The framing of relative performance feedback: Seeing the glass as half empty or half full. *Journal of Personality and Social Psychology, 66,* 1061–1073.

Miyake, K. (1993). Social comparison, and level and stability of self-esteem: Self-esteem management through social comparison. Ph.D. dissertation, University of Rochester.

Oldersma, F. L., Buunk, B. P., & de Dreu, C. K. W. (1997). Downward comparison as a relationship-enhancing mechanism: The moderating roles of relational discontent and individual differences in social comparison orientation. Manuscript submitted for publication.

Olson, B. D., & Evans, D. L. (1999). The role of the big five personality dimensions in the direction and affective consequences of everyday social comparisons. *Personality and Social Psychology Bulletin, 25,* 1498–1508.

Pietromonaco, P. R., & Feldman-Barrett, L. (1997). Working models of attachment and daily social interactions. *Journal of Personality and Social Psychology, 73,* 1409–1423.

Pinkley, R., Laprelle, J., Pyszczynski, T., & Greenberg, J. (1988). Depression and the self-serving search for consensus after success and failure. *Journal of Social and Clinical Psychology, 6,* 234–244.

Reis, H. T., & Gable, S. L. (2000). Event sampling and other methods for studying daily experience. In H. T. Reis & C. Judd (Eds.), *Handbook of research methods in social and personality psychology* (pp. 190–222). New York: Cambridge University Press.

Reis, T. J., Gerrard, M., & Gibbons, F. X. (1993). Social comparison and the pill: Reactions to upward and downward comparison on contraceptive behavior. *Personality and Social Psychology Bulletin, 19,* 13–20.

Reis, H. T., & Wheeler, L. (1991). Studying social interaction with the Rochester Interaction Record. In M. P. Zanna (Ed.), *Advances in experimental social psychology* (Vol. 24, pp. 270–312). San Diego, CA: Academic Press.

Roney, C. J. R., & Sorrentino, R. M. (1995). Uncertainty orientation, the self, and others: Individual differences in values and social comparison. *Canadian Journal of Behavioural Science, 27,* 157–170.

Sedikides, C. (1994). Incongruent effects of sad mood on self-conception valence: It's a matter of time. *European Journal of Social Psychology, 24,* 161–172.

Smith, R. H., & Insko, C. A. (1987). Social comparison choice during ability evaluation: The effect of comparison publicity, performance feedback, and self-esteem. *Personality and Social Psychology Bulletin, 13,* 111–122.

Smith, R. H., Parrott, W. G., Diener, E. F., Hoyle, R. H., & Kim, S. H. (1999). Dispositional envy. *Personality and Social Psychology Bulletin, 25,* 1007–1020.

Sorrentino, R. M., Hanna, S. E., & Roney, C. J. R. (1992). A manual for scoring need for uncertainty. In C. P. Smith (Ed.), *Motivation and personality: Handbook of thematic content analysis.* Cambridge: Cambridge University Press.

Sorrentino, R. M., Hodson, G. L., & Huber, G. L. (In press). Uncertainty orientation and the social mind. In J. P. Forgas, K. D. Williams, & L. Wheeler (Eds.), *The social mind: Cognitive and motivational aspects of interpersonal behavior.* Cambridge: Cambridge University Press.

Spence, J. T., Helmreich, R. L., & Stapp, J. (1974). The Personal Attributes Questionnaire: A measure of sex role stereotypes and masculinity–femininity. *Journal Supplement Abstract Service Catalog of Selected Documents in Psychology, 4,* 43–44.

Stone, A. A., Schwartz, J. E., Neale, J. M., Shiffman, S., Marco, C. A., Hickcox, M., Paty, J., Porter, L. S., & Cruise, L. J. (1998). A comparison of coping assessed by ecological momentary assessment and retrospective recall. *Journal of Personality and Social Psychology, 74,* 1670–1680.

Swallow, S. R., & Kuiper, N. A. (1988). Social comparison and negative self-evaluation: An application to depression. *Clinical Psychology Review, 8,* 55–76.

Swallow, S. R., & Kuiper, N. A. (1992). Mild depression and frequency of social comparison behavior. *Journal of Social and Clinical Psychology, 11,* 167–180.

Swallow, S. R., & Kuiper, N. A. (1993). Social comparison in dysphoria and nondysphoria: Differences in target similarity and specificity. *Cognitive Therapy and Research, 17,* 103–122.

Swap, W. C., & Rubin, J. Z. (1983). Measurement of interpersonal orientation. *Journal of Personality and Social Psychology, 44,* 208–219.

Van der Zee, K., Buunk, B., & Sanderman, R. (1998). Neuroticism and reactions to social comparison information among cancer patients. *Journal of Personality, 62(2),* 175–194.

Van der Zee, K., Oldersma, F., Buunk, B. P., & Bos, D. (1998). Social comparison preferences among cancer patients as related to neuroticism and social comparison orientation. *Journal of Personality and Social Psycholoy, 75,* 801–810.

Watson, D., & Friend, R. (1969). Measurement of social evaluative anxiety. *Journal of Consulting and Clinical Psychology, 33,* 448–457.

Wenzlaff, R. M., & Prohaska, M. L. (1989). When miser prefers company: Depression, attributions, and responses to others' moods. *Journal of Experimental Social Psychology, 25,* 220–233.

Wheeler, L., & Miyake, K. (1992). Social comparison in everyday life. *Journal of Personality and Social Psychology, 62,* 760–773.

Wheeler, L., & Reis, H. T. (1991). Self-recording of everyday life events: Origins, types, and uses. *Journal of Personality, 59,* 339–354.

Wills, T. A. (1981). Downward comparison principles in social psychology. *Psychological Bulletin, 90,* 245–271.

Wills, T. A. (1991). Similarity and self-esteem in downward comparison. In J. Suls & T. A. Wills (Eds.), *Social comparison: Contemporary theory and research* (pp. 51–74). Hillsdale, NJ: Lawrence Erlbaum.

Wilson, S. R., & Benner, L. A. (1971). The effects of self-esteem and situation upon comparison choices during ability evaluation. *Sociometry, 34,* 381–397.

Wood, J. V. (1996). What is social comparison and how should we study it? *Personality and Social Psychology Bulletin, 22,* 520–537.

Wood, J. V., Michela, J. L. & Giordano, C. (In press). Downward comparison in everyday life: Reconciling self-enhancement models with the mood-cognition priming model. *Journal of Personality and Social Psychology.*

Wood, J. V., Giordano-Beech, M., & Ducharme, M. J. (1999). Compensating for failure through social comparison. *Personality and Social Psychology Bulletin, 25,* 1370–1386.

Wood, J. V., Giordano-Beech, M., Taylor, K. L., Michela, J. L., & Gaus, V. (1994). Strategies of social comparison among people with low self-esteem: Self-protection and self-enhancement. *Journal of Personality and Social Psychology, 67,* 713–731.

Wood, J. V., & Lockwood, P. (1999). Social comparisons in dysphoric and low self-esteem people. In R. Kowalski & M. Leary (Eds.), *The social psychology of emotional and behavioral problems: Interfaces of social and clinical psychology* (pp. 97–135). Washington, DC: APA Books.

9

Among the Better Ones

Upward Assimilation in Social Comparison

REBECCA L. COLLINS

Since the first empirical tests of Festinger's (1954) social comparison theory, theorists have been concerned with the "direction" of comparisons: whether people compare with persons superior or inferior to themselves and under what conditions (Wheeler, 1991). This focus on comparison direction was maintained by theorists exploring how exposure to superior versus inferior others influences well-being (Wills, 1981). Comparison direction was considered important to study because it supposedly indicated whether one was looking for (or responding to) favorable or unfavorable information about the self. With the exception of two early studies (Wheeler, 1966; Thornton & Arrowood, 1966), the literature made two assumptions: (1) that the evaluative implications of comparison are intrinsic to its direction, and (2) that the comparison process involves contrasting one's abilities or attributes with those of others. Accordingly, it was thought that upward comparison is used to learn how much one falls short of one's superiors and lowers self-evaluations.

Upward assimilation theory (Collins, 1996) challenges both assumptions. Studies of other relativistic judgments have shown them to be influenced by both assimilation and contrast effects (Manis & Paskewitz, 1984; Parducci, 1964), and I have argued that the same is true of social comparisons. Sometimes, comparisons have clear implications. Extreme information suggesting a large difference between self and target, relative to the subjective distribution of the comparison dimension, may automatically evoke contrast (Herr, 1986). However, large differences of this sort typically result in the cessation of social comparison (Wood, 1989), and the contrast may never affect self-evaluations (Gilbert, Giesler, & Morris, 1995).

More often, social comparison involves moderate differences in ability. Information of this sort is often ambiguous, just as the proverbial glass is half full or half empty. Under such circumstances, an objective difference in ability or attribute can indicate likeness to a comparison target as well as difference from him or her. Webster's dictionary defines the verb "to compare" as:

REBECCA L. COLLINS • RAND Corporation, Santa Monica, California 90407.

Handbook of Social Comparison: Theory and Research, edited by Suls and Wheeler. Kluwer Academic/Plenum Publishers, New York, 2000.

1: to represent as similar: LIKEN, 2: to examine the character or qualities of esp. in order to discover resemblances or differences ... COMPARE implies an aim of showing relative values or excellences by bringing out characteristic qualities whether similar or divergent. (*Webster's New Collegiate Dictionary*, 1988, p. 267)

The lay usage of "compare" is interesting because it points out what comparison theorists have often given short shrift: Comparison may involve a search for and perception of similarity to a target, as well as difference. Thus, responses to upward comparisons may follow either of two paths. The comparer may see his or her ability as similar to the target's and evaluate him- or herself more positively as a result. However, if the comparer focuses on the differences between him- or herself and the target, upward comparison should be ego deflating.

Upward assimilation theory (Collins, 1996) predicts that the evaluative implications of social comparison depend on two factors: the direction of the comparison and the comparer's expectation that he or she will be similar to the target on the characteristic being evaluated. Much of social cognition is driven by expectations. The top-down processing of information influences what information we seek, what we attend to, and how we interpret what we encounter (Fiske & Taylor, 1991). Comparative judgments are no exception to this: People are more likely to perceive similarity when they expect to find it (Manis & Paskewitz, 1984). In a set of studies, Manis and colleagues induced a "short" or "tall" expectancy by exposing participants to a series of either short or tall individuals (Manis, Biernat, & Nelson, 1991). When asked to make a subsequent judgment of height, the strength and direction of the expectancy created by this previous exposure positively predicted perceptions of subsequent targets' heights. These studies involved perceptions of others, rather than of self, but the task was otherwise identical to that of social comparison. Manis and colleagues' results suggest that expectations that the self will be similar to another person enhance the likelihood of assimilation to that person's characteristics.

What promotes expectations of similarity? Manis' research demonstrates that the mere existence of the comparison other can be enough to achieve a minimal expectation of likeness, but it is probable that other aspects of the comparison context can further enhance this expectation. Contributors to expectations have not been studied, but some likely candidates can be identified from among the variables known to influence the comparison process in other ways. The most obvious of these is actual similarity, relative to the possible range of the ability or characteristic under evaluation. People expect to be most similar to those who rank close to themselves in the population distribution. The comparison literature has long noted that people compare only to those within range of their own abilities (Wood, 1989), and this may explain why. People are not interested in comparing their basketball playing with Michael Jordan's, because most people do not expect to play as well as he does. Instead, they compare to persons only slightly better than themselves (Gruder, 1971). Upward assimilation theory predicts that, to the extent that comparers expect to be similar to these persons, consequent self-evaluations are more likely to be positive.

A second factor that may promote expected similarity on the comparison dimension is similarity on other dimensions (sometimes referred to as "related attributes"). People prefer to compare with individuals of the same gender or race, or those who share their interests and training (Gruder, 1977; Wood, 1989). Presumably, these individuals' abilities are considered relevant self-standards because people expect those who are similar to them in some ways to be similar to them in others (Goethals & Darley, 1977). Medin, Goldstone, and Gentner (1993) suggest that when people are asked the question "How similar are X and Y?" they hear, in effect, "how are X and Y similar?" Aspects of similarity are then integrated to draw a more general conclusion about similarity. Importantly, this general conclusion "creates an expectation for new commonalities to be discovered" (pp. 258–259).

To the extent that similarity to people with the same background is expected, upward assimilation theory predicts that upward comparison with them will lead to more positive self-evaluations. There appears to be a contradiction between this prediction and previous findings that comparison with similar individuals has a greater impact (Wood, 1989). Traditionally, this has meant that people react more *negatively* to upward comparison with others who are similar in background or related attributes. This can be resolved by assuming that comparison with persons at very low levels of expected similarity has no impact; neither an assimilation nor a contrast effect takes place. At moderate levels of expected similarity, comparisons should have a contrast effect, and as expectations reach higher levels, the likely outcome of comparison is assimilation (see Chapters 2 and 3, this volume, for further discussion of the role of related attributes in comparison).

Three additional factors may influence expectations of similarity; all are related to the individual's precomparison belief about his or her ability level. First, because most people believe they possess positive characteristics rather than negative ones (Alicke, 1985), expectations of similarity to someone doing poorly are likely to be rare (Collins, 1996). Thus, the direction of comparison should influence expectations of similarity. Although it is possible for people to assimilate to worse-off others under the assumptions of upward assimilation theory, the theory suggests that downward assimilation is a relatively rare occurrence. Second, self-esteem threat should influence expected similarity. Feedback suggestive of poor standing or prior negative experience with the comparison dimension probably undermines the comparer's expectation of similarity to superior others. The third factor—chronic low self-esteem—should have a similar effect. While most people may expect to be similar to "the better ones," this is not likely to be true of persons with more negative self-views. In summary, positive beliefs about the self should promote expectations of similarity to upward targets and consequently promote upward assimilation.

A schematic diagram of upward assimilation theory is provided in Fig. 1. In addition to the processes articulated above, the figure indicates the outcomes of assimilation and contrast effects—improvements and decrements in self-evaluated ability or attributes. These predicted effects are a matter of degree rather than absolutes. Each factor in the model increases the probability of the responses shown but does not necessitate this response. Indeed, it is possible that both assimilation and contrast occur simultaneously during comparison and that evaluative outcomes are determined by the relative strength of these two responses (Manis & Paskewitz, 1984). Although simultaneous assimilation and contrast has not been shown in social comparison, it has been demonstrated for similar judgments (Biernat, Manis, & Kobrynowicz, 1997; Manis et al., 1991). Manis and colleagues (1991) obtained evidence of simultaneous assimilation and contrast in the aforementioned study involving judgments of height. Through the use of path analysis, the researchers were able to show a positive effect of induction height on perceived target height (i.e., assimilation) and a negative effect (i.e., contrast) occurring as part of the same trial. The assimilation effect was mediated by expectations regarding the height of the target individuals, as noted earlier, and was evident only when the mediating path was included in the model. It was also necessary that the direct contrast effect of induction on judgments be statistically controlled, before the assimilation effect could be observed.

In interpreting Fig. 1, it is also important to remember that assimilation and contrast are part of a larger comparison process. Other outcomes and processes are likely to occur in concert with those shown. For example, individuals often react to comparison with changes in

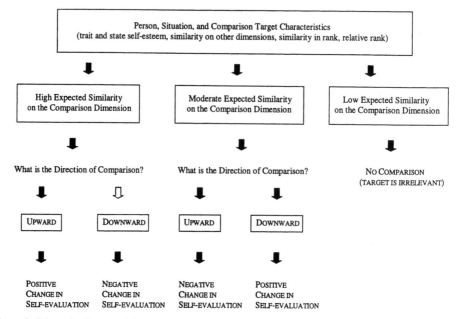

Figure 1. Schematic diagram of the upward assimilation process. White arrow indicates less-probable pathway.

affect. These reactions may flow directly from self-evaluation (and represent feelings about one's abilities and characteristics), may stem from other information gained through comparison [e.g., the possibility of self-improvement (Buunk, Collins, Taylor, & VanYperen, 1990; Lockwood & Kunda, 1997; Major, Testa, & Bylsma, 1991)], or may be the result of a process other than comparison [e.g., basking in the reflection of the target's high ability (Tesser, 1988)]. Thus, affect may not match an individual's evaluative reaction to comparison and cannot be used to determine whether either assimilation or contrast has taken place.

The claim that affect is a poor indicator of assimilation highlights an important distinction between upward assimilation theory and other recent theories of upward comparison. The best-known of these was presented by Taylor and Lobel (1989). In it, they draw a distinction between comparative evaluation and comparative contact. According to their theory, upward evaluation is ego deflating, but contact with better-off others is inspiring and mood elevating. Others have argued that upward comparison can cause people to feel good even without contact. People can draw inspiration from those doing better than themselves when standing on the comparison dimension is changeable and controllable (Major et al., 1991). For example, cancer patients and persons with marital difficulties feel better after upward comparison, as long as they feel in control of their situations (Buunk et al., 1990). Unlike upward assimilation theory, these theories do not predict changes in self-view as a result of upward comparison. They predict improvement in mood. A theory that does predict evaluative change has been proposed by Lockwood and Kunda (1997). They argue that upward comparison can improve self-views, but the hypothesized process is quite different from upward assimilation. According to their theory, upward comparison makes people feel good because of what *might* be in the future, not because of their current standing on the comparison dimension. In contrast, upward assimilation theory hypothesizes a basic perceptual bias that influences self-evaluations, regardless of expected future status.

In the remaining pages of this chapter, I discuss previous studies in the context of this upward assimilation framework. I will begin at the heart of the model: the premise that upward comparisons can be perceived as indicating similarity to better-off others rather than difference.

PERCEIVED SIMILARITY TO BETTER-OFF OTHERS

The upward assimilation model rests on the assumption that comparers can see themselves as having the same ability or attributes as persons who are objectively better-off than they. For example, David should be able to conclude that he is about the same height as Nancy, although David is 5'3" and Nancy 5'4". Similarly, Megan might believe she is as fit as her hiking companion, Tom, even though Megan tires more quickly. Previous studies of the comparison process, while not designed to test this assumption, have collected data consistent with it. One of these is a study of the social comparisons made by bridge players (Nosanchuk & Erickson, 1985). In the study, bridge players were given several different hypothetical situations and asked to indicate whether they would compare to someone similar in ability, a slightly worse player, or a better player than themselves in each instance. They were also asked to list the names of actual people with whom they would compare in each situation. Although participants indicated a preference for comparison with similar others, a statistical comparison of the objective bridge-playing abilities of participants and those of their comparison targets showed that these targets were actually significantly better players than were the study participants. It appears that participants perceived upward comparison targets as similar to themselves in ability, rather than better.

Because Nosanchuk and Erickson did not ask bridge players to report on the objective skill levels of their comparison targets, we cannot be sure that participants were aware of their inferiority to the targets they designated as "similar." For self-perceptions to be elevated by upward comparison, it is necessary for comparers to perceive, at least unconsciously, the objectively superior standing of the target. Comparison to someone perceived to be of exactly the same ability as oneself should not elevate self-worth. Instead, it must be perceived that "he is good, and because I am pretty much the same, I must be good, too." DeVellis et al. (1991) collected data that suggest just such a pattern. In their study, they asked women with rheumatoid arthritis to view a series of slides and listen to an audiotape describing the story of another woman with arthritis. Participants separately rated their own coping and that of the woman, and then rated how well they were coping in comparison with the woman. According to the separate ratings of self and other, participants viewed their own coping more negatively than they viewed the woman's. However, when the comparative rating was examined, they rated themselves as similar to this same woman (0.19 on a scale ranging from −2 to +2, where 0 indicated equivalence). The difference between the comparative rating and the separate ratings was highly statistically significant.

DeVellis and colleagues also presented data that broke their sample into groups with different perceptions. Looking at the separate ratings of self and target, 42% of the sample rated themselves and the target identically, 50% rated themselves as inferior to the target, and 8% rated themselves as superior to the other woman. According to the comparative rating, however, 78% of participants perceived themselves to be the same as the woman, 5.5% saw themselves as inferior, and 17% saw themselves as superior to the target. Together, these data indicate that 95% of the sample viewed their coping ability as similar to or better than the other woman's, even though half the sample rated their coping as worse than hers when responding to two separate rating scales. Thus, people can be aware of a difference between their own standing and that of their superiors and at the same time perceive it as insignificant. These are exactly the conditions that should result in upward assimilation.

Assimilation also may occur in less extreme forms. Instead of perceiving the self and someone who is better-off as "the same," the better-off individual may provide an interpretive frame for viewing the self, an anchor that pulls judgments toward more positive evaluations. Judgments involving nonsocial stimuli show this effect (Parducci, 1964), as do judgments of other people (Martin, Seta, & Crelia, 1990). For example, an object will be perceived as heavier when judged as part of a series of heavy objects rather than light ones. The object is "framed" by the heavy objects preceding and is perceived to be part of a "heavy" class (Parducci, 1964). Assimilation biases judgments of the object in the direction of greater weight in this example, but does not cause all objects in the series to be perceived as identically heavy. Thus, an individual may perceive two entities as different on a given dimension but make judgments of their characteristics in the direction of assimilation.

The very act of comparison implies some level of similarity, some perception that the objects or people involved are members of a category. Thus, there always may be some expectation of similarity and some level of assimilation involved in comparative judgments. The question is whether a contrast effect will emerge that outweighs this. Upward assimilation theory predicts that the relative strength of assimilation and contrast processes depends on the degree of similarity expected by the comparer. No studies of social comparison have directly tested this; however, a number have looked at other factors that determine whether upward comparison results in assimilation or contrast, and their results reflect on the validity of the expected similarity hypothesis.

STUDIES OF UPWARD ASSIMILATION
AND CONTRAST EFFECTS ON SELF-EVALUATIONS

In the first study to examine assimilation in social comparison, Brown, Novick, Lord, and Richards (1992) showed female college students photos of attractive or unattractive women and then asked them to rate their own attractiveness. In this basic condition, results replicated earlier studies using a similar methodology (Cash, Cash, & Butters, 1983; Thornton & Moore, 1993). Women who looked at attractive photos rated their own looks somewhat more negatively than did the control group, and women who looked at the unattractive photos viewed themselves more positively—a contrast effect. However, under other conditions (tested in additional studies described below), upward assimilation effects were obtained. In each case, the effect of comparison depended on the level of similarity between the target and the participant on dimensions other than attractiveness.

In one of these studies, the target supposedly had expressed either very different attitudes from the participant on a pretest or attitudes similar to the participant's (Brown et al., 1992). In the attitude-dissimilar condition, upward comparison produced a lower attractiveness rating than did downward comparison. However, when the comparer and target were purportedly very similar in their beliefs, upward and downward comparison had similar effects on self-perceptions. Indeed, participants' ratings of their own attractiveness were (nonsignificantly) higher after upward comparison than after downward. In two additional studies, comparisons were made either with persons who purportedly shared the comparer's birthday or with those who did not. In the birthday-unmatched conditions, self-evaluations did not change in response to upward comparison, relative to a precomparison measure (an effect Brown and colleagues attribute to a self-enhancing tendency to overlook negative information). However, in the birthday-matched conditions, attractiveness ratings increased in response to upward comparison. Brown et al. (1992) attributed the upward assimilation effect to participants' perceptions that they shared a rare attribute with the target.

Another investigation (Brewer & Weber, 1994) obtained assimilation effects using a very different procedure, but one that, like the manipulation used by Brown et al. (1992), indicated that a distinctive characteristic was shared by comparer and target. In this research, Brewer and Weber used a minimal group procedure to create social categories. Following this, they showed undergraduates a videotape of another student who was portrayed as either more or less academically competent than most undergraduates. Some students were informed that this individual was a member of the same group as themselves, others were told that the individual was a member of the outgroup. In addition, half the participants were led to believe that members of their group were in the minority and half thought they were majority group members. Upward comparison led to more positive self-evaluations than did downward comparison when members of minority groups compared themselves with other in-group members. Downward comparisons were more self-enhancing than upward when majority group members made in-group comparisons.

A second study in the same report also exposed participants to better-off others who were fellow members of a minority group. Its results suggested that such comparisons are more self-enhancing than upward or downward comparison to outgroup majorities. The findings also suggested that assimilation to in-group targets is more likely when group membership is related to target status.

Brewer and Weber did not, unfortunately, include a no-comparison control group in their study. This makes it impossible to determine why different comparison conditions had different effects. Upward comparison may have produced more favorable self-evaluations than did downward because both comparisons had a (differentially) negative effect or because upward comparison had no effect and downward comparison lowered self-evaluations. Neither finding would support upward assimilation theory. However, Brewer and Weber did report the average self-evaluation of individuals in the population from which study participants were drawn, and it is possible to make a nonstatistical comparison of this number with self-evaluations in each of their conditions. When comparers and targets shared a distinctive attribute, upward comparisons increased self-evaluations above this baseline. When this was not the case, upward comparison lowered self-evaluations. Thus, both assimilation and contrast effects appear to have been obtained, depending on shared distinctiveness.

Pelham and Wachsmuth (1995) also demonstrated how variations in comparison conditions can produce both assimilation and contrast reactions. Instead of shared distinctiveness, their interest was in the combined effects of self-certainty (knowing one's ability level prior to comparison) and closeness [feeling that the target and self are highly similar or linked in some way (Tesser, 1988)]. In study 1, participants' self-views increased with exposure to a roommate who had poor abilities and decreased with exposure to a roommate who was highly skilled, but only when participants were relatively uncertain of their own ability level. When self-views were highly certain, the reverse was true. Exposure to a highly skilled roommate improved self-perceptions in this case and exposure to a less skilled roommate decreased self-evaluations. In study 2, individuals who had received prior feedback about their own abilities (and so were high in self-certainty) evaluated themselves more positively after an acquaintance received favorable feedback and more negatively after the acquaintance received negative feedback—an assimilation effect. Contrast effects were obtained when participants were uncertain of their self-views, having received no prior feedback concerning their own abilities.

The results of these three investigations are consistent with upward assimilation theory. Clearly, the self-evaluative effects of social comparison were not intrinsic to its direction, and comparison did not always evoke contrast. In each experiment reported, the same comparison information led to different effects, depending on the context in which it was presented. Upward comparison produced contrast effects under some conditions but led to assimilation effects in others. According to upward assimilation theory, contrast and assimilation are determined by expectations of similarity. These studies also provide indirect support for this contention.

FACTORS INFLUENCING ASSIMILATION, AND THEIR ASSOCIATION WITH EXPECTED SIMILARITY

One of the factors that predicted assimilation was sharing a rare attribute with the comparison target. Note that similarity on any given attribute was not enough to produce assimilation in any of these studies. Instead, assimilation emerged when individuals compared with someone who was similar to them in some highly unique manner. Although neither Brown et al. (1992) nor Brewer and Weber (1994) measured participants' beliefs or expectations about their similarity to the comparison target, it is quite plausible that expected similarity was higher under shared distinctiveness conditions. Indeed, this presumption was the basis for Brewer and Weber's use of the manipulation (they were studying needs for similarity and uniqueness).

In the Pelham and Wachsmuth (1995) investigation, the role of expectations is less clear. Self-certainty and closeness might combine to create an expectation of similarity, but this is in no way obvious. The authors conducted a third study that was reported in the same article as the two studies previously described. In it, they assessed perceived similarity to the comparison other as their dependent measure. The procedures were otherwise parallel to those in the other two studies. They found that perceived similarity was indeed predicted by a significant interaction between self-certainty and relationship closeness. While self-certainty was unrelated to perceived similarity when the comparer and target were not close, certainty and similarity were highly related when closeness was strong. When both closeness and self-certainty were high (the conditions under which an assimilation effect had been obtained in the other studies), the correlation between participants' ratings of their own attributes and those of the comparison others was .62. When either certainty or closeness was low, correlations ranged from −.12 to .18. Although we cannot be sure that expectations of similarity to friends actually mediated the assimilation effects Pelham and Wachsmuth obtained in their other studies, we can conclude that assimilative self-evaluation occurred under conditions in which perceived similarity to the target on other attributes was quite high.

Similarity to targets on other dimensions is not the only factor likely to promote expected similarity on the comparison dimension. The direction of comparison also should influence expected similarity. Specifically, upward assimilation should be more common than downward assimilation. The studies just reviewed support this hypothesis, although they provide relatively little evidence on this issue. In one of the Brewer and Weber studies and two of those conducted by Brown and colleagues, participants had weak or nonsignificant reactions to downward comparison information about highly similar others—downward assimilation did not occur. Although not a study of assimilation and contrast, the De Vellis study of rheumatoid arthritis patients discussed earlier also suggests an asymmetry in reactions to upward and downward comparison. Recall that participants rated an upward comparison target more highly than themselves using two separate scales, but also indicated on another measure that they were similar or superior to the same patient. Some participants were exposed instead to a worse-off target. These participants perceived themselves as superior to the comparison target, whether separate ratings or direct comparisons of similarity were examined. Again, we cannot know from any of these studies that upward targets produce assimilation more often because expected similarity is higher, but this evidence is suggestive of that hypothesis.

At the outset of this chapter it was suggested that normative beliefs concerning the superiority of one's own abilities (Alicke, 1985) are responsible for a tendency to assimilate upward rather than downward. It was argued that persons with high self-esteem therefore should be most vulnerable to upward assimilation effects. Of this there is not yet supportive evidence. Only one study has explored this idea (Brown et al., 1992), and it found just the opposite. In that investigation, persons with low trait self-esteem were more likely to inflate their self-evaluations following upward comparison to a highly similar other. Brown and colleagues predicted this effect, arguing that upward assimilation is an indirect method of self-enhancement, and that such indirect methods are more often used by persons low in self-esteem (Brown, Collins, & Schmidt, 1988). Such a motivated use of upward comparison would not necessarily be inconsistent with upward assimilation theory, but would certainly qualify its predictions regarding self-esteem. Perhaps persons high in self-esteem benefit from a straightforward perceptual bias such as that discussed herein, while those with low self-esteem are most likely to use upward comparison in a deliberate, motivated attempt to self-enhance.

No study has yet explored the influence of situational threats to self-esteem on assimilation and contrast processes. If upward assimilation proves in future research to be less likely under conditions of threat, this may explain why people are less likely to make upward comparisons in such circumstances (Collins, 1996). It is important that such work be conducted, because interest in how social comparisons are involved in the maintenance of self-esteem is central to contemporary social comparison theory (Wills, 1981; Wood, 1989).

IMPLICATIONS FOR COMPARISON SELECTIONS

Breaking the link between comparison direction and comparison effects has important implications for comparison behavior. It means that, when an individual chooses to compare with someone who is superior, either of two motives may be in play. The goal of the comparison may be to demonstrate the likeness between the individual's ability and that of the target. In this case, upward comparison is driven by self-enhancement needs. Alternatively, the goal of the upward comparison might be to determine the degree of change in the self or the target that would be necessary to equalize ability. In this case, upward comparison is motivated by self-evaluative and perhaps self-improvement needs.

Using upward comparisons to self-enhance does not require the comparer to realize that the assimilation process will influence his or her self-perceptions. Nor must the individual be cognizant of his or her desire to self-enhance. The social comparer need only expect to be similar to particular people, and use that information to choose a comparison target. In one of the first studies of the social comparison process, Wheeler (1966) suggested that people make upward comparisons to self-enhance and presented evidence that this behavior is based on assumptions of similarity. Participants in the study were run in groups. Each took a test, was given an ambiguous score, and was told that his or her performance ranked at the middle of the distribution for that test session. Each was then given an opportunity to view the score associated with any other rank in the session. The dependent measure was the rank chosen for this comparison. Wheeler found that most participants wished to compare with someone better. He also found that most who chose an upward comparison target (75%) assumed they were more similar to this person than to someone worse than themselves. Few people who chose a downward comparison target (36%) made this assumption. Wheeler concluded that upward comparison is used to confirm that one is "almost as good as the very good ones" (Wheeler, 1966, p. 30).

We found even stronger evidence of this in a replication of Wheeler's study (Collins & Di Paula, 1996, study 4). Like Wheeler, we found that most people picked a higher-ranked individual with whom to compare. Indeed, most of our participants chose the highest scorer as their comparison target. Those who did so rated their probable similarity to this individual significantly higher than did participants who chose someone else with whom to compare. When we examined the association between expected similarity to the high scorer and level of interest in comparing with him or her, the correlation just reached significance ($r = .21$, $p = 0.05$). Does this correlation reflect a desire to self-enhance? The association between expected similarity and the comparer's belief that learning the top score would lead him or her to "feel good about" his or her own score was also significant ($r = .25$, $p = 0.03$), as was the correlation between expected self-enhancement and interest in comparing to the highest scorer ($r = .41$, $p = 0.001$).

Thus, expected similarity apparently influences the direction of comparisons, as well as their interpretation. Individuals are more likely to compare to better-off others if they expect these comparisons to reveal similarity in ability level and to result in more positive self-perceptions. Conversely, high expectations of similarity to worse-off others may deter people from engaging in downward comparison. Indeed, this might account for cancer patients' aversion to interaction with those who are doing poorly (Collins, Dakof & Taylor, 1988; Taylor & Lobel, 1989). Shared membership in the group "people with cancer" may constitute shared uniqueness, and this may prompt avoidance of downward comparison.

Expected similarity's moderation of the comparison process creates some problems for the comparison researcher. If the effects that comparisons produce are not intrinsically linked to their direction, it becomes necessary to expand our paradigms for studying the comparison process. There may still be reason to test the preferred direction of comparison under varying circumstances [for example, to predict with whom people will affiliate (Festinger, 1954)]. However, if a theorist's goal is to understand the motives reflected by comparison behavior, it may be necessary to assess these motives directly or to ask comparers what results they anticipate from making a particular comparison. Alternatively, researchers may wish to manipulate or assess expected similarity to the target on the dimension of comparison, in addition to assessing whether the target is better- or worse-off than the comparer. This would enable the moderating effect of similarity to be taken into account in one's predictions.

IMPLICATIONS FOR THE INFLUENCE
OF SOCIAL ENVIRONMENT ON SELF-EVALUATIONS

It is clear from the studies reviewed in this chapter that the effects of social comparisons on self-evaluations are not intrinsically linked to their direction. This is not unlike the earlier findings of my colleagues and myself, arguing that the affective consequences of social comparison are not intrinsic to their direction (Buunk et al., 1990). In earlier research, however, we argued that affect varies as a function of one's belief about probable future status. Lockwood and Kunda (1997) have made a similar argument. In contrast, upward assimilation does not depend on the expectation of future change. Through upward assimilation, people can feel better about themselves following upward comparison without making reference to their future status.

Although it is clear that this can occur, it is less certain that it happens with any frequency. Studies looking at the impact of an environment that presents more frequent opportunities for upward than downward comparison indicate that this has a detrimental effect on life satisfaction (Crosby, 1976). This implies that contrast effects are more prevalent than tendencies to assimilate to comparison others. Similar effects of the comparison environment also have been obtained for evaluations of academic achievement. Marsh and Parker (1984) demonstrated that youth who attend schools with high achievers perceive their own academic abilities more negatively than do those who attend low-achieving schools.

Of course, judgments of satisfaction may be quite differently affected by comparative information than are evaluations of ability or other characteristics. A person can perceive him- or herself to have very high ability or very good life circumstances and nonetheless feel dissatisfied with this status. Marsh and Parker's (1984) data, while it speaks directly to self-evaluated ability, also may be a special case. Academic environments tend to focus on relative achievement and to provide constant feedback regarding relative rank. They may promote contrast by creating a competitive environment that is not typical of ability domains. More-over, the relative prevalence of assimilation and contrast depends ultimately on the specifics of one's social environment. While it is clear that people typically interact with similar others, the extent of this similarity and perceptions of its uniqueness are critical in determining whether assimilation or contrast will predominate. Do people spend most of their time with persons they see as uniquely like themselves (social psychologists who do the Lindy Hop) or persons with whom they share only a mundane similarity (fellow academicians)? Finally, it is possible that the social context has very little to do with the comparisons that people make. People appear to actively seek, select, and even construct comparison information to fit their goals (Wood, 1989), although they are not able to completely avoid reacting to comparisons that are thrust on them (Gilbert et al., 1995). Thus, the emphasis on the total social environment in these studies may be misplaced.

To understand how assimilation and contrast processes influence social comparisons as they actually occur, we probably need to do more naturalistic studies that measure individual perceptions of similarity and difference, patterns of interaction, *and* the objective attributes of the social environment. More diary studies like Wheeler and Miyake's (1992) are clearly called for, but we must take care in such research not to rely solely or even heavily on self-report. Perceptions of similarity and difference are likely to be elusive prey in our hunt for the social and cognitive sources of self-evaluation. It appears that the assimilation process is automatic and occurs outside of consciousness. People are aware of the outcomes of their comparisons, not of how they process comparative information. In an early paper describing the psychophysics of judging objects to be heavy or light, Parducci (1983) aptly describes how evaluations emerge from the comparative context without individuals' awareness:

> If one asks subjects after an experimental session to describe how they selected an appropriate category for each stimulus, their answers are usually disappointing: "It was just how the weight felt, that's what I called it." When an occasional subject becomes more expansive, there are likely to be obvious discrepancies between his conjectures and the data he has just produced. For example, successive contrast is frequently reported: "The same weight feels heavier to me when it follows a lighter weight than when it follows a heavier weight." However, the actual ratings are in the opposite direction, successive assimilation rather than contrast. (p. 263)

This insight into the phenomenology of the social comparer also suggests why comparison researchers for so long focused only on comparative contrast. Use of others as an interpretive frame through which to view oneself occurs outside of our consciousness, as well as that of the persons we study.

CONCLUSIONS

I have argued that the process of comparing involves a search for similarities. When people compare themselves to better-off others they look for and expect to find congruence. Comparers' self-evaluations are anchored by these expectations, and thus by the abilities of their superiors. As a result, self-evaluations may increase in response to upward comparison, allowing comparers to conclude that they are "among the better ones."

REFERENCES

Alicke, M. D. (1985). Global self-evaluation as determined by the desirability and controllability of trait adjectives. *Journal of Personality and Social Psychology, 49,* 1621–1630.

Biernat, M., Manis, M., & Kobrynowicz, D. (1997). Simultaneous assimilation and contrast effects in judgments of self and others. *Journal of Personality and Social Psychology, 73,* 254–269.

Brewer, M. B., & Weber, J. G. (1994). Self-evaluation effects of interpersonal versus intergroup social comparison. *Journal of Personality and Social Psychology, 66,* 268–275.

Brown, J. D., Collins, R. L., & Schmidt, G. W. (1988). Self-esteem and direct vs. indirect forms of self-enhancement. *Journal of Personality and Social Psychology, 55,* 445–453.

Brown, J. D., Novick, N. J., Lord, K. A., & Richards, J. M. (1992). When Gulliver travels: Social context, psychological closeness, and self-appraisals. *Journal of Personality and Social Psychology, 62,* 717–727.

Buunk, B., Collins, R., Taylor, S., & VanYperen, N. (1990). The affective consequences of social comparison: Either direction has its ups and downs. *Journal of Personality and Social Psychology, 59,* 1238–1249.

Cash, T. F., Cash, D. W., & Butters, J. W. (1983). "Mirror, mirror, on the wall...?": Contrast effects and self-evaluations of physical attractiveness. *Personality and Social Psychology Bulletin, 9,* 351–358.

Collins, R. L. (1996). For better or worse: The impact of upward social comparisons on self-evaluations. *Psychological Bulletin, 119,* 51–69.

Collins, R. E., Dakof, G., & Taylor, S. E. (1988). Social comparison and adjustment to a threatening event. Unpublished manuscript, University of California, Los Angeles.

Collins, R. L., & Di Paula, A. W. (1996). Unpublished data. University of British Columbia.

Crosby, F. (1976). A model of egoistical relative deprivation. *Psychological Review, 83,* 85–113.

DeVellis, R. F., Blalock, S. J., Holt, K., Renner, B. R., Blanchard, L. W., & Klotz, M. L. (1991). Arthritis patients' reactions to unavoidable social comparisons. *Personality and Social Psychology Bulletin, 17,* 392–399.

Festinger, L. (1954). A theory of social comparison processes. *Human Relations, 7,* 117–140.

Fiske, S. T., & Taylor, S. E. (1991). *Social cognition.* New York: McGraw-Hill.

Gilbert, D. T., Giesler, R. B., & Morris, K. A. (1995). When comparisons arise. *Journal of Personality and Social Psychology, 69,* 227–236.

Goethals, G. R., & Darley, J. (1977). Social comparison theory: An attributional approach. In J. Suls & R. L. Miller (Eds.), *Social comparison processes: Theoretical and empirical perspectives* (pp. 259–278). New York: Hemisphere.

Gruder, C. L. (1971). Determinants of social comparison choices. *Journal of Experimental Social Psychology, 7,* 473–489.

Gruder, C. L. (1977). Choice of comparison persons in evaluating oneself. In J. Suls and R. L. Miller (Eds.), *Social comparison processes: Theoretical and empirical processes* (pp. 21–41). New York: Hemisphere.

Herr, P. M. (1986). Consequences of priming: Judgment and behavior. *Journal of Personality and Social Psychology, 51,* 1106–1115.

Lockwood, P., & Kunda, Z. (1997). Superstars and me: Predicting the impact of role models on the self. *Journal of Personality and Social Psychology, 73,* 91–103.

Major, B., Testa, M., & Bylsma, W. (1991). Responses to upward and downward social comparisons: The impact of esteem-relevance and perceived control. In J. Suls & T. A. Wills (Eds.), *Social comparison: Contemporary theory and research* (pp. 237–260). Hillsdale, NJ: Lawrence Erlbaum.

Manis, M., Biernat, M., & Nelson, T. F. (1991). Comparison and expectancy processes in human judgment. *Journal of Personality and Social Psychology, 61*, 203–211.

Manis, M., & Paskewitz, J. (1984). Judging psychopathology: Expectations and contrast. *Journal of Personality and Social Psychology, 20*, 217–230.

Marsh, H. W., & Parker, J. W. (1984). Determinants of student self-concept: Is it better to be a relatively large fish in a small pond even if you don't learn to swim as well? *Journal of Personality and Social Psychology, 47*, 213–231.

Martin, L. L., Seta, J. J., & Crelia, R. A. (1990). Assimilation and contrast as a function of people's willingness and ability to expend effort in forming an impression. *Journal of Personality and Social Psychology, 59*, 27–37.

Medin, D. L., Goldstone, R. L., & Getner, D. (1993). Respects for similarity. *Psychological Review, 100*, 254–278.

Nosanchuk, T. A., & Erickson, B. H. (1985). How high is up? Calibrating social comparison in the real world. *Journal of Personality and Social Psychology, 48*, 624–634.

Parducci, A. (1964). Sequential effects in judgment. *Psychological Bulletin, 61*, 163–167.

Parducci, A. (1983). Category ratings and the relational character of judgment. In H. G. Geissler, H. F. J. M. Buffort, E. L. J. Leuwenberg, & V. Sarris (Eds.), *Modern issues in perception* (pp. 262–282). Berlin: VEB Deutscher Verlag der Wissenschaften.

Pelham, B. W., & Wachsmuth, J. O. (1995). The waxing and waning of the social self. *Assimilation and Contrast in Social Comparison, 69*, 825–838.

Taylor, S. E., & Lobel, M. (1989). Social comparison activity under threat: Downward evaluation and upward contacts. *Psychological Review, 96*, 569–575.

Tesser, A. (1988). Toward a self-evaluation maintenance model of social behavior. In L. Berkowitz (Ed.), *Advances in experimental social psychology* (Vol. 20, pp. 181–227). New York: Academic Press.

Thornton, D., & Arrowood, A. J. (1966). Self-evaluation, self-enhancement, and the locus of social comparison. *Journal of Experimental Social Psychology, 2 (Suppl. 1)*, 40–48.

Thornton, D., & Moore, S. (1993). Physical attractiveness contrast effect: Implications for self-esteem and evaluations of the social self. *Personality and Social Psychology Bulletin, 19*, 474–480.

Webster's Ninth New Collegiate Dictionary. (1988). Springfield, MA: Merriam-Webster, Inc.

Wheeler, L. (1966). Motivation as a determinant of upward comparison. *Journal of Experimental Social Psychology, 2 (Suppl. 1)*, 27–31.

Wheeler, L. (1991). A brief history of social comparison theory. In J. Suls & T. A. Wills (Eds.), *Social comparison: Contemporary theory and research* (pp. 3–22). Hillsdale, NJ: Lawrence Erlbaum.

Wheeler, L., & Miyake, K. (1992). Social comparison in everyday life. *Journal of Personality and Social Psychology, 62*, 760–773.

Wills, T. A. (1981). Downward comparison principles in social psychology. *Psychological Bulletin, 90*, 245–271.

Wood, J. V. (1989). Theory and research concerning social comparisons of personal attributes. *Psychological Bulletin, 106*, 231–248.

10

Assimilative and Contrastive Emotional Reactions to Upward and Downward Social Comparisons

RICHARD H. SMITH

Henry Fleming, the central character of Stephen Crane's (1952/1895) Civil War novel, *The Red Badge of Courage*, eagerly joins the Union army although he knows little about war. Only much later does he realize how ignorant he is about whether he will run when the fighting starts. This uncertainty about himself sets off a disguised but full-scale search for social comparisons until, through the gut check of battle, he can "... watch his legs discover their merits and their faults" (Crane, 1952/1895, p. 21). Much of the classic and current social comparison theory would find support in how Fleming uses social comparisons during the several days portrayed in the novel (Suls & Miller, 1977; Suls & Wills, 1991). Festinger (1954) emphasized the role of uncertainty in motivating a person's interest in social comparisons, and it is Fleming's ignorance about his own capacity for bravery that first prompts him to probe for fears among the other soldiers so as "... to measure himself by his comrades" (Crane, 1952/1895, p. 21). Even the seemingly objective test of battle is confounded by social comparisons. In an early battle, Fleming panics and runs, but it is the sight of other soldiers turning tail first that induces his behavior, creating in social comparison terms a form of social validation (Cialdini, 1993) that spurs him to "... speed toward the rear in great leaps" (Crane, 1952/1895, p. 47).

Perhaps the novel's most striking use of social comparisons, however, is the degree to which the many swings in Fleming's emotions seem determined by how he compares himself with other soldiers. Although he fears that his running from battle proves he is a coward, Fleming can occasionally find brief emotional comfort in noticing that many others ran, often with even greater zeal. He sees a roadway cluttered with fearful, retreating troops, and these downward comparisons produce pleasure rather than pity (e.g., Wills, 1981). But, just as frequently, upward comparisons intrude, creating unpleasant feelings (e.g., Brickman & Bulman, 1977; Salovey & Rodin, 1984). He sees an advancing group of infantry looking proud

RICHARD H. SMITH • Department of Psychology, University of Kentucky, Lexington, Kentucky 40506.

Handbook of Social Comparison: Theory and Research, edited by Suls and Wheeler. Kluwer Academic/Plenum Publishers, New York, 2000.

and resolute, quite the opposite of the retreating soldiers he saw earlier. This depresses him, and, as he watches them pass, he grows envious and wishes he could "... exchange lives with one of them" (Crane, 1952/1895, p. 69). Perhaps the key theme of the novel is the shame Fleming feels as he begins to squarely address the fact that so many other soldiers actually have their "red badge of courage," whereas he does not. Take away the social comparisons that impinge on Fleming's awareness and there would be little texture or bite to his emotional experience.

Stephen Crane's literary intuitions in *The Red Badge of Courage* make a powerful case for the range, frequency, and consequences of emotional responses to social comparisons. It seems that at every pivotal turn in the novel, social comparisons play a principal role in Fleming's various emotional states. Yet, how accurately do Crane's literary intuitions reflect people's actual affective responses to social comparisons? The general purpose of the chapter is to attempt to map out a way of examining the many possible emotions that might arise from social comparisons. Using insights taken largely from current theoretical and empirical work on social comparison processes, I will try to isolate the social comparison-based emotions that seem most important and prevalent and suggest the factors that can help explain their distinctive qualities.

GENERAL ANALYTIC STRUCTURE

Social Comparison- versus Social Reflection-Based Emotions

The variety of familiar and more subtle emotions resulting, at least in part, from social comparisons is considerable. Thus, mapping the territory is a complex task (e.g., Heider, 1958; Major, Testa, & Bylsma, 1991; Ortony, Clore, & Collins, 1988; Tesser, 1991). I will constrain my analysis to social comparisons directly relevant to a person's important goals, a criterion often assumed necessary for strong emotions to arise (e.g., Campos, Barrett, Lamb, Goldsmith, & Stenberg, 1983; Lazarus, 1991; Ortony et al., 1988). In terms of social comparison theory and research, this means that the comparisons will involve someone *similar* on attributes related to the comparison (e.g., Gastorf & Suls, 1978; Goethals & Darley, 1977; Major et al., 1991; Miller, Turnbull, & McFarland, 1988; Wood, 1989) and on comparison domains important and *relevant* to the self (e.g., Major et al., 1991; Salovey & Rodin, 1984; Tesser, 1991). Similarity on comparison-related attributes and high self-relevance appear to enhance both the likelihood of comparison being made and the resulting impact of the comparison on the self (Lockwood & Kunda, 1997). The impact of the comparison on the self links it most directly to emotions.

Constraining this analysis to social comparisons directly relevant to a person's important goals harmonizes well with Tesser's characterization of explicitly social comparison-based emotions. Tesser's (1991) self-evaluation maintenance model (see Chapter 7, this volume) contrasts emotions resulting from social *comparison* processes with those resulting from social *reflection* processes. According to Tesser's model, comparison processes occur when we are confronted with another person's performance on a domain of high relevance to ourselves, particularly when this person is psychologically close. Tesser's intended meaning of closeness is broad, but it incorporates the sense of similarity on comparison-related attributes noted above. Social reflection processes also occur when the other person is psychologically close. However, unlike social comparison processes, the other person's performance is on a domain of *low* relevance to the self.

Social reflection processes represent an important and innovative broadening of social comparison theory's initial casting by Festinger (1954). There is clear evidence that reflection processes do produce emotions, especially when the other person outperforms the self (Brewer & Weber, 1994; Cialdini, Borden, Thorne, Walker, Freeman & Sloan, 1976; Tesser, 1988, 1991). Furthermore, reflection emotions do appear to involve some sort of comparison between the self and another person. However, I will restrict my analysis to emotions following most directly from social comparisons.

Direction of Comparison

One familiar and telling distinction to make among types of social comparison-based emotions is that they can differ based on whether the emotion-eliciting comparison is with someone superior or inferior. In other words, these emotions often result from either upward comparisons (superior other) or downward comparisons (inferior other). Research on affective reactions to social comparisons usually can be classified in terms of whether it focuses on one or more of these two directions of comparison (e.g., Buunk & Gibbons, 1997; Suls & Miller, 1977; Suls & Wills, 1991). Clearly, the direction of social comparison has heuristic value for understanding affective reactions, and my analysis will adopt this distinction, as Figure 1 shows.

Desirability for the Self

Another useful distinction among social comparison-based emotions concerns their desirable or undesirable consequences for the self. Initial research on affective reactions to social comparisons focused on negative affective reactions to upward comparisons and positive affective reactions to downward comparisons. However, more recent research indicates that either direction of comparison can have "its ups and downs" (e.g., Buunk, Collins, Taylor, VanYperen, & Dakof, 1990). Both upward and downward comparisons can be either desirable or undesirable for the self (Brewer & Weber, 1994; Brown, Novick, Lord, & Richards, 1991; Buunk et al., 1990; Buunk & Ybema, 1997; Collins, 1996; Leach, Webster, Smith, Kelso, Brigham, & Garonzik, 2000; Lockwood & Kunda, 1997; Major et al., 1991; Taylor & Lobel, 1989; Tesser, 1988; Wood & VanderZee, 1997). Thus, upward comparisons can produce a broad range of emotions from those that are pleasant experiences, such as inspiration and admiration (e.g., Brickman & Bulman, 1977; Lockwood & Kunda, 1997) to those that are unpleasant, such as envy and resentment (e.g., Crosby, 1976; Folger, 1987; Salovey & Rodin, 1984; Silver & Sabini, 1978; Sullivan, 1953). Downward comparisons can produce another varied set of emotions, from those that are pleasant, such as pride (e.g., Tesser, 1991) and *schadenfreude* (e.g., Smith et al., 1996) to those that are unpleasant, such as worry and pity (e.g., Wood & VanderZee, 1997). As Fig. 1 also indicates, a large part of my analysis will make use of the 2 × 2 descriptive structure defined by considering both the upward or downward direction of the comparison and the desirable or undesirable implications of the comparison for the self.

Desirability for the Other

Another aspect of my analysis will concern the desirable or undesirable implications of the comparison for the other person. Social comparison-based emotions are made more complex by the fact that a social comparison involves the fortunes of not only the self but also

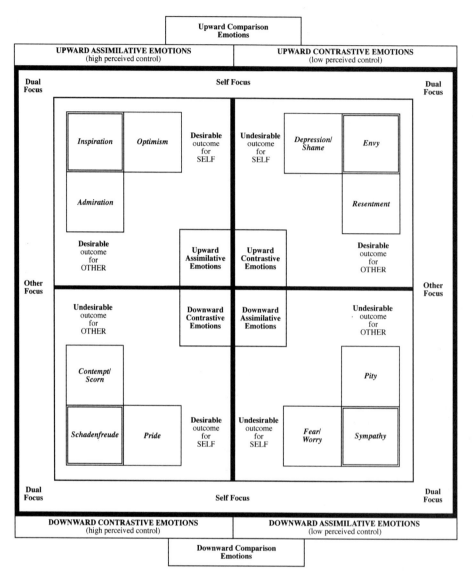

Figure 1. Social comparison-based emotions.

another person. The traditional social comparison perspective emphasizes how knowledge of others' opinions and abilities affects self-evaluations and affective reactions to such self-evaluations. Thus, an analysis of affective reactions to social comparison information could be confined narrowly to examining affect-inducing inferences about the self that follow simply from knowing where one stands compared to other people. However, it is also the case that the relative standing of other people represents outcomes for them to which one can respond with emotion. An upward comparison for the self, in a relative sense, represents a positive outcome (advantage or superiority) for the other person, whereas a downward comparison for the self represents a negative outcome (disadvantage or inferiority). Though created by relative differences, these are outcomes happening to another person about which one can feel positively or negatively.

Affective reactions to the fortunes of others need not involve relativistic considerations, as Heider (1958) and Ortony et al. (1988) point out in their analyses of four basic types of emotional responses to the fortunes of others. These four types entail either pleased or displeased reactions to events assumed to have either desirable or undesirable consequences for another person. For example, according to Ortony et al. (1988), the fact that we like a person could be one reason why a desirable event happening to him or her could make us pleased. Our sense of how deserved the outcome also could be important, deserved outcomes being more pleasing than undeserved ones. Because of our basic value system, we might simply be pleased when "virtue is rewarded ... and justice prevails" (Ortony et al., 1988, p. 94). The assessment of deservingness might have little or no association with how we compare with the other person. However, Ortony et al. (1988) emphasize that it is more typical for the social comparison context to exert a heavy influence on our reactions to the fortunes of others. Not only will the desirability of another's fortune be determined by whether it is relatively more or less desirable than our own situation, but judgments of liking and deservingness also may have relativistic origins. Especially when the relatively advantaged person is a member of our own social group, there may be a strong tendency to feel resentful over this advantage and to dislike this person because of it, as research on relative deprivation would indicate (e.g., Crosby, 1976; Davis, 1959; Folger, 1987; Runciman, 1966). As Ortony et al. (1988) contend, "People cannot help but evaluate the fortunes of others at least in part with reference to their own situations, this is a perfectly reasonable conclusion" (p. 105).

Again, the task of understanding social comparison-based emotions is complex. Take envy as an example. It is perhaps the prototype of the social comparison-based emotion as it so clearly requires a social comparison for it to take place. We feel envy when the relative good fortune or advantage of another person makes us feel discontent and ill will (e.g., Foster, 1972; Salovey & Rodin, 1984; Silver & Sabini, 1978; Smith, 1991). Why do we feel discontent? It is probably because of the unflattering implications of the comparison for the self in an area that is important to us (e.g., Salovey and Rodin, 1984; Salovey, 1991; Smith, Parrott, Ozer, & Moniz, 1994). But, why do we feel ill will? There may be many reasons (e.g., Montaldi, 1998), but one reason is that the very fact of the advantaged person's superiority can affect our evaluation of him or her. For example, research suggests that invidious comparisons will often create a subjective sense that the envied person's advantage is unfair (Smith et al., 1994), which, in turn, creates feelings of ill will. The key point here is that the sense of injustice seems inspired by the relative advantage enjoyed by the envied person, rather than in response to more objective, absolute criteria.

As Dunning and his colleagues have shown (see Chapter 17, this volume), social judgment is often closely linked to social comparison. Both processes are relational. Dunning distinguishes between social comparison and egocentric comparison. Social comparison involves using information about other people to learn about the self. Egocentric comparison involves using information about the self to make a judgment about others. It is clear that both social comparison and egocentric comparison are ubiquitous phenomena and that they often proceed hand in hand. The situations in which we are motivated to judge ourselves through social comparisons seem to overlap considerably with those situations in which we are motivated to judge others through egocentric comparisons. Thus, an understanding of social comparison-based emotions must take into account the relation basis both for evaluating the self and for evaluating other people.

My analysis will attempt to incorporate both the self- and other-evaluative components of affective responses to social comparisons. Thus, within the descriptive structure created by considering the direction of the comparison and its desirability for the self, I also include the desirability of the comparison for the other person. In general, an upward comparison will mean desirable implications for the other and a downward comparison will mean undesirable implications for the other, as Fig. 1 suggests.

Focus of Attention

An additional feature to my analysis involves the claim that social comparison-based emotions differ in terms of whether the self or the other person receives the greater focus of attention (Master & Keil, 1987). Emotions typically concern the self in relation to the external world. We feel fear because something in the external world frightens us, and our concern about what will happen to us then creates the emotion. However, as Solomon (1976) argues, it also seems "... obvious that the various emotions do not pay equal attention to these 'poles' of subjectivity" (p. 254). Some emotions appear to involve a predominant "outer" focus on the external world. When we feel resentful or angry, for example, we seem largely focused on the other person who is the cause of our anger. Other emotions involve a predominant "inner" focus on the self. In shame, for example, the focus of attention is often on our own inferiority or misconduct. Other people's evaluation of us may provide the impetus for the feeling, but the focus is on the self's inferiority or misconduct. Finally, there may be circumstances in which the focus has more of a dual or "bipolar" quality in which the focus shifts back and forth between the self and the other. Solomon (1976) suggests that love may often fit this class of emotions, as it involves a "... certain relationship between oneself and the other" (p. 256).

With social comparison-based emotions, the two "poles" of subjectivity involve the self and another person. On the one hand, these emotions follow from the self-evaluative implications of the comparison. On the other hand, these emotions follow from how we evaluate the other person. As reflected in Fig. 1, I will argue that useful distinctions among social comparison-based emotions can in part be explained by considering the balance of attention given to the self and to the other in a particular emotion-inducing social comparison.

Contrastive versus Assimilative Reactions and Perceived Control

Heider (1958) claimed that social comparisons can often play "... role of background or surrounding, which, through the effects of contrast, can serve to enhance p's lot or impair it" (p. 285). He also argued that in other situations assimilation processes explain people's reactions to social comparisons, as when, "the fact that o [the other] has x makes it seem possible that p [the person] can realize it also" (p. 288). This distinction between contrast ["displacement away from the values of contextual stimuli" (Wedell, 1994, p. 1007)] and assimilation ["displacement of judgments toward the contextual standard" (Wedell, 1994, p. 1007)] figures prominently in recent theoretical developments in social comparison theory (e.g., Brewer & Weber, 1994; Buunk & Ybema, 1997; Collins, 1966; Wood & VanderZee, 1997) (see Chapter 9, this volume). I will also adopt this distinction and will try to show that it captures, at least in part, the different processes underlying various social comparison-based emotions. In line with Major and co-workers' (1991) more general model of reactions to social comparisons, I also will argue that perceived control is a key determinant for whether assimilative or contrastive reactions occur.

To summarize, my aim in this chapter is to differentiate social comparison-based emotions using a number of distinctions. I will argue that each emotion can be categorized in terms of whether it results from an upward or a downward comparison, whether it produces a positive or negative experience for the self and whether it produces a positive or negative experience for the other. I also will suggest that each emotion involves a characteristic focus of attention—either on the self, the other, or a dual focus on the self and the other. In addition, I will claim that each emotion can be broadly characterized as having either an assimilative or contrastive nature, largely following from perceptions of control. Overall, four general types of social comparison-based emotions emerge from this analysis, based on whether the comparison is upward or downward and whether it is assimilative or contrastive in nature. Finally, after describing each general type of emotion and suggesting possible subtypes within each general category, the remainder of the chapter will consider a number of implications of this analysis.

UPWARD COMPARISON EMOTIONS

Upward Contrastive Emotions

> As the youth looked at them the black weight of his woe returned to him. He felt that he was regarding a procession of chosen beings. The separation was as great to him as if they had marched with weapons of flame and banners of sunlight. He could never be like them. He could have wept in his longings. (Crane, 1952/1895, p. 68)

In the hours following his running from battle, Fleming tries to deny the enormity of his behavior, but the recurring sight of other soldiers who acted bravely makes this painfully difficult. His reactions share a number of features often found in negative emotional reactions to upward social comparisons. Possibly the defining feature of such comparisons is that they seem linked to *contrastive* judgmental processes (e.g., Brewer & Weber, 1994; Collins, 1996; Heider, 1958). The comparison puts in high relief what one lacks, and the result is impairment. If the domain of comparison is important and the advantaged person is similar on comparison-related attributes, an unpleasant jolt of feeling is likely to follow (e.g., Brickman & Bulman, 1977; Major et al., 1991; Salovey & Rodin, 1984; Tesser, Millar, & Moore, 1988; Wheeler & Miyake, 1992; Wills, 1981).

Why would another person's advantage necessarily bring about a contrastive judgment? As noted earlier, a key explanation appears linked to beliefs about whether the discrepancy is changeable (Aspinwall, 1997; Buunk & Ybema 1997; Collins, 1996; Lockwood & Kunda, 1997; Major et al., 1991; Weiner, 1986; Wood & VanderZee, 1997). Discrepancies that seem unchangeable bring about contrastive reactions. Fleming feels miserable when observing the other soldiers because he believes that "he could never be like them" (Crane, 1952/1895, p. 68). Social comparison researchers have found various ways to convey or demonstrate this point. Major and colleagues, in a theoretical analysis of behavioral, cognitive, and affective reactions to social comparison (Major et al., 1991) and in an empirical demonstration (Testa & Major, 1988), note how *perceived control* "... alters the meaning and significance of these discrepancies and the comparer's responses to them" (Major et al., 1991, p. 246). Negative affective reactions result when people believe they are unable to close the gap between themselves and the advantaged person.

Research on counterfactual thinking also suggests the importance of perceived control in people's reactions to upward comparisons (see Chapter 18, this volume). An upward comparison, especially with someone who shares comparison-related attributes, should easily create an imagined, better alternative to one's current situation. Typically, negative affect should result from the contrastive nature of this personified, counterfactual (Folger, 1987; Markman, Gavanski, Sherman, & McMullen, 1993; Roese & Olson, 1995). Negative affect should be especially likely, however, if the counterfactual creates little sense that the discrepancy can be undone (Folger, 1987; McMullen & Markman, 1994; McMullen, Markman, & Gavinski, 1995). McMullen et al. (1995) report three studies, for example, in which upward counter-factuals tended to produce contrast effects. Negative affect resulting from these contrast effects was reduced, however, when participants had a sense of perceived control. McMullen et al. (1995) conclude that *without* an enhanced sense of control, people will "… experience the full brunt of the negative affect associated with considering how things could have been better" (p. 157).

TYPES OF UPWARD CONTRASTIVE EMOTIONS

Most research on negative affective reactions to upward comparisons has not differenti-ated among types of negative emotions, at least not in a systematic way. It has only been a recent theme to suggest that such reactions can be either positive or negative (e.g., Buunk et al., 1990; Taylor & Lobel, 1989). However, separate traditions of research show that useful distinctions can be made. Research in relative deprivation focuses on upward social compari-sons producing resentment (e.g., Crosby, 1976; Folger, 1987). Another tradition of research links social comparison with depressive affect (e.g., Ahrens & Alloy, 1997; Gilbert, 1992; Swallow & Kuiper, 1992). Still another tradition examines envy (e.g., Salovey & Rodin, 1984; Silver & Sabini, 1978; Smith et al., 1994). Resentment refers to angry feelings resulting from the perception that another's advantage is unfair. Depressive feelings are more likely to result when another's advantages creates a sense of inferiority. Envy, as already noted, is the combination of both discontent and hostility resulting from another person's advantage. Clearly, these are different emotions, despite the overlapping contrastive character that they appear to share. How can one understand the distinctiveness of these emotions?

Self-Focus: Depressive Feelings and Shame

Depressive Feelings.   I claimed earlier that social comparison-based emotions might differ in the balance of attention given to the self and to the other. Certain upward contrastive comparisons seem to point toward the self as anchoring the contrast. The other person's superiority stimulates the emotional reaction, but it is the comparison's conspicuous implica-tions for the self that dominate one's thoughts and stir one's feelings. Fleming's reaction to the many soldiers who acted bravely is a good example. His woeful feelings are initiated by comparing himself with these soldiers, but the upshot of these comparisons causes him to dwell on the depressing possibility that he is a coward.

An upward contrastive comparison carries potentially huge evaluative and attributional weight. Not only can it create a sense of inferiority, but it also can localize the cause of inferiority within the self. A contrastive social comparison is a form of low consensus information, which implies an internal attribution for one's disadvantage (e.g., Kelley, 1967, 1972). Self-caused inferiority, especially if it seems stable and irrevocable, is a reliable prescription for lowered self-esteem and associated unpleasant, depressive feelings (e.g., Abramson, Seligman, & Teasdale, 1978; Beck, 1967; Gilbert, 1992; Smith et al., 1994; Weiner, 1986). It may be the internal causal attribution of inferiority that helps bring about the perceptions of low personal control so characteristic of upward contrastive comparisons. Furthermore, internal causal attributions may make it more likely that the focal point of the comparison will be on the self rather than on the other.

A number of recent models of depression emphasize the role of self-focus in creating and maintaining depressive responses to stressful events (e.g., Pyszczynski & Greenberg, 1987; Wood, Saltzberg, Neale, Stone, & Rachmiel, 1990). Depressive feelings have been found to be correlated with self-focus in both clinical and nonclinical samples (Ingram, Lumry, Cruet, & Seiber, 1987; Ingram & Smith, 1984; Smith & Greenberg, 1981; Smith, Ingram, & Roth, 1985). Inducing an external focus in depressed people appears to reduce their depressive affect (Nix, Watson, Pyszczynski, & Greenberg, 1995) and attenuates their pessimistic views (Pyszczynski, Holt, & Greenberg, 1987). Chronically self-focused people appear to react with more negative affect and dysfunctional negative thoughts in response to failure feedback compared to non–self-focused people (Ingram, Johnson, Bernet, & Dombeck, 1992). Furthermore, self-focus appears to be associated with a style of coping with stress that perpetuates depressive feelings (Wood et al., 1990). Whereas nondepressed people will try to escape self-focus after failure (e.g., Gibbons & Wicklund, 1976; Gibbons, 1990), depressed people often seem unable to break free from a chronic self-focusing style (Pyszczynski & Greenberg, 1986, 1987).

There also is evidence from research on asymmetries in self–other judgments that a focus of attention on the self might amplify contrast effects (e.g., Holyoak & Gordon, 1983; Srull & Gaelick, 1983). In Holyoak and Gordon's (1983) research, participants were asked to compare themselves to another person, under conditions in which either the participant or the other person was the focus of the comparison. When the participant was the focus (e.g., "How similar are you to your friend in shyness?"), contrast effects were greater (they perceived themselves as less similar) than when the other person was the focus ("How similar is your friend to you in shyness?"). Presumably, contrastive affective reactions to another person's advantage should also be enhanced by a focus on the self.

Shame.   As noted earlier, perhaps the key theme of Crane's novel is the shame that Fleming feels as he contrasts his own cowardly behavior with the bravery of other soldiers. Fleming is lucky that this early behavior went unnoticed, but his shame is so strong that when he later walks amid the other wounded soldiers, he flushes and feels that "his shame could be viewed" (Crane, 1952/1895, p. 59). Shame is another emotion associated with a focus on the self that also can result from an upward contrastive social comparison (e.g., Gilbert, 1992; Lewis, 1971; Solomon, 1976). The research literature on shame highlights a number of possible features of the emotion, but there is general agreement that shame results from the diminishment of the self (e.g., Lewis, 1971; Niedenthal, Tangney, & Gavinski, 1994; Tangney, 1998), often in the imagined or actual eyes of others whose opinions matter (e.g., Ausubel, 1955; Gibbons, 1990; Higgins, 1987; Smith, Webster, & Parrott, 2000). The typical counterfactual bringing about shame is, "If only I were not a certain kind of person" (Niedenthal et al., 1994), consistent with the irrevocable character of an upward contrastive emotion. Shame also appears more likely if the self can be blamed for this diminishment (e.g., Lazarus, 1991; Ortony et al., 1988; Weiner, 1986).

Shame is clearly an underresearched emotion in the social comparison literature and deserves much more attention (e.g., Gilbert, 1998). It arises not only when a person's nonmoral attributes suggest inferiority, such as in the case of an uncontrollable stigma (e.g., Goffman, 1963; Smith et al., 2000), but also when a person's actions fall short of norms of moral behavior (e.g., Lewis, 1971; Smith et al., 2000; Tangney, 1998). Thus, it can surface in a broad range of circumstances in which social comparisons play an important role. If a person feels shame, it is a likely sign that a self-relevant social comparison is at work.

The connection between shame and the public exposure of inferiority suggests that publicity also may play an important general role in social comparison processes. For example, there is clear evidence in studies using the rank order paradigm that public comparisons have strong effects on comparison choices (Smith & Insko, 1987; Wilson & Benner, 1971). Typically, participants who believe they have scored in the middle rank on an ability test will be most interested in learning how the top-ranked scorer has done (e.g., Wheeler et al., 1969). This choice appears most informative about the meaning of their own score. However, as was particularly evident in the study by Smith and Insko (1987), participants expressed much less interest in learning this score, if doing so required that they actually meet with this top performer to compare scores. Public comparison can bring with it a variety of unpleasant consequences (see also Brickman & Bulman, 1977), and the painful emotion of shame is the common marker of these consequences.

Other Focus: Resentment

Other upward contrastive emotions seem to point to the other as anchoring the contrast. In these situations, the fact of the other's advantage or superiority is the focal point, and resentment, rather than depressive feelings or shame, may be the more likely emotion to result (Solomon, 1976). Resentment occurs when another person's relative advantage or superiority is perceived as undeserved or unjustified (e.g., Folger, 1987; Ortony et al., 1988; Weiner, 1986). The hub of emotion will center around the fact that this other person does not deserve his or her advantage. As Folger (1987) notes, "… resentment is an emotion with an outwardly directed target, an implicit accusation of wrongdoing" (p. 204). The contrastive nature of resentment is suggested by findings indicating that the emotion is associated with a reduced sense of control. Resentment is most likely to occur if the prospects for obtaining an outcome, unfairly enjoyed by another person, seem remote (Folger, Rosenfield, Rheaume, & Martin, 1983b; Folger, Rosenfield, & Rheaume, 1983a; Folger, Rosenfield, & Robinson, 1983c; Folger, 1987).

A focus on the other person's undeserved advantage has a number of associated features. Whereas the cause of the discrepancy may seem internal in the case of self-focus, it may seem less so in the case of other-focus. It is more the other person's unjust actions and unfair advantages that cause, and are to blame, for one's inferior status rather than one's personal qualities. Also, an external focus should decrease the chances of depressive reactions (e.g., Abramson et al., 1978; Beck, 1967). As noted earlier, one of the reasons that a self-focused style following failure is associated with depression is that this style may prevent the normal coping response of shifting to an external focus (Pyszczynski & Greenberg, 1986, 1987). The perception of unfair advantage may be an especially effective inducement away from self-focus as attention shifts to the reason for one's resentment, the other's enjoying unfair advantage. Resentment, when it is based on a flagrant injustice, becomes indignation and would involve even less of a self-focus. As Solomon (1976) argues, indignation "… presents itself as a matter of selfless principle; 'it is not for myself that I am concerned, but rather because of the *principle* of the matter' " (p. 255). Thus, hostility and resentment result rather than depressive feelings and shame.

A focus on the other person also means that the degree to which one likes or dislikes this person now becomes an important factor in determining the precise quality of one's emotions

(Heider, 1958; Ortony et al., 1988). When the focus is on the self, the likeable or dislikeable attributes of the advantaged person may have little effect on one's feelings of inferiority. However, as Ortony et al. (1988) argue, emotions resulting from the fortune of others will be affected by the degree to which the other person is liked. Resentment will probably be mitigated if we like the advantaged person but will be aggravated if we dislike this person. It is harder to resent intensely the advantaged person when the person is modest and unassuming. Arrogance in the unfairly advantaged person can enrage, as research on aggressive responses to various forms of insult indicates (Baron & Richardson, 1994).

Fleming's resentment is usually directed at the high-ranked but incompetent officers who "perch tranquilly" in positions that allow them to avoid the dangers confronting the regular soldiers (Crane, 1952/1895). But he is powerless to change the situation, and this makes him furious. Fleming clearly resents their advantaged position because he believes them unworthy of this advantage and because he realizes that hc can do nothing to prevent them from sending him into some foolish battle.

Dual Focus: Envy

Is there an emotion that fits a dual focus on both what the self lacks and what the other possesses? Envy is a possibility. Its experience can be understood as a combination of both a focus on one's own disadvantage and on the other person's advantage. The focus on one's disadvantage brings about a sense of inferiority (Smith et al., 1994), thus producing depressive feelings. The focus on the other's advantage brings about a sense that the advantage is undeserved, thus producing resentment (Smith et al., 1994).

In envy, there may be an inherent shifting back and forth between self and other focus. For one thing, it may be less clear-cut that the other person's advantage is actually undeserved. Heider (1958) claimed that envy arises in part from an "ought" force that requires that people should have equality in outcomes, especially if they appear similar in most other respects. However, the typical advantages enjoyed by the envied person do not violate obvious, societal standards of justice. In fact, certain societal norms require that we "smile at the fortune of another" (Heider, 1958, p. 289) rather than envy the good fortune. Thus, envy-based resentment enjoys only subjective validity and rarely holds up to public scrutiny. If it met more severe, objective standards of injustice, then, the emotion would be resentment proper rather than envy (Smith et al., 1994). Thus, in envy, there are usually insufficient grounds for a heavy focus on the undeserved advantage of the other person. One must at least dwell as often on the fact of one's inferiority, created and highlighted by the other person's advantage.

Envy is a complex emotion (Parrott, 1991). Its dual focus may bring with it the array of possible feelings normally associated with either self or other focus in addition to feelings that might arise from shifting back and forth between self and other focus. Thus, it is not surprising to see some authors note the connections between envy and shame (e.g., Berke, 1988; Gilbert, 1992). There is shame inherent in inferiority and there is shame inherent in feeling hostile toward another person simply because of his or her advantage. Because of its shameful nature, envy is often a private and hidden emotion. Envy-produced hostility manifests itself in indirect ways, such as derogation of the envied person to a third party (Salovey & Rodin, 1984; Silver & Sabini, 1978). Because it involves a focus on the other, envy is also affected by whether the other person is liked or disliked. Although envy may motivate one to find reasons to dislike the advantaged person (to justify ill will), it is probably true that it is more difficult to envy someone we like than someone we dislike.

Upward Assimilative Emotions

> The tall soldier, for one, gave him some assurance. This man's serene unconcern dealt him a measure of
> confidence, for he had known him since childhood, and from his intimate knowledge he did not see
> how he could be capable of anything that was beyond him. (Crane, 1952/1895, p. 21)

Although most of the initial upward comparisons that Fleming makes lead to unpleasant emotions, not all of them do. When he sees the calmness of this childhood friend, this actually makes him feel greater confidence in himself. This kind of comparison seems linked to assimilative rather than contrastive judgmental processes in which, as noted earlier, there is displacement of judgments toward a contextual standard. The apparent difference between the self and the other person, far from suggesting separation as in the case of contrastive reactions, generates a sense of similarity or newfound self-enhancement (Buunk & Ybema, 1997; Collins, 1996; Lockwood & Kunda, 1997; Wood & VanderZee, 1997). Because the comparison is in a domain important to the self, pleasant feelings result.

How can another's advantage bring about assimilative reactions? In some cases, the perception of similarity in other respects may simply redefine the discrepancy as not representing a discrepancy in the first place (e.g., Collins, 1996; Wheeler, 1966). In effect, the comparison person serves as a proxy (Wheeler, Martin, & Suls, 1997), informing us that we can and will perform similarly. Fleming feels assured when noticing the tall soldier's greater confidence because he believes, based on knowing the soldier since childhood, that they were at least equally capable in many other respects. In other cases, this perception of similarity indicates that the prospects for eliminating the discrepancy are good (e.g., Aspinwall, 1997; Brickman & Bulman, 1977; Buunk & Ybema 1997; Collins, 1996; Lockwood & Kunda, 1997; Major et al., 1991; Meichenbaum, 1971; Seta, 1982; Testa & Major, 1990; Weiner, 1986; Wood & VanderZee, 1997). As with contrastive reactions, perceived control seems important, although perceived control tends to be high rather than low in the case of assimilative reactions. Upward comparisons coupled with high perceived control "... increase self-efficacy and inspire and motivate performance rather than induce helplessness or anger" (Major et al., 1991, p. 247).

TYPES OF UPWARD ASSIMILATIVE EMOTIONS

Research on assimilative affective reactions to upward comparisons is less extensive (e.g., Brickman & Bulman, 1977, experiment 3) than on contrastive affective reactions (e.g., Morse & Gergen, 1970; Salovey & Rodin, 1984; Smith et al., 1996). What this research has shown is that positive emotions of any kind can occur rather than showing that there may be useful distinctions to be made among types of positive emotions (e.g., Buunk et al., 1990). However, as with upward contrastive emotions, self or other focus may help suggest some possibilities.

Self-Focus: Optimistic Feelings

In certain situations, the advantage of the other person may bring about a predominant focus on the positive implications for the self. The comparison person establishes the attractive possible outcome, but once this possible outcome seems within reach, it is this prospect, rather than its existing attainment by the other person, that is the focus and that generates pleasant, optimistic feelings (Ortony et al., 1988). This seems to be the case with Fleming when he examines the tall soldier (Crane, 1952/1895). The comparison he makes with this soldier serves to inform him about his own capacity to cope with battle, and it is this gain in self-knowledge that makes him feel good. One key to the creation of optimistic feelings is that the target person shares similarities on comparison-related attributes other than the comparison dimension itself (Brickman & Bulman, 1977, experiment 3). This similarity allows for the easy construal that the apparent advantage actually represents something possible for the self. If the domain of comparison is important, then it is quite natural for the upward redefining of the self to create pleasant, optimistic feelings (Collins, 1996). The future self is now full of newfound *and* well-founded possibilities (Markus & Nurius, 1986).

The study by Brickman and Bulman (1977, experiment 3) just cited is good evidence for the possibility of optimistic feelings in response to upward comparisons. Participants examined files on past students from their university. Aspects of these files were manipulated to describe a former student who was either from a similar or dissimilar background to the participant and who was either of the same (recent graduate) or previous (graduated "years ago") generation. For participants sharing a similar background to the person described in the file, successful achievements by this person produced greater personal satisfaction when this person was from a previous generation than from the same generation. Assimilation effects presumably occurred when achievements were made by someone of a previous generation because participants could expect similar success for themselves in due course.

Some of the research on the social comparisons made by cancer patients also is supportive (Taylor & Lobel, 1989; Wood & VanderZee, 1997), especially with regard to comparisons based on the important dimension of survival. If people suffering from cancer learn that another person (similar to them in ways that seem relevant to health) has overcome this disease, then this knowledge leads to positive rather than negative reactions.

Other Focus: Admiration

Are there also situations in which the predominant focus of the upward assimilative comparison is on the other person? What kind of emotion would result? Admiration is a good candidate. Admiration occurs when another person arouses a sense of wonder, delight, and pleased approval (*Webster's New World Dictionary*, 1982). It is perhaps the prototype of what Ortony et al. (1988) call the *appreciation* emotions, in which one reacts with "… approval for some praiseworthy action, the more praiseworthy, the more intense" (p. 145). We feel admiration when someone does something praiseworthy, especially when it is out of the ordinary (thus, an upward comparison). Unlike in the case of resentment, where the advantage seems undeserved, with admiration the advantage seems quite deserved. Also, in contrast to resentment, the other person is probably likeable rather than dislikeable (Ortony et al., 1988), in part because of his or her praiseworthy actions. Extraordinary and praiseworthy actions, performed by a likeable person, attract our positive attention and focus, and this creates admiration.

If a person's actions are so extraordinary, it might seem that this would reduce the sense that the comparer shares a basic similarity to this person; thus, reducing the impact and relevance of the comparison (Festinger, 1954; Mettee & Smith, 1977). This might be especially true if these actions seemed dispositionally caused. However, if the typical source of admiration is an action that one person could hope to emulate, then there should be some sense of similarity preserved.

A study by Lockwood and Kunda (1997, experiment 2) is consistent with these conclusions. In this study, first or fourth year undergraduates read a newspaper article about an outstanding graduating student. This student not only was very bright but also was involved in numerous volunteer activities. Paralleling the Brickman and Bulman (1977) study just noted, only first-year students found reading this article to enhance their own self-evaluations. But, more to the point, first-year students, when asked to focus on characteristics of the graduating student, also rated him or her more positively than the fourth-year students. Presumably, because first-year students could assume that they had enough time to replicate both the achievements and actions of good will displayed by the graduating student, they may have both raised their own self-evaluations and felt more positively toward this student as well.

Dual Focus: Inspiration

What affective reaction might occur when an upward assimilative comparison creates a dual focus on both the positive implications for the self and the admirable attributes of the other person? Perhaps inspiration matches such a case. Feelings of inspiration, like optimism, imply enhanced expectations for the future and a positive redefining of one's capabilities, created by another person's superior example (e.g., Berger, 1977; Meichenbaum, 1971). However, unlike optimism, they also seem to require that the advantaged person be expressly admired. The praiseworthy actions of the advantaged person suggest a particular road map for how one can model a similar advantage (e.g., Lockwood & Kunda, 1997). Optimism can result from the knowledge that a certain positive outcome can occur, discovered because someone similar in other respects enjoys this outcome. Inspiration suggests that the impressive actions of another person can provide the model for achieving this outcome.

Some of the research on social comparisons among cancer patients may reflect inspiration (Wood & VanderZee, 1997). As noted earlier, as long as an upward comparison suggests positive expectations for the future progress of the disease (because of similarity in relevant attributes), a cancer patient can feel optimistic about his or her own prospects. Inspiration should occur if the other person's praiseworthy coping actions seem to help explain why the disease has taken a healthy course, thus providing a guide for one's own coping efforts.

The study by Lockwood and Kunda (1997) also provides especially good evidence for inspiration. In addition to rating the graduating student described in the newspaper article and providing self-evaluations, participants also responded to open-ended questions about why the student may have been a relevant person for comparison. These responses, in a sense, required that participants think directly how the student, as a comparison other, was relevant to their own goals, thus encouraging a dual focus. These responses were coded for the presence of inspiration, denigration of the comparison process, and similarity to the student on dimensions other than the intended career goal. A remarkable 82% of the first-year participants described themselves as inspired and excited by the comparison (e.g., "I almost want to work superhard so that I can get that award she got ... I just decided that I will go to the ... meeting tomorrow now because it is probably a good idea to get involved like Jennifer did") compared to 6% of the fourth-year participants. Also, only 6% of the first-year participants denigrated the comparison process (e.g., "you can't compare 'success' between any two people on the planet because we are all different and successful in our own right") compared to 50% of the fourth-year participants. Finally, 53% of the first-year participants noted similarities they shared with the student (e.g., "She seems very similar to me ... She also participates in activities other than academic related like myself. Similarly, I like to help those in need") compared to only 19% of the fourth-year participants. Lockwood and Kunda suggest that the first-year participants, unlike fourth-year participants, could expect to attain the accomplishment of the graduating student by the time they themselves graduated. Therefore, similarities between this student and themselves were highlighted, and the comparison process was embraced as means of inspiring them to follow this person's lead.

DOWNWARD COMPARISON EMOTIONS

Downward Contrastive Emotions

> His friend at his side seemed suffering great shame. As he contemplated him, the youth felt his heart grow more strong and stout. He had never been compelled to blush in such a manner for his acts; he was an individual of extraordinary virtues. (Crane, 1952/1895, p. 92)

Fortunately for Fleming, no survivors detected his early cowardice. Later, he does act bravely, which allows him to slowly rebuild a good feeling about himself. He also compares himself to others whose shameful actions did *not* escape public notice. Typically, these comparisons provide easy opportunities for self-enhancement and bring him pleasure. This type of comparison seems to have a contrastive character, but downward rather than upward in direction (e.g., Gibbons & Gerrard, 1991; Wills, 1981). In such cases, the disadvantage of another person creates a background that highlights one's own advantage rather than disadvantage (Heider, 1958) or reveals superiority previously unnoticed. The result is pleasing.

As with other comparison-based emotions, the perception of control over the discrepancy appears to be a key predictor of contrastive reactions. However, unlike with upward comparisons of a contrastive tenor, one feels a high rather than low sense of control. Whereas with upward contrastive comparisons one's inferiority seems a stable unalterable state, with downward contrastive comparisons one's superiority seems a stable and controllable state (Major et al., 1991). In the example above, Fleming could look back on his own behavior and see no instances of the childish panic and blushing like that displayed by his friend. Fleming believed that he had never, would never, behave quite in this way, and so the difference between himself and his friend seemed ironclad, thus building a more positive and pleasing sense of himself.

TYPES OF DOWNWARD CONTRASTIVE EMOTIONS

Useful distinctions also can be made among types of downward contrastive emotions, although research on these distinctions is particularly sparse (Ortony et al., 1988; Wills, 1891). As with upward comparison emotions, social comparison researchers examining specific types of emotions have focused more on demonstrating either generally positive or negative reactions than on distinguishing types of emotions within each general category. Thinking in terms of self and other focus may suggest possibilities here as well.

Self-Focus: Pride

Some downward contrastive comparisons may involve the self as the focal point of the comparison. The other person's disadvantage induces the comparison, but the direct implications for the self receive one's main attention. This may be especially likely to occur if a positive internal characteristic seems to cause the discrepancy. In terms of self-evaluation and causal inferences, the processes may be similar to upward contrastive comparisons, except that the conclusions are positive rather than negative for the self. Pride is perhaps the best emotion term to characterize the pleasant feelings that result (Major et al., 1991; Tesser, 1991; Weiner, 1986). Fleming's reaction to his shame-ridden friend appears to be of this type. This downward comparison allows Fleming his first bit of reclaiming of the positive identity that had been threatened by his cowardly behavior the previous day. Indeed, immediately after this incident he imagines the now-reasonable prospect of his returning home a hero to boast about his experience.

The role of publicity in social comparison-based emotions was noted earlier. Shame was an obvious example. Publicity also may play an important role in social comparison-based pride. Just as our inferior, blameworthy attributes create less shame if they are kept private, our superior praiseworthy attributes create greater pride if they are made public (Webster, Weeter, & Smith, 2000). Near the end of the novel, Fleming's bravery arouses in him his deepest feelings of pride. These feelings are especially intense because his bravery is witnessed by many others. When the fighting is over, he reflects on his public deeds in his mind's eye and finds deep satisfaction in studying these "guilded images of memory."

Other Focus: Contempt–Scorn

The further removed Fleming is from his early cowardice, the more his confidence is renewed. One way he achieves this is to distance himself from other soldiers who seemed weak and timid compared to himself (e.g., Gibbons & Gerrard, 1991). He allows his thoughts to dwell on how others had also run with particular terror. Whereas he had escaped the earlier battle with his dignity intact, these other soldiers were weak men who only deserved his "scorn." In these cases, Fleming's reactions are clearly contrastive in nature. And, the implications for his own self-evaluation are usually part of his thinking. But, the source of his emotional reactions seems to be the perceived inferiority of other people. Emotions that we label contempt and scorn fit this situation.

Contempt and scorn involve feelings toward someone whom one considers low, worthless, or beneath notice (*Webster's New World Dictionary*, 1982). Ortony et al. (1988) characterize these types of emotions as *reproach* emotions in which one disapproves of someone else's blameworthy action. Contempt and scorn do not require a social comparison. One could reproach another person simply because he or she has violated a basic social norm without regard to how this person's behavior compares to one's own behavior (Ortony et al., 1988). However, there often seems a clear sense in which these emotions follow a perception that another person is inferior to the self in some important way. Furthermore, this person's inferiority seems deserved because of his or her blameworthy actions. As with other emotions resulting from a focus on the other, liking and disliking also seem important in contempt and scorn, as it is much easier to feel this way for people we dislike (Heider, 1958; Ortony et al., 1988). And, contemptible actions probably breed disliking in turn.

It is even possible to feel contempt for people who are our superior in certain important ways, if they are "contemptible" people. The perception of such moral inferiority may become a means of coping with this superiority (Montaldi, 1998), as research and theory on active downward comparisons might suggest (e.g., Gibbons & Gerrard, 1991; Wills, 1981). Active downward comparisons involve a more purposeful and selective focus on the real or imagined inferior attributes of another person. Possibly, such perceptions are especially effective for coping with another's superiority because they shift the focus away from one's own inferiority. Instead, the apparent moral inferiority of this person holds center stage. Also, like Fleming, people are capable of getting considerable pleasure out of heaping scorn on others, perhaps most readily when their self-esteem could do with a boost (Gibbons & Gerrard, 1991; Wills, 1981).

Dual Focus: *Schadenfreude*

Is there a downward contrastive emotion following from a dual focus? The pleasure resulting from recognizing one's superiority may sometimes come evenly blended with the contempt derived from noticing the blameworthy inferiority of the other person. Emotion terms are scarce for this type of situation (Ortony et al., 1988), but one possibility is *schadenfreude*, pleasure at the misfortunes of others (Brigham, Kelso, Jackson, & Smith, 1997; Heider, 1958; Smith et al., 1996). In the case of pride, the other person's disadvantage establishes one's superiority, but there is little sense that one is pleased by the other person's disadvantageper se. With contempt, one may receive a benefit to the self from noticing the other's contemptible actions, but this benefit is not the salient feature of the emotion. *Schadenfreude*, however, seems to involve both features. The self-enhancing aspect of the downward comparison provides the pleasure (Brigham et al., 1997), and the apparently contemptible aspects of the person may produce the malicious edge that also seems part of the emotion. *Schadenfreude* is clearly part of Fleming's repertoire of emotions. As mentioned earlier, he felt pleasure rather than pity when he witnessed a group of fearful, retreating soldiers. Part of this pleasure had a scornful flavor. As they passed, he noted to himself that they reassembled "soft, ungainly animals" (Crane, 1952/1895, p. 68). Another part of his pleasure followed from self-enhancement, as the sight of these soldiers let him conclude that "perhaps, he was not so bad after all" (Crane, 1952/1895, p. 68).

Downward Assimilative Emotions

> The battle reflection that shone for an instant in the faces on the mad current made the youth feel that forceful hands from heaven would not have been able to have held him in place if he could have got intelligent control of his legs. (Crane, 1952/1895, p. 39)

When Fleming sees the fearful retreating troops *after* his own cowardly actions, he feels *schadenfreude*. However, much earlier in the novel, *before* he has experienced battle, he is fraught with uncertainty about whether he will run, and so he has a very different reaction to a similar sight. He sees the chaotic stampede of retreating soldiers, and this makes him worry about how he will react. He fears that "composite monster" of battle will cause him to "... run better than the best of them" (Crane, 1952/1895, p. 39), as indeed it does. Untested as he was and seeing no obvious differences between these men and himself, Fleming found it difficult to conclude that he would react much differently. This type of reaction can be described as generally *assimilative*, but, unlike its upward counterpart, the implications are *negative* rather than *positive* for the self. As Heider (1958) phrases it, "... with the reality of *o's* [the other's] lot the possibility of *p's* [the person's] is given ... *o's* misfortune brings the possibility to *p's* mind that he [or she] also might suffer" (p. 288). The comparison between the self and the other, rather than suggesting contrast, creates a sense of impending similarity in fate (e.g., Aspinwall, 1997; Brickman & Bulman, 1977; Brown & Inouye, 1978; Buunk & Ybema, 1997; Collins, 1996; Gibbons & Gerrard, 1991; Wood & VanderZee, 1997).

Once again, expectations about whether one will become like the disadvantaged person, based on one's sense of control, appear especially important in understanding such assimilative reactions. Whereas downward comparisons produce contrast effects when perceived control is high, when perceived control is low the uninviting possibilities produce assimilative effects (e.g., Major et al., 1991; Wood & VanderZee, 1997).

TYPES OF DOWNWARD ASSIMILATIVE EMOTIONS

What useful distinctions can be made among types of downward assimilative emotions? Little theory and research have examined this question. Until recently, the major focus of research on downward comparisons has been on their beneficial contrastive effects. As noted above, the more recent research has involved demonstrating that the effects can be generally either positive or negative. Examining the implications of self versus other focus may suggest possibilities here as well.

Self-Focus: Worry and Fear

Fleming's realization that he probably will run when confronted by battle (made evident by seeing the other fearful soldiers) is an example of a downward assimilative comparison, in which the focus of the comparison seems to be on the negative implications for the self. In such cases, the other person establishes the negative possible outcome, but it is the prospect of a similar outcome for the self, rather than its unfortunate attainment by the other person, that anchors one's thoughts and generates negative feelings. What labels do we have for such feelings? They seem to fit the category of fear or anxiety emotions in which one is upset about the prospect of an undesirable event (Lazarus, 1991; Ortony et al., 1988). Certainly such emotions fit the examples emerging from the research on downward comparisons made by cancer patients (Taylor & Lobel, 1989), in particular those that involve the domain of actual physical condition as opposed to coping behavior (Wood & VanderZee, 1997).

The fear and worry resulting from a downward assimilative comparison may have uniquely powerful qualities. Linking the negative outcome to a specific person, especially someone similar in other key respects, brings the negative prospects close to home. When Fleming first joined the army, he felt superior to his school friends who had to remain at home. But, this view of things dissipated soon enough when he found himself near the battle lines and he sees his first dead soldier. At this sight he assumed "... the demeanor of one who knows he is doomed" (Crane, 1952/1895, p. 32). People are often unrealistically optimistic in assessing their relative risk for various negative outcomes (e.g., Weinstein, 1980). However, learning that someone very similar to ourselves has suffered a negative outcome may effectively shake us free from excessive forms of biased thinking. For example, in a series of studies by Alicke, Klotz, Breitenbecher, Yurak, and Vredenburg (1995), unrealistic optimism was systematically reduced as the target of comparison became more individuated; that is, when participants compared themselves with an actual person rather than the "average person." This reduction was most successful when participants had personal contact with this person.

Other Focus: Pity

What emotion might follow from a downward assimilative comparison focusing more on the other person? Pity seems a good candidate here. When we feel pity, we feel sorrow for another's suffering or misfortune (e.g., Lazarus, 1991; Ortony et al., 1988; Weiner, 1986). Pity is especially intense if the suffering is unusual (Ortony et al., 1988), if the person appears undeserving of his or her misfortune (Ortony et al., 1988; Weiner, 1986), if we have reason to like the person (Ortony et al., 1988), and if the cause of the other person's misfortune appears uncontrollable (Weiner, Graham, & Chandler, 1982). In the case of social comparison-based pity, the same factors that intensify pity in general also might serve to keep the focus of the comparisons on the suffering person rather on the implications of this suffering for one's own future outcomes. Although one's general reaction is assimilative in nature, and thus one feels a downward pull of similarity with the other on the dimension of comparison, the extraordinary nature of this undeserved suffering (in a person who is liked) may tighten a focus on this suffering.

Further contributing to a focus on the other person in social comparison-based pity is that this person is suffering in a *relative* sense. Research on altruism is instructive on this point. Thompson, Cowan, and Rosenhan (1980) induced either egocentric sadness (self-focused) or empathic sadness (other focused) in participants who were then placed in a position to act altruistically toward another person. Empathic sadness produced much more altruism than egocentric sadness. Noting these earlier findings, Rosenhan, Salovey, and Hargis (1981) suggest that the decision to help another person often involves a "tacit" social comparison in which a person assesses whether his or her plight is greater or less than that of the other person. Determining that the other person's situation is worse than one's own leads to thoughts focused on this person's situation. This direction of attention makes helping more likely.

Dual Focus: Sympathy

What type of emotion might result from a downward assimilative comparison having a dual focus? The feeling would need to incorporate both the worry and fear over one's future outcomes plus a pity for the current disadvantaged condition of the other person. Perhaps sympathy fits best. Although sympathy is often used synonymously with pity (Lazarus, 1991; Ortony et al., 1988), there also is a sense in which it is different from pity. Whereas definitions of pity clearly focus on the concern and sorrow over another person's situation, definitions of sympathy emphasize the kinship in feeling that enables a person to share in the misfortune of another person (*Webster's New World Dictionary*, 1982). In other words, in contrast to pity, sympathy involves a clearer sense of similarity between the self and the other person. With sympathy, the sense of potential similarity in outcomes is evident and at the same time one feels concerned over the misfortune currently being experienced by the other person. As part of sympathy involves a focus on the other person, deservingness and liking will play an important role in determining the precise nature of the feeling (e.g., Brigham et al, 1997; Heider, 1958; Ortony et al., 1988; Weiner, 1986). For example, in the study by Brigham et al. (1997), sympathy toward the person experiencing the misfortune was measured in addition to *schadenfreude*. Participants' sympathy was positively correlated with their perceptions that the misfortune was undeserved.

REVIEW OF THE MAIN CONCEPTUAL THEMES

Assimilation, Contrast, and Perceived Control

Guided by classic and more recent empirical work on social comparisons, my analysis began with the assumption that emotional reactions to social comparisons come in at least four general forms resulting from upward or downward comparisons that can be either a pleasant or an unpleasant experience. I have tried to make the further point that emotional reactions to social comparison can be either assimilative or contrastive in nature. Predicting these two different reactions may come down to whether the comparer can expect to have control over the discrepancy, either closing the gap in the case of upward comparisons or maintaining it in the case of downward comparisons. This theme emerges graphically in Fig. 1 in the form of diagonals: The assimilative diagonal runs from inspiration across and down to sympathy, while the contrastive diagonal runs from *schadenfreude* up and across to envy.

Focus of Attention in the Context of Relativistic Judgments

Another main theme of this analysis is that these emotions may tend to differ in terms of focus, either on the self, the other, or a dual focus. This is a tricky claim to make because, to the extent that each of these emotions can be social comparison-inspired, the focus will always be a matter of proportion, Without a degree of dual focus, they would lack relativistic roots. However, one advantage of making this claim is that it suggests interesting complexities in these emotions. On the one hand, a social comparison-based emotion results from the implications of the comparison for the self. Does this other person's bravery mean that *I* am a coward? Yes, I ran in battle, but look at these others that did the same or worse. Perhaps, I am not so bad. Social comparison theory is, first and foremost, a theory of *self*-evaluation, and part of the reason why social comparisons create emotions is that they can contribute so heavily to self-evaluations. On the other hand, social comparison-based emotions also are about the "fortunes of others." Thus, to this extent, they involve reactions to a positive or negative event happening to another person. As noted earlier, our reactions to the comparison are affected by how much we like the other person and how much we perceive the comparison difference to be deserved. Thus, a particular social comparison-based emotion, depending on the focus of the comparison and the proportion of focus, can produce a mixture of feelings linked to a complex set of contributing factors. Of course, the dual focus roots of social comparison-based emotions also show that the basic perception of whether an event is positive or negative, or either the self or the other, will always be relativistic in nature.

ADDITIONAL THEMES

Outcome Interdependence

The fact that a social comparison can affect a person's self-evaluation and emotional state establishes an interdependence of outcomes between the self and the other person. Contrastive reactions to social comparisons involve *noncorrespondent* outcomes between the self and the other person (Kelley & Thibaut, 1978). What this means is that what is good for the other person has negative implication for the self. In Fig. 1, this is represented by the contrastive diagonal. These reactions can also be described as "ill will emotions" in which "... the desirability of the event for the self is not congruent with the desirability of the event for the other" (Ortony et al., 1988, p. 92). In Heider's (1958) terms, these represent *discordant* reactions.

The notion of noncorrespondence is a particularly useful one because it highlights the fact that tangible outcomes emerging from social comparisons often play a major role in determining reactions. Regardless of liking and deservingness, for example, if another person's gain directly leads to our own disadvantage, then displeasure is a natural response. And if another person's disadvantage directly leads to our own advantage, pleasure is a natural response. As many scholars have pointed out, competitive, zero-sum situations are ideal breeding grounds for various feelings of ill will (e.g., Elster, 1989; Foster, 1972; Russell, 1930; Schoeck, 1969). When there is competition for limited, important resources, another person's success is usually at one's own expense. In general, the vicissitudes in one person's fortunes will have immediate incongruent effects on the fortunes of another person, bringing about the contrastive feelings of pride, scorn, and *schadenfreude* or depression, resentment, and envy, depending who has gained or lost the advantage.

Whereas the contrastive diagonal tends to involve noncorrespondent outcomes, the assimilative diagonal tends to involve *correspondent* outcomes (Kelley & Thibaut, 1978), meaning that what is good for the other person will translate into something pleasant for the self, and what is bad for the other person is unpleasant for the self. Goodwill emotions, rather than ill will emotions, usually result (Ortony et al., 1988). In Heider's (1958) terms, these represent *concordant* reactions. Variations in either person's outcomes will have immediate congruent effect on the other person, bringing about the assimilative feelings of admiration, optimism, and inspiration or fear, pity, and sympathy, depending on whether the outcomes are good or bad.

Connections among Emotions

To a degree, the laying out of the four general types of emotions following from social comparison may create the impression that these emotions are unconnected, operating separately from one another. This is far from the case. For example, one emotion may set the stage for another. My collaborators and I have done a series of studies examining the link between envy and *schadenfreude* (Brigham et al., 1997; Smith et al., 1996). At first glance, these emotions may seem quite independent from each other. For one thing, envy results from a painful upward comparison, while *schadenfreude* results from a pleasurable downward comparison. However, they are both contrastive in kind (as well as noncorrespondent and discordant). The pain of envy is caused by another person's good fortune and the pleasure of *schadenfreude* is caused by another's bad fortune. The positive outcomes for one person seem to actually lead to negative outcomes for the other (with envy) and vice versa (with *schadenfreude*).

In these studies we reasoned that the conditions associated with envy would create circumstances ripe for *schadenfreude*, if a misfortune allows the envy-producing upward comparison to be transformed into a downward comparison. First of all, as noted earlier, a facet of envy often includes a sense that the envied person is undeserving of his or her advantage. And so, if this person subsequently suffers a misfortune, it may be natural to feel pleased. At least in a subjective sense, things are now how they "ought" to be (Heider, 1958). Envy also involves hostility and dislike aimed at the advantaged person, and thus a misfortune befalling the envied person appeases this antipathy as well. Finally, there are at least two senses in which the misfortune might benefit the person feeling envy. In competitive situations, this misfortune might lead to this person's direct gain, which should be pleasing to some degree. Also, the misfortune may go far in eliminating the basis for the invidious comparison. In fact, if the misfortune is of sufficient magnitude, the unpleasant feelings derived from a contrastive and seemingly irrevocable upward comparison can be transformed into the pleasing feelings derived from a contrastive downward comparison. The pleasure of release from invidious feelings also is all the more robust because it is compatible with the sense that the misfortune befalls a dislikeable person who now appears to be getting what he or she deserves.

In the first study (Smith et al., 1996), participants watched a videotaped interview of another student who was applying for medical school. Envy was manipulated by having this student appear either average or superior in terms of academic achievements and social life. At the end of the interview, an epilogue informed participants that the student had to delay plans for medical school because of an infraction he had committed. This misfortune suffered by the superior student created greater *schadenfreude* than when it was suffered by the average student. Furthermore, this effect was largely mediated by envious feelings measured before the misfortune. A second study (Brigham et al., 1997) replicated this effect and generalized it to situations in which the misfortune was undeserved. Even when the person suffering the misfortune played no role in this outcome, as long as participants envied this person, they tended to feel happy as a result.

THE SIGNIFICANCE OF SOCIAL COMPARISON-BASED EMOTIONS

An Evolutionary Perspective

One way of making a case for the importance of social comparison-based emotions is to suggest their role in human evolution (Buunk & Ybema, 1997; Gilbert, 1992). Festinger (1954) linked social comparison processes with adaptive behaviors, but his emphasis was not on emotions but on accurate self-assessment. Gilbert (1992) has made a particularly strong case for the evolutionary underpinnings of our capacities to compare ourselves with others and also has discussed the various emotions that often result from these comparisons. It appears that one of our basic motivations is desire for social status and prestige, if only because this leads to prevailing in the realm of sexual selection. Social success in the pursuit of important resources translates into reproductive success (Barash, 1977; Gilbert, 1992; Krebs, Davies, & Parr, 1993). One key to operating in an environment where there is competition for dominance is that one must be able to recognize where one stands. The ability to recognize the true features of a social hierarchy and act accordingly (either submissively or dominantly) is highly adaptive, which appears to be why one sees this ability in many animal species as well as human beings. The ability to make reasonably accurate social comparison must be at the core of the ability, and thus it is likely to be "... phylogenetically very old, biologically powerful" (Gilbert, Price, & Allan, 1995, p. 149). Indeed, the capacity to make such comparisons may have gone hand in hand with the development of sense of self. With humans, the consequences of where one falls in the social hierarchy (given one's relative share of important reproduction-enhancing resources) appear to contribute powerfully to self-esteem. Social comparison-based emotions are possibly the clearest markers for how well or poorly we believe we rank on attributes that matter in important social hierarchies.

Rousseau on Social Comparsion-Based Emotions

A particularly interesting perspective on social comparison-based emotions that in some way presaged evolutionary ideas was outlined by Rousseau (1984/1754) in his classic work, *A Discourse on Inequality*. Rousseau notes that the most important differences among people are artificial. This is because they are based on societal processes that exaggerate the effects of natural inequalities, such as difference in intelligence and strength. If we were to live in solitary state, these natural inequalities would be of no consequence, as long as we were strong and savvy enough to find food and shelter. Rousseau argues that over the course of human history, we have increased our interactions with other people, and as a result social comparisons begin to dominate our perceptions and emotions:

> People become accustomed to judging different objects and to making comparisons; gradually they acquire ideas of merit and of beauty, which in turn produce feelings of preference ... Each began to look at the others and to want to be looked at himself; and public esteem came to be prized. He who sang or danced the best; he who was the most handsome, the strongest, the most adroit or the most eloquent became the most highly regarded, and this was the first step toward inequality and at the same time toward vice. From those first preferences there arose, on the one side vanity and scorn, on the other shame and envy, and the fermentation produced by these new leavens finally produced compounds fatal to happiness and innocence. (p. 114)

Rousseau also claims that our sense of self shifted with the progression as well. Whereas in the "state of nature" people possessed a self-love simply flowing from finding sustenance, shelter, and avoiding physical injury, people in the society of others developed *amour propre*, a kind of self-pride born of a developing desire to be superior to others and be admired by them. Rousseau tries to claim that human beings, by nature, are free from relativistic concerns. It is only when we started living in groups that these relativistic concerns, and the emotions resulting from them, began emerging. Current thinking would emphasize the way in which our proclivities have always evolved in a social, group context. If this is true, then we have always evolved as organisms that acknowledge and adapt to the relativistic and emotion-inducing facts of everyday life.

CONCLUSION

The developing theory and empirical evidence suggest that social comparison-based emotions are wide-ranging, consequential, and frequent. Yet, it is also the case that my analysis has focused only on what I considered to be the most obvious cases of social comparison-based emotions. Not only may other candidate emotions fit better, but, within each category of emotion, a finer-grained analysis could have been conducted. For example, one largely unexplored type of emotion arises when one's superiority is perceived as threatening to others (e.g., Brigham, 1996; Brickman & Bulman, 1977; Exline & Lobel, 1999; Foster, 1972). Fear of envy, as this emotion is sometimes labeled (Brigham, 1996), has been the basis for an extensive, anthropological analysis of human behavior (Foster, 1972), but has received little attention in social psychology. In fact, fear of envy is just one of a variety of interesting emotions that can result from recognizing one's relative advantage and thinking about how this advantage is being received (Leach, Iyer, & Snider, in press). These and other social comparison-based emotions represent unchartered, fertile territory for future social psychological research.

My analysis has relied heavily on Stephen Crane's novel to augment the existing theoretical and empirical research on social and comparison-based emotions. It seems fitting to conclude with a few additional facts about the novel. *The Red Badge of Courage* was published before Crane reached the age of 25. Although Crane had no experience in war, what was most remarkable about the novel was that it struck readers as being so true to what war must be like. Just as the photography of Mathew Brady had documented the external realities of the Civil War, it seemed to convey in an original way the psychological realities of war. His insights into human nature appear no less accurate for the contemporary reader. Certainly, when it comes to a subtle understanding of how our emotions are affected by social comparisons, the developing scientific evidence shows that Crane was right on the mark.

REFERENCES

Abramson, L. Y., Seligman, M., & Teasdale, J. D. (1978). Learned helplessness in humans: Critique and reformulation. *Journal of Abnormal Psychology, 87*, 49–74.

Ahrens, A. H., & Alloy, L. B. (1997). Social comparison processes in depression. In B. P. Buunk & F. X. Gibbons (Eds.), *Health, coping, and well-being* (pp. 389–410). Mahwah, NJ: Lawrence Erlbaum.

Alicke, M. D., Klotz, M. L., Breitenbecher, D. L., Yurak, T. J., & Vredenburg, D. S. (1995). Personal contact, individuation, and the better-then-average effect. *Journal of Personality and Social Psychology, 68*, 804–825.

Aspinwall, L. G. (1997). Future-oriented aspects of social comparisons: A framework for studying health-related comparison activity. In B. P. Buunk & F. X. Gibbons (Eds.), *Health, coping, and well-being* (pp. 125–166). Mahwah, NJ: Lawrence Erlbaum.

Ausubel, D. P. (1955). Relationships between shame and guilt in the socialization process. *Psychological Review, 67*, 378–390.

Barash, D. P. (1977). *Sociobiology and behavior.* New York: Elsevier.

Baron, R. A., & Richardson, D. R. (1994). *Human aggression* (2nd ed.). New York: Plenum Press.

Beck, A. T. (1967). *Depression: Clinical, experimental, and theoretical aspects.* New York: Harper & Row.

Berger, S. M. (1977). Social comparison, modeling, and perseverance. In J. M. Suls & R. L. Miller (Eds.), *Social comparison processes: Theoretical and empirical perspectives,* (pp. 209–234). Washington, DC: Hemisphere.

Berke, J. (1988). *The tyranny of malice: Exploring the dark side of character and culture.* New York: Summit Books.

Brewer, M. B., & Weber, J. G. (1994). Self-evaluation effects of interpersonal versus intergroup comparison. *Journal of Personality and Social Psychology, 66*, 268–275.

Brickman, P., & Bulman, R. J. (1977). Pleasure and pain in social comparison. In J. M. Suls & R. L. Miller (Eds.), *Social comparison processes: Theoretical and empirical perspectives* (pp. 149–186). Washington, DC: Hemisphere.

Brigham, N. L. (1996). The effects of invidious comparisons on modest self-presentation. Unpublished doctoral dissertation, University of Kentucky.

Brigham, N. L., Kelso, K. A., Jackson, M. A., & Smith, R. H. (1997). The roles of invidious comparisons and deservingness in sympathy and *schadenfreude. Basic and Applied Social Psychology, 19*, 363–380.

Brown, I., Jr., & Inouye, D. K. (1978). Learned helplessness through modeling: The role of perceived similarity in competence. *Journal of Personality and Social Psychology, 36*, 900–908.

Brown, J. D., Novick, N. J., Lord, K. A., & Richards, J. M. (1992). When Gulliver travels: Social context, psychological closeness, and self-appraisals. *Journal of Personality and Social Psychology, 62*, 717–727.

Buunk, B. P., Collins, R. L., Taylor, S. E., VanYperen, N. W., & Dakof, G. A. (1990). The affective consequences of social comparison: Either direction has it ups and downs. *Journal of Personality and Social Psychology, 59*, 1238–1249.

Buunk, B. P. & Gibbons, F. X. (Ed). (1997). *Health, coping, and well-being: Perspectives from social comparison theory.* Mahwah, NJ: Lawrence Erlbaum.

Buunk, B. P., & Ybema, J. F. (1997). Social comparisons and occupational stress: The identification-contrast model. In B. P. Buunk & F. X. Gibbons (Eds.), *Health, coping, and well-being* (pp. 359–388). Mahwah, NJ: Lawrence Erlbaum.

Cialdini, R. B. (1993). *Influence: Science and practice* (3rd ed.). Glenview, IL: Scott Foresman.

Cialdini, R., Borden, R., Thorne, A., Walker, M., Freeman, S., & Sloan, L. (1976). Basking in reflected glory: Three (football) field studies. *Journal of Personality and Social Psychology, 34*, 366–375.

Collins, R. L. (1996). For better or worse: The impact of upward social comparison on self-evaluations. *Psychological Bulletin, 119*, 51–69.

Campos, J. J., Barrett, K. C., Lamb, M. E., Goldsmith, H. H., & Stenberg, C. (1983). Socioemotional development. In P. H. Mussen (Ed.). *Handbook of child psychology* (Vol. 2, pp. 783–915). New York: Wiley.

Crane, S. (1952/1895). *The red badge of courage,* New York: Signet.

Crosby, R. (1976). A model of egoistic relative deprivation. *Psychological Review, 83*, 85–113.

Davis, J. A., (1959). A formal interpretation of the theory of relative deprivation. *Sociometry, 22*, 280–296.

Elster, J. (1989). *The cement of society.* New York: Cambridge University Press.

Exline, J. J., & Lobel, M. (1999). The perils of outperformance: Sensitivity about being the target of a threatening upward comparison. *Psychological Bulletin, 125*, 307–337.

Festinger, L. A. (1954). A theory of social comparison processes. *Human Relations, 7*, 117–140.

Folger, R. (1987). Reformulating the preconditions of resentment: A referent cognition model. In J. C. Masters & W. P. Smith (Eds.), *Social comparison, social justice and relative deprivation: Theoretical, empirical, and policy perspectives* (pp. 183–215). Hillsdale, NJ: Lawrence Erlbaum.

Folger, R., Rosenfield, D., & Rheaume, K. (1983a). Role-playing effects of likelihood and referent outcome on relative deprivation. *Representative Research in Social Psychology, 13*, 2–10.

Folger, R., Rosenfield, D., & Rheaume, K., & Martin, C. (1983b). Relative deprivation and referent cognitions. *Journal of Experimental Social Psychology, 19*, 172–184.

Folger, R., Rosenfield, D., & Robinson, T. (1983c). Relative deprivation and procedural justice effects. *Journal of Personality and Social Psychology, 45*, 268–273.

Foster, G. M. (1972). The anatomy of envy: A study in symbolic behavior. *Current Anthropology, 13*, 165–202.

Gastorf, J. W., & Suls, J. (1978). Performance evaluation via social comparison: Performance similarity versus related attribute similarity. *Social Psychology, 41*, 297–305.

Gibbons, F. X. (1986). Social comparison and depression: Company's effect on misery. *Journal of Personality and Social Psychology, 51*, 140–148.

Gibbons, R. X. (1990). The impact of focus of attention and affect on social behaviour. In W. R. Crozier (Ed.), *Shyness and embarrassment: Perspective from social psychology* (pp. 119–143). Cambridge: Cambridge University Press.

Gibbons, F. X., & Gerrard, M. (1991). Downward comparison and coping with threat. In J. Suls & T. A. Wills (Eds.), *Social comparison: Contemporary theory and research* (pp. 317–346). Hillsdale, NJ: Lawrence Erlbaum.

Gibbons, F. X., & Wicklund, R. A. (1976). Selective exposure to the self. *Journal of Research in Personality, 10*, 98–106.

Gilbert, P. (1992). *Depression: The evolution of powerlessness*. New York: Guilford Press.

Gilbert, P. & Andrews, B. (Eds.) (1998). *Shame: Interpersonal behavior, psychopathology, and culture*. New York: Oxford University Press

Gilbert, P., Price, J., & Allan, S. (1995). Social comparison, social attractiveness and evolution: How might they be related? *New Ideas in Psychology, 13*, 149–165.

Goethals, G. R. & Darley, J. (1977). Social comparison theory: An attributional approach. In J. M. Suls & R. L. Miller (Eds.), *Social comparison processes: Theoretical and empirical perspectives* (pp. 259–278). Washington, DC: Hemisphere.

Goffman, E. (1963). *Stigma*. Englewood Cliffs, NJ: Prentice-Hall.

Heider, F. (1958). *The psychology of interpersonal relations*. New York: John Wiley.

Higgins, E. T. (1987). Self-discrepancy: A theory relating self and affect. *Psychological Review, 94*, 319–340.

Holyoak, K. J., & Gordon, P. C. (1983). Social reference points. *Journal of Personality and Social Psychology, 44*, 881–887.

Ingram, R. E., Lumry, A. E., Cruet, E., & Sieber, W. (1987). Attentional processes in depressive disorders. *Cognitive Therapy and Research, 11*, 351–360.

Ingram, R. E., Johnson, B. R., Bernet, C. Z., & Dombeck, M. (1992). Vulnerability to distress: Cognitive and emotional reactivity in chronically self-focussed individuals. *Cognitive Therapy and Research, 16*, 451–472.

Ingram, R. E., & Smith, T. W. (1984). Depression and internal versus external focus of attention. *Cognitive Therapy and Research, 8*, 139–152.

Kelley, H. H. (1967). Attribution in social psychology. *Nebraska Symposium on Motivation, 15*, 192–238.

Kelley, H. H. (1972). Causal schemata and the attribution process. In E. E. Jones, D. E. Kanouse, H. H. Kelley, R. E. Nisbett, S. Valins, & B. Weiner (Eds.), *Attribution: Perceiving the causes of behavior* (pp. 151–174). Morristown, NJ: General Learning Press.

Kelley, H. H., & Thibaut, J. W. (1978). *Interpersonal relations*. New York: John Wiley & Sons.

Krebs, J. R., Davies, N. B., & Parr, J. (1993). An introduction to behavioural ecology (3rd ed.). Oxford, England: Blackwell Scientific Publications.

Lazarus, R. S. (1991). *Emotion and adaptation*. New York: Oxford University Press.

Leach, C. W., Iyer, A., & Snider, N. (In press). Spoiling the consciences of the fortunate: The experience of relative advantage and support for social equality. In I. Walker & H. J. Smith (Eds.), *Relative deprivation: Specification, development, and integration*. New York and Cambridge: Cambridge University Press.

Leach, C. W., Webster, J. M., Smith, R. H., Kelso, K., Brigham, N., & Garonzik, R. (2000). The social comparison style questionnaire: Assessing tendencies to contrast or assimilate upward and downward comparisons. Manuscript submitted for publication.

Lewis, H. B. (1971). *Shame and guilt in neurosis*. New York: International Universities Press.

Lockwood, P., & Kunda, Z. (1997). Superstars and me: Predicting the impact of role models on the self. *Journal of Personality and Social Psychology, 73*, 91–103.

Major, B., Testa, M., & Bylsma, W. H. (1991). Responses to upward and downward comparisons: The impact of esteem-relevance and perceived control. In J. Suls & T. A. Wills (Eds.), *Social comparison: Contemporary theory and research* (pp. 237–260). Hillsdale, NJ: Lawrence Erlbaum.

Markman, K. D., Gavanski, I., Sherman, S. J., & McMullen, M. N. (1993). The mental simulation of better and worse possible worlds. *Journal of Experimental Social Psychology, 29*, 87–109.

Markus, H., & Nurius, P. (1986). Possible selves. *American Psychologist, 41*, 954–969.

Master, J. C., & Keil, L. J. (1987). Generic comparison processes in human judgment and behavior. In J. C. Master & W. P. Smith (Eds.), *Social comparison, social justice and relative deprivation: Theoretical, empirical, and policy perspectives* (pp. 11–54). Hillsdale, NJ: Lawrence Erlbaum.

McMullen, M. N., Markman, K. D., & Gavinski, I. (1995). Living in neither the best nor worst of all possible worlds: Antecedents and consequences of upward and downward counterfactual thinking. In N. J. Roese & J. M. Olson (Eds.), *What might have been: The social psychology of counterfactual thinking* (pp. 133–167). Mahwah, NJ: Lawrence Erlbaum.

Meichenbaum, D. H. (1971). Examination of model characteristics in reducing avoidance behavior. *Journal of Personality and Social Psychology, 17*, 298–307.

Mettee, D. R., & Smith, G. (1977). Social comparison and interpersonal attraction: The case for dissimilarity. In J. M. Suls & R. L. Miller (Eds.), *Social comparison processes: Theoretical and empirical perspectives* (pp. 69–101). Washington, DC: Hemisphere.

Miller, D. T., Turnbull, W., & McFarland, C. (1988). Particularistic and universalistic evaluation in the social comparison process, *Journal of Personality and Social Psychology, 55*, 908–917.

Montaldi, D. (1998). Review of research on the envy concept. Unpublished manuscript.

Morse, S., & Gergen, K. J. (1970). Social comparison, self-consistency, and the concept of self. *Journal of Personality and Social Psychology, 40*, 624–634.

Niedenthal, P. M., Tangney, J. P., & Gavanski, I. (1994). "If only I weren't" versus "If only I hadn't": Distinguishing shame and guilt in conterfactual thinking. *Journal of Personality and Social Psychology, 67*, 585–595.

Nix, G., Watson, C., Pyszczynski, T., & Greenberg, J. (1995). Reducing depressive affect through external focus of attention. *Journal of Social and Clinical Psychology, 14*, 36–52.

Ortony, A., Clore, G. L., & Collins, A. (1988). *Cognitive structure of emotions*. New York: Cambridge University Press.

Parrott, W. G. (1991). The emotional experiences of envy and jealousy. In P. Salovey (Ed.), *The psychology of jealousy and envy* (pp. 3–30). New York: Guilford.

Pyszczynski, T., & Greenberg, J. (1986). Evidence for a depressive self-focussing style. *Journal of Research in Personality, 20*, 95–106.

Pyszczynski, T., & Greenberg, J. (1987). Self-regulatory perseveration and the depressive self-focussing style: A self-awareness theory of the development and maintenance of depression. *Psychological Bulletin, 102*, 122–138.

Pyszczynski, T., Holt, K., & Greenberg, J. (1987). Depression, self-focussed attention and expectancies for future positive and negative events for self and others. *Journal of Personality and Social Psychology, 52*, 994–1001.

Roese, N. J., & Olson, J. M. (1995). *What might have been: The social psychology of counterfactual thinking*. Mahwah, NJ: Lawrence Erlbaum.

Rosenhan, D. L., Salovey, P., & Hargis, K. (1981). The joys of helping: Focus of attention mediates the impact of positive affect on altruism. *Journal of Personality and Social Psychology, 40*, 899–905.

Rousseau, J. (1984). *A discourse on inequality*. New York: Viking Penguin. (originally published in 1754) (translated by Maurice Cranston)

Runciman, W. G. (1966). *Relative deprivation and social justice: A study of attitudes to social inequality in twentieth-century England*. London: Routledge & Kegan Paul.

Russell, B. (1930). *The conquest of happiness*. New York: Liveright.

Salovey, P. (1991). Social comparison processes in envy and jealousy. In J. Suls & T. A. Wills (Eds.), *Social comparison: Contemporary theory and research* (pp. 261–285) Hillsdale, NJ: Lawrence Erlbaum.

Salovey, P., & Rodin, J. (1984). Some antecedents and consequences of social-comparison jealousy. *Journal of Personality and Social Psychology, 47*, 780–792.

Schoeck, H. (1969). *Envy: A theory of social behavior*. New York: Harcourt, Brace, and World.

Seta, F. (1982). The impact of comparison processes on coactors' task performance. *Journal of Personality and Social Psychology, 42*, 281–291.

Silver, M., & Sabini, J. (1978). The perception of envy. *Social Psychology Quarterly, 41*, 105–117.

Smith, R. H. (1991). Envy and the sense of injustice. In P. Salovey (Ed.), *The psychology of jealousy and envy* (pp. 79–99). New York: Guilford.

Smith, R. H., Diener, E., & Garonzik, R. (1990). The roles of comparison level and alternative comparison domains in the perception of envy. *British Journal of Social Psychology, 29*, 247–255.

Smith, R. H., & Insko, C. A. (1987). Social comparison choices during ability evaluation: The effects of comparison publicity, performance feedback, and self-esteem. *Personality and Social Psychology Bulletin, 13*, 111–122.

Smith, R. H., Parrott, W. G., Ozer, D., & Moniz, A. (1994). Subjective injustice and inferiority as predictors of hostile and depressive feelings in envy. *Personality and Social Psychology Bulletin, 20,* 705–711.

Smith, R. H., Turner, T. J., Garonzik, R., Leach, C. W., Druskat, V. U., & Weston, C. M. (1996). Envy and *schadenfreude. Personality and Social Psychology Bulletin, 22,* 158–168.

Smith, R. H., Webster, J. M., & Parrott, W. G. (2000). The role of publicity in guilt and shame. Manuscript submitted for publication.

Smith, T. W. & Greenberg, J. (1981). Depression and self-focused attention. *Motivation and Emotion, 5,* 323–331.

Smith, T. W., Ingram, R. E., & Roth, D. L. (1985). Self-focussed attention and depression: Self-evaluation, affect and life stress. *Motivation and Emotion, 9,* 381–389.

Solomon, R. C. (1976). *The passions.* Garden City, NY: Anchor Press.

Srull, T. K., & Gaelick, L. (1983). General principles and individual differences in the self as a habitual reference point: An examination of self-other judgments of similarity. *Social Cognition, 2,* 108–121.

Sullivan, H. S. (1953). *Clinical studies in psychiatry.* New York: Norton.

Suls, J. & Miller, R. L. (Eds.) (1977). *Social comparison processes: Theoretical and empirical perspectives.* New York: Hemisphere.

Suls, J. M., & Miller, R. L. (Eds.) (1977). *Social comparison processes.* Washington DC: Hemisphere.

Suls, J., & Wan, C. K. (1987). In search of the false-uniqueness phenomenon: Fear and estimates of social consensus. *Journal of Personality and Social Psychology, 52,* 211–217.

Suls, J. M., & Wills, T. A. (Eds.) (1991). *Social comparison: Contemporary theory and research.* Hillsdale, NJ: Lawrence Erlbaum.

Swallow, S. R., & Kuiper, N. A. (1992). Mild depression and frequency of social comparison behavior. *Journal of Social and Clinical Psychology, 11,* 167–180.

Tangney, J. P. (1998). How does guilt differ from shame? In J. Bybee (Ed.), *Guilt and children* (pp. 1–17). New York: Academic Press.

Taylor, S. E., & Lobel, M. (1989). Social comparison activity under threat: Downward evaluation and upward contacts. *Psychological Review, 96,* 569–575.

Tesser, A. (1988). Toward a self-evaluation maintenance model of social behavior. In L. Berkowitz (Ed.), *Advances in experimental social psychology* (Vol. 20, pp. 181–227). New York: Academic Press.

Tesser, A. (1991). Emotion in social comparison and reflection processes. In J. Suls & T. A. Wills (Eds.), *Social comparison: Contemporary theory and research* (pp. 115–145). Hillsdale, NJ: Lawrence Erlbaum.

Tesser, A., Millar, M., & Moore, J. (1988). Some affective consequences of social comparison and reflection processes: The pain and pleasure of being close. *Journal of Personality and Social Psychology, 54,* 49–61.

Testa, M., & Major, B. (1990). The impact of social comparison after failure: The moderating effects of perceived control. *Basic and Applied Social Psychology, 11,* 205–218.

Thompson, W. C., Cowan, C. L. & Rosenhan, D. L. (1980). Focus of attention mediates the impact of negative affect on altruism. *Journal of Personality and Social Psychology, 38,* 291–300.

Webster, J. M., Weeter, C., & Smith, R. H. (2000). Does praise mean better than others? Manuscript in preparation.

Webster's new world dictionary (2nd ed.). (1982). New York: Simon & Schuster.

Wedell, D. H. (1994). Contextual contrast in evaluative judgments: A test of pre- versus postintegration models of contrast. *Journal of Personality and Social Psychology, 66,* 1007–1019.

Weiner, B. (1986). *An attributional theory of motivation and emotion.* New York: Springer-Verlag.

Weiner, B., Graham, S., & Chandler, C. (1982). Pity, anger, and guilt: An attributional analysis. *Personality and Social Psychology Bulletin, 8,* 226–232.

Weinstein, N. D. (1980). Unrealistic optimism about future life events. *Journal of Personality and Social Psychology, 39,* 806–820.

Wheeler, L. (1966). Motivation as a determinant of upward comparison. *Journal of Experimental Social Psychology, 2*(Suppl. 1), 27–31.

Wheeler, L., Martin, R., & Suls, J. (1997). The proxy model of social comparison for self-assessment of ability. *Personality and Social Psychology Review, 1,* 54–61.

Wheeler, L., & Miyake, K. (1992). Social comparison in everyday life. *Journal of Personality and Social Psychology, 62,* 760–773.

Wheeler, L., Shaver, K. G., Jones, R. A., Goethals, G. R., Cooper, J., Robinson, J. E., Gruder, C. L., & Butzine, K. W. (1969). Factors determing choice of a comparison other. *Journal of Experimental Social Psychology, 5,* 219–232.

Wills, T. A. (1981). Downward comparison principles in social psychology. *Psychological Bulletin, 90,* 245–271.

Wilson, S. R., & Benner, L. A. (1971). The effects of self-esteem and situation upon comparison choices during ability evaluation. *Sociometry, 34,* 381–397.

Wood, J. V. (1989). Theory and research concerning social comparison of personal attributes. *Psychological Bulletin*, *106*, 213–248.

Wood, J. V., Saltzberg, J. A., Neale, J. M., Stone, A. A., & Rachmiel, T. B. (1990). Self-focused attention, coping responses, and distressed mood in everyday life. *Journal of Personality and Social Psychology*, *58*, 1027–1036.

Wood, J. V., & VanderZee, K. (1997). Social comparisons among cancer patients: Under what conditions are comparisons upward and downward? In B. P. Buunk & F. X. Gibbons (Eds.), *Health, coping, and well-being* (pp. 299–328). Mahwah, NJ: Lawrence Erlbaum.

11

Examining Social Comparisons with the Test Selection Measure

Opportunities for the Researcher and the Research Participant

JOANNE V. WOOD

Imagine that you and a colleague have both been nominated for a prestigious, university-wide teaching award. In the end, your colleague wins the teaching award and you are crushed. If your goal is self-enhancement—to feel better about yourself—or at least to ensure that you do not feel any worse than you already do, what strategies of social comparison could you use? One possibility is that you could avoid comparing yourself with your colleague, to prevent further injury to your ego. A second possibility is that you could seek new comparisons with your colleague on the dimension of teaching ability, in an effort to convince yourself or others that you actually are the better teacher. For example, you could attend her class and see whether she can hold an audience of undergraduates as spellbound as you can. Or you could focus on your ability to nurture the creative talents of graduate students, a quality your colleague lacks. Alternatively, you could concede that your colleague is the better teacher, and you could seek out comparisons on dimensions other than teaching ability. Is she as happily married as you are? Is she as good at gardening?

Now imagine that you would like to use such comparative strategies, but you are a research participant in a study conducted by a social comparison researcher. What possibility for these comparative strategies would be available to you? In most social comparison studies conducted in the laboratory, you would have no opportunity to avoid comparisons altogether. And virtually no studies would offer you an opportunity to try to reverse your failure by seeking new comparisons on a dimension on which you failed, or to seek further comparisons on new dimensions unrelated to the failure. Instead, in the typical comparison study, you would be allowed to engage in only one strategy of comparison: selecting a comparison target. You would be presented with potential comparison targets, and you would choose between them. A typical finding would be that people who have just received some threat to their self-

JOANNE V. WOOD • Department of Psychology, University of Waterloo, Waterloo, Ontario, Canada N2L 3G1.

Handbook of Social Comparison: Theory and Research, edited by Suls and Wheeler. Kluwer Academic/Plenum Publishers, New York, 2000.

esteem would select targets who are "downward"—inferior to oneself—or at least, less "upward"—superior to oneself—than would people who have not been threatened (e.g., Smith & Insko, 1987).

This focus on target selection has flowed naturally from the dominant theoretical perspectives in social comparison. Festinger's (1954) central hypothesis was that people seek to compare themselves with others who are similar. His concept of a "unidirectional drive upward" also suggested that people may be biased to seek targets that are in the upward direction. Wills's (1981) downward comparison theory proposed that when people are threatened, they seek downward comparisons for self-enhancement. Target selection studies have been indispensable to testing such theoretical perspectives, and hence have been essential to the growth of social comparison theorizing.

At the same time, social comparison researchers' focus on target selections also has stunted that growth in two ways. First, target selection studies fail to capture a social comparison context that is prevalent and very consequential in everyday life, namely, one in which one fails or succeeds relative to another specific person. As in the teaching award scenario, that person may be a fixture in one's life, such as a colleague, and comparisons with him or her may be inevitable. In such cases, the target may be almost a given; selecting a different target may not be satisfactory or even possible. A second way in which researchers' almost exclusive focus on target selection has stunted theoretical development is that the kinds of comparative strategies that one might want to use in such social comparison circumstances—avoiding comparisons, selecting new comparison dimensions, and seeking new comparisons on the same dimension—have received little attention.

In this chapter, first I describe these comparative strategies in more detail. Then I briefly review methods that have been used to examine social comparisons and discuss why they largely have not permitted participants to use such comparative strategies. Then I devote the bulk of this chapter to describing a method that does allow participants to use such comparative strategies, results we have obtained with this method, and what this method has taught us about comparison process and function.

THREE RELATIVELY NEGLECTED SOCIAL COMPARISON STRATEGIES

Avoiding Comparisons

Social comparisons can be uncomfortable, even painful. As Brickman and Bulman (1977) wrote, "If two people compare themselves on a valued dimension ... Someone will feel bad, and both parties ... must be concerned with coping with these negative feelings" (p. 152). Brickman and Bulman (1977) provided many examples of how such discomfort may sometimes lead people to avoid social comparisons altogether. For example, friends may refrain from initiating discussions that will lead to mutual self-disclosure, academics may avoid circulating their curriculum vitae, and people often choose not to attend their high school reunions.

Avoiding comparisons may be more properly seen as a self-protective strategy than as a true self-enhancement strategy. That is, avoiding comparisons is not likely to make one feel better, but merely to prevent or lessen one's pain. The distinction between self-protection and self-enhancement has become important in the literature on self-esteem. Baumeister, Tice, and Hutton (1989) proposed that for people with high self-esteem, the primary goal is self-enhancement, whereas for people with low self-esteem, the primary goal is self-protection (cf. Arkin, 1981; Schlenker, Weigold, & Hallam, 1990). That is, whereas highs are oriented toward achieving gains for their self-esteem, lows are oriented primarily toward avoiding losses. Hence, lows try to avoid exposing their failures and weaknesses. Whereas highs are bold and willing to take risks to achieve gains for their self-esteem, lows are more risk-averse (cf. Josephs, Larrick, Steele, & Nisbett, 1992a). Evidence is accumulating that supports this view of low self-esteem people as cautious and self-protective (e.g., Steele, Spencer, & Lynch, 1993; Tice, 1991).

Despite the relevance of self-protection to the literatures on coping strategies and self-esteem, and despite the relevance of the avoidance of social comparison to the development of social comparison theory, researchers have devoted little empirical attention to social comparison avoidance. Some studies have examined the avoidance of certain types of comparisons. For example, when individuals believe that their ability is particularly low, they tend to avoid highly upward comparisons (e.g., Smith & Insko, 1987). What participants may really prefer, however, is to avoid comparisons altogether.

Selecting New Comparison Dimensions

When people fail or receive a threat to self-esteem in one domain, they may counteract that threat by focusing on their other assets or talents. For example, Baumeister and Jones (1978) found that participants who had received a negative evaluation rated themselves very favorably on dimensions unrelated to that evaluation. Similarly, participants who had failed a test of intellectual ability were especially likely to offer to help another person (Brown & Smart, 1991). The idea that people may counteract a threat in one domain by drawing on strengths in other domains is central to Steele's (1988) theory of self-affirmation. Self-affirmation theory holds that when people encounter a threat to some domain of self, they need not counter that threat specifically. Rather, they need to restore their overall self-worth. Hence, after a failure, one may restore one's self-image by affirming important aspects of oneself, aspects that may be unrelated to the domain in which one failed.

This strategy of focusing on dimensions unrelated to the dimension on which one has been threatened also may be useful as a social comparison strategy. My colleagues and I first became aware of this possibility in an interview study of women who had been diagnosed with breast cancer. We noticed that during the course of their interviews, respondents often drew comparisons between themselves and other people. These remarks, which offered a gold mine of unanticipated comparison data, were coded into categories (Wood, Taylor, & Lichtman, 1985). One of these categories was "dimensional comparisons," in which the focus seemed to be not on a specific comparison target but on a dimension of comparison. Many respondents appeared to focus selectively on dimensions on which they were advantaged. For example, women who had undergone lumpectomies, a less disfiguring surgery, drew comparisons with others who had had mastectomies, but mastectomy patients did not voice comparisons with women who had had lumpectomies. Older women compared themselves favorably with younger women (e.g., "That's a terrible, terrible thing for a young girl to face. It's different if you're an older woman like me"), but younger women did not compare themselves with older women. All these women could have focused their comparisons on people who did not have cancer, but they focused instead on ways in which they were more fortunate than others or superior to others.

The interview method permitted such "dimensional comparisons" because the researchers did not confine respondents' comparisons to a single dimension. This was not because the researchers possessed special insight; they had asked specific comparison questions about a single dimension, namely, coping ability, near the end of the interview. The richness of the comparative data that respondents spontaneously offered throughout their interviews (i.e., not in response to any question about comparison) became apparent only after the interviews were transcribed. It was then that the researchers noticed that when respondents were free to compare on any dimension they desired, they seemed to be selective about the dimensions on which they did so.

Seeking New Comparisons on the Same Dimension

When one's self-esteem is threatened by receiving unfavorable feedback in one domain, another strategy is to try to disconfirm that feedback directly. If one has failed a test, for example, one may study hard and take the test again. One also may try to behave in ways that contradict the negative feedback. For example, participants who had been told earlier that they were "self-oriented and apathetic to the concerns of others," were especially willing to be helpful to other people (Steele, 1975), and participants who had been told that they were "exploitative and competitive" behaved especially cooperatively (Baumeister, 1982).

This strategy of disconfirming negative feedback directly could be accomplished through social comparisons, by seeking new comparisons on the same dimension. In the teaching award example, I suggested that one could seek further comparisons with one's colleague's teaching ability, But in the social comparison literature, this strategy has received even less attention than the other two strategies. In the typical laboratory study, participants receive a score on a test that they have already taken and have no opportunity to try to reverse that feedback. They cannot take the test again or seek new comparisons on the dimension tapped by the test or on related dimensions.

Significance of These Three Strategies

Investigating these strategies would be valuable not only because it would provide a more comprehensive understanding of social comparison processes. The strategies of avoiding comparisons, selecting comparison dimensions, and seeking new comparisons on the same dimension also paint a new portrait of the individual seeking social comparisons. Target selection studies have portrayed the individual comparison seeker as selective, but that selectivity has been assumed to be constrained by the availability of comparison targets. These other comparison strategies allow the individual more flexibility than does target selection, because the individual is not limited by whatever comparison targets happen to be available (cf. Wood et al., 1985; Wood, 1989).

These strategies also have implications that go beyond the social comparison literature. Recently, my colleagues and I, writing about self-enhancement strategies in general, grouped together the two general strategies of disconfirming the self-esteem threat and focusing attention on dimensions unrelated to the threat (Wood & Dodgson, 1996; Wood, Giordano-Beech, & DuCharme, 1999). In the context of social comparisons, "disconfirming the self-esteem threat" would be accomplished by seeking new comparisons on the same dimension and "focusing attention on dimensions unrelated to the threat" would be accomplished by seeking new dimensions for comparison. We identified the two general strategies as two types of "compensation." By compensation, we mean "attempts to generate an experience that will reflect positively on the self and thereby counterbalance the self-esteem threat" (Wood et al., 1999, p. 3).

We are intrigued by compensation as a coping strategy for two main reasons. First, compensation need not involve illusions or distortions of reality. In contrast, well-studied strategies such as externalizing blame or discrediting negative feedback (see Blaine & Crocker, 1993), seem to distort reality to some degree. Although such reality-distorting strategies may not always be maladaptive (see Colvin & Block, 1994; Taylor & Brown, 1988), they are almost certainly maladaptive under some circumstances or if used excessively (Baumeister, Heatherton, & Tice, 1993). in contrast, compensation attempts involve generating a new experience to cast the self in a positive light. Generating a new experience need not involve distorting the old. Even compensation attempts aimed at disconfirming negative feedback do not need to involve denying reality, because they may involve trying harder in a second attempt after a poor performance, or a change in actual behavior.

The second reason that we are intrigued by compensation is that it may be a strategy that distinguishes people with high self-esteem from people with low self-esteem. Identifying such distinguishing strategies is an important pursuit for self-esteem researchers, because it points to mechanisms that may underlie the maintenance of self-esteem. Compensation strategies should appeal to highs' interest in self-enhancement but should violate lows' need for self-protection. Compensation attempts can be risky, because attempts to overturn a failure may be unsuccessful, and hence may compound one's humiliation, and comparisons involving one's other talents may reveal that one is not superior but inferior. People with high self-esteem appear to be more willing to take risks (Josephs et al., 1992a; Baumeister et al., 1989, 1993), whereas lows are more risk averse (Josephs et al., 1992a; Tice, 1991).

A few studies outside of social comparison are consistent with this suggestion that people with high self-esteem are more likely than people with low self-esteem to engage in compensatory strategies (Baumeister, 1982; Brown & Smart, 1991; Dodgson & Wood, 1998; Josephs, Markus, & Tafarodi, 1992b: experiment 3). Would the same self-esteem differences hold true for compensation attempts that involve social comparison? Indeed, do people engage in social comparisons for compensation? If so, social comparison may provide an especially effective means of compensating, because one may not only shed positive light on oneself, one may see oneself as superior to another person, which would afford a downward comparison. In addition, when a threat to self-esteem occurs in a social comparison context—as in the teaching award scenario—social comparisons that reverse one's inferiority with that very person may be particularly satisfying.

RESEARCH GOALS THAT LED TO THE CREATION
OF TEST SELECTION MEASURE

Investigating these three strategies, then, has the potential to enrich the literatures on social comparison, self-esteem, and coping and self-enhancement strategies. Several years ago, my colleagues and I sought to address questions pertinent to these literatures. We wanted to study social comparisons as a means of coping with threat. We also wanted to examine self-esteem differences in the use of social comparisons as a coping strategy, and hence we wanted to permit multiple comparison strategies that might be used differentially by high and low self-esteem people. We were focused at that time on two comparison strategies: comparison avoidance and the selection of comparison dimensions. We were not mindful at that time of the possibility that people could seek new comparisons on the same dimension on which they had been threatened, but we did know that by providing a rich context that afforded participants flexibility and choice in their comparison making, we might discover new comparison strategies.

We had learned this lesson from the breast cancer study. As mentioned earlier, the very unconstrained context in that study fostered the discovery of "dimensional comparisons"— the strategy of being selective about the dimensions in which to compare. In addition, we also identified a strategy that I have not talked about in this chapter, which we called, "manufacturing normative standards of adjustment." In this case, the respondent contrasted her own adjustment with a hypothetical standard of adjustment that was worse than her own. In addition, the unconstrained context also enriched our understanding of other comparative phenomena. For example, our respondents talked about ways in which they avoided painful comparisons, such as by making appointments with their oncologists early in the day, so as to avoid facing fellow patients whose conditions were worsening. This example also illustrates something we learned about downward comparisons, namely, that comparing with others who are worse off is not necessarily self-enhancing; it can be frightening (cf. Wills, 1981).

In short, the unconstrained context of the "free response" method that we used in the breast cancer study, as well as similar methods that followed (Wood, 1996), yielded a new richness of detail about comparison processes, a richness that has led to a greater appreciation of the complexity and subtlety of social comparison processes. Researchers have learned that the comparison process is exquisitely flexible, perhaps even involving processes of construction (Goethals, 1986; Wood et al., 1985), and that the individual making social comparisons may be more active than previously thought (Wood, 1989).

Thus, we knew that an unconstrained context could lead to new developments in social comparison theory. However, we chose not to use the free response method again, because we wanted to study these processes experimentally. Such methods as free responses are ambiguous about causal direction, for a couple of reasons. First, threat is not manipulated in such studies. The reasoning has been that in the laboratory, people tend to make upward comparisons when they are not threatened (Wood, 1989), and hence, if they make downward comparisons under threat—and victim populations are certainly threatened—it must be the threat that prompted the downward comparisons. Because of experimental evidence that comparisons are more downward in direction under conditions of threat (e.g., Smith & Insko, 1987), this reasoning was not unfounded but it clearly was not airtight.

In addition, in the breast cancer study, we assumed that each participant's motive for making downward comparisons was self-enhancement, but inferring motives from direction of comparison is hazardous (Wood, 1996). Victims may well harbor motives other than self-enhancement, such as self-improvement (Taylor & Lobel, 1989). Moreover, a single comparison target may serve multiple motives and have multiple effects (Buunk, Collins, Taylor, VanYperen, & Dakof, 1990; Major, Testa, & Bylsma, 1991). For example, as noted earlier, a downward comparison may be threatening rather than self-enhancing (Taylor & Lobel, 1989). And people sometimes may seek upward comparisons for self-enhancement, rather than downward comparisons, because assuming similarity with or identifying with an upward target can make one feel good about oneself (Collins, 1996; Taylor & Lobel, 1989).

Not only did we want to manipulate threat, we also wanted to know what comparison targets were available to our participants, as well as what information was available about those targets. In the breast cancer research, our argument that participants were being selective about their comparisons rested on the assumption that they had upward and downward targets available to them, and hence their focus on downward targets was selective. We based this assumption, in part, on evidence that our sample's physical and psychological adjustment was typical for the population of breast cancer patients. The fact that respondents' dimensional comparisons were always with people who were worse off, rather than with people who did not have cancer, points to selectivity in their comparisons. However, we did not truly know which comparisons they had to choose from.

All these goals, then, argued for an experimental study in the laboratory that contained two elements: a manipulation of threat and a measure/context that would not only permit participants to select rich comparative information but that would permit the strategies of avoiding comparisons and selecting comparison dimensions. The two main categories of camparison selection measures available to us were the rank order paradigm and "looking" measures (Wood, 1996).

PREVIOUS MEASURES OF COMPARISON SELECTION

The Rank Order Paradigm

The traditional paradigm in social comparison research involves the rank order method, invented by Ladd Wheeler in the 1960s. In that paradigm, participants complete a bogus test of some attribute and are given bogus information about how they and several co-participants performed on the test. They are told that their own score ranks in the middle of the others' scores. Then they are given the opportunity to see the score received by a person occupying another rank. The question is which score will participants choose—that of someone who is ranked higher than themselves (an upward comparison), lower than themselves (a downward comparison), or close to themselves (a similar comparison)? And how close or distant in the rank orders do they select? An example is a study in which participants took a personality test and were told that their score ranked fourth out of seven. Participants overwhelmingly chose to see the scores of others ranked second and third; that is, others who were upward but still close in the rank order (Wheeler, 1966).

The rank order method does not permit participants to engage in the three strategies I identified earlier. Participants cannot choose to avoid comparisons; they must choose which score they would like to see, even if they would rather not. Nor can they hope to reverse a failure by making new comparisons on the dimension of failure. For example, they cannot take a new test of that dimension; they can see only another person's score on a test already completed. Participants also cannot choose to make comparisons on new dimensions, dimensions that might afford them a chance to prove their superiority.

Moreover, despite certain advantages of the rank order method, it has been criticized for the poverty of social comparison information that it provides to participants (see Wood, 1996). Participants have been told their score and their standing in the rank order. Hence, they know their standing along the dimension and they know the standing of any comparison target relative to their own. What can they gain by learning only the specific score of that target? The only purpose seems to be to find out exactly how far away they are from others (Wheeler & Zuckerman, 1977). Such information is not likely to be useful very often. Instead, as other authors have pointed out, when people receive a score in real life, they want to find out the average score and the whole distribution of scores, rather than a single score (e.g., Suls & Tesch, 1978).

Looking Methods

In "looking" measures, the researcher provides an opportunity for participants to examine social comparison information and then measures the degree to which participants take that opportunity. For example, in a study of students who had taken a test, the investigators made available other students' scores on the test and counted the number of such scores that participants wanted to see (Brickman & Berman, 1971).

The social information provided by looking methods is richer than that provided by the rank order method. Participants may see more than another person's specific score on a distribution on which they already know their own and the target's relative standing. They may see a whole distribution of scores or actually observe another person. For example, in one study, children learning a new task had an opportunity to watch another child performing the same task (Ruble, Feldman, & Boggiano, 1976). Using looking measures, researchers can measure participants' overall interest in social comparisons or they can examine participants' interest in particular targets of comparison by inducing expectations about what the information available to them will reveal and then measuring participants' interest in seeing that information. For example, participants who had received feedback on a test were led to expect that the information available to them would reveal that most other participants had failed (in one condition) or had succeeded (in another condition). Participants who had failed preferred to see information about others who also had failed (Pyszczynski, Greenberg, & LaPrelle, 1985).

Looking measures allow participants to engage in the strategy of avoiding comparisons, because they can choose to look at the information available to them or not. A few looking studies have suggested that people do choose to avoid comparisons when those comparisons are likely to be unfavorable. For example, when nondysphoric participants believed that their own performance was poor, they decreased their overall comparison seeking, whereas dysphoric participants did not (Swallow & Kuiper, 1992).

Looking methods have not been used to examine the strategies of seeking new comparisons on the same dimension or of selecting new dimensions of comparison. The information available to participants typically concerns only a single dimension. Moreover, like the rank order paradigm, it often includes only other people's scores on a test on which participants already have received feedback. However, the looking method could be adapted to measure the strategies of seeking further comparisons on the same dimension or on new dimensions. In fact, some looking measures may already have permitted such strategies, even if they did not examine them. In Ruble and co-workers's (1976) study, for example, in which children could watch another child performing a task, the children could have been interested in multiple dimensions—not only how the other child performed the task, but how long he or she persevered at the task, or even dimensions such as the sex and age of the other child. To actually measure participants' interest in such dimensions, the researcher somehow must distinguish between those dimensions and allow participants to select from different dimensions.

That is what we sought to do. We wanted a context that would permit research participants flexibility and choice in their social comparison-seeking, while still permitting the control and precision required to address our research questions. Enter the test selection measure.

THE TEST SELECTION MEASURE

With these goals in mind, several years ago Kathryn Taylor and I developed a new measure of social comparison selection that we call the test selection measure. We present to participants a list of tests, from which we ask them to select tests for a co-participant to complete and for themselves to complete. Participants could choose the same or entirely different tests for the other person as for themselves, or some combination of the same and different tests. We led participants to believe that they would receive their own and their co-participant's results of the tests. Hence, if participants selected the same tests for themselves and their co-participant, they could expect to make comparisons with that person; if they selected different tests, they could avoid comparisons. For example, in one study we gave participants a list of 20 tests, including such dimensions as "social sensitivity" and "creativity," and we asked them to select five tests for the other person and five tests for themselves (Wood, Giordano-Beech, Taylor, Michela, & Gaus, 1994: Experiment 2). Thus, participants could choose to make between zero and five comparisons; about 15% of the participants chose zero, about 21% chose two, about 19% chose five. The average across all participants was about 2.21 comparisons.

We typically present the test selection measure under the guise of an impression formation task. Participants are led to believe that their task is to form an impression of the other person. Receiving the other person's test scores on a variety of tests ostensibly will help them to form that impression. We get participants to select tests for themselves by pretending that we need "normative information." Would they mind completing some tests themselves, the experimenter asks, while they are waiting for the other person to complete his or her tests? All participants have agreed to do so. We make it clear that they should choose any tests for their co-participant that will help them to form their impression of him or her and that they are free to select any tests for themselves that they would like to take. Participants never actually complete the tests; our question is whether they choose matching tests for themselves and the other person, how many they choose, and which particular tests they select.

Could participants choose matching tests for reasons other than to make social comparisons? One possibility is that they are merely interested in the domains that certain tests purportedly assess. In an effort to do a good job on the impression formation task, they might choose tests for their co-participant that tap into domains they regard as especially important, and they could select the same tests for themselves because they wish to evaluate themselves in the same important domains, not because they are seeking social comparisons per se. Although interest in particular domains no doubt influences participants' choices, interest cannot account for the differences that we obtain between conditions, differences that I describe shortly.

Another possible explanation for the selection of matching tests is that participants may select matching tests by chance. Even if participants select tests for themselves and their co-participant completely randomly, they might sometimes select matching tests. Accordingly, we typically compare the rates of match-picking not only between experimental groups but also with a chance baseline. Later in this chapter, I discuss this issue in more detail.

Could participants seek comparisons but not choose matching tests? If participants believed, for instance, that the domain that test A taps into is correlated with the domain that test B taps into, they could select A for the self and B for the other and still expect to receive comparative information In this sense, counting only matching tests as comparisons may underestimate comparison seeking. In one study, we collected data to assess the seriousness of this possibility. We calculated new comparison scores not based on number of matching tests selected, but based on the degree of relatedness between the tests selected, as rated by independent judges. Results based on these new relatedness scores did not differ from those for matching tests. Hence, we concluded that our method of simply counting matching tests does capture the important comparative tendencies (see Wood et al., 1994, p. 722, for more detail).

We believe that the test selection measure more closely parallels naturalistic circumstances of comparison than do most previous measures of comparison selection. The information that participants can hope to obtain through the test selection measure is very rich and meaningful. Unlike the rank order paradigm and like looking measures, the test selection measure does not force participants to choose comparisons. Participants can avoid comparisons simply by choosing different tests for themselves and their co-participant. Unlike both types of previous measures, it also offers participants great flexibility in choosing the dimensions on which to compare. But the test selection measure has its drawbacks too, which I describe later.

RESULTS OBTAINED WITH THE TEST SELECTION MEASURE

In our first two studies using the test selection measure, we manipulated threat by presenting feedback to participants concerning their performance on a bogus test or tests (tests that were not part of the test selection measure). In one study, we told them that they had taken tests that were indicative of their suitability for their chosen career (Wood et al., 1994: Experiment 1). In the second study, participants completed a bogus test of "social accuracy," which ostensibly concerned their ability to understand the feelings and motivations of other people, and which was described as a very important dimension, predictive of success in relationships and life (Wood et al., 1994: Experiment 2; cf. McFarland & Ross, 1985). Undergraduates participated with a same-sex co-participant who was unknown to them. When participants were led to believe that they had performed poorly, they believed that their co-participant had performed well; when they were led to believe that they had performed well, they believed that their co-participant had performed poorly.

Although our original intention was simply to manipulate threat, the context of that threat was clearly a socially comparative one: Participants not only succeeded or failed in an absolute sense; they succeeded or failed relative to another person participating in the study at the same time. In this respect, our studies resemble a program of research conducted by Tesser and colleagues (see Chapter 7, this volume). They have presented participants with information about how they performed on some dimension relative to another person (see Tesser, 1986, for a review), and have manipulated three variables: the relative performance of the two participants, the similarity or "closeness" of the co-participant, and the personal importance of the performance dimension to the participant. The investigators' main focus has been on the strategies that participants use to benefit their self-esteem. For example, when participants fail relative to a similar co-participant on a dimension that they cherish, they often try to reduce their similarity to the other person or to devalue the importance of the dimension (see Tesser, 1986, for a review).

Like Tesser, we were interested in the strategies that people use after they receive a threat to their self-esteem, strategies seemingly designed to restore or boost their self-esteem. However, unlike Tesser's work, we were interested in strategies involving social comparison selections, whether participants wanted to make further comparisons with the other person or avoid further comparisons and on what dimensions they sought comparisons, if any. Although the social comparative nature of the threat context was almost beside the point initially, it has proved to be useful. It enabled us to capture a social comparison context—in which one fails or succeeds relative to another specific person—that, as mentioned earlier, is common and uncomfortable in everyday life. In such situations, strategies other than target selection may be preferable.

To examine participants' comparison selections, we used the test selection measure. To set the stage for the test selection measure, the experimenter drew a link between the cover story and the impression formation task. In one study, for example, participants were told that the purpose of the study was to examine the association between social accuracy and the ability to form accurate first impressions (Wood et al., 1994: Experiment 2). Then participants selected tests for themselves and for their co-participant to complete. Recall that we interpreted the selection of matching tests to represent selections of comparisons. Our participants who were low in self-esteem exhibited quite a different pattern of test selections than did those who were high in self-esteem, as I describe next.

TEST SELECTIONS BY LOW SELF-ESTEEM PARTICIPANTS

In an extension of the view that low self-esteem people are self-protective (e.g., Baumeister et al., 1989), Wood et al. (1994) predicted that lows would be especially likely to avoid comparisons after failure. As predicted, low self-esteem participants chose to make fewer comparisons with their co-participant when they had just failed than when they had just succeeded. When they had just failed, their co-participant had just outperformed them on a very important dimension, so further comparisons would have invited further damage to their self-esteem. Clearly, the self-protective course of action was to refrain from comparing in that condition. However, low self-esteem–failure participants did not appear to truly avoid comparisons, relative to a chance baseline (Experiments 1 and 2) or relative to a no-feedback group (Experiment 2). Later I describe these baselines in more detail, as well as their weaknesses. These weaknesses suggest that lows may in fact have avoided comparisons after they failed.

Wood et al. (1994) proposed that although people with low self-esteem are primarily self-protective, they may venture beyond their usual self-protectiveness when they have an opportunity for self-enhancement that is relatively "safe." Safe opportunities for self-enhancement are those in which a favorable outcome is virtually guaranteed. The idea that people with low self-esteem will engage in self-enhancement when they have safe opportunities to do so is similar to the idea that lows engage in strategies of self-enhancement that are indirect. For example, whereas high self-esteem people brag about matters with which they are directly associated, lows are more likely to brag about matters that are associated with groups to which they belong (Brown, Collins, & Schmidt, 1988). Such circuitous routes to self-enhancement are less likely to be disconfirmed and to lead to personal humiliation, and hence should appeal to the self-protective goals of people with low self-esteem (Baumeister, 1993).

In our test selection context, we predicted that lows would seek comparisons after they had succeeded with a person they had just outperformed on an important dimension. Such comparisons promise success more than the typical comparison, and hence should be relatively safe. This prediction was confirmed in two studies; low self-esteem participants were especially likely to select matching tests for themselves and their co-participant when they had outperformed that co-participant on the important dimensions of "success in future career" (Wood et al., 1994: Experiment 1) and "social accuracy" (Experiment 2).

People with low self-esteem, then, may venture beyond their usual self-protectiveness when they have a safe opportunity for self-enhancement. But this raises a puzzling question: Why would they seek self-enhancement after success, when they are presumably feeling good about themselves? Wills's (1981) theory of downward comparison and the literature on self-enhancement more generally has assumed that people seek self-enhancement when they are feeling bad, rather than when they are feeling good. Wood et al. (1994) argued that lows were reveling in their success; by seeking further comparisons with someone they knew to be inferior to themselves on an important dimension, they were taking advantage of a relatively rare opportunity to feel good about themselves.

This finding has a parallel in other research that we have completed recently. Using a modified version of a social comparison diary method introduced by Wheeler and Miyake (1992), university student participants recorded the comparisons that they made in their everyday lives (Wood, Michela, & Giordano, in press). We asked participants to report their motive for social comparison each time they recorded a comparison. According to these self-reports, low self-esteem participants sought social comparisons for self-enhancement and downward comparisons in particular, when they were happy more than when they were unhappy.

We make sense of these findings by drawing from Wills' (1981) idea that people with low self-esteem probably are chronically needy of self-enhancement. However, this need probably frequently collides with their need for self-protectiveness, and their self-protectiveness probably typically wins out. Low self-esteem people are keenly averse to risks (Josephs et al., 1992a), and their most important goal seems to be to guard whatever precious self-esteem resources they have (Baumeister et al., 1989; Steele et al., 1993). Hence, they can rarely fulfill their needs for self-enhancement. But it appears that people with low self-esteem will seize opportunities to self-enhance when they are emboldened by relatively good feelings about themselves and when those opportunities are relatively risk-free.

TEST SELECTIONS BY HIGH SELF-ESTEEM PARTICIPANTS

What did high self-esteem participants do in these studies? What we found initially surprised us. Highs exhibited a pattern that was opposite to that of lows: They chose to compare with the other person more when they had failed and less when they had succeeded. Not comparing much in the success condition made sense; previous research had indicated that people are not typically interested in making comparisons with others who are clearly inferior to themselves (e.g., Gastorf, Suls, & Lawhon, 1978). Unlike people with low self-esteem, who may revel in the opportunity to make further comparisons with someone who is clearly inferior, high self-esteem participants may have been uninterested in doing so.

More puzzling were the comparison choices of the high self-esteem participants who had failed. They had just learned that their co-participant was highly superior to themselves on an important dimension—and in that sense was a highly upward comparison—yet they sought further comparisons with that person. This result contradicts the previous literature. Although previous studies may not always have shown that threatened people make truly downward comparisons (Wheeler & Miyake, 1992), they have certainly indicated that under threat, people make comparisons that are less upward, not more upward (e.g., Smith & Insko, 1987). Here were high self-esteem participants making highly upward comparisons when threatened.

Why? We considered the possibility that high self-esteem people were seeking to compensate for their failure. Recall that people with high self-esteem appear to be more likely than people with low self-esteem to engage compensatory strategies, at least those not involving social comparison (Baumeister, 1982; Brown & Smart, 1991; Dodgson & Wood, 1998; Josephs et al., 1992b). In the Wood et al. (1994) research, high self-esteem participants could have believed that, although their co-participant had outperformed them on the "social accuracy" test, they would perform better than their co-participant on the tests that they selected. Other research suggests that even after high self-esteem people have failed, they expect to perform successfully on a second try, and they exert more effort than do low self-esteem people (McFarlin & Blascovich, 1981; McFarlin, Baumeister, & Blascovich, 1984). In keeping with these ideas, Wood and co-workers' (1994) high self-esteem participants predicted that they would perform better than the other person on the upcoming tests. But can we be sure that high self-esteem people who failed were seeking comparisons so as to compensate in the Wood et al. (1994) research? Several alternative explanations are plausible. One applies to both low self-esteem–success participants and high self-esteem–failure participants: Both groups may have been surprised or puzzled about their feedback and may have sought further comparisons to help them to understand it. In one study, we found evidence against this possibility (Wood et al., 1994: Experiment 2). Specifically, the low self-esteem–success participants and high self-esteem–failure participants were not especially puzzled by their feedback, relative to other participants in their respective conditions, and measures of puzzlement and skepticism were not correlated with comparison seeking. Although this evidence convinced us that this "puzzled–skeptical" alternative explanation could not account for the results (Wood et al., 1994: Experiment 2), several other alternative explanations remained. For example, people under threat sometimes seek upward comparisons to improve themselves (Taylor & Lobel, 1989). Because participants expected to see the other person's test responses on a variety of dimensions, they may have expected to learn something from their highly competent co-participant.

To rule out such alternative explanations, we conducted more studies of high self-esteem people (Wood et al., 1999). In one of these studies, for example, we attempted to manipulate the motivations of high self-esteem people who failed. We reasoned that, if their goal in seeking comparisons after failure is self-enhancement through compensation, they should not seek comparisons if that goal had been satisfied already. Hence, after participants experienced a failure on the social accuracy test, we offered half of them an opportunity to compensate via a self-affirmation task. Participants completed a scale that concerned a value, such as religion or politics, that they held to be especially impartant. This task has been shown to be an effective means of self-affirmation (e.g., Steele & Liu, 1983).

We expected that completing a self-relevant value scale would reduce the desire for comparison seeking in high self-esteem failure participants because it would satisfy their need for compensation. High self-esteem failure participants who had not self-affirmed, in contrast, were expected to seek comparisons in hopes of compensating for the failure. After failing and then engaging in the self-affirmation task or not, we asked participants to again select five tests for their co-participant and for themselves from a list of 20 tests, supposedly tapping into such dimensions as athletic ability, intelligence, and appreciation of the fine arts. As predicted, participants in the no-affirmation condition sought more comparisons than did participants in the affirmation condition; the no-affirmation group sought an average of 3.76 and the affirmation group sought an average of 2.00 out of a possible 5.

This result supports the view that high self esteem people sought comparisons after failure in an effort to compensate for their failure. If they sought comparisons with their co-participant because they were seeking self-improvement rather than self-enhancement, that goal should not have been satisfied through the self-affirmation task. This result and others (Wood et al., 1999) suggest that our high self-esteem participants sought comparisons after they failed with a person who had outperformed them in an effort to turn an upward comparison into a downward one.

MODIFYING THE TEST SELECTION MEASURE
TO EXAMINE SOCIAL COMPARISON GOALS AND STRATEGIES

My colleagues and I have modified our test selection measure in various studies to try to gather further evidence for the motives of high and low self-esteem participants, as well as to study the three strategies further.

Avoiding Comparisons

Wood et al. (1994) examined the strategy of comparison avoidance further in a study of low self-esteem participants who had succeeded. Wood and co-workers examined whether low self-esteem–success participants would avoid comparisons if they did not know that their co-participant had failed. We predicted that participants who did not know that the other had failed would self-protectively seek fewer comparisons than participants who knew that they had surpassed the other. To test this idea, we told only half the low self-esteem participants how their co-participant scored on the social accuracy test. This group selected more matching tests than did the group who did not learn of the other's inferiority on social accuracy. This method illustrates that researchers using the test selection measure may manipulate the comparison targets available to participants; some participants received certain information about their co-participant, whereas others did not. Thus, the test selection measure offers another way of revealing the motives behind social comparison.

Seeking New Comparisons on the Same Dimension and Selecting New Comparison Dimensions

In one study, we attempted to see whether participants would choose dimensions that were related or unrelated to a dimension on which they just received success or failure feedback (Wood et al., 1994: Experiment 2). Although we were not successful in our specific operationalization of related and unrelated dimensions (participants may have perceived some demand to select from each category equally), future attempts might be more successful. Researchers could then study which strategy participants prefer: to make comparisons on the same dimension to reverse their failure (a form of "direct" compensation) or to choose new dimensions for comparison (a form of "indirect" compensation). Participants' preferences may depend on their self-esteem and other features of the comparison context.

We also have modified our procedure to examine whether participants choose to compare on their own strengths or weaknesses (Wood et al., 1999: Experiment 1). In one of our compensation studies, we predicted that high self-esteem participants who failed would prefer to compare on dimensions on which they were strong rather than weak. Only comparisons involving their talents and assets would offer an opportunity to outperform the other and thereby compensate. To test this idea, we had obtained information about participants' self-perceived strengths and weaknesses through earlier mass testing. Later, when participants had received success or failure feedback in the laboratory and were about to select tests for the "impression formation" task, we told them that they could select any of the tests for their co-participant. However, rather than allow them to choose any tests for themselves, we asked participants whether they would mind taking certain tests themselves—tests on which we supposedly were especially in need of "normative information." For participants in the "weakness" condition, we asked them to take the tests they had identified as their weakest; for the "strength" condition, we asked them to take the tests they had identified as their strongest. The experimenter did not let on that she knew that they were the participant's own strengths or weaknesses. Comparisons were scored as the number of tests that participants chose for their co-participant that matched those they were asked to take themselves. As predicted, participants who had failed and who were allowed to compare on their strengths chose more matches than those who were allowed only to compare on their weaknesses.

To help rule out the possibility that these failure participants were seeking comparisons on their strengths not to compensate but simply because they were more interested in their strengths, we compared them with participants who had succeeded and who were allowed to compare on their strengths. The success–strength participants should have had less interest in seeking comparisons because they had no need to compensate. Results supported this prediction, albeit weakly; failure–strength participants sought somewhat more comparisons than did success–strength participants.

Hence, we conducted another study in which we manipulated the availability of the co-participant's strengths and weaknesses, rather than the participant's own strengths and weaknesses (Wood et al., 1999: Experiment 2). To do so, we drastically altered our test selection context and borrowed a measure that Tesser and Campbell (1980) had developed. Tesser and Campbell (1980) gave participants two "sample tests," supposedly reflecting two different personality dimensions. On one test, participants learned that they had performed at the same "below average" level as a confederate, and on the other, they learned that their own performance was "average" but that the confederate's was "clearly above average." When participants then had a choice of which test to continue working on, they preferred the one on which they had performed the same as the other. Thus, participants preferred the test on which they had performed worse (below average vs. average), apparently to avoid the dimension on which they had performed worse than the confederate.

My colleagues and I predicted that high self-esteem participants who failed would be especially likely to choose for comparison their co-participant's weakness. We gave high self-esteem participants success or failure feedback and then provided information about how a co-participant performed on two short "sample" tests, unrelated to the success or failure feedback. Participants were asked to choose between these two test dimensions for further testing—one that the co-participant had performed only "average" on in the "sample" tests, and one that he or she had performed at the highest possible level in the "sample" tests. The test they chose would be given to both the participant and the co-participant, thus providing an opportunity for social comparison. If participants who had received failure feedback sought to compensate for their failure, they should choose the test on which their co-participant performed only average. As predicted, 78% of those who failed chose the other person's weaker dimension, whereas only 37% of those who had succeeded chose the other's weaker dimension. It appears, then, that failure participants chose the test that would allow them an opportunity to compensate.

Using the Test Selection Measure to Examine Other Comparison Goals

In our research using the test selection measure, our focus has been on how social comparison strategies may serve the motive of self-enhancement. But what about the two other main motives served by social comparison, namely self-evaluation and self-improvement (Wood, 1989)? In the teaching award scenario, for example, the professor who did not win the award may seek social comparisons for the purpose of reevaluating her teaching ability. She also may socially compare in hopes of improving her teaching ability. There is no reason why the test selection measure could not be used to examine such motives as well.

The test selection measure may be especially useful for examining the motive of self-improvement, which has received less attention than the other two motives (Wood, 1989). The test selection method has two features that seem crucial for observing self-improvement: a reason for seeking improvement and comparative information that will facilitate improvement. Because participants are asked to complete new tests, they may be motivated to try to improve in the study context itself, and the new tests provide an opportunity to try to improve or to demonstrate improvement. There is little need to provide an opportunity for improvement in the study context itself if the dimension under consideration is one that is personally important in participants' lives outside the laboratory. In such cases, participants would be motivated to improve. For example, student participants may be especially interested in comparisons involving academic ability, and they can hope to apply what they have learned from their comparisons after they leave the laboratory. When the dimension is unfamiliar or unimportant to participants, however, the study context itself must involve a task on which participants will continue to work after they receive social comparative feedback.

Even more important to capturing self-improvement motives, however, is the second feature that the test selection measure can provide. Specifically, the information it offers through social comparisons should be instructive or inspiring. Because participants expect to see their co-participant's test responses on a variety of dimensions, they may hope to learn something. Contrast this information with that provided by the rank order method. When a person wants to improve him- or herself, little can be gained by simply learning the score of someone else. Imagine Roy, a ballet dancer, who is continually trying to improve his technique and grace. He cannot learn anything from finding out that the critics gave a principal dancer more praise than he received. Rather, he would probably try to improve his dancing by watching those dancers practice and perform. In addition, finding out the exact score of an upward target offers little in the way of inspiration, which is another way in which upward comparisons facilitate self-improvement goals (Wood, 1989). The test selection method could be adjusted so as to provide information that could be inspiring. For example, rather than choosing new tests to take, participants could select to see biographical information about their co-participant.

Other Potential Uses of the Test Selection Measure

Perhaps the rank order paradigm's greatest asset is its capacity to measure preferences for comparison direction very precisely; participants are told explicitly what their score is, and then they have the opportunity to learn the score of someone else at a rank higher, lower, or about the same as their own. When participants at rank four select a target at rank seven, for example, they are making a clearly upward comparison, and that comparison is three ranks away from their own. In contrast, in other paradigms it can be difficult to know whether participants perceive the target to be truly upward or downward relative to themselves. As Wheeler and Miyake (1992) have pointed out, researchers have called certain target choices "downward" that may not have been downward relative to participants' self-perceptions.

This potential for error is present in the test selection measure. Participants presumably have general expectations for their own and their co-participant's performance on the upcoming tests, based on the earlier manipulation of success or failure. However, they are not given explicit information about how the other person will perform on the tests they choose from the test selection measure. Hence, we do not know for certain whether they are choosing comparisons that they expect to be downward or upward. Wood et al. (1994) attempted to assess participants' expectations by asking them to rate how they thought they and their co-participant would perform on the upcoming tests. However, this method is not perfect because participants' ratings may not reflect their true expectations; their ratings may be colored by other motives and biases. For example, because participants have yet to complete the tests, they may be especially modest (Schlenker et al., 1990).

A better way to learn how the participants expect to perform on the tests is to ask for self-ratings in the pertinent domains several weeks before the laboratory session, as we did in the strength–weakness study described earlier. And with a bit of stage management, participants could be led to have certain expectations for how their co-participant will perform on the dimensions, as we did in the study involving a choice between the co-participant's strong and weak dimensions. In these ways, the test selection method may be altered to examine people's preferences for direction and target of comparison, whether they are seeking upward or downward comparisons.

Thus far, we have used the test selection measure to assess comparisons with a single person: the participant's co-participant. But the measure could be altered to permit comparisons with multiple targets. For example, the experimenter could tell participants that they will receive information about many other people on any dimension they select. Indeed, we usually do tell participants that they will receive normative information for any test that they select, so that they will not be motivated to compare solely to get such information.

Researchers interested in examining comparison strategies that can be assessed with the test selection method but whose research contexts are not well-suited for the taking of tests could provide other types of tests or comparative information to choose from rather than tests per se. In short, the test selection method has the potential to be adapted in many ways to suit researcher's needs.

FURTHER OBSERVATIONS ABOUT THE TEST SELECTION MEASURE

What Is an Appropriate Baseline?

With the test selection measure, we have focused primarily on the degree to which comparison-seeking differs between conditions (e.g., whether low self-esteem participants who have failed seek fewer comparisons than do lows who have succeeded). Sometimes, however, we have been interested in whether participants avoid or seek comparisons in an absolute sense. Do low self-esteem participants who have failed truly avoid comparisons or merely seek fewer than those who have succeeded? To address such questions, a baseline is required, but deciding what is the appropriate baseline has been difficult.

One baseline that we have used is a chance baseline. As mentioned earlier, if participants made their choices on the test selection measure completely randomly, they might sometimes select the same tests for themselves and the other person. For example, in one study we offered participants a list of 12 tests and asked them to select three for themselves and three for the other person (Wood et al., 1994: Experiment 1). We calculated the expected frequencies for each of the possible outcomes—between zero and three matches—under a random model in which three tests were chosen independently for self and other from a list of 12 tests. If participants chose tests completely randomly, they would have selected an average of 0.692 matches. Yet the sample selected an average of 1.73 matches. We compared each group's number of matches with the expected mean of 0.692, and learned that all groups, including low self-esteem–failure participants, sought comparisons at rates above chance.

However, chance may not be the appropriate baseline for determining whether participants sought or avoided comparisons, for a couple of reasons (Wood et al., 1994). First, if participants are especially interested in some test dimensions and not in others, the number of dimensions from which they could choose would be smaller than the total number of tests. Suppose, for example, that participants chose randomly not from the list of 12 but from the 9 they were especially interested in. Then the number of expected matches would be higher than the calculation based on all 12 dimensions. A second problem with the chance baseline is that it assumes that if participants approached the task mindlessly, they would only choose matching tests "accidentally." However, if participants were uninvolved in the test selection task, they may well select more matches rather than fewer, because they may not bother to pick different tests for the self and the other. For example, they may choose the first three tests for both. Both problems would result in a chance baseline that is too low. Hence, our conclusion that participants compared at above-chance rates may be inaccurate, and low self-esteem–failure participants may have avoided comparisons after all.[1]

A second type of baseline, more familiar to all of us, is a neutral condition. For example, Wood et al. (1994: Experiment 2) employed not only success and failure conditions, but a condition in which participants completed the social accuracy test but received no feedback. Low self-esteem participants who had succeeded selected more matching tests than did this no-feedback group, but low self-esteem–failure participants did not avoid comparisons relative to this no-feedback group. However, the low self-esteem–no-feedback group may again underestimate low self-esteem people's baseline rates of comparison seeking. A no-feedback condition may not be a neutral experience for people with low self-esteem, who are likely to assume that they have failed. Some other results of our study suggested that this was true. If low self-esteem–no-feedback participants believed that they had not done well on the social accuracy test, they may have avoided comparisons, in their typical self-protective fashion. Hence, it would have been difficult to see a difference between the low self-esteem failure and no-feedback groups in their avoidance of comparisons.

We also have used a third type of baseline. This one attempts to control for a large contributor to differential interest in domains, namely culturally shared values (Wood et al.,

---

[1]Calculating the chance baseline requires some sophisticated mathematical know-how. It falls within the area of combinatorial mathematics, and the problem—determining what is the expected number of matching tests chosen if participants choose X tests for themselves and X for another person from a list of Y tests—involves what is called a "hypergeometric series." I have required the help of mathematics professors at the University of Waterloo, especially Dr. David Jackson.

1999). For example, intelligence is highly valued in our culture, and hence many participants may prefer to complete and to have the co-participant complete a test of intelligence. One way to gauge the extent to which culturally shared preferences influence the degree of match picking is to pair each participant's own selections for the self with every other participant's selections for the other. If interest in certain domains is culturally shared, these pairings should yield some matches.[2]

Although the cultural baseline takes into account differential interest in test dimensions, a major weakness is that this baseline seems to imply that only numbers of matches that exceed the cultural baseline represent true comparison seeking. Yet people are likely to be especially interested in making comparisons in domains that are valued by the culture, and hence such comparisons should be considered to be true comparisons. Because of such problems, we offered the cultural baseline not as a substitute for previous baselines, but as a supplementary one.

Social Desirability Concerns

Norms operate against appearing to be too eager to compare oneself with other people (Brickman & Bulman, 1977). Concerns about social desirability can sometimes interfere with researchers' attempts to measure social comparisons (Wood, 1996). One advantage of the test selection measure is that it disguises participants' interest in comparisons under the cloak of an "impression formation" task. They need not be embarrassed about selecting matching tests, because doing so may be a sensible strategy for forming an impression of another person.

During debriefings, we often have asked participants why they selected the tests that they selected and why they selected matching tests in particular. Participants typically claim that they simply selected the tests that most interested them or that would be most informative about their co-participant. We know that these self-reports cannot tell the whole story, because they do not account for why some groups seek more comparisons than do other groups. It is telling that when we asked uninvolved participants—people who had not participated in the test selection studies—why people would select matching tests in our procedure, they all came up with social comparison explanations (Wood et al., 1994: "interview study"). About 37% of these naïve respondents mentioned self-evaluative or self-improvement motives for making comparisons and 94% described self-enhancement motives. Several respondents specifically mentioned that people who had failed want to compare themselves further with their co-participant to compensate for the failure.

These results suggest that participants easily recognize the test selection measure as offering an opportunity to make social comparisons. The differences between the answers given by these uninvolved participants and our actual participants suggests to us that actual participants harbor social comparison motives, but that they do not wish to reveal them to the experimenter and perhaps even to themselves.

We believe that such social desirability concerns probably inhibited participants' interest in social comparison in a recent study, in which we shed the "impression formation" cover story. Recall the compensation study described earlier that asked participants to choose between another person's strong or weak dimensions (Wood et al., 1999: Experiment 2). That measure forced participants to choose a test for both themselves and the other person, and hence forced them to select a comparison. However, we also included an "unforced" measure in that study. Participants were asked to select a test for themselves and a test for their co-

---

[2]For example, in the self-affirmation study, the average number of matches yielded by this procedure was 1.55. As expected, this "cultural baseline" was higher than the chance baseline of 1.25. Although both the no-affirmation and affirmation groups sought comparisons at rates above the chance baseline, only the no-affirmation group sought more comparisons than the expected number based on the "cultural" baseline.

participant and this time were not required to select the same tests for both; they could choose different tests if they desired. The tests they could choose between were the same as those offered in the "forced" measure. They supposedly tapped into the same domains tapped into by "sample tests," which had suggested that the co-participant's ability was "average" in one case and "superior" in the other case. Thus, on this measure, participants could choose to compare or not, and if they chose to compare, they could do so on the other's average or superior dimension. On this measure, in contrast to the forced measure, failure participants did not show a preference for comparing on the other's weakness; they preferred not to compare at all.

This unforced measure resembled our usual test selection measure, with three important exceptions: (1) there was no impression formation "cover" for their interest in social comparisons; (2) it offered only a choice between two tests, instead of the usual 12–20; and (3) participants had information about how the other person could be expected to perform on those two tests. These features created a very bald context for social comparison, indeed, a blatantly competitive context. Failure participants may have feared that if they chose the other's weak dimension, they would appear to be especially competitive and to be taking pleasure in another person's weakness (Brickman & Bulman, 1977; Wills, 1981). Thus, we believe that this context made participants feel self-conscious about their choices and made the option of not comparing more appealing than usual. Clearly, further research is needed to confirm this hunch.

LESSONS FROM THE TEST SELECTION MEASURE CONCERNING SOCIAL COMPARISON

Beyond the topics I have already discussed, the test selection measure has taught us two main lessons about social comparison. One concerns the three strategies highlighted in this chapter, and the second concerns the research contexts that investigators use to address their questions, which constrain the conclusions that they draw.

Comparison Strategies

Our studies using the test selection measure have confirmed that target selection is not the only social comparison strategy that people may use. As has been argued but rarely examined empirically, people may avoid comparisons (Brickman & Bulman, 1977). They may do so to protect themselves from possibly unfavorable comparisons (as our low self-esteem–participants may have done), and they may do so simply because they are not interested in comparisons (as our high self-esteem success participants may have felt).

As we learned in the breast cancer research, people need not seek downward comparisons on the dimension on which their self-esteem has been threatened; they may focus instead on other dimensions on which they have a greater chance of emerging as superior. The test selection measure has enabled us to examine such dimension selection more systematically. This strategy may be particularly well suited to self-enhancement attempts, because finding a downward comparison on the dimension on which one has been threatened may be difficult. In addition, when a threat to self-esteem comes from being surpassed by a specific other person, sometimes choosing a different comparison target is not satisfying. However downward that different target, the comparison may not remedy the threat as much as besting the very person who surpassed oneself, and one may be able to surpass that person only on a dimension that is different from the original comparison.

The strategy of seeking new comparisons on the same dimension is one that has received virtually no previous attention. Nor have we fully exploited the potential of the test selection measure to capture this strategy. But the possibility that people may engage in this strategy seems very likely. Reversing an earlier failure against a rival may be particularly satisfying.

The Importance of the Comparison Context

Results obtained with the test selection measure point to contextual boundaries of widely held assumptions about social comparison selection. One assumption that has guided social comparison research since the beginning is that social comparison consists of selecting comparison targets. But as the test selection measure has confirmed, target selection is not the sine qua non of social comparison. If the context permits, people may use comparison strategies other than target selection.

A second widely held assumption has been that people choose comparisons that are more downward in direction when they are under threat than when they are not threatened. This assumption had achieved almost the status of a truism (e.g., Wood, 1989), yet it may be true only for certain contexts—contexts in which making a downward comparison (or a less upward comparison) is the only route for self-enhancement that one has. Wood and co-workers' (1994) high self-esteem–failure participants made highly upward comparisons, apparently for self-enhancement (Wood et al., 1999). They made highly upward comparisons in the following sense. As in many previous social comparison studies, participants took a test, learned that they performed poorly on it, and then were presented with an opportunity to compare themselves with someone who had strongly outperformed them on that test, indeed, who had achieved the highest possible score (in most studies, participants have other potential targets as well). Wood and co-workers' (1994) high self-esteem participants chose to compare themselves further with this highly superior person, whereas previous target selection studies suggest that people are unlikely to make such highly upward comparisons after threat (e.g., Smith & Insko, 1987). This discrepancy seems likely to be due to differences in the comparison context; whereas most previous studies have allowed participants only to compare their scores on the test they already took, our context allowed participants to perform on new tasks, which provided an opportunity to overturn the earlier failure or too focus on alternative domains.

Another illustration of the contextually bound nature of our conclusions (and hence, our theories) is the finding that some people seek self-enhancement and downward comparisons in particular when they are happy rather than when they are threatened (Wood et al., 1994; Wood et al., in press, cf. Wheeler & Miyake, 1992). This finding was revealed only when the research participants were low in self-esteem, and when the context under study included two features: (1) circumstances that were not only not threatening but were especially positive—involving success or positive mood—which may embolden people with low self-esteem, and (2) an opportunity for self-enhancement that was "safe"—relatively free of the risk of failure or humiliation.

In summary, the contexts that we as researchers provide for comparisons can determine which conclusions we draw. No doubt, future researchers will identify contextual limitations of the conclusions we have drawn from the test selection measure.

CONCLUSION

Social comparison offers many opportunities for fulfilling goals such as self-enhancement and self-improvement. To fully appreciate the ways in which social comparison provides these opportunities, researchers themselves must provide participants with more opportunities— more comparison options—than traditional comparison selection measures have allowed.

Although methods such as the rank order paradigm have revealed a great deal about the selection of comparison targets, researchers need other methods to learn about comparative strategies other than target selection. Methods that are less constrained and that allow participants more flexibility, such as the test selection measure, offer researchers new opportunities to examine the processes and functions of social comparison.

REFERENCES

Arkin, R. M. (1981). Self-presentational styles. In J. I. Tedeschi (Ed.), *Impression management theory and social psychological research* (pp. 311–333). San Diego, CA: Academic Press.

Baumeister, R. F. (1982). Self-esteem, self-presentation, and future interaction: A dilemma of reputation. *Journal of Personality, 50,* 29–45.

Baumeister, R. F. (1993). Understanding the inner nature of low self-esteem: Uncertain, fragile, protective and conflicted. In R. F. Baumeister (Ed.), *Self-esteem: The puzzle of low self-regard* (pp. 201–218). New York: Plenum Press.

Baumeister, R. F., Heatherton, T. F., & Tice, D. M. (1993). When ego threats lead to self-regulation failure: Negative consequences of high self-esteem. *Journal of Personality and Social Psychology, 64,* 141–156.

Baumeister, R. F., & Jones, E. E. (1978). When self-presentation is constrained by the target's knowledge: Consistency and compensation. *Journal of Personality and Social Psychology, 36,* 608–618.

Baumeister, R. F., Tice, D. M., & Hutton, D. G. (1989). Self-presentational motivations and personality differences in self-esteem. *Journal of Personality, 57,* 547–579.

Blaine, B., & Crocker, J. (1993). Self-esteem and self-serving biases in reactions to positive and negative events: An integrative review. In R. F. Baumeister (Ed.), *Self-esteem: The puzzle of low self-regard* (pp. 55–85). New York: Plenum Press.

Brickman, P., & Berman, J. J. (1971). Effects of performance expectancy and outcome certainty on interest in social comparison. *Journal of Experimental Social Psychology, 7,* 600–609.

Brickman, P., & Bulman, R. J. (1977). Pleasure and pain in social comparison. In J. M. Suls & R. L. Miller (Eds.), *Social comparison processes: Theoretical and empirical perspectives* (pp. 149–186). Washington, DC: Hemisphere.

Brown, J. D., & Smart, S. A. (1991). The self and social conduct: Linking self-representations to prosocial behavior. *Journal of Personality and Social Psychology, 60,* 368–375.

Brown, J. D., Collins, R. L., & Schmidt, G. W. (1988). Self-esteem and direct versus indirect forms of self-enhancement. *Journal of Personality and Social Psychology, 55,* 445–453.

Buunk, B. P., Collins, R. L., Taylor, S. E., VanYperen, N. W., & Dakof, G. A. (1990). The affective consequences of social comparison: Either direction has its ups and downs. *Journal of Personality and Social Psychology, 59,* 1238–1249.

Collins, R. L. (1996). For better or worse: The impact of upward social comparison on self-evaluations. *Psychological Bulletin, 119,* 51–69.

Colvin, C. R., & Block, J. (1994). Do positive illusions foster mental health? An examination of the Taylor and Brown formulation. *Psychological Bulletin, 116,* 3–20.

Dodgson, P., & Wood, J. V. (1998). Self-esteem and the cognitive accessibility of strengths and weaknesses after failure. *Journal of Personality and Social Psychology, 75,* 178–197.

Festinger, L. (1954). A theory of social comparison processes. *Human Relations, 7,* 117–140.

Gastorf, J. W., Suls, J., & Lawhon, J. (1978). Opponent choices of below average performers. *Bulletin of the Psychonomic Society, 12,* 217–220.

Goethals, G. R. (1986). Fabricating and ignoring social reality: Self-serving estimates of consensus. In J. M. Olson, C. P. Herman, & M. P. Zanna (Eds.), *Relative deprivation and social comparison: The Ontario symposium* (Vol. 4, pp. 135–157). Hillsdale, NJ: Lawrence Erlbaum.

Josephs, R. A., Larrick, R. P., Steele, C. M., & Nisbett, R. E. (1992a). Protecting the self from the negative consequences of risky decisions. *Journal of Personality and Social Psychology, 62,* 26–37.

Josephs, R. A., Markus, H. R., & Tafarodi, R. W. (1992b). Gender and self-esteem. *Journal of Personality and Social Psychology, 63,* 391–402.

Major, B., Testa, M., & Bylsma, W. H. (1991). Responses to upward and downward social comparisons: The impact of esteem-relevance and perceived control. In J. Suls & T. A. Wills (Eds.), *Social comparison: Contemporary theory and research* (pp. 237–260). Hillsdale, NJ: Lawrence Erlbaum.

McFarland, C., & Ross, M. (1982). Impact of causal attributions on affective reactions to success and failure. *Journal of Personality and Social Psychology, 43,* 937–946.

McFarlin, D. B., Baumeister, R. B., & Blascovich, J. (1984). On knowing when to quit: Task failure, self-esteem, advice, and nonproductive persistence. *Journal of Personality, 52,* 138–155.

McFarlin, D. B., & Blascovich, J. (1981). Effects of self-esteem and performance feedback on future affective preferences and cognitive expectations. *Journal of Personality and Social Psychology, 40,* 521–531.

Pyszczynski, T., Greenberg, J., & LaPrelle, J. (1985). Social comparison after success and failure: Biased search for information consistent with a self-serving conclusion. *Journal of Experimental Social Psychology, 21,* 195–211.

Ruble, D. N., Feldman, N. S., & Boggiano, A. K. (1976). Social comparison between young children in achievement situations. *Developmental Psychology, 12,* 192–197.

Schlenker, B. R., Weigold, M. E., & Hallam, J. R. (1990). Self-serving attributions in social context: Effects of self-esteem and social pressure. *Journal of Personality and Social Psychology, 58,* 855–863.

Smith, R. H., & Insko, C. A. (1987). Social comparison choice during ability evaluation: The effects of comparison publicity, performance feedback, and self-esteem. *Personality and Social Psychology Bulletin, 13,* 111–122.

Steele, C. M. (1975). Name calling and compliance. *Journal of Personality and Social Psychology, 31,* 361–369.

Steele, C. M. (1988). The psychology of self-affirmation: Sustaining the integrity of the self. In L. Berkowitz (Ed.), *Advances in experimental social psychology* (Vol. 21, pp. 261–302). San Diego, CA: Academic Press.

Steele, C. M., & Liu, T. J. (1983). Dissonance processes as self-affirmation. *Journal of Personality and Social Psychology, 45,* 5–19.

Steele, C. M., Spencer, S. J., & Lynch, M. (1993). Self-image resilience and dissonance: The role of affirmational resources. *Journal of Personality and Social Psychology, 64,* 885–896.

Suls, J., & Tesch, F. (1978). Students' preferences for information about their test performance: A social comparison study. *Journal of Applied Social Psychology, 8,* 189–197.

Swallow, S., & Kuiper, N. A. (1992). Mild depression and frequency of social comparison behavior. *Journal of Social and Clinical Psychology, 11,* 167–180.

Taylor, S. E., & Brown, J. D. (1988). Illusion and well-being: A social psychological perspective on mental health. *Psychological Bulletin, 103,* 193–210.

Taylor, S. E., & Lobel, M. (1989). Social comparison activity under threat: Downward evaluation and upward contacts. *Psychological Review, 96,* 569–575.

Tesser, A. (1986). Some effects of self-evaluation maintenance on cognition and action. In R. M. Sorrentino & E. T. Higgins (Eds.), *The handbook of motivation and cognition: Foundations of social behavior* (pp. 435–464). New York: Guilford.

Tesser, A., & Campbell, J. (1980). Self-definition: The impact of the relative performance and similarity of others. *Social Psychology Quarterly, 43,* 341–347.

Tice, D. M. (1991). Esteem protection or enhancement? Self-handicapping motives and attributions differ by trait self-esteem. *Journal of Personality and Social Psychology, 60,* 711–725.

Wheeler, L. (1966). Motivation as a determinant of upward comparison. *Journal of Experimental Social Psychology, Suppl. 1,* 27–31.

Wheeler, L., & Miyake, K. (1992). Social comparison in everyday life. *Journal of Personality and Social Psychology, 62,* 760–773.

Wheeler, L., & Zuckerman, M. (1977). Commentary. In J. M. Suls & R. L. Miller (Eds.), *Social comparison processes: Theoretical and empirical perspectives* (pp. 335–357).

Wills, T. A. (1981). Downward comparison principles in social psychology. *Psychological Bulletin, 90,* 245–271.

Wood, J. V. (1989). Theory and research concerning social comparisons of personal attributes. *Psychological Bulletin, 106,* 231–248.

Wood, J. V. (1996). What is social comparison and how should we study it? *Personality and Social Psychology Bulletin, 22,* 520–537.

Wood, J. V., & Dodgson, P. G. (1996). When is self-focused attention an adaptive coping response? Rumination and overgeneralization versus compensation. In I. G. Sarason, B. R. Sarason, & G. R. Pierce (Eds.), *Cognitive interference: Theories, methods, and findings* (pp. 231–259). Hillsdale, NJ: Lawrence Erlbaum.

Wood, J. V., Giordano-Beech, M., Taylor, K. L., Michela, J. L., & Gaus, V. (1994). Strategies of social comparison among people with low self-esteem: Self-protection and self-enhancement. *Journal of Personality and Social Psychology, 67,* 713–731.

Wood, J. V., Taylor, S. E., & Lichtman, R. R. (1985). Social comparison in adjustment to breast cancer. *Journal of Personality and Social Psychology, 49,* 1169–1183.

Wood, J. V., Giordano-Beech, M., & DuCharme, M. J. (1999). Compensating for failure through social comparison. *Personality and Social Psychology Bulletin, 25,* 1370–1386.

Wood, J. V., Michela, J. L., & Giordano, C. (in press). Downward comparison in everyday life: Self-enhancement models versus the mood-cognition priming model. *Journal of Personality and Social Psychology.*

12

Social Comparison

Lessons from Basic Research on Judgment

DOUGLAS H. WEDELL AND ALLEN PARDUCCI

Social comparisons may be thought to serve two basic functions: (1) to provide a check on one's version of reality, and (2) to serve as a basis for self-evaluation. The former function is demonstrated in the classic Schacter (1959) experiments on affiliation and in the social comparison mechanisms mediating bystander intervention (Latane & Darley, 1970). The latter is exemplified by the typical finding that regardless of the absolute level of one's performance, one is happier being near the top rather than the bottom of the relevant referent group (Brickman & Campbell, 1971; Marsh & Parker, 1984; Smith, Diener, & Wedell, 1989). Common to both functions is the idea that social comparisons can provide norms or standards with which to evaluate the situation or oneself. In this chapter we will focus on the cognitive processes underlying the formation of these judgmental standards. We examine basic judgment research from both social and nonsocial domains, with an aim to explicate some of the principles underlying the comparison process and consider the import of these principles for social comparisons.

We begin with a discussion of Parducci's (1965, 1995) range–frequency theory of judgment, as this theory provides a good description of how standards relate to the contextual set under consideration in a wide variety of judgment situations. Social comparisons can be viewed from the perspective of judgment situations in which the context is defined by the members of the relevant comparison group. Range–frequency theory provides a detailed description of how such comparisons are made and why downward comparisons so often lead to positive feelings of success, happiness, or self-esteem and upward comparison the reverse (Crosby, 1972; Marsh & Parker, 1984; Wills, 1991).

We then consider several elaborations of the range–frequency model and their import for social comparisons. The first elaboration concerns how the number of categories used in thinking about a situation may lead to different evaluations. We review research on how

DOUGLAS H. WEDELL • Department of Psychology, University of South Carolina, Columbia, South Carolina 29208.   ALLEN PARDUCCI • Department of Psychology, University of California at Los Angeles, Los Angeles, California 90024.

Handbook of Social Comparison: Theory and Research, edited by Suls and Wheeler. Kluwer Academic/Plenum Publishers, New York, 2000.

increasing the number of categories moderates contextual effects and consider implications for social comparisons. Another elaboration we consider is the ideas that the contexts for social comparisons may be separate from the contexts for intrapersonal experiences. We consider how these two types of contexts may interact and how people may make of use them. We then consider how imagined events and experiences might be included in the context for judgment. Such imagined events may be elicited through counterfactual thinking (Kahneman & Miller, 1986), daydreaming, or rumination.

Next we consider implications of how the multidimensional nature of the context for social comparison may lead to different self-evaluations. We review literature illustrating range–frequency effects in multidimensional contexts and consider how these might apply in social comparisons. In addition to basic range–frequency effects of context, we consider how weighting of dimensions and examination of higher–order relational information within a multidimensional context may affect evaluations. We then move on to consider how the contexts for social comparison may shape preferences in Aristotelian domains where more is not always better, but rather where it is a more moderate value along the dimension, a "golden mean," that is valued highest. We argue that in such domains, context serves the role of establishing norms used in both reality monitoring and self-evaluation.

Finally we consider how a broader conception of the self might affect the comparison process. For example, fans and auxiliary members of sports teams are clearly extremely pleased when their teams win, even though team members would represent an upward comparison to these spectators. An individual's group identity may lead to a different context for evaluation, a concept related to the idea of collective self-esteem (Luhtanen & Crocker, 1991). Thus through the identification process, upward comparisons can in such cases produce more positive self-evaluations, as described by Tesser and colleagues (Tesser, 1991; Tesser, Miller, & Moore, 1988).

RANGE–FREQUENCY THEORY OF JUDGMENT

The history of thinking about the relational character of judgment, including the special case of social comparisons, goes back at least to the Greek philosophers, Plato and Aristotle. The same conditions that arouse pleasure at one time may at another time prove disappointing or even painful, depending on changes in the context in which they are experienced. With social comparisons, the context typically includes other people with whom one's own conditions can be compared.

The rise of experimental psychology in the late 19th and early 20th centuries produced various alternative measures of experience, typically reports by human observers of what they were experiencing. These reports almost always include category ratings, like "slightly pleasant" or "extremely disappointing." Ratings expressed in such terms continue to serve as widely employed dependent variables in psychological research, because they are the means by which we most often express the dimensional judgments of events in our own everyday lives. To facilitate the development of scientific understanding of how such judgments are made, researchers associate numbers with the respective categories, for example, restricting their experimental subjects to a rating scale from "1—extremely unpleasant" to "9—extremely pleasant." To improve experimental control, researchers also try to specify the context in which such dimensional judgments are made.

Much of our understanding of dimensional judgments has grown out of experimental research using simple psychophysical stimuli. For example, the experimental subject might be presented a series of squares that vary in size, under instructions to rate the size of each square in comparison with the other squares presented in the same experimental session. The selection of these comparison sizes is systematically manipulated to determine the effects of different features of the context. The measure of theoretical understanding is then how well the resulting shifts in ratings can be predicted.

Systematic manipulation of the set of stimuli to be presented produces dramatic effects on the rating of any particular stimulus: The rating will be lower when most of the other stimuli are greater and higher when most of the other stimuli have lesser values on the dimension of judgment. Different theories of judgment explain the separate ratings in terms of relationships between each stimulus and different statistical features of the whole set of presented stimuli. Thus Volkmann's (1951) range theory of social judgement emphasized the relationship between what was being judged and the two extreme values of the stimulus context. Helson's (1964) theory of adaptation level singled out the mean of the contextual stimuli as the standard for judgment, with the rating of each stimulus depending on its difference from this mean or adaptation level. In the present chapter, we shall be concentrating on implications of range–frequency theory (Parducci, 1995), which emphasizes the relationship of what is being judged to the two endpoints of the context and also to the relative frequency of presentations exceeded by what is being judged, that is, its percentile rank in the context. We shall be employing range–frequency theory in our efforts to explain the effects of social comparisons.

This theory is easiest to grasp using numerical examples. Indeed, the research that led to the original development of the theory used abstract numbers as stimuli, the subject's task being to rate each of a set of 48 numbers printed in order of increasing value, from 100 to 1000, on a single page (Parducci, Calfee, Marshall, & Davidson, 1960). Each rating was restricted to one of six categories, from "1—very small" to "6—very large."

The Context for Judgment

Each judgment compares what is being judged to a set of related objects or stimuli that vary on the dimension of judgment. For example, such a dimensional judgment might answer the question: "How large is this particular number in comparison with the other numbers printed on the same page?" In this case, the context is a prescribed set of stimuli chosen by the experimenter. In other cases, it might be those similar stimuli to which the person making the judgment recently has been exposed. The context might also include imaginary stimulus values, counterfactuals that are evoked by actual presentations but never actually presented themselves, or stimulus values suggested by cognitive information presented in verbal form (such as, "imagine a number larger than any of those on the page"). In this chapter, we are particularly concerned with social comparisons, as when at least some components of the context represent attributes of other people. Since the contextual stimuli are often not present at the time of judgment, or even consciously recalled, they must somehow be represented cognitively so that they can provide the basis for judgment. Because the size of the effective context is limited by the cognitive capacities for processing such information, even some recently presented stimuli might have dropped out of the set currently represented as context (see Parducci & Wedell, 1986). Understanding the judgment is often a problem of identifying its context.

The Range Principle

Insofar as a judgment reflects the range principle, it describes what proportion of the contextual range falls below the stimulus being judged. The total range in the example of judging numbers was 900 (1000–100) so that the lowest sixth of the range extended from 100 to 250, a subrange of 150 (900/6). Following the range principle, any number between 100 and 250 would be rated "1–very small," those falling within the next subrange, 250 to 400, would be rated "2–small," and so forth. More generally, the range value of any stimulus corresponds to the proportion of the contextual range that it exceeds. In the special case where the stimuli are themselves abstract numbers, the range values are assumed to be linear to the presented stimulus numbers; when the stimuli do not themselves come in numerical form, as, for example, auditory tones of varying intensity, the relationship can instead be logarithmic. In practice, certainly with social stimuli, range values are themselves inferred from the ratings in best-fit analyses of the data.

Although the range principle may be stated in terms of category subranges, range values themselves are conceived on a continuous 0–1 scale that denotes the proportion of the contextual range falling below the stimulus being judged. The range value (R_{ik}) of a given stimulus i in context k is described by the following equation:

$$R_{ik} = (S_i - S_{min,k})/(S_{max,k} - S_{min,k}) \tag{1}$$

where S_i is the context invariant scale value of the stimulus, and the minimum and maximum values defining the range are designated $S_{min,k}$ and $S_{max,k}$, respectively. For example, a stimulus that is halfway between the extreme values receives a range value of 0.5, denoting that half the contextual range falls below that value. Range values thus denote a convenient way to describe the location of a stimulus with regard to the contextual range.

The Frequency Principle

Insofar as judgments follow the frequency principle, the same number of contextual stimuli are assigned to each of the available categories. In the research using abstract numbers as stimuli, the 48 numbers are divided between the six categories, with eight numbers (48/6) assigned to each category; thus, the first eight numbers would be assigned to the lowest category, the next eight to the second category, and so on. If the numbers are closely packed at the lowest end, for example, 100, 102, 105, 109, 114, 121, 128, 139, the frequency principle would produce a lowest category that spanned only a narrow subrange, in this case 39 (139–100); if they are widely spaced, for example, 100, 206, 289, 331, 362, 397, 425, 500, the lowest category would span a much wider subrange, in this case 400 (500–100).

More generally, the frequency value (i.e., the judgment according to the frequency principle) is equal to the percentile rank of that stimulus divided by 100 (to put it on the same 0-to-1 proportion scale as the range value). The equation describing the frequency value of stimulus i in context k is given below:

$$F_{ik} = (rank_{ik} - 1)/(N_k - 1) \tag{2}$$

where N_k is the number of contextual stimuli and represents the maximum contextual rank, $rank_{ik}$ is the rank of the stimulus in that contextual set, and 1 represents the minimum rank. Thus the frequency value describes the proportion of contextual stimuli lying below the stimulus value. For example, a frequency value of 0.75 means that 75% of the stimulus distribution falls below the stimulus value.

The Range–Frequency Compromise

Unless the stimuli are uniformly spaced across the contextual range, range and frequency values are likely to differ for any particular stimulus. The resulting judgment then falls between these two values and is represented as their weighted average:

$$J_{ik} = wR_{ik} + (1 - w)F_{ik} \qquad (3)$$

where J_{ik} is the judgment of the ith stimulus in context k, w is the weighting of the range value, R_{ik}, and $(1 - w)$ is the weighting of the frequency value, F_{ik}, of this stimulus. With abstract numbers as stimuli, the compromise is close to halfway, so that range and frequency principles receive about equal weighting, that is, close to 0.5. In a variety of experimental situations, w is found to be close enough to 0.5 that this equal weighting of range and frequency values is sometimes assumed in tests of the theory (Parducci et al., 1960; Wedell, Parducci, & Roman, 1989).

From Judgments to Ratings

Each judgment is assumed to be an internal experience that can be expressed overtly as a category rating. When ratings are expressed in numerical terms or when verbal categories are converted to numbers by the researcher (customarily by rank in the set of available categories), the relationship between category rating and judgment is given by the following equation:

$$C_{ik} = bJ_{ik} + a \qquad (4)$$

where the category rating of the ith stimulus in context k, is a linear function of its judgment, with the multiplicative constant, b, equal to one less than the number of categories (i.e., the range of their ranks) and with the additive constant, a, equal to the value assigned the lowest category (customarily 1).

Application to Social Comparisons

Figure 1 provides a schematic illustration of the application of the range frequency model to several distributions. In these diagrams, variations of height are used to illustrate variations of the attribute of interest. Comparison groups representing the relevant contexts are identified by whether they are full range, low range, or high range and whether the distribution is uniform, positively skewed, or negatively skewed. Numbers under each person describe the range frequency judgments (on a 0–100 scale), assuming the range is defined strictly by the comparison group and range and frequency principles are equally weighted (i.e., $w = .5$). Our primary focus will be on the rating of the shaded individual in each group. This target person has the same moderate attribute value in each of the five comparison groups, but receives different evaluations due to the different distributions in which he appears.

The seven persons in the full-range uniform (FU) condition are spaced at equal intervals so that range and frequency values will agree. For example, the target has a height halfway between the tallest and shortest persons in this set and also is at the median of the distribution. Hence this individual receives a rating of 50. Now consider the evaluation of the target when placed in different comparison contexts. In the low-range uniform (LU) distribution, he receives a rating of 100 because he is the tallest person in the contextual set. Alternatively, he receives a rating of 0 in the high-range uniform (HU) distribution because he is now the shortest person in the set. In both LU and HU distributions, range and frequency effects are perfectly confounded. In order to see the independent operation of frequency effects, we hold the range constant. This is illustrated in the last two sets. In the full-range positively skewed (FP) set, the target is at the midpoint of the range (i.e., $R_{ik} = 0.5$) but has a frequency value of 0.75. Averaging these two values and converting to the 0–100 point scale results in a rating of 63. Conversely, the target has a frequency value of only 0.25 in the full-range negatively skewed (FN) set and so receives a rating of 37. Because range is held constant, the difference in the

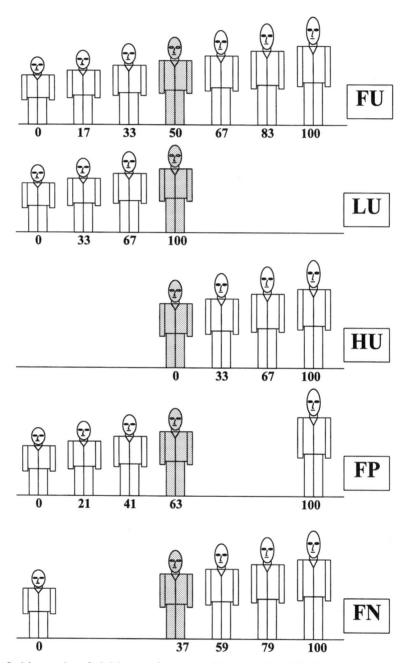

Figure 1. Social comparisons for height across five contexts: full-range uniform (FU), low-range uniform (LU), high-range uniform (HU), full-range positive skew (FP), and full-range negative skew (FN). Numbers represent range–frequency predictions (on a 0–100 scale) assuming $w = .5$ and the range is defined by the comparison set. The shaded target individual is common to all sets.

ratings of the targeted individual across FP and FN sets is simply due to differences of the individual's ranks across the comparison group.

We have focused our description of the context effects shown in Fig. 1 on how an individual's self-evaluation may be affected by being compared to sets with different ranges and frequency distributions. Qualitatively, these are the same predictions given by Helson's (1964) adaptation-level theory in which judgments simply reflect deviations from the mean or adaptation level. One qualitatively different prediction between these two theories emerges when we consider the combined evaluations of all members of the group. In particular, consider the FP and FN distributions. According to adaptation-level theory, the average of the ratings in these two contexts will be the same because the sum of deviations from the mean is always zero (Brickman & Campbell, 1971; Parducci, 1968). On the other hand, range–frequency theory entails a higher average rating in the negatively skewed distribution. This is because range values are typically higher in the negatively skewed distribution, so that more persons have values above the midpoint of the distribution. Specifically, Parducci (1995) has shown that the mean of judgments (on a 0–1 scale) is given by the following equation:

$$\bar{J} = .5 + w(\text{Mean} - \text{Midpoint})/\text{Range} \qquad (5)$$

where Mean $= \Sigma S_i/N$, Midpoint $= (S_{max,k} + S_{min,k})/2$, and Range $= (S_{max,k} - S_{min,k})$. Note that if judgments are entirely based on frequency values (i.e., $w = 0$), then the average of the judgments will always be 0.5, a neutral value, regardless of the skewing of the distribution. On the other hand, if judgments are entirely based on range values ($w = 1.0$), then the model reduces to Volkmann's (1951) range model and the average of the judgments will rise above 0.5 as the distribution becomes more and more negatively skewed (so that the mean is above the midpoint). Thus, the mean of the ratings for the FN distribution would, according to pure range theory, be higher than that for the FP distribution at the same time the ratings of the common target stimuli will be the same across contexts. However, range–frequency theory implies that the target stimulus would be rated lower in the FN set.

Clearly, according to range–frequency theory, effects of a particular social comparison context may have different implications for satisfaction of a particular individual than for satisfaction of the group as a whole. The group as a whole is on average more satisfied when the distribution is negatively skewed, but the same individual will be more satisfied in a positively skewed distribution (equated in range), due to that person's higher rank within the group. This is an important implication of range–frequency theory that often has been misunderstood. How can the judgment of any particular stimulus or individual be lower when the overall mean of all judgments is higher? Again, this is because so many more stimuli or people are closer to the top of a negatively skewed distribution.

In this regard, it is also important to note that the predictions in Fig. 1 are all based on the simple assumption that the context is completely determined by the characteristics of the group to which one is a member. It is as if members of the LU group had no idea of the existence of members of the HU group, or at least did not consider this other group when evaluating themselves. This may seem reasonable according to the well-supported tenet of the social comparison theory that we compare ourselves only to similar others (Festinger, 1954; Goethals & Darley, 1977). For example, one may compare one's softball-playing ability primarily with others playing in the same recreation league, and it seems unlikely that one would include major league baseball players in the comparison set. It is such highly dissimilar contextual groups that would produce the theoretical social comparison judgments shown in Fig. 1 for LU and HU sets. However, if groups are not so distinct or dissimilar, then our target person in the LU group might consider joining the HU group. In this situation, we might expect the range to extend to include the higher values in the HU group. The consequence would be that our target individual would now rate himself much lower, as his range value would have dropped from 1.0 to 0.50. Thus, critical to how we apply range–frequency theory is the issue of what exactly constitutes the context for comparison. We discuss this issue in more detail later in this chapter.

Validation of the Model

As we have just pointed out, range–frequency theory leads to different predictions about the effects of context than those generated by other basic contextual theories, such as Volkmann's (1951) range theory and Helson's (1947) adaptation-level theory. In this section we briefly review the evidence in favor of the range–frequency model.

The psychophysical arena has provided the strongest tests of the range–frequency theory in comparison to its competitors. One way to characterize the differences among these theories is in terms of how they assign values to represent the context. Adaptation-level theory uses a single value (the mean or the adaptation level). Range theory uses the minimum and maximum values defining the range. Range–frequency theory takes the specific shape of the distribution into account (as represented through the frequency principle) and also the range (as represented through the range principle).

Figure 2 illustrates patterns of data correctly predicted by range–frequency theory but inconsistent with both range and adaptation-level theories. The left panel shows predictions for positively and negatively skewed distributions. Note that the functions pinch at the ends but differ widely in the middle. The pinching at the end can be interpreted as evidence that the two distributions generate the same range of values, and thus range theory predicts no differences in the ratings for positive and negative sets. On the other hand, adaptation-level theory does predict higher ratings for the positive set, but it does not predict the pinching of the functions at the end stimuli. Only range–frequency theory predicts the pattern of data shown and experimentally verified with a wide variety of stimuli and judgment tasks, as demonstrated in dozens of experiments (Mellers & Birnbaum, 1983; Parducci & Perrett, 1971; Smith et al., 1981; Parducci & Wedell, 1986; Wedell, 1994, 1996).

With auxiliary assumptions, adaptation-level theory could perhaps be made to fit the data in the left panel (for example, one might assume artificial ceiling and floor effects that cause the pinching of the functions). Thus, several experiments have been run comparing bell and U-shaped distributions, as shown in the middle panel of Fig. 2. In this case, the adaptation level as defined by the stimulus falling at the middle of the judgment scale is identical across contexts. Consequently, adaptation-level theory predicts no differences in ratings of the same stimuli in these two contexts. Contrary to this prediction, the systematic effects of context predicted by range–frequency theory and shown in the middle panel of Fig. 2 have been repeatedly demonstrated for a variety of stimuli and judgment dimensions (e.g., Parducci & Perrett, 1971; Wedell & Parducci, 1988; Wedell et al., 1989). However, once again, one might invoke auxiliary assumptions to explain the data within adaptation-level and range theories. For example, if the unit on the judgment scale were proportional to the standard deviation of the contextual distribution, then some of the differences observed for bell and U-shaped distributions could be explained within the adaptation-level framework. Thus, as a very stringent test of the theories, Birnbaum (1974) created distributions similar to those shown in the right panel of Fig. 2. These distributions resulted in the double crossover of the rating

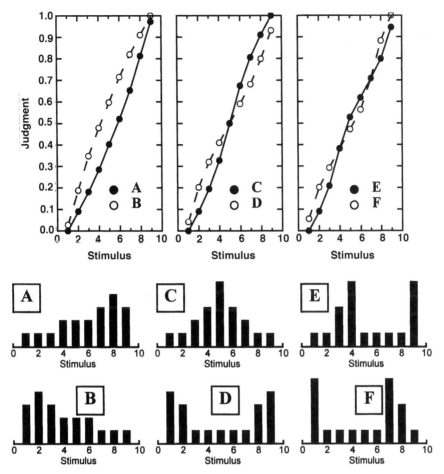

Figure 2. Range–frequency predictions for different distributions based on $w = .5$ and an experimentally defined range. Left panel compares (A) negatively skewed and (B) positively skewed sets. Middle panel compares (C) bell and (D) U-shaped sets. Right panel represents a double crossover interaction using offset bimodal distributions (E and F). Each pattern of judgment has been demonstrated experimentally.

functions predicted by range–frequency theory that was clearly inconsistent with adaptation-level theory.

In addition to psychophysical judgments, range–frequency models have been fit successfully to a wide variety of judgment dimensions, including judgments of attractiveness of faces (Wedell, Parducci, & Geiselman, 1987), attractiveness of apartments (Mellers & Cooke, 1994), attractiveness of consumer products (Wedell & Pettibone, 1996), psychopathology of abstracted clinical case histories (Wedell, Parducci, & Lane, 1990), evaluations of test scores (Mellers & Birnbaum, 1983; Wedell et al., 1989), happiness of life events (Parducci, 1968; Wedell & Parducci, 1988), equity of salary allocations (Mellers, 1986), and likability of persons described by trait adjectives (Wedell, 1994). Thus, it seems appropriate to employ range–frequency theory to characterize how people generally construct contextual standards of judgment.[1]

Process Considerations

One issue that often arises when discussing the nature of context effects is whether the changes in judgment so regularly observed with changes in context correspond to "real" changes in the psychological impression of the stimulus or whether they are simply an artifact of how responses are generated and communicated (Krantz & Campbell, 1961; Manis, 1967). One answer to the challenge posed by asserting context effects are merely labeling effects is to point out how even if this were true, labels appear to have a strong psychological impact on evaluations and performance (e.g., the change in standard effect described by Higgins & Lurie, 1983). However, in addition to effects of context created by remembering and using prior labels, we believe there is good evidence that range–frequency effects reflect changes not just in the overt responses but also in subjective impressions. For example, the basic contrast effects described by range–frequency theory occur across a wide variety of responses, from category ratings to physiological measures of anxiety (Krupat, 1974) to the speed with which rats run toward a reward (Crespi, 1944). It also is clear that range–frequency theory effects occur even when none of the contextual stimuli are overtly rated (Parducci & Wedell, 1986; Smith et al., 1989), so that these effects do not depend on simple response processes as proposed by some researchers (Haubensak, 1992).

Perhaps the most convincing evidence of the psychological reality of the contrast effects described by range–frequency theory is found when range–frequency values serve as the basis of other operations, such as determining equity (Mellers, 1986), preference (Mellers & Cooke, 1994; Cooke & Mellers, 1998; Wedell, 1998), or similarity (Wedell, 1996). Because similarity

---

[1]Another often-cited theory of contextual standards is Sherif and Hovland's (1961) social judgment theory. According to this theory, one's own position on the attitude continuum acts as a contextual standard; attitudes close to one's position are assimilated, whereas attitudes further away are contrasted. The model was based initially on psychophysical research with lifted weights (Sherif, Taub, and Hovland, 1958) in which an unjudged standard weight was assigned the end category on a rating scale and its effects on ratings of the other weights were observed. Relative to ratings made without such standards, ratings of stimuli nearest the standard shifted (assimilated) toward the value of the standard and those further away shifted in the opposite direction (contrast). Subsequent research within the psychophysical realm (Parducci & Marshall, 1962) demonstrated that this assimilation and contrast pattern was mainly an artifact of the method used (reserving a category for the standard) along with the well-documented memory drift of the remembered value of the standard toward the mean of all stimulus values. Thus, the assimilation component of the model is found in psychophysical judgment only under very restrictive conditions.

Sherif and Hovland's (1961) model has persisted in the literature, largely because there have been several studies that show that persons with extreme anchors produce a pattern of judgment similar to assimilation and contrast (for a review, see Eiser, 1990). Unlike the psychophysical judgment situation, these results appeared to be dependent on individuals having strong affective responses to the attitudinal positions being judged. Several researchers have demonstrated that rather than represent assimilation and contrast effects, these effects of own anchor are best understood as accentuation or polarization effects in which those who are affectively involved with an attitude domain tend to use their affective reactions to stimuli to accentuate differences among them (Eiser and van der Pligt, 1982; Judd & Harackiewicz, 1980). Thus, for example, Lambert and Wedell (1991) found a person who is high in sociability will rate a high sociability target as higher in sociability and a low sociability target as lower in sociability than a person who is moderate on that trait. The former effect is suggestive of assimilation and the latter of contrast, but both can be explained as a result of people who are highly involved in a dimension accentuating differences along the scale. The accentuation interpretation of this pattern of results was supported by the demonstration that own-position did not predict this effect when affective involvement was partialed out but that affective involvement in the dimension did predict the effect even when own-position was partialed out. These affectively based accentuation effects are beyond the scope of the present discussion.

is an important construct mediating social comparisons, we will review the evidence that demonstrates how similarity relationships are determined by a range–frequency process. Wedell (1996) used a psychophysical judgment paradigm in which participants rated the similarity in size of pairs of squares drawn from either a positively skewed or negatively skewed distribution. If similarity were independent of context, then the similarity relationships among common target pairs should not differ across contexts. However, if similarity were based on range–frequency altered values, then different similarity relationships should emerge across contexts. Wedell (1996) found that similarity was typically based on the range–frequency-altered values rather than on context-independent values.

To get a feel for this effect, consider once again the FP and FN distributions shown in Fig. 1. The two end persons and our shaded target person are common to the two distributions. If similarity were based simply on context-independent values, then the target person's similarity to the highest- and lowest-valued individuals would be the same in the two contexts. However, what if similarity were based on the range–frequency judgments shown below each individual? In the FP condition the target receives a rating of 63 and in the FN condition he receives a rating of 37, while lowest- and highest-valued persons are rated 0 and 100, respectively. If similarity is based on the difference in the contextually altered ratings, then the target person would be seen as more similar to the tallest person rather than the shortest person in the FP condition. This similarity relationship would be reversed in the FN condition. And this, indeed, is the empirical finding (Wedell, 1996).

The finding of contextually altered similarity relationships is particularly important to social comparisons because similarity is thought to moderate the comparison process (Festinger, 1954). In particular, there is good evidence that persons who are dissimilar to ourselves are unlikely to be included in the social comparison set (Major, Testa, & Bylsma, 1991). the context-dependent similarity relationships described by Wedell (1996) can be combined with the moderating function of similarity in determining the comparison context to predict a reduction and even a reversal of context effects described in Fig. 1. For example, because the highest-valued person is less similar to the target person in the FN rather than the FP condition, he is more likely to be excluded from the comparison set in the FN condition. Similarly, the lowest-valued person is less likely to be included in the comparison set in the FP than in the FN set. These effects would combine to reduce the effects of skewing as demonstrated by Sarris (1967).

If we take an extreme example, we can even see conditions in which the effects of context would reverse. For example, let us assume that the comparison set consists of only the persons one rank above and one rank below the target person. In the FP condition, the context would consist of the tallest person and a person only slightly shorter than the target. In this context, the target would be below average on the rating scale. In the FN condition, the context would consist of the shortest person and a person only slightly taller than the target. In this context, the target would be above average on the rating scale.

The upshot of this analysis is that a critical determinant of social comparison effects is what gets included in the comparison context. Because range–frequency processes have been shown to work on similarity relations (Wedell, 1996) and similarity has been shown to moderate what gets included in the context (Brown, 1953; Festinger, 1954; Goethals & Darley, 1977; Sarris, 1967), the comparison set may be less skewed than the reference distribution, thereby moderating (and even possibly reversing) the expected effects of context. Unfortunately, it is difficult to determine the contents of the social comparison context directly. Moreover, dimensions other than the dimension on which judgments are based would affect similarity, and hence, inclusion in the context of social comparison. For example, Miller

(1982) demonstrated that people tend to select others similar in physical attractiveness for comparison, even when this dimension is irrelevant to the attribute of comparison. Clearly, the determination of the set of individuals making up the social comparison context is vital to the understanding the effects of social comparisons.

ELABORATIONS OF RANGE–FREQUENCY THEORY

In this section, we discuss several elaborations of the basic range–frequency model that seem applicable to social comparisons.

Number of Categories Used in Making Evaluations

Although we noted earlier that range–frequency effects occur across a wide variety of response modes, there are response factors that appear to affect the impact of the recently experienced context on judgment. One of the more interesting of these is the number of categories used in making judgments (Parducci, 1982). In most scientific research, the number of rating categories is prescribed by the researcher. However, it is reasonable to assume that people differ in the number of categories they naturally use to evaluate life events. Some of these differences may be due to general differences in cognitive style: Some people tend to see the world in black and white and some in many variations of gray (Bieri et al., 1966; Gardner & Schoen, 1962). Other differences may be domain specific, so that people tend to use more categories when making judgments within a domain of expertise rather than a domain with which they are unfamiliar (Murphy & Wright, 1984; Tanaka & Taylor, 1991). The research on number of categories asks the question of whether such differences in the prescribed number of categories used in evaluating stimuli lead to differences in the nature of the contextual dependency of judgment. It general, we have found two basic tendencies: Increases in number of categories lead to (1) diminished effects of repeated stimulus values, and (2) extension of the stimulus range to include a broader set of stimulus values than those presented for judgment.

In a series of experiments, Parducci and Wedell (1986) investigated how effects of manipulating frequency values depended on the number of categories and the method for manipulating frequency values. One way to manipulate frequency values is to vary the number of times the different stimuli are repeated. The histograms of Fig. 2 illustrate this method. Here, the same stimuli are presented in the two contexts but with different frequencies. A second way to manipulate frequency values is to manipulate the spacing rather than the frequencies of the stimuli. This manipulation is illustrated in the FP and FN sets of Fig. 1. Here, each person is represented only once, but the spacing of people's heights differ so that the target person is ranked fourth shortest in the FP context but second shortest in the FN context. Parducci and Wedell found that when frequency values were manipulated by presenting the same small number of stimuli with unequal frequencies, the weighting of frequency values $(1 - w)$ appeared to diminish systematically with increase in number of categories. This result is illustrated in the first row of Table 1. When only two or three categories were used to rate the five squares, the relatively high values of $1 - w$ indicate that ratings strongly depended on whether the distribution was positively or negatively skewed. However, when ratings were made on a 100-point scale, the manipulation of context had little effect on the stimulus ratings.

The results described above were based on the situation in which the number of categories was prescribed by the experimenter. Parducci and Wedell (1986) also investigated the situation in which people could generate their own categories. In these open category condi-

Table 1. Inferred Frequency Weighting (1 − w) as a Function of Method of Skewing, Number of Stimuli, Type of Stimuli, and Number of Categories

Type of stimuli	N	Skewing	Judgment	Number of categories					
				2	3	5	7	9	100
Squares[a]	5	Unequal frequencies	Size	.69	.45	.25	—	.20	.07
Squares[a]	9	Unequal frequencies	Size	.87	.51	.46	.51	.33	.14
Squares[a]	5	Unequal spacing	Size	—	.39	—	—	.39	.26
Squares[a]	9	Unequal spacing	Size	—	.38	—	—	.37	.12
Schematic faces[b]	9	Unequal frequencies	Emotion	—	.40	—	.31	—	.14
Case histories[c]	20	Unequal spacing	Mental disturbance	—	.75	—	.44	—	.40
Photos of faces[d]	48	Unequal spacing	Attractiveness	—	—	.24	—	—	.24

[a]Parducci & Wedell (1986)
[b]Wedell & Parducci (1988)
[c]Wedell, Parducci, & Lane (1990)
[d]Wedell, Parducci, & Geiselman (1987)
Abbreviation: N, number of stimuli.

tions, participants were told that they could use whatever phrases or descriptors they wished to describe the variations in size that they saw. In one condition, two example categories were given ("small" and "large"). In another condition, six example categories were given (e.g., "very very small," "small," "slightly larger than average," etc.). As one might expect, the number of example categories given to participants influenced the number of categories they decided to use in rating the stimuli, with the two-example instructions leading to the use of about five categories on average and the six-example instructions leading to the use of about six categories on average. Parallel to the results from the prescribed category situation, participants in the two-example condition showed significantly greater skewing effects than those in the six-example condition. Of greater consequence to the generality of the category effect are the results that compared those who used fewer than five spontaneously generated categories to those who used greater than five categories. When analyzed in this manner, average results for those using fewer than five categories looked nearly identical to results from prescribing three categories; results from those using five or more categories looked very similar to results from prescribing nine categories. Thus, these results suggest that the category effect generalizes to the situation in which the number of categories are spontaneously generated by the subject.

The second row of Table 1 illustrates results of an unequal frequencies manipulation conducted using nine rather than just five square sizes. Although increasing the number of categories once again leads to diminished context effects (as indexed by 1 − w), overall, the effects of skewing are greater for the nine-stimulus sets. Parducci and Wedell (1986) argued that the effects of number of categories and number of stimuli had a common basis, namely, that the frequency principle can conflict with a consistency principle when stimuli are repeated many times. When a stimulus is repeated often and there are relatively large numbers of categories, the frequency principle essentially will lead to the same stimulus being assigned to more than one category. However, a basic principle for reliability of judgment is to assign consistently the same stimulus to the same category, a consistency principle. Apparently when these conflict, the consistency principle is given precedence over the frequency principle. As the number of categories increases relative to the number of stimuli, the frequency principle is more likely to conflict with the consistency principle, and hence effects of skewing are diminished.

One consequence of this explanation is that it should make a difference whether skewing is achieved through manipulating stimulus frequencies or stimulus spacing. When stimulus spacing is manipulated, there is less likely to be a conflict between the frequency and consistency principles so that skewing should be less dependent on the number of categories or number of stimuli. The third and fourth rows of Table 1 illustrate the results for unequal spacing manipulations in judgments of square size. As predicted, the frequency weighting is nearly identical for three and nine category scales regardless of whether there were five or nine stimulus values. However, the 100-point scale produced markedly reduced effects of skewing in both stimulus conditions. This latter result may be tied to the task of judging square size, because skewed spacing manipulations for other psychophysical judgments and social judgment domains show large effects of context for 100-point scales and even magnitude estimation scales that are virtually boundless (Mellers, 1983; Wedell et al., 1990).

The dependence of the category effect on whether stimuli are skewed by manipulating frequencies or by manipulating spacing leads to the question of whether increasing the number of categories matters outside the psychophysical laboratory. The last three rows of Table 1 describe data that speak to this question. Data in the fifth row show that when schematic faces are judged in terms of how happy or sad they appear, the category effect is still present (Wedell & Parducci, 1988). Data in the sixth row correspond to ratings of the psychopathology of abstracted clinical case histories (Wedell et al., 1990). Despite the fact that skewing was obtained via unequal spacing, there was a significant decrease in the effects of skewing from 3 to 7 categories, but no additional decrease from 7 to 100 categories. The final row shows a lack of effect of increasing number of categories for judgments of the attractiveness of photographs of faces with unequal spacing (i.e., skewing was achieved by showing different faces rather than the same faces with different frequencies). These results are generally consistent with the psychophysical judgment data in which the category effect is more likely to occur when contextual stimuli or events vary in their frequency rather than in their spacing along the dimension of judgment.

Overall, as shown in Table 1, increasing the number of rating categories often can lead to a decrease in the sensitivity of judgments to contextual skewing. This decreased sensitivity is greatest when the stimuli are relatively few, the number of categories are relatively large, and skewing is achieved by manipulating the relative frequencies with which different stimuli are repeated. In such circumstances, a person who thinks in terms of just two categories (e.g., large or small, good or bad, friendly or unfriendly) will tend to be very sensitive to changes in the ranks of stimuli, whereas those who use a more fine-grained scale will be less sensitive.

Although the effects of varying the number of categories on sensitivity to skewing were not large in the research on attractiveness and psychopathology, another interesting effect emerged in both of these studies. As the number of categories increased, the inferred range likewise appeared to increase. Thus, when considering the relative attractiveness of photographs of faces on a five-point scale, mean ratings for the extreme cases spanned roughly three fourths of the rating scale, whereas ratings of these stimuli on the 100-point scale spanned only about half of the rating scale. The most obvious interpretation is that this flattening of the slope of the rating functions is due to greater extension of the contextual range with more categories. When an individual has only a few categories, reserving extreme categories for extreme stimuli outside the present range would prevent use of the scale to discriminate differences in the experimental set. However, when many categories are available, the scale can be anchored to a wider range without loss of discrimination.

As a practical application, consider an example of a person who recently has had a severe accident and who can no longer function as he or she once did (for example, a victim of a stroke, a heart attack, or a spinal injury). At this point, the individual is facing a period of adjustment to a new context. Failure to adjust would result in strong negative feelings of depression and anger, as that person's current capabilities are now so far down and so far below that of others. In this case, it may be very discouraging to use many categories in judging one's progress, abilities, and self-image. A large number of categories will encourage comparisons to a broader range, which in this situation would mean strong upward extension of the range, and hence more negative evaluation of oneself. On the other hand, using just two or three categories to rate oneself could restrict the range to a more plausible set of achievable behaviors. Also, the large number of categories may lead to a discounting of any progress one is making day by day, whereas, restriction to just a few categories would result in greater sensitivity to this type of slow but steady progress in behavioral abilities, enhancing self-image and self-esteem.

Intrapersonal versus Social Comparison Context

Smith et al. (1989) conducted a study to determine whether intrapersonal and social comparisons both followed the same process. Participants viewed either negatively or positively skewed distributions of numbers, described as representing tips (for waiting tables) received either by others at the same restaurant (social comparisons) of by the participant over different occasions at the restaurant (intrapersonal comparison). Participants then rated how happy they would feel if they received each of six different tips (target stimuli). The results for both intrapersonal and social comparisons followed the same range–frequency predictions, conforming to the general pattern shown in the left panel of Fig. 2 for positively and negatively skewed distributions. However, participants gave significantly greater weight to the frequency principle when making evaluations based on intrapersonal comparisons ($1 - w = 0.71$) than when making evaluations based on social comparisons ($1 - w = 0.47$). This means that happiness or satisfaction was more affected by how people's performances ranked with their own past performances than with how their performances ranked with the performances of others. A consequence of the greater weighting of the frequency principle in the intrapersonal context is that overall happiness, conceived as the mean of all judgments, will vary less as a function of skewing in this context. As Eq. (5) indicates, overall happiness will depend on the skewing of the distribution of events only to the extent that the range principle is weighted. When frequency values receive full weight (i.e., $1 - w = 1.0$), then the mean of all the judgments (i.e., happiness) must equal the neutral point on the happiness scale. The greater weighting of frequency values in the intrapersonal context suggests a strategy that may serve to buffer individuals from large swings in overall happiness as a function of their distributions of outcomes. It also may reflect a tendency of people to be more willing to compare themselves to their own performances rather than to the performances of others.

Although not studied by Smith et al. (1989), it is possible to manipulate both intrapersonal and social comparison contexts for the same individual. For example, in a typical classroom setting, one can compare one's performance on a test or quiz to the performance of the class, a social comparison, or to one's own past test scores, an intrapersonal context (Albert, 1977; Suls & Mullen, 1982). Within attribution theory (Kelley, 1967), the former would be the basis for consensus information and the latter for consistency and distinctiveness information. The attributional analysis emphasizes the reality-checking function of social comparisons. However, both sources can be used to influence the evaluation of one's performance. A poor student who scores a C+ may be happy with that performance if it is above past performances, despite still being low for the class. A top student might still be pleased with a B+, if it were the top score in the class, even though it represented his or her own lowest score. In the former case, greater weight was given to intrapersonal comparisons, whereas in the latter case it was social comparisons that got greater weight. It would be instructive to examine how individuals weigh these two sources of contextual information. One would expect individual differences to interact with situational differences; however, there has been little work on how intrapersonal and social comparison domains are integrated.

In addition to determining how these two sources of information are weighted when the information is equally available, we also might ask under what conditions individuals seek out these different types of information. A study by Levine and Green (1984) suggests that the type of social comparison information sought may depend on the intrapersonal context one experiences. In that study, elementary school students were given false feedback on a task that suggested they were doing increasingly worse or increasingly better (a manipulation of intrapersonal context). The intrapersonal context variable was crossed with social comparison context, the low context represented by a tendency for comparison others to perform more poorly than the participant and the high context represented by the opposite tendency. After the feedback on each trial, participants were permitted to look at a score of a peer who had performed worse or better than they did on that trial. The basic finding was that those in the positive intrapersonal context made equal numbers of upward and downward social comparisons and those in the negative intrapersonal context made more downward social comparisons. Thus, when the intrapersonal context results in negative self-evaluation, one may be more likely to seek out a social comparison context that will bolster self evaluations (i.e., downward comparisons).

Applications of range–frequency theory to happiness and satisfaction have tended to concentrate on the intrapersonal context (Parducci, 1995). Social comparisons have been modeled as imagined events that might skew the context or extend the range. More research is needed to determine whether these two sources of information tend to be considered independently (as when the student is alternatively pleased that he got the top score and disappointed because he usually scores better) or if they are blended into one general context (as when he experiences the good and bad as their average, that is, indifferent).

Imaginary Social Comparisons

When we concentrate our attention on those experiences most saturated with affect, that is, with pleasure or pain, they seem largely imaginary: hopes for future success, memories of past failures, or pure fantasies that are related only tenuously to external events. Many of our social comparisons occur in this subjective world of the imagination. We imagine what it would be like to outperform out closest rivals, we relive the disappointment we felt when they outperformed us, or we create a Walter Mitty world in which we are the star performers in activities that we have never been so foolish as to actually attempt in the real world.

Because these most subjective of experiences have long been considered outside the realm of objective science, there are few studies attempting to bring them under experimental control: Our knowledge in this arena comes largely from reflecting on our own daydreaming. However, this commonsense type of knowledge can be abetted by what has been learned about judgments in the laboratory and, with our present concern, about the particular kinds of judgment involving social comparisons. For example, consider the pleasures we get from an imagined victory in competition with other people. This is what we call an imagined downward social comparison. We fantasize that we are outperforming relevant others, our colleagues, other researchers working on the same problems, or perhaps just acquaintances with whom we have a pleasant rivalry in some sport. In each case, the pleasure comes from judging ourselves better on whatever dimension underlies the comparison, amount of recognition or fame, success at problem solving, speed in an athletic competition. The better we do in comparison with these relevant others, the greater our delight.

In the absence of contrary evidence, one can assume that the same principles of judgment operate in these imaginary comparisons as in the well-controlled judgments elicited in psychophysical experiments. Thus, for each imaginary social comparison there is a context that includes the performances of these relevant others, whether the context represents their actual performances or instead the imaginary performances that we have assigned them in our fantasies. More often, it may contain some of both, with their actual performances stimulating what we imagine for them. Like any judgment, each imaginary experience depends on its place in a context of related experiences, its place in the contextual range, and the proportion of contextual experiences that fall below it on the dimension of judgment.

The assumption that imaginary social comparisons follow the contextual rules of judgment precludes the possibility of a fantasy life that is pure pleasure, one in which we are forever delighted by how we are outperforming our competitors. For there must be a worst in any context, the lower end point of its range, and that worst will be experienced as painful indeed. If we could succeed in focusing our fantasy life completely on imaginary successes, the relevant context would come to include only these successes. Any particular success might no longer be high in this highly restricted context, and the lesser among these imaginary successes would cease to be pleasant, eventually becoming painful as the imagined failures were excluded from the context. This is why the construction of contexts so isolated that their component experiences were always pleasurable, as envisioned by Brickman and Campbell (1971), and variously cited by others, must be psychological impossibilities.

More realistically, we might envision contexts in which imaginary experiences are mostly pleasant, only rarely unpleasant or painful. As with the experimentally controlled contexts for judgments of stimuli actually presented, these would be contexts in which the better or more preferred experiences came relatively often, that is, in negatively skewed distributions.

Stimulating the Imagination.   Our imaginations are often stimulated by external sources, such as conversations with colleagues, reading, or watching television. In each, we can exert some degree of control over the skewing of the contexts of imaginary social comparisons invoked. For example, if we find that remarks by a certain colleague regularly cause us to imagine ourselves outperformed, we can turn to other colleagues for our conversations of this type. Similarly with books: We can choose books with whose heroes we can identify and experience vicariously their successes; or, more creatively, the books can serve as catalysts, providing the materials from which we ourselves can fashion happy scenarios featuring, for example, downward social comparisons. This is more difficult with television because the programs go on in real time with little opportunity for us to develop our own imaginative scenarios. Watching sports, we can identify with the home team or with particular athletes, experiencing their successes as our own. But this use of our imagination does not leave us much control. Even superathletes often perform far enough below their personal bests and the home team may endure miserable losing streaks. Sometimes, as with certain sitcoms, the characters provide the social context for our own superiority: Compared with such losers, we can imagine ourselves to be real winners.

Thinking like Pollyanna. A special case in which downward social comparisons provide the context for evaluating our own superior position is that of the famous "game" played by the fictional Pollyanna. In spite of her own misfortune, this young girl was supposedly able to make herself feel better by imagining the more terrible misfortunes of others. Which of us has not, as a child, stared at the Brussels sprouts while a well-meaning mother assured us that starving children in remote parts of the world would eagerly devour what we were rejecting. This did not improve the taste of the sprouts; and, more generally as adults, we smile condescendingly when someone tries to be a Pollyanna. Experience makes us skeptical. To work, the downward social comparisons must became part of the context for what we are judging. The starving children are just too remote. Perhaps we must actually experience some of their hunger before they can enter our context for social comparison. And as Faye Crosby (1972) argued from her survey of upward comparisons, the possibility of achieving the higher level must seem likely and we must feel entitled to it. These conditions are unlikely to be met when the mother invokes the comparison at the dinner table.

Is there any particular attitude that serves to facilitate a happy balance of pleasure over pain in social comparisons? What is needed is an approach to life that keeps the possibility of something very much worse within the context for judging one's own conditions. A tragic sense of life might serve this function. It would include occasional suffering, perhaps the vicarious suffering of the miseries of others, understanding that this might well be one's own lot. This would establish the lower endpoint of one's scale, enhancing the judgments of whatever is higher in the same context. Of course, restraint must be exercised to avoid extending upward the other end of one's contextual range, for any upward extension lowers the judgment of whatever is lower in the same context. The caveat here is that these matters are quantitative, depending on how frequently the respective endpoints are experienced. A little misery may enhance the quality of one's life, but dwelling on the awful possibilities tips the overall quality of life to the negative. At the other end, there can hardly be too much of a good thing. The trick is to be satisfied with what is best in one's context, providing that one continues to experience it with high frequency. Range–frequency theory implies that although such highs do lower the judgment of any lesser event, they can more than counterbalance this loss if they are themselves experienced frequently enough (Parducci, 1995, pp. 133–136). What is crucial, as suggested by the range–frequency analysis, is that the worst of the social comparisons be experienced only rarely and the best relatively often. For then, regardless of the absolute levels of one's conditions, the miseries would be rare and the joys common.

Counterfactuals and Social Comparison. Beyond deliberately imagining different worlds, possible worlds may be spontaneously generated by considerations of experienced outcomes. Kahneman and Miller (1986) introduced the idea that a stimulus event may often elicit a counterfactual, especially when the event is unusual. Thus, a tragic event is all the more tragic when it occurs during an exceptional sequence of events rather in the normal routine, for the exceptional is more easily undone in the counterfactual world. In an application of counterfactual reasoning to social comparisons, Medvec, Madey and Gilovich (1995) found that Olympic silver medal winners were, on average, less pleased with their performance than were bronze medal winners. They presented evidence that this was due to different counterfactual comparisons. The silver medalists tended to make an upward comparison because of the ease with which they could generate counterfactual worlds in which they had done that one little extra thing that would have pushed them from silver to gold. The bronze medalists, on the other hand, were often happy to have made a medal at all. Their counterfactual thinking was centered on how they might not have won any medal, a downward comparison. These illustrations once again suggest that one key to understanding social comparison processes is to develop a more complete understanding of just what gets included in the context for judgment.

Multidimensional Contexts

Thus far, our discussion of how the context of social comparisons affects evaluations of the self has focused on unidimensional comparisons or judgments. However, experiences outside the laboratory are typically more complex, differing along many dimensions. Even a simple social comparison judgment of efficacy within a given domain may be determined by comparing one's performance to that of others along many different dimensions, such as intelligence, attractiveness, success, and so forth. How are multidimensional comparisons made and what role does context play in such comparisons?

Consider the simplest case in which people differ on two dimensions. Using a sports analogy, think of baseball players who may be evaluated in terms of batting ability and fielding ability. The overall evaluation of these players should depend primarily on two factors: (1) the contextual valuation of each player's performance along each dimension, and (2) the relative weighting of batting ability versus fielding ability. Table 2 shows that player A is slightly better in batting than B but slightly worse in fielding. Would the overall evaluation of these two players differ in the two social comparison contexts depicted in the table? Although this research question has not been answered using social comparisons themselves, several studies have examined it for evaluations of various stimuli within different multidimensional contexts (Mellers & Cooke, 1994, 1996; Cooke & Mellers, 1998; Simonson & Tversky, 1992; Wedell, 1998). A common experimental manipulation, illustrated in Table 2, widens the range of values on one dimension and narrows the range on the other dimension. In Table 2, the wide–narrow context refers to the situation in which there is a wide range of values on the batting dimension but a narrow range on the fielding dimension (with the narrow–wide context representing the opposite situation). Given equal weighting of the batting and fielding dimensions, range–frequency theory predicts that player B will be judged more favorably than player A in the wide–narrow context, because the wide range of values on the batting dimension will effectively diminish the advantage of A over B along this dimension and the narrow range on the fielding dimension will enhance the advantage of B over A. The narrow–wide context predicts the opposite pattern, favoring A over B. These types of effects have been observed both for ratings of the attractiveness of apartments (Mellers & Cooke, 1994) and also direct choices between apartments and between other alternatives (Mellers & Cooke, 1996; Simonson & Tversky, 1992; Wedell, 1998). They also have been found for attractiveness ratings when frequency rather than range is manipulated (Cooke & Mellers, 1998).

Table 2. Multidimensional Manipulation of Context

Player	Wide–narrow context		Narrow–wide context	
	Batting	Fielding	Batting	Fielding
A	6	5	6	5
B	5	6	5	6
C	2	7	7	2
D	10	4	4	10

Although the observed effects could simply be described in terms of a change in the weighting of batting versus fielding across the two contexts, this does not appear to be the case. Wedell (1998) noted that weights measured by subjective ratings of importance actually increased for the dimension with the widest context, thus working against the observed effect. Mellers and Cooke (1994) also found evidence contrary to a change in weighting explanation. However, it should be noted that this type of experiment has not been conducted within the realm of social comparisons. Those players who know themselves to be better batters than fielders may give greater weight to the batting dimension in social comparisons (or at least in their self-serving public pronouncements). This type of self-serving weighting scheme could occur regardless of context.

Clearly the relative weighting of the different dimensions becomes an important determinant of judgments made within a multidimensional context. Tversky and colleagues (Gati & Tversky, 1984; Tversky, 1977) have provided convincing evidence that shared features within a context receive greater weight in similarity comparisons. Roberts and Wedell (1994) demonstrated a similar effect in judgments of emotion words. When emotion words were uniformly sampled from a two-dimensional circumplex, similarity relationships based on a sorting task were consistent with a two-dimensional representation of emotion as described by Russell and colleagues (Russell, 1980; Russell & Fehr, 1987). However, when the set of emotion terms heavily sampled those from the second quadrant, a third dimension emerged that represented the differences between terms such as "anger" and "fear" (both negative valence and high arousal, but differing in potency). In essence, the context that included little variation along this dimension resulted in minimal weighting of that dimension. Similarly, the variation along dimensions within a referent group on which social comparisons are based may provide a weighting scheme for judgments of similarity and perhaps preference. Dimensions along which individuals are relatively homogenous would receive less weight.

Thus far, our discussion of multidimensional context has focused primarily on weights and values as the determinants of the comparison process. This is clearly the traditional view as described in expected utility theory and multiattribute utility theory. However, research on decoy effects in choice have revealed that relational properties among the stimuli being compared can play an important role in the attractiveness of alternatives within the contextual set (Huber, Payne, & Puto, 1982). Table 3 illustrates a commonly used contextual manipulation. Here the stimuli being compared are cars that vary along two dimensions: ride quality (rated on a 0–100 scale) and miles per gallon. The choice data from Wedell (1991) reflect a

Table 3. Effects of a Range Extension for Asymmetrically and Symmetrically Dominated Decoys on Choice Percentages[a]

Car	Values		Asymmetric sets		Symmetric sets	
	RQ	MPG	{A,B,R_A}	{A,B,R_B}	{A,B,RS_A}	{A,B,RS_B}
A	80	33	79.2	29.2	67.0	63.4
B	100	27	18.8	68.8	31.0	34.6
R_A	60	33	2.0	—	—	—
R_B	100	21	—	2.0	—	—
RS_A	60	27	—	—	2.0	—
RS_B	80	21	—	—	—	2.0

[a]From Wedell (1991).
Abbreviations: RQ, ride quality; MPG, miles per gallon.

situation in which the participant was presented with sets of three cars and asked to choose the most attractive within each set. Car A had moderate ride quality but high miles per gallon, whereas car B had excellent ride quality but low miles per gallon. Thus, the attributes trade off, making choice more difficult.

As shown in Table 3, choice percentages differed dramatically depending on which third alternative was included in the choice set. Car R_A extended the range downward on the poorer dimension of car A—ride quality. According to range–frequency theory, this downward extension should reduce the negative impact of car A's poor ride quality and enhance its attractiveness. Similarly, car R_B extended the range downward on the poorer dimension of car B—miles per gallon—enhancing its attractiveness. In addition to extension of the range, these decoy alternatives are asymmetrically dominated within the set. Dominance occurs when an alternative is clearly superior to another alternative on one dimension and at least as good on all other dimensions. People key in on dominance relations, rarely ever choosing a dominated alternative. This is reflected in the data in Table 3, with dominated alternatives R_A and R_B being chosen only 2% of the time. In this situation, car R_A was dominated by A but not B, and car R_B was dominated by B and not A. These asymmetric dominance relations appear to be important to the obtained effect.

In the second set of data shown in Table 3, the decoys extend the range in a similar way as in the first data set, but they are symmetrically dominated by both A and B (that is, RS_A and RS_B decoys are both unambiguously worse than both alternatives A and B). Here the dramatic effect on choice proportions goes away. These data clearly show the important role of asymmetric dominance in moderating attractiveness. Subsequent research by Wedell and Pettibone (1996) has gone on to provide evidence that both range–frequency valuation processes and relational valuing of asymmetric dominance are operating in these situations.

The idea of relational valuation seems important for understanding how social comparisons operate with multiattribute stimuli. Table 3 suggests that one's self-evaluation should be bolstered considerably when one can asymmetrically dominate others in a comparison set. Focusing on persons whom one asymmetrically dominates makes it easier to justify one's enhanced status. For example, Simonson (1989) showed that when individuals had to provide justifications of their choices, the effects of asymmetric dominance increased rather than decreased, pointing to the justification role of such comparisons. Furthermore, Wedell and Pettibone (1996) showed that not only are the asymmetrically dominated alternatives rated more attractive, they also are rated as easier to justify. This is because one may use a qualitative rather than quantitative argument about the alternative's worth. For example, car A clearly is better than car R_A, but car B is not clearly better than car R_A; therefore, car A must be superior to car B.

As the number of relevant dimensions for judgment increases, it becomes less likely that any one stimulus will dominate another. Thus, we would expect that people who focus on a large set of attributes will be less likely to enhance self-evaluations through dominance relationships. On the other hand, there is plenty of evidence that people tend to make decisions on a greatly reduced attribute set (Payne, Bettman & Johnson, 1993). Thus it would be interesting to determine how the key dimensions of comparison are selected. Individuals who structure their comparisons to include a set of attributes in which they clearly dominate others in the set should perceive themselves more favorably than those who do not. For example, consider persons A, B, C, and D who vary on dimensions of success as shown in Table 4. None of these individuals dominates the other when all dimensions are considered; however, each dominates at least one other when the number of comparison dimensions is reduced. For example, if person A leaves out the excitement dimension (i.e., gives it no weight), then A

**Table 4. Values of Comparison Set Along
Four Dimensions of Job Satisfaction**

Person	Benefits	Salary	Intellectual	Excitement
A	6	6	4	4
B	5	6	3	6
C	7	5	3	5
D	6	3	4	6

dominates B and D and should feel relatively satisfied. On the other hand, if person D focuses only on intellectual stimulation and excitement, then D dominates the other three persons. More generally, how dimensions are weighted appears very important to the type of comparison made. What is unclear at this point is the degree to which individuals can themselves determine which dimensions they emphasize and which they ignore. It seems likely, though, that variations within the comparison group on any given dimension receive greater weight as the degree of variation on that dimension increases (Wedell, 1998).

Contextually Determined Ideals

Thus far, our discussion has focused primarily on dimensions that are monotonically related to evaluative judgments. For example, we tend to like jobs that pay more money, have higher benefits, are more exciting, and so on. However, many dimensions do not follow this "more is better" rule. Instead, there is an intermediate level that is perceived as ideal. For example, one's soup may be too salty or not salty enough. In such cases, there are separate contexts for stimuli above and stimuli below the ideal (e.g., soups that are too salty, soups that are too bland); and to predict how the different levels will be judged, range–frequency theory must be applied separately to each (Parducci, 1989). That stimuli can be perceived as having too much or too little of a given attribute is at the heart of Coombs' (1964) ideal point theory of preference. What is not well specified within that theory is how the ideal may be contextually determined. There is growing evidence that context plays an important role in determining ideals (Riskey, Parducci, & Beauchamp, 1979), and doctors confidently advise patients that after a few weeks on a reduced-salt diet previously preferred levels will taste too salty. We examine these context effects and their implications for social comparisons in this section.

In a recent set of experiments, Wedell and Pettibone (1999) demonstrated how preferences for facial configurations were influenced by the recent context. In this research, schematic faces that varied in the width of nose or the gap between the eyes were presented to participants and rated on a descriptive scale (very narrow feature to very wide feature) and a pleasantness scale (very unpleasant configuration to very pleasant configuration). The usual range–frequency effects were obtained for descriptive ratings so that the same nose width was judged wider when the context consisted of faces with very narrow nose widths. Moreover, preferences for faces depended strongly on context. When comparison faces had mostly narrow noses, the most preferred face had a narrower nose than when the comparison faces had mostly wide noses. Thus, the ideal migrated toward the center of the comparison set, a more short-term instance of the general finding that people are most attracted to those faces that are closest to the average of faces (Langlois & Roggman, 1990). Thus, people have contextually determined ideals for faces.

The data of Wedell and Pettibone (1999) are well described by assuming that people prefer a face with a nose that they would rate moderate sized or a 5 on the 9-point rating of nose width. When several narrow-nosed faces are added to the context, the range–frequency judgment process leads to assigning the value of moderate (5) to a face with a narrower nose. If the face judged moderate corresponds to the ideal, then people will prefer faces with narrower noses. Wedell and Pettibone (1999) found these systematic effects on preference for both unidimensional and multidimensional manipulations of context and also using both rating scale and choice paradigms.

The contextual determination of ideals through a range–frequency process has implications for how people establish social norms. For example, how people view their body shapes will depend on the set of individuals to which they compare themselves. If this set is mostly very thin, then a thin ideal will be established so that a person of moderate weight may view himself or herself as overweight. Similarly, one may use social comparisons to establish norms for behavior. If one goes out with people who drink a lot of alcohol, then the norm for drinking might be 4 or 5 beers a night; whereas, if one hangs out with teetotalers, that much beer would seem excessive. The establishment of norms in this manner may serve as a partial basis for the reality-monitoring function of social comparisons. The question, "Am I drinking too much?" is likely to be answered by a comparison to a norm based on one's context of social comparison.

The establishment of contextually determined norms also may have a powerful influence on other behaviors besides judgment and choice. People with anorexia nervosa compare themselves to a "thin ideal" (Stice, Schupak, Shaw, & Stein, 1994). This thin ideal may represent a contextual comparison set skewed by overexposure to models in fashion magazines who then predominate in social comparisons. Unfortunately, this extreme ideal for weight has proven hard to correct. Exposure to persons who are overweight or in the normal range of weight may not have much influence because their lack of similarity to the anorexic herself may exclude them from the comparison set.

A Broader Conception of Self

Much of the literature on upward and downward social comparisons is consistent with the basic range–frequency application in which upward comparisons produce more negative self-evaluations and downward comparisons more positive self-evaluations (Parducci, 1995). However, there are clear exceptions to this rule. For example, Tesser and colleagues (1988) have provided convincing evidence that upward comparisons can sometimes lead to more positive evaluations. This can result from a process of basking in the reflected glory of others. Thus, when our baseball hero hits a home run, our own self-esteem shoots up because we identify with our heroes, as though we had hit the home run ourselves. Our hero is evaluated in the context of other players, just as we more typically evaluate ourselves in the context of people like us. But insofar as we identify with our hero, we average his high rating with our own otherwise lesser rating, resulting in a higher self evaluation. More generally, we average the self-rating based on our own performance with that of the person or group with which we identify, both ratings being determined by the range–frequency compromise.

This conception of social comparison seems applicable to the broader question: Would you rather have the best house in a poor neighborhood or the worst house in a rich neighborhood? Realtors would advise choosing the latter, for lenders and future buyers tend to rate the house higher when it is in a better neighborhood. More generally, the idea behind the averaging of self and group evaluations is that people can have a broader conception of themselves. Thus, when sufficiently close to others, as in strong friendships or family relationships, "the success of my brother is also my success." The broader identification of the self also can occur when identifying with a referent group. The worst player in a world series can still identify with his winning team, and thus evaluate himself positively. The idea of an expanded self could be seen as consistent with Collins' (1996) evaluation that upward social comparisons should lead to enhanced self-evaluations when the target of comparison is seen as being in the same class or category as oneself. Thus, living in the wealthy neighborhood allows me to categorize myself with my wealthy neighbors and average their success with my own.[2]

APPLICATION TO INDIVIDUAL HAPPINESS

It is tempting to apply these ideas about social comparisons to the improvement of our most crucial decision processes. How can we tip life's hedonic balance more toward pleasure? This may seem dangerously speculative, but let us live dangerously!

Our lives sometimes can be characterized as a tug-of-war between success and happiness. Each new success seems to bring happiness, but we quickly adapt to our new level of achievement; it may take scarcely a month before a raised salary is already being overdrawn at the bank. Failures require a much longer period of adaptation. This difference was demonstrated long ago in laboratory experiments where extensions of the range of contextual stimuli produce immediate adaptation while restrictions of the range resulted in only a very slow rebalancing of the scale of judgment (e.g., Parducci, 1956). In terms of range–frequency theory, this is because any higher level is represented immediately as a new upper end point of the contextual range. Even when this higher level ceases to be experienced, it continues to define the upper end point so that range values do not change until it disappears from the context.

In domains where higher levels of success become increasingly difficult to achieve, where there is a pyramid of success with only a few at the top, most people become trapped at lower levels, as described by the Peter Principle (Peter, 1969). This becomes especially disappointing for the more ambitious whose social comparisons include others who have achieved the highest levels. Although these models for success can motivate higher absolute levels of performance, they also reduce satisfaction with lower levels.

What makes it so difficult to drop these upward-looking social comparisons is our belief that the highest levels of achievement produce the highest levels of satisfaction. This belief is contrary to the relational approach to judgment. The greatest satisfactions are experienced at the top of any contextual range, regardless of how high or low that top may be. The fact that higher levels are always satisfying within any particular context reinforces the false inference that the same higher levels will be satisfying when the context changes. The banker makes more money, on average, than the research scientist. However, the banker's context of social comparisons is likely to include those whose earnings have reached the dizzying heights

[2]The positive effects of upward comparisons are often referred to as assimilation effects. The current widespread use of the terms assimilation and contrast to describe the effects of context can be deceptive when assumed to be explanatory principles rather than just descriptive labels for directions of shift. Given a unidimensional scale, a particular judgment can be displaced in only one of two directions—assimilation or contrast—depending on whether toward or away from contextual stimuli. However, there are many different processes that can explain either assimilation or contrast. Range–frequency theory explains contrast as a result of changes in the contextual distribution. It produces assimilation only in conjunction with supplementary considerations, such as the special attributions, identifications, stimulus averaging, memory drifts, or other processes that we have evoked in trying to account for everyday judgments.

possible in high finance. Research scientists, having little chance of earning so much, are unlikely to compare themselves with bankers. Thus, researchers are more likely to be satisfied with their incomes than are bankers. Of course, in other domains, such as depth of understanding, the researcher may suffer by comparing himself with the deepest thinkers, something the banker is unlikely to do.

The range–frequency analysis of the comparison process that we have described in this chapter bears some similarities to the widely cited approach to hedonic relativism described by Brickman and Campbell (1971). In their analysis, they reached the discouraging conclusion that in the long run our pleasures and pains must be evenly balanced, referred to as "the hedonic treadmill." As we have seen, this discouraging conclusion is implied by the theory of adaptation level (Helson, 1964): because algebraic deviations from the mean must sum to zero, any theory of judgment that centers the scale of judgment upon the mean, with judgments proportional to the deviations, entails an even balance. We have rejected this implication because the experimental research shows that the scale is only artifactually centered at the mean and that judgments are typically not proportional to deviations from the mean. Because range–frequency theory entails that the hedonic balance tips in proportion to the skewing of the contextual distribution, it offers hope for an overall balance tipped markedly toward happiness.

Brickman and Campbell (1971), although operating within the assumption of adaptation level theory, did leave the door open for an escape from the even balance; and they have been cited approvingly for this by others (e.g., Kahneman & Varey, 1991). Their escape hatch is the possibility of extreme pleasures that are isolated from the hedonic treadmill. For example, they propose special holidays or feasts that are so isolated as not to enter the context for judging lesser events. But axiomatic to the relational approach is that such a holiday would be experienced as wonderfully pleasurable only if it were experienced in the context of lesser events, such as lesser holidays or even days of fasting. The range–frequency analysis (e.g., Parducci, 1995, p. 167) leaves no room for context-free dimensional judgments. As members of some context, these holidays could be pleasant indeed. And if experienced with sufficient frequency, whether in actuality, in memory, or in anticipation, they will help tip the overall balance toward the side of pleasure in spite of their negative effect on lesser events judged within the same context.

More generally, we would caution that the range–frequency effects on evaluations we have discussed in this chapter need to be considered with regard to several other psychological processes that may be operating concurrently. Unless there is a tendency for the individual to identify with the object of comparison, range–frequency theory predicts that downward comparisons lead to more positive self-evaluations and upward comparisons to more negative self-evaluations. These effects occur because such comparisons alter the range and ranks of the relevant contextual distribution. However, whether these comparisons lead to the predicted changes in self-evaluation depend on what other psychological processes the individual brings to bear on the problem. For example, Brickman and Bullman (1977) pointed out that downward comparisons might lead to negative feelings because one may experience conflict from feeling better at someone else's expense. If this attributional process generates negative interpretations of one's own behaviors, these behaviors will be lower in the context of social comparisons, with the resulting range–frequency compromise producing lower self-evaluations.

In a similar vein, Taylor and Lobel (1989) point out that the positive effects of downward comparisons for cancer patients generally occur in situations in which evaluations are based on indirect contact or imagined groups. When given a chance to choose with which persons they prefer to spend time, these patients overwhelmingly choose to be with those better off than themselves, referred to by Taylor and Lobel (1989) as tendency toward upward contacts. We believe the preference for upward contacts does not contradict range–frequency theory predictions concerning the effects of comparisons, but it reflects additional processes that may be operating. For example, upward contacts may be preferred because they provide better opportunities for problem solving (Lazarus & Folkman, 1984), they are a source of motivation, inspiration, and hope (van den Borne, Pruyn, & van Dam-de Mey, 1986), or the actual inter-actions with healthier patients are simply more enjoyable. Furthermore, people often choose as goals upward comparisons that enhance their motivation for achievement, even at the cost of some immediate loss of self-esteem (Parducci, 1995).

CONCLUDING REMARKS

To better understand social comparisons, this chapter has expanded beyond the basic range–frequency analysis of unidimensional ratings. With this goal, we have attempted to integrate recent work on a variety of research fronts. One of these concerned the effects of multidimensional contexts. There is now compelling evidence that range–frequency processes generalize to the integration of multiple dimensions so that differences along one dimension may be enhanced relative to differences along another dimension, due to differences between the respective ranges and ranks of stimuli on each dimension (Cooke & Mellers, 1998; Mellers & Cooke, 1994; Wedell, 1998). What is less well understood is how much control individuals have in determining the weights of different dimensions. Such control might be crucial to social comparisons. For example, if one compares unfavorably to a roommate on five of seven dimensions or domains, comparisons will be predominantly upward, and thus negative. However, if the two dimensions of downward comparison are given greater weight, the resulting self-evaluation may be positive.

The multidimensional structure of comparisons also suggests the potential importance of relational information. For example, decoy effects imply that preferences may be dramatically altered by introducing an asymmetrically dominated decoy. This suggests that downward comparisons to an individual whom one dominates on all relevant dimensions of comparisons will boost self-evaluations by a greater degree than predicted by range–frequency theory alone. Conversely, comparisons to "Mr. Perfect" who dominates one's own traits and perfor-mances on all relevant dimensions might be particularly devastating.

Finally, our contextual analysis of social comparisons emphasizes the more general problem of what constitutes context for particular comparisons. Psychophysical experiments typically employ stimuli that are unidimensional and disconnected from real-world objects (i.e., squares that vary in size, random dot patterns that vary in number); with such stimuli we can often assume that the context is simply the particular values presented for judgment. It is under these conditions that the relationship between context and judgment has been studied most rigorously and the range–frequency theory has been developed and tested most thor-oughly. But even in these simple cases, the participant sometimes constructs a context that goes beyond the stimulus values actually presented for judgment, as when background values are included in the context (Brown, 1953; Parducci & Wedell, 1986). Furthermore, the effective context may consist primarily of just those stimuli from the most recent trials and not the full set presented during the experimental session.

Judgments and comparisons made in our everyday lives can be enormously more complex. Most everyday stimuli are multifaceted and multidimensional so that the outcome of the comparison process hinges on which facet one is attending to and how the various contexts for the different dimensions are integrated. Stimuli themselves can evoke counterfactuals that become a part of the contextual set guiding comparison. One's personal history of experiences also becomes a primary source for generating a context for comparison, and imaginary events may be the prime components of a context, especially for contexts affecting our pleasures and pains. From the relativistic point of view in which experiences take on meaning only in relationship to the context of other experiences, these additional factors ought not to be ignored simply because they complicate the analysis of judgment. Fuller understanding of how social comparisons determine our value experiences requires a better understanding of what constitutes the context for everyday judgments.

REFERENCES

Albert, S. (1977). Temporal comparison theory. *Psychological Review, 84,* 485–503.

Bieri, J., Atkins, A. L., Briar, S., Leaman, R. L., Miller, H., & Tripodi, T. (1966). *Clinical and social judgment: The discrimination of behavioral information.* New York: Wiley.

Birnbaum, M. H. (1974). Using contextual effects to derive psychophysical scales. *Perception and Psychophysics, 15,* 89–96.

Brickman, P., & Bullman, R. (1977). Pleasure and pain in social comparison. In J. Suls & R. L. Miller (Eds.), *Social comparison processes: Theoretical and empirical perspectives* (pp. 149–186). New York: Hemisphere.

Brickman, P., & Campbell, D. T. (1971). Hedonic relativism and planning the good society. In M. H. Appley (Ed.), *Adaptation-level theory* (pp. 287–302). New York: Academic Press.

Brown, D. R. (1953). Stimulus similarity and the anchoring of subjective scales. *American Journal of Psychology, 66,* 199–214.

Collins, R. L. (1996). For better or worse: The impact of upward social comparison on self-evaluations. *Psychological Bulletin, 119,* 51–69.

Coombs, C. H. (1964). *A theory of data.* New York: Wiley.

Cooke, A. D. J., & Mellers, B. A. (1998). Multiattribute judgment: Attribute spacing influences single attributes. *Journal of Experimental Psychology: Human Perception and Performance, 24,* 496–504.

Crespi, L. P. (1944). Quantitative variation of incentive and performance in the white rat. *American Journal of Psychology, 55,* 467–520.

Crosby, F. (1972). A model of egoisticial relative deprivation. *Psychological Review, 83,* 84–113.

Eiser, J. R. (1990). *Social judgment.* Pacific Grove, CA: Brooks-Cole.

Eiser, J. R., & van der Pligt, J. (1982). Accentuation and perspective in altitudinal judgment. *Journal of Personality and Social Psychology, 42,* 224–238.

Festinger, L. (1954). A theory of social comparison processes, *Human Relations, 7,* 117–140.

Gardner, R. W., & Schoen, R. A. (1962). Differentiation and abstraction in concept formation. *Psychological Monographs* (Whole No. 560).

Gati, I., & Tversky, A. (1984). Weighting common and distinctive features in perceptual and conceptual judgments. *Cognitive Psychology, 16,* 341–370.

Goethals, G. R., & Darley, J. M. (1977). Social comparison theory: An attributional approach. In J. Suls & R. Miller (Eds.), *Social comparison processes: Theoretical and empirical perspectives* (pp. 259–278). Washington, DC: Hemisphere.

Haubensak, G. (1992). The consistency model: A process model for absolute judgments. *Journal of Experimental Psychology: Human Perception and Performance, 18,* 202–209.

Helson, H. (1947). Adaptation-level as a frame of reference for prediction in psychophysical data. *American Journal of Psychology, 60,* 1–29.

Helson, H. (1964). *Adaptation-level theory.* New York: Harper & Row.

Higgins, E. T., & Lurie, L. (1983). Context, categorization and recall: The "change-of-standard" effect. *Cognitive Psychology, 15,* 525–547.

Huber, J., Payne, J. W., & Puto, C. (1982). Adding asymmetrically dominated alternatives: Violations of regularity and similarity hypothesis. *Journal of Consumer Research, 9,* 90–98.

Judd, C. M., & Harackiewicz, J. M. (1980). Contrast effects in attitude judgment, An examination of the accentuation hypothesis. *Journal of Personality and Social Psychology, 41,* 26–36.

Kahneman, D., & Miller, D. T. (1986). Norm theory: Comparing reality to its alternatives. *Psychological Review, 93*, 136–153.

Kahneman, D., & Varey, C. (1991). Notes on the psychology of utility. In J. Elster & J. E. Roemer (Eds.), *Interpersonal comparisons of well-being*. Cambridge, England: Cambridge University Press.

Kelley, H. H. (1967). Attribution theory in social psychology. In D. Levine (Ed.), *Nebraska symposium on motivation* (pp. 192–238). Lincoln: University of Nebraska Press.

Krantz, D. L., & Campbell, D. T. (1961). Separating perceptual and linguistic effects of context shifts upon absolute judgments. *Journal of Experimental Psychology, 62*, 35–42.

Krupat, E. (1974). Context as a determinant of perceived threat. *Journal of Personality and Social Psychology, 29*, 731–736.

Lambert, A. J., & Wedell, D. H. (1991). The self and social judgment: The effects of affective reaction and "own position" on judgments of unambiguous and ambiguous information about others. *Journal of Personality and Social Psychology, 61*, 884–897.

Langlois, J. H., & Roggman, L. A. (1990). Attractive faces are only average. *Psychological Science, 1*(2), 115–121.

Latane, B., & Darley, J. M. (1970). *The unresponsive bystander: Why doesn't he help?* New York: Appleton Century Crofts.

Lazarus, R. S., & Folkman, S. (1984). *Stress, appraisal and coping*. New York: Springer.

Levine, J., & Green, S. M. (1984). Acquisition of relative performance information: The roles of intrapersonal and interpersonal comparison. *Personality and Social Psychology Bulletin, 10*, 385–393.

Luhtanen, R., & Crocker, J. (1991). Self esteem and intergroup comparisons: Toward a theory of collective self-esteem. In J. Suls & T. A. Wills (Eds.), *Social comparison: Contemporary theory and research* (pp. 211–234). Hillsdale, NJ: Lawrence Erlbaum.

Major, B., Testa, M., & Bylsma, W. H. (1991). Responses to upward and downward social comparisons: The impact of esteem-relevance and perceived control. In J. Suls & T. A. Wills (Eds.), *Social comparison: Contemporary theory and research* (pp. 237–260). Hillsdale, NJ: Lawrence Erlbaum.

Manis, M. (1967). Context effects in communication. *Journal of Personality and Social Psychology, 5*, 326–334.

Marsh, H. W., & Parker, J. W. (1984). Determinants of student self-concept: Is it better to be a relatively large fish is a small pond even if you don't learn to swim as well? *Journal of Personality and Social Psychology, 14*, 213–231.

Medvec, V. H., Madey, S. F., & Gilovich, T. (1995). When less is more: Counterfactual thinking and satisfaction among Olympic medalists. *Journal of Personality and Social Psychology, 69*, 603–610.

Mellers, B. A. (1983). Evidence against "absolute" scaling. *Perception and Psychophysics, 33*, 523–526.

Mellers, B. A. (1986). "Fair" allocations of salaries and taxes. *Journal of Experimental Psychology: Human Perception and Performance, 12*, 80–91.

Mellers, B. A., & Birnbaum, M. H. (1983). Contextual effects is social judgment. *Journal of Experimental Social Psychology, 19*, 157–171.

Mellers, B. A., & Cooke, A. D. J. (1994). Trade-offs depend on attribute range. *Journal of Experimental Psychology: Human Perception and Performance, 20*, 1055–1067.

Mellers, B. A., & Cooke, A. D. J. (1996). The role of task and context in preference measurement. *Psychological Science, 7*, 76–82.

Miller, C. (1982). The role of performance-related similarity on social comparison of abilities: A test of the related attribute hypothesis. *Journal of Experimental Social Psychology, 18*, 513–523.

Murphy, G. L., & Wright, J. C. (1984). Changes in conceptual structure with expertise: Differences between real-world experts and novices. *Journal of Experimental Psychology: Learning, Memory and Cognition, 10*, 144–155.

Parducci, A. (1956). Direction of shift in the judgment of single stimuli. *Journal of Experimental Psychology, 51*, 169–178.

Parducci, A. (1965). Category Judgment: A range–frequency model. *Psychological Review, 72*, 407–418.

Parducci, A. (1968). The relativism of absolute judgments. *Scientific American, 219*, 84–90.

Parducci, A. (1982). Category Ratings: Still more context effects. In B. Wegener (Ed.), *Social attitudes and psychophysical measurement* (pp. 262–282). Hillsdale, NJ: Lawrence Erlbaum.

Parducci, A. (1989). Hedonic judgments for Aristotelian domains. In G. Canevet, B. Scharf, A.-M. Bonnel, & C.-A. Possamai (Eds.), *Fechner Day 89* (pp. 36–41), Cassis, France: International Society for Psychophysics.

Parducci, A. (1995). *Happiness, pleasure and judgment: The contextual theory and its applications*. Mahwah, NJ: Lawrence Erlbaum.

Parducci, A., Calfee, R. C., Marshall, L. M., & Davidson, L. P. (1960). Context effects in judgment: Adaptation level as a function of mean, midpoint, and median of the stimuli. *Journal of Experimental Psychology, 60*, 65–77.

Parducci, A., & Marshall, L. M. (1962). Assimilation versus contrast in the anchoring of perceptual judgment of weight. *Journal of Experimental Psychology, 63*, 426–437.

Parducci, A., & Perrett, L. F. (1971). Category rating scales: Effects of relative spacing and frequency. *Journal of Experimental Psychology Monograph, 89*, 427–452.

Parducci, A., & Wedell, D. H. (1986). The category effect with rating scales: Number of categories, number of stimuli, and method of presentation. *Journal of Experimental Psychology: Human Perception and Performance, 12*, 496–516.

Payne, J. W., Bettman. J. R., & Johnson, E. J. (1993). *The adaptive decision maker.* New York: Cambridge University Press.

Peter, L. J. (1969). *The Peter principle.* New York: Morrow.

Roberts, J. S. & Wedell, D. H. (1994). Context effects on similarity judgments of multidimensional stimuli: Inferring the structure of the emotion space. *Journal of Experimental Social Psychology, 30*, 1–38.

Riskey, D. R., Parducci, A., & Beauchamp, G. K. (1979). Effects of context in judgments of sweetness and pleasantness. *Perception and Psychophysics, 26*, 171–176.

Russell, J. A. (1980). A circumplex model of affect. *Journal of Personality and Social Psychology, 39*, 1161–1178.

Russell, J. A., & Fehr, B. (1987). Relativity of perception of emotion in facial expressions. *Journal of Experimental Psychology: General, 116*, 223–237.

Sarris, V. (1967). Adaptation-level theory: Two critical experiments on Helson's weighted-average model. *American Journal of Psychology, 80*, 331–334.

Schacter, S. (1959). The psychology of affiliation. Stanford. CA: Stanford University Press.

Sherif, M., & Hovland, C. I. (1961). *Social judgment: Assimilation and contrast effects in communication and attitude change.* New Haven, CT: Yale University Press.

Sherif, M., Taub, D., & Hovland, C. I. (1958). Assimilation and contrast effects of anchoring stimuli on judgment. *Journal of Experimental Psychology, 55*, 150–155.

Simonson, I. (1989). Choice based on reasons: The case of attraction and compromise effects. *Journal of Consumer Research, 16*, 158–174.

Simonson, I., & Tversky, A. (1992). Choice in context: Trade-off contrast and extremeness aversion. *Journal of Marketing Research, 29*, 281–895.

Smith, R. H., Diener, E., & Wedell, D. H. (1989). Intrapersonal and social comparison determinants of happiness: A range–frequency analysis. *Journal of Personality and Social Psychology, 56*, 317–325.

Stice, E., Schupak, N. E., Shaw, H. E., & Stein, R. I. (1994). Relation of media exposure to eating disorder symptomatology: An examination of mediating mechanisms. *Journal of Abnormal Psychology, 103*, 836–840.

Suls, J., & Mullen, B. (1982). From the cradle to the grave: Comparison and self-evaluation across the life-span. In J. Suls (Ed.), *Psychological perspectives on the self* (Vol. 1, pp. 97–125). Hillsdale, NJ: Lawrence Erlbaum.

Tanaka, J. W., & Taylor, M. (1991). Object categories and expertise: Is the basic level in the eye of the beholder? *Cognitive Psychology, 23*, 457–482.

Taylor, S. E., & Lobel, M. (1989). Social comparison activity under threat: Downward evaluation and upward contacts. *Psychological Review, 96*, 569–575.

Tesser, A. (1991). Emotion in social comparison and reflection processes. In J. Suls & T. A. Wills (Eds.), *Social comparison: Contemporary theory and research* (pp. 115–145). Hillsdale, NJ: Lawrence Erlbaum.

Tesser, A., Miller, M., & Moore, J. (1988). Some affective consequences of social comparison and reflection processes: The pain and pleasure of being close. *Journal of Personality and Social Psychology, 54*, 49–61.

Tversky, A. (1977). Features of similarity. *Psychological Review, 84*, 327–352.

van den Borne, H. W., Pruyn, J. F. A., & van Dam-de Mey, K. (1986). Self-help in cancer patients: A review of studies on the effects of contacts between fellow-patients. *Patient Education and Counseling, 9*, 33–51.

Volkmann, J. (1951). Scales of judgment and their implications for social psychology. In J. H. Roherer & M. Sherif (Eds.), *Social psychology at the crossroads* (pp. 279–294). New York: Harper & Row.

Wedell, D. H. (1991). Distinguishing among models of contextually induced preference reversals. *Journal of Experimental Psychology: Learning, Memory, and Cognition, 17*, 767–778.

Wedell, D. H. (1994). Contextual contrast in evaluative judgments: Test of pre- versus postintegration models of contrast. *Journal of Personality and Social Psychology, 66*, 1007–1019.

Wedell, D. H. (1996). A constructive–associative model of the contextual dependence of unidimensional similarity. *Journal of Experimental Psychology: Human Perception and Performance, 22*, 634–661.

Wedell, D. H. (1998). Testing models of tradeoff contrast in pairwise choice. *Journal of Experimental Psychology: Human Perception and Performance, 24*, 49–65.

Wedell, D. H., & Parducci, A. (1988). The category effect in social judgment: Experimental ratings of happiness. *Journal of Personality and Social Psychology, 55*, 341–356.

Wedell, D. H., Parducci, A., & Geiselman, R. E. (1987). A formal analysis of ratings of physical attractiveness: Successive contrast and simultaneous assimilation. *Journal of Experimental Social Psychology, 23*, 230–249.

Wedell, D. H., Parducci, A., & Lane, M. (1990). Reducing the dependence of clinical judgment on the immediate context: Effects of number of categories and type of anchors. *Journal of Personality and Social Psychology, 58,* 319–329.

Wedell, D. H., Parducci, A., & Roman, D. (1989). Student perceptions of fair grading: A range–frequency analysis. *American Journal of Psychology, 102,* 233–248.

Wedell, D. H., & Pettibone, J. C. (1996). Using judgments to understand decoy effects in choice. *Organizational Behavior and Human Decision Processes, 67,* 326–344.

Wedell, D. H., & Pettibone, J. C. (1999). Preference and the contextual basis of ideals in judgment and choice. *Journal of Experimental Psychology: General, 128,* 346–361.

Wills, T. A. (1991). Similarity and self-esteem in downward comparison. In J. Suls & T. A. Wills (Eds.), *Social comparison: Contemporary theory and research* (pp. 51–78). Hillsdale, NJ: Lawrence Erlbaum.

13

Consequences of Social Comparison

Selective Accessibility, Assimilation, and Contrast

THOMAS MUSSWEILER AND FRITZ STRACK

Almost all our achievements are relative, in that their merit depends on the achievements of others. This becomes especially clear in situations that are competitive in nature. For example, Sammy Sosa may be proud of the fact that he hit 66 homeruns in 1998, and thus surpassed the old record by a margin of 5. However, it may be difficult for him not to compare his 66 to the 70 home runs hit by Mark McGuire in the very same season. Similarly, you may be fairly content with your own athletic achievements, but still, after signing up for a competitive sports event, will probably start to compare your abilities to those of your rivals. What do you think would be the consequences of such comparisons? Would they make you feel better or worse? Would they change your own evaluation of your qualities? Would they boost or sabotage your performance?

Although it often has been lamented that social comparison research has traditionally focused too little attention on such questions (Wood, 1989), in recent years numerous studies have investigated the consequences social comparisons have for self-evaluations (e.g., Brewer & Weber, 1994; Brown, Novick, Lord, & Richards, 1992; Lockwood & Kunda, 1997; Pelham & Wachsmuth, 1995), affect (e.g., Aspinwall & Taylor, 1993; Buunk, Collins, Taylor, Van-Yperen, & Dakof, 1990; Gibbons & Gerrard, 1989; Reis, Gerrard, & Gibbons, 1993; Tesser, Millar, & Moore, 1988), and behavior (e.g., Seta, 1982; Taylor, Wayment, & Carrillo, 1996). These studies have demonstrated that social comparisons sometimes produce assimilation (e.g., more positive evaluations after an upward comparison), and at other times produce contrast (e.g., more negative evaluations after an upward comparison). Which of these two opposing effects occurs depends on a host of moderating variables such as self-esteem (e.g., Aspinwall & Taylor, 1993; Buunk et al., 1990; Gibbons & Gerrard, 1989) psychological closeness (e.g., Brewer & Weber, 1994; Brown et al., 1992; Pelham & Wachsmuth, 1995; Tesser et al., 1988), the relevance of the comparison dimension (Tesser, 1988), and the

THOMAS MUSSWEILER AND FRITZ STRACK • Universitaet Wuerzburg, Psychologie II, 97070 Wuerzburg, Germany.

Handbook of Social Comparison: Theory and Research, edited by Suls and Wheeler. Kluwer Academic / Plenum Publishers, New York, 2000.

attainability of the comparison standard (Lockwood & Kunda, 1997) (for a discussion of additional moderating variables, see Taylor et al., 1996).

In spite of these insights, our understanding of the consequences of social comparison remains incomplete. In particular, little is known about the judgmental processes that underlie the effects of social comparisons (see Wills & Suls, 1991; Wood, 1989). To remedy this shortcoming, it may be fruitful to invoke conceptualizations of assimilation and contrast that were developed in other research paradigms. One paradigm in which the underlying processes of assimilation and contrast have been intensively investigated is social cognition research. In the present chapter, we will attempt to apply some of the basic notions of this research in order to allow for a more complete understanding of the consequences of social comparison.

A SOCIAL COGNITION PERSPECTIVE ON ASSIMILATION AND CONTRAST: THE SELECTIVE ACCESSIBILITY MODEL

One of the most fundamental principles of social cognition research is the accessibility principle (for recent reviews, see Higgins, 1989, 1996; Sedikides & Skowronski, 1991; Wyer & Srull, 1989), which holds that when making any kind of judgment, people focus on knowledge that comes to mind easily. Recently, we have suggested that this basic principle may be fruitfully invoked to understand the consequences of making a comparison. Specifically, we proposed a selective accessibility model (Mussweiler, 1997; Mussweiler & Strack, 1999a,b, 2000a; Mussweiler, Förster, & Strack, 1997; Strack & Mussweiler, 1997) that assumes that making a comparison alters the accessibility of knowledge about the comparison target. In particular, we suppose that judges compare a target to a given standard by selectively generating knowledge that is consistent with the notion that the target is similar to the standard (the selectivity hypothesis). Generating such knowledge increases its accessibility, so that it influences subsequent evaluations of the target (the accessibility hypothesis) (for a detailed description of the selective accessibility model, see Mussweiler & Strack, 1999b).

In social comparisons, the self typically constitutes the target of the comparison and a salient other constitutes the comparison standard. From a selective accessibility perspective, a person would thus compare himself or herself to a given standard by generating evidence indicating that he or she is similar to the standard. Doing so increases the accessibility of this evidence, which is likely to influences subsequent self-evaluations.

The Selectivity Hypothesis

In order to compare a target to a given standard, participants have to relate their stored knowledge about the target to this task. Such active retrieval of judgment-relevant knowledge is accomplished through hypothesis testing (Trope & Liberman, 1996), which is typically based on diagnostic evidence (i.e., evidence that helps decide whether the tested hypothesis is true or false) (e.g., Trope & Bassok, 1982). In many cases, evidence is most diagnostic if it is consistent with the tested hypothesis (Trope & Liberman, 1996). Specifically, adopting a positive test strategy (i.e., examining cases in which the target characteristic is present) is often the most critical test when a single hypothesis is under consideration (Klayman & Ha, 1987).

In linking this notion to the process of making a comparison, we (Mussweiler, 1997; Mussweiler & Strack, 1999a,b; Strack & Mussweiler, 1997) suggested that judges compare a target to a given standard by testing the hypothesis that the target's value on the judgmental dimension is, in fact, equal to the standard. To do so, judges engage in a "positive test strategy" and selectively retrieve knowledge from memory that is consistent with this assumption. In other words, judges consider the possibility that the target and the standard are equal (see also Koehler, 1991) by initiating a selective search for evidence about the target that is consistent with this assumption (for empirical evidence supporting this assumption, see Mussweiler & Strack, 1999a, 2000a).

Take the following example as an illustration of this mechanism: Assume you have just signed up for a local tennis tournament. You are a pretty good player and you are vain enough to care about winning the trophy. However, you know that your neighbor Donald who is also going to compete is an excellent player as well. In fact, Donald won the last three tournaments. In this situation, you will have to compare your tennis skills to those of Donald in order to find out whether you have a realistic chance to win the trophy. Specifically, you will have to decide whether you play better or worse than Donald. The selective accessibility model holds that in this situation, you would assume to be similar to the comparison standard. Specifically, you would make the critical comparison, by testing the hypothesis that you do in fact play as well as Donald. To do so, you would try to retrieve knowledge from memory that is consistent with this assumption. That is, you would selectively generate information indicating that you are as good a player as your standard of comparison. For example, you may recall that you have recently improved your backhand considerably, that your serve and volley is irresistible, that your new racquet helps a lot, and so forth.

The Accessibility Hypothesis

How does testing the hypothesis that the target is similar to the standard influence subsequent evaluations of the target? How does testing the hypothesis that you are as good a tennis player as Donald change your evaluation of your own tennis skills? Within the selective accessibility model, we assume that this influence is mediated by knowledge accessibility. Research on this topic has repeatedly demonstrated that activating knowledge (e.g., by using a priming task) may influence subsequent evaluations (e.g., Higgins, Rholes, & Jones, 1977; Srull & Wyer, 1979). Generating knowledge in the course of making a comparison may exert an influence in a similar way. Specifically, generating knowledge increases its accessibility, so that it is more likely to be used for a subsequent judgment. However, in adopting a positive test strategy, judges do not generate a representative set of knowledge about the target. Rather, they recall it selectively. Thus, making a comparison selectively increases the accessibility of standard-consistent knowledge about the target. This easily accessible knowledge is then primarily used for subsequent evaluations of the target, so that these evaluations are based on standard-consistent knowledge (for empirical support of this assumption, see Mussweiler & Strack, 1999a, 2000a; Strack & Mussweiler, 1997). In our example, comparing yourself to Donald selectively increases the accessibility of knowledge indicating that you are a good player (e.g., your serve and volley is irresistible). As a consequence, you are likely to use this knowledge for subsequent evaluations of your tennis skills.

Consequences of Selective Accessibility: The Role of Applicability and Representativeness

Research on the determinants of knowledge accessibility effects further suggests that the influence this easily accessible standard-consistent knowledge has on later evaluations of the target depends on its applicability and representativeness. Specifically, the extent to which accessible knowledge influences a given judgment depends on its applicability (e.g., Higgins

& Brendl, 1995; Higgins et al., 1977). That is, the more relevant the implications of accessible knowledge are for the judgment at hand, the more likely it is to be used in the judgment process. Thus, the more applicable accessible knowledge is, the stronger its effects on judgment will be. For example, accessible knowledge indicating that you are a good tennis player is likely to have the strongest effects on evaluations of your tennis skills because it is highly relevant for this evaluation. The same knowledge, however, is likely to have less influence on judgments of your soccer skills. Although both activities require similar abilities to some extent, they also are different in important aspects, so that knowledge about one's tennis skills is of limited relevance for evaluations of one's soccer skills. Finally, this knowledge is unlikely to have any influence on evaluations of your cooking skills, because playing tennis and cooking have very little in common, so that knowledge about the first is irrelevant for evaluations of the latter (for experimental evidence examining the role of knowledge applicability in comparisons, see Strack & Mussweiler, 1997).

How applicable knowledge is used in the judgment process is determined by its representativeness. It has been suggested (e.g., Martin & Achee, 1992; Strack, 1992) that people do not invariably use knowledge that is accessible and applicable to the current judgment. Rather, they engage in a representativeness check (Strack, 1992) and determine whether using easily accessible knowledge is appropriate to reach an accurate judgment. To the extent that accessible knowledge is similar to the judgmental target or pertains to the same overall category or time period (Strack, 1992), it is likely to be seen as representative for the judgment. Representative knowledge is used as a judgmental basis, which leads to an assimilation of the judgment toward the implications of this knowledge. Nonrepresentative knowledge, however, may be excluded from the judgment (Martin, 1986; Schwarz & Bless, 1992) or used a comparison standard (Schwarz & Bless, 1992) in evaluations of the target. This leads to contrast of the judgment away from the implications of accessible knowledge.

For example, accessible knowledge about your present tennis skills is representative for evaluations of your present tennis skills, because it pertains to the same target and the same time period as the evaluation. In this case, your evaluation is likely to be based on and be consistent with the implications of this knowledge, which produces an assimilation effect. The same knowledge, however, is nonrepresentative for evaluation of your tennis skills in your first year of playing tennis, because presumably you played much worse as a beginner. As a consequence, this knowledge is unlikely to be used as a judgmental basis. Instead, it may function as a comparison standard, which is likely to yield a contrast effect: In comparison to your excellent present play, your skills as a beginner appear even more dilettante. Note that in the latter case, although accessible knowledge is nonrepresentative for the judgment, it is still applicable. Specifically, it pertains to the same domain, and thus entails relevant information for your evaluation by providing a comparison standard. Consequently, it is likely to be used to make the evaluation.

SELECTIVE ACCESSIBILITY IN SOCIAL COMPARISON

According to the selective accessibility model, engaging in a comparison involves a selective search for evidence indicating that the comparison target (i.e., the self) is similar to the comparison standard. This notion is in line with the literature on social comparison. In fact, the selective accessibility model is in accord with the two core notions of Festinger's (1954) original theory, namely the assumption that people engage in social comparison in order to obtain diagnostic feedback about their abilities and that in order to do so, they compare primarily with similar others.

Diagnosticity in Social Comparison

As we have pointed out before, selectively searching for hypothesis-consistent evidence is likely to provide judges with the most diagnostic evidence for the critical comparison (Klayman & Ha, 1987; Trope & Liberman, 1996). Thus, hypothesis-consistent testing may constitute a quest for diagnostic information. Similarly, Festinger (1954) assumed that people engage in social comparison in order to obtain diagnostic information about their abilities. He argued that such diagnostic information is important because people require realistic appraisals of their skills in order to select activities that match their level of competence. As Festinger put it, " ... holding ... inaccurate appraisals of one's abilities can be punishing or even fatal" (1954, p. 117). In line with this reasoning, it has been demonstrated that people are often motivated to obtain diagnostic information about their abilities: When given the opportunity to choose between different tasks, they often opt for the task that promises to be the most diagnostic about their abilities (for a review, see Trope, 1986). In fact, they may even do so when this choice is likely to entail unfavorable feedback. This suggests that veridical self-assessment is an important motive in social comparison (for a discussion of different motives in social comparison, see, for example, Taylor et al., 1996; Wood, 1989; Wood & Taylor, 1991). Thus, social comparisons are at least partly motivated by the same quest for diagnostic evidence that is assumed to underlie the judgmental processes specified in the selective accessibility model.

Similarity in Social Comparison

This motive to assess one's veridical standing relative to the comparison standard may be best achieved by considering the possibility that one's own standing on the judgmental dimension is equal to that of the comparison standard (Wheeler, 1966; Collins, 1996). To see the diagnostic advantages of testing this similarity hypothesis, take our introductory example as an illustration. Imagine that you want to find out whether you have a realistic chance to beat Donald in your prestigious local tennis tournament and win the trophy. To do so, you are likely to compare your own athletic achievements with those of Donald. The most diagnostic way to make this comparison appears to be that you first find some critical features that are indicative of your competitor's abilities and then test whether you possess these features as well. For example, you may know that Donald is regarded as one of the top three players in town and may test the possibility that you do belong to the top three as well. To make this test, you may assume for a while that you are, in fact, one of the top three and try to muster evidence that supports this assumption. In this case the presence as well as the absence of the critical feature (i.e., belonging to the top three) is diagnostic for the judgment to be made. Specifically, no matter what the result of this hypothesis test, you have obtained valuable information to make the critical judgment. If the feature is present, this suggests that you may indeed be equally skilled as your competitor, if the feature is not present, you may not be quite as good. Thus, because you explicitly tested whether you possess the feature that characterizes the standard, the evidence that was generated to test this possibility allows you to judge how your abilities measure up to those of the comparison standard.

This, however, is not true for hypothesis tests that involve features that do not represent the standard's standing on the judgmental dimension. For example, suppose you found the idea of belonging to the top three too farfetched, and thus would test a more modest alternative hypothesis. For example, you may test the possibility that you belong to the top 10. Now, in contrast to testing the critical hypothesis itself (i.e., you belong to the top 3), the results of this test are not necessarily informative with respect to the critical judgment. For example, if you come to the conclusion that you are probably better than top 10, it is difficult to derive direct implications for the critical judgment. In this case, you still do not know how your achievements measure up to those of your competitor.

This example suggests that testing whether a critical feature that is indicative of the standard's position on the judgmental dimension also characterizes the comparison target provides the most diagnostic information for the critical comparison. That is, testing the possibility that the comparison target is equal to the standard appears to be the most diagnostic way to assess the target's standing in comparison to the standard.

Consistent with this assumption that testing for similarity between the target and the standard constitutes the most diagnostic way to make a comparison, social comparison theory traditionally has stressed the importance of similarity in the process of selecting a comparison standard. In fact, Festinger's original formulation already acknowledges the diagnostic advantages of comparing with similar others. Specifically, he states that "if some other person's ability is too far from his own ... it is not possible to evaluate his own ability accurately by comparison with this other person" (Festinger, 1954, p. 120). Similarly, Goethals and Darley (1977) have argued that a comparison with a standard that is similar to oneself on dimensions that are related to the critical ability allows for the clearest evaluation of one's ability (cf. Wheeler, Martin, & Suls, 1997). In support of this notion, research has demonstrated that people often select similar others as comparison standards (e.g., Wheeler, 1966). Extending these original formulations we assume that a quest for similarity not only influences the selection process. In addition to selecting similar others as comparison standards, judges also may focus on the ways in which they are similar to a given comparison standard.

Empirical evidence also exists that is suggestive of the assumed focus on similarity in social comparison (e.g., DeVellis et al., 1991; Lockwood & Kunda, 1997; Miyake & Zuckerman, 1993; Nosanchuk & Erickson, 1985). For example, Nosanchuk and Erickson (1985) demonstrated that bridge players who were given a choice of comparison standards chose to compare with others who were objectively superior to themselves. Subjectively, however, participants perceived the selected standards to be at a similar level of competence. This suggests that participants did in fact construe themselves to be similar to the standard (Collins, 1996). More direct evidence in support of this possibility is provided by Lockwood and Kunda (1997). These researchers had students read descriptions of an outstanding graduate student before they asked them to evaluate themselves on a number of dimensions that were related to general career success. Subsequently, they rated how relevant this student was as a comparison standard and then justified these ratings in an open-ended statement. An analysis of these statements revealed that participants focused primarily on features that they had in common with the comparison standard. For example, they stated to be similar to the standard with respect to preferred hobbies, social activities, academic aspirations, and so on.

Taken together, this evidence demonstrates that similarity is an important factor in the social comparison process. Furthermore, it suggests that—consistent with the selective accessibility model—social comparisons may involve testing the hypothesis that the comparison target (i.e., oneself) is similar to the given standard.

Testing for Selective Accessibility in Social Comparison

The selective accessibility model predicts that testing this similarity hypothesis increases the accessibility of evidence that implies actual similarity with the standard of comparison. Thus, comparing oneself to an upward standard should increase the accessibility of knowledge about the self that indicates that one also is high on the critical dimension. By the same token, comparing oneself to a downward standard should increase the accessibility of knowledge indicating that one is low on the critical dimension.

We tested these predictions in a recent study (Mussweiler & Strack, 2000b) in which we used a lexical decision task (see Neely, 1991, for a review) to assess the accessibility of self-related knowledge (see Dijksterhuis et al., 1998). Specifically, we had participants compare themselves with either a moderately athletic (the former race car driver Nicki Lauda) or a moderately unathletic (Bill Clinton) celebrity.[1] In particular, participants were instructed to indicate whether they thought they were more or less athletic than the respective comparison standard. After making this comparison, they received a lexical decision task that included words associated with being athletic (e.g., dynamic, athletic), words associated with being unathletic (e.g., weak, heavy), neutral words (e.g., postcard, jacket), and nonwords. For each of the presented words, the participants' task was to determine whether these words do or do not constitute a German word. In order to distinguish between the accessibility of semantic knowledge in general and the accessibility of self-related knowledge, we followed a procedure developed by Dijksterhuis et al. (1998). Specifically, half the lexical decisions were preceded by the subliminal presentation of a word that is closely associated with the self-concept (I, my, me). The other half was preceded by a word unrelated to the self (and, or, when). Subliminal presentation of self-related words has been demonstrated to activate the self-concept, so that lexical decision trials that are preceded by such primes assess the specific accessibility of self-related knowledge (Dijksterhuis et al., 1998).

Our results demonstrate that after a comparison with Nicki Lauda (i.e., the moderately athletic standard), participants were faster in recognizing words associated with being athletic than words associated with being unathletic. In contrast, after comparing with Bill Clinton (the moderately unathletic standard), they were faster in recognizing words associated with being unathletic. This relation, however, only held for those trials that were preceded by the subliminal presentation of self-related primes. Thus, comparing with a given standard appears to have increased the accessibility of standard-consistent knowledge about the self (i.e., knowledge suggesting that one is similar to the standard on the judgmental dimension).

Limits of Selective Accessibility

From the current perspective, a social comparison increases the accessibility of standard-consistent knowledge about the target because judges assume that they are similar to the standard of comparison and selectively search for evidence that is consistent with this assumption. However, judges are only likely to engage in this process if being similar to the standard of comparison constitutes a realistic possibility. For instance, in our introductory example, you may well consider the possibility that you play tennis as well as your neighbor Donald, because both of you are at similar levels of excellence. For more extreme standards (e.g., Pete Sampras), however, you are unlikely to engage in this similarity test. In this case, in which it is obvious that the target (i.e., the self) is dissimilar from the standard, judges are more likely to make the comparison using categorical knowledge about the target and the standard (see Mussweiler & Strack, 2000a). Specifically, if you were to compare your tennis skills with those of Grand Slam champion Pete Sampras, you would most likely acknowledge that he belongs to a specific subcategory of tennis players (i.e., professionals) and make the comparison by excluding yourself from this category. In particular, you may ascribe yourself to the

---

[1]Pretesting revealed that our research participants saw Nicki Lauda and Bill Clinton as moderately high and low standards in the domain of athletics.

negation of the standard's category (e.g., hobby tennis players) and make the comparison based on the attributes associated with both categories. Thus, rather than testing the possibility that you play as well as Pete Sampras, you may conclude right away that you play worse, because tennis professionals are typically better than hobby players. As a consequence, the evaluation of your tennis skills is likely to be based on your membership in an inferior group (i.e., hobby players). Conceivably, this leads to less favorable evaluations (i.e., a contrast effect).

Thus judges may not always be inclined to engage in the presumed similarity test. Under specific circumstances (e.g., when the standard is too extreme) they may resort to different judgmental strategies (e.g., categorical differentiation). Notably, assimilation is only likely to be the result of social comparison, if similarity between the target and the standard is assumed. If this is not the case, contrast is the more likely outcome (see Collins, 1996, for a more elaborate discussion).

This perspective on assimilation and contrast is consistent with the factors that have been found to moderate the effects of social comparison. One central moderator is psychological closeness. If judges feel close to the comparison standard, they tend to assimilate. If closeness is low, however, contrast is the more likely outcome (e.g., Brewer & Weber, 1994; Brown et al., 1992; Pelham & Wachsmuth, 1995; Tesser et al., 1988). This may be the case because judges only test the hypothesis that they are similar to the standard when the other is close to them. Similarly, attainability of the standard's status may lead to assimilation (e.g., Buunk et al., 1990; Lockwood & Kunda, 1997; Taylor et al., 1996) because it allows for inclusion in the category of the standard and thus facilitates testing the similarity hypothesis.

Thus, social comparisons may not always involve testing the hypothesis that the target is similar to the standard. However, there is reason to believe that the similarity test is the more likely alternative. Specifically, because judges typically select similar others as comparison standards (Wheeler, 1966), they are likely to entertain the possibility that they are, in fact, similar to these standards.

IMPLICATIONS FOR SOCIAL COMPARISON

The evidence that we have presented so far indicates that social comparisons increase the accessibility of standard-consistent knowledge, which is then likely to be used for later judgments about the comparison target. From this perspective, the effects that are produced by social comparison can be conceptualized as knowledge-accessibility effects. Doing so enables us to apply the basic principles of knowledge accessibility (see Higgins, 1996, for a review) to the realm of social comparison. This approach promises to shed new light on the judgmental processes that underlie social comparison.

Applicability in Social Comparison

Current conceptualizations of knowledge accessibility effects (e.g., Higgins, 1996; Martin & Achee, 1992; Schwarz & Bless, 1992; Strack, 1992) typically assume that the effects of accessible knowledge depend on how this knowledge is used in the judgment process. As outlined before, the first determinant of knowledge use is its applicability. Specifically, it has been demonstrated that accessible knowledge will only be used for a judgment if it is applicable (e.g., Higgins et al., 1977). As a consequence, applicability determines the magnitude of knowledge accessibility effects.

Applying this principle to social comparisons suggests that the magnitude of the influence that a comparison will have on subsequent self-evaluations depends on how applicable the knowledge that has been rendered easily accessible in the comparison process is to this evaluation. In particular, a comparison will have no influence if accessible knowledge is not applicable. Consistent with this reasoning, it has been demonstrated that the consequences of social comparisons depend on how self-relevant the comparison dimension is (e.g., Lockwood & Kunda, 1997; Salovey & Rodin, 1984; Tesser, 1988). For example, self-evaluations were only affected by a comparison with an upward standard, if the standard's domain of excellence is relevant to the self. If it is irrelevant, however, self-evaluations remained unchanged (Lockwood & Kunda, 1997). For instance, students who were planning to become teachers evaluated their own qualities to be better after reading about an excellent teacher. However, reading about an excellent accountant did not influence these evaluations.

From the current perspective, one possible interpretation for these results is that comparing oneself to an upward standard increases the accessibility of standard-consistent knowledge about the self. To the extent that this comparison is carried out for self-relevant as well as irrelevant dimensions (e.g., because it is explicitly asked for), such increased accessibility should result regardless of the relevance of the comparison dimension. However, relevance is likely to determine whether the accessible knowledge is used to make the self-evaluative judgment. Because self-evaluations are likely to be based only on self-relevant knowledge, increasing accessibility on an irrelevant dimension is unlikely to have an effect. Thus, a comparison on an irrelevant dimension may not influence self-evaluations because the knowledge that is rendered easily accessible is not applicable to these evaluations.[2]

Representativeness in Social Comparison

The second moderator of knowledge accessibility effects is representativeness. If accessible knowledge is representative for the current judgment, it will be used as a judgmental basis, so that assimilation will result. If, however, accessible knowledge is not representative, it may be excluded from the judgment (Martin & Achee, 1992; Schwarz & Bless, 1992) or used as a standard of comparison (Schwarz & Bless, 1992; Strack, 1992), which is likely to produce contrast.

From the current perspective the effects of social comparison are mediated by the increased accessibility of standard-consistent knowledge about the self. Thus, in the social comparison paradigm, accessible knowledge typically pertains to the same target as the critical evaluation. Because representativeness is determined by similarity (Kahneman & Tversky, 1972), knowledge that pertains to the judgmental target itself is likely to be representative for judgments about this target. Consequently, accessible knowledge is likely to be used as a judgmental basis, so that assimilation occurs (e.g., Herr, 1986).

In some cases, however, accessible knowledge may be nonrepresentative for the critical judgment, although both pertain to the self. For example, if easily accessible knowledge pertains to a different period of life, it may be nonrepresentative for the critical evaluation. As was demonstrated by Strack, Schwarz, and Gschneidinger (1985), increasing the accessibility of self-related knowledge that pertains to the past yields contrast effects on judgments about the present. Specifically, listing positive past life events induced participants to judge their

---

[2]Note that unlike much of the social comparison literature (Wood, 1989) this reasoning does not focus on how self-relevance influences the selection of a comparison standard. Rather, it concentrates on the consequences a given comparison will have, presupposing that this comparison was in fact carried out. This, of course, is not to say that self-relevance does not influence the selection process as well.

current well-being to be lower. This suggests that increasing the accessibility of self-related knowledge during a social comparison that pertains to a different time period as the critical evaluation may lead to similar contrast effects. For example, comparing one's present athletic abilities to those of Bill Clinton may produce a contrast effect on evaluations of one's athletic abilities in college. Specifically, in order to compare with Bill Clinton (i.e., a low standard of comparison) one may selectively search for evidence indicating that one is fairly unathletic at the moment. One's current level of fitness, however, is likely to be nonrepresentative of one's fitness in college. As a consequence, one may exclude this information from the judgment or use it as a standard of comparison, which is likely to produce a contrast effect (Strack & Mussweiler, 1997).

Because in most cases the critical judgment pertains to the same time period as accessible knowledge, however, representativeness is likely to constitute the default in social comparison. As a consequence, judgments may typically be assimilated to the implications of accessible knowledge.

Affective Consequences of Accessible Knowledge

Another intriguing implication of the present framework pertains to the affective consequences of social comparison. Recent conceptualizations (e.g., Buunk et al., 1990) typically assume that affect is determined by the target's relative standing on the comparison dimension. Specifically, "learning that another is better off than yourself provides at least two pieces of information: (a) that you are not as well off as everyone and (b) that it is possible for you to be better than you are at present" (Buunk et al., 1990, p. 1239). From this perspective, the affective consequences of a comparison depend on which piece of information one focuses on. Specifically, a person may feel worse if he or she focuses on the fact that the comparison standard is better off, and this person may feel better if he or she focuses on the fact that the superior state of the standard may be obtained. Consistent with this assumption, it has been demonstrated that people who are able to focus on the possibility of self-improvement (e.g., due to their high self-esteem) are more likely to experience positive affect after an upward comparison (e.g., Buunk et al., 1990).

From a selective accessibility perspective, however, an additional mechanism appears to contribute to the affective consequences of social comparison. Specifically, independent of the implications a specific comparison has for one's relative standing on the comparison dimension, self-related knowledge that is generated in order to make this comparison has its own affective qualities. For example, thinking about one's athletic achievements when comparing to Nicki Lauda is likely to elicit more positive affect than thinking about one's failures when comparing to Bill Clinton. Consequently, more positive affect is likely to be elicited by an upward than by a downward comparison. The affective consequences of the implications concerning one's relative standing on the judgmental dimension, however, are likely to go in the opposite direction. Specifically, realizing that one is less athletic than Nicki Lauda produces more negative affect than realizing that one is better than Bill Clinton. This suggests that generating standard-consistent knowledge about the self and assessing one's position along the judgmental dimension relative to the comparison standard may yield opposing affective consequences.

Which of both tendencies is more influential depends on their relative intensity. One factor that influences how intensive the affective consequences of generating knowledge are is the vividness of this knowledge. For example, it has been demonstrated that thinking about negative or positive past events may yield an assimilation effect on judgments of current well-being if participants focus on how this event occurred, rather than on why it happened (Strack et al., 1985). Presumably, focusing on how the event occurred induces participants to draw a more vivid image, which is likely to elicit event-congruent affect. That is, vividly thinking about a positive life event is likely to elicit positive affect, whereas thinking about a negative life event is likely to produce negative affect. This affect then may be used as a judgmental basis for judgments about current well-being (Schwarz & Clore, 1983) so that assimilation results. In contrast, the causal analysis ("why") of the events is unlikely to elicit congruent affect, so that here the contrast effect described before is more likely to persist. Similarly, vividly thinking about standard-consistent knowledge about the self is likely to have strong affective consequences that may offset the opposing effects that result from assessing one's relative standing on the judgmental dimension (for an experimental illustration of this possibility in the realm of counterfactual thinking, see McMullen, 1997).

Automatic Behavior Activation

Finally, conceptualizing social comparison in a selective accessibility framework affords a new perspective on the behavioral consequences of comparisons. Recent research (Bargh, Chen, & Burrows, 1996; Carver, Ganellen, Froming, & Chambers, 1983; Chartrand & Bargh, 1996; Chen & Bargh, 1997; Dijksterhuis et al., 1998; Dijksterhuis & van Knippenberg, 1998; Mussweiler & Förster, 2000) has demonstrated that the effects of accessible knowledge are not limited to social judgment. Rather, increasing the accessibility of knowledge also may "activate particular feelings and even specific action tendencies" (Berkowitz, 1984, p. 412). That is, because behavior corresponds to mental representations that obey the same laws as purely semantic concepts (see Carlston, 1994; Prinz, 1990), they may be activated in a similar fashion (for a more elaborate discussion of this point, see Bargh, 1997; Bargh et al., 1996; Dijksterhuis & van Knippenberg, 1998).

In line with this assumption, it has been demonstrated that increasing the accessibility of a specific concept leads participants to behave in a manner that is consistent with this concept (e.g., Bargh et al., 1996; Carver et al., 1983; Dijksterhuis et al., 1998). For example, increasing the accessibility of the aggressiveness concept by having participants unscramble sentences (Srull & Wyer, 1979) with aggressive content induced them to administer stronger shocks to a confederate who failed to solve a learning task (i.e., to behave more aggressively) (Carver et al., 1983).

Applying this insight to the realm of social comparison suggests that comparing oneself with a given standard may automatically trigger behavior that is consistent with the knowledge that has been rendered easily accessible during the comparison process. Direct support for this assumption stems from a recent study by Dijksterhuis et al. (1998). Here, participants were instructed to imagine Albert Einstein (a high standard of comparison for intelligence) and list all the attributes about his typical behaviors, lifestyle, and appearance that came to their minds. The authors assumed that doing so would trigger an implicit comparison process. Because Albert Einstein constitutes a maximally extreme standard of intelligence, participants who compare themselves with Einstein are unlikely to test the hypothesis that they are as intelligent as he is (i.e., they will not engage in a similarity test). Rather, this comparison is likely to produce a contrast effect on self-evaluations and induce participants to see themselves as fairly *un*intelligent. Consistent with this assumption Dijksterhuis et al. (1998) demonstrated that the accessibility of self-related knowledge that indicated low levels of intelligence was increased.[3] More importantly, participants also were found to behave less intelligently. Specifically, given a trivial pursuit test, they answered fewer questions correctly than a group that had previously thought about a low standard of comparison (i.e., Claudia Schiffer, who as a supermodel is stereotypically seen as unintelligent). This finding suggests that social comparisons may directly trigger behavior that is consistent with the implications of self-related knowledge that has been rendered easily accessible during the comparison process.

In summary, conceptualizing social comparison within a selective accessibility framework affords a number of intriguing implications. First, the consequences of social comparison are likely to depend on the applicability and the representativeness of the self-related knowledge that was generated during the comparison process. Second, this knowledge has affective implications, which may influence affective reactions to a given comparison. Finally, selectively increasing the accessibility of self-related knowledge not only may influence judgments about the self but also may trigger corresponding behavior.

SELECTIVE ACCESSIBILITY AND REFERENCE POINT USE: SIMULTANEOUS ASSIMILATION AND CONTRAST

So far, we have focused our analysis on the consequences that making a comparison has for the accessibility of self-related knowledge. Because in most cases comparing increases the accessibility of standard-consistent knowledge, the described selective accessibility mechanism typically leads to assimilation. The evidence we have reviewed demonstrates that selective accessibility is one consequence of social comparison. It is, however, not the only consequence. Specifically, a social comparison not only increases the accessibility of standard-consistent knowledge. It also provides a reference point against which the implications of this knowledge can be evaluated. For example, comparing with Nicki Lauda not only leads one to consider the ways in which one is athletic, it also suggests a reference point (i.e., Nicki Lauda) against which to evaluate the implications of this knowledge.

Research in psychophysics (Brown, 1953; Helson, 1964) and social judgment (Ostrom & Upshaw, 1968) repeatedly has demonstrated that the latter mechanism typically produces contrast effects (for a detailed discussion, see Wyer & Srull, 1989). For example, a target stimulus is typically judged to be lighter in the context of a heavy stimulus than in the context of a light stimulus (e.g., Helson, 1964). Applied to the context of social comparison, this suggests that one should judge oneself to be lower on the critical dimension after a comparison with a high standard than after a comparison with a low standard. In fact, such contrast effects have been found in a host of studies (e.g., Brown et al., 1992; Cash, Cash, & Butters, 1983; Morse & Gergen, 1970; Thornton & Moore, 1993).

Although the two mechanisms of selective accessibility and reference point use are clearly dissociable because they are mediated by different judgmental processes, they both are

[3]Thus, Dijksterhuis et al. (1998) found the accessibility of standard-inconsistent knowledge to be increased after a social comparison, whereas our own research (Mussweiler & Strack, 2000b) found increased accessibility of standard-consistent knowledge. This difference may be due to the use of differentially extreme comparison standards in both studies. Whereas Dijksterhuis and co-workers used the most extreme standard available (i.e., Albert Einstein for intelligent), we deliberately selected moderate standards (Nicki Lauda and Bill Clinton for athletic). As outlined before, it may be difficult to test the hypothesis that one is equal to a maximally extreme standard. Consequently, the accessibility of standard-inconsistent knowledge may be increased as a result of the comparison.

likely to operate in parallel in most cases. Consequently, assimilation and contrast may be simultaneous effects of social comparison. This possibility is supported by the results of a recent study (Mussweiler & Strack, 2000b) in which we used different judgment formats to assess the effects of social comparison. It has been suggested (Biernat, Manis, & Nelson, 1991; Biernat, & Manis, 1994; Biernat, Manis, & Kobrynowicz, 1997) that the contrast effects that result from reference point use are primarily apparent on dimensional judgments for which participants may use a reference point to interpret the end point of the given scale. For example, in order to indicate how large one's drug consumption is on a scale from 1 ("not at all large") to 9 ("very large") one first has to interpret the given scale labels. That is, one has to determine what a drug consumption of 9 is supposed to stand for. In this situation, judges are likely to use salient standards to "anchor" the response scale. Doing so typically yields a contrast effect (see Wyer & Srull, 1989, for a more elaborate discussion). For example, using an extreme upward standard (e.g., the musician Frank Zappa) to anchor the response scale may lead judges to assume that this upward standard represents the upper end of the response scale (e.g., 9 is equivalent to Zappa's drug consumption). Compared to this high standard, judges own standing on the judgmental dimension is likely to appear fairly low, so that they will ascribe a low value to themselves. In contrast, using an extreme downward standard (e.g., the tennis professional Steffi Graf) to anchor the response scale (e.g., 1 is equivalent to Steffi Graf's drug consumption) may lead them to ascribe a fairly high value to themselves. Thus, different response scale anchoring is likely to produce a contrast effect.

Such response scale anchoring, however, is unlikely to influence absolute judgments (e.g., "How often do you use drugs per week?"). Because these judgments pertain to objective numeric quantities, the underlying response scale does not have to be interpreted by the judge. Consequently, the mechanism that is responsible for contrast on dimensional judgments is not operating, so that contrast effects are unlikely to occur. Hence, absolute judgments are likely to be based on the implications of accessible knowledge. Consistent with this assumption, our research on judgmental anchoring (Tversky & Kahneman, 1974) has demonstrated that absolute judgments reflect the consequences of selective accessibility (see Mussweiler & Strack, 1999b, for an overview).

This reasoning suggests that a social comparison may simultaneously lead to assimilation on an absolute judgment and to contrast on a dimensional judgment. Our results are consistent with this assumption. Specifically, we asked participants whether they used drugs (e.g., alcohol, marihuana) more or less frequently than a presumably high social standard (Frank Zappa) or a presumably low social standard (Steffi Graf). Subsequently, we asked them to indicate how often they use such drugs. Consistent with our previous research in the anchoring paradigm (for an overview, see Mussweiler & Strack, 1999b), participants who had compared with the high standard indicated that they used drugs more often than participants who had compared with the low standard. Thus, we found assimilation on the absolute judgment. Subsequently, participants indicated on a 9-point scale (1 = "not at all large"; 9 = "very large") how large their drug consumption is. For this dimensional judgment, we found a contrast effect. That is, participants judged their drug consumption to be lower after comparing with the high standard than after comparing with the low standard (Mussweiler & Strack, 2000b).

Note, however, that in order for this contrast effect to occur, a given standard has to be seen as relevant for the current judgment. An irrelevant standard is unlikely to be used to interpret the given response scale and should not exert an effect on a dimensional judgment. This reasoning is consistent with the results of a study on psychophysical judgment (Brown, 1953) in which participants were asked to judge a series of test weights that were preceded by a context weight (a tray of weights). The context weight was either introduced as a part of the stimulus set by explicitly asked participants to judge its weight or participants were made to believe that it is not part of the stimulus set by asking them to hold the tray as a favor for the experimenter. Results showed that contrast effects only occurred if the context stimulus is seen as a part of the stimulus set, and thus was relevant for the critical judgment. If this was not the case, however, the very same context stimulus did not influence judgments of the target (for a more elaborate discussion, see Wyer & Srull, 1989).

This suggests that a comparison with a social standard will only produce a contrast effect if it is seen as relevant for the critical judgment. To explore this possibility, we (Mussweiler & Strack, 2000c) manipulated the relevance of the given standard. In particular, we did or did not explicitly ask participants to compare themselves with the standard. Explicitly asking participants to engage in a comparison is likely to increase the relevance of the standard. Not asking them to do so is likely to undermine relevance. In one study, we presented participants with a description of a student who either adjusted very well to college or who had problems in adjusting. Half the participants were explicitly asked whether they adjusted better or worse to college than the given standard (relevant). In contrast, the other half was simply asked to rate the quality of the description of the standard (irrelevant). Following the logic of our previous experiment, we then asked participants to judge their own adjustment to college using absolute (e.g., "How many weeks did it take you to adjust to college?") and dimensional judgment formats (e.g., "How well did you adjust to college?" 1 = not at all well; 9 = very well). Our results demonstrate that absolute judgments were assimilated to the comparison standard regardless of its relevance. That is, reading about the standard that adjusted well to college induced participants to see themselves as also adjusting well. Similarly, reading about the standard that adjusted badly induced them to see themselves as adjusting badly too. In contrast, the dimensional judgment was influenced by the relevance manipulation. The typical contrast effect only occurred if the standard appeared relevant for the critical judgment because an explicit comparison was asked for. If this was not the case, the contrast effect did not hold.

The implications of these findings are twofold. First, they indicate that in order to be used as a reference point, a given standard has to be seen as relevant for the current judgment. Second, they demonstrate that the mechanisms of selective accessibility and reference point use are moderated by different variables. This suggests that although both mechanisms occur in parallel, they are clearly dissociable.

In contrast to the existing literature on social comparison, these findings indicate that assimilation and contrast may be simultaneous rather than mutually exclusive consequences of social comparison (for a discussion of simultaneous assimilation and contrast effects in social judgment, see Manis & Paskewitz, 1984). Presumably, the absolute and the dimensional judgment tapped two different judgmental processes. Selective accessibility is apparent on the absolute judgment, whereas reference point use is apparent on the dimensional judgment. Thus, although both effects occur simultaneously, they appear to be caused by different underlying mechanisms.

SUMMARY AND CONCLUSION

In this chapter, we have attempted to conceptualize the consequences of social comparison as knowledge accessibility effects. The basic assumption of this conceptualization is that comparing with a social standard involves a selective increase in the accessibility of knowledge about the comparison target. This knowledge then mediates the judgmental, affective, and behavioral consequences of the social comparison. From this perspective, the effects of a specific comparison depend on (1) which knowledge about the comparison target is rendered accessible during the comparison process, and (2) how this knowledge is used for subsequent self-evaluations.

In most cases, judges appear to make a comparison by testing the hypothesis that they are similar to the comparison standard. Consequently, a social comparison typically increases the accessibility of standard-consistent knowledge about the self. How accessible knowledge influences subsequent self-evaluations depends on how this knowledge is used. Specifically, the direction of the effect depends on whether or not accessible knowledge is representative for the critical judgment. Because the knowledge that was generated during the comparison pertains to the target of the subsequent judgment itself, it is likely to be representative for this judgment in most of the cases. As a consequence, evaluations will be assimilated to the implications of easily accessible knowledge. How strong this influence is, however, depends on the degree to which this knowledge is applicable to the critical evaluation.

Selectively increasing the accessibility of knowledge about the comparison target, however, not only influences judgments about the target, but is also likely to have direct affective and behavioral consequences. Specifically, because accessible knowledge also has affective implications, affective responses to social comparisons will be assimilated to these implications. Similarly, behavior that is consistent with accessible knowledge is likely to be triggered.

The present analysis demonstrates that to reach a complete understanding of social comparisons, it is necessary to examine their underlying cognitive mechanisms. As our research suggests, such insights are particularly important to understand the effects of social comparisons on cognitive, affective, and behavioral dimensions.

REFERENCES

Aspinwall, L. G., & Taylor, S. E. (1993). Effects of social comparison direction, threat, and self-esteem on affect, self-evaluation, and expected success. *Journal of Personality and Social Psychology, 64*, 708–722.

Bargh, J. A. (1997). The automaticity of everyday life. In R. S. Wyer (Ed.), *Advances in social cognition* (Vol. 10, pp. 1–61). Hillsdale, NJ: Lawrence Erlbaum.

Bargh, J. A., Chen, M., & Burrows, L. (1996). Automaticity of social behavior: Direct effects of trait construct and stereotype activation on action. *Journal of Personality and Social Psychology, 71*, 230–244.

Berkowitz, L. (1984). Some effects of thoughts on anti- and prosocial influences of media events: A cognitive–neoassociation analysis. *Psychological Bulletin, 95*, 410–427.

Biernat, M., & Manis, M. (1994). Shifting standards and stereotype-based judgments. *Journal of Personality and Social Psychology, 66*, 5–20.

Biernat, M., Manis, M., & Kobrynowicz, D. (1997). Simultaneous assimilation and contrast effects in judgments of self and others. *Journal of Personality and Social Psychology, 73*, 254–269.

Biernat, M., Manis, M., & Nelson, T. E. (1991). Stereotypes and standards of judgment. *Journal of Personality and Social Psychology, 60*, 485–499.

Brewer, M. B., & Weber, J. G. (1994). Self-evaluation effects of interpersonal versus intergroup social comparison. *Journal of Personality and Social Psychology, 66*, 268–275.

Brown, D. R. (1953). Stimulus-similarity and the anchoring of subjective scales. *American Journal of Psychology, 66*, 199–214.

Brown, J. D., Novick, N. J., Lord, K. A., & Richards, J. M. (1992). When Gulliver travels: Social context, psychological closeness, and self-appraisals. *Journal of Personality and Social Psychology, 62*(5), 717–727.

Buunk, B. P., Collins, R. L., Taylor, S. E., VanYperen, N. W., & Dakof, G. A. (1990). The affective consequences of social comparison: Either direction has its ups and downs. *Journal of Personality and Social Psychology, 59*, 1238–1249.

Carlston, D. E. (1994). Associated systems theory: A systematic approach to cognitive representations of persons. In R. S. Wyer, Jr. (Ed.), *Advances is social cognition* (pp. 1–78). Hillsdale, NJ: Lawrence Erlbaum.

Carver, C. S., Ganellen, R. J., Froming, W. J., & Chambers, W. (1983). Modeling: An analysis in terms of category accessibility. *Journal of Experimental Social Psychology, 19*, 403–421.

Cash, T. F., Cash, D., & Butters, J. W. (1983). "Mirror, mirror, on the wall …?": Contrast effects and self-evaluations of physical attractiveness. *Personality and Social Psychology Bulletin, 9*(3), 351–358.

Chartrand, T. L., & Bargh, J. A. (1996). Automatic activation of impression formation and memorization goals: Nonconscious goal priming reproduces effects of explicit task instructions. *Journal of Personality and Social Psychology, 71*, 464–478.

Chen, M., & Bargh, J. A. (1997). Nonconscious confirmation processes: The self-fulfilling consequences of automatic stereotype activation. *Journal of Experimental Social Psychology, 33*, 541–560.

Collins, R. L. (1996). For better or worse: The impact of upward social comparison on self-evaluations. *Psychological Bulletin, 119*(1), 51–69.

DeVellis, R. F., Blalock, S. J., Holt, K., Renner, B. R., Blanchard, L. W., & Klotz, M. L. (1991). Arthritis patients' reactions to unavoidable social comparison. *Personality and Social Psychology Bulletin, 17*, 392–399.

Dijksterhuis, A., Spears, R., Postmes, T., Stapel, D. A., Koomen, W., van Knippenberg, A., & Scheepers, D. (1998). Seeing one thing and doing another: Contrast effects in automatic behavior. *Journal of Personality and Social Psychology, 75*, 862–871.

Dijksterhuis, A., & van Knippenberg, A. (1998). The relation between perception and behavior, or how to win a game of Trivial Pursuit. *Journal of Personality and Social Psychology, 74*(4), 865–877.

Festinger, L. (1954). A theory of social comparison processes. *Human Relations, 7*, 117–140.

Gibbons, F. X., & Gerrard, M. (1989). Effects of upward and downward social comparison on mood states. *Journal of Social and Clinical Psychology, 8*, 14–31.

Goethals, G. R., & Darley, J. M. (1977). Social comparison theory: An attributional approach. In J. M. Suls & R. L. Miller (Eds.), *Social comparison processes: Theoretical and empirical perspectives* (pp. 259–278). Washington, DC: Hemisphere.

Helson, H. (1964). *Adaptation level theory: An experimental and systematic approach to behavior.* New York: Harper.

Herr, P. M. (1986). Consequences of priming: Judgment and behavior. *Journal of Personality and Social Psychology, 51*, 1106–1115.

Higgins, E. T. (1989). Knowledge accessibility and activation: Subjectivity and suffering from unconscious sources. In J. S. Uleman & J. A. Bargh (Eds.), *Unintended thought* (pp. 75–123). New York: Guilford.

Higgins, E. T. (1996). Knowledge activation: Accessibility, applicability, and salience. In E. T. Higgins & A. W. Kruglanski (Eds.), *Social psychology: Handbook of basic principles* (pp. 133–168). New York: Guilford Press.

Higgins, E. T., & Brendl, C. M. (1995). Accessibility and applicability: Some "activation rules" influencing judgment. *Journal of Experimental Social Psychology, 31*, 218–243.

Higgins, E. T., Rholes, W. S., & Jones, C. R. (1977). Category accessibility and impression formation. *Journal of Experimental Social Psychology, 13*, 141–154.

Kahneman, D., & Tversky, A. (1972). Subjective probability: A judgment of representativeness. *Cognitive Psychology, 3*, 430–454.

Klayman, J., & Ha, Y. W. (1987). Confirmation, disconfirmation, and information in hypotheses testing. *Psychological Review, 94*, 211–228.

Koehler, D. J. (1991). Explanation, imagination, and confidence in judgment. *Psychological Bulletin, 110*, 499–519.

Lockwood, P., & Kunda, Z. (1997). Superstars and me: Predicting the impact of role models on the self. *Journal of Personality and Social Psychology, 73*, 91–103.

Manis, M., & Paskewitz, J. R. (1984). Specifity in contrast effects: Judgments of psychopathology. *Journal of Experimental Social Psychology, 20*, 217–230.

Martin, L. L. (1986). Set/reset: Use and disuse of concepts in impression formation. *Journal of Personality and Social Psychology, 51*, 493–504.

Martin, L. L., & Achee, J. W. (1992). Beyond accessibility: The role of processing objectives in judgment. In L. L. Martin & A. Tesser (Eds.), *The construction of social judgment* (pp. 252–271). Hillsdale, NJ: Lawrence Erlbaum.

McMullen, M. N. (1997). Affective contrast and assimilation in counterfactual thinking. *Journal of Experimental Social Psychology, 33*, 77–100.

Miyake, K., & Zuckerman, M. (1993). Beyond personality impressions: Effects of physical and vocal attractiveness on false consensus, social comparison, affiliation, and assumed and perceived similarity. *Journal of Personality, 61*, 411–437.

Morse, S., & Gergen, K. J. (1970). Social comparison, self-consistency, and the concept of self. *Journal of Personality and Social Psychology, 16*, 148–156.

Mussweiler, T. (1997). *A selective accessibility model of anchoring: Linking the anchoring heuristic to hypothesis-consistent testing and semantic priming.* Lengerich, Germany: Pabst.

Mussweiler, T., & Förster, J. (2000). The sex-aggression link: A perception-behavior dissociation. *Journal of Personality and Social Psychology*, in press.

Mussweiler, T., & Strack, F. (1999a). Hypothesis-consistent testing and semantic priming in the anchoring paradigm: A selective accessibility model. *Journal of Experimental Social Psychology*, *35*, 136–164.

Mussweiler, T., & Strack, F. (1999b). Comparing is believing: A selective accessability model of judgmental anchoring. In W. Stroebe & M. Hewstone (Eds.), *European review of social psychology* (Vol. 10, pp. 135–167). Chichester, England: Wiley.

Mussweiler, T., & Strack, F. (2000a). The use of category and exemplar knowledge in the solution of anchoring tasks. *Journal of Personality and Social Psychology*, *78*, 1038–1052.

Mussweiler, T., & Strack, F. (2000b). The relative self: Informational and judgmental consequences of comparative self-evaluation. *Journal of Personality and Social Psychology*, *79*.

Mussweiler, T., & Strack, F. (2000c). Unpublished data. University of Würzburg, Würzburg, Germany.

Neely, J. H. (1991). Semantic priming effects in visual word recognition: A selective review of current findings and theories. In D. Besner & G. W. Humphreys (Eds.), *Basic processes in reading* (pp. 264–337). Hillsdale, NJ: Lawrence Erlbaum.

Nosanchuk, T. A., & Erickson, B. H. (1985). How high is up? Calibrating social comparison in the real world. *Journal of Personality and Social Psychology*, *48*, 624–634.

Ostrom, T. M., & Upshaw, H. S. (1968). Psychological perspectives and attitude change. In A. G. Greenwald, T. C. Brock, & T. M. Ostrom (Eds.), *Psychological foundations of attitudes* (pp. 217–242). New York: Academic Press.

Pelham, B. W., & Wachsmuth, J. O. (1995). The waxing and waning of the social self: Assimilation and contrast in social comparison. *Journal of Personality and Social Psychology*, *69*, 825–838.

Prinz, W. (1990). A common coding approach to perception and action. In O. Neumann & W. Prinz (Eds.), *Relationships between perception and action: Current approaches* (pp. 167–201). Berlin: Springer.

Reis, T. J., Gerrard, M., & Gibbons, F. X. (1993). Social comparison and the pill: Reactions to upward and downward comparison of contraceptive behavior. *Personality and Social Psychology Bulletin*, *19*, 13–20.

Salovey, P., & Rodin, J. (1984). Some antecedents and consequences of social comparison jealousy. *Journal of Personality and Social Psychology*, *47*, 780–792.

Schwarz, N., & Bless, H. (1992). Constructing reality and its alternatives: An inclusion/exclusion model of assimilation and contrast effects in social judgment. In H. Martin & A. Tesser (Eds.), *The construction of social judgment* (pp. 217–245). Hillsdale, NJ: Lawrence Erlbaum.

Sedikides, C., & Skowronski, J. J. (1991). The law of cognitive structure activation. *Psychological Inquiry*, *2*, 169–184.

Seta, J. J. (1982). The impact of comparison processes on coactors' task performance. *Journal of Personality and Social Psychology*, *42*, 281–291.

Srull, T. K., & Wyer, R. S. (1979). The role of category accessibility in the interpretation of information about persons: Some determinants and implications. *Journal of Personality and Social Psychology*, *37*, 1660–1672.

Strack, F. (1992). The different routes to social judgments: Experiential versus informational strategies. In L. L. Martin & A. Tesser (Eds.), *The construction of social judgment* (pp. 249–275). Hillsdale, NJ: Lawrence Erlbaum.

Strack, F., & Mussweiler, T. (1997). Explaining the enigmatic anchoring effect: Mechanisms of selective accessibility. *Journal of Personality and Social Psychology*, *73*, 437–446.

Strack, F., Schwarz, N., & Gschneidinger, E. (1985). Happiness and reminiscing: The role of time perspective, affect, and mode of thinking. *Journal of Personality and Social Psychology*, *49*, 1460–1469.

Taylor, S. E., Wayment, H. A., & Carrillo, M. (1996). Social comparison, self-regulation, and motivation. In R. M. Sorrentino & E. T. Higgins (Eds.), *Handbook of motivation and cognition* (pp. 3–27). New York: Guilford Press.

Tesser, A. (1988). Toward a self-evaluation maintenance model of social behavior. In L. Berkowitz (Ed.), *Advances in experimental social psychology* (Vol. 20, pp. 181–227). New York: Academic Press.

Tesser, A., Millar, M., & Moore, J. (1988). Some affective consequences of social comparison and reflection processes: The pain and pleasure of being close. *Journal of Personality and Social Psychology*, *54*, 49–61.

Thornton, D., & Moore, S. (1993). Physical attractiveness contrast effect: Implications for self-esteem and evaluations of the social self. *Personality and Social Psychology Bulletin*, *19*, 474–480.

Trope, Y. (1986). Self-assessment and self-enhancement in achievement motivation. In R. Sorrentino & E. T. Higgins (Eds.), *Handbook of motivation and cognition: Foundations of social behavior* (Vol. 1, pp. 350–378). New York: Guilford Press.

Trope, Y., & Bassok, M. (1982). Confirmatory and diagnostic strategies in social information gathering. *Journal of Personality and Social Psychology*, *43*, 22–34.

Trope, Y., & Liberman, A. (1996). Social hypothesis testing: Cognitive and motivational factors. In E. T. Higgins & A. W. Kruglanski (Eds.), *Social psychology: Handbook of basic principles* (pp. 239–270). New York: Guilford Press.

Tversky, A., & Kahneman, D. (1974). Judgment under uncertainty: Heuristics and biases. *Science, 185,* 1124–1130.
Wheeler, L. (1966). Motivation as a determinant of upward comparison. *Journal of Experimental Social Psychology,*
   2, 27–31.
Wheeler, L., Martin, R., & Suls, J. (1997). The proxy model of social comparison for self-assessment of ability.
   Personality and Social Psychology Review, 1, 54–61.
Wills, T. A., & Suls, J. (1991). Commentary: Neo-social comparison theory and beyond. In J. Suls & T. A. Wills (Eds.),
   Social Comparison: Contemporary theory and research (pp. 395–411). Hillsdale, NJ: Lawrence Erlbaum.
Wood, J. V. (1989). Theory and research concerning social comparisons of personal attributes. *Psychological Bulletin,*
   106, 231–248.
Wood, J. V., & Taylor, K. L. (1991). Serving self-relevant goals through social comparison. In J. Suls & T. A. Wills
   (Eds.), *Social comparison: Contemporary theory and research* (pp. 23–49). Hillsdale, NJ: Lawrence Erlbaum.
Wyer, R. S., & Srull, T. K. (1989). *Memory and cognition in its social context.* Hillsdale, NJ: Lawrence Erlbaum.

14

Evaluating Social Comparison Targets

MARK D. ALICKE

Social comparison is the process by which people establish, maintain, refine, or embellish their self-concepts. The early history of social comparison research emphasized the comparisons people select to evaluate their abilities and opinions (Latane, 1966). In particular, this research assessed whether people preferred to elucidate their performance outcomes by comparing with superior or inferior others. The emphasis on comparison selections as opposed to comparison outcomes derived from Festinger's (1954) conjecture that people evaluate their abilities by comparing with targets who are similar to themselves.

The emphasis on comparison selections was parlayed into the most popular design in the initial stages of social comparison research, namely, the rank order paradigm. In rank order research, participants learn their distributional position on an ability test (usually in the middle) and then indicate their preference for viewing higher- or lower-ranked scores. Prior to the 1980s, social comparison researchers focused predominately on situations in which people select specific referents to diagnose their characteristics. Since then, researchers have recognized that social comparisons cannot always be orchestrated (Mettee & Smith, 1977; Suls, 1986; Wheeler & Miyake, 1992; Wood, 1989). Many, if not most, social comparison opportunities are foisted upon us, such as when siblings are compared by their parents and peers, students receive grade distributions, employees are evaluated for pay raises, or athletic teams compete. Although people have some control over the social situations they enter and the associates they encounter, it seems fair to say that both transitory and stable self-views are shaped largely through the outcomes of spontaneous, inadvertent comparisons (Gilbert, Giesler, & Morris, 1995).

Another relatively recent offshoot of traditional social comparison research is the idea that people compare themselves with hypothetical or "generalized" others as well as with specific referents. Patients suffering from serious illnesses, for example, sometimes construct comparisons with hypothetical worse-off targets (Wood, Taylor, & Lichtman, 1985). Other research shows that people buttress their attitudes or opinions by constructing hypothetical peer groups who share their views (Goethals, 1986; Suls & Wan, 1987). Besides comparing with hypothetical or generalized targets, people also may hold "context-free" conceptions of

MARK D. ALICKE • Department of Psychology, Ohio University, Athens, Ohio 45701-2979.

Handbook of Social Comparison: Theory and Research, edited by Suls and Wheeler. Kluwer Academic/Plenum Publishers, New York, 2000.

their standing on various characteristics relative to these targets. The most extensive literature on this topic involves studies on the "optimistic bias," or more generally, the "better than average" effect. Participants in this research compare their prospects or characteristics with those of an average peer. Research on the better-than-average effect consistently shows that people evaluate themselves or their prospects more favorably than those of an average peer on most judgment dimensions (Alicke, 1985; Alicke, Klotz, Breitenbecher, Yurak, & Vredenburg, 1995; Dunning, Meyerowitz, & Holzberg, 1989; Weinstein, 1980).

SOCIAL COMPARISON TARGETS

Besides contributing to self-concept formation and maintenance, social comparisons contribute to impressions of the comparison target. Self-assessment and target assessment are interdependent in the sense that self-perceptions influence target impressions and target impressions shape the comparison's meaning for the self. That the self-concept is molded by comparison feedback is, of course, the central tenet of traditional social comparison theory. Much less attention has been directed, however, to the ways in which social comparisons influence perceptions of the comparison target.

Perceptions of others are complicated by their self-concept implications. Admitting that other people are morally, socially, intellectually, or physically superior may require downgrading self-conceptions. Conversely, acknowledging the incompetence of the people we outperform negates the benefit the comparison could potentially confer. A "fundamental social comparison dilemma" arises, therefore, when performance data or social feedback threaten a desired self-image. The dilemma people face is between accurately assessing others' abilities and characteristics and risking self-concept damage. Impressions of social comparison targets, therefore, cannot be divorced from their self-concept implications. Our impressions of superior and inferior targets are ultimately related to the self-conceptions we wish to achieve or maintain.

This chapter addresses the impressions people form of social comparison targets as a result of comparing favorably or unfavorably to those targets. In particular, I assess how self-perceptions and ego enhancement motives influence impressions of comparison targets' abilities and traits. Consistent with most social comparison analyses, I classify comparisons as lateral, upward, or downward (comparison direction). I also consider favorable and unfavorable comparisons of each type (comparison outcome). This classification scheme is depicted in Table 1. Classifying comparisons by direction and outcome is consistent with the common experience of having one's performance expectations confirmed or disconfirmed by task or social feedback.

The comparisons depicted in Table 1, in which people expect the target to be superior, worse, or about the same as themselves on the comparison dimension are expectancy-driven comparisons. In this scheme, upward, lateral, and downward comparisons refer to the subject's[1] expectation about the target's standing prior to receiving comparison feedback. Expectancy-driven comparisons contrast with data-driven comparisons in which comparison direction is ascertained solely by learning whether one compares favorably or unfavorable to the target. Data-driven comparisons in which the subject (i.e., the person making the comparison) outperforms the target are downward comparisons and those in which the target outper-

---

[1] I use the term "subjects" rather than "participants" throughout this chapter to delineate between the person who is making the comparison and the target of the comparison. Because both subject and target are participants in experiments, the term participant does not adequately distinguish between the two.

**Table 1. Favorable and Unfavorable Outcomes in Comparisons
with People Expected To Be Superior (Upward), Inferior (Downward),
or about the Same as Oneself (Lateral) on the Comparison Dimension**

	Upward	Downward	Lateral
Favorable	Outperform a person who you expect to be superior	Outperform a person who you expect to be inferior	Outperform a person who you expect to be about equal
Unfavorable	Underperform a person who you expect to be superior	Underperform a person who you expect to be inferior	Underperform a person who you expect to be about equal

forms the subject are upward comparisons. Lateral comparisons occur when subject and target perform about equally. Although I focus primarily on expectancy-driven comparisons in this chapter, one particular type of data-driven comparison (which I have called the "genius effect") is considered at length in the section on unfavorable upward comparisons.

Expectancy-driven comparisons are based on either focal or related (also called background) attributes (Goethals & Darley, 1977; Suls, Gastorf, & Lawhon, 1978). Although Festinger (1954) emphasized focal abilities in his original social comparison paper, researchers have since recognized that comparisons often are predicated on attributes that are predictive of the focal attribute, especially when people are uncertain of their standing on the focal characteristic. For example, in the absence of specific ability-related information, people may choose to compare with others of the same age, sex, and background, assuming that these characteristics are related to the ability being diagnosed. Furthermore, the outcomes of focal comparisons can engender inferences about related attributes (Wood, 1989). Learning that a fellow student receives a better grade in a physics course, for example, may lead to the inference that she also will perform better in a mathematics course. In some instances, the need to restore or maintain self-esteem may encourage derogatory related attribute inferences, such as that a more attractive person is less intelligent (Ehrlich, 1973; Wills, 1981).

As the scheme represented in Table 1 suggests, this chapter deals primarily with situations in which behavior or performance feedback is available for both the subject and the comparison target. This accords with the social comparison tradition in which comparisons are linked directly to behavioral outcomes. As noted above, however, more recent social comparison research has addressed circumstances in which people compare themselves to generalized others, abstracted from specific performance contexts. In this research, represented primarily by the better-than-average effect, comparisons are made with an average peer who may or may not represent an actual person. Research on the better-than-average effect is considered in a separate section at the end of the chapter.

Four moderators of target impressions are discussed at various points throughout this chapter. These moderators include the comparison's ambiguity, the importance of the comparison dimension for the subject's self-concept, the nature of the subject's and target's relationship, and the subject's need for accuracy. The first moderator, comparison ambiguity, determines whether conditions are conducive for self-enhancement. Objectively based comparisons, such as those predicated on indisputable facts or prevailing consensus, are relatively unambiguous and therefore difficult to manipulate for self-enhancement purposes. It would be difficult, for example, to deny another's superior job status or salary. On the other hand, many if not most dispositional characteristics are imperfectly linked to specific behavioral episodes (Reeder & Brewer, 1979) and therefore are highly ambiguous. It would be relatively easy, for example, to disavow another's seemingly superior honesty by using idiosyncratic definitions of honesty (Dunning et al., 1989) or by proffering self-serving excuses for dishonest behavior.

Second, comparisons on central self-concept dimensions encourage motivationally-based revisions more than peripheral comparisons (Miller, 1984). As Tesser's (1988, 1991) self-evaluation maintenance model implies, people find it more difficult to admit inferiority on important self-concept dimensions. Thus, the degree to which target attributions are moderated by ego-related concerns depends on whether the comparison dimension represents an essential aspect of the subject's identity.

Third, the comparison target's closeness can affect the way comparisons are construed. Tesser's self-evaluation maintenance model predicts that people are more likely to form favorable impressions of close others on peripheral than on central self-concept dimensions. According to this view, the threat to the self-concept posed by continued interaction with superior performers leads people to distance themselves from those performers or to derogate them. As will be described in the section on unfavorable upward comparisons, however, recent research suggests that positive views of superior performers are formed even on important self-concept dimensions, at least when the comparison is unambiguous.

Fourth, the contrasting needs for self-esteem maintenance and accurate assessment that underlie the fundamental social comparison dilemma can instigate a cost-benefit analysis in which subjects weigh the benefits of personal advancement against the potential costs of self-concept decline. If the target were a prospective group member whose performance could enhance the group's prospects, for example, it would be counterproductive to deny her superior ability. Conversely, if the target's performance had no palpable benefits, self-esteem maintenance concerns might override accuracy needs.

POST COMPARISON SHIFTS

The foregoing discussion suggests that self-perception and social perception are interdependent in the sense that the target's perceived abilities and characteristics help define the self, and self-perceptions, in turn, influence target attributions. This interdependence creates numerous possibilities for shifts in self- and target perception as the result of social comparison outcomes. These shifts can be cognitively or motivationally based. Cognitively based effects on target assessments derive from the use of the self as an anchor or comparison standard. If I consider myself to be a good tennis player, for example, the person who trounces me may seem like a prospective Wimbledon champion (contrast effect), whereas the person who beats me less severely may seem unrealistically close in ability (assimilation effect). Ego-related needs dictate perceiving others more positively or negatively depending on which direction reflects most favorably on the self. A person who wishes to be perceived as cooperative, for example, may underestimate the target's cooperativeness to elevate her own position on that trait. Conversely, a person who wishes to avoid being perceived as dishonest may exaggerate the target's dishonesty, thereby appearing more honest by comparison. This chapter emphasizes motivationally based effects, although it is important to note that establishing these effects requires eliminating alternative, cognitive explanations.

Figures 1–4 depict some of the most typical shifts that are hypothesized to occur after favorable and unfavorable upward and downward comparisons. (Lateral comparisons are not shown to avoid undue complexity.) Each figure depicts three types of shifts. In general, social comparison outcomes may induce changes in self-evaluation, target evaluation, or both, and

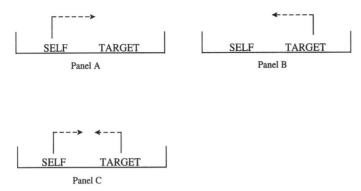

Figure 1. Favorable upward comparisons.

these changes can occur in various directions.[2] For example, a comparison may result in the self being moved toward or away from the comparison target or in the comparison target being moved toward or away from the self. In addition to these individual shifts, both people can move simultaneously in the same or opposite directions. The specific possibilities delineated in Figures 1–4 are discussed further under the appropriate subheadings below.

One complicating factor that Fig. 1 does not account for is that individual and simultaneous shifts can occur on either focal or inferred attributes. As a result of comparing unfavorably to the target on an intellectual task (focal attribute), for example, subjects may shift perceptions of their social skills (inferred attribute) upward while shifting perceptions of the target's social skills downward. This type of compensation effect is discussed most extensively in the section on unfavorable comparisons.

FAVORABLE COMPARISONS

Upward Comparisons

Favorable upward comparisons are potentially the most ego-enhancing of all social comparisons. Nothing is more satisfying to athletes, for example, than to defeat top performers in their field. Similarly, outperforming outstanding class members on a test is ego-enhancing to students of lesser ability. As shown in Fig. 1 (panel A), a natural consequence of such comparisons is to shift oneself upward toward and perhaps beyond the target. Another possibility (panel B) is to shift the target downward toward oneself. In other words, favorable upward comparisons would indicate that one has improved or that the target has regressed. The third main possibility (panel C) is for both shifts to occur simultaneously; that is, for the self to be shifted upward and the target downward. Panel A represents the most desirable shift from an ego-enhancement perspective because it represents the greatest self-concept gain relative to the target.

Outperforming reputedly superior targets may also raise questions about the comparison's reliability, especially if the outperformance is extreme. Instead of adjusting their own or

---

[2]Another possibility, of course, is for no shift to occur in self or target positions, but this possibility is unnecessary to show on the graphs.

276   MARK D. ALICKE

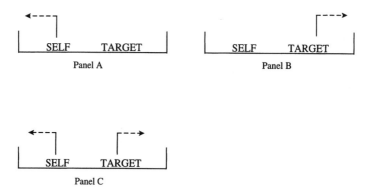

Figure 2. Favorable downward comparisons.

the target's standing, people could instead question the likelihood of repeating the outperformance in similar circumstances. Although this tactic would be disadvantageous from a self-enhancement perspective, accuracy concerns sometimes might override self-enhancement needs and lead people to seek further comparison data. A mediocre chess player who beats an expert, for example, might question whether the expert was paying attention or really trying.

One possible response to favorable but potentially unreliable upward comparisons is to handicap oneself in future comparisons. Self-handicapping research suggests that people will sabotage their future performances when they are uncertain about the basis of their initial successes (Berglas & Jones, 1978; Higgins, Snyder, & Berglas, 1990). A person who is unexpectedly asked on a date by an extremely desirable partner, for example, might get drunk to provide an excuse for potential rejection. In the context of social comparison, stacking the deck against oneself provides a ready excuse for being outperformed. Thus, self-handicapping can obviate the need to relinquish one's improved standing. Self-handicapping research suggests that people will construct obstacles to success when further comparisons with the target are inevitable and they are unconfident in repeating the outperformance.

Because favorable upward comparisons indicate that the comparer is unexpectedly superior to the target on the comparison dimension, such comparisons present an interesting

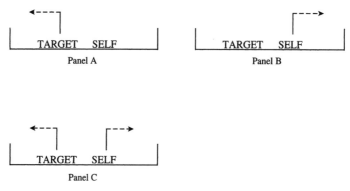

Figure 3. Unfavorable upward comparisons.

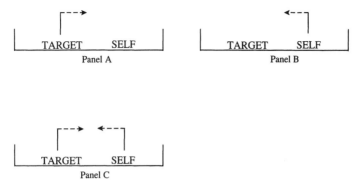

Figure 4. Unfavorable downward comparisons.

dilemma in close personal relationships, particularly when interpersonal values are involved. A partner may be surprised and dismayed, for example, to learn that his spouse is less honest than himself. Another example involves one's parents, who have always proclaimed racial tolerance, discouraging interracial relationships. Such expectancy violations introduce complex attributional problems. Because of their cognitive availability and emotional impact, negative expectancy violations might be expected to produce downward shifts in target evaluations. Research shows, however, that people strive to exaggerate their partners' virtues, perhaps because of the difficulties inherent in recognizing their faults (Murray, 2000; Murray & Holmes, 1997). Elevating morally inferior relationship partners is consistent with the basic self-enhancement rule that it is best to view people we outperform as favorably as possible. In close personal relationships, however, elevating the partner might negate one's superiority on the comparison dimension. Such attributional tendencies would help explain outsiders' perplexity in trying to understand why more virtuous members maintain relationships with far less virtuous partners.

Lateral Comparisons

The fundamental tenet of Festinger's (1954) original social comparison theory is that people prefer to compare their abilities with similar others. As Goethals and Darley (1977) noted, Festinger's hypothesis applies best to related attributes similarity. According to the related attributes view, people seek comparisons with others who are similar to them on characteristics that are useful for predicting their standing on the focal attribute. In terms of comparison outcomes, favorable lateral comparisons based on related attributes are informative because they suggest that the subject, who should be about equal to the target based on related attributes, may actually be superior.

Festinger's assumption that comparisons with similar others (i.e., lateral comparisons) are more informative for assessing abilities than comparisons with dissimilar others (i.e., upward or downward comparisons) holds true for comparison selections but not for comparison outcomes. Specifically, favorable lateral comparisons on focal attributes are considerably less informative than favorable upward comparisons. In other words, learning that you have outperformed someone who is close to you in ability is less surprising than learning that you have outperformed someone who is reputedly superior. Two equally matched tennis partners, for example, expect to trade wins and loses, whereas an inferior partner expects only an occasional victory. Lateral comparison victories might lead to a slight upward self-concept revision or a slight downward adjustment of the partner.

Downward Comparisons

Outperforming inferior targets is generally uninformative of one's own or the other's capabilities. Comparing favorably to targets who are expected to be inferior may lead to a slight downward adjustment of the target, a slight upward self-adjustment, or a simultaneous upward movement of the self and downward movement of the target (Fig. 2). Ego-enhancement needs are generally best served by attributing the most ability possible to inferior performers. The better the inferior performer, the better is one's superior performance by comparison. Thus, favorable downward comparisons are likely to lead subjects to exaggerate targets' abilities and may in some circumstances even improve self-evaluations (Alicke, LoSchiavo, Zerbst, & Zhang, 1997).

Downward comparisons are most informative when the margin of outperformance is greater or less than expected. Engaging in a close competition with a reputedly inferior performer may lead to a diminished perception of one's abilities or to an enhanced view of the target. Self-enhancement perspectives predict target aggrandizement, although when accuracy concerns predominate, people may adjust their ability downward as a result of favorable, but unexpectedly close, comparisons.

An unexplored implication of self-enhancement perspectives, however, is that subjects may elevate their self-views via nondiagnostic downward comparisons. For example, although there is little to be learned from lifting heavier weights than a much smaller person, the superior performer may undercorrect for this difference and thereby exaggerate his weight-lifting ability. People may even search actively for nondiagnostic downward comparisons. An example is provided by older children who interact and compare with younger ones to inflate their perceived abilities. In such cases, older children may simply discount their advantage on related attributes or exaggerate the younger children's competence on the focal dimension, thereby enhancing the comparison's value.

UNFAVORABLE COMPARISONS

Upward Comparisons

From the perspective of comparison selections, upward comparisons are intriguing because they bring the fundamental social comparison dilemma into sharp relief: When given the opportunity, will people compare themselves to superior performers who can provide valuable self-improvement data, or avoid such comparisons for the potential ego-deflating information they may convey? Even if people do not consciously select upward comparisons, the sheer number of social comparison opportunities that spontaneously arise virtually guarantees that people will sometimes compare unfavorably with superior others. As Festinger (1954) recognized, targets who are far superior on the comparison dimension may simply be dismissed as irrelevant for self-evaluation. However, comparisons with superior targets are not easily dismissible when the subject wishes to excel on the comparison dimension. A graduate student who learns of a peer's superior vita, for example, may despair of his or her ability to succeed in a research career (Lockwood & Kunda, 1997). As panels A and D of Fig. 3 show, one prominent but disagreeable consequence of unfavorable social comparisons is a downward shift in one's perceived standing on a judgment dimension. As will be discussed below, self-concept decrements can, at least in some circumstances, be avoided by shifting perceptions of the comparison target's ability (panel B of Fig. 3).

Tesser's (1988, 1991) self-evaluation maintenance model (SEM) provides the most thorough treatment of reactions to unfavorable comparisons. According to Tesser, unfavorable comparisons engender a reflection or a comparison process. The reflection process occurs when the comparison target is close to the subject and the comparison dimension is relatively unimportant to the subject's self-concept. Under these conditions, subjects can indirectly enhance their self-esteem by evaluating the target favorably and "basking" in the target's superior attributes. The comparison process occurs when subjects are outperformed on important dimensions by close others. When the comparison process is engaged, subjects tend to deemphasize their closeness to the target, downgrade the relevance of the comparison dimension, or hinder the target's performance. (See Chapter 7, this volume, for a more detailed description of the SEM model.)

The SEM assumes that superior performers generally will be denigrated or avoided except when the inferior performer has a close relationship with the superior performer and the performance dimension is relatively trivial. These predictions accord with other perspectives on social comparison that assume upward social comparisons tend to evoke defensive attributional strategies (e.g., Brickman & Bulman, 1977; Morse & Gergen, 1970; Wills, 1981). However, in a recent review of the upward social comparison literature, Collins (1996) has argued that upward comparisons are preferable to downward comparisons when they can be construed to negate the implications of inferior performance. Thirty years earlier, Wheeler (1966) suggested that inferior performers can benefit from upward comparisons by concluding they are in the same league with high performers and that they could, with requisite effort, attain a similar performance level. Upward comparisons also help people estimate how much they must improve to achieve a superior performance level. From this vantage, therefore, the key to resolving the fundamental social comparison dilemma is not to avoid superior comparison targets but to make attributions about oneself and the target that satisfy self-esteem needs without flagrantly disregarding accuracy needs.

Because most social comparison theories (e.g., Wills, 1981; Wood, 1989) have assumed that people deal defensively with unfavorable upward comparisons by avoiding them, distorting their meaning, or derogating the target, the conditions under which people form positive impressions of superior performers have been largely unexplored. One exception is a study by Gould, Brounstein, and Sigall (1977) that evaluated the attributions of subjects who *anticipated* competing against potentially superior performers. Subjects in their research first learned they had attained average performance on a tactile perception task. In some conditions, subjects expected to compete for money against a person who had previously competed successfully on this task. Subjects then estimated the potential competitor's ability. Attributions were made either publicly (names and social security numbers were required on the questionnaires) or privately (responses were placed in a sealed envelope without names or social security numbers and taken to the department secretary). Results showed that higher ability was ascribed to the potential competitor when attributions were made publicly.

Gould and colleagues were concerned with the self-presentational aspect of ability attributions. Thus, their primary comparisons were between public and private response conditions. The absence of an external standard for evaluating the competitor's performance makes it impossible to determine whether participants' ratings of the competitor in the public condition were generally favorable, or whether they were favorable only in relation to the private response condition. Furthermore, Gould and co-workers' findings are limited by the fact that their subjects never interacted with the competitors and, therefore, did not know if the competitions were more competent.

The Genius Effect. A recent set of studies on what I have termed the "genius" effect was designed to assess the effects on comparison target attributions of actually being outperformed. This research was stimulated by the obvious fact that even people with exceptional abilities or attributes eventually encounter someone who is smarter, more attractive, happier, friendlier, more likable, or wealthier than themselves. When the conditions under which these upward comparisons occur are sufficiently ambiguous, the subject has recourse to a variety of identity-repairing excuses. A college student, for example, who is outperformed by a roommate on a test might convince herself that her roommate studied harder, that the test was unfair, that she studied the wrong material, or that she had a bad day. However, plausible excuses can be difficult to find. The aforementioned student might be well aware that she studied harder than her roommate, that the test was fair, and that she studied the right material. When people are unambiguously outperformed, they can still salvage favorable self-images by employing a potent construal mechanism, namely, exaggerating the superior performer's ability.

Aggrandizing the superior performer helps resolve the fundamental social comparison dilemma. By viewing the outperformer as unusually talented, inferior performers can appreciate the outperformer's competence without suffering undue damage to their own perceived competence. The genius effect suggests a more salutary and pervasive role for upward comparisons than has generally been recognized. Intuitively, it seems more adaptive to exaggerate the ability of superior performers than to derogate or avoid them. Furthermore, unrealistically favorable evaluations are probably more beneficial to social relationships than derogatory ones.

The genius effect also helps to explain how people maintain unrealistically favorable self-images. As the literature on the better-than-average effect indicates, people evaluate themselves more favorably than an average peer on most dimensions (Alicke, 1985; Alicke et al., 1995; Dunning et al., 1989). Relatively little research has been directed, however, toward discovering how people maintain these self-images in the face of contradictory social comparisons. The genius effect suggests what may be a pervasive strategy for maintaining an unrealistically favorable self-image following upward comparisons, namely, to exaggerate the talents of people who fare better on the comparison dimension.

The hypothesis that people exaggerate the ability of superior performers requires a comparison of the ability attributions made by people who are and who are not outperformed. Furthermore, the outperformance should be clear and by a significant margin, thereby reducing the plausibility of excuses. Four recent studies were conducted to meet these conditions (Alicke et al., 1997). Participants in each study completed a perceptual intelligence test with a confederate and subsequently learned that the confederate's performance exceeded their own. The test comprised ten items from Raven's (1965) progressive matrices in which participants were shown an incomplete figure and asked to identify which of eight segments would complete the figure. Based on pretesting, the test was constructed so that the average student would answer three items correctly. By prearrangement, the confederate always answered seven items correctly. Comparisons with the confederate were primarily data-driven rather than expectancy-driven in that subjects were given no specific information upon which to base expectancies about the target's ability.

Subjects and confederates scored each other's tests so that the subject would be aware of the confederate's performance. An observer witnessed the subject's and confederate's performance from behind a one-way window and was informed of each person's score. The hypothesis that people exaggerate the outperformer's ability was tested by comparing the attributions of the confederate's perceptual intelligence made by the subject who was outperformed and by the observer who simply watched the performance and learned of the scores.

The results of study 1 are shown in Fig. 5. As predicted, subjects rated the confederate more favorably than did observers. In addition, a significant interaction was obtained between the rater (subject or observer) and the person being rated (subject or confederate): Whereas subjects did not rate their perceptual intelligence more favorably than did observers, they did rate the confederate's perceptual intelligence more favorably. The finding that subjects did not rate their perceptual intelligence more favorably is important because it eliminates the possibility that their increased ratings of the target were an artifact of their elevated self-ratings.

A second study increased the primacy of responding to assess whether the tendency to exaggerate an outperformer's ability could be explained by self-presentational concerns. Because the previously described research of Gould et al. (1977) was concerned with the self-presentational aspect of ability attributions, their primary comparisons were between public and private response conditions. Thus, they did not include controls (such as our observers) against which to compare subjects' attributions. For this reason, it is impossible to ascertain whether the tendency to exaggerate a potential outperformer's ability in their study was limited to public response conditions or was simply magnified in such conditions.

Although neither names nor other forms of identification were attached to the questionnaires in our first study, it is possible, nevertheless, that participants were concerned that the experimenter or confederate would see their ratings. In addition to replicating the findings of the previous study, therefore, the purpose of study 2 was to see whether the tendency to exaggerate the outperformer's ability would be obtained when responses were more carefully hidden from the experimenter and confederate. Subjects and confederates in study 2 performed the task individually in separate rooms. Responses were placed in sealed envelopes without identification and dropped into a large box. The observer watched each person take

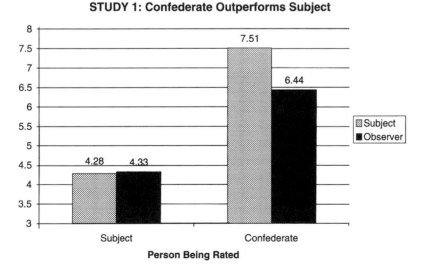

Figure 5. Perceptual intelligence ratings.

the test individually and was subsequently provided with each person's score. The results of this study were consistent with the previous one, thus suggesting that the tendency to exaggerate outperformers' ability cannot be explained by the motivation to appear modest to public audiences.

A third study assessed the assumption that exaggerating the outperformer's ability helps people maintain their perceived competence at a relatively high level. My explanation for the genius effect assumes that exaggerating an outperformer's ability helps people maintain a relatively favorable assessment of their competence. This explanation suggests that people who are outperformed and given the opportunity to aggrandize the target should view their competence more favorably than those who receive similar performance outcomes but who are not given the opportunity to evaluate the target.

We expected self-elevation to occur on a related attribute (specifically, general intelligence) rather than on the focal attribute (i.e., perceptual intelligence). The reason for this is that after being outperformed on perceptual intelligence, subjects have little choice but to rate the outperformer higher than themselves on this dimension if they want to appear credible to themselves and others. Even if subjects wished to exaggerate their perceptual intelligence, this assessment would be difficult to justify. Consistent with expectation, the results of study 3 showed that subjects who were given the opportunity to aggrandize the outperformer subsequently rated their own general intelligence higher than subjects who did not have this opportunity. Thus, subjects who explicitly evaluated the outperformer raised their self-perceptions on a related attribute.

A final study showed that people also exaggerate the ability of those they outperform. As suggested in the previous section on favorable downward comparisons, the self-enhancement perspective predicts that outperformers should attribute the highest plausible ability to the people they outperform because outperforming a competent person is more ego-enhancing than outperforming an incompetent one. Participants in study 4 received an average of seven items correct (easier items were pretested and used to ensure better performance) and learned that the inferior performer had answered three items correctly. Consistent with the self-enhancement perspective, Fig. 6 shows that participants evaluated the inferior performer more favorably than did observers.

To date, subjects in genius effect studies have had no specific basis for predicting whether the comparison target is superior, inferior, or about the same as themselves on focal or related dimensions. In this sense, the genius effect is a data-driven rather than an expectancy-driven phenomenon. As research on the better than average effect (discussed in the final section) suggests, however, people generally evaluate themselves more favorably than others, although this tendency is minimized on ability-related dimensions. If people do expect to outperform the target, the genius effect could be classified as a comparison in which subjects expected to be superior but turned out to be inferior (unfavorable downward comparison). The effects of expectancy confirmation and disconfirmation on target evaluations is an important topic for future genius effect investigations.

Lateral Comparisons

Assuming that performance outcomes are traded between people with equivalent ability, unfavorable lateral comparisons (i.e., comparisons in which people expect to be equal but turn out to be inferior) should be as expected as favorable lateral ones. Self-esteem maintenance perspectives, however, raise the possibility that people whose performance is equivalent over the long run will be disproportionately swayed by individual performance episodes in a

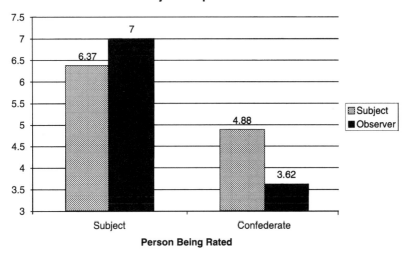

Figure 6. Perceptual intelligence ratings.

manner that enhances their self-concepts. For example, a single favorable performance outcome might lead subjects to exaggerate their superiority to the target, whereas a single unfavorable performance outcome will be discounted.

Because people generally expect to vanquish their inferiors or lose to their superiors, comparisons in which people underperform targets who they expect to be equal, based on past performance or background attributes, may evoke more negative emotions than upward or downward comparisons. This assumption can be understood in terms of Crosby's (1976) relative deprivation theory. Crosby hypothesizes that relative deprivation occurs under conditions in which the subject feels entitled to, but unlikely to obtain, something the target possesses (Bernstein & Crosby, 1980). Although relative deprivation research has tended to focus on material possessions, the same analysis can be extended to personal attributes. In the case of unfavorable lateral comparisons, the target possesses an attribute the subject wishes he or she possessed but feels unlikely to attain. Because the lateral target is similar to the subject on related attributes, their disparity on the focal attribute seems especially inequitable. This disparity may lead subjects to denigrate or distance themselves from the target.

One example in which lateral comparisons invite invidious target perceptions involves perceptions of wealthy athletes. When players go on strike, fans seem to unleash their wrath more on the players than on the owners. Perhaps this is because fans, while appreciating the players superiority on the focal attribute, believe that players are more similar to themselves than owners on what Wood (1989) calls "surrounding attributes"; that is, similar background factors that are unrelated to the focal task. Thus, fans may view players as lateral comparison targets on surrounding attributes but owners as upward comparisons. Fans may feel more relatively deprived, therefore, in comparing themselves to players, whose monetary good fortune is believed to be unjustified. Feelings of envy aroused by players' good fortune may encourage a variety of derogatory impressions (Smith et al., 1994, 1996; see also Chapter 10, this volume). Stereotypes such as the dumb athlete or dissolute Hollywood star may be propagated partly to compensate for these individuals' superior wealth or fame.

Downward Comparisons

Unfavorable downward comparisons are potentially the most threatening of all social comparisons because they suggest a deterioration in one's abilities (panels B and C of Fig. 4). Alternatively, such comparisons could be attributed to luck or to an improvement in the target's ability (panel A of Fig. 4). Attributions to luck are desirable from a self-esteem maintenance standpoint because they counter the assumption that one's abilities have deteriorated. Such excuses are most likely to occur when performance outcomes are ambiguous, such as if the subject were physically or psychologically stressed, or if there were no danger of further comparisons in which the subject might again be outperformed.

When unfavorable performance outcomes are unambiguous and ostensibly reliable, self-esteem maintenance perspectives predict that subjects will favor target improvement attributions over deterioration of their abilities to explain their unexpectedly inferior performance. If the target has substantially improved, the subject's perceived competence can be salvaged. This reasoning suggests that the genius effect also is likely to occur in unfavorable downward comparisons. An example is losing a competition to a younger sibling after years of comfortable superiority. When there is little choice but to acknowledge the superiority of a heretofore inferior performer, target aggrandizement is an attractive construal mechanism that minimizes the degree of perceived slippage in one's abilities.

Interesting problems arise when the subject has an advantage over the target on related attributes but compares unfavorably on focal ones. Consider an example in which a job candidate learns that she has a better educational background than her closest competitor. Assuming that educational background is highly related to the focal dimension, the candidate's superior education confers a competitive advantage. However, if she ultimately loses the job, she may suffer more significant self-concept decrements than if her educational background were equal or inferior. This assumption can be understood in terms of attribution theory's augmentation principle (Kelley, 1972), which stipulates that stronger dispositional inferences are made when behavior is inconsistent rather than consistent with external forces. In this example, losing a job when you have a distinct advantage indicates a lower ability level than losing one for which you are disadvantaged. The augmentation principle, therefore, suggests that favorable comparisons on related attributes are a liability when unfavorable outcomes on focal attributes occur. One strategy for deflecting unfavorable self-concept implications in such cases is to downplay one's advantage or to identify unforeseen opponent advantages. In contrast to the general self-esteem maintenance assumption that it is best to elevate the perceived ability of those we outperform, this strategy would have the opposite effect of diminishing the opponent's perceived ability. Downgrading inferior performers seems most likely to occur in highly competitive situations in which competitive needs negate the self-esteem benefits to be accrued from exaggerating the opponent's ability.

Shifts in self and target perceptions also may occur following unfavorable comparisons on dimensions that disclose personal values. Consider the dilemma, for example, of a person who discloses an extramarital affair or an illegal financial dealing to a presumably corrupt colleague and then learns that the colleague never committed either of these misdeeds. Even if people react to their own moral failings with face-saving excuses, they may subsequently empathize more with the target. When excuses are difficult to maintain, subjects may have no recourse but to shift their self-conceptions downward toward the target. Self-concept decrements such as these can be the precursors of major attitudinal and behavioral changes, such as a former racist altering his prejudiced attitudes and discriminatory behavior.

Another possible response to an unfavorable downward comparison is to find an even more unfavorable target for comparison (Wills, 1981). An unfaithful spouse, for example, may highlight downward comparisons with people who have had multiple or longer-lasting affairs. Politicians caught in lies or scandals frequently highlight the triviality of their misdeeds compared to those of their predecessors. One of President Clinton's most compelling arguments against conviction in the Senate was to proclaim the insignificance of his offenses in comparison to those committed by Nixon in the Watergate scandal.

NONEVENT COMPARISONS: THE BETTER-THAN-AVERAGE EFFECT

The preceding sections addressed circumstances in which people learn that they have performed worse than, about the same as, or better than, a comparison target. As noted in the introduction, people also harbor general conceptions of where they stand relative to others on performance for behavior dimensions. These comparisons are context-free in the sense that they do not involve reactions to specific task-related feedback. A preponderance of the literature pertaining to context-free comparisons with hypothetical or generalized others comprises studies on the better-than-average effect (Alicke, 1985; Alicke et al., 1995; Codol, 1975; Dunning et al., 1989). In the better-than-average paradigm, participants are asked to compare themselves to an average peer on various trait or behavior dimensions. The main conclusion gleaned from numerous studies on this topic is that people evaluate themselves more favorably than their peers on most characteristics. Although the better-than-average effect is one of the most perdurable findings in the social–psychological canon, no generally accepted explanation for these findings has emerged. Current explanations can be distinguished as to whether they assume that subjects recruit concrete targets or behavioral instances for each comparison, or whether better-than-average judgments are made without reference to specific comparison targets or behavioral episodes. I will refer to the former position as the "concrete comparison view" and to the latter as the "abstract comparison view."

One source of evidence for the concrete comparison view derives from research showing that the optimistic bias—the tendency to assume one's prospects of experiencing misfortune are less than an average peer's—is diminished when subjects are given specific information to suggest that others are no more predisposed to misfortune than themselves (e.g., Weinstein, 1980, 1983; Weinstein & Lachendro, 1982). Perloff and Fetzer (1986) have suggested that in comparing the likelihood that they will experience misfortune to that of an average peer people select comparison targets who are especially at risk for these events, thereby enhancing their chances of comparing favorably. Presumably, this tendency to select favorable comparison targets is impeded by explicit data suggesting that others are no more susceptible to these unfortunate events than oneself.

Another possible concrete strategy for comparing one's characteristics or prospects to those of others is to sample a biased set of behaviors (Weinstein, 1980). For example, when asked to assess their honesty, people may think selectively about instances in which they were extremely honest and then limit the comparison to these instances, effectively ignoring times when they were less honest. Similarly, in comparing the possibility that they will get divorced to that of the average peer, people may think of behavioral tendencies that make divorce unlikely (e.g., that they are cooperative and understanding) and then base the comparison on these positive characteristics.

The abstract comparison view, however, questions whether subjects typically recruit specific comparison targets or behavioral episodes in comparing themselves to an average peer. Instead of conjuring specific comparisons to make such judgments, the abstract comparison perspective suggests that subjects evaluate their characteristics independently of others and apply a constant elevation factor for self-enhancement purposes (Alicke et al., 1995). This perspective depicts better-than-average comparisons in terms of a linear model in which each trait is accorded a scale value and weight and in which the grand mean component (i.e., the elevation factor) is a positive constant based on a globally positive self-concept.

Although the abstract comparison perspective has yet to be directly tested, it is indirectly supported by studies that question the plausibility of the concrete comparison view. For example, the better-than-average effect has been obtained when participants make an extremely large number of trait comparisons in a relatively short time, and it seems implausible that they recruit individual people or behaviors for each comparison (Alicke, 1985). Furthermore, the better-than-average effect is neither reduced nor eliminated when subjects are precluded from making specific comparisons by cognitive load manipulations (Alicke et al., 1995, study 7), such as being required to count backward by three digit numbers while making their judgments. Finally, participants rarely report recruiting specific individuals or specific behaviors when asked how they made these comparisons during debriefing. In Alicke and co-workers' (1995) study 7, none of the 65 subjects in the cognitive load condition and only 2 of 67 subjects in the no-cognitive load condition reported making such comparisons.

Another source of evidence against the view that people recruit exemplars for each comparison comes from recent research on the "better-than-myself" effect (Alicke & Vredenburg, 2000). In these studies, participants in a pretesting session estimate the percentage of times they engage in trait-representative behaviors (e.g., acting cooperatively verus uncooperatively) when the opportunities to display these behaviors arise. After each percentage estimate, participants make corresponding trait ratings (e.g., cooperativeness–uncooperativeness) on bipolar rating scales. Later in the semester, participants receive another set of behavioral estimates, this time purportedly from a randomly selected student, and are asked to estimate this student's traits on the same scales. Behavioral estimates are tailored for each subject so that they are identical to those the subject completed earlier in the semester. Thus, comparisons with the randomly selected peer's percentage estimates actually represent comparisons with their own. The better-than-myself effect is reflected in the finding that people consistently rate the hypothetical student lower on the traits than they had rated themselves based on identical behavioral estimates. The better-than-myself effect, therefore, provides another basis for questioning whether concrete behavior calculations underlie the better-than-average effect.

The contention that trait and behavior comparisons are made abstractly rather than on the basis of concrete behavioral analyses is also supported by research showing that the better-than-average effect is diminished or eliminated when subjects are induced to make their judgments more concretely. Studies have shown, for example, that the magnitude of the better-than-average effect is consistently smaller on objectively-based judgment dimensions (e.g., those involving abilities) (Alicke, 1985; Allison, Messick, & Goethals, 1989; Messick, Bloom, Boldizar, & Samuelson, 1985) than on subjectively based ones. Furthermore, research has shown that the better-than-average effect is greater when subjects are permitted to provide their own trait definitions than when the traits are defined for them (Dunning et al., 1989).

The foregoing studies focus on the comparison dimension's ambiguity. Another source of ambiguity in average peer comparisons derives from the nature of the comparison target. In contrast to comparisons with real-life individuated targets, the average peer is an amorphous, hypothetical comparison standard. If the better-than-average effect is facilitated by the abstractness of the comparison, then inducing subjects to compare themselves with specific, concrete referents should diminish the better-than-average effect. Put another way, if the better-than-average effect requires a high level of comparison target ambiguity, thereby allowing people to apply an abstract elevation factor, then this bias should be attenuated or eliminated in comparisons with concrete, individuated targets.

This assumption was tested in seven studies by Alicke et al. (1995). In the first and simplest study, participants were first separated into two large rooms. Students in one room were asked to be sure they were sitting next to someone they had never met. They were next asked to look at the person they were sitting next to and then to move their seats. Participants then compared themselves to the person they had sat next to on 20 positive and 20 negative trait dimensions. Students in the adjoining room simply compared themselves to the average college student on the same scales. Results showed that the better-than-average effect was significantly diminished in comparisons with real people on 31 of the 38 trait dimensions on which the effect was obtained. Thus, simply comparing oneself to a real person is generally sufficient to reduce the better-than-average effect. These findings lend support to the notion that the better-than-average effect does not typically involve concrete comparisons with real people or with specific behaviors.

Six more studies were conducted to isolate the aspects of comparisons with real people that differentiate them from average peer comparisons. Study 2 tested the possibility that students may view the "average" student pejoratively, based on a dislike of being perceived as average. Participants in this study were asked to estimate the percentage of their peers who fell into nine labeled categories ranging from, for example, extremely dependable to extremely undependable. These percentage estimates were made for each of 12 bipolar trait dimensions. This procedure allowed us to construct distributions of each trait dimension showing the percentage of peers that subjects placed in each of the nine categories, ranging from the least favorable to the most favorable end of the trait dimension. In the second part of the study, one third of the participants located themselves in one of the nine categories for each trait dimension, another third estimated where they believed the person they had been sitting next to fell, and the final third estimated where the average college student fell. This study yielded three primary results. First, the average person was not generally viewed pejoratively: On most dimensions, participants placed the average student above the distribution mean for that trait. Second, specific people were again rated more favorably than the average college student. Third, self-evaluations were consistently above both the average and the specific person.

A common paradigm was developed for the remaining studies. In each study, participants watched an interaction in which a target was asked various mundane questions by an interviewer. The person being interviewed was the comparison target in all experimental conditions. Comparisons were made on a series of traits as well as on likelihood estimates that they and the target would experience various unfortunate events. Study 3 included five subject conditions: one in which the subject was the person conducting the interview (interviewer condition); a second in which the subject was an observer who watched the interview take place in the same room (live observer condition); a third in which subjects watched the interview on videotape; a fourth in which subjects read a verbatim transcript of the interview; and a fifth in which subjects compared themselves to the average college student.

The results of study 3 can be summarized in two main findings. The first finding was that the better-than-average effect was larger when people compared themselves to the average college student than in any other condition. This finding suggests that target individuation is one factor that differentiates comparisons with real people from comparisons with an average peer. In other words, the better-than-average effect is reduced whenever people compare themselves to a real human being, even one about whom they possess no specific information. The second main finding was that the conditions involving live personal contact with the target (i.e., the interviewer and live observer conditions) resulted in a reduced better-than-average effect in comparison to the conditions in which there was no live contact (i.e., in the transcript and videotape conditions). Interacting with the target did not affect the better-than-average effect independently of live personal contact as shown by the absence of a difference between the interviewer and live observer conditions. Based on these findings, we concluded that live personal contact is a second factor that differentiates real comparisons from average peer comparisons.

Subsequent studies were conducted to assess alternatives to the live personal contact factor. One important finding from these studies was that the live personal contact conditions (i.e., interviewer and live observer) produced lower better-than-average ratings than comparisons in which participants watched the interview take place from behind a one-way mirror. This finding was obtained although subjects who viewed the interview from behind a one-way mirror had an identical visual vantage to that of the live observer who witnessed the interview from the same room. Thus, the simple barrier of a mirror was sufficient to eradicate the effects produced by live personal contact.

Other studies in this series showed that reductions in the better-than-average effect in the interviewer and live observer conditions were equivalent regardless of whether observers saw the target's face or the back of the target's head. Furthermore, no differences were obtained among conditions in which participants watched a videotape, a video presentation they thought represented a contemporaneous presentation of the interview, an audiotape of the interview, or a still videotaped image of the target without the interview. In each of these conditions, the better-than-average effect was larger than in the live personal contact conditions. Thus, neither verbal nor visual cues seemed to be an important component of differences between the live personal contact and nonlive personal contact conditions.

Research on the better-than-average effect, therefore, suggests that unless people are explicitly forced to compare themselves with specific individuals, they tend to maintain abstract conceptions of themselves as better than average. Individuated social comparisons reduce this tendency but generally do not eliminate it. The better-than-average effect raises interesting questions about the general self-concept effects of everyday social comparisons. Even when people process information about specific social comparisons objectively, these comparisons may have minimal effect on their self-concepts. In other words, once people develop fairly stable notions of their traits, abilities, and characteristics, specific social comparisons may be insufficient to override abstract positive self-conceptions. Thus, it may take an inordinate amount of discrepant social comparison data to alter the self-conceptions people wish to maintain.

SUMMARY AND FUTURE DIRECTIONS

Research on social comparison processes originally emphasized the types of comparisons people select to diagnose their abilities and opinions. As argued at the outset, social comparison in its original guise probably overemphasized people's ability to select comparisons to suit self-evaluation needs. Many if not most social comparisons occur inadvertently in the course of receiving behavioral and performance feedback. Accordingly, recent social comparison research has focused more on the consequences than on the antecedents of the comparison process (e.g., Alicke et al., 1997; Gibbons, Persson, & Gerrard, 1994; Kulik & Gump, 1997; Major, Sciacchitano, & Crocker, 1993; Ybema & Buunk, 1993, 1995).

Identifying a comparison target is only the first step in the comparison process. Arguably, the most important aspect of social comparison is learning whether one fares better or worse than the target on the comparison dimension. Comparison outcomes are useful not only for informing subjects about their own standing but also for forming impressions of the target. Because social comparison research has focused overwhelmingly on the temporary and chronic effects of comparisons on the self-concept, the comparison's effects on target evaluations are only beginning to be explored.

In this chapter, I have portrayed comparisons as varying along two dimensions: comparison direction (upward, lateral, or downward) and comparison outcome (favorable or unfavorable). This depiction applies to expectancy-driven comparisons, in which subjects have reason to believe that the target is superior, about the same, or inferior to themselves on the comparison dimension, and in which these expectancies are confirmed or disconfirmed by the comparison's outcomes. This cross-classification of comparison direction and outcome has the virtue of combining two major aspects of social comparisons that have been treated separately in previous studies and in delineating problems in self- and target evaluation that have yet to be investigated. Because researchers have not previously conceptualized social comparisons in this manner, much of the discussion on this topic was based on speculation about how self-enhancement motives would influence self- and target evaluations.

Of the various comparison possibilities enumerated, unfavorable upward comparisons have been studied most extensively. Impromptu encounters with more fortunate others occur routinely in social life. Sooner or later, we all meet others who are smarter, more physically attractive, more popular, wealthier, and happier than ourselves. A variation on the "fundamental social comparison dilemma" applied to target attributions involves the competing desires to evaluate the target accurately while avoiding threats to one's perceived competence. Accurate target appraisals are beneficial in assessing which targets are likely to foster or hinder one's personal goals and also in gauging one's relative abilities and attributes. These benefits are countermanded by the potential for self-concept diminution. Target attributions, therefore, represent a compromise between the desire for accurate evaluation and the need to maintain the self-concept at the highest believable level.

The pervasiveness of unfavorable upward comparisons suggests that it is impossible always to derogate or distance oneself from the target. Furthermore, the need to coexist harmoniously with superior others often precludes shunning them. The "genius effect" is a powerful construal mechanism that enables people to appreciate superior targets' abilities without suffering undue self-concept damage. The genius effect is consistent with a growing literature in social comparison theory that underscores the benefits of upward social comparison (e.g., Collins, 1996; Gastorf, Suls, & Sanders, 1980; Seta, 1982; Wood, 1989; Wood & Taylor, 1991). To date, however, the genius effect has been demonstrated in specific circumstances, namely, when the target is a stranger who has unambiguously outperformed the subject on a relatively novel intelligence task. Future research is required to ascertain whether the genius effect occurs when subjects have stronger expectancies about their own and the target's performance, when there is less discrepancy between the subject's and target's performance, thereby introducing greater ambiguity, and on other comparison dimensions such as those involving attitudes or opinions, social traits, and interpersonal values.

Another direction for future research on target evaluations involves circumstances in which comparisons involve the opinions of a third party, such as when a parent compares two siblings, a teacher two students, or an employer two employees. Third-party evaluations can be highly ambiguous. As an example, consider a situation in which person A selects person B as a dating partner over person C. Because there are many potential bases for person A's preference, person C faces a difficult task in identifying which one was the prepotent cause of person A's selection. Among the possible dimensions person C might consider are physical attractiveness, intelligence, personality, and background. Jones and Davis's (1965) discussion of noncommon effects suggests that person C will identify the factor that most differentiates him from person B. Thus, if persons B and C are about equal in physical attractiveness, intelligence, and background, but person B is an extravert, whereas person C is an introvert, person C should identify personality as the primary cause of person A's choice. A complicating factor, however, is that these dimensions have different self-esteem implications. If intelligence is more important to person C than physical attractiveness, person C is less likely to conclude that intelligence was the basis of the dating decision. Furthermore, person C's inferences are relevant to his evaluation of the comparison target (person B). If person C concludes that person B was selected for his physical attractiveness, he may exaggerate person B's physical attractiveness and underestimate his standing on other dimensions. The factors involved in making attributions about third-party preferences are complex and worthy of attention in future research.

The extant literature on target evaluations focuses only on a comparison's implications for a specific social comparison target. In some circumstances, however, subjects may generalize target evaluations to other group members. For example, the morally disillusioning behavior of a political or religious leader may diminish opinions of all politicians or religious leaders. Consistent with this possibility, research has shown that the misdeeds of high-profile minority group members result in negative stereotype revisions of those groups (Feather, 1994). This research suggests, for example, that O. J. Simpson's transformation from star athlete and pop icon to double-murderer might have altered African-American stereotypes among whites.

The present classification scheme can be extended to intergroup comparisons. The genius effect, for example, suggests circumstances in which people will exaggerate the ability of outgroups, namely, when they are unambiguously outperformed by those groups. Group-level analyses introduce a series of complicating factors that are worthy of future research. For example, competition between groups may diminish the tendency to acknowledge the outperforming group's superiority (Brewer & Weber, 1984; Major et al., 1993). Ironically, however, the genius effect might be exacerbated in comparisons with negatively stereotyped groups. A racist, for example, who is outperformed by the minority group member is especially likely to view that person as an unusual exemplar and to exaggerate the person's competence on the performance dimension. Thus, research on the genius effect raises a number of intriguing questions about the conditions under which in-group members will exaggerate the abilities of ostensibly superior out-groups.

Finally, research on the better-than-average effect extends social comparison beyond its original boundaries to include context-free comparisons with hypothetical or generalized others. Numerous studies show that people evaluate themselves more favorably than an average peer on most dimensions, although the effect is attenuated on relatively objective (such as ability) judgment dimensions (Allison et al., 1989), when comparisons are made more objective by providing participants with specific trait definitions (Dunning et al., 1989), or when participants are forced to compare with specific individuals rather than hypothetical peers (Alicke et al., 1995). Better-than-average effect research raises important questions about the relationship between specific social comparisons and more global self-evaluations. If people evaluate their characteristics by comparing themselves to others and if many if not most social comparisons are encountered rather than selected, how can people consistently perceive themselves to be better than average on almost every characteristic imaginable? Although part of the better-than-average conundrum can be explained by the abstractness of the average person as a comparison target, the effect still emerges consistently, albeit less extremely, in comparisons with real individuals. Apparently, people harbor positive self-images that are highly resistant to the unfavorable implications of upward social comparisons. Strategic deployment of self-serving construal mechanisms provides one explanation for people's ostensible immunity to unfavorable comparisons. This chapter has highlighted one such mechanism—aggrandizing the superior performer—that provides an especially powerful means for maintaining a positive self-concept in the face of objectively unflattering data. The genius effect provides a way out of the fundamental social comparison dilemma by allowing people to appreciate and even benefit from superior performers without letting the air out of their inflated self-concepts.

REFERENCES

Alicke, M. D. (1985). Global self-evaluation as determined by the desirability and controllability of trait adjectives. *Journal of Personality and Social Psychology, 49*, 1621–1630.

Alicke, M. D., Klotz, M. L., Breitenbecher, D. L., Yurak, T. J., & Vredenburg, D. S. (1995). Personal contact, individuation, and the better-than-average effect. *Journal of Personality and Social Psychology, 68*, 804–825.

Alicke, M. D., LoSchiavo, F. M., Zerbst, J. I., & Zhang, S. (1997). The person who outperforms me is a genius: Esteem maintenance in upward social comparison. *Journal of Personality and Social Psychology, 73*, 781–789.

Alicke, M. D., & Vredenburg, D. S. (1999). The better than myself effect. Unpublished manuscript.

Allison, S. T., Messick, D. M., & Goethals, G. R. (1989). On being better but not smarter than others: The Muhammad Ali effect. *Social Cognition, 7*, 275–296.

Berglas, S., & Jones, E. E. (1978). Drug choice as a self-handicapping strategy in response to non-contingent success. *Journal of Personality and Social Psychology, 36*, 405–417.

Bernstein, M., & Crosby, F. (1980). An empirical examination of relative deprivation theory. *Journal of Experimental Social Psychology, 16*, 442–456.

Brewer, M. B., & Weber, J. G. (1994). Self-evaluation effects of interpersonal versus intergroup social comparisons *Journal of Personality and Social Psychology, 66*, 268–275.

Brickman, P., & Bulman, R. J. (1977). Pleasure and pain in social comparison. In J. M. Suls & R. L. Miller (Eds.), *Social comparison processes: Theoretical and empirical perspectives* (pp. 149–186). Washington, DC: Hemisphere.

Codol, J. P. (1975). On the so-called "superior conformity of the self" behavior: Twenty experimental investigation. *European Journal of Social Psychology, 5*, 457–501.

Collins, R. L. (1996). For better or worse: The impact of upward social comparison on self-evaluations. *Psychological Bulletin, 119*, 51–69.

Crosby, F. (1976). A model of egoistic relative deprivation. *Psychological Review, 83*, 85–113.

Dunning, D., Meyerowitz, J. A., & Holzberg, A. D. (1989). Ambiguity and self-evaluation: The role of idiosyncratic trait definitions in self-serving assessments of ability. *Journal of Personality and Social Psychology, 57*, 1082–1090.

Ehrlich, H. J. (1973). *The social psychology of prejudice.* New York: Wiley.

Feather, N. T. (1994). Attitudes toward high achievers and reactions to their fall: Theory and research concerning tall poppies. In M. P. Zanna (Ed.), *Advances in experimental social psychology* (Vol. 26, pp. 1–73). New York: Academic Press.

Festinger, L. (1954). A theory of social comparison processes. *Human Relations, 7*, 117–140.

Gastorf, J. W., Suls, J., & Sanders, G. S. (1980). Type A coronary-prone behavior pattern and social facilitation. *Journal of Personality and Social Psychology, 38*, 773–780.

Gibbons, F. X., Persson, B., & Gerrard, M. (1994). From top dog to bottom half: Social comparison strategies in response to poor performance. *Journal of Personality and Social Psychology, 67*, 638–652.

Gilbert, D. T., Giesler, B. R., & Morris, K. A. (1995). When comparisons arise. *Journal of Personality and Social Psychology, 69*, 227–236.

Goethals, G. R. (1986). Fabricating and ignoring social reality: Self-serving estimates of consensus. In J. M. Olson, C. P. Herman, & M. P. Zanna (Eds.), *Relative deprivation and social comparison: The Ontario Symposium* (Vol. 4, pp. 135–158). Hillsdale, NJ: Lawrence Erlbaum.

Goethals, G. R., & Darley, J. M. (1977). Social comparison theory: An attributional approach. In J. M. Suls & R. L. Miller (Eds.), *Social comparison processes: Theoretical and empirical perspectives* (pp. 259–278). Washington, DC: Hemisphere Publishing.

Gould, R., Brounstein, P. J., & Sigall, H. (1977). Attributing ability to an opponent: Public aggrandizement and private denigration. *Sociometry, 40*, 254–261.

Higgins, R., Snyder, C. R., & Berglas, S. (1990). *Self-handicapping: The paradox that isn't.* New York: Plenum Press.

Jones, E. E., & Davis, K. E. (1965). From acts to dispositions: The attribution process in person perception. In L. Berkowitz (Ed.), *Advances in experimental social psychology* (Vol. 2, pp. 219–262). New York: Academic Press.

Kelley, H. H. (1972). Causal schemata and the attribution process. In E. E. Jones, D. E. Kanouse, H. H. Kelley, R. E. Nisbett, S. Valins, & B. Weiner (Eds.), *Attribution: Perceiving the causes of behavior* (pp. 151–174). Morristown, NJ: General Learning Press.

Kulik, J. A., & Gump, B. B. (1997). Affective reactions to social comparison: The effects of reactive performance and related attributes information about another person. *Personality and Social Psychology Bulletin, 23*, 452–468.

Latane, B. (1966). Studies in social comparison—Introduction and overview. *Journal of Experimental Social Psychology, 2*(Suppl. 1), 1–5.

Lockwood, P., & Kunda, Z. (1997). Superstars and me: Predicting the impact of role models on the self. *Journal of Personality and Social Psychology, 73*, 91–103.

Major, B., Sciacchitano, A., & Crocker, J. (1993). In-group versus out-group comparisons and self-esteem. *Personality and Social Psychology Bulletin, 19*, 711–721.

Messick, D. M., Bloom, S., Boldizar, J. P., & Samuelson, C. D. (1985). Why we are fairer than others. *Journal of Experimental Social Psychology, 21*, 480–500.

Mettee, D. R., & Smith, G. (1977). Social comparison and interpersonal attraction: The case for dissimilarity. In J. M. Suls & R. L. Miller (Eds.), *Social comparison processes: Theoretical and empirical perspectives* (pp. 69–101). Washington, DC: Hemisphere Publishing.

Miller, C. T. (1984). Self-schemas, gender, and social comparison: A clarification of the related attributes hypothesis. *Journal of Personality and Social Psychology, 46*, 1222–1228.

Morse, S., & Gergen, K. J. (1970). Social comparison, self-consistency, and the concept of self. *Journal of Personality and Social Psychology, 16*, 148–156.

Murray, S. L. (2000). The quest for conviction? Motivated cognition in romantic relationships. *Psychological Inquiry, 110*, 502–510.

Murray, S. L., & Holmes, J. G. (1997). A leap of faith? Positive illusions in romantic relationships. *Personality and Social Psychology Bulletin, 23*, 586–604.

Perloff, L. S. & Fetzer, B. K. (1986). Self-other judgments and perceived vulnerability to victimization. *Journal of Personality and Social Psychology, 50*, 502–510.

Raven, J. C. (1965). *Advanced progressive matrices, sets I and II.* London: Lewis.

Reeder, G. D., & Brewer, M. B. (1979). A schematic model of dispositional attribution in interpersonal perception. *Psychological Review, 86*, 61–79.

Seta, J. (1982). The impact of comparison processes on coactors' task performance. *Journal of Personality and Social Psychology, 42*, 281–291.

Smith, R. H., Parrott, W. G., Ozer, D., & Moniz, A. (1994). Subjective injustice and inferiority as predictors of hostile and depressive feelings in envy. *Personality and Social Psychology Bulletin, 20*, 705–711.

Smith, R. H., Turner, T. J., Garonzik, R., Leach, C. W., Druskat, & Weston, C. M. (1996). Envy and *schadenfreude*. *Personality and Social Psychology Bulletin, 22*, 158–168.

Suls, J. M. (1977). Social comparison theory and research: An overview from 1954. In J. M. Suls & R. L. Miller (Eds.), *Social comparison processes: Theoretical and empirical perspectives* (pp. 1–19). Washington, DC: Hemisphere Publishing.

Suls, J. M. (1986). Notes on the occasion of social comparison theory's thirtieth birthday. *Personality and Social Psychology Bulletin, 12*, 289–296.

Suls, J. M., Gastorf, J., & Lawhon, J. (1978). Social comparison choices for evaluating a sex- and age-related ability. *Personality and Social Psychology Bulletin, 4*, 102–105.

Suls, J. M., & Wan, C. K. (1987). In search of the false-uniqueness phenomenon: Fear and estimates of social consensus. *Journal of Personality and Social Psychology, 52*, 211–217.

Tesser, A. (1988). Toward a self-evaluation maintenance model of social behavior. In L. Berkowitz (Ed.), *Advances in experimental social psychology* (Vol. 21, pp. 181–227). New York: Academic Press.

Tesser, A. (1991). Emotion in social comparison and reflection processes. In J. Suls & T. A. Wills (Eds.). *Social comparison: Contemporary theory and research* (pp. 115–145). Hillsdale, NJ: Lawrence Erlbaum.

Weinstein, N. D. (1980). Unrealistic optimism about future life events. *Journal of Personality and Social Psychology, 39*, 8-6-820.

Weinstein, N. D. (1983). Reducing unrealistic optimism about illness susceptibility. *Health Psychology, 2*, 11–20.

Weinstein, N. D., & Lachendro, E. (1982). Egocentrism as a source of unrealistic optimism. *Personality and Social Psychology Bulletin, 8*, 195–200.

Wheeler, L. (1966). Motivation as a determinant of upward comparison. *Journal of Experimental Social Psychology, Suppl. 1*, 27–31.

Wheeler, L., & Miyake, K. (1992). Social comparison in everyday life. *Journal of Personality and Social Psychology, 62*, 760–773.

Wills, T. A. (1981). Downward comparision principles in social psychology. *Psychological Bulletin, 90*, 245–271.

Wood, J. V. (1989). Theory and research concerning social comparisons of personal attributes. *Psychological Bulletin, 106*, 231–248.

Wood, J. V., & Taylor, K. L. (1991). Serving self-relevant goals through social comparison. In J. Suls & T. A. Wills (Eds.), *Social comparison: Contemporary theory and research* (pp. 23–49). Hillsdale, NJ: Lawrence Erlbaum.

Wood, J. V., Taylor, S. E., & Lichtman, R. R. (1985). Social comparison in adjustment to breast cancer. *Journal of Personality and Social Psychology, 49*, 1169–1183.

Ybema, J. F., & Buunk, B. P. (1993). Aiming at the top: Upward social comparison of abilities after failure. *European Journal of Social Psychology, 23*, 627–645.

Ybema, J. F., & Buunk, B. P. (1995). Affective responses to social comparison of abilities after failure. *British Journal of Social Psychology, 20*, 277–288.

15

Social Comparison, Affiliation, and Emotional Contagion under Threat

JAMES A. KULIK AND HEIKE I. M. MAHLER

In this chapter we will be concerned primarily with the extent to which social comparison processes influence a person's face-to-face affiliative behaviors and emotional reactions when faced with a novel, threatening situation. To provide some theoretical and historical background to these issues, we will begin by selectively reviewing some of the classic work relevant to affiliation choices made in the face of acute threat (see Cottrell & Epley, 1977; Wheeler, 1974, for more extensive reviews). In doing so, we will focus on several of the central concepts presented by Schachter (1959) in his seminal book that extended social comparison theory to the domain of affiliation and emotion. Of particular interest will be what we believe were erroneous conclusions regarding the part that desires for emotional comparison and cognitive clarity play in affiliation preferences under threat. Drawing heavily on our own work, we then will consider in some detail recent studies that have gone beyond traditional fear and affiliate-choice paradigms to examine the extent to which social comparison principles account for how people actually affiliate with each other in acute, threat situations. Finally, we will present a conceptual model of emotional contagion that considers, as an integral part, Schachter's (1959) notion that social comparison processes also should influence the likelihood that people will "catch" the emotions of others.

THREAT AND AFFILIATE PREFERENCES

Psychologists have long been interested in the affiliation preferences of people who are faced with a novel, threat situation. A theoretical cornerstone of this stress and affiliation research has been Festinger's (1954) social comparison theory. Festinger argued that people have a basic need for accurate appraisal of their opinions and abilities, and that lacking an objective standard for reference, individuals will compare themselves to other people. Festin-

JAMES A. KULIK AND HEIKE I. M. MAHLER • Department of Psychology, University of California, San Diego, La Jolla, California 92093-0109.

Handbook of Social Comparison: Theory and Research, edited by Suls and Wheeler. Kluwer Academic/Plenum Publishers, New York, 2000.

ger proposed further, in his "similarity hypothesis," that people prefer to compare themselves to others of relatively similar ability or opinion. Purportedly, similar others provide a more accurate and stable gauge for evaluating one's relative standing than do people of very different ability or opinion.

Implicit in Festinger's original formulation was the potential relevance of social comparison processes for efforts to cope with stressful situations (Taylor, Buunk, & Aspinwall, 1990). That is, as a part of coping with a novel, threatening, or challenging situation, individuals are likely to have a need to evaluate the nature of the situation, their resources, and their emotional reactions. It was Schachter (1959), however, who explicitly extended social comparison theory to the domain of stress and emotion by proposing that people who face novel threats will experience an increased desire to affiliate with others, particularly with others who currently are facing the same threat. As Schachter (1959) phrased it, "misery doesn't love just any kind of company, it loves only miserable company" (p. 24).[1]

Consistent with this idea, several laboratory experiments, conducted primarily in the 1960s and early 1970s, found that individuals made fearful by the threat of electric shock generally preferred to wait with similarly threatened others rather than alone or with others not facing the threat (e.g., Darley, 1966; Firestone, Kaplan, & Russell, 1973; Sarnoff & Zimbardo, 1961; Schachter, 1959: experiments 1 and 2; see Cottrell & Epley, 1977; Wheeler, 1974, for reviews). More recent naturalistic studies, although lacking the comparison groups needed for a direct test, also can be interpreted as broadly consistent with this notion. For example, Buunk, VanYperen, Taylor, and Collins (1991) conducted a survey of 634 married individuals and found that the greater the respondent's marital stress, the greater the interest in talking with others about the marriage (cf. Molleman, Pruyn, & van Knippenberg, 1986). It is largely on the basis of such studies of affiliate choice that the summary conclusion was reached that threat increases need for affiliation with others awaiting a similar threat.

The reason that fear might increase desire to affiliate with similarly threatened others has been the subject of considerable theoretical interest. Schachter (1959) considered various possibilities but, in an extension of basic social comparison theory, clearly favored a self-evaluation explanation. According to this view, novel threats evoke uncertainty regarding resultant bodily arousal. This uncertainty purportedly motivates us to affiliate with similarly threatened others, because such individuals are thought to provide the best gauge for evaluating the intensity, nature, or appropriateness of our emotional state. Thus Schachter proposed what we will call the "emotional similarity hypothesis," wherein needs for emotional self-evaluation are induced by novel threat and are met through social comparison or, more specifically, through emotional comparison with similarly threatened others.

Gerard and Rabbie (1961) tested the emotional comparison notion by exposing groups of subjects either to threat of high- or low-level shock and then providing: (1) (fictitious) feedback indicating the subject's arousal level, as well as that of each member in the group; (2) feedback indicating only the subject's arousal level; or (3) no feedback indicating subject

[1]A classic study by Sarnoff and Zimbardo (1961) indicated threats that produce fear, such as physical threats, are likely to produce increases in desires for affiliation with similar others, whereas threats that produce embarrassment reduce desires for affiliation (see also Morris et al., 1976; Navar & Helmreich, 1971). Inasmuch as the distressing aspect of a potentially embarrassing situation is presumably predicated on there being witnesses to one's plight, it is not surprising that threat of embarrassment would reduce the desire to be in the presence of additional potential witnesses (i.e., affiliates). The point of the study, however, is that we cannot rightly assume that threats that produce different emotions will have the same effects on affiliation desires. Because the great majority of research, including our own, has involved fear-affiliation relationships, our focus and our use of the term "threat" in this chapter will involve specifically threats that evoke fear or concern for one's physical well-being.

or others' arousal levels. The results provided mixed support for the emotional comparison hypothesis. As predicted, subjects with feedback concerning their own and others' emotional reactions indicated less desire to wait with the others than did subjects who had only information indicating their own arousal levels. However, inconsistent with an emotional comparison prediction, the group with information about their own arousal levels also expressed lower desire for affiliation than the group with no arousal information. Also inconsistent, higher threat failed to produce significantly more decisions to affiliate than lower threat, either separately or in interaction with the arousal information conditions (cf. Darley & Aronson, 1966; Gerard, 1963; Zimbardo & Formica, 1963).

Schachter also considered briefly the possibility that affiliation with similar others under threat could be motivated by a desire for fear reduction (either directly through reassurances or indirectly through distraction), but this possibility has received relatively little empirical study (Helgeson & Mickelson, 1995). Schachter's affiliation choice results never did completely rule out a fear reduction motivation as a partial explanation, and several studies have indicated that threatened individuals who chose to wait with similarly threatened others gave primarily the belief that the others might reduce their anxiety as a reason (Sarnoff & Zimbardo, 1961; Teichman, 1973; Zimbardo & Formica, 1963). Unfortunately, the few studies that have offered participants different affiliate options under threat in an effort to pit emotional comparison explanations against fear reduction explanations have produced divergent results (Darley & Aronson, 1966; Rabbie, 1963). So while it seems reasonably clear that people frequently believe they choose to affiliate with similarly threatened others for anxiety reduction, the degree to which this is an actual cause of their choices is less clear (cf. Nisbett & Wilson, 1977).

Finally, Schachter also considered the possibility that a desire to increase cognitive clarity, that is, to reduce uncertainty regarding the nature and dangerousness of the situation, might motivate affiliation with similarly threatened others. In doing so, he acknowledged that emotional comparison can be viewed as a special case of cognitive clarity efforts. That is, part of reducing uncertainty about a novel threat situation may involve reducing uncertainty about how one should respond emotionally. Schachter, however, preferred to differentiate cognitive clarity, which he viewed in nonsocial terms as threat-relevant information gathering, from emotional comparison processes, which are inherently interpersonal and intended to evaluate one's feelings.

Thus defined, Schachter argued against cognitive clarity as an important determinant of affiliation, based largely on the results of one of his classic studies (Schachter, 1959: experiment 3). Subjects who faced either high or low (shock) threat were asked to make their affiliation choice (to wait with fellow subjects or alone), either under conditions in which all verbal affiliation would be prohibited (no-talk condition) or verbal affiliation would be permitted for threat-irrelevant topics only (irrelevant-talk condition). Schachter argued that verbal affiliation about the threat is not essential for meeting emotional comparison needs, but is essential for gaining cognitive clarity for the situation. He therefore expected to find that high-threat individuals exhibit greater desires to affiliate in no-talk and irrelevant-talk conditions alike. However, the subjects' affiliation choices did not conform to predictions; subjects in the high-threat condition did not choose to wait with the similar others more than low-threat subjects in either talk condition (1959, pp. 34, 37). It was only when Schachter performed internal analyses that disregarded experimental conditions (and thus sacrificed the ability to draw causal inferences) that he found a positive relationship between fear level and affiliative tendency. It was based on such internal analyses that Schachter argued desire for cognitive clarity had been ruled out "as any sort of potent motive" for affiliation under threat (p. 39), and that emotional comparison needs (and perhaps anxiety reduction needs) were more likely the primary motivation for affiliation with similar others when fearful.

Results based on internal analyses, in the context of null experimental effects, obviously provide less than optimal support for Schachter's (1959) conclusion that desire for cognitive clarity is a relatively unimportant determinant of affiliation desires in the face of acute threat. Less obvious, Schachter's conclusion is called further into question when we consider the lack of experimental effects found in his experiment 3 in relation to his experiment 1 results. The major procedural difference was that in experiment 1 high- and low-threat subjects had a choice to wait alone or with a similarly threatened other without any restrictions imposed on verbal affiliation. Under such circumstances, high-threat subjects did choose more often than low-threat subjects to wait with others. So what we see is that threat failed to increase affiliation when people would be prohibited from discussion of the threat (experiment 3), but threat did increase affiliation if there were no such restrictions (experiment 1). Therefore, if anything, Schachter's own experimental results actually seem to suggest the considerable importance of cognitive clarity desires as a determinant of desires for affiliation under threat.

Seemingly stronger support for the importance of emotional comparison desires as a motivater of affiliation under threat was provided by Zimbardo and Formica (1963). But here again a close reading renders the conclusions suspect. Zimbardo and Formica found that under higher threat (of shock), individuals indicated a greater preference for awaiting the threat in the presence of someone likewise facing the threat (similar emotional state) rather than with someone who had already experienced the threat (dissimilar emotional state). On the surface, this finding suggests that affiliation choices were more likely motivated by desires for emotional comparison than for cognitive clarity, if one assumes that a potential affiliate who is awaiting threat would provide the better gauge for emotional comparison, and a potential affiliate who has already experienced a particular threat the greater cognitive clarity. However, a critical procedural point in the Zimbardo and Formica experiment is that subjects' affiliation choices were made with the proviso that they would not be allowed to discuss the experiment with the potential affiliate. This prohibition was imposed in an effort to rule out cognitive clarity a priori as an explanation for the anticipated tendency for high-threat subjects to want to affiliate more with others awaiting the same threat. As we have noted elsewhere (Kulik & Mahler, 1990), however, eliciting an affiliate choice preference, while experimentally removing any chance for one's desire for cognitive clarity to operate, does not rule out the possibility that a desire for cognitive clarity normally is an important motivator of affiliation under threat. Thus, what the Zimbardo and Formica results actually suggest is that when the motivation for cognitive clarity is blocked by features of the situation, affiliation choices in the face of threat then may be determined by desires for emotional comparison (or fear reduction). This clearly is not the same as saying affiliation choices under threat are motivated principally, or routinely, by desires for emotional comparison, particularly when one considers how infrequently threat-relevant affiliation is likely prohibited in real-world contexts.

Indeed, more recent studies that have examined affiliation choices made in the face of imminent physical threats, absent "no-talking" constraints, suggest a more prominent role of cognitive clarity as a motivator of affiliation choices. Kirkpatrick and Shaver (1988), for example, found that individuals asked to imagine facing strong versus weak electric shock were more apt to choose to wait with someone who had already experienced the shock rather than someone likewise awaiting shock when their verbal interactions would not be restricted; but if verbal interactions were to be restricted, higher threat increased preferences for the emotionally similar affiliate relative to the experienced other (see also Rofe, 1984). Consistent with this, Kulik and Mahler (1989) found in a sample of hospitalized patients awaiting the threat of coronary bypass surgery that 60% preferred assignment to a roommate who was already recovering from bypass surgery compared to only 17% who preferred a roommate awaiting bypass surgery (23% had no preference). Although a preoperative roommate is apt to be more similar in emotional status, and therefore presumably a better referent for emotional comparison, patients who preferred the postoperative roommate indicated a belief that such a roommate would have greater potential for providing cognitive clarity, that is, for reducing their uncertainty about what was to come.

As we have argued elsewhere (e.g., Kulik & Mahler, 1990, 1997), the early fear and affiliate choice research thus appears to have underemphasized the importance of desires for cognitive clarity in favor of desires for emotional comparison as determinants of affiliation choices made under acute threat. More comprehensive reviews of the early literature appear at least implicitly to reach similar conclusions (see Cottrell & Epley, 1977; Rofe, 1984; Shaver & Klinnert, 1982; Suls, 1977). Rofe (1984) is perhaps most explicit, arguing that when facing threat, the desirability of a potential affiliate will depend on the perceived ability of that individual to reduce the stressfulness or uncertainty of the situation, not on the emotional comparison potential of the affiliate per se. This conclusion is quite compatible with current conceptualizations of stress and coping that emphasize the importance of cognitive appraisal processes (e.g., Cohen & Lazarus, 1983; Lazarus & Folkman, 1984, cf. Kirkpatrick & Shaver, 1988). According to these models, when we encounter a novel situation, we engage in a primary appraisal process to assesses the extent to which the situation is likely to cause us harm. Efforts to obtain cognitive clarity for a situation can be viewed as central to primary appraisal efforts.

Seeking information about the nature of the situation also is believed to play a role in subsequent problem-focused coping efforts, which are aimed at improving one's situation, and/or emotion-focused coping efforts, which are aimed at controlling the emotional response to the situation as it exists (Cohen & Lazarus, 1979; cf. Taylor & Lobel, 1989). Thus when we are faced with a novel threat, we experience as a part of coping an increased desire for information relevant to the threat, and we are likely to choose an affiliate substantially according to the ability of the other to reduce uncertainty or fear about the threat situation. When the possible affiliate choices do not appear to differ in their cognitive clarity value, we may choose on the basis of fear reduction value and/or emotional comparison value. So we believe the early work was probably correct that fear-provoking threat is likely to increase our predilection to seek out others who face the same threat. But, if the choice is between waiting with someone who has already been through the fear-producing experience or someone who is facing it still, and we will not be prevented from talking about the situation, we are apt to choose the veteran, at least in part because of his or her greater potential to provide cognitive clarity for the threat.

Although interesting, none of the work on fear and affiliation choice, nor more recent extensions that involve reports indicating with whom individuals generally affiliate or about whom they want information (see reviews by Buunk, 1994; Taylor, Buunk, Collins, & Reed, 1992), indicate the extent to which social comparison processes determine actual affiliative behaviors in an acute threat situation. Clearly, what determines initial affiliation desires is not necessarily what determines how people actually affiliate in a face-to-face threat situation. It is well known that attitudes and behavior toward an object are often divergent (Ajzen & Fishbein, 1977; Wicker, 1969), and the correspondence between a stated desire to be in the presence of another person, which is essentially an attitude, may not necessarily predict actual affiliative behaviors with that person. This seems particularly so given that our affiliative behavior is presumably dependent to some degree on our own motivation and also on the behavior of the affiliate. We now turn to a consideration of the evidence that social comparison processes are relevant to actual affiliative behaviors with others.

AFFILIATIVE BEHAVIORS IN THE FACE OF ACUTE THREAT

Nonverbal Affiliation

We can affiliate nonverbally or verbally. Facial gaze has been used by social interaction researchers as a primary indicator of nonverbal affiliation (e.g., Argyle & Dean, 1965). There are only a few studies that have examined such nonverbal affiliation in an acute threat situation. Buck and Parke (1972) compared facial gaze of subjects who faced either threat of shock or threat of embarrassment (sucking on infantile oral objects). Threatened subjects waited alone or in the presence of a confederate who ostensibly was not faced with the same situation. The confederate acted either nonsupportively (said nothing) or supportively (made a supportive remark before "remembering" the prohibition against talking). The results of primary interest indicated that subjects made fearful by threat of shock increased their looking to both supportive and nonsupportive confederates, whereas subjects faced with embarrassment appeared to increase their looking only when the confederate appeared explicitly supportive.

These results are broadly consistent with the affiliate choice results of Sarnoff and Zimbardo (1961) and Navar and Helmreich (1971), which suggest that desire for affiliation with similar others is greater when fearful than when embarrassed. However, given that the affiliate in the Buck and Parke (1972) study was not a fellow sufferer, it is not clear that these results involve social comparison processes per se. What would be needed is evidence that affiliation was greater specifically with a fellow sufferer. Also, given that there was not a low- or no-threat condition, we cannot tell whether fear increased affiliation, embarrassment reduced affiliation, or both.

A laboratory study by Kulik, Mahler, and Earnest (1994) was intended to test more explicitly Schachter's (1959) emotional similarity hypothesis in the context of both nonverbal and verbal affiliation (results involving the latter will be discussed separately when we take up the topic of verbal affiliation). Individuals were videotaped while awaiting either a high or low threat (the prospect of strong vs. negligible cold pressor pain) with someone who was either awaiting or who had already experienced the same threat. Of interest here was the emotional similarity prediction that facial gaze should be greater under high than low threat principally with the similarly inexperienced affiliate. The results indicated that facial glances were significantly greater under high than low threat and separately that there were more facial glances in pairs that included an *experienced* partner compared to pairs in which partners were inexperienced. It seems to us quite possible that the relatively frequent looks directed at experienced partners reflect a desire to obtain cognitive clarity for the situation. The facial expressions of experienced others could provide cues, beyond words, that suggest how bad an imminent, novel threat situation is. This possibility is supported by the results of a study in which subjects, asked to imagine the prospect of awaiting electric shock, expressed the belief that simply observing experienced others would provide useful information with which to gauge the aversiveness of the shock (Kirkpatrick & Shaver, 1988).

Two recent laboratory studies of nonverbal affiliation by Gump and Kulik (1997) did find support for the emotional similarity hypothesis under slightly different circumstances. Similarity was operationalized in terms of the type of threat faced by potential affiliates (same vs.

different threat) rather than, as in Kulik et al. (1994), in terms of the prior experience of potential affiliates (similarly inexperienced versus experienced). In their first study, Gump and Kulik (1997) had participant pairs listen over headphones to audiotaped instructions in which an ischemia task that they were to perform was described as either innocuous (low-threat condition) or as quite painful (high-threat condition). Independent of threat level, participants also were led to believe either that their "partner" would be performing the same task or a different task. According to the emotional similarity hypothesis, emotional comparison needs should be greater under high than low threat and served principally by affiliation with someone facing the *same* high threat situation.

Videotaped recordings that were made while subjects listened to the audiotape indicated that high-threat pairs demonstrated greater nonverbal affiliation than low-threat pairs. Independent of the effect of threat, pairs facing the same situation also spent more time looking at each other than pairs facing dissimilar situations. Finally, and most interesting, further analyses revealed that high-threat (fearful) subjects looked more at the affiliate who they believed faced a similar compared to dissimilar situation, whereas low-threat (calm) subjects looked at their potential affiliate about the same regardless of whether the affiliate was facing the same or a different situation. This pattern held regardless of the specific emotional reaction of affiliates.

A second study (Gump & Kulik, 1997: study 2) used a slightly different procedure, but produced a similar pattern of nonverbal affiliation. In this study, the same manipulations of threat (high vs. low) and similarity of other's situation (similar vs. dissimilar) were used, but the affiliate was a confederate who exhibited either a calm or fearful reaction while listening to the audiotape. The results indicated that high-threat participants spent significantly more time looking at their affiliates than did low-threat participants. More interesting, a planned comparison provided support for the pattern predicted by the emotional similarity hypothesis, in that high-threat participants with affiliates who were facing the same situation exhibited significantly greater affiliation than participants in the other three conditions (see Fig. 1). As in the initial study, there was no evidence that the emotional reaction conveyed by the affiliates moderated these effects.

Together, these studies constitute the strongest evidence to date that the emotional similarity hypothesis has some predictive utility for the domain of face-to-face affiliation

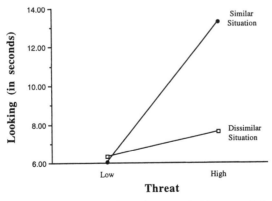

Figure 1. The effect of threat and situational similarity on time spent looking at an affiliate. From Gump and Kulik (1997: study 2).

under threat. The pattern of results also helps clarify a long-standing ambiguity in the proper interpretation of "similar" other. Over the years, some researchers have operationalized similarity in terms of the similarity of the others' apparent emotional response to the situation (e.g., Darley & Aronson, 1966; Firestone et al., 1973;a Zimbardo & Formica, 1963), whereas others have interpreted similarity in terms of the situation faced by the other (e.g., Goethals & Darley, 1977). Frequently the two dimensions have been confounded, as when threatened participants have had to choose between waiting with someone facing the same threat (and presumably therefore also in a relatively similar emotional state) versus someone facing a different, nonthreatening situation [and presumably therefore also in a dissimilar emotional state, e.g., Darley, (1966); Schachter (1959); Sullins (1991); Zimbardo & Formica (1963)]. Viewed in this context, it is noteworthy that both Gump and Kulik (1997) studies indicated that the effect of threat on affiliation was moderated by the situational similarity of the affiliate, regardless of the emotional reaction of the affiliate. Thus, for example, there was no indication that fearful participants affiliated more with affiliates who appeared fearful (similar emotion) compared to calm (dissimilar emotion). These results suggest that under threat, affiliative behavior increases as a function of the perception that the other person is facing the same situation rather than as a function of the perception that the other person is expressing the same emotional state. We suspect this is what Schachter (1959) meant all along in his reference to "miserable company."

It should be noted that the Gump and Kulik (1997) affiliation results do not enable us to conclude that differences in desires for emotional comparison per se motivated the obtained differences in looking behavior. That is possible, but so too are other motivations. One alternative possibility is that something about imminent threat makes an individual more apt to like someone facing the same threat, and this greater interpersonal attraction (rather than desire for emotional comparison), increases nonverbal affiliation (cf. Miller & Zimbardo, 1966). Note too that even if the differences in nonverbal affiliation observed in the Gump and Kulik (1997) studies were motivated by emotional comparison desires, this in itself would not argue that the need for emotional comparison is a more important determinant of nonverbal affiliation under threat than is the desire for cognitive clarity. First, it seems plausible that more cognitive clarity information can be gleaned from the expressions of someone who awaits the same rather than a different threat. Second, and more important, the Kulik et al. (1994) results that indicated more nonverbal affiliation with a threat-experienced compared to threat-inexperienced partner further suggest the relative importance of cognitive clarity desires as a motivation.

Verbal Affiliation

Morris et al. (1976) were the first to take a social comparison approach to the study of verbal affiliation patterns that occur in acute threat situations. Their study was not intended specifically to test Schachter's emotional similarity hypothesis, in that there was no explicit comparison of verbal affiliation under high versus low threat or with a similar versus dissimilar other. Instead, they examined the hypothesis that individuals facing a fear-inducing situation would spend more time affiliating for purposes of social comparison than would individuals facing either embarrassing or ambiguous situations. In their experiment, groups of individuals arrived at the experimental room where they found props and materials intended to create fear (electric shock generators and "shock release" forms), embarrassment (contraceptive devices, nude photos), or ambiguity (two cardboard boxes filled with unidentified computer cards). The results indicated that time spent in "verbal information seeking" (e.g., asking others if they know what is going on) was the greatest for the fear groups, least for the embarrassment groups, and intermediate for the ambiguity groups. Although not mentioned specifically by the authors, it is worth noting that the results also indicated that the greatest proportion of time in all three conditions was spent in threat-irrelevant affiliation (e.g., talking about a recent movie).

The difference that Morris et al. (1976) found between the affiliation patterns of participants who were embarrassed compared to fearful is again roughly consistent with the affiliate choice studies by Sarnoff and Zimbardo (1961) and Navar and Helmreich (1971), both of which suggest fear increases the desire to wait with others who face the same situation, whereas embarrassment diminishes the desire. However, because the Morris et al. study did not include a no- or low-threat control group, the results do not demonstrate directly that fear increased verbal affiliation or that embarrassment decreased verbal affiliation, only that the two types of threat differ somehow in their effects. Also, the aggregated manner in which verbal interaction was coded does not indicate whether fear subjects were affiliating for purposes of emotional comparison, cognitive clarity, or other reasons.

The laboratory study by Kulik et al. (1994), mentioned in our previous discussion of nonverbal affiliation, was intended to test more explicitly the emotional similarity hypothesis in the context of verbal affiliation. To accomplish this, the verbal affiliations were recorded of subjects who faced either high or low threat (the prospect of strong vs. negligible cold pressor pain) with someone who was either awaiting the same threat or who had already experienced the threat. Of interest was whether verbal affiliation would be greater under high than low threat principally with the similarly inexperienced affiliate. The study also was designed to explore the nature of the interactions that took place, that is, for example, the extent to which topics of conversation and questions focused on details of the experiment proper, emotions, or "irrelevant" topics. The emotional similarity hypothesis in strongest form predicts that higher threat should increase overall affiliation particularly with someone currently facing the same threat, or in weaker form that affiliation for purposes of emotional comparison should be greatest with such a person under higher threat. On the other hand, if the desire for cognitive clarity is normally an important determinant of affiliation under threat when discussion is not artificially constrained, one might anticipate the most discussion specifically about the experiment when higher-threat subjects wait with an experienced rather than inexperienced partner.

As was the case with the Morris et al. (1976) study, the results indicated that in absolute terms more time was spent talking about threat-irrelevant topics than threat-relevant topics (see also Kulik, Moore, & Mahler, 1993). Of more immediate interest, the results also generally did not support the emotional similarity hypothesis, and in certain respects ran counter to it. First, although the threat manipulation differentially induced fear as intended, there was no evidence that high compared to low threat produced greater verbal affiliation either overall or specifically with a similarly threatened other; this was the case whether affiliation was defined in terms of total time talking or separated into time talking about threat-relevant versus threat-irrelevant topics. Second, threat-relevant affiliation did differ as a function of partner characteristics, but such that subjects and their partners engaged in more threat-relevant affiliation when the partners were threat experienced rather than inexperienced. More fine-grained analyses generally produced an overall picture with respect to threat-relevant affiliation that showed subjects asking more factual (e.g., how long does it last?) and evaluative (how bad is it?) questions related to the threat situation and receiving more threat-relevant responses from experienced partners compared to inexperienced partners. Given that experienced partners would be expected to have greater information value than inexperienced partners, this pattern appears generally consistent then with the hypothesis that cognitive clarity concerns differentiated actual verbal affiliations under threat. The desire for emotional comparison, which purportedly is best served by affiliation with others currently facing similar threat (Schachter, 1959), does not seem to be a viable explanation for these results.

Finally, in an effort to assess the role of a more naturalistic threat on verbal affiliation patterns, Kulik and Mahler (1997) recently compared the hospital roommate affiliations of 73 patients scheduled to undergo a major (coronary bypass) surgery with those of 83 patients scheduled to undergo a relatively minor (prostate) surgery. Patients were assigned before surgery to a roommate who had either a similar or dissimilar surgical problem, and who was either similar (preoperative) or dissimilar (postoperative) in surgical status. The night before their surgery, patients also completed privately a measure of anxiety. As expected, prostate patients reported significantly less preoperative anxiety than bypass patients ($P > .01$), and we therefore may consider the prostate patients to have faced a relatively low-threat situation.

Patients also completed a questionnaire the night before surgery that was designed to determine overall affiliation (minutes spent talking to the roommate) and, relevant to the current topic, the extent to which patients had engaged in affiliations involving emotional caparison (e.g., had mentioned to their roommate how nervous they were feeling) and cognitive clarity (e.g., had a better idea of what to expect because of their roommate). For present purposes, the issue of primary interest is the extent to which patients engaged in such affiliations as a function of their threat level (i.e., major vs. minor surgery), the similarity of the roommate's surgical problem, and the similarity of the roommate's surgical status. In this context, the emotional similarity hypothesis predicts that affiliation (either overall or specifically involving emotional comparison) should be highest for coronary bypass (high threat) patients paired with a roommate who is likewise preoperative and cardiac. A somewhat different pattern would be expected for affiliation involving efforts to achieve cognitive clarity or information about the threat situation. Because a roommate who already has been through the same surgery is believed to have the greatest information value with respect to the threat (Kulik & Mahler, 1989), we might expect that affiliations directed toward obtaining cognitive clarity would be greatest for patients paired with roommates already recovering from a similar surgery. If desire for cognitive clarity increases with threat, we also might expect this pattern to be more pronounced for the bypass patients compared to the prostate patients.

Kulik and Mahler (1997) found no support for the strongest form of the emotional similarity hypothesis, in that there were no significant effects on total affiliation. With respect to affiliations relevant to emotional comparison, however, high-threat patients were more likely than low-threat patients to have mentioned their nervousness to their roommates and to have been informed of the roommate's nervousness ($P < .05$). Patients also were more apt to have mentioned how nervous they felt to a roommate who had a similar compared to dissimilar surgical problem ($P < .02$). However, there was no evidence that threat increased discussion of emotions particularly with someone who was awaiting the same surgical threat (and who therefore presumably was most relevant for emotional comparison).

A similar pattern was found for cognitive clarity affiliations (indexed by the average of 5 items), in that there was evidence of more cognitive clarity affiliation when patients faced high than low threat ($P < .01$) and when roommates had similar compared to dissimilar surgical problems ($P < .0001$). However, in this case, there also was evidence of an interaction ($P < .02$), which indicated that the tendency to engage in more cognitive clarity affiliation with a roommate who had a similar rather than dissimilar problem was greater under high than low threat. This effect held regardless of whether or not the roommate was still awaiting the surgical threat (see Fig. 2).

As can be seen in Fig. 3, Kulik and Mahler (1997) also found that high-threat patients engaged in more cognitive clarity affiliation with someone who was threat-experienced

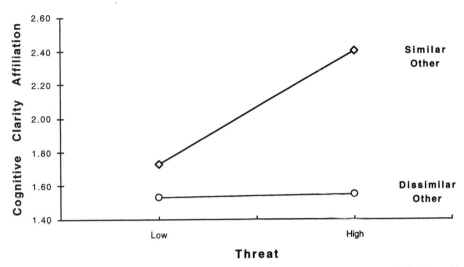

Figure 2. Cognitive clarity affiliation as a function of threat level and similarity of roommate's health problem. Values can range from 1 to 4. From Kulik and Mahler (1997).

(postoperative) rather than inexperienced (preoperative) ($P < .05$), whereas under lower threat no such difference was evident. Finally, there was evidence that across threat levels, patients engaged in significantly ($P < .05$) more cognitive clarity affiliations with roommates who already were recovering from similar surgeries than with those awaiting similar surgery, awaiting a different surgery, or recovering from a different surgery.

The finding that the higher-threat patients engaged in significantly more affiliation concerning their emotional status than did the lower-threat patients may constitute the most

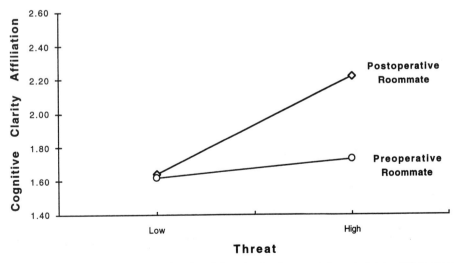

Figure 3. Cognitive clarity affiliation as a function of threat level and roommate's surgical status. Values can range from 1 to 4. From Kulik and Mahler (1997).

direct evidence to date that threat prompts verbal affiliation for purposes of emotional comparison. However, the fact that higher threat did not appear to increase discussions of emotional state specifically with others who were awaiting the same threat is not consistent with even the weaker form of the emotional similarity hypothesis. As Kulik and Mahler (1997) noted, one interesting possibility is that under such high threat, patients view anyone who is facing or has recently faced surgery as able to provide feedback that would be helpful for determining the appropriateness of their emotional response to the situation. That is, perhaps when we face severe threat, we are not so sensitive to the finer distinctions between affiliate characteristics as is implied by the emotional similarity hypothesis. An alternative possibility is that the greater discussion of emotions found in the higher-threat situation does not actually reflect emotional comparison efforts per se. Perhaps one of the things greater fear does is to increase the likelihood that individuals will mention their nervousness inadvertently to an affiliate, because the fear is so salient that it "slips out." Or perhaps high-threat patients mention how nervous they feel hoping for sympathy or reassurance from any source. Clearly more work is needed to clarify these issues.

The separate finding that patients were more apt to discus their emotions with someone who had a similar compared to dissimilar health problem is somewhat easier to reconcile with the emotional similarity hypothesis, if certain assumptions are made. First, it may be that beyond a certain level of threat, increasing levels of threat simply do not monotonically increase desires for emotional comparison. Even the low-threat patients in this analysis were faced with a level of threat that substantially exceeds anything that can be created in a laboratory.

Second, and more important from a theoretical standpoint, there has been a long-held presumption that emotional comparison requires the potential affiliate to be currently facing the same threat, and thereby to be in an emotionally similar state (Schachter, 1959). As Kulik and Mahler (1997) noted, however, perhaps this assumption is false when verbal affiliation is not restricted. Normally, a potential affiliate who already has experienced the same threat that an individual currently faces can still tell the threatened person how he or she *had* felt emotionally, prior to the threat. There is no obvious reason for such information to be any less valid or useful for determining the appropriateness of one's emotional reactions than if obtained from someone who currently faces the same threat.

As noted previously, fear and affiliation choice studies have tended to require threatened subjects to choose an affiliate under conditions where verbal affiliation would be prohibited or limited to threat-irrelevant topics. In so doing, researchers removed the potential for engaging in emotional comparison through verbal affiliation and, as a result, they may have over-emphasized the necessity of emotional similarity at the moment of affiliation. That is, if we wish to engage in emotional comparison, but we are prohibited from direct discussion of emotions, the nonverbal expressions of someone who currently faces the same threat might well provide a better emotional gauge than the nonverbal expressions of someone who already has experienced the threat. However, so long as verbal affiliation is not restricted, which seems more the norm, it may be that the key to whether discussion of emotions ensues is more simply whether or not the potential affiliate has firsthand experience with a similar threat. Such affiliates, whether they currently face or have already experienced the threat may be viewed as capable of reducing uncertainties about the appropriateness of one's emotional reactions, and thereby motivate relevant verbal affiliation for emotional comparison purposes.

And what of cognitive clarity affiliations? The Kulik and Mahler (1997) results suggest that if the "ideal" affiliate from a cognitive clarity standpoint is present (i.e., someone who already has experienced the same situation that we await), the level of threat we face may not matter so much. Regardless of threat level, patients engaged in the greatest amount of cognitive clarity affiliation with others who were already recovering from a similar operation. This result is consistent with the Kulik et al. (1994) laboratory study, which found that regardless of threat levels, participants exhibited more cognitive clarity affiliation with a person who already had experienced a similar threat than with a person who still awaited a similar threat. It may be that a potential affiliate who already has experienced the novel situation we await is such an optimal resource for gaining a better understanding of what to expect and do that little or no threat is necessary to stimulate cognitive clarity affiliations.

Threat may exert a stronger moderating influence on cognitive clarity affiliations, however, when the affiliate's information value is less than ideal. Thus, Kulik and Mahler (1997) found that under higher threat, patients engaged in more cognitive clarity affiliation if the affiliate had a relatively similar problem, whether or not the affiliate already had experienced the threat. Higher threat likewise produced more cognitive clarity affiliation if the affiliate was threat-experienced rather than inexperienced, whether or not the affiliate's surgical problem was the same. All else equal, a patient who faces or has faced a similar threat will have more threat-relevant information than someone who faces or has faced a dissimilar threat. Likewise, all else equal, someone who has recently experienced surgery is likely to have more information value for a preoperative patient than someone who is waiting to have surgery. Thus, when we are under substantial threat, perhaps we are not so inclined to "hold out" for the perfect affiliate from which to get cognitive clarity for the situation. Under higher threat, it may be more adaptive to seek cognitive clarity even from those whose relevant information may be only partial (so long as it is accurate as far as it goes). In other words, when one faces a high threat situation, it may be especially important to gain some cognitive clarity, even if incomplete.

HOW IMPORTANT IS EMOTIONAL COMPARISON AS A DETERMINANT OF FACE-TO-FACE AFFILIATIVE BEHAVIOR UNDER THREAT?

Judging by the implicit message of early fear and affiliate choice work, we might have expected that people facing a novel physical threat in the presence of another would affiliate to the extent that the affiliate could provide a basis for emotional comparison, and correspondingly that the preponderance of affiliation would involve emotional comparison. We have argued here and elsewhere (Kulik & Mahler, 1990), however, that some of the classic work within the fear and affiliate choice paradigm used methods that likely led to an overemphasis on the importance of emotional comparison and to a premature dismissal of the importance of cognitive clarity as a determinant of affiliate choices under threat. The more recent efforts to study how people actually affiliate under threat in a face-to-face situation likewise suggest a relatively modest role of emotional comparison. The best evidence for an affiliation pattern in a face-to-face situation that would be predicted by the emotional similarity hypothesis is provided by Gump and Kulik (1997), who found that under higher threat, people spent more time looking at someone who was waiting for the same rather than a different threat. It is not clear that these differences were motivated by emotional comparison desires, but the pattern at least is consistent with this possibility.

There also is some evidence that threat may increase verbal affiliations that involve emotions (and perhaps emotional comparisons), and so too does having an affiliate who faces a relatively similar situation, independent of threat (Kulik & Mahler, 1997). But to date, efforts to examine the degree to which cognitive clarity versus emotional comparison desires influence verbal affiliation under threat suggest, if anything, that efforts to achieve cognitive clarity may account for more of the variance (Kulik et al., 1994; Kulik, Mahler, & Moore, 1996). As noted previously, this conclusion is quite compatible with current conceptualizations of stress and coping that emphasize the importance of cognitive appraisal processes (e.g., Cohen & Lazarus, 1983; Lazarus & Folkman, 1984), and with models of social comparison that propose threat increases desire for affiliation for purposes of self-improvement (Taylor & Lobel, 1989; cf. Rofe, 1984). This is not to say, however, that desires for cognitive clarity are the sole, or even a major, determinant of affiliative behavior in face-to-face threat situations. In the three studies that provide relevant results (Morris et al., 1976; Kulik et al., 1993, 1994), for example, it is noteworthy that in absolute terms, most of the verbal affiliation that occurred was not explicitly threat or emotion-related. Thus, we should keep in mind that neither cognitive clarity nor emotional comparison motivations are likely to account for the bulk of the verbal affiliation that actually occurs under threat. A more precise characterization might be to suggest that one factor that distinguishes the threat-relevant verbal affiliation that does occur is a desire for cognitive clarity, and this desire may increase with threat.

Although the amount of variance in verbal affiliation under threat that can be accounted for by cognitive clarity or emotional comparison desires may not be large in absolute terms, affiliation for such purposes may nonetheless be quite important in functional terms, that is, for its influence on the person's well-being. For example, Kulik et al. (1996) have found that gaining cognitive clarity from fellow surgical patients may directly influence hospital recovery time. It has long been known that affiliation before surgery with a health care practitioner for the purpose of reducing the patient's uncertainty about the nature of the surgery and what to expect (i.e., to provide cognitive clarity) can benefit recovery (Mumford, Schlesinger, & Glass, 1982; Suls & Wan, 1989, for relevant reviews). The Kulik et al. (1996) study suggests that affiliations with fellow patients that provide cognitive clarity may have similar benefit. As is the case for affiliations with professionals, it may be that the amount of time needed to achieve a beneficial degree of cognitive clarity from a fellow patient is not large. Perhaps just a few well-chosen words from the "right" person will do. If so, the proportion of the total affiliation with a fellow patient that is aimed at achieving cognitive clarity would not have to be large for the amount of cognitive clarity obtained to have important benefits. Similar issues may apply to affiliations for purposes of emotional comparison, although to date there is no evidence to suggest, for example, that emotional comparisons influence the physical recoveries of surgical patients (Kulik et al., 1996). We might expect, however, that emotional comparison processes under threat would influence emotional reactions to the situation. It is to this issue that we now turn.

AFFILIATION AND EMOTIONAL CONTAGION

Even if emotional comparison processes do play a more limited role than was once assumed in determining the degree of affiliative behavior that people exhibit under threat, it remains possible that emotional comparison processes can exert a significant influence on emotional responses to threat situations. This follows from another interesting aspect of Schachter's (1959) thought about emotional comparison. As we have already discussed, Schachter believed that the reason for affiliating when facing novel threat situations is to use the emotional responses of others as a gauge for evaluating the intensity, nature, or appropriateness of one's emotional responses. In order to enable maximally informative and stable self-evaluations, the comparison others should be facing a similar threat situation and reacting emotionally in a fairly similar manner (cf. Festinger, 1954). One interesting implication of this idea, suggested by Schachter, is that if discrepancies in emotional responses to the same situation exist (so long as the responses are not "too" discrepant), there will be pressures toward reducing those discrepancies, that is, toward convergence in emotional responses among affiliates. Thus Schachter proposed (but did not test) the notion that if affiliation exposes discrepant emotional responses to a novel situation, there will be "attempts to influence others and bring them closer to one's own position … " (p. 115).[2]

The nature of these hypothesized "attempts to influence" the emotional reactions of others have never received much research attention. One possibility, of course, is that people may discuss their respective reactions and thereby achieve some degree of convergence. As we saw in our discussion of the verbal affiliation studies, however, explicit discussion of emotional reactions may not be so prevalent as we might at first think. There may be "costs," for example, to admitting openly to a stranger that one is (or is not) apprehensive about a situation (cf. Cottrel & Epley, 1977). Thus another more subtle possibility is that people use their facial expressions to communicate what they consider to be the "correct" emotional response to a situation. Someone who perceives the situation as threatening can signal this to an affiliate by frowning or grimacing frequently, smiling infrequently, and so on. This expressive information could in turn influence affiliates' appraisals of the situation, and thereby lead to convergent emotional reactions, that is, produce a contagion effect. In some ways this may be analogous to the classic bystander intervention studies, wherein people who faced an ambiguous emergency situation in the presence of a stranger tended not to discuss the appropriate behavioral reaction, but instead shot glances at their partners' expressions in an effort to clarify the situation (e.g., Latane & Rodin, 1969).

If emotional comparison does include pressures to establish a common social reality, we would expect the patterns of emotional contagion to follow the predicted patterns of emotional comparison affiliation. That is, a "social comparison model" of contagion would predict that our emotional reactions to a situation will be influenced by another person's emotions specifically when we are aroused by a novel threat, and we face a similar situation as the affiliate (cf. Schachter, 1959). Under such circumstances, we should be especially apt to use our perception of the other's emotional response as a guide for our own emotional response. If we are not facing a novel threat situation, emotional comparisons would presumably be unnecessary, and if we are facing a novel threat but with an affiliate who faces an altogether different situation, emotional comparisons presumably would be largely irrelevant and contagion therefore relatively unlikely.

An interesting alternative view of when and how emotional contagion might occur is suggested by the recent theory of primitive emotional contagion (Hatfield, Cacioppo, & Rapson, 1992, 1993, 1994). According to this theory, we quite generally and spontaneously mimic the facial expressions (e.g., Bavelas, Black, Lemery, & Mullett, 1987; Bernieri, Reznick, & Rosenthal, 1988; Haviland & Lelwica, 1987), body movements (Chapple, 1982),

---

[2]As we noted earlier, Schachter (1959) considered fear reduction a secondary motivation for increased desires to affiliate with similarly threatened others; he felt that this was so because the mere presence of someone who currently faces the same threat (i.e., a fellow sufferer) would serve to reduce fear. Evidence that is directly relevant to the notion that the mere presence of such a fellow sufferer reduces fear is quite equivocal, however (see Cottrell & Epley, 1977, for a detailed review). Note that if social comparison processes of the sort described by Schachter do mediate emotional reactions to novel threat situations, we would expect that affiliation with a calm fellow sufferer might indeed reduce one's fear, but affiliation with a fearful fellow sufferer would, if anything, increase one's fear. An interesting and somewhat ironic possibility then is that some of the inconsistency in the fear reduction studies may stem from the social-comparison-based contagion effects that Schachter also hypothesized.

and speech duration (Matarazzo, Weitman, Saslow, & Wiens, 1963) of affiliates. Theoretically, self-perception processes (Laird & Bresler, 1991; cf. Bem, 1972) and/or afferent feedback from such postural or facial mimicry, as captured in the facial feedback hypothesis, then create a corresponding feeling of emotion (e.g., Adelman & Zajonc, 1989; Duclos et al., 1989; Izard, 1990; Laird, 1984; Strack, Martin, & Stepper, 1988; Zajonc, Murphy, & Inglehart, 1989; cf. James, 1890), and emotional contagion is thereby produced.

Because of its speed and complexity, behavioral mimicry is thought to be an automatic and nonconscious activity (Davis, 1985; Hatfield et al., 1992, 1993, 1994), and there is no apparent implication that either threat or the similarity of the situation faced by the affiliate should influence the amount of mimicry or emotional contagion that will occur. Thus, the primitive contagion view would predict, for example, that we should quite generally smile more with a calm, smiling affiliate than with a nervous, frowning affiliate, and *because* we smile more and frown less we should be calmer with the calm affiliate.

Although a social comparison model and the primitive contagion model of emotional contagion make somewhat different predictions for when and how contagion should occur, it is entirely possible that each has some predictive utility. In Fig. 4 we have outlined a model of contagion that combines elements of both the social comparison and the primitive contagion views (and adds a few other factors for good measure). As implied by the figure, we assume that affiliation generally plays a central role in the creation of emotional contagion. At the very least, a person must be exposed to the emotions of another in some fashion before his or her emotional state can be said to have been influenced by the other. It is possible of course that simply receiving information about the emotional state of another person could influence one's own emotional state, as for example, when we hear secondhand that a friend is sad, happy, or upset about some matter; no direct affiliation with the other person need be involved. We suspect, however, that emotional contagion occurs more typically when there is actual inter-personal contact, and so here we are primarily concerned with the determinants of affiliation and how that affiliation might lead to emotional contagion.

Before considering the determinants of affiliation, we begin by noting that affiliation, like all social behavior, is multiply determined and multidimensional. One potentially useful distinction that was mentioned in our previous discussion of threat and affiliation studies is between situation-irrelevant and situation-relevant affiliation. Within the fear and affiliation literature, the little evidence that exists suggests the bulk of verbal affiliation that occurs likely does not focus on the particulars of a given situation, even a threat situation (Kulik et al., 1993; Kulik, Mahler, & Earnest, 1994; Morris et al., 1976). This prevalence point is implied by the greater area devoted in the figure to situation-irrelevant affiliation.

With respect to the determinants of affiliation, the model proposes first that how much one affiliates, particularly about situation-irrelevant topics, should depend on a variety of factors, including individual differences in general affiliative tendencies, for example, need for affiliation (Craig, Koestner, & Zuroff, 1994; Hill, 1987), and the similarity of the affiliate's personal characteristics, for example, race, age, attitudes, personality, and so on (e.g., Byrne, 1961; Cappella & Palmer, 1990; Newcomb, 1961).

In comparison, we hypothesize that affiliation about the situation itself (specifically, affiliation for purposes of achieving cognitive clarity and emotional comparison) is more likely determined by the similarity of the situation faced by the other, threat, and their interaction (the latter depicted in the figure by the "X" between the respective boxes). The best evidence for these propositions comes from the Kulik and Mahler (1997) analysis that showed that emotional comparison and cognitive clarity affiliation levels were greater under

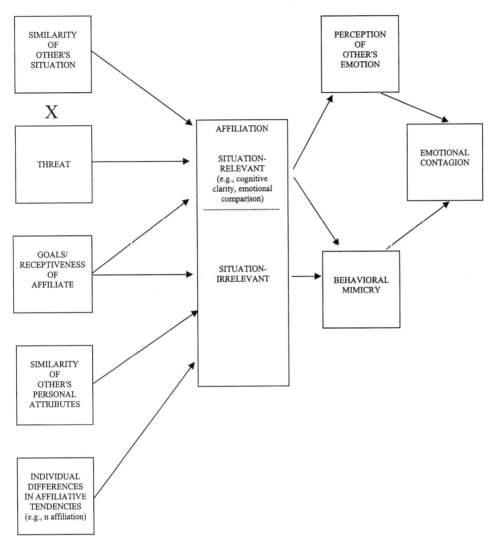

Figure 4. Model of emotional contagion.

higher threat and separately with others in relatively similar situations; in the case of cognitive clarity affiliation, there also was evidence that threat increased affiliation especially with similar others (see also Gump & Kulik, 1997, for a similar interaction pattern with nonverbal affiliation).

The amount of face-to-face affiliation that occurs, of course, also should depend significantly (and perhaps interactively) on the receptiveness and goals of the affiliate. There has been very little attention devoted to this issue. Inasmuch as verbal affiliation is presumably more difficult, if not impossible, to maintain with someone who does not wish to affiliate, the receptiveness of the affiliate should serve as an important moderator, regardless of whether the conversation focuses on the situation or not. (The receptiveness of the affiliate may have less of a moderating influence on nonverbal affiliation, in that it seems easier to watch than to maintain a conversation with an unreceptive affiliate.) In actual social interactions, social comparison processes presumably flow both ways, producing at times complementary needs and at other times conflicting needs among potential participants. An interesting possibility is that a person who has recently experienced a novel threat situation that another awaits will recognize his or her uniquely relevant attributes, and as a result feel some sense of obligation or increased desire to assume the role of informant (cf. Kulik et al., 1994) or emotional supporter (cf. Helmreich & Collins, 1967; Kulik & Mahler, 1997). If so, such a person may be more apt to steer conversation toward the situation in an effort to provide cognitive clarity, emotional comparison, and/or emotional support (cf. Kulik et al., 1996). Clearly, to address such issues, it will be necessary to have more detailed verbal affiliation data than are currently available.

Continuing with the model, affiliation can then lead to emotional contagion via at least two mechanisms: behavioral mimicry and emotional comparison. The theory of primitive contagion, because of an automatic tendency to mimic the behavior of others (Hatfield et al., 1992), implies that a significant amount of emotional contagion likely occurs whether or not a person is experiencing threat and regardless of the similarity of the situation faced by affiliates. To the extent that our emotions thereby are influenced without any awareness of the other's emotional state, emotional comparison conceptually would not be involved.

Separate from the foregoing, the model also incorporates the social comparison view that emotional contagion is especially likely in a person who faces a novel threat and the presence of similar-situation others. Theoretically, this would occur through emotional comparison, which as indicated in the figure, would seem to involve some degree of awareness of the affiliate's emotional state (how else do we make an emotional comparison?) and perhaps through behavioral efforts to influence the other person, as outlined above.

An interesting possibility proposed by the model that has not been considered by social comparison theorists is that a mimicry mechanism also could contribute to greater contagion under threat with a similar other; that is, if threat increases, in particular how much individuals look at and talk to an affiliate who faces the same situation, we might expect that mimicry likewise would be greater under such conditions. More time spent looking and talking (perhaps in hopes of obtaining cognitive clarity, emotional comparison, ideas for escape or coping) allows for greater opportunity to mimic. If so, the question then would be whether the pattern of emotional contagion predicted by the social comparison model, if obtained, might actually work through such a mimicry mechanism or instead through the emotional comparison mechanism.

We have no doubt that the proposed contagion model is underspecified. We could have added many more boxes and hypothetical moderators, for example, individual differences for the tendency to mimic others (Hatfield et al., 1992, Hatfield et al., 1994) and for the effects of mimicry on emotions (e.g., Laird et al., 1994). But for present purposes, and as a general framework, we believe the proposed model may offer some organizational and heuristic value.[3] In keeping with the main focus of this chapter, therefore, our primary concern from this point will be to evaluate the evidence to date that social comparison processes play a part in emotional contagion phenomena.

---

[3]The model also may have some heuristic value for research on mass psychogenic illness, wherein there is widespread reporting of physical symptoms among a group but no detectable organic pathology. Triggering conditions include high stress (threat), uncertainty, and affiliation with similar others (e.g., Kerckhoff & Back, 1968; Suls, Martin, & Leventhal, 1997).

Social Comparison and Emotional Contagion

An early study by Wrightsman (1960) represents the first empirical effort to test Schachter's view that social comparison processes mediate emotional contagion. Wrightsman began by threatening multiple groups of subjects with the prospect of painful injections. Group members then waited either together or separately (alone). Anxiety ratings that were obtained after the waiting period showed some evidence of greater uniformity of anxiety reactions among those individuals who waited together compared to those who waited alone. The evidence was modest, however, in that the obtained effects were limited to firstborns; and when certain procedural confounds were eliminated in a subsequent study by MacDonald (1970), the effects were not replicated. For present purposes, it also is important to note that because threat was not varied, the specific role that threat may have played is unknown. Likewise, because all subjects faced the same threat, the impact of affiliate similarity was not assessed. As such, Wrightsman's (1960) results also are consistent with a primitive emotional contagion view that would emphasize a mimicry mechanism rather than an emotional comparison mechanism (cf. Schachter & Singer, 1962; Reisenzein, 1983).

A study by Sullins (1991) addressed one of the limitations of the Wrightsman study by examining whether emotional contagion is greater with an affiliate facing a similar as opposed to dissimilar situation. Before completing an opinion survey, participants waited either alone, with someone believed to be "a second subject" (similar other), or with someone believed to be "taking a makeup exam" (dissimilar other). The results suggested that emotional contagion occurred only in the similar-partner condition. This finding is consistent with the contagion pattern that would be predicted by the emotional comparison hypothesis, but because threat was not varied, the specific role that threat may have played is again unknown.

Studies of people's responses to naturalistic threats also have provided some support for the notion that social comparison processes contribute to emotional contagion. Three studies by Kulik and colleagues, for example, found that preoperative patients were more fearful if their roommate was likewise preoperative rather than postoperative (Kulik & Mahler, 1987; Kulik et al., 1993, 1996). This pattern *may* reflect emotional contagion, if one assumes that roommates who are preoperative are generally more fearful than roommates who are postoperative (cf., Auerbach, 1973). Interestingly, however, there was no evidence in these studies that the patient's anxiety level depended on the similarity of the roommate's health problem. Thus, if contagion was occurring in these naturalistic studies, the pattern of results is more consistent with a primitive emotional contagion than a social comparison prediction.

Although relevant, none of the foregoing studies manipulated both threat level and the similarity of the affiliate's situation, the minimum set of conditions needed to differentiate patterns that suggest social comparison derived emotional contagion from primitive emotional contagion. Recent work by Gump and Kulik (1997), described previously in our discussion of nonverbal affiliation, sought to provide such a test and also to test for evidence of social comparison and behavioral mimicry mechanisms. To review, in study 1, pairs of participants were told over headphones that they would be performing an ischemia task, which was described either as quite painful (high threat) or as a mild pressure sensation (low threat). Independent of threat level, participants also were led to believe either that the other participant would be performing the same task or a completely different task. Videotaped recordings of participants' facial expressions were made while they listened to the audiotapes. As noted previously, manipulation checks supported both the threat and situational similarity manipulations. More interesting, participants were more anxious the more their affiliates were anxious. This evidence of emotional contagion was not qualified significantly either by threat level or situational similarity, a pattern more suggestive of primitive emotional contagion than social-comparison-based contagion.

In an effort to understand the mechanisms that might have produced the observed contagion, three possible mediators were examined (see Gump & Kulik, 1997, study 1, for details of analyses). Briefly, results suggested that the observed relationship between a participant's anxiety level and that of the affiliate may have been mediated partially but not substantially by how much time participants looked at the affiliate; that is, there was some indication that participants spent more time watching affiliates who were more anxious, but there was little evidence that participants' anxiety levels were higher with more anxious affiliates specifically *because* anxious affiliates were more watched. Additional analyses produced evidence that a social comparison mechanism also may have partially mediated emotional contagion; participants' own anxiety levels were higher the more they perceived the affiliate as anxious, and the strength of the positive relationship between participant and affiliate anxiety levels appeared to depend partly on these perceptions of the affiliate's anxiety. Finally, there also was evidence that behavioral mimicry had occurred; independent of experimental conditions, there was a substantial, positive relationship between the facial expressions of participants and affiliates (defined as time spent smiling minus the time spent frowning). However, inasmuch as there was no significant relationship between participants' facial expressions and their own anxiety levels, there was no direct support for the idea that such facial mimicry directly contributed to contagion.

Because affiliates in this first study were not randomly assigned to their emotional reactions, but instead were allowed to respond as they chose, it is not possible to conclude that the observed positive relationship between affiliate and participant anxiety was causal. To address this issue, in a second experiment Gump and Kulik (1997) used the same manipulations of threat (high versus low) and similarity of other's situation (similar versus dissimilar) but changed the dyads so that each consisted of one actual participant and one confederate affiliate who was trained to respond either in a relatively calm or fearful manner. With respect to the question of contagion, as can be seen in Fig. 5, there was evidence that high-threat participants tended to be less anxious with an affiliate who appeared calm compared to nervous ($P = .05$), whereas low-threat participants remained equally nonanxious with a calm or nervous affiliate. Thus, the evidence for contagion was specific to higher threat situations. Also noteworthy, this interaction effect showed no evidence of being moderated by the situational similarity of the affiliate.

Thus, the pattern of contagion observed falls somewhere between what would be predicted by the primitive contagion and social comparison perspectives. The finding that contagion was evident regardless of the similarity of the affiliate's situation is in keeping with a primitive contagion view; the finding that contagion occurred under threat but not under no-threat conditions is not. The effect of threat on contagion is consistent with the social comparison prediction that novel threat will enhance the tendency for people's emotions to be influenced by the emotions of others; but the lack of a moderating influence of the other's situational similarity is not consistent with the idea that threat should increase contagion specifically with those who face the same situation (Schachter, 1959; cf. Cottrell & Epley, 1977).

As they did in their first study, Gump and Kulik (1997) also analyzed participants' facial expressions to determine whether there was evidence of behavioral mimicry. As in the first study, there was evidence of mimicry but with a twist; participants did exhibit more positive expressions with the smiling (calm) affiliate compared to the frowning (nervous) affiliate, but interestingly, this mimicry effect was more pronounced under high- than low-threat condi-

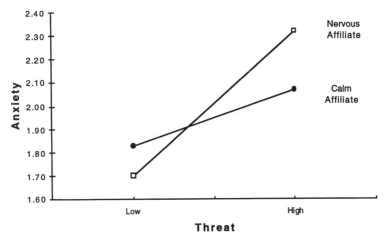

Figure 5. The effect of threat and affiliate emotion on participant self-reported anxiety. Values can range from 1 to 4. From Gump and Kulik (1997: footnote 7).

tions. In fact, as can be seen in Fig. 6, high-threat participants' expressions were significantly more positive with the smiling than frowning affiliate ($P < .005$), whereas low-threat participants did not differentiate ($P > .30$).

Although there was intriguing evidence that contagion and behavioral mimicry were both greater under high than low threat, unfortunately (for those who like simple stories), formal mediational analyses provided no direct support for the notion that contagion was actually a by-product of the mimicked behavior; as in Gump and Kulik's first study (1997), the expressive behavior of participants was not reliably related to their reported emotional reactions. Although such a null relationship is inconsistent with what would be predicted by the facial feedback hypothesis (see Laird, 1984), it is possible that more fine-grained analyses of expressions would have yielded some relationship. At the same time, it is worth noting that null relationships between facial expressions and reported emotion have been found even under what would seem to be extremely sensitive measurement conditions, that is, when individual expressions are experimentally manipulated (e.g., Cacioppo, Bush, & Tassinary, 1992; Matsumoto, 1987; Tourangeau & Ellsworth, 1979), so it is not certain that more fine-grained analyses would have produced stronger relationships. All that can be concluded safely is that there was no direct evidence that expressive mimicry, as operationalized, mediated the effect of threat on contagion.

In considering the Gump and Kulik (1997) studies then, we see a pattern of contagion in the first study that is relatively consistent with the prediction of primitive emotional contagion theory (i.e., an effect that holds across threat level and the similarity of other's situation), and in the second study a pattern that is more consistent with a social comparison view (i.e., contagion specifically under higher threat conditions). In neither study did the similarity of the situation faced by the affiliate moderate contagion, a null effect that also has been observed in preoperative patients assigned roommates who had either similar or dissimilar health problems (Kulik & Mahler, 1987; Kulik et al., 1993, 1996). It may be that even if an affiliate is to perform a different task (or have a different surgery), the fact that the affiliate also is in an experiment (or hospital) makes his or her situation fairly similar in a broader sense. If so, it is possible that contagion will be found yet to be greater with similar compared to dissimilar-

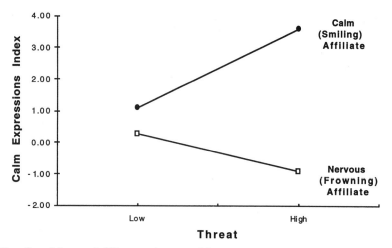

Figure 6. The effect of threat and affiliate emotion on participants' expressions. Positive values indicate more time spent smiling than frowning and negative values the reverse. From Gump and Kulik (1997: study 2).

situation others, if there is even greater divergence between the affiliates' respective situations [e.g., if the dissimilar-situation affiliate is not even in an experiment (cf. Schachter, 1959: experiments 1 and 2)]. At the same time, it is interesting to note that the Gump and Kulik studies showed that participants did perceive their situation to be more similar to that of the similar compared to dissimilar other and, perhaps more importantly, did affiliate nonverbally more with the similar other. This suggests the interesting possibility that emotional contagion, relative to affiliation, may be less strongly determined by the similarity of the affiliate's situation. Additional work will be needed to determine whether this is generally the case.

The more immediate question concerns the role that threat plays in emotional contagion phenomena. Why was there evidence of contagion in the first Gump and Kulik (1997) study, regardless of threat level, but evidence of contagion only under high threat in the second study? One possibility is that the more controlled conditions of the second study simply provide a more refined picture of contagion effects. Perhaps we are quite generally more susceptible to influence when we are under threat. On the other hand, the tighter control exercised over the affiliate's behavior in study 2 may have worked against more general contagion effects. That is, in the first study, all participants were actual participants, and their behaviors vis-à-vis each other were allowed to vary fairly naturally. When behavior is allowed to vary naturally, there is likely to be more of a give-and-take quality to the affiliation. One person smiles, the other person returns the smile, and perhaps adds a grimace or shrug of the shoulders, and so on. Such an interactive process may be part of the influence process that Schachter (1959) hypothesized occurs when there is a divergence among people in initial emotional responses to a situation. This give-and-take quality of affiliation may serve to increase our involvement with the other person and make it more likely that the other's emotional reactions will influence us. In contrast, the emotional behaviors exhibited by the confederate affiliates in the second study occurred, by design, as a function of auditory cues on a tape. Thus the affiliate's emotional behaviors were completely noncontingent with respect to the participant's behaviors, that is, they occurred independently of what participants did. Perhaps if another person's emotional reactions are completely asynchronous to our own, our emotional involvement and therefore our susceptibility to contagion is reduced, particularly if we are not in a state of threat. These seem to us fascinating issues for future work on social comparison and emotional contagion to explore.

CONCLUSIONS

Schachter (1959) sought to disambiguate the old saying that "misery loves company" with what surely has become one of the more famous quotes in all of social psychology, namely, that "Misery doesn't love just any kind of company, it loves only miserable company" (p. 24). He further argued in his "emotional similarity hypothesis," that novel threat increases the desire to affiliate specifically with others who are facing the same threat (i.e., with miserable company), because such individuals provide the necessary basis for emotional comparisons. We believe Schachter may have had it partially correct in that the evidence generally does support the notion that novel threat is likely to increase stated desires to be in the presence of others awaiting the same situation, relative to waiting alone or with someone who faces a totally different situation. However, when there are no anticipated restrictions imposed on verbal affiliation (which is likely the vast majority of the time), and the choice is between a person who is awaiting the same novel threat or a person who has already experienced the same threat one awaits, people are more apt to choose the threat-experienced person and to talk about the nature of the situation with such a person. Thus it does not appear that misery "loves only miserable company," unless one wants to expand the concept of miserable to include those who previously were "miserable" in the same situation.

The reason a threat-experienced other tends to be chosen over someone who theoretically is ideally suited for emotional comparison (i.e., someone currently facing the same threat) appears to be because a threat-experienced person is believed to be better able, by virtue of firsthand information, to reduce uncertainty regarding what to expect in the situation, that is, to provide cognitive clarity (Kirkpatrick & Shaver, 1988; Kulik & Mahler, 1989; cf. Rofe, 1984). The fact that a threat-experienced person also can provide emotional comparison information if allowed to speak is an added bonus (Kulik & Mahler, 1997). We have argued, therefore, that Schachter (1959) and the early fear and affiliate choice research overemphasized the importance of desires for emotional comparison and underestimated the importance of desires for cognitive clarity as determinants of affiliation choices made under acute threat. A largely similar conclusion can be drawn from more recent efforts to examine the actual affiliative behaviors exhibited in acute threat situations.

We also have argued that just because one might choose an affiliate based on a certain motivation, it does not follow that subsequent face-to-face affiliative behavior will be exclusively (or even predominantly) directed by that motivation. In part this is because once in the face-to-face situation, additional factors are likely to come into play, for example, the goals, motivations, and personal qualities of the affiliate, and so forth. More subtly, it also is unclear exactly how much affiliative behavior is needed to achieve cognitive clarity, emotional comparison, or any other goal. It may well be that a few key words or facial expressions are sufficient in a given instance. Thus it is important to keep in mind that the desires for cognitive clarity and for emotional comparison may not account for the bulk of the affiliative behavior displayed under threat. However, in functional terms, even small amounts of such affiliations may be quite important for efforts to cope with the situation. Gaining cognitive clarity from an affiliate may benefit such outcomes as surgical recovery, whereas engaging in emotional comparison (and perhaps behavioral mimicry) under threat with similar others may influence one's emotional reactions, for better or worse.

ACKNOWLEDGMENTS

We thank Nicko Christenfeld, Ladd Wheeler, and Jerry Suls for their helpful comments.

REFERENCES

Adelman, P. K., & Zajonc, R. B. (1989). Facial efference and the experience of emotion. *Annual Review of Psychology, 40,* 249–280.
Ajzen, I., & Fishbein, M. (1977). Attitude-behavior relations: A theoretical analyses and review of empirical research. *Psychological Bulletin, 84,* 888–918.
Argyle, M., & Dean, J. (1965). Eye-contact, distance, and affiliation. *Sociometry, 28,* 289–304.
Auerbach, S. M. (1973). Trait–state anxiety and adjustment to surgery. *Journal of Consulting and Clinical Psychology, 40,* 264–271.
Bavelas, J. B., Black, A., Lemery, C. R., & Mullett, J. (1987). Motor mimicry as primitive empathy. In N. Eisenberg & J. Strayer (Eds.), *Empathy and its development* (pp. 317–338). New York: Cambridge University Press.
Bem, D. J. (1972). Self-perception theory. in L. Berkowitz (Ed.), *Advances in experimental social psychology* (Vol. 6, pp. 1–62). New York: Academic Press.
Bernieri, F. J., Reznick, J. S., & Rosenthal, R. (1988). Synchrony, pseudosynchrony, and dissynchrony: Measuring the entrainment process in mother–infant interactions. *Journal of Personality and Social Psychology, 54,* 243–253.
Buck, R. W., & Parke, R. D. (1972). Behavioral and physiological response to the presence of a friendly or neutral person in two types of stressful situations. *Journal of Personality and Social Psychology, 24,* 143–153.
Buunk, B. P. (1994). Social comparison processes under stress: Towards an integration of classic and recent perspectives. In W. Stroebe & M. Hewstone (Eds.), *European Review of Social Psychology* (Vol. 5, pp. 211–241). New York: Wiley.
Buunk, B. P., VanYperen, N. W., Taylor, S. E., & Collins, R. L. (1991). Social comparison and the drive upward revisited: Affiliation as a response to marital stress. *European Journal of Social Psychology, 21,* 529–546.
Byrne, D. (1961). Interpersonal attraction and attitude similarity. *Journal of Abnormal and Social Psychology, 62,* 713–715.
Cacioppo, J. T., Bush, L. K., & Tassinary, L. G. (1992). Microexpressive facial actions as a function of affective stimuli: Replication and extension. *Personality and Social Psychology Bulletin, 18,* 515–526.
Cappella, J. N., & Palmer, M. T. (1990). Attitude similarity, relational history, and attraction: The mediating effects of kinesic and vocal behaviors. *Communication Monographs, 57,* 161–183.
Chapple, E. D. (1982). Movement and sound: The musical language of body rhythms in interaction. In M. Davis (Ed.), *Interaction rhythms: Periodicity in communicative behavior* (pp. 31–52). New York: Human Sciences Press.
Cohen, F., & Lazarus, R. S. (1979). Coping with the stresses of illness. In G. C. Stone, F. Cohen, & N. E. Adler (Eds.), *Health psychology—A handbook* (pp. 77–112). San Francisco: Jossey-Bass.
Cohen, F., & Lazarus, R. S. (1983). Coping and adaptation in health and illness. In D. Mechanic (Ed.), *Handbook of health, health care, and the health professions* (pp. 608–635). New York: Free Press.
Cottrell, N. B., & Epley, S. W. (1977). Affiliation, social comparison and socially mediated stress reduction. In J. M. Suls & R. L. Miller (Eds.), *Social comparison processes: Theoretical and empirical perspectives* (pp. 43–68). New York: Hemisphere.
Craig, J. A., Koestner, R., & Zuroff, D. C. (1994). Implicit and self-attributes intimacy motivation. *Journal of Social and Personal Relationships, 11,* 491–507.
Darley, J. M. (1966). Fear and social comparison as determinants of conformity behavior. *Journal of Personality and Social Psychology, 4,* 73–78.
Darley, J. M., & Aronson, E. (1966). Self-evaluative vs. Direct anxiety reduction as determinants of the fear-affiliation relationship. *Journal of Experimental Social Psychology, 2*(Suppl. 1), 66–79.
Davis, M. R. (1985). Perceptual and affective reverberation components. in A. B. Goldstein & G. Y. Michaels (Eds.), *Empathy: Development, training, and consequences* (pp. 62–108). Hillsdale, NJ: Lawrence Erlbaum.
Duclos, S. E., Laird, J. D., Schneider, E., Sexter, M., Stern, L., & Van Lighten, O. (1989). Emotion-specific effects of facial expressions and postures on emotional experience. *Journal of Personality and Social Psychology, 57,* 100–108.
Festinger, L. A. (1954). A theory of social comparison processes. *Human Relations, 7,* 117–140.
Firestone, I. J., Kaplan, K. J., & Russell, J. C. (1973). Anxiety, fear, and affiliation with similar-state versus dissimilar-state others: Misery sometimes loves nonmiserable company. *Journal of Personality and Social Psychology, 26,* 409–414.
Gerard, H. B. (1963). Emotional uncertainty and social comparison. *Journal of Abnormal and Social Psychology, 66,* 568–573.

Gerard, H. B., & Rabbie, J. M. (1961). Fear and social comparison. *Journal of Abnormal and Social Psychology*, *62*, 586–592.

Goethals, G. R., & Darley, J. M. (1977). Social comparison theory: An attributional approach. In J. M. Suls & R. L. Miller (Eds.), *Social comparison processes: Theoretical and empirical perspectives* (pp. 259–278). Washington, DC: Hemisphere.

Gump, B., & Kulik, J. A. (1997). Stress, affiliation, and emotional contagion. *Journal of Personality and Social Psychology*, *72*, 305–319.

Hatfield, E., Cacioppo, J. T., & Rapson, R. L. (1992). Primitive emotional contagion. In M. S. Clark (Ed.), *Review of personality and social psychology* (pp. 151–177). Newbury Park, CA: Sage.

Hatfield, E., Cacioppo, J. T., & Rapson, R. L. (1993). Emotional contagion. *Current Directions in Psychological Science*, *2*, 96–99.

Hatfield, E., Cacioppo, J. T., & Rapson, R. L. (1994). *Emotional contagion*. New York: Cambridge University Press.

Haviland, J. M., & Lelwica, M. (1987). The induced affect response: 10-week-old infants' responses to three emotion expressions. *Developmental Psychology*, *23*, 97–104.

Helgeson, V. S., & Mickelson, K. D. (1995). Motives for social comparison. *Personality and Social Psychology Bulletin*, *21*, 1200–1209.

Helmreich, R. L., & Collins, B. E. (1967). Situational determinants of affiliative preference under stress. *Journal of Personality and Social Psychology*, *6*, 79–85.

Hill, C. A. (1987). Affiliation motivation: People who need people but in different ways. *Journal of Personality and Social Psychology*, *52*, 1008–1018.

Izard, C. E. (1990). Facial expressions and the regulation of emotions. *Journal of Personality and Social Psychology*, *58*, 487–498.

James, W. (1890). *Principles of psychology*. New York: Holt.

Kerckhoff, A. C., & Back, K. W. (1968). *The June Bug: A study of hysterical contagion*. New York: Appleton-Century-Crofts.

Kirkpatrick, L. A., & Shaver, P. (1988). Fear and affiliation reconsidered from a stress and coping perspective: The importance of cognitive clarity and fear reduction. *Journal of Social and Clinical Psychology*, *7*, 214–233.

Kulik, J. A., & Mahler, H. I. M. (1987). Effects of preoperative roommate assignment on preoperative anxiety and postoperative recovery from coronary-bypass surgery. *Health Psychology*, *6*, 525–543.

Kulik, J. A., & Mahler, H. I. M. (1989). Stress and affiliation in a hospital setting: Preoperative roommate preferences. *Personality and Social Psychology Bulletin*, *15*, 183–193.

Kulik, J. A., & Mahler, H. I. M. (1990). Stress and affiliation research: On taking the laboratory to health field settings. *Annals of Behavioral Medicine*, *12*, 106–111.

Kulik, J. A., & Mahler, H. I. M. (1997). Social comparison, affiliation, and coping with acute medical threats. In F. X. Gibbons & B. P. Buunk (Eds.), *Health and coping: Perspectives from social comparison theory* (pp. 227–261). Mahwah, NJ: Lawrence Erlbaum.

Kulik, J. A., Mahler, H. I. M., & Earnest, A. (1994). Social comparison and affiliation under threat: Going beyond the affiliate-choice paradigm. *Journal of Personality and Social Psychology*, *66*, 301–309.

Kulik, J. A., Mahler, H. I. M., & Moore, P. J. (1996). Social comparison and affiliation under threat: Effects on recovery from major surgery. *Journal of Personality and Social Psychology*, *71*, 967–979.

Kulik, J. A., Moore, P., & Mahler, H. I. M. (1993). Stress and affiliation: Hospital roommate effects on preoperative anxiety and social interaction. *Health Psychology*, *12*, 119–125.

Laird, J. D. (1984). The real role of facial response in the experience of emotion: A reply to Tourangeau and Ellsworth, and others. *Journal of Personality and Social Psychology*, *47*, 909–917.

Laird, J. D., Alibozak, T., Davainis, D., Deignan, K., Fontanella, K., Hong, J., Levy, B., & Pacheco, C. (1994). Individual differences in the effects of spontaneous mimicry on emotional contagion. *Motivation and Emotion*, *118*, 231–247.

Laird, J. D., & Bresler, C. (1991). The process of emotional experience: A self-perception theory. In M. S. Clark (Ed.), *Review of Personality and Social Psychology*, (Vol. 13, pp. 213–234). Newbury Park, CA: Sage.

Latane, B., & Rodin, J. (1969). A lady in distress: Inhibiting effects of friends and strangers on bystander intervention. *Journal of Experimental Social Psychology*, *5*, 189–202.

Lazarus, R. S., & Folkman, S. (1984). *Stress, appraisal, and coping*. New York: Springer.

MacDonald, A. P. (1970). Anxiety affiliation and social isolation. *Developmental Psychology*, *3*, 242–254.

Matarazzo, J. D., Weitman, M., Saslow, G., & Wiens, A. N. (1963). Interviewer influence on durations of interviewee speech. *Journal of Verbal Learning and Verbal Behavior*, *1*, 451–458.

Matsumoto, D. (1987). The role of facial response in the experience of emotion: More methodological problems and a meta-analysis. *Journal of Personality and Social Psychology*, *52*, 769–774.

Miller, N., & Zimbardo, P. G. (1966). Motives for fear-induced affiliation: Emotional comparison or interpersonal similarity? *Journal of Personality*, *34*, 481–503.

Molleman, E., Pruyn, J., & van Knippenberg, A. (1986). Social comparison process among cancer patients. *British Journal of Social Psychology, 25,* 1–13.

Morris, W. N., Worchel, S., Bois, J. L., Pearson, J. A., Rountree, C. A., Samaha, G. M., Wachtler, J., & Wright, S. L. (1976). Collective coping with stress: Group reactions to fear, anxiety, and ambiguity. *Journal of Personality and Social Psychology, 33,* 674–679.

Mumford, E., Schlesinger, H. J., & Glass, G. V. (1982). The effects of psychological intervention on surgery and heart attacks: An analysis of the literature. *American Journal of Public Health, 72,* 141–151.

Navar, I., & Helmreich, R. (1971). Prior social setting, type of arousal, and birth order as determinants of affiliative preference for a working situation. *Representative Research in Social Psychology, 2*(2), 32–42.

Newcomb, T. M. (1961). *The acquaintance process.* New York: Holt, Rinehart, and Winston.

Nisbett, R. E., & Wilson, T. D. (1977). Telling more than we can know: Verbal reports on mental processes. *Psychological Review, 84,* 231–259.

Rabbie, J. M. (1963). Differential preference for companionship under threat. *Journal of Abnormal and Social Psychology, 67,* 643–648.

Reisenzein, R. (1983). The Schachter theory of emotion: Two decades later. *Psychological Bulletin, 94,* 239–264.

Rofe, Y. (1984). Stress and affiliation: A utility theory. *Psychological Review, 91,* 235–250.

Sarnoff, I., & Zimbardo, P. G. (1961). Anxiety, fear, and social isolation. *Journal of Abnormal and Social Psychology, 62,* 356–363.

Schachter, S. (1959). *The psychology of affiliation.* Stanford, CA: Stanford University Press.

Schachter, S., & Singer, J. E. (1962). Cognitive, social, and physiological determinants of emotional state. *Psychological Review, 69,* 379–399.

Shaver, P., & Klinnert, M. (1982). Schachter's theories of affiliation and emotions: Implications of developmental research. In L. Wheeler (Ed.), *Review of personality and social psychology* (Vol. 3, pp. 37–71). Beverly Hills, CA: Sage.

Strack, F., Martin, L. L., & Stepper, S. (1988). Inhibiting and facilitating conditions of facial expressions: A non-obtrusive test of the facial feedback hypothesis. *Journal of Personality and Social Psychology, 54,* 768–776.

Sullins, E. S. (1991). Emotional contagion revisited: Effects of social comparison and expressive style on mood convergence. *Personality and Social Psychology Bulletin, 17,* 166–174.

Suls, J. M. (1977). Social comparison theory and research: An overview from 1954. In J. M. Suls & R. L. Miller (Eds.), *Social comparison processes: Theoretical and empirical perspectives* (pp. 1–20). Washington, DC: Hemisphere.

Suls, J., Martin, R., & Leventhal, H. (1997). Social comparison, lay referral, and the decision to seek medical care. In F. X. Gibbons & B. P. Buunk (Eds.), *Health and coping: Perspectives from social comparison theory* (pp. 195–226). Mahwah, NJ: Lawrence Erlbaum.

Suls, J., & Wan, C. K. (1989). Effects of sensory and procedural information on coping with stressful medical procedures and pain: A meta-analysis. *Journal of Consulting and Clinical Psychology, 57,* 372–379.

Taylor, S. E., Buunk, B., & Aspinwall, L. (1990). Social comparison, stress, and coping. *Personality and Social Psychology Bulletin, 16,* 74–89.

Taylor, S. E., Buunk, B., Collins, R. L., & Reed, G. M. (1992). Social comparison and affiliation under threat. In L. Montada (Ed.), *Life crisis and experiences of loss in adulthood* (pp. 213–227). Hillsdale, NJ: Lawrence Erlbaum.

Taylor, S. E., & Lobel, M. (1989). Social comparison activity under threat: Downward evaluation and upward contacts. *Psychological Review, 96,* 569–575.

Teichman, M. (1973). Emotional arousal and affiliation. *Journal of Experimental Social Psychology, 9,* 591–605.

Thornton, D. A., & Arrowood, A. J. (1966). Self-evaluation, self-enhancement, and the locus of social comparison. *Journal of Experimental Social Psychology, 2*(Suppl. 1), 40–48.

Tourangeau, R., & Ellsworth, P. C. (1979). The role of facial response in the experience of emotion. *Journal of Personality and Social Psychology, 37,* 1519–1531.

Wheeler, L. (1974). Social comparison and selective affiliation. In T. L. Huston (Ed.), *Foundations of interpersonal attraction* (pp. 309–329). New York: Academic Press.

Wicker, A. W. (1969). Attitudes versus action: The relationship of verbal and overt behavior responses to attitude objects. *Journal of Social Issues, 25,* 41–78.

Wrightsman, L. S. (1960). Effects of waiting with others on changes in level of felt anxiety. *Journal of Abnormal and Social Psychology, 61,* 216–222.

Zajonc, R. B., Murphy, S. T., & Inglehart, M. (1989). Feeling and facial efference: Implications of the vascular theory of emotion. *Psychological Review, 96,* 395–416.

Zimbardo, P. G., & Formica, R. (1963). Emotional comparison and self-esteem as determinants of affiliation. *Journal of Personality, 31,* 141–162.

III

Related Social Phenomena

16

The Projective Perception of the Social World

A Building Block of Social Comparison Processes

JOACHIM KRUEGER

TO COMPARE AND TO PROJECT

Corollary IIIA: Given a range of possible persons for comparison, someone close to one's own ability or opinion will be chosen for comparison. (Festinger, 1954, p. 121)

Festinger (1954) proposed that people seek accurate knowledge of the self, and that to find it, they compare themselves with similar others. He peppered his paper with references to the idea that people have some notion as to who is similar to them and who is not. His followers agree: "Looking for or identifying a similarity or a difference between the other and the self on some dimension [is a] core feature [of the theory]; the majority of comparison researchers implicitly seem to share this definition" (Wood, 1997, p. 521). But how do perceptions of similarity and dissimilarity arise?

Incomplete Comparisons

It may seem paradoxical that people should be uncertain about who they are, while at the same time they know enough to distinguish between similar and dissimilar others. If they did not know themselves at all, they could not determine the similarity of others. To jump start their social comparison processes, participants in early research received a little information about themselves (e.g., a test score and a rank in a small group) and the opportunity to obtain the score of another person (Wheeler, 1966). In such a situation, people tend to choose the score of somebody with a similar (and slightly better) rank. But they cannot learn much from it. The overall distribution of scores remains unknown, and so the degree of similarity with the other person remains ambiguous.

What complicates judgments of similarity is that focused comparisons between two

JOACHIM KRUEGER • Department of Psychology, Brown University, Providence, Rhode Island 02912.

Handbook of Social Comparison: Theory and Research, edited by Suls and Wheeler. Kluwer Academic/Plenum Publishers, New York, 2000.

objects or two people reveal little. Sound judgments require a representation of the whole class to which the two objects belong. What is the meaning of saying that Jack and Jill are similar to each other if it is unknown how similar couples are on the average? A comparison between two people requires an implicit comparison between this particular comparison and all others (or their average). In short, knowledge of individuals depends on knowledge of a relevant population. Where does this knowledge originate? In the social world, people often possess only limited sample information, and in the laboratory they tend to learn only a little (if anything) about the characteristics of others. How then do they make comparisons? The possibility that is of greatest interest here is that people simply make up some of the necessary information by "guess, conjecture, or rationalization" (Goethals, Messick, & Allison, 1991, p. 154). This "fabrication" (Goethals, 1986) of social knowledge is the topic of this chapter. My thesis is that people come to know the population in part through processes of social projection. By projecting their own characteristics to the population, people find (or fantasize) many other individuals who are (or seem to be) sufficiently similar to make social comparisons informative.

Projection means that judgments about others are anchored on the self, and this anchoring enhances perceptions of similarity. When judgments about individual or collective others serve as the anchors for judgments about the self, perceptions of similarity are reduced (Catrambone, Beike, & Niedenthal, 1996). This asymmetry has a startling implication: Seeking comparisons and making comparisons are separate processes involving different reference points. These processes occur sequentially and produce assimilation and contrast, respectively. Either way, some initial knowledge of the self is necessary so that social comparisons can shape the self-concept further. Self-knowledge has primacy; it is more often revised than created by knowledge of others (Felson, 1993; see also Chapter 17, this volume).

Early Projectors

Floyd Allport's (1924) insights into the psychology of crowds brought social projection to the attention of psychologists. He suggested that individual crowd members succumb to an "illusion of universality," which is the belief that all other crowd members respond to the situation (e.g., the crowd leader) as they themselves do.[1] But Allport did not think that projection is restricted to the crowd situation. A person may project the "consciousness of himself into those about him" (p. 307) at any time. Allport recalled that "as a boy [he] was harassed by the belief that other people, through some telepathic process, were aware of his inmost thoughts" (p. 307). This private form of projection soon emerged in empirical research (Katz & Allport, 1931). Among the findings concerning students' attitudes was a classification of the students into five groups according to their confessed frequency of academic cheating (not at all, on quizzes, on one exam, on more than one exam, and "extremely"). Each student also estimated the prevalence of cheating on a 7-point scale (0%, 20%, 33%, 50%, 67%, 80%, 100%). The correlation between the admitted frequency of cheating and the median prevalence estimates was .93 (Katz & Allport, 1931, Table LXIV, p. 227).

Over the decades, projection was demonstrated in many contexts and explained in the light of many theories. The theory of cognitive dissonance, for example, suggested that the discovery of negative characteristics within the self would create psychological tension (i.e., a

---

[1]Allport's "illusion of universality" differs sharply from Festinger's "pressure towards uniformity." Festinger believed that "if uniformity is achieved there is a state of social acquiescence" (p. 125). To Allport, uniformity meant turmoil.

drive state). If people could not deny or eliminate these negative characteristics, they might resort to projecting them to others. Doing this, they presumably felt better (e.g., Bramel, 1962).

More recent work can be classified along three theoretical perspectives. Each perspective stresses the role of information processing rather than motivated consistency seeking, but each evaluates the processes and outcomes of projection differently. As part of the heuristics and biases approach to social cognition, the *false consensus paradigm* claims that any significant perception of consensus reveals a fallacy of thought (Ross, Greene, & House, 1977). By contrast, the *induction paradigm* holds that projection, however biased it may be, is defensible if understood as a generalization from a small sample (Hoch, 1987). Finally, the *egocentrism paradigm* views projection as an irrational yet adaptive form of perception. This paradigm locates error in the failure to generalize the behaviors of other individuals to the group (Krueger & Clement, 1994). I first review the theory and the evidence for each paradigm. Then, I sharpen the distinctions between the induction and the egocentrism paradigms, and I comment on the relevance of projection for other social–cognitive biases, social behavior, and social comparison processes

FALSE CONSENSUS

In a landmark article, Ross et al. (1977) labeled projection the "false consensus effect" (FCE) and demonstrated its pervasiveness in dozens of tests. Each test consisted of the presentation of a stimulus item (e.g., an opinion, a personality trait, or a behavioral intention), which participants decided to either endorse or reject. They also estimated social consensus as the percentage of people who endorse the item. For each item, the FCE was assessed as the difference between the consensus estimates made by endorsers and the estimates made by nonendorsers. When the difference between the two means was significant—as most were— consensus estimates were said to have been projective and thus false.

Projection as a Stimulus Characteristic

Table 1 displays the results of a replication of the Ross et al. study. The stimulus items are 14 trait-descriptive terms. Thirteen of the 14 comparisons indicate projection and seven are reliable. As one would expect, people tend to expect others to share their own personality traits. The degree to which they do this can be expressed by the raw difference between the two mean consensus estimates (i.e., the FCE), by a standardized measure of effect size (Cohen's d or a point-biserial r), or by a test statistic (t).

The FCE paradigm suggests that half the consensus effects are false and that half are not. These judgments follow from decisions about statistical significance. This method-driven strategy to appraise the rationality of social judgment has two important characteristics. The first characteristic is that judgments concerning rationality depend not only on the averages of the consensus estimates but also their number. The more estimates there are, the more likely it is that bias is detected. Even with a fixed number of estimates, variations in actual consensus rates create differences in statistical power. Estimates are most likely to be judged false if the percentage of actual endorsement is close to 50%. The data displayed in Table 1 illustrates this. Across items, the extremity of actual consensus (i.e., its distance from 50%) is negatively related to the test statistic ($r = -.34$) and to the correlational effect size ($r = -.24$); but it is unrelated to the raw ($r = .12$) and the standardized effect size ($r = .02$). The variability of actual consensus biases judgments about the falsity of perceived consensus only when people's own

**Table 1. Average Consensus Estimates
and Statistical Effects ($N = 164$)**

		Estimated consensus				
	Actual	Endorsement				
Traits[a]	consensus	Yes	No	d	r	t
1. Alert	91	75	65	.62	.19	2.21
2. Argumentative	50	64	53	.50	.25	3.19
3. Candid	76	51	51	−.01	−.002	−.03
4. Christian	34	42	41	.07	.03	.39
5. Discontented	36	48	33	.73	.35	4.43
6. Gluttonous	15	34	19	.88	.33	3.73
7. Imaginative	88	70	67	.15	.05	.58
8. Loud	37	46	43	.16	.08	1.66
9. Meticulous	46	52	41	.53	.26	3.39
10. Neat	55	48	44	.26	.13	1.69
11. Sly	28	36	28	.40	.19	2.17
12. Smoker	15	40	37	.21	.07	.95
13. Smug	12	41	33	.38	.14	1.46
14. Suggestible	33	46	35	.49	.23	2.87
Combined[b]	44	49	42	.39	.16	1.93

[a]Twelve traits were selected using normative values of observability and favorability
(Rothbart & Park, 1986). Three traits (1, 9, 10) were both easy to observe and favorable,
three (2, 6, 8) were easy to observe and unfavorable, three (3, 7, 14) were difficult to
observe and favorable, and three (5, 11, 13) were difficult to observe and unfavorable. The
trait "Christian" was added because it previously yielded a false uniqueness effect (FUE)
(Bosveld et al., 1996). The trait "smoker" yielded an FCE that was attributed to selective
exposure (Sherman et al., 1983).
[b]The combined values are means, except the t, which is a median.

item endorsements serve as a status variable. This bias is avoided when item endorsements are manipulated experimentally (e.g., Agostinelli, Sherman, Presson, & Chassin, 1992).

The second characteristic of the standard item-by-item assessment is that it underestimates the strength of projection. Consider the first two items in Table 1. The average FCE (10.5%) can be obtained by averaging the two mean estimates made by endorsers ($Ms = 75\%$ and 64%, for "alert" and "argumentative," respectively) and then subtracting the average of the two mean estimates made by nonendorsers ($Ms = 65\%$ and 53%). But more people claim to be "alert" (91%) than "argumentative" (50%). When the averages are weighted by the differences in actual consensus, the FCE increases ($16\% = .91 \times 75\% + .5 \times 64\% − .09 \times 65\% + .5 \times 53\%$). Across all items, the weighted FCE ($M = 18.22\%$) as well as the other three statistical indices are greater than the unweighted FCE ($d = .83$, $t = 19.90$, $r = .38$).

How to be Rational in the FCE Paradigm

What can perceivers do to escape the verdict of irrationality? They must either estimate consensus accurately or ignore their own responses when they are not sure how much consensus there actually is. The first possibility is rarely an option. Having to estimate what everyone knows reveals little about the process of consensus estimation under uncertainty. For this reason, questions such as "Would people agree to carry a sandwich board to propagate the ominous "Repent!' " have become classic (Ross et al., 1977). Strange items minimize the role of relevant social knowledge. There could only be indirect knowledge such as beliefs concerning the likelihood of compliance in general. But regardless of such knowledge, each participant's response is merely a sample of one that he or she should ignore.

Why is the neglect of available sample information regarded as the best way to make a judgment? During the 1970s, many social psychologists felt that "laypeople" operated more or less like they themselves did, basing judgments about reality on systematically collected and analyzed data. This view suggested that people make consensus estimates by testing a null hypothesis (Krueger, 1998b). People were expected to estimate social consensus in a way similar to the way scientists decided whether these estimates were false. When the statistical tool of null hypothesis significance testing (NHST) became a model of mind (Gigerenzer, 1991), the question became whether this tool was used right.

No Exposure. To judge social consensus by NHST, perceivers need a hypothesis and relevant data. But it is unclear what consensus value people entertain as the null hypothesis or to what extent they agree on its location (e.g., 50% or any other). Whatever this hypothesis may be, a single observation (however outlying it might be) is not enough to reject it. If perceivers knew this, researchers could not reject *their* null hypothesis of no projection no matter how many perceivers they sampled.

Random Exposure. Perhaps people have other information besides their own responses. One possibility is that this extra information is unbiased by the perceiver's own response. If so, NHST is possible but again it guarantees the retention of the null hypothesis. Consider perceiver A, who endorses the item and perceiver B who does not. Both know the same two other individuals, but they do not know each other. One of the others endorses the item, and so the sample available to A consists of two thirds endorsers, whereas the sample available to B is one third endorsers. If A and B project their observed proportions, the difference between them (33%) is substantial. Because the sample is small, however, the standard error of the difference is so large (27%) that the null hypothesis survives. An increase in sample size does not change this. If, for example, A and B know 50 people who endorse the item and 50 who reject it, their own responses hardly matter. If they project their observed proportions (including the self) to the group, the FCE is minute (.99%). The standard error, although reduced (4.97%), does not threaten the null hypothesis.

In short, people's own responses do not affect consensus estimation if their thinking is in any way related to NHST. Because their estimates *do* covary with their own responses, however, it seems that perceivers do not apply NHST correctly or not at all, and thus must be considered irrational. This verdict overlooks the fact that NHST itself is a melange of mathematical rules and social conventions. People who do not subscribe to .05 conservatism can easily reject a null hypothesis that is contradicted by a few data points. This rejection would not make them less rational, but only more adventurous.

Selective Exposure. A final possibility is that individual responses are related to available sample observations. If people fail to recognize the selectivity of their exposure to similar others, their consensus estimates are biased. This view does not question people's ability to test hypotheses, but their ability to avoid or correct sample bias. In a typical study, perceivers judge how many of their friends behave a certain way (e.g., smoke; Sherman, Presson, Chassin, Corty, & Olshavsky, 1983). Although these judgments about individual friends predict consensus estimates, this need not mean that people infer group consensus from biased samples. They might simply infer both individual behaviors and group consensus from their own behaviors (Bosveld, Koomen, & van der Pligt, 1994). This interpretation is plausible because people exaggerate the similarities between themselves and other individuals (Kenny, Bond, Mohr, & Horn, 1996). In other words, selective exposure may itself be a projective perception, and actual exposure within a group need not be selective. The personality profiles of college students, for example, are no more similar among roommates than among randomly paired students (Fuhrman & Funder, 1995). If actual exposure is unbiased, it cannot explain biased estimates, and the self returns as the most likely source of projection. Indeed, the FCE occurs even when there is no exposure to others. It occurs, for example, when the meaning of a behavior is obscure ("Eat at Joe's!") or when people learn they have an attribute they did not know they had (e.g., success or failure at a strange task).

INDUCTIVE REASONING

In the FCE paradigm, social perceivers and investigators both tend to reject the null hypothesis of no difference, and the latter think that the former are irrational for doing so. This conclusion would be justified if perceivers benefited from statistical power as much as investigators do. If exposed to a large random sample, perceivers might make accurate and unbiased estimates. That is, an increase in power would enhance their chances of appearing rational. Having to respond to obscure items, however, robs research participants of this possibility.

Thus, the question remains of whether perceivers should ignore their own responses when they have little or no information about the behaviors or others (i.e., in the case of no exposure). According to the FCE paradigm, the answer is yes because single observations cannot precipitate the rejection of a hypothesis. What if, however, consensus estimation is an attempt to *generate* rather than to test a hypothesis? When perceivers feel uncertain about social consensus—as they often do—they may assume that their own responses are those of the majority. Consider a reversal of the typical estimation task. Rather than asking how common a behavior is in a group given a single observation, the question is what a single behavior will be given its prevalence in the group. Suppose Dr. Data knows that 80% of professors prefer experimental over postmodern psychology. Knowing this, and having temporarily lost her introspective faculties, Data infers *deductively* that she is probably an old-fashioned experimentalist. Having recovered memory, Data also realizes that she prefers lecture-style over seminar-style teaching and that 80% of her peers prefer one method. She can now infer *inductively* that hers is probably the majority position. Both modes of inference are valid. The majority implies the self and the self implies the majority.[2]

If projection is a form of induction, a single observation is informative. Rather than seeking the rejection of a false null hypothesis, this view of induction stresses the value of point estimation. Consider again the person who is aware of two desirable behaviors and one undesirable behavior. Rather than asking whether the null hypothesis of no difference is false, this person may realize that the sampled proportion is the best estimate of the population proportion, and therefore that desirable behavior is more common than undesirable behavior. Instead of testing a hypothesis, this person generates one. The weakness of NHST is its disinterest in alternative hypotheses, but this is what perceivers must explore when estimating

[2]When a group is characterized by multiple behaviors with different base rates, inductive inferences are more regressive (i.e., less variable) than deductive inferences.

consensus. By point estimation, they can infer that the most likely consensus distribution in the group is the one they have preserved in the sample.

Bayesian Induction

If only one observation exists, it would be reckless to assume that all other instances, yet to be observed, will be the same. This would mean that all groups are perfectly homogeneous, a possibility that is contradicted by experience. Dawes (1989) suggested that the social perceiver does not begin with one specific null hypothesis but with a family of hypotheses. In the simplest case, known as the *principle of indifference*, these hypotheses are equally likely at the outset (LaPlace, 1814). In other words, the social perceiver begins in a state of ignorance regarding social consensus. All possible percentages, ranging from 0% to 100%, seem equally applicable. Attempting to make a numerical prediction, the perceiver assumes that the consensus for one option is 50%. This estimate is not, however, a unitary null hypothesis, but the result of an effort to minimize the error that is almost certain to occur when the true percentage is revealed. Errors greater than 50% are not possible.

When observations appear, such as the perceiver's own response, the probabilities of the 101 hypotheses are no longer the same. Hypotheses stating that this response is that of a minority are now less likely, and hypotheses stating that this response is that of a majority are more likely. The hypothesis that this particular response does not exist is eliminated, and the hypothesis that all group members show this response is now the most probable. But clearly, this hypothesis is not the only one. To estimate consensus, the perceiver needs to integrate the probabilities of the remaining 100 hypotheses by weighting each hypothesis with its probability of being true. Accepting the principle of indifference, the aggregate posterior probability of the response is $(k + 1)/(n + 2)$, where k is the number of responses of a certain kind (e.g., preference for A rather than B), and n is the size of the sample (see also Gigerenzer & Murray, 1987; Krueger & Clement, 1996). If there is only one observation, its probability is $\frac{2}{3}$. As sample size increases, the prediction approaches the proportion observed in the sample.[3]

The Bayesian rationale allows perceivers to predict the probability of a hypothesis given the observed data, $P(H|D)$, whereas NHST only provides the probability of the data given the null hypothesis, $P(D|H)$. Which conditional probability do social perceivers care about? Their task is not to make a judgment about the null hypothesis but to estimate consensus (i.e., to make a point estimation). Aside from offering a realistic platform for evaluating the rationality of consensus estimation, Bayesian induction provides a mechanism for projection that is both necessary and sufficient: Use of one's own (and any other) response.

Brunswikian Induction

A limitation of the Bayesian approach is that social reality, with its variable distributions of responses, plays no role in the assessment of the perceivers' rationality. Brunswik's (1955) lens model offers an approach to induction that takes actual consensus into account. It suggests that perceivers use more or less valid cues and that they use these cues more or less reliably. Across observations, perceivers can detect which cues covary with a reality criterion. They can detect the covariation between their own behaviors and those of the majorities, and thus recognize their own responses as valid cues for group consensus. Perceivers who understand

[3]Own endorsements predict group consensus regardless of the distribution of the prior probabilities. The assumption of uniform priors (the "principle of indifference") is attractive because it (1) captures the psychological state of ignorance, and (2) simplifies the mathematical prediction of the posterior probabilities.

this project and thereby increase the accuracy of their predictions (Hoch & Loewenstein, 1989).

Consider the simple case of four behaviors, two shown by a majority and two shown by a minority. There are 16 possible patterns in which behaviors of individual group members may coincide with the behaviors of the majority or with the behaviors of the minority. There also are 16 possible patterns of predictions, ranging from assuming that all behaviors are majority behaviors to assuming that none is. The 256 intersections of these profiles yield scores for projection and accuracy. Projection can be expressed by the percentage (0%, 25%, 50%, 75%, or 100%) of behaviors in which the person expects the majority to behave as he or she does, while accuracy is the percentage of behaviors in which the prediction (majority behavior versus minority behavior) matches reality.

The key to the Brunswikian perspective is the realization that some patterns of endorsement are more likely than others. Suppose the actual endorsement probability is ⅔ for each majority item and ⅓ for each minority item. If responses to the items are independent, it is far more likely that all of the individual's responses match the responses of the majority ($P = .1975$) than that all match the responses of the minority ($P = .0123$). Figure 1 shows the probability of each validity score. The behaviors of most individual group members are associated with the behaviors of the majority. Their own behaviors are valid cues for majority behavior even if there is no other sample information. The most important consequence of this relationship is that the correlation between projection and accuracy increases with validity.

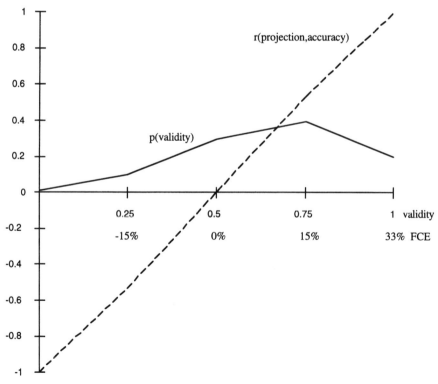

Figure 1. The probability of validity coefficients and their effect on the correlation between projection and accuracy.

When the correlation between projection and accuracy is weighted by the probability with which it occurs (i.e., validity), its mode is .53. On the average, a person can assume that the group agrees with him or her in three out of four cases.

If most individuals project in this reasonable fashion, FCEs appear for most behaviors. If, for example, everyone projects at the level of the most likely validity, the average probability that an endorser expects the majority to also endorse the item is .74. The corresponding value for nonendorsers is .29.[4] The average size of the FCE now depends on the size of the consensus estimates. If people follow the logic of Bayesian prediction (and the principle of indifference), their estimates are 58% for their own behaviors and 43% for the alternatives.[5] The FCE (15%) obtained from these theoretical considerations is remarkably similar to the average (unweighted) FCE obtained in meta-analyses (Mullen & Hu, 1988).

If people projected all their responses to the group, as the Bayesian model would predict, accuracy and the FCE would increase further. This rarely happens, however, and Brunswik's approach describes more realistically what people actually do. Noting that validity tends to be positive but not perfect, they project roughly at the level of the average expected validity (Krueger & Clement, 1997). By doing this, they attain greater predictive accuracy than they would have if they had not projected at all, and as a group they produce FCEs as a statistical byproduct.

Individualized Projection

When the FCE is computed item by item, the average strength of projection within a person and differences between people remain unknown. To overcome this limitation, the Brunswikian approach suggests that item endorsements and estimated and actual consensus be intercorrelated across items and within individual people. The correlation between endorsements and actual consensus expresses the validity of each set of responses for the aggregated group responses. In the illustrative data set (see Table 1), these correlations are high ($M = .57$), because most individuals are indeed similar to the group average. Given this substantial validity correlation, perceivers are right to project; and they do, as expressed by the correlation between endorsements and estimated consensus ($M = .45$). Finally, the correlation between estimated and actual consensus reveals considerable accuracy ($M = .62$). The key claim of the induction paradigm is that projection increases accuracy. Indeed, accuracy is reduced when endorsements are controlled (partial $M = .49$). However, it is also clear that perceivers do not only rely on self-related knowledge. If they did, the partial accuracy would be zero, and the raw accuracy correlation would not be larger than the validity correlation (Dawes & Mulford, 1996; Krueger, 1998a).

Also consistent with the induction paradigm, projection ($r = .47$) and validity ($r = .40$) are positively related to accuracy across people. The effect of projection is reduced but not eliminated when validity is controlled (partial $r = .34$). Again, information unrelated to the self also appears to affect consensus estimates. Similarly, the effect of validity does not disappear when projection is controlled (partial $r = .22$). The most typical group members predict consensus most accurately regardless of their own projection. Finally, typical group members (i.e., those with the most valid responses) project more than atypical members do ($r = .49$). These findings illustrate the need to examine projection not only for individual items, but also

[4]These values were computed by summing the predicted majority endorsements for each item and each level of validity. This sum yields the probability of predicted majority endorsement when divided by the total number of predictions.
[5]For endorsers, $.7363 \times \frac{2}{3} + .2911 \times \frac{1}{3} = .5788 \times 100$; for nonendorsers, $.2911 \times \frac{2}{3} + .7363 \times \frac{1}{3} = .4304 \times 100$.

within and across people. When this is done, the benefits of projection and the limitations of the FCE paradigm become apparent.

EGOCENTRIC PERCEPTION

The first two approaches to the study of projection have emphasized statistical reasoning by viewing consensus estimation as a form of hypothesis testing (FCE) or hypothesis generation (induction). Neither paradigm explains, however, why projection occurs in the first place. The FCE paradigm shows which variables are sufficient to increase projection, but not which are necessary (Krueger, 1998a). The induction paradigm models empirical consensus estimates well, but it is vague about underlying psychological processes.

The third view of projection abandons the notion of statistical reasoning and instead tries to understand projection as a facet of perception. This view assumes that a person's own response to a stimulus—be it approach or avoidance—automatically generates the idea that others respond similarly. Automatic approach–avoidance tendencies are well-documented. When presented, most stimuli elicit primitive responses that tell perceivers how they feel about the stimulus (Niedenthal & Kitayama, 1994). Most simply, they accept their perceptions as being realistic. Trust in sense perception usually works so well (this snarling Doberman is aggressive ... better get out) that it generalizes to social perception. Often, our interactants are what they appear to be and they mean what they say. Clearly, however, social perception and interaction is also fraught with deception and error. Communication and rhetoric beget gullibility. Statements that ring true enjoy instant credence and false ones need to be "unbelieved" by laborious scrutiny (Gilbert, 1991). Nevertheless, approach and avoidance are *about* the stimulus, and thus, every response involves at least some degree of stimulus attribution (Higgins, 1997). Once a quality, be it positive or negative, has been attributed to the stimulus, other people can be expected to be similarly affected by it (Gilovich, Jennings, & Jennings, 1983).

Adaptiveness

> We start with the bare observation that a number of persons will in a given situation perceive objects
> and happenings within it in a similar way and that their modes of action in the situation will also have a
> basic similarity. (Asch, 1952, p. 128)

Perceivers not inclined to make rapid stimulus attributions suffer in most environments. Although seeing a charging hound, tasting bitter herbs, or relishing the joys of sex are deeply subjective experiences, they emanate from reality. This reality may not determine perception, but it constrains it. Reality is objective in the sense that others who face the same stimulus feel similarly. Asch (1952) understood that "we discover that the surroundings are accessible to all; they are open to inspection [and that] we discover a basic unity in our perceptions, motives, thoughts, and purposes" (pp. 129–130). Asch knew that trust in this unity is the foundation of human relations. Much of communication, for example, is the mutual confirmation of what we already know others know. The power of faith in "common ground" is unmasked whenever it breaks down unexpectedly. Autism and some psychoses, for example, severely limit the sharing of that which is already agreed upon. A hallucinated voice, for example, is an idiosyncratic event. If the hallucinator wishes to discuss what he or she has heard, frustration is inevitable because others cannot respond with the expected empathy. Some forms of psychotherapy that discourage stimulus attributions regardless of what it is that the client experiences ("It's all in your head!") work against the natural grain of the perceptual apparatus. It is a difficult task for the human mind to find comfort in the conviction that its sensations, perceptions, and feelings are controlled by mysterious inner forces rather than being healthy responses to what is out there.

Social projection saves mental energy while still producing adaptive results (as shown by its fit with inductive algorithms). These qualities have long been recognized, but have not influenced research on projection itself. Hume, Wundt, James, and Freud were among the many thinkers who used introspection and self-analysis to generate hypotheses about how minds (and not only their own) work. Their contributions were not definitive, however, because they went beyond the projection of individual responses. Instead, some of their predictions involved complex sequences of events that, in conjunction, were not likely to be found in others. Added details increase the perceived representativeness of a scenario, but they also reduce its generalizability (Tversky & Kahneman, 1974). Freud, for example, thought he had discovered a universal conflict between fathers and sons. He may have been right, but the details of his own conflict and its presumed mythical origins were too intricate to be a probable experience among others. In other words, egocentric projection is useful when restricted to individual stimuli. Complex patterns, especially when their components do not covary, become rapidly idiosyncratic.

Projected Minds

> After prolonged research on myself, I brought out the fundamental duplicity of the human being.
> (Camus, cited in Bok, 1989, p. xv)

Why would the pioneers of psychological science bother with introspection? Laziness or lack of access to empirical sampling methods hardly satisfy as explanations. More likely, they anticipated Asch's axioms or more recent philosophies of mind: "Whatever else a mind is, it is supposed to be something like our minds; otherwise we wouldn't call it a mind" (Dennett, 1996, p. 4). As self-evident as the projection of mind may seem, it is not without challenge. Solipsists believe that only their own minds exist. Because there is more than one solipsist, one might wonder—as Wittgenstein did—why they do not talk to each other. Indeed, they avidly talk to nonsolipsists, thus exposing their belief that there are other minds that need education in solipsism. To say this may be unfair because some solipsists simply doubt that the existence of other minds can be proven. And in that, they are correct. Although it is impossible to prove the existence of other minds (as it is impossible to prove that the sun will set), the assumption that they do has been useful (Nagel, 1967).

Projective faith in the existence of other minds is an adaptive premise that permits the gathering of empirical knowledge. Although nobody needs to worry about proving the premise itself, the inferences that follow from it can readily be modified by experience. Humphrey (1978) suggested that this is the primary function of consciousness:

> The trick which nature came up with was *introspection*: it proved possible for an individual to develop a model of the behaviour of others by reasoning by analogy from his own case, the facts of his own case being revealed to him by "examination of the contents of consciousness." (p. 901)

Many inner experiences find overt expression. If others have minds like ours (premise), we expect them to respond to stimuli as we do (prediction), and can then note their behavior (test). What is being tested is not the premise but the prediction. The founders of psychology knew this, but many of their successors abandoned this form of hypothesis generation at great loss: "Nature's psychologists succeed where academic psychologists have failed because the former make free use of introspection" (Humphrey, 1978, p. 901).

Testing hypotheses about other minds is a costly diversion unless there is something to be gained. Sometimes others feel differently from us, which is important to know, especially when there is a threat of deception. Deceivers seek illicit gains and to realize these gains they have to outmaneuver their own projections. The con man who draws a mark into his game has to feign disappointment about initial but intended losses. He then can up the ante and liberate his victim of financial assets. This is difficult because the con man's projection is that the mark can detect his inner sense of glee. The con man, much like young Allport, is likely to endure the illusion of transparency (Gilovich, Savitsky, & Medvec, 1998). Awareness of one's own lies may bring unbidden arousal, at least if there is a smidgen of compunction. Not surprisingly then, those who deceive best are those who manage to deceive themselves (Mele, 1997). As Costanza said to Seinfeld: "Remember Jerry, it's not a lie if you believe it."

When self-deception does not work, the con artists may fear that their arousal is visible, which increases arousal further. Expecting others to know their private states, they may ultimately choose honesty. To avoid detection, they deceive less than they could have. People cannot detect the inner states of others as well as they think they can (DePaulo & Friedman, 1998). If they exaggerate both their own and others' detective ability, projection limits deception in general.

INDUCTION AND EGOCENTRISM COMPARED

The standard tests of consensus estimation do not distinguish between induction and egocentrism. Both paradigms predict that most people project most of the time. How can we know whether projection is primarily a matter of reasoning or perception? Recent research has created conditions under which the two paradigms make different predictions. One procedural innovation is to vary the target of projection so that the perceiver is either a member of the group or not. The other innovation is to vary the source of the behavioral information so that the available response is either the perceiver's own or that of another individual.

Social Categorization

The surest way to eliminate projection is to ask people to estimate social consensus for a group to which they do not belong. At first blush, this negative finding appears to support the idea that people reason inductively. After all, induction is an inference from a sample to the population from which this sample was drawn. If the characteristics of two populations or groups are known to be unrelated, a sample of observations obtained from one group is diagnostic with respect to that group but not the other. When this situation is created experimentally with urns representing groups and chips of varying color representing sample characteristics, participants draw the proper inferences (Krueger & Clement, 1996).

The lack of projection to social out-groups seems to replicate this experimental situation, but this similarity is deceiving. Humanity is broken up into multiple groups, usually by a small number of distinctive characteristics. Catholics, for example, revere the Virgin Mother, whereas Jews do not. But how else do these groups differ? Social categorization does not mean that other characteristics are independent (or even opposite) of each other. Enjoyment of the outdoors, poetry, or overpriced space-age coffee varies more across people than between groups. Nevertheless, group predictions depend on the self only when the self belongs to the group (Cadinu & Rothbart, 1996). People seem not to realize that both groups are subsumed under a shared population (Sloman, 1997). Failing to project to the out-group, they neglect population base rates. *The real error is not projection, but the lack thereof.* It is difficult to explain the lack of projection to out-groups as part of inductive reasoning without introducing further assumptions, such as base rate neglect.[6]

The lack of projection to out-groups is also puzzling from the perspective of the egocentrism paradigm. Why do men fail to generalize their own responses to women and vice versa (Brown, 1996; Krueger & Zeiger, 1993)? It is as if people treat members of out-groups as members of different species. People rarely attribute consciousness as they experience it to other animals. Surely, they would not go as far as to deny consciousness to members of the opposite sex or other out-groups, but they seem to believe that theirs are different kinds of mind. In sum, the powerful moderating effect of social categorization on projection presents a challenge to both paradigms. But testable hypotheses do suggest themselves. For example, projection may occur automatically (and egocentrically) with respect to both in-groups and out-groups, but be effortfully inhibited for out-groups.

Self versus Other

The clearest way to discriminate between the two paradigms is by looking at variations in the source of the behavioral information. From the point of view of inductive reasoning, the source of a behavioral sample is irrelevant. *Any* observation is a valid cue for prediction, unless it is clearly discredited as being biased. In contrast, egocentric perception implies that people are more sensitive to those responses that emanate from themselves. They experience their own responses directly, subjectively, and thus believably. What they learn about the behaviors of others is superficial in comparison. When I prefer the House Italian over Newman's salad dressing, I am certain that I do, but I cannot be sure that Newman himself likes the dressing that bears his name. When appraising the behaviors of others, people must make greater allowances for deception and error than when appraising their own (in part, because they are— by definition—unaware of their own self-deceptions).

The significant partial accuracy correlations presented earlier (which controlled own responses) suggest that perceivers possess valid knowledge about the behavior of other individuals. However, this method does not reveal how many pieces of information they use, nor does it reveal the strength of induction from the self (projection) relative to the strength of induction from individual others. Although projection is inductively conservative, it would be egocentrically biased if induction from others' responses is even more conservative.

The use of self-related and individual other-related information is directly compared in "bogus stranger" experiments. After learning whether another person endorses or rejects the stimulus, participants make their own responses and they estimate social consensus. The size of the FCE is then compared depending on whether the two responses (own and other) are the same or different. Inductive reasoning demands that both responses receive the same weight, and the FCE should disappear when the stranger gives a discrepant response. But this does not happen. Consider a case in which participants read the Minnesota Multiphasic Personality Inventory-2 item "Criticism or scolding hurts me terribly," and learn that another student, whose response is ostensibly sampled randomly from a database, either endorses or rejects this statement (Krueger & Clement, 1994). Consensus bias is twice as large when the other agrees rather than disagrees. Still, the latter FCE indicates that endorsement by one and rejection by

---

[6]The moderation of projection by social categorization is consistent with the finding that people seek comparisons with members from their own social categories (e.g., sex or age). A good deal of similarity is assumed before the assessment itself is made (Wood, 1989).

the other do not cancel each other out as induction theory requires. Even the responses of many unanimous others do not override a single person's response. If extended to a whole list of items, the result is much the same. When consensus estimates for multiple items are regressed on the participant's own and the stranger's responses, the weight for the own responses is more than twice as large than the weight for the stranger's responses (Clement & Krueger, 2000).

It is reassuring, however, that the stranger's responses do not go entirely unheeded. If that were not the case, social learning and social comparisons would be all but impossible. People who happen to be atypical group members are most likely to encounter attitudes, behaviors, and preferences different from their own. If they ignore this important information, they run the risk of perceiving the group inaccurately, of failing to conform when conformity is adaptive, and perhaps of being ostracized.

But why do the responses of other individuals carry comparatively little weight? Besides having possible concerns about the truthfulness of others, people may simply perform conservatively on *any* task that they understand as being inductive. In classic research on the revision of beliefs, participants infer the composition of urns from samples of colored balls. They imagine two urns, one filled with 70% red balls and 30% blue balls, and the other filled with 30% red balls, and 70% blue balls. The prior probability of each urn to be sampled is .5. Next, participants learn that eight red and four blue balls were sampled, and their task is to estimate the probability that the balls came from the predominantly red urn. The typical answer $(P = .75)$ is lower than the correct one $(P = .97)$ (Peterson & Beach, 1967).[7]

When they face multiple plausible hypotheses, people also hesitate to revise their beliefs. Recall that when people are ignorant about the prevalence of a feature in a category, their best guess is 50%. When a single datum (feature present or feature absent) is sampled, its posterior probability is $\frac{2}{3}$. People ignore single data and other small samples, however, not realizing that belief revision does not increase but decrease with each successive observation (Krueger & Clement, 1996). In consensus estimation, people appear to treat the responses of others in the same way as they treat balls drawn from an urn. They apply the same inductive conservatism.

The induction paradigm is an incomplete account of consensus estimation because neither its theoretical tenets nor its empirical findings explain both the strong projection from the self and the limited generalization from the other. The former satisfies mathematical norms, whereas the latter fits the standard finding of conservatism. The egocentrism paradigm attempts to account for the self–other discrepancy. Its focus is again on the self. Why do

---

[7]For normative belief revision (see Gigerenzer & Murrary, 1987), the probability of the data given the hypothesis (red urn) is

$$P(D|H) = \binom{n}{x} p_r^x (1 - p_r)^{n-x}.$$

The probability p_r is the percentage of red balls in the predominantly red urn U_r, and p_r^x is the probability of drawing a sequence of x (i.e., 8) red balls from that urn. Analogously, $(1 - p_r)^{n-x}$ is the probability of drawing $n - x$ (i.e., 4) blue balls from that urn. The product of these probabilities is the probability of drawing a sequence of x red and $n - x$ blue balls from the predominantly red urn. The binomial coefficient $\binom{n}{x}$ gives the number of possible sequences of this kind. The outcome of 8 reds and 4 blues has a probability of .231 if the predominantly red urn is sampled, and a probability of .008 if the predominantly blue urn is sampled. The posterior probability of the predominantly red urn follows from Bayes's rule as

$$p(U_r|D) = p(U_r) \times \frac{p(D|U_r)}{p(U_r) \times p(D|U_r) + p(U_b) \times p(D|U_b)} = .967$$

people not show their usual conservatism when inferring group consensus from their own responses? What makes the self special?

BELIEF FORMATION VERSUS BELIEF REVISION

Immediacy

A great deal of self-related knowledge is highly accessible (Bargh, 1982; Wood & Cowan, 1995). When a stimulus appears, one's own initial response—however tentative it might be—leaps into consciousness. At the same time, it is clear that most others respond similarly to the same stimulus. But how do people project their internal states or traits to others? The likely answer is that trait attributions to the self depend in part on simple and immediate responses to the lexical stimulus: the trait word. At minimum, people extract desirability information from trait words, and thus have a ready cue as to whether the trait is descriptive of themselves and most others (Pratto & John, 1991). One's own responses rush in with the stimulus, and even dispositional stimuli may be automatically associated with group characteristics (Clement & Krueger, 1998).

The high accessibility of one's own responses poses a problem for inductive reasoning. Induction means that observations lead to revisions of beliefs that already exist. In other words, the social perceiver needs to have a belief about the popularity of a stimulus item *before* even considering his or her own response as a piece of relevant data. To make consensus estimates, however, people need to know what the stimulus is, and if they do, their own responses force themselves to mind. Thus, consensus estimates are always posterior beliefs because they already involve a sampling observation. If so, the logic of induction, which suggests a sequence of prior belief, sampling, and posterior belief, lacks its crucial first element. This means that consensus estimates derived from one's own response serve to *form* rather than revise beliefs. *Egocentric perception takes place before raters can ask themselves what the priors would have been had they not encountered this particular stimulus.*[8]

In contrast, responses of other individuals enter the picture *after* beliefs have already been formed egocentrically. Sampling others fits the three-step inductive sequence, and subsequent consensus estimates are revisionary rather than formative. If conservatism is a robust feature of belief revision, it is here that it should be seen. Projection is less conservative, and thus seemingly more normative, because it is free of prior beliefs resisting revision. This perspective suggests that the role of other-related information is equivalent to that of self-related information only when presented independently. Hansen and Donoghue (1977) created such a situation by having some participants (actors) sip an unfamiliar drink, while allowing others (observers) to look on. Not surprisingly, actors inferred population preferences from their own experience with the drink. More importantly, observers also used the actors' appraisals of the drink to infer how most others would feel, but observers who also had an opportunity to taste the drink themselves ignored the apparent preference of the other participant and only used their own response to predict consensus.

Unless the stimulus is entirely unfamiliar, self-related associations can creep in before the identity of the specific stimulus has been revealed. Suppose my friend Jack raves about the latest movie with Eastwood. Can I infer the popularity of this movie from his reaction alone?

---

[8]Mathematically, of course, it is possible to apply Bayes's rule backward and to estimate the prior probability of consensus given the data (own response) and the posterior probability (consensus estimate).

Even if I have not seen the movie, I know my feelings about actors-turned-politicians, Eastwood himself, his type of movies, movies in general, and a wealth of other related issues. Through lateral induction from these related beliefs, my knowledge of Jack's response is egocentrically contaminated, and thus will not stand alone as I predict the movie's popularity. It is thus unlikely that the observed responses of others create beliefs de novo.

Anchoring

If Bayesian belief revision cannot adequately describe egocentric projection, what can? The use of self-related information as a formative rather than a revisionary datum recalls the judgmental heuristic of anchoring and insufficient adjustment (Tversky & Kahneman, 1974).[9] A typical study involves obscure questions presented along with possible but patently arbitrary answers. For example, the question might be what percentage of African countries are former British colonies. A high arbitrary anchor (e.g., 60%) leads to higher estimates than a low anchor (e.g., 20%). But there is a fundamental difference between the anchoring heuristic and belief revision. An anchor is not a piece of data. Participants do not learn, for example, that a randomly selected country (e.g., Zambia) was a former British colony. If that were the case, one could compare prior and posterior estimates. Instead, the anchoring task provides an arbitrary prior probability, which participants then fail to ignore.

Projection is egocentric in that people anchor their consensus estimates on their own responses and adjust insufficiently when observing someone else's response. Rather than starting out at the 50% mark (which they may never consider) and then revising upward to their own response, they may start at the 100% mark for consensus with the self and then adjust (insufficiently) downward toward the 50% mark. The anchoring heuristic operates rather automatically, as one would expect if projection is a perceptual phenomenon (Wilson, Houston, Etling, & Brekke, 1996). People who attempt to disregard their own responses are unable to reduce projection (Krueger & Clement, 1994).

Good evidence for anchoring and insufficient adjustment comes from a study on interpersonal communication (Keysar, Barr, & Balin, 1998). Much of the time, communicators can plan utterances by relying on the common ground shared with their interlocutors. The common ground in communication resembles the notions of "validity" or "actual similarity" in the induction paradigm. What happens, however, when a communicator knows that the interlocutor does not share a crucial piece of information? The anchoring heuristic suggests that initial, reflexive attempts at forming an utterance will be egocentric. To appreciate the interlocutor's divergent perspective and to correct (adjust) the utterance takes time and may produce errors.

Keysar et al. (1998: experiment 1) devised a question-and-answer game in which one participant (the communicator) learned that "John read the newspaper." The other participant (the interlocutor) asked "Did he read the novel?" The communicator also received privileged information, which was either independent of the question ("Mary read a novel") or interfered with it ("Ralph read a novel"). When the privileged sentence interfered with the correct answer (no!) because of the shared pronoun, communicators' responses were slowed down by 170 msec and they involved 10% more errors. Similar egocentric anchoring occurred in an eye movement study (Keysar et al., 1998: experiment 2). Here communicators had to help "artists" (actually Keysar's confederates) complete a picture of a plane. The artists could see only an incomplete sketch, whereas communicators saw the full picture. Again, however, the

---

[9]The term "anchoring and insufficient adjustment" is redundant. If adjustment were sufficient, the initial numerical value would not be called an anchor because it had been forgotten or otherwise mentally deactivated.

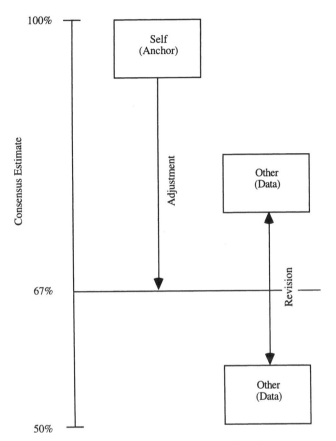

Figure 2. Self-anchoring (projection) and conservative induction from other data as a two-stage process of belief formation and belief revision.

communicators were exposed to some foils, including a bird. Some of the time, and under a pretext, communicators were instructed to "look at the bird" just before the artists asked them what color the wings were. The foil (the bird), which was not part of the common ground, delayed the saccade launch to the plane by an average of 180 msec. These findings are convergent evidence that initial responses are unrestricted by knowledge about other individuals. Only with time and effort can these egocentric anchors be adjusted toward the perspective of others.[10]

Consistent with Keysar's model, consensus estimation now may be understood as the two-stage process displayed in Fig. 2. In the first stage, perceivers automatically generate an extreme hypothesis based on their own response. Realizing that not everyone agrees with them, they adjust this estimate toward a more moderate value, allowing for variability. In the second stage, they use the responses of individual others for a conservative revision of their

[10]Using a similar design, Newton (1990, cited in Ross & Ward, 1996) found that people fail to appreciate that their self-generated embellishments to auditory stimuli are not available to others. Participants who knew which tune was being fingertapped greatly overestimated the degree to which uninformed others could identify the tune.

adjusted egocentric hypothesis. If the first other individual encountered disagrees with the perceiver, belief revision is conservative to the extent that it is smaller than the preceding adjustment.

The Curse of Knowledge

The processes of self-anchoring and inductive use of other-related information can work jointly or in opposition to each other. Their interplay can be seen when people predict what consensus estimates others will make. They realize that another person who endorses a stimulus item will probably make a higher consensus estimate than a person who rejects the same item (Krueger & Zeiger, 1993). But predictions of others' consensus estimates also covary with the anchor of the predictors' own responses. People who themselves would have endorsed the item expect the other person to give a higher estimate than people who would have rejected the item. In principle, this anchoring is rational because own responses are related to actual consensus values (own validity), which are related to others' responses (others' validity), which are related to others' estimates (others' projection).[11] The size of this rational anchoring is small because it is the product of three regression weights. Against this background, empirical anchoring effects are too strong. Perceivers' own endorsements predict the consensus estimates they attribute to others as much as the perceived endorsements of those others do. In other words, perceivers act as if the others knew their own (the perceivers' responses) and used them adequately (Krueger, 1998a).

The failure to suppress irrelevant knowledge creates biases of commission. The over-weighting of a self-referent sample response is egocentric because people *are* able to ignore other-referent sample information. The hindsight bias nicely illustrates the curse of egocentric knowledge. People with outcome knowledge not only fail to ignore the outcome when making their own predictions (hindsight), but also project their own biased predictions to other forecasters who lack outcome knowledge (Fischhoff, 1975). Similarly, people who gain facility with a task, thanks to practice, expect unpracticed individuals to be proficient too (Kelley & Jacoby, 1996). In communication, privileged semantic knowledge can be a curse. People who have learned the meaning of obscure linguistic idioms assume that this meaning is transparent to uninformed others (Keysar & Bly, 1995). These expectations concerning the performance of others violate rules of induction. One's own knowledge should not be reflected in the performance of others who lack this knowledge. Even those of us who study these effects are entrapped by them. When writing lectures, it is difficult to predict how much students already know; and when writing chapters, it is equally difficult to predict how much the readers know.[12]

When Induction and Egocentrism Converge

The evidence from the bogus stranger studies casts doubt on the claim that social perceivers treat self- and other-related information equivalently. But the self and the stranger differ in many ways. The self has the advantage of being salient, familiar, and enduring, whereas others are incorporeal data points presented in the sparsest manner. The justification

---

[11] I am grateful to Robyn Dawes for pointing this out.

[12] To test the idea that it is difficult to know what others know, average student evaluations of 167 courses were analyzed. As expected, ratings of the instructors' awareness of the students' level of understanding were lower than ratings of preparedness, clarity, enthusiasm, and receptiveness to questions. They were equal only to ratings concerning the use of instructional aids, and higher only than ratings of interest.

for the bogus stranger method is that it tests the strong form of the induction hypothesis. It should not matter what else is known about the other aside from the critical endorsement information. Psychologically, it may matter a great deal, however, and the egocentrism hypothesis offers a perspective on these self–other differences. According to the strong form of this hypothesis, there is a categorical difference between the self and the other, which stems from the inescapable subjectivity of the self and its experiences. According to the weak form, another person can become more selflike through processes such as individuation, familiarity, or love. The question is whether under some conditions another person's responses receive as much weight as one's own.

One way to approach this question is to individuate the other person. In one study, the other person was either represented by a mere identification number or by a name and a brief description. Although participants found it easier to form an impression about the named other, they did not give him or her more inductive weight than the anonymous other (Clement & Krueger, 2000). An alternative approach is to allow participants to predict the responses of someone they know well, and to use those predictions as information for the estimation of group consensus. When tested individually, college students relied both on their own responses to trait terms and on the responses they expected of their roommates (Krueger & Stanke, in press). But even these expected responses carried less weight than their own. In a follow-up study, students were tested along with their roommates in their dormitory apartments. This method not only replicated the high familiarity of the other, but also made him or her visually salient. These conditions were sufficient to eliminate the differences between self- and other-related correlations with consensus estimates. The roommates' responses were not provided by the investigators but were estimated, and these estimates were, in part, projective. For example, the assumed similarity of the roommates was greater than their actual similarity. Indeed, roommates were no more similar to one another than were two randomly paired students. Nevertheless, when students felt that their roommates would respond differently than they themselves would, egocentric projection disappeared.

The equivalence of the self and the familiar other raises the question of whether the underlying mechanisms are the same. According to the egocentrism hypothesis, projection from the self depends on processes of perceptual anchoring and downward adjustment, whereas generalization from the other depends on processes of data sampling and upward revision. Do the roommate data imply that students anchor on their familiar other's responses as much as they anchor on their own? A cluster of ancillary results indicates that representations of the self continue to enjoy egocentric primacy over representations of the familiar other even when both are perceived to be equally similar to the group. In particular, ratings about the self were made faster (see also Dunning & Hayes, 1996), were more stable over time (see also Granberg & Brent, 1983), and were experienced as being easier than ratings about either another person or the group (see also Biernat, Manis, & Kobrynowicz, 1997).

IMPLICATIONS FOR OTHER SOCIAL PERCEPTUAL BIASES AND BEHAVIOR

The implications of projection for some other social judgmental biases have been examined (correspondence bias: Hansen & Donoghue, 1977; actor–observer bias: Krueger, Ham, & Linford, 1996; hindsight bias and overconfidence: Stanovich & West, 1998). Of greatest theoretical interest are the relationships between projection and other egocentric biases. The two biases I consider here—false uniqueness and self-enhancement—both imply a contrast rather than projective assimilation between the self and the other.

(False) Uniqueness and Self-Enhancement

> We're all individuals!
> (Crowd in Monty Python's *Life of Brian*)

The perception of the self as being unique, as being differentiated from others, has been considered a basic psychological function and need, at least in the Western world (Markus & Kitayama, 1991). On the face of it, any attempt to see the self as being unique would limit or even overturn the effects of social projection. Indeed, psychologists have offered four different perspectives on uniqueness bias. The following review is guided by the question of whether these biases challenge the idea that projection is the primary perceptual orientation.

Reversals of the FCE. As its name suggests, the false uniqueness effect (FUE) is a negative FCE. Occasionally, consensus estimates are *lower* among those participants who endorse the item than among those who reject it (Agostinelli et al., 1992; Bosveld, Koomen, & van der Pligt, 1996; Klar, 1996; Suls, Wan, Barlow, & Heimberg, 1990). Some of these FUEs are serendipitous and some fail to replicate. Relative to the number of published FCEs, their number is so small that they may just represent sampling variability.

Aside from the possibility that the FUE is a statistical oddity, it is difficult to interpret. For example, the size of the Asian-American ethnic group is estimated to be smaller by Asian Americans themselves than by members of other ethnic groups (Krueger & Clement, 1997). It is tempting to attribute this FUE to the Asian minority. Caucasians, blacks, and Hispanics each show an FCE, believing that their own group is larger than it is believed to be by other groups. The idea that Asians are uniquely prone to uniqueness bias can only be tentative, however, because members of collectivistic cultures and their descendants are the least interested in the individualistic notion of uniqueness (Markus & Kitayama, 1991). From a methodological point of view, one might wonder what would happen if members of other ethnic groups decreased their estimates of the size of the Asian group (perhaps because they projectively increased estimates of the size of their own groups). Increased projection among other groups could eliminate the FUE for Asians despite the fact that no change occurred in the perceptions or motivations of that group.

Estimation Errors. An alternative interpretation of false uniqueness is less ambiguous. Often, people do not realize how common their own behaviors are (Nickerson, Baddeley, & Freeman, 1987). In the case of ethnic population estimates, for example, Caucasians underestimate the size of their own group (50% vs. 74%), while blacks (26% vs. 12%), Hispanics (21% vs. 10%), and Asians (8% vs. 3%) overestimate the size of theirs. Depending on one's interpretation of bias, conflicting biases seem to exist within the Caucasian and the Asian group. Caucasians project in that they think there are more Caucasians than other groups do (FCE), but they underestimate the size of their own group relative to its actual size (uniqueness). Asians, by contrast, exhibit the FUE when their estimates are compared with those made by other groups, but they overestimate the actual size of their own group. This apparent paradox is resolved when over- and underestimation biases are understood as regression effects (Krueger & Clement, 1997; Stone & Kamiya, 1957). The size of a large group (e.g., an ethnic majority) is more easily underestimated than overestimated by members of *any* group, and the reverse is true for the size of a small group. In other words, differences between estimated and actual consensus on a particular item say little about projection or uniqueness.

Biased Perceivers. To avoid the pitfalls of single-item analyses, perceptions of (false) uniqueness can be understood and assessed as a property of individual people. There is little research on the question of whether certain personality traits predict individual differences in perceptions of consensus and uniqueness. In one rare attempt to locate such predictors, Fenigstein and Abrams (1993) found that public self-consciousness is related to projection. Low public self-consciousness, when measured as a trait or a state, does not create FUEs, however, but only reduces the strength of projection. Following the idiographic approach preferred in the induction paradigm, one can ask if there are any individual perceivers who generate negative correlations between their own item endorsements and their consensus estimates. Such patterns of absolute uniqueness bias are rare. In the sample presented earlier, only 8% of the correlations were negative.[13] It is thus possible that there are a few people who systematically believe their own characteristics (whatever they may be) to be uncommon in the group. It remains to be seen whether these perceptions are stable person characteristics, or whether they are statistical oddities (i.e., type I errors against the true claim that all people project).

Better than Average. The common finding that most people believe they are better than average is occasionally interpreted as evidence for an FUE. Most people enhance the self above the group average (see Armor & Taylor, 1998; Krueger, 1998c, for reviews), which raises the question of whether they can simultaneously feel different (i.e., better) and similar to others. Self-enhancement suggests a favorable contrast between the self and others, whereas projection suggests assimilation. The solution to this paradox is simple. Self-enhancement is a positive difference between the location of the self and the location of the average person on a continuous scale. Like most people, Joe may enhance himself by thinking he is more satisfied with his life than most others are with theirs. At the same time, Joe may project his own level of satisfaction onto others (Klar & Giladi, 1999). His estimate of the proportion of satisfied people may be larger than the estimate given by somebody who is rather dissatisfied.

Ratings of personality traits reveal the coexistence of these two common biases. The illustrative data set also comprises ratings of a randomly chosen student and the social desirability of each trait. In Fig. 3, the average self- and other ratings are plotted against the 14 traits, which are sorted from left to right according to their average (social) desirability ratings. The high correlation between the two sets of ratings ($r = .88$) reflects projection.[14] Traits that people claim for themselves, they also tend to attribute to others. This correlation between self- and other descriptions is largely a product of social desirability (see also Bosveld, Koomen, & Vogelaar, 1997). People are more likely to claim positive than negative traits for the self *and* for another person.[15] The more they project, the less room for self-enhancement they have. Still, positive traits are judged to be more descriptive (by .57 standard units) and negative traits to be less descriptive (by .16 standard units) of the self than of the other person. As illustrated by the hypothetical motorist, people tend to feel similar to others, yet superior.

Some traits are more conducive to projection (FCE) than self-enhancement and vice versa ($r = -.57$). The motivational view of egocentrism suggests that differences in trait desirability mediate this correlation. It seems plausible that people project their negative traits onto others, while at the same time claiming that positive traits are more descriptive of them than of others. If so, the correlation between the two biases should disappear when social desirability is controlled. This, however, does not happen (partial $r = -.50$). Last, when the two biases are assessed idiographically, no relationship emerges, again supporting the view that self-enhancement cannot be construed as a uniqueness bias.

---

[13]Most raters with absolute false uniqueness scores had positive validity scores (7%).
[14]Self- and other ratings were jointly standardized; desirability ratings were standardized separately.
[15]Still, some projection occurs independent of social desirability (partial $r = .19$).

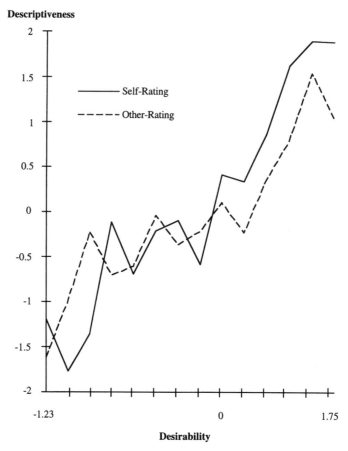

Figure 3. Projection and self-enhancement across 14 personality traits.

Personal Validation. A final perspective on false uniqueness derives from Forer's (1949) classic work on the "Barnum effect." Forer administered a personality inventory, but instead of preparing individualized personality sketches based on actual test scores, he wrote one moderately positive and vague sketch. Most of his participants felt that this sketch captured their personalities well. When they learned that everyone had received the same sketch, most of them were surprised, amused, and embarrassed. It was this emotional reaction that suggested that participants understood their ratings of the sketch's accuracy to mean *unique* accuracy. In other words, it was only implicit that they felt that the sketch captured their personality as it differed from the personalities of others.

But does the recognition of oneself in a vague description mean that the described characteristics are seen as unique in the sense of being rare? In a recent study, participants completed a personality inventory, and they were informed that, among other things, they were "enthusiastic, high-spirited, ingenious, [and] imaginative" (Krueger & Clement, 1996, p. 60). The Barnum effect emerged in that the sketch was rated as more accurate by those whom it was said to describe ($M = 7.26$, an a 9-point scale) than by those whom it was not said to describe ($M = 5.58$). However, estimates about the percentage of people who fit the description did not vary depending on whether the person him- or herself was described by it.

The skeptical tone of this review is not meant to suggest that people have no sense of uniqueness. It merely seems that perceptions of exaggerated or false uniqueness are rare and unstable. Next, I consider some surprising consequences of projection for social behavior. After all, as social animals, humans cannot get by with perception and contemplation alone; they also must act.

Behavior

A single universal soul resides in everyone; the wise man sees himself in all and all in him. (*Bhagavad Gita*, cited in Wright, 1994, p. 375)

Collective behavior depends in part on what the constituent individuals expect the collectivity will do. If individuals have a choice between acting and doing nothing, their perceptions of what others will do create a dilemma. If the considered action is costly but desirable, people are motivated to leave it to others to realize the common good. But then, if they sit back to enjoy a free ride, projection suggests that others will do likewise. Hence, each individual is caught in a loop of preparing and halting action with shifting perceptions that others will do the same.

Competition and Cooperation. Most participants in Prisoner's Dilemma games show rational self-interest when they know what their partners will do. They realize that competition maximizes their own gains regardless of the other's behavior. When they do not know yet, however, what the other will do, one out of three cooperates (Shafir & Tversky, 1992). This cooperation is puzzling because it defies rationality. The notion of projection can contribute to the demystification of cooperation. When players do not know the other's behavior, they can compete or cooperate depending on what feels right to them. Either way, they will expect the other to reciprocate their behavior (Kerr, 1989; Mulford, Orbell, Shatto, & Stockard, 1998; but see Gifford & Hine, 1997). Competitors who expect competition are reassured that they are not suckers. Cooperators can take pride in maximizing the joint payoff. Note that projection cannot occur when the other's behavior is known before the players themselves act. Here, their own behaviors are reactive rather than projective. Regardless of what the other has done, it is clear that competition maximizes their own gain.

Voting. Many political scientists consider voting irrational because it presents more costs than benefits to the individual (Meehl, 1977). A single vote is rarely decisive but casting it requires time and effort. Some have suggested that people derive other benefits from voting, such as the satisfaction that comes from expressing an attitude, doing one's civic duty, or nurturing a reputation of responsibility (Overbye, 1995). Others believe that voters expect that they can induce like-minded others to vote as well (Quattrone & Tversky, 1984). This is a strong claim of magical thinking, but perhaps noncausal processes of projection suffice to make people vote. Initially, potential voters who project their own preferences to the electorate should be reluctant to vote because they expect a favorable outcome. If they decide to refrain from voting, however, they establish a behavioral intention (i.e., to stay at home) that is also projectible. Being more inclined to project to in-groups than out-groups, they may now fear that political allies are more likely to abstain than opponents. This, in turn, should motivate them to vote after all.[16] Thus, the effect of projection on abstention is self-eradicating.

[16]Deciding for and against voting could become a loop that may be broken by the realization that the cost of voting is smaller than the cost of losing an election despite one's belief that public opinion is on one's side. Defeated politicians like to point out that they were unable to mobilize their supporters.

Consistent with this idea, voters are more confident of victory after they have resolved their conflict in favor of voting (Regan & Kilduff, 1988).

Ethical Conduct. Cooperation and voting are instances of socially desirable behavior, and projection can help explain why these behaviors do not disappear. But the effect of projection on desirable behavior remains tentative.[17] Many people, obeying the rational dictate of selfishness, do not cooperate, do not vote, or deceive others. Perhaps because of this, some teachers of ethics think it necessary to urge their disciples to behave well in spite of potential costs. Still, their appeals to selflessness are rooted in egocentrism. Jesus Christ suggested that you "Do unto others as you want them to do unto you." Rabbi Hillel asked that you "Don't do unto others what you don't want them to do unto you." Not surprisingly, there are no allocentric rules, such as "Do unto yourself as others want to do unto you (or unto themselves)," or "Don't do unto yourself what you don't want others to do unto you (or unto themselves)."

Ethical rules that are projective stimulate reciprocal altruism, but a crucial difference should be noted (see Kaufman, 1961; Nørretranders, 1998, for a philosophical and a neuropsychological discussion, respectively). It matters what it is that people are asked to project. By focusing on likes or gains, Christ's prescriptive rule allows errors. Because likes are less uniform than dislikes (preferences for sweet or dry vintages vary, whereas almost everyone dislikes a wine turned sour), would-be benefactors take the risk of doing unto others what those others do not like. When that happens, the resulting pain is larger than the intended pleasure (Kahneman & Tversky, 1984). Hillel's proscriptive rule minimizes the regret that follows from hurting others unwittingly. The errors that may arise from following this rule are not only fewer but also less serious (i.e., failing to identify and deliver a benefit).

PROJECTION, INTROJECTION, AND SOCIAL COMPARISON

Depending on one's theoretical orientation, social perceivers appear to be either irrational (FCE), statistically sophisticated (induction), or self-absorbed (egocentrism). All theories of social projection share the assumption, however, that a person's own responses not only predict consensus estimates but also *cause* them to be consistent with own responses. This is a strong claim, and objections to it must be considered. It is accepted, for example, that sometimes the direction of the causal path is inverted. Theories of social identity, self-categorization, and conformity seek to identify the conditions under which such "introjection" occurs (e.g., Oakes, Haslam, & Turner, 1994). When there is a correlation between own responses and consensus estimates, it is not clear to what extent it is produced by projection, introjection, or a combination of the two.

Perceptions of life span personality development illustrate this mix (Heckhausen & Krueger, 1993). When predicting (or postdicting) stability and change in their own personalities, people rely in part on normative expectations about life span development. Adults of all ages judge their own development as being similar to the development of "most other people." Introjection can be plausibly expected from young adults. They may find it relatively easy to forecast their own late-life development from the development of aging others whom they observe. Relevant egocentric information is truly missing. For older individuals, how-

---

[17]Sometimes projection is detrimental to interpersonal behavior and communication. Negotiators who project their own preferences onto their opponents often miss benefits because they fail to accommodate the other's divergent needs (Bottom & Paese, 1997).

ever, the assumed similarity with most others may be more projective. The elderly may find it easier to postdict normative developmental trends from their own remembered development.

Separating Projection from Introjection

To determine the relative strength of projection and introjection, Granberg and Brent (1983) studied the link between political preferences and expectations concerning the outcome of Presidential elections over time. Consistent with projection, expectations (i.e., consensus estimates) were more malleable than preferences. Preferences at time 1 predicted expectations at time 2 when preferences at time 2 were controlled (partial $r = .26$). In contrast, there was no evidence for a "bandwagon effect" (i.e., introjection). Expectations at time 1 did not predict preferences at time 2 when expectations at time 2 were controlled (partial $r = -.05$). Similarly, Bauman and Ennett (1996) found that when initial alcohol and tobacco use was controlled, peer behavior had little effect on subsequent substance use (rs about .10). Using experimental procedures, Cadinu and Rothbart (1996) provided some members of laboratory groups with self-relevant information (i.e., how they had scored on four types of tasks) and others with information about how the group had scored as a whole. The former relied heavily on self-relevant information to infer group scores (projection), whereas the latter relied only modestly on the group scores to predict their own (introjection).

These findings show that projection is stronger than introjection when both have an opportunity to occur at the same time. In some social situations, however, their interplay is dynamic, and the question is whether a projective bias still occurs after the attitudes of individual members have been changed by group pressures. When people have been recruited into a majority and know that they have, their projections might merely be accurate reflections of reality. Using small interacting groups, Latané and L'Herrou (1996) demonstrated the endurance of projection. Exchanging persuasive e-mail messages with four others, participants expected rewards for adopting the majority attitude. Most came to believe that they had joined the majority including many of those who had not. The inverse error was less frequent.

Projection as a Basis for Comparison

Since Festinger's (1954) original formulation, interpersonal similarity has been recognized as being necessary for comparison processes to unfold. I opened the present chapter with the claim that the *perception* of similarity is critical. The perception of similarities (and differences) permits the selection of some individuals for comparison (and the rejection of others). Armed with information about selected similar others, people can then appraise, evaluate, and adjust their self-concepts. The conundrum is how the similarity of others is judged when the self-concept is still unstable.

The evidence for social projection suggests that people already have some self-knowledge, although some of this knowledge may consist only of tentative feelings, hunches, or hypotheses. This knowledge, when it is projected onto others, constrains and complements social comparison processes (Suls, 1986). Without much thought, people assume most others to be similar to themselves so that they exclude only a minority of others from further comparisons. Depending on the motivational state of the perceiver, the expectation of similarity then leads to one of two conclusions. Either no further comparisons seem necessary, or they seem useful of the fine-tuning of the self-concept. The latter route may reveal the (in)accuracy of the projective perception. Perceivers need to take a closer look at the characteristics of others to determine whether they are as similar to themselves as they think they are

(Orive, 1988). If projection turns out to be false and the others are indeed quite different from the self, the social comparison process may be aborted; if projection turns out to be correct (as it should be in most cases), social comparison can proceed.

ACKNOWLEDGMENTS

I am indebted to Robyn Dawes for stimulating my thinking about social projection, to Rosamel Benavides and Judith Schrier for correcting my projective illusions about the readability of the first draft, and to Talia Ben-Zeev for reminding me that we can all be eccentric.

REFERENCES

Agostinelli, G., Sherman, S. J., Presson, C. C., & Chassin, L. (1992). Self-protection and self-enhancement biases in estimates of population prevalence. *Personality and Social Psychological Bulletin, 18*, 631–642.
Allport, F. H. (1924). *Social psychology.* Boston, MA: Houghton Mifflin.
Armor, D., & Taylor, S. E. (1998). Situated optimism: Specific outcome expectancies and self-regulation. *Advances in Experimental Social Psychology, 30*, 309–379.
Asch, S. E. (1952). *Social psychology.* New York: Prentice-Hall.
Bargh, J. A. (1982). Attention and automaticity in the processing of self-relevant information. *Journal of Personality and Social Psychology, 43*, 425–436.
Bauman, K. E., & Ennett, S. T. (1996). On the importance of peer influence for adolescent drug use: commonly neglected considerations. *Addiction, 91*, 185–198.
Biernat, M., Manis, M., & Kobrynowicz, D. (1997). Simultaneous assimilation and contrast effects in judgments of self and others. *Journal of Personality and Social Psychology, 73*, 254–269.
Bok, S. (1989). *Lying: Moral choice in public and private life* (2nd. ed.). New York: Vintage.
Bosveld, W., Koomen, W., & van der Pligt, J. (1994). Selective exposure and the false consensus effect: The availability of similar and dissimilar others. *British Journal of Social Psychology, 33*, 457–466.
Bosveld, W., Koomen, W., & van der Pligt, J. (1996). Estimating group size: Effects of category membership, differential construal and selective exposure. *European Journal of Social Psychology, 26*, 523–535.
Bosveld, W., Koomen, W., & Vogelaar, R. (1997). Construing a social issue: Effects on attitudes and the false consensus effect. *British Journal of Social Psychology, 36*, 263–272.
Bottom, W., & Paese, P. W. (1997). False consensus, stereotypic cues, and the perception of integrative potential in negotiation. *Journal of Applied Social Psychology, 27*, 1919–1940.
Bramel, D. (1962). A dissonance theory approach to defensive projection. *Journal of Abnormal and Social Psychology, 64*, 121–129.
Brown, C. E. (1996). False consensus bias and gender: The case of Judge Clarence Thomas. *Psychological Reports, 78*, 144–146.
Brunswik, E. (1955). Representative design and probabilistic theory. *Psychological Review, 62*, 236–242.
Cadinu, M. R., & Rothbart, M. (1996). Self-anchoring and differentiation process in the minimal group setting. *Journal of Personality and Social Psychology, 70*, 661–677.
Catrambone, R., Beike, D., & Niedenthal, P. (1996). Is the self-concept a habitual referent in judgments of similarity? *Psychological Science, 7*, 158–163.
Clement, R. W., & Krueger, J. (1998). Liking persons versus liking groups: A dual-process hypothesis. *European Journal of Social Psychology, 28*, 457–469.
Clement, R. W., & Krueger, J. (2000). The primacy of self-referent information in perceptions of social consensus. *British Journal of Social Psychology, 39*, 279–299.
Dawes, R. M. (1989). Statistical criteria for a truly false consensus effect. *Journal of Experimental Social Psychology, 25*, 1–17.
Dawes, R. M. (1990). The potential nonfalsity of the false consensus effect. In R. M. Hogarth (Ed.), *Insights in decision making: A tribute to Hillel J. Einhorn* (pp. 179–199). Chicago: University of Chicago Press.
Dawes, R. M., & Mulford, M. (1996). The false consensus effect and overconfidence: Flaws in judgment, or flaws in how we study judgment? *Organizational Behavior and Human Decision Processes, 65*, 201–211.
Dennett, D. C. (1996). *Kinds of minds.* New York: Basic Books.

DePaulo, B. M., & Friedman, H. S. (1998). Nonverbal communication. In D. T. Gilbert, S. T. Fiske, & G. Lindzey (Eds.), *Handbook of social psychology* (Vol. 2, pp. 3–40). Boston, MA: McGraw-Hill.

Dunning, D., & Hayes, A. F. (1996). Evidence for egocentric comparison in social judgment. *Journal of Personality and Social Psychology, 71,* 213–229.

Felson, R. B. (1993). The (somewhat) social self: How others affect self-appraisals. In J. M. Suls (Ed.), *The self in social perspective* (pp. 1–26). Hillsdale, NJ: Lawrence Erlbaum.

Fenigstein, A., & Abrams, D. (1993). Self-attention and the egocentric assumption of shared perspectives. *Journal of Experimental Social Psychology, 29,* 287–303.

Festinger, L. (1954). A theory of social comparison processes. *Human Relations, 7,* 117–140.

Fischhoff, B. (1975). Hindsight ≠ foresight: The effect of outcome knowledge on judgment under uncertainty. *Journal of Experimental Psychology: Human Perception and Performance, 1,* 288–299.

Forer, B. R. (1949). The fallacy of personal validation: A classroom demonstration of gullibility. *Journal of Abnormal and Social Psychology, 44,* 118–123.

Fuhrman, R. W., & Funder, D. C. (1995). Convergence between self and peer in the response-time processing of trait-relevant information. *Journal of Personality and Social Psychology, 69,* 961–974.

Gifford, R., & Hine, D. W. (1997). "I'm cooperative but you're greedy": Some cognitive tendencies in a commons dilemma. *Canadian Journal of Behavioural Science, 29,* 257–265.

Gigerenzer, G. (1991). From tools to theories: A heuristic of discovery in cognitive psychology. *Psychological Review, 98,* 254–267.

Gigerenzer, G., & Murray, D. J. (1987). *Cognition as intuitive statistics.* Hillsdale, NJ: Lawrence Erlbaum.

Gilbert, D. T. (1991). How mental systems believe. *American Psychologist, 46,* 107–119.

Gilovich, T., Jennings, D. L., & Jennings, S. (1983). Causal focus and estimates of consensus. *Journal of Personality and Social Psychology, 45,* 550–559.

Gilovich, T., Savitsky, K., & Medvec, V. H. (1998). The illusion of transparency: Biased assessments of others' ability to read one's emotional states. *Journal of Personality and Social Psychology, 75,* 332–346.

Goethals, G. R. (1986). Fabrication and ignoring social reality: Self-serving estimates of consensus. In J. M. Olson, C. P. Herman, & M. P. Zanna (Eds.), *Relative deprivation and social comparison: The Ontario symposium* (Vol. 4, pp. 135–158). Hillsdale, NJ: Lawrence Erlbaum.

Goethals, G. R., Messick, D. M., & Allison, S. T. (1991). The uniqueness bias: Studies of constructive social comparison. In J. Suls & T. A. Wills (Eds.), *Social comparison: Contemporary theory and research* (pp. 149–176). Hillsdale, NJ: Lawrence Erlbaum.

Granberg, D., & Brent, E. (1983). When prophecy bends: The preference–expectation link in US Presidential elections, 1952–1980. *Journal of Personality and Social Psychology, 45,* 477–491.

Hansen, R. D., & Donoghue, J. M. (1977). The power of consensus: Information derived from one's own and others' behavior. *Journal of Personality and Social Psychology, 35,* 294–302.

Heckhausen J., & Krueger, J. (1993). Developmental expectations for the self and most other people. *Developmental Psychology, 29,* 109–121.

Higgins, E. T. (1997). Biases in social cognition: "Aboutness" as a general principle. In C. McGarty & S. A. Haslam, *The message of social psychology: Perspectives on mind in society* (pp. 182–199). Oxford, England: Blackwell.

Hoch, S. J. (1987). Perceived consensus and predictive accuracy. *Journal of Personality and Social Psychology, 53,* 221–234.

Hoch, S. J., & Loewenstein, G. F. (1989). Outcome feedback: Hindsight and information. *Journal of Experimental Psychology: Learning, Memory, and Cognition, 15,* 605–619.

Humphrey, N. (June 1978). Nature's psychologists. *New Scientist, 29,* 900–904.

Kahneman, D., & Tversky, A. (1984). Choices, values, and frames. *American Psychologist, 39,* 331–350.

Katz, D., & Allport, F. (1931). *Students' attitudes.* Syracuse: Craftsman Press.

Kaufman, W. (1961). *The faith of a heretic.* New York, NY: Doubleday.

Kelley, C. M., & Jacoby, L. L. (1996). Adult egocentrism: Subjective experience versus analytic bases for judgment. *Journal of Memory and Language, 35,* 157–175.

Kenny, D. A., Bond, C. F., Jr., Mohr, C. D., & Horn, E. M. (1996). Do we know how much people like one another? *Journal of Personality and Social Psychology, 71,* 928–936.

Kerr, N. L. (1989). Illusions of efficacy: The effects of group size on perceived efficacy on social dilemmas. *Journal of Experimental Social Psychology, 25,* 287–313.

Keysar, B., Barr, D. J., & Balin, J. A. (1998). Definite reference and mutual knowledge: Process models of common ground in comprehension. *Journal of Memory and Language, 39,* 1–20.

Keysar, B., & Bly, B. (1995). Intuitions of the transparency of idioms: Can one keep a secret without spilling the beans? *Journal of Memory and Language, 34,* 89–109.

Klar, Y. (1996). Dysphoria and consensus estimates for behavioral choices: Equally inaccurate but in opposite directions. *Journal of Research in Personality, 30,* 278–289.

Klar, Y., & Giladi, E. E. (1999). Are most people happier than their peers or are they just happy? *Personality and Social Psychology Bulletin, 25,* 585–594.

Krueger, J. (1998a). On the perception of social consensus. *Advances in Experimental Social Psychology, 30,* 163–240.

Krueger, J. (1998b). The bet on bias: A foregone conclusion? *Psycoloquy, 9*(46). http://www.cogsci.soton.ac.uk/cgi/psyc/newpsy?9.46

Krueger, J. (1998c). Enhancement bias in the description of self and others. *Personality and Social Psychology Bulletin, 24,* 505–516.

Krueger, J., & Clement, R. W. (1994). The truly false consensus effect: An ineradicable and egocentric bias in social perception. *Journal of Personality and Social Psychology, 67,* 596–610.

Krueger, J., & Clement, R. W. (1996). Inferring category characteristics from sample characteristics: Inductive reasoning and social projection. *Journal of Experimental Psychology: General, 128,* 52–68.

Krueger, J., & Clement, R. W. (1997). Consensus estimates by majorities and minorities: The case for social projection. *Personality and Social Psychology Review, 1,* 299–319.

Krueger, J., Ham, J. J., & Linford, K. M. (1996). Perceptions of behavioral consistency: Are people aware of the actor-observer effect? *Psychological Science, 7,* 259–264.

Krueger, J., & Stanke, D. (in press). The role of self-referent and other-referent knowledge in perceptions of group characteristics. *Personality and Social Psychology Bulletin.*

Krueger, J., & Zeiger, J. S. (1993). Social categorization and the truly false consensus effect. *Journal of Personality and Social Psychology, 65,* 670–680.

LaPlace, P. S. (1814). *Essai philosophique sur les probabilites.* Paris: Courcier.

Latané, B., & L'Herrou, T. (1996). Spatial clustering in the conformity game: Dynamic social impact in electronic groups. *Journal of Personality and Social Psychology, 70,* 1218–1230.

Markus, H., & Kitayama, S. (1991). Culture and the self: Implications for cognition, emotion, and motivation. *Psychological Review, 98,* 224–253.

Meehl, P. E. (1977). The selfish voter paradox and the thrown-away vote argument. *American Political Science Review, 71,* 11–30.

Mele, A. R. (1997). Real self-deception. *Behavioral and Brain Sciences, 20,* 91–136.

Mulford, M., Orbell, J., Shatto, C., & Stockard, J. (1998). Physical attractiveness, opportunity, and success in everyday exchange. *American Journal of Sociology, 103,* 1565–1592.

Mullen, B., & Hu, L. (1988). Social projection as a function of cognitive mechanisms: Two meta-analytical integrations. *British Journal of Social Psychology, 27,* 333–356.

Nagel, T. (1967). *What does it all mean?* New York: Oxford University Press.

Nickerson, R. S., Baddeley, A., & Freeman, B. (1987). Are people's estimates of what other people know influenced by what they themselves know? *Acta Psychologica, 64,* 245–259.

Niedenthal, P. M., & Kitayama, S. (1994). *The heart's eye: Emotional influences in perception and attention.* San Diego, CA: Academic Press.

Nørretranders, T. (1998). *The user illusion..* New York: Viking.

Oakes, P. J., Haslam, S. A., & Turner, J. C. (1994). *Stereotyping and social reality.* Oxford, England: Blackwell.

Orive, R. (1988). Social projection and social comparison of opinions. *Journal of Personality and Social Psychology, 54,* 953–964.

Overbye, E. (1995). Making a case for the rational, self-regarding, "ethical" voter … and solving the "paradox of not voting" in the process. *European Journal of Political Research, 27,* 369–396.

Peterson, C. R., & Beach, L. R. (1967). Man as an intuitive statistician. *Psychological Bulletin, 68,* 29–46.

Pratto, F., & John, O. P. (1991). Automatic vigilance: The attention-grabbing power of negative social information. *Journal of Personality and Social Psychology, 61,* 380–391.

Quattrone, G. A., & Tversky, A. (1984). Causal versus diagnostic contingencies: On self-deception and on the Voter's Illusion. *Journal of Personality and Social Psychology, 46,* 237–248.

Regan, D. T., & Kilduff, M. (1988). Optimism about elections: Dissonance reduction at the ballot box. *Political Psychology, 9,* 101–107.

Ross, L., Greene, D., & House, P. (1977). The "false consensus effect": An egocentric bias in social perception and attribution processes. *Journal of Experimental Social Psychology, 13,* 279–301.

Ross, L., & Ward, A. (1996). Naïve realism in everyday life: Implications for social conflict and misunderstanding. In E. S. Reed, E. Turiel, & T. Brown (Eds.), *Values and norms: The Jean Piaget symposium* (pp. 103–135). Mahwah, NJ: Lawrence Erlbaum.

Rothbart, M., & Park, B. (1986). On the confirmability and disconfirmability of trait concepts. *Journal of Personality and Social Psychology, 50*, 131–142.

Shafir, E., & Tversky, A. (1992). Thinking through uncertainty: Nonconsequential reasoning and choice. *Cognitive Psychology, 24*, 449–474.

Sherman, S. J., Presson, C. C., Chassin, L., Corty, E., & Olshavsky, R. (1983). The false consensus effect in estimates of smoking prevalence: Underlying mechanisms. *Personality and Social Psychological Bulletin, 9*, 197–207.

Sloman, S. A. (1997). Categorical inference is not a tree: The myth of inheritance hierarchies. *Cognitive Psychology, 35*, 1–33.

Stanovich, K. E., & West, R. F. (1998). Individual differences in rational thought. *Journal of Experimental Psychology: General, 127*, 161–188.

Stone, P., & Kamiya, J. (1957). Judgments of consensus during group discussion. *Journal of Abnormal and Social Psychology, 55*, 171–175.

Suls, J. (1986). Notes on the occasion of social comparison theory's thirtieth birthday. *Personality and Social Psychology Bulletin, 12*, 289–296.

Suls, J., Wan, C. K., Barlow, D. H., & Heimberg, R. G. (1990). The fallacy of uniqueness: Social consensus perceptions of anxiety disorder patients and community residents. *Journal of Research in Personality, 24*, 415–432.

Tversky, A., & Kahneman, D. (1974). Judgment under uncertainty. Heuristics and biases. *Science, 185*, 1124–1131.

Wheeler, L. (1966). Motivation as a determinant of upward comparison. *Journal of Experimental Social Psychology* (Suppl. 1), 27–31.

Wilson, T., Houston, C. E., Etling, K. M., & Brekke, N. (1996). A new look at anchoring effects: Basic anchoring and its antecedents. *Journal of Experimental Psychology: General, 125*, 387–402.

Wood, J. V. (1989). Theory and research concerning social comparisons of personal attributes. *Psychological Bulletin, 90*, 245–271.

Wood, J. V. (1997). What is social comparison and how should we study it? *Personality and Social Psychology Bulletin, 22*, 520–537.

Wood, N., & Cowan, N. (1995). The cocktail party phenomenon revisited: How frequent are attention shifts to one's name in an irrelevant auditory channel? *Journal of Experimental Psychology: Learning, Memory, and Cognition, 21*, 255–260.

Wright, R. (1994). *The moral animal.* New York: Pantheon.

17

Social Judgment as Implicit Social Comparison

DAVID DUNNING

At first blush, this chapter will appear to be in the wrong book. The volume focuses on what theorists and researchers know and sometimes suspect about social comparison processes. By definition, these are processes by which people come to know and understand themselves through comparing themselves and their behavior with other people. Over the years, researchers have discovered quite a bit about what spurs people on to make social comparisons, the processes by which they make those comparisons, the people that they choose to compare themselves with, and the consequences of this comparison activity (for reviews beyond this volume, see Collins, 1996; Suls & Wills, 1991; Wills, 1981; Wood, 1989). These researchers have discovered that social comparison is a frequent and ubiquitous activity in the mental life of the social animal, with consequences for how people think about themselves and their social worlds. Indeed, these discoveries began with Leon Festinger's classic article on the topic in 1954, and the decades have diminished neither the importance nor the value of theories of social comparison.

However, in this chapter I am going to focus on the reverse. Instead of focusing on how people come to understand themselves via their comparisons with others, I will suggest that people often come to an understanding of other people by comparing those other people with themselves. I will argue that this egocentric comparison process in social judgment is a ubiquitous and frequent one, and that it carries many implications for how people come to understand their peers, their social worlds, and even themselves.

Thus, in the chapter, I set myself a threefold mission. The first part of the mission is to document that people do, indeed, commonly compare other people with themselves when striving toward understanding and evaluating them. The second part of the mission will be to explore why people so commonly engage in these egocentric comparison processes. The third part of the mission will be to explore contradictions and convergences between research on egocentric comparison processes and themes that arise from work on social comparison.

To presage my final argument a touch, I will ultimately suggest that research showing that

DAVID DUNNING • Department of Psychology, Cornell University, Ithaca, New York 14853-7601.

Handbook of Social Comparison: Theory and Research, edited by Suls and Wheeler. Kluwer Academic / Plenum Publishers, New York, 2000.

people often engage in egocentric comparison, the opposite of social comparison, actually increases the importance we as researchers place on social comparison processes, as well as the importance practitioners and laypersons should assign to these processes. That is, peel away the surface of social judgment a bit and one finds underneath an act of social comparison. Social judgment is often an implicit form of social comparison. As a consequence, the factors, processes, and mechanisms that influence social comparison also are those that influence social judgment. To understand social judgment, thus requires understanding social comparison.

EVIDENCE FOR EGOCENTRIC COMPARISON

Before Leon Festinger (1954) articulated the first tenets of social comparison theory, scholars and researchers in psychology had begun to see hints that the act of understanding others depends significantly on the self. Judgments of others tend to carry a heavy dose of the self. Such an observation came easily to early psychological theorists such as Hall (1898), James (1915), McDougall (1921), and Mead (1934). Other researchers asserted that the self was the central touchstone in the psychological field of the individual, and as such served as an important, if not *the* important, organizing principle of their understanding of the social world (Murphy, 1947; Rogers, 1951; Sullivan, 1947). Other theorists made more specific statements. For example, Baldwin (1902) ventured that people came to understand the personalities of others by coming to understand their own. Freud (1924/1956) suggested that people protected their own self-image by projecting unwanted aspects of the self onto others. Some theorists even speculated that judgments of others were commonly, if not always, influenced by how those others related to or compared with the self (Combs & Snygg, 1949; Krech & Crutchfield, 1948).

Patterns of Social Judgment Related to the Self

Empirical evidence soon began to align with these speculations about the self and social judgment. Over the decades, several phenomena emerged that suggested the self was related to, if not a pervasive influence over, social judgment (for a review, see Dunning, 1998).

For example, people tend to see others as similar to themselves. When describing other individuals, people tend to use the same trait terms as they do to describe themselves (Dornbusch, Hastorf, Richardson, Muzzy, & Vreeland, 1965; Lemon & Warren, 1974; Lewicki, 1984). They also tend to overestimate the commonness of their own responses and behaviors among the general population, in a phenomenon that became known as the *false consensus effect* (Ross, Greene, & House, 1977; for a review, see Marks & Miller, 1987), often seeing the behavior of others who act differently as strange or peculiar. Not even notions of abstract social concepts were immune to the presumed influence of the self. When people are asked to describe their prototype of what, for example, a leader or an intelligent person is, their descriptions tend to resemble themselves and their idiosyncratic strengths (Dunning & McElwee, 1995; Dunning, Meyerowitz, & Holzberg, 1989; Dunning, Perie, & Story, 1991).

In addition, in their impressions of others, people tend to emphasize those attributes that they believe they possess themselves. For example, those who believe that they are extraverted, relative to their less extraverted peers, tend to give more weight to whether or not another person is extraverted in their evaluations of that person. People also make more extreme, polarized, and confident judgments of others along a trait dimension if they feel they possess that trait themselves (Eiser & Mower White, 1974, 1975; Lambert & Wedell, 1991;

Markus & Smith, 1981). They also make many more inferences about other traits when given information on whether a person possesses a trait they consider self-descriptive than they do when given information about a trait they fail to consider self-descriptive (Alicke, 1993; Carpenter, 1988; Catambone & Markus, 1987; Markus, Smith, & Moreland, 1985).

Indeed, people's self-descriptive traits tend to be more "central" in their impressions of other people, in a phenomenon that has come to be known as the *self-image bias* (Lewicki, 1983). By central, I mean that a person's impression of another individual along that specific trait dimension in question is more closely correlated with his or her impressions along all other trait dimensions. To a person who holds extraversion to be central, his or her evaluation of another person's extraversion is more highly correlated with his or her evaluations of the other person's intelligence, social skill, ethics, and creativity, for example.

Taken together, these phenomena suggest that the self is related to social judgment in a common and pervasive way. If one wants to know how one person will judge another, one would go a long way toward anticipating those judgments by knowing how the person describes himself or herself. These phenomena also suggest, albeit more indirectly, that the self plays a causal role in how people reach social judgments. However, that last suggestion must be considered tentative, despite the voluminous data showing that the self is related to social judgment. Given the correlational data of the research reviewed above, conclusions about the causal role of the self in social judgment are made with some jeopardy.

How are we to conclude that the self, indeed, does influence social judgment? More to the point, how are we to conclude the central assertion that I make in this chapter, that the self influences social judgment because people compare the behavior of others to their own behavior as they evaluate those others? The research reviewed above only indirectly hints that people engage in egocentric comparison when making social judgments.

Egocentric Contrast Effects

I believe that the causal nature of the self in social judgment can be documented by focusing on one of the earliest and most repeatedly documented phenomenon in research on self and social judgment. Closely investigating this phenomenon provides the best evidence for the assertion that people ubiquitously compare others to themselves as they judge their ability and character.

The phenomenon in question is the egocentric contrast effect in social judgment. In the 1940s, researchers began to notice that the judgments people made about the attributes and behavior of others seemed related to their own. For example, among African Americans, judgments of the lightness or darkness of another's skin color depended on their own skin color (Marks, 1943). Judgments about whether another person was tall or short depended on the height of the person making the judgment (Hinckley & Rethlingshafer, 1951). Most typically, judgments were inversely correlated with the person's attributes. A short person, for example, tended to rate other people as tall. A tall person tended to rate other people as short.

Soon, such contrast effects were observed, accidentally, in the domain of attitudes. In trying to select items for a "Thurstone scale" on attitudes toward civil rights, Hovland and Sherif (1952), among others, discovered that perception of whether scale items were "pro-" or "anti-civil rights" depended importantly on the individual's own "pro" or "anti" attitudes. For example, given a moderate but tame statement in support of civil rights, individuals who considered themselves very "pro-civil rights" tended to see the statement as rather "anti." Individuals who were "anti-civil rights" tended to see the statement as "pro." Contrast effects were observed in a number of attitude domains, such as prohibition (Hovland, Harvey, &

Sherif, 1957; Sherif & Jackman, 1966), abortion (Corenblum & Corfield, 1976; Romer, 1983), the Arab–Israeli conflict (Prothro, 1955), and environmentalism (Bruvold, 1975).

In the 1990s, such contrast effects again were uncovered in completely different domains of social judgment. In their studies of traits and abilities, Dunning and Cohen (1992) found that a person's impression of the behavior and ability of others depended on his or her own behavior. Confronted with a target individual who occasionally arrived at their classes a little late, people who were never late to their classes found the target to be less punctual than did those who frequently came late to class. Those who studied roughly 6 hours every day saw a person who studied only 3 hours a day to be less studious than did those who studied only 1 hour per day. Again, contrast effects were observed in a number of studies in a wide variety of domains, such as math skill, studiousness, punctuality, and athletics.

But how are these contrast effects the best evidence that people think of themselves and their behaviors, achievements, and habits when judging those of others? In the 1960s, several researchers proposed explanations for the contrast effect that invoked some vague notion of egocentric comparison. For example, Sherif and Hovland (1961) suggested that the self serves as some sort of "anchor" in social judgment. However, that explanation seems to serve as more of a redescription of the effect than it does an explanation for it. Helson (1964) suggested that the self served as a neutral point that a person had adapted to. But again, there was little explication of how that adaptation took place, what it meant for the self to serve as a neutral point, and how this neutral point was evoked when it was time to judge someone.

Perhaps the most specific and clearly articulated explanation of the contrast effect came from Upshaw (1974) in his variable perspective account. This perspective focused on people who held extreme attitudes on an issue. He suggested that when these people rated the attitude statements of others and noticed that the rating scale failed to capture their own extreme attitude, they "stretched" the rating scale to include their own stance. The net effect of this strategy was to provide ratings of others that looked dissimilar from the self. However, again, this explanation was imperfect, in that it did not anticipate the ubiquity of the effect, specifically its operation in the judgments of people who did not hold extreme abilities.

Direct Evidence

It was with this background that Andrew Hayes and I decided to document, once and for all, the specific cognitive processes underlying the contrast effect (Dunning & Hayes, 1996). In doing so, we thought we could show that people were explicitly thinking of themselves while they judged others. We took our inspiration from recent work on *norm theory* (Kahneman & Miller, 1986), and proposed that when people judge others, they do not do so in isolation. They must compute some reference point or "norm" to compare the other person's behavior with. That is, they must think about other exemplar individuals and consider whether the target's behavior was more or less impressive than this comparison set. Further, we suggested that this norm or collection of individuals often includes information about the self and one's own behavior, since self-behavior is some of the most cognitive available information that people have in the social realm (Prentice, 1990).

Asking People.   We then conducted three studies demonstrating that people think about themselves and their own behavior as they judge the behavior of others. First, we did the simplest study to test our proposals (Dunning & Hayes, 1996: study 1). We presented participants with a description of a target individual. Strewn throughout the description was quantitative information about how the target behaved in several domains [e.g., the target played intramural basketball 3 hours every week, was late to class once per week, had gotten a 620 on his or her quantitative Scholastic Assessment Test (SAT) before entering college].

We asked participants to judge the target along a number of personality dimensions relevant to this quantitative data (e.g., athleticism, punctuality, math ability) and collected comparable information on how participants themselves performed in these domains. As expected, judgments of the target were correlated with participants' own behavior. For example, participants who spent several hours a week in athletic pursuits rated the target as less athletic than did those who had few fitness activities.

Of key concern was how participants answered two questions immediately after they had judged the target. In one vague question, we asked participants what they had thought of when providing judgments. Although the question contained no more explicit prod than this, 39% of participants explicitly stated that they thought about their own behavior as they judged the target. They also mentioned other comparison points, such as their acquaintances, population norms, and people similar to the target, but the primary type of information included in their "norm" was self-information. Buttressing the importance of thinking about the self, when we split participants into two groups based on whether or not they mentioned comparing the target to themselves on this question, those who mentioned such comparisons displayed stronger contrast effects than did those who did not.

The importance of egocentric comparison was further highlighted in a follow-up question. In a question that pointedly asked whether participants had compared the target with "anyone or anything," a full 70% of participants mentioned comparing the target to the self. To be sure, and again, participants mentioned other comparisons points (acquaintances, population norms, people similar to the target, people who exemplified the trait), but the self was the most frequently cited comparison person by far in answers to this query.

Reaction Time Evidence. However, Andy Hayes and I were leery of resting our case for egocentric comparison in social judgment with only the data from this one study. To be sure, asking participants how they reached their conclusions can be useful, but it has been well known for at least 20 years that people are far from perfect in their ability to describe the factors that influence their decisions (Nisbett & Wilson, 1977). Thus, we decided to see if we could find more "on-line" evidence of egocentric comparison that did not rely on explicit mentions of the process.

In two studies, we looked for evidence of egocentric comparison by observing the reaction times of people making self-reports. We surmised that if people think of their own behavior as they judge others in some domains, then asking them to judge another person in a domain should speed up their ability to report their own behavior in that domain. For example, after judging whether someone who studies 19 hours a week is studious, people should respond more quickly to a query about their own study habits.

The two studies we conducted that followed this logic proved supportive. In the first (Dunning & Hayes, 1996: study 2), participants judged a target in two critical domains (e.g., athletics, math skill). Afterward, when asked about their behavior, participants gave significantly quicker responses than they did in two control domains in which they offered no judgments (e.g., punctuality, studiousness). Again, overall, participants displayed contrast effects in their judgments.

More importantly, the contrast effect was stronger among participants who showed evidence of thinking about self-behavior as they judged the targets. That is, in each trait domain in which they had judged the target, we split participants into two equal-sized groups based on the reaction times they posted as they reported their own behavior. One group consisted of those who reported their own behavior quickly, and we presupposed that they had done so because they had thought of their own behavior as they judged the behavior of the target. The other group consisted of those who reported their behavior more slowly, and we presumed that these participants had been less likely to think of their own behavior than their faster peers. Thus, we expected the fast group, because they had more likely engaged in egocentric comparison, would exhibit greater contrast effects than the slow group. That was, indeed, what we found. The fast group, the one that had presumably thought about the self, showed a bigger degree of contrast than did the slow group. Figure 1 shows this difference by averaging the results we obtained across four different trait domains.

In a follow-up study (Dunning & Hayes, 1996: study 3), we provided more direct evidence that it was the self and the self's behavior that was recruited during the social judgment process. Critics looking over the study above could plausibly suggest that we had not observed "activation" of self-information but rather the operation of a general priming effect. That is, thinking about behavior in a certain domain (e.g., athletics) should make any type of information related to that domain more cognitively available. As a consequence, people should be quicker to answer *any* question related to that domain. Thus, we asked some participants to answer questions about a distant acquaintance after judging a target individual. A priming

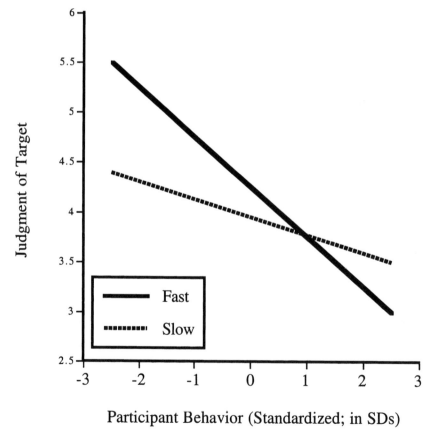

Figure 1. Relationship between self-performance and judgments of another person's traits, depending on speed with which participant's could report their own behavior. Derived from data in Dunning and Hayes (1996: study 2).

account of our results predicted that providing judgments of others would speed people up in their reports about this acquaintance. Our account predicted that no facilitation in reaction times would occur, because these distant acquaintance (unlike the self) would rarely appear in the norm people constructed to judge the behavior of the target.

The data suggested that we were right. Providing judgments of the target failed to speed subsequent reports of an acquaintance's behavior. However, and again, providing judgments of another person caused people to report their own behavior more quickly, furnishing evidence once again that people thought about their own behavior as they judged that of others.

WHY EGOCENTRIC COMPARISON?

So far, so good. Indeed, so straightforward. Evidence from studies of the contrast effect and the specific evidence of direct egocentric comparison in Dunning and Hayes (1996) suggests that people commonly think of themselves and their own behavior as they judge others.

However, if one steps back from these data and considers the totality of research in social psychology over the past 30 years, one soon finds a mystery that at first is difficult to explain. In many different studies done in many different ways, researchers have found that people ignore or at best give little weight to a type of information that is like self-information but is clearly more informative for social judgment. That type of information is consensus information, which traditionally is defined as information about what other people do in relevant situations (Kelley, 1967). For example, when hearing that Arnold tripped over Linda's feet at a dance and fell down, the listener might consider the question as to whether Arnold is clumsy. To answer that question accurately, Arnold should find out and consider how many other people who have danced with Linda have tripped over her feet. If few have, then Arnold is clumsy. If many have, then the problem may rest with Linda and not with Arnold.

Several studies concerning consensus information have shown that people give it short shrift. People give little weight to consensus information when making attributions for another person's behavior (McArthur, 1976; Nisbett & Borgida, 1975), making predictions about how a person might behave (Dunning, Griffin, Milojkovic, & Ross, 1990; Vallone, Griffin, Lin, & Ross, 1990), and when judging the confidence with which they make those predictions (Dunning et al., 1990; Vallone et al., 1990). To be sure, some researchers have dissented from this overall conclusion, showing that people do pay attention to consensus information in some situations (Smith, Hilton, Kim, & Garonzik, 1992), or when the information is presented in a certain way (Kassin, 1979; Wells & Harvey, 1977), or for some tasks (Windschitl & Wells, 1997). Others have suggested that consensus information should be ignored in the evaluation of the traits of others (Windschitl & Wells, 1997).

However, despite these critiques, the same puzzle emerges: Why do people use information about their own behavior so commonly in judgments of others in situations in which they give little or no weight to consensus information, even when it is provided for them? More to the point, why do they so commonly use self-information when what the self does provides only one data point of what people do in a given situation? Consensus information, by definition, must be a more accurate statistical norm of how people react to common situations and everyday domains, yet people appear not to think about this type of information or tend to use it when it is proffered to them. Thus, why all the enthusiasm about what is only a pale shadow of consensus information (what the self does) and the lack of enthusiasm for the real thing?

For example, the neglect of consensus information in deference to self is evident in one of our early studies on egocentric contrast effects. In that study (Dunning & Cohen, 1992: study 6) we decided to see whether providing people with consensus information would stop them from using the self in social judgment. Thus, for roughly half our participants, we provided them information about the behavior of students at their university in the trait domains we asked them about. For example, we told them that 90% of students received at least a 610 on the quantitative SAT, 75% more than 635, 50% more than 680, 25% more than 710, and 10% more than 740. We then presented them with a target whose behavior fell exactly on the 50th percentile in each domain. We then asked them to judge the target and also collected information on their own behavior.

Once again, across all participants in the study, judgments of the target were correlated with the participant's own behavior. More importantly, the correlation failed to be any weaker (mean $r = -.25$) among participants giving consensus information than it was among a control group of participants who received no consensus information (mean $r = -.27$). More to the point, participants correctly perceived the target's behavior to fall in the 50th percentile (we asked them), but knowing this fact failed to undo the relationship between self and social judgment.

Some Candidate Explanations

There, then, is the mystery: If people so often avoid using consensus information in their social judgments, why do they so commonly use a piece of information that arguably is a questionable proxy for that information? There are many possible ways to explain away this mystery. Consider the following candidates.

Normative Considerations.   First, people might use self-information because it is normative and appropriate to do so. In order to disambiguate and evaluate the meaning of another person's behavior, one must consider how other people would behave in the same environment. Thus, it is normative to consider one's own behavior because it provides a data point on how people behave. Statistical analyses have borne out the wisdom of this normative analysis (Dawes, 1989; Krueger, 1998; Chapter 16, this volume), and studies have shown that people make more accurate predictions of others if they presume that others will behave as they do themselves (Dunning et al., 1990). More than that, assuming that other people would behave differently not only increases error, but also unanticipated error (Dunning et al., 1990).

However, the observation that it is normative to use the self as a data point against which to judge the behavior of others does little to answer the specific question under consideration here. If it is normative to use the self as a data point, then it also must be normative to use consensus information as well, yet people more enthusiastically employ self-information than they do consensus information (e.g., Dunning & Cohen, 1992: study 4). So why the selective use of only self-information?

In addition, in other research in which the power of self and consensus information has been compared, self-information tends to have an influence over social judgment that goes beyond its status as a single data point. As data points go, some data points are more equal than others, and self-information is given more weight than comparable information about other people. For example, in recent studies of the false consensus effect, which refers to the tendency to overestimate the prevalence of one's own behaviors and preferences, people tend to give their own behavior more weight in estimates of consensus than they do any other. For example, if a person prefers Chinese food over Italian food and learns that another individual in his or her social group prefers the opposite, his own preference is given more weight in estimates of what other people will prefer than will the data point coming from the other person (Krueger & Clement, 1994). Thus, the normative status of self-information does not explain its use over the use of consensus information.

Availability.   Second, one could propose that people want to use consensus information in their everyday lives but that it is often unavailable to them. As a consequence, they use what is available and that is their own behavior (Prentice, 1990). This explanation is akin to the old joke of the person who comes across a friend who is on hands and knees on Eighth Avenue scouring the sidewalk for something. When the person asks her friend what he is doing, he replies that he lost his contact on Sixth Avenue. Puzzled, the person asks "Then why are you looking here?" To which the friend replies that the light is better over here.

However, this availability explanation fails as a complete explanation of the use of self-information over consensus information. It implies that people would stop using self-information and would instead embrace consensus information if that information were made available. Unfortunately, that is not what occurs (e.g., Dunning & Cohen, 1992: study 4). In studies in which people are explicitly provided consensus information, they often ignore it in their attributions, judgments, and predictions (for a review, see Kassin, 1979).

A Bias toward Upward Comparisons.   Third, the neglect of consensus information and the enthusiasm for self-information may lie in other considerations. Consider the following thought experiment. If you wanted to know if Johnny studies enough at college, which comparison person would you want information about to aid in your judgment: the student who just made Phi Beta Kappa or a student who just dropped out?

My intuition is that you would want to know about the successful student more than the dropout, and this may explain why people ignore consensus information. When judging others, people may not want to know how "any" other person behaved in the relevant situation. Rather, they may only want to know how reasonable, successful, proficient, and moral individuals respond. This reasoning receives some indirect support in work on social comparison. When people wish to evaluate themselves objectively on some task and are given the chance to compare themselves with others who completed the same task, they show a bias toward selecting people who turned in performances that are superior to their own and away from people who turned in inferior performances (e.g., Gruder, 1977; Wheeler, 1966). That is, there is a general bias toward "upward" comparison, or rather toward people who show some competence or facility in the domain under consideration.

This bias toward comparisons with competent individuals may explain the bias toward egocentric comparison and the relative neglect of consensus information. When given consensus information, one does not know the degree to which the responses come from reasonable and honorable people. However, for the self, the picture is clearer. People tend to think of themselves as lovable and capable people, more so than they should really allow themselves to think (Alicke, 1995; Dunning et al., 1989; Weinstein, 1980), and so they may think that comparing others to the self ensures an upward comparison to a proficient and reasonable individual, and thus a comparison that is more informative than one to anybody.

Causal Information.   As well, consider the fact that people fail to consider consensus information when it is presented to them as a simple statistical summary, but do use it when causal explanations for the consensus data are provided. For example, in making judgments about a student who failed an exam, people will give little weight to the fact that 75% of students in the class failed the exam until it is pointed out to them that this means the exam was difficult, and thus a likely causal agent of anybody's failure (Ajzen, 1977).

A similar process may explain why people use the self in social judgment. Being told that 50% of university students study more than 19 hours per week may strike people as a pallid statistical factoid. However, when considering how much they themselves study, students recognize that statistic as coming from a web of situational and personal factors that produce it (e.g., you have to study a lot, the classes are so hard; professors ask for so much reading; there isn't that much else to do on a Sunday night). Thus, that is a statistic that has a causal explanation, which can then be brought to bear on judgments of other people (e.g., how can that person study only 5 hours a week; how do they expect to do well?).

The Symbolic Management of Social Judgment

However, there is one explanation for the use of self-information and the neglect of consensus information that I feel is important and that has been supported by data from our laboratory. That explanation centers on *who* exactly is being judged when people proffer judgments of others. In our experiments, the answer to that question would seem to be obvious beyond belief. We asked participants to judge the target individual we presented to them and provided the scales that specified which traits were to be judged and how their impressions were to be reported, and our participants complied with our requests.

However, I wish to suggest that the target was not the only person being judged as participants confronted our questionnaires and struggled with their answers. Through their ratings of the target, participants were not only making statements about the target but also about themselves. Even though we did not ask participants to describe or judge themselves, participants understood that the conclusions they reached about the target said something about their own habits and achievements. As a consequence, they managed or fashioned their judgments of the target to insure that the (hidden) judgment about the self would be a positive one. They made sure that the judgments they made about the target reflected back on the self.

I would term this activity the *symbolic management* of social judgment. People are wary of what their judgments say about themselves, even when the self is not being evaluated in any explicit or public way, and so tailor their judgments to portray an image of the self that they want to portray. This symbolic management perspective accounts for many of the nuances of how the self is related to and presumably influences social judgment (for a review, see Dunning, 1998).

For example, consider the false consensus effect described above. It is a pervasive phenomenon, save one exception. Whereas people grossly overestimate the commonness of their own shortcomings, they fail to do so for attributes that they consider their strengths (Campbell, 1986; Marks, 1984; Mullen & Goethals, 1990; although see how Krueger & Clement, 1997, have appropriately called some empirical demonstrations of this assertion into question). From a symbolic management perspective, such a waxing and waning of the false consensus effect is to be expected. By claiming that their shortcomings are common, people diminish the importance of those failings. By claiming that their strengths are unusual, people maintain self-impressions that they are uniquely competent individuals.

Evidence from Egocentric Contrast Effects.   The symbolic management perspective also explains the waxing and waning of the contrast effect in social judgment. Take as an example the results of study 4 of Dunning and Cohen (1992). In this study, we explored whether the contrast effect would be the strongest when people confronted a target individual who posted a low, medium, or high performance. For example, in the domain of athleticism, we presented participants with a target who spent only an hour a week in athletic pursuits (low target), or a target who spent 3 hours per week in such pursuits (medium target), or one who spent 12 hours (high target). We had some modest expectations that the medium target would elicit the strongest contrast effect (after all, the high target was obviously high and the low one was obviously low), but that is not what we found.

What we found is displayed in Fig. 2, based loosely on data we gathered in the domains we examined of athleticism, math skill, and studiousness. As seen in the figure, it was the low target that elicited the strongest contrast, followed by the medium target. The high target was viewed favorably by all participants and did not elicit a contrast effect.

Why did low target elicit the strongest contrast effect? A symbolic management perspective can explain this result rather easily by contrasting the responses of participants whose behavior fell on the low end of the scale with those whose behavior fell on the high end. Consider those on the low end and how their responses reflect back on themselves. They rated all targets favorably, regardless of performance. In doing so, they could preserve their own claim to possess the traits in question themselves. They could continue to think of themselves as athletic, studious, and skilled in math (see Chapter 14, this volume; Alicke, LoSchiavo, Zerbst, & Zhang, 1997, for similar data and analysis). No such preservation need take place for participants whose behavior fell at the high end of the scale. They know they are mathematically skilled or athletic. To heighten their own sense of competence and achievement, they

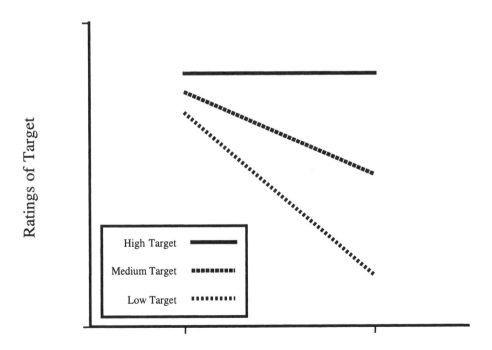

Perceiver's Own Performance

Figure 2. Typical relationship between self-performance and judgments of other people, depending on whether those other people post high, medium, or low performances.

must emphasize the exclusivity of their behavior and performances. They can do this by denigrating the performances of others to the extent that those performances allow. As could be seen in the data from Dunning and Cohen (1996: study 4), that is exactly what they did.

Evidence from Threats to Self-Esteem.   More recently, we have collected data that more directly implicates the desire to think well of one's self in the production of the contrast effect. Keith Beauregard and I (Beauregard & Dunning, 1998) decided to test whether threatening self-esteem would exacerbate the contrast effects we observed, compared with a situation in which we bolstered self-esteem. If the contrast effect occurs because people are buttressing or maintaining favorable self-images of themselves, then this tendency should be especially apparent when those favorable self-images have been called into question. I had employed this strategy successfully in another series of studies looking at the motivational bases of self-serving definitions of traits (Dunning, Leuenberger, & Sherman, 1995).

In three studies, Beauregard and I exposed participants to either a success or failure experience (Beauregard & Dunning, 1998). In particular, in the first two studies we asked participants to take a short test of their "integrative orientation ability," an intellectual skill that was not assessed via standard tests of intelligence. (Of course, there is no such thing as integrative orientation ability in reality). We told participants that having the skill might prove important to them in the future, since tests of the ability were just about to be added to exams (e.g., the Graduate Record Examination, Law Scholastic Aptitude Test, Medical College Admissions Test) that helped students qualify for graduate or professional schools after their undergraduate days. Roughly half the participants were given an easy version of the test and they did quite well. Roughly half were given a very difficult version of the test, on which they rarely answered more than one item correctly.

Of key interest was how these failure and success experiences would influence participants' judgments of a target individual while they took a break before confronting a second version of the integrative orientation test. Participants were given a description of a target individual that included, among a number of other pieces of information, data on his or her score on the SAT. Among the many personality judgments participants were asked to make of the target was a question on how "intelligent" they found the target to be. Of course, for all participants, we had data on their own scores on the SAT test, and thus could assess the extent to which they judged the intelligence of the target based on how well his or her SAT scores compared with their own.

In the failure conditions of both studies, we found strong contrast effects, in that judgments of the target's intelligence depended significantly on the participant's own SAT score. Participants who possessed low SAT scores themselves rated the target as rather intelligent (implicitly preserving their own claim to intelligence); high SAT participants rated the target as more unintelligent (thus emphasizing their exclusivity and meaningfulness of their own SAT score). After success in both studies, no such contrast effect arose. Instead, all participants, regardless of their own SAT score, rated the target as intelligent.

Extension to Attitudes.   A third study extended this symbolic management perspective to judgments of attitude (Beauregard & Dunning, 1998: study 3). We hypothesized that attitudes for many people act like abilities, in that people like to see themselves as unique and accomplished in the attitudes they adopt as a way of bolstering or maintaining self-esteem. They wish to think of themselves as part of an elect who have found the true and objective way to think about the world. In this regard, seeing another person who thinks a little bit differently might be enough to cause people who care about their attitudes to see this other person as "different." Indeed, we may go so far as to label the person as inferior.

We decided to test these ideas by seeing how judgments of another person's attitudes were influenced by failure and success experiences. Relative to those confronting a success experience, would people experiencing failure see another person who adopted a moderate attitudinal stance as more different from and inferior to themselves? In several psychology and human development classes at Cornell University, we identified a number of individuals who viewed themselves as very "pro-choice" on the issue of abortion rights and who felt the attitude was an important part of their self-definition. We then exposed some of these pro-choice participants to failure and some to success experiences with the integrative orientation test.

While on a break waiting to take a second version of the test, we asked them to pass the time by passing some judgments on a target individual. In particular, this target had written an essay explaining his or her position on abortion rights. The position the target had adopted was rather a complex, nuanced, and tortured one that endorsed the right to have an abortion but that also the idea of several limits on obtaining one (e.g., parental notification for minors, a 24-hour waiting period). Participants were asked first how "pro-choice" or "pro-life" the essay was. Participants in the failure condition were more likely to view the essay as different from their own stance, rating it as more pro-life than did their success counterparts. They also rated it directly as less similar to their own stance on the issue. Moreover, they rated the essay as less reasonable and more biased than did their success peers.

A Side Note: On Abilities and Attitudes.   Beyond affirming our analysis that people manage their judgments of others in order to maintain desired impressions of self, study 3 of Beauregard and Dunning (1998) made another point of some relevance to work on social comparison. From the days of Festinger (1954), theorists made a bright line distinction between abilities on the one hand and attitudes (or opinions) on the other. People are motivated to think their abilities are distinct and superior from others (Wills, 1981), or at least work toward that end (Festinger, 1954). However, with attitudes, people are motivated to think of others as being similar to themselves. That is, to validate one's attitudes, one would want to believe that everyone else thought the same way (Campbell, 1986; Marks, 1984; Tesser & Campbell, 1983).

Beauregard and Dunning (1998: study 3) called the firmness of this distinction between abilities and attitudes into question (echoing comments made in classic reviews of social psychology, such as Jones & Gerard, 1967). In that study, we showed that people at times handle their attitudes just like they handle their abilities: They are motivated to think of themselves as distinct and superior. That is, we threatened the self-esteem of some partici-pants, and their response was not to validate their attitudes by seeing another person as similar to themselves but to see that person as different, as well as biased and misguided. Thus, attitudes can act like abilities. At times, in order to affirm their self-worth, people can see themselves as distinctly correct and able in their ability to hold uniquely the correct attitude toward important issues. This observation should hardly be read as an argument for abolishing the distinction between attitudes and abilities, but it does suggest that that researcher should be mindful that at times the distinction does not hold.

Another Side Note: Emotional Consequences.   It should be mentioned that these studies of the egocentric contrast effect under self-esteem threat leave open one question that we have not yet addressed but that is of the highest importance. We presume that people judge others in a self-serving way to bolster self-esteem, but as of yet we have not demonstrated that judging others in this way actually influences or changes self-esteem. After denigrating the behavior of others, do people feel good (or at least better) about themselves, either in terms of the image they possess of themselves or the emotions they feel?

To date, there has been only one study, related to our work, that looks at the consequences of self-serving judgment for self-image and affect. This study comes from the work of Alicke and colleagues (Chapter 14, this volume; Alicke et al., 1997) on the "genius effect," or the tendency people have of extolling the virtues of those who outperform them in order to give themselves room to rate themselves as "pretty good." In one clever study, Alicke and colleagues compared the self-images of participants who had been given the chance to praise the intelligence of a person who had outperformed them in an intellectual task against the self-images of participants given no such chance. Participants given the chance to judge the other person reported feeling more intelligent themselves than did participants not given such a chance, suggesting that judgments of others can have consequences for judgments of self.

However, to date, we know of no study that has looked at the opposite situation of comparison, that is, how people will feel about themselves after being given the chance to denigrate the talents of a person whom they outperform? Will people rate themselves more positively after judging an inferior other, and what emotions will they feel? In regards to emotion, it is instructive to consider the thoughts outlined by Smith (Chapter 10, this volume) on the emotional fallout of social comparison. In essence, when people denigrate the skills of inferior performers, they are constructing downward social comparisons. According to Smith, there are a wealth of emotions that an individual can feel after engaging in downward comparisons. They can feel pride toward themselves and contempt for the other.

More intriguing, they can feel a syndrome of emotions that he labeled *schadenfreude*, which is a sense of pleasure at the misfortune of others. Tellingly, Smith reports that feelings of *schadenfreude* are evoked the most by downward comparisons if a person had been feeling aversive emotions (e.g., jealousy) just before the comparison took place. In this regard, it would be interesting to see what emotions were felt by participants in our failure conditions above (Beauregard & Dunning, 1998). They had just experienced an aversive event that called their intellectual skills into question. Does seeing the inferior performance of another on the SAT cause them to feel a sort of pleasure that comes from viewing the "misfortune" of another? This is a hypothesis worthy of further study.

The Role of Favorable Self-Views.   Finally, we have conducted an experiment that provided convergent evidence that people validate themselves through their judgments of others, and that it is this self-validational activity that produces the contrast effect in social judgment. My central thesis is that people shape their perceptions of other people to preserve favorable images they have of themselves. Of course, this presupposes that people have favorable self-images. But what about those who fail to have such favorable self-images to maintain? If the symbolic management perspective is correct, these individuals should fail to reach judgments that reflect favorably on themselves. As a consequence, the pattern of judgments these people display should differ from their peers who do possess positive self-images.

Thus, Beauregard and I set out to see whether only people with positive self-images would show self-validational contrast effects in their judgments of others (Dunning & Beauregard, in press). Our starting point was the specific pattern of contrast effects found in study 4 of Dunning and Cohen (1992). Recall that in that study, we found that targets posting low performances tended to elicit the largest contrast effect, with low-achieving participants rating those targets positively and high-achieving ones rating the target more negatively. All participants saw targets who posted high performances in a favorable light. We wondered whether we could replicate this pattern only among participants who judged themselves favorable in the relevant trait domain. Among participants who viewed themselves negatively, we expected no such pattern. Indeed, we expected no contrast effect at all.

Thus, we pretested hundreds of Cornell University undergraduates on the Texas Social Behavior Inventory, a test of a person's beliefs about his or her social competence. We identified a number of people who scored high on this scale and a number who scored low. We brought them into the laboratory to have them take a test of social skill. The test consisted of looking at 25 pairs of suicide notes. In each pair, one of the suicide notes was authentic and one was fake, and participants had to decide which was which. Their score on the test was rigged, and they achieved a score of either 21 or 13 on the test.

After completing the test and receiving their score, participants rated themselves on a number of follow up questions, including questions of how socially perceptive, a good judge of character, socially competent, and socially confident they themselves were. They then were asked to give "control ratings" for two other individuals who had completed the social skills test earlier in the day. One of the individuals had posted a score of 19; the other had posted a score of 15.

Table 1 displays the responses of positive and negative self-view participants as a function of their own self-view, their performance on the test, and the performance of the target individuals. As can be seen in the table, positive self-view participants replicated the pattern uncovered in Dunning and Cohen (1992: study 4). The low-performing target elicited the strongest contrast effect, with participants who themselves scored low rating the target more favorable than did their counterparts who scored high. In short, participants with low scores rated both targets high, presumably to preserve their claim of possessing social skills themselves. Participants with high scores rated the target less favorably, presumably to heighten the distinctiveness of their own score and their own ability in social domains.

Table 1. Ratings of High and Low Target's Social Skills as a Function of Participants' Self-Views on Social Skills and Their Performance on the Suicide Note Task[a]

	Participant performance[b]		
Target performance	Low	High	Difference
High self-view participants			
High	6.2	5.9	0.3
Low	5.8	4.7	1.1*
Low self-view participants			
High	5.7	5.2	0.5
Low	5.0	4.7	0.3

[a]From Dunning & Beauregard (in press).
[b]Ratings of target social skill could range from 1 to 7, with higher numbers indicating more skill.
*$p < .0001$.

For negative self-view participants, a simpler picture emerged. Nothing happened. Judgments of the targets were not influenced by the participant's own performance on the suicide note task. There was no disparagement of the target who performed more poorly than the participants themselves did. The only effect to emerge was that the low performing target was viewed less favorably than the high performing one, which is not a surprise.

Summary.   In sum, the research reviewed above all converges toward two main conclusions. First, people commonly engage in egocentric comparison as they judged others. This was revealed first by the contrast effects we observed in social judgment. It was more directly revealed in studies in which we explored whether people explicitly thought of their own behavior as they judged others. They could more quickly report their own behavior after judging that of others, indicating that they had compared their own behavior to that of others when they provided evaluations of those others. They also explicitly admitted that they engaged in egocentric comparison.

Second, people fashion their judgments of others to maintain positive images of self and enhance self-esteem. Participants extolled the virtues of those who outperformed them, presumably to permit them to enhance their own self-image as much as possible. They denigrated the performances of those who performed more poorly than they themselves did, presumably to enhance the exclusivity of their own achievements. Importantly, this management of social judgment in the service of self-regard was greater when self-esteem was threatened. It was also evident only among participants who had positive self-images to maintain.

CONTRADICTIONS AND CONVERGENCES WITH SOCIAL COMPARISON RESEARCH

As noted at the outset of this chapter, the work reviewed above presents a direct prima facie contradiction with work on social comparison. We have suggested that a common activity that people engage in is the act of egocentric comparison. Given information about other people, people evoke information about themselves to reach a judgment. However, social comparison work has suggested the exact opposite, that the common activity people engage in is gathering information about other people to learn about the self.

Needless to say, this basic contradiction is more apparent than real. People can commonly engage in both self- and social comparison processes. The fact that social comparison is ubiquitous does not preclude people from frequently engaging in egocentric comparison processes. People have opportunities to do both many times each and every day.

When Do People Engage in Egocentric versus Social Comparison?

But given this, what activity do people engage in when there is a choice between engaging in a self- or a social comparison process? What will determine when people will decide to judge the other person (thus engaging in egocentric comparison) and when they decide to think about or rethink the self (and thus engage in social comparison)? There are many plausible factors to consider.

The Mandate of the Situation.   First, sometimes people are thrust into situations that mandate one type of comparison over the other. Sometimes, people are obligated to judge others. An academic department starts a job search for a new faculty and interviewees are selected to visit. In that situation, each faculty person is compelled to judge the qualifications and potential of each interviewee. In the process, each is likely to engage in some egocentric comparison. However, at other times, people are compelled to evaluate themselves. Graduate students who are about to apply for academic jobs may compare themselves to their peers and to the faculty around them to gauge their chances at employment. In so doing, they engage in social comparison.

Self-Certainty.   Other factors may influence when people engage in self- versus social comparison more indirectly. The central principle that guided Festinger's (1954) original proposal was the belief that people wish to reduce any uncertainty they possess about their skills and opinions. As subsequent work has shown, the desire to reduce uncertainty about one's self is a powerful determinant of the search for information about the self (Trope, 1986). Thus, it is likely that people are the most likely to engage in social comparison when they are the most uncertain about themselves; when they have little sense of whether they are competent or incompetent in the trait domain under consideration.

It also is this instance in which people are least likely to engage in egocentric comparison. Two reasons suggest that people will not engage in egocentric comparison when they are uncertain about themselves. First, self-behavior in the face of uncertainty is uninformative in social judgment. If someone does not know whether he or she is competent in a trait domain, then information about his or her behavior will not help in any evaluation of others. Second, people engage in egocentric comparison in order to validate images they already possess of themselves (Beauregard & Dunning, 1998; Dunning & Beauregard, in press). If a person does not possess a clear image of his or her ability, then that person has no self-impression to maintain or bolster through egocentric comparison.

Self-Favorability.   Notions of self-validation suggest that the favorability of one's self-image will play a role similar to that of certainty. That is, people may engage in egocentric comparison when they have a favorable view of themselves. By so doing, they can evoke a sense of self-esteem and competence. However, when they possess unfavorable views of self, they may avoid egocentric comparisons. Recall that the pattern of data we saw in Dunning and Beauregard (in press) suggested that this analysis may be valid. When participants had positive views of their own social skills, their performance on a test of social skills had a significant impact on their evaluations of the social skills of others, in ways that suggested they were striving to validate their positive self-images. When participants possessed more negative views of their own social skills, no evidence of egocentric comparison was found in the judgments they rendered about others. Instead, their judgments of the social skills of others were driven primarily by how well those others had performed on tests of social skills, without being "contaminated" by how well they themselves had performed on the same tests.

Lessons from Social Comparison Work for Research on Social Judgment

The work above also suggests that social comparison research has much to say to researchers focused on social judgment. Curiously, work on how people come to judge themselves (e.g., social comparison) and research on how they come to evaluate others have often started from different premises, developed along different avenues, and sometimes come to different conclusions about how people carry out their cognitive tasks. In looking at social comparison research in general and the specific empirical studies reviewed above, one sees many lessons that research on social judgment could earn from social comparison theorists. Consider the following.

Social Judgment Is Relational.   The genius in the original proposals by Festinger (1954) on social comparison was the recognition that people do not judge themselves in isolation, but must compare their behavior with either objective or social standards. Self-judgment is relational. Such judgments rest on how the self compares in relation to some standard. The notion that judgment is relational is one that has been made in a number of research domains, often with important implications. For example, prospect theory showed how economic decisions are often significantly influenced by the specific reference points that people compare their economic options with (Kahneman & Tversky, 1979). People's emotional reactions are shaped not so much by the events they encounter, but by the counterfactual alternatives that these events evoke (Roese & Olson, 1995).

Curiously, the observation that judgment is often relational has largely been absent in work on judgments of others. Rarely do researchers ask what standards or norms people use to compare target individuals as they judge them (for an exception, see Higgins & Lurie, 1983). Our work on egocentric contrast effects suggests that social cognitive researchers should take the relational nature of social judgment more seriously and strive to find the standards, norms, and comparison points that people use as they judge others. In our work, we found that the self was a common reference point, but is that the only one? Do other common or important reference points exist? Are reference points like the self used when clear objective standards are available? Our research has only scratched a number of issues related to the relational nature of social judgment.

Social Judgment Is Motivated.   Glancing through the literature on social comparison, one is struck by how much of it is guided by concerns over motivation. What motives prompt people to compare themselves with others? Researchers have found many candidates. People engage in social comparison to learn about themselves (Festinger, 1954; Wood, 1989). They compare upward with superior performers in order to improve themselves (Wood, 1989). They compare downward (and occasionally upward) to bolster a sense of self-mastery and esteem (Wills, 1981). They compare to verify beliefs, either positive or negative, they possess about themselves (Hegelson & Mickelson, 1995). They compare to forge a common bond with others (Helgeson & Mickelson, 1995) or to bask in some sort of reflected glory (Pelham & Wachsmuth, 1995; Tesser, 1988). In short, social comparison work has focused to a large extent on what goals people wish to fulfill as they judge others.

Motives Attending Judgment.   Curiously, research on social judgment has neglected work on how motivations influence judgments of others. To be sure, some explorations on the motivational basis of social cognition has been done (for reviews, see Dunning, in press; Pittman, 1998), but for the prototypical social cognitive experiment, the issue of motivation is not emphasized or addressed. Commonly, researchers just assume that people judge others to satisfy a simple appetite for knowledge (Dunning, 1999). Or, they assume nothing. The issue of motivation is subverted by handing participants questionnaires specifying some judgments to be made, and then furnishing the target to be judged. In these circumstances, the primary motivation at work is the desire to comply with the experimenter's requests.

The research we described above on egocentric contrast effects, and the work of social comparison more generally, suggests that researchers should take the issue of motivation more seriously in research on social judgment. If evaluations of the self are so laden with motivations and goals, then it is likely that evaluations of others also are shaped by these same motivations. For example, the studies above on egocentric contrast effects, as well as other research from my laboratory (Dunning et al., 1989, 1991, 1995; Dunning & McElwee, 1995; Hayes & Dunning, 1997) suggests that the motive to validate positive self-images has a pervasive influence on judgments of other people. That is, the same motive that has played a large role in the evolution of social comparison, namely, self-enhancement, plays a potentially significant role in social cognition more generally.

Thus, research on social comparison suggests that researchers could profit by examining how the same motives that influence self-evaluation also influence judgments of others. Beyond the simple need to know and the ubiquitous need to self-affirm, motives toward improvement, self-verification, and the forging of common bonds might carry many implications for the way people evaluate their friends and neighbors, peers and colleagues, elders and underlings.

Different Motives at Play for Self- versus Social Judgment. But there are other payoffs to thinking about social cognition from a motivational perspective. The motives that surround self-judgment may differ from those circling social judgment, in ways that may explain the different conclusions people reach about themselves versus others. The motive to self-enhance, for example, is an obvious one. This motive obviously attaches itself more to self-judgment than it does to social judgment, with the usual conclusion that people hold more favorable impressions of themselves than they do of their peers (Alicke, 1985; Brown, 1986; Dunning et al., 1989; Weinstein, 1980).

But there are other motives that may influence self and social judgment differently. For example, consider the motivation for improvement. The motive for self-improvement is strong (Taylor, Neter, & Wayment, 1995) and one can safely assume that people are more concerned about improving themselves than they are about improving others. As such, the motive for self-improvement may shape what data people pay attention to and what conclusions they reach about themselves than any comparable motive does for the judgments they reach for others. For example, when I was in graduate school, I used to play tennis frequently with another graduate student of roughly equal ability. However, each of us had the firm impression that he was the superior tennis player, albeit not by much. Over beers one day, we confessed our comparative evaluations of each other and started to speculate on why we had such a disagreement when we were clearly working from the same evidence.

It became evident to us quickly that it was the motive toward self-improvement that caused our divergent evaluations of each other. Because we were each motivated to improve our games, we paid close attention to our flaws (because they needed work) but also to instances in which we had made spectacular shots. We each paid attention to these successes because we took them to reveal our "true potential," the one we were working to fulfill each time we walked on the tennis court. Thus, these successes were remembered and given great weight in our assessment of our own abilities. However, we took no such note of the successes of the other person when assessing his ability. We were not interested in improving his game (leave it to them), or discovering his true potential. Instead, each of us just wanted to get a sense of how the other person played "on average" and gave no special weight to their spectacular successes. Thus, the goal of self-judgment (self-improvement) and the aim of social judgment (determining the others' typical level of play) differed, with concomitant differences in the conclusions reached about the self versus others.

More scientific evidence for the impact of self-improvement on producing differences between self and social judgment comes from Jones, Rock, Shaver, Goethals, and Ward

(1968), who presented participants with a series of puzzles and varied whether participants succeeded brilliantly over the first few trials and then met with increasing failure (a *descending* pattern of performance) or first met failure and then ended with a spectacular series of successes (an *ascending* pattern). They found that participants rated themselves more positively on their own ability when their performance ascended rather than when it declined. That is, participants were sensitive to whether they were improving on the task; the motive of self-improvement had influenced how they reached their judgment.

However, concerns about improvement failed to influence judgments of others in the same way. When judging the performances of others, people rated targets with descending performance patterns, namely, success up front that was followed by failure, more positively than they did targets with ascending performance patterns. When judging others, it appeared that people were more interested in assessing their average level of performance, giving weight to the first few pieces of data, and not in whether those others were improving in their achievements.

Social Judgment Is Selective.   Social comparison theorists discovered a long time ago that people do not compare themselves with anybody. Social comparison is selective (although see Gilbert, Giesler, & Morris, 1995, for a dissenting note). Depending on the circumstance, people may compare upward to superior individuals (Wheeler, 1966) or downward to inferior ones (Hakmiller, 1966). They may seek out similar individuals (Festinger, 1954; Wheeler, Martin, & Suls, 1997) or dissimilar ones (Mettee & Smith, 1971). They may compare themselves with individuals who are like them on attributes that are related to the ability or attitude in question (Zanna, Goethals, & Hill, 1975). They may compare themselves with those they feel close to (Tesser, 1988) or those who share some characteristic that they consider self-defining (Miller, 1984). People are discriminating in who they compare themselves with, depending on their goals in the particular situation they confront.

Again, in this regard, research on social judgment presents a curiosity. People in their everyday life must be selective in who they judge and what they judge them on. There are simply too many opportunities each and every day for social judgment, and people would be overwhelmed by a paralyzing cognitive activity if they decided to judge every person they met on every conceivable trait domain. However, in research on social cognition, this issue of selection is not addressed. Instead, the issue is finessed in the laboratory by having the experimenter specify who must be judged and on what trait dimensions.

Thus, in general, work on social comparison points out the general lesson that people must be selective in their cognitive activity. But more than that, work in my laboratory, combined with research on social comparison, provides many clues about who people select to judge and who they choose to ignore.

Consider one of the central principles that guided the work in my laboratory on egocentric contrast effects. The principle was that people shaped or managed their judgments of others in order to maintain positive images of self. More generally, what that principle suggests is that social judgment is driven by concerns for self. We have emphasized the concern of self-validation, but many other self-concerns have been pointed out by social comparison theorists, such as the need to gain information about the self and the desire toward self-improvement.

What this line of thinking suggests is that people may be the most motivated to judge others in exactly those situations in which people wish to judge themselves, namely, when they are drawn toward engaging in social comparison. That would mean that they are driven to judge people who are superior to them when they wish to self-improve, ignoring people who are inferior. It would mean that they form strong impressions of inferior others but not superior ones when they wish to validate themselves. It would suggest that people are most concerned about forming elaborate and sophisticated impressions of people who are similar to themselves, either in the trait domain under consideration or in terms of related attributes. It would suggest that people are driven to form complex and nuanced impressions of the people they are close to, such as friends and family, because those individuals are so influential in forming their sense of self (Tesser, 1988).

Thus, work on social comparison may contain many clues about who people "obsess" about when engaging in social judgment and on what dimensions they obsess about. With this in mind, it is instructive to recall that people tend to make more confident and extreme judgments of others along trait dimensions they hold to be self-defining (Eiser & Mower White, 1974, 1975; Lambert & Wedell, 1991; Markus & Smith, 1981). What is more, they tend to make many more inferences about other people when given information about those others in these self-defining trait dimensions (Alicke, 1993; Carpenter, 1988; Catambone & Markus, 1987; Markus et al., 1985).

That result naturally follows from the idea that these are the trait domains in which people compare themselves with others the most. People may come to judge others the most on these trait domains because they are the ones in which they have engaged in the most social comparison. The social comparison activity has led them to become expert in those domains, and so it would these domains that become the ones on which they judge others the most. As well, continued enthusiasm for social comparison along these domains may provide people with a great number of opportunities to consider the talents and failings of others in these domains, and thus opportunities to make judgments of those others.

Methods from Social Judgment Work Relevant to Social Comparison

The cross talk between research on social judgment and that on social comparison can also flow in the reverse direction. There is at least one idea from the work reviewed above on social judgment that could be profitably transferred to research on social comparison. The idea centers on a potential method of assessing when people have engaged in spontaneous social comparisons.

As Wood (1996) has noted, there is a panoply of methods used to assess when and with whom people engage in social comparisons. These methods each have strengths and weaknesses. Some, for example, require that the researcher give participants an explicit chance to compare themselves with others and then see who they select to compare themselves with. Of course, because participants are presented with an explicit chance at social comparison, the researcher does not know whether participants even would be interested in that social comparison opportunity of the experiment had not provided it so transparently. Other methods involve presenting participants with some potentially important comparative information and then seeing whether the judgments of participants are subsequently influenced by it, which then is taken as evidence of social comparison. Unfortunately, this method at times is open to alternative explanations that do not involve social comparison.

In the work reviewed above, we presented an additional method that could be used to assess when people engage in social comparison, even when not explicitly prompted to do so. It is the reaction time methodology used in two of the three studies in Dunning and Hayes (1996). Recall that in those two studies, we explored whether people compare target individuals with themselves by examining the speed with which they could report their own behaviors. Faster speeds were taken to indicate thinking about the self and were evidence of egocentric comparison. Such a methodology could easily be transported to studies of social comparison. For example, a group of students could be convened to talk about personal issues, and one could mention how many alcoholic drinks he or she had consumed over the last week. Later, students could be asked to report their own level of alcoholic consumption. To the extent that students can report their own consumption quickly, and more quickly than a situation in which alcohol is not mentioned at all, the researcher would have evidence of comparison activity. Of course, in this situation one does not know whether students thought of their own alcoholic consumption in order to judge their own behavior (social comparison) or the behavior of the person reporting their own consumption (egocentric comparison), but one is aware that comparison activity took place.

The reaction time methodology also can be used in situations that more clearly involve social comparison. For example, students could be asked to judge whether they are heavy or light drinkers. They then could be asked to report how many alcoholic drinks they consume, as well as how many drinks each of their friends consumes. A researcher could look for social comparison by assessing the speed with which participants report the behavior of their friends, relative to a situation in which no alcohol-related questions are asked. To the extent that participants report their friends' behavior quickly, it could be taken as evidence of social comparison. More than that, researchers could pinpoint who exactly participants tended to compare themselves with. Did they compare themselves with their best friends, or ones of their own gender, or the one who is most prototypic of college students? To be sure, any researcher interested in using reaction time measures to assess comparison activity should be mindful of a number of control conditions and questions that I have not outlined here (see Dunning & Hayes, 1996). But properly thought out reaction time experiments could profitably address a host of questions concerning social comparison.

CONCLUDING REMARKS

I began this chapter by suggesting that it might be in the wrong volume. Instead of focusing on how people learn about themselves by judging others, I focused on how people learn about others by focusing on the self. Along the way, I reviewed evidence that people spontaneously think about themselves as they judge others. I also reviewed data suggesting that people think of themselves because they wish to make sure that their judgments of others honor and obey certain ideas, usually favorable ones, they have of themselves. Thus, social judgment is often just a form of social comparison, done implicitly to be sure, but social comparison just the same.

I hope that by now the reader, like me, realizes that my initial suggestion about this chapter was wrong. The work I have reviewed on social judgment has much relevance for work on social comparison. Far from challenging the importance and usefulness of social comparison work, the research I reviewed suggests that the assumptions and principles of social comparison carry many implications for how we as psychologists should think about social judgment. Social judgment is relational. It is motivated. And it is selective. All these principles were recognized, whether explicitly or implicitly, very early on by social comparison theorists. In exploring these principles, theorists came a long way toward understanding how people come to understand themselves. In this chapter, I have suggested that thinking about these principles would help us to better understand how people come to evaluate and perceive others.

That is, what I am suggesting for psychological researchers is a little social comparison.

Researchers in one tradition (e.g., social judgment) could stand to look at researchers in another (e.g., social comparison) and ask how they compare to theorists in that other tradition, not in terms of number of publications or visibility, but rather in how that other tradition has come to understand the human being in his or her social environment. The insights of other traditions often can add to the insights of one's own. Festinger (1954) said that the need for social comparison was often prompted by a "unidirectional upward drive" (p. 125). In the case of understanding people in their environment, there can be few more efficient and informative ways to fulfill that upward drive than by considering the wisdom and knowledge of other research traditions.

ACKNOWLEDGMENT

Preparation of this chapter was supported financially by NIMH Grant RO1 56072.

REFERENCES

Ajzen, I. (1977). Intuitive theories of events and the effects of base-rate information on prediction. *Journal of Personality and Social Psychology, 35,* 303–314.

Alicke, M. D. (1985). Global self-evaluation as determined by the desirability and controllability of trait adjectives. *Journal of Personality and Social Psychology, 49,* 1621–1630.

Alicke, M. D. (1993). Egocentric standards of conduct evaluation. *Basic and Applied Social Psychology, 14,* 171–192.

Alicke, M. D., LoSchiavo, F. M., Zerbst, J., & Zhang, S. (1997). The person who outperforms me is a genius: Maintaining perceived competence in upward social comparison. *Journal of Personality and Social Psychology, 72,* 781–789.

Baldwin, J. E. (1902). *Social and ethical interpretations in mental development.* New York: Macmillan.

Beauregard, K. S., & Dunning, D. (1998). Turning up the contrast: Self-enhancement motives prompt egocentric contrast effects in social judgment. *Journal of Personality and Social Psychology, 74,* 606–621.

Brown, J. D. (1986). Evaluations of self and others: Self-enhancement biases in social judgment. *Social Cognition, 4,* 353–376.

Bruvold, W. H. (1975). Judgmental bias in the rating of attitude statements. *Educational and Psychological Measurement, 35,* 605–611.

Campbell, J. D. (1986). Similarity and uniqueness: The effects of attribute type, relevance, and individual differences in self-esteem and depression. *Journal of Personality and Social Psychology, 50,* 281–294.

Carpenter, S. L. (1988). Self-relevance and goal-directed processing in the recall of weighting of information about others. *Journal of Experimental Social Psychology, 24,* 310–322.

Catambone, R., & Markus, H. (1987). The role of self-schemas in going beyond the information given. *Social Cognition, 5,* 349–368.

Collins, R. L. (1996). For better or worse: The impact of upward social comparison on self-evaluation. *Psychological Bulletin, 119,* 51–69.

Combe, A. W., & Snygg, D. (1949). *Individual behavior: A perceptual approach to behavior.* New York: Harper & Brothers.

Corenblum, B., & Corfield, V. K. (1976). The effect of attitude and statement of favorability upon the judgment of attitude statements. *Social Behavior and Personality, 4,* 249–256.

Dawes, R. M. (1989). Statistical criteria for a truly false consensus effect. *Journal of Experimental Social Psychology, 25,* 1–17.

Dornbusch, S. M., Hastorf, A. J., Richardson, S. A., Muzzy, R. E., & Vreeland, R. S. (1965). The perceiver and the perceived: Their relative influence on the categories of interpersonal cognition. *Journal of Personality and Social Psychology, 1,* 671–684.

Dunning, D. (1998). *Linking self to social judgment: On the symbolic management of social judgment.* Unpublished manuscript. Cornell University.

Dunning, D. (1999). A newer look: Motivated social cognition and the schematic representation of social concepts. *Psychological Inquiry, 10,* 1–11.

Dunning, D. (in press). On the motives underlying social cognition. In N. Schwarz & A. Tesser (Eds.), *Blackwell handbook of social psychology: Volume 1: Intrapersonal processes.* New York: Blackwell.

Dunning, D., & Beauregard, K. S. (in press). Regulating impressions of others to affirm images of the self. *Social Cognition.*

Dunning, D., & Cohen, G. L. (1992). Egocentric definitions of traits and abilities in social judgment. *Journal of Personality and Social Psychology, 63,* 341–355.

Dunning, D., Griffin, D. W., Milojkovic, J. H., & Ross, L. (1990). The overconfidence effect in social prediction. *Journal of Personality and Social Psychology, 58,* 568–592.

Dunning, D., & Hayes, A. F. (1996). Evidence for egocentric comparison in social judgment. *Journal of Personality and Social Psychology, 71,* 213–229.

Dunning, D., Leuenberger, A., & Sherman, D. A. (1995). A new look at motivated inference: Are self-serving theories of success a product of motivational forces? *Journal of Personality and Social Psychology, 69,* 58–68.

Dunning, D., & McElwee, R. O. (1995). Idiosyncratic trait definitions: Implications for self-description and social judgment. *Journal of Personality and Social Psychology, 68,* 936–946.

Dunning, D., Meyerowitz, J. A., & Holzberg, A. D. (1989). Ambiguity and self-evaluation: The role of idiosyncratic trait definitions in self-serving assessments of ability. *Journal of Personality and Social Psychology, 57,* 1082–1090.

Dunning, D., Perie, M., & Story, A. L. (1991). Self-serving prototypes of social categories. *Journal of Personality and Social Psychology, 61,* 957–968.

Eiser, J. R., & Mower White, C. J. (1974). Evaluative consistency and social judgment. *Journal of Personality and Social Psychology, 30,* 349–359.

Eiser, J. R., & Mower White, C. J. (1975). Categorization and congruity in attitudinal judgment. *Journal of Personality and Social Psychology, 31,* 769–775.

Festinger, L. (1954). A theory of social comparison processes. *Human Relations, 7,* 117–140.

Freud, S. (1924/1956). Further remarks on the defense neuropsychoses. In *Collected papers of Sigmund Freud* (Vol. 1, pp. 155–182). London: Hogarth Press.

Gilbert, D. T., Giesler, R. B., & Morris, K. A. (1995). When comparisons arise. *Journal of Personality and Social Psychology, 69,* 227–236.

Gruder, C. L. (1977). Choice of comparison persons in evaluating oneself. In J. M. Suls & R. C. Miller (Eds.), *Social comparison processes: Theoretical and empirical perspectives* (pp. 21–42). Washington, DC: Hemisphere.

Hackmiller, K. L. (1966). Threat as a determinant of downward comparison. *Journal of Experimental Social Psychology, 2* (Suppl. 1), 32–39.

Hall, G. S. (1898). Some aspects of the early sense of self. *American Journal of Psychology, 9,* 351–395.

Hayes, A. F., & Dunning, D. (1997). Construal processes and trait ambiguity: Implications for self–peer agreement in personality judgment. *Journal of Personality and Social Psychology, 72,* 664–677.

Helgeson, V. S., & Mickelson, K. D. (1995). Motives for social comparison. *Personality and Social Psychology Bulletin, 21,* 1200–1209.

Helson, H. (1964). *Adaptation-level theory.* New York: Harper & Row.

Higgins, E. T., & Lurie, L. (1983). Context, categorization, and memory: The "change-of-standard" effect. *Cognitive Psychology, 15,* 525–547.

Hinckley, E., & Rethlingshafer, D. (1951). Value judgments of heights of men by college students. *Journal of Psychology, 31,* 257–296.

Hovland, C. I., Harvey, O. J., & Sherif, M. (1957). Assimilation and contrast effects in reactions to communications and attitude change. *Journal of Abnormal and Social Psychology, 55,* 244–252.

Hovland, C. I., & Sherif, M. (1952). Judgmental phenomena and scales of attitude measurement: Item displacement in Thurstone scales. *Journal of Abnormal and Social Psychology, 47,* 822–832.

James, W. (1915). *Psychology: Briefer course.* New York: Holt.

Jones, E. E., & Gerard, H. B. (1967). *Foundations of social psychology.* New York: John Wiley & Sons.

Jones, E. E., Rock, L., Shaver, K. G., Goethals, G. R., & Ward, L. M. (1968). Pattern of performance and ability attribution: An unexpected primacy effect. *Journal of Personality and Social Psychology, 10,* 317–340.

Kahneman, D., & Miller, D. T. (1986). Norm theory: Comparing reality to its alternatives. *Psychological Review, 93,* 136–153.

Kahneman, D., & Tversky, A. (1979). Prospect theory: An analysis of decision under risk. *Econometrika, 47,* 263–291.

Kassin, S. M. (1979). Consensus information, prediction, and causal attribution: A review of the literature and issues. *Journal of Personality and Social Psychology, 37,* 1966–1981.

Kelley, H. H. (1967). Attribution theory in social psychology. In D. Levine (Ed.), *Nebraska symposium on motivation* (Vol. 15, pp. 192–240). Lincoln: University of Nebraska Press.

Krech, D., & Crutchfield, R. S. (1948). *Theory and problems of social psychology.* New York: McGraw-Hill.

Krueger, J. (1998). On the perception of social consensus. In M. Zanna (Ed.), *Advances in experimental social psychology* (Vol. 30, pp. 163–240). San Diego: Academic Press.

Krueger, J., & Clement, R. W. (1994). The truly false consensus effect: An ineradicable and egocentric bias in social perception. *Journal of Personality and Social Psychology, 67,* 596–610.

Krueger, J., & Clement, R. W. (1997). Consensus estimates by majorities and minorities: The case for social projection. *Personality and Social Psychology Review, 1,* 299–319.

Lambert, A. J., & Wedell, D. H. (1991). The self and social judgment: Effects of affective reaction and "own position" on judgments of unambiguous and ambiguous information about others. *Journal of Personality and Social Psychology, 61,* 884–898.

Lemon, N., & Warren, N. (1974). Salience, centrality, and self-relevance of traits in construing others. *British Journal of Social and Clinical Psychology, 13,* 119–124.

Lewicki, P. (1983). Self-image bias in person perception. *Journal of Personality and Social Psychology, 45,* 384–393.

Lewicki, P. (1984). Self-schema and social information processing. *Journal of Personality and Social Psychology, 47,* 1177–1190.

Marks, E. (1943). Skin color judgments of Negro college students. *Journal of Abnormal and Social Psychology, 388,* 370–376.

Marks, G. (1984). Thinking one's abilities are unique and one's opinions are common. *Personality and Social Psychology Bulletin, 10,* 203–208.

Marks, G., & Miller, N. (1987). Ten years of research on the false-consensus effect: An empirical and theoretical review. *Psychological Bulletin, 102,* 72–90.

Markus, H., & Smith, J. (1981). The influence of self-schemas on the perception of others. In N. Cantor & J. F. Kihlstrom (Eds.), *Personality, cognition, and social interaction* (pp. 233–262). Hillsdale, NJ: Lawrence Erlbaum.

Markus, H., Smith, J., & Moreland, R. L. (1985). Role of the self-concept in the social perception of others. *Journal of Personality and Social Psychology, 49,* 1494–1512.

McArthur, L. Z. (1976). The lesser influence of consensus than distinctiveness information on causal attribution. *Journal of Personality and Social Psychology, 33,* 733–742.

McDougall, W. (1921). *An introduction to social psychology.* Boston: Luce.

Mead, G. H. (1934). *Mind, self, and society.* Chicago: University of Chicago Press.

Mettee, D. R., & Smith, G. (1977). Social comparison and interpersonal attraction: the case for dissimilarity. In J. M. Suls & R. L. Miller (Eds.), *Social comparison processes: Theoretical and empirical perspectives* (pp. 69–101). Washington, DC: Hemisphere.

Miller, C. T. (1984). Self-schemas, gender, and social comparison: A clarification of the related attributes hypothesis. *Journal of Personality and Social Psychology, 46,* 1222–1228.

Mullen, B., & Goethals, G. R. (1990). Social projection, actual consensus and valence. *British Journal of Social Psychology, 29,* 279–282.

Murphy, G. (1947). *Personality: A biosocial approach to origin and structure.* New York: Harper.

Nisbett, R. E., & Borgida, E. (1975). Attribution and the psychology of prediction. *Journal of Personality and Social Psychology, 32,* 932–943.

Pelham, B. W., & Wachsmuth, J. O. (1995). The waxing and waning of the social self: Assimilation and contrast in social comparison. *Journal of Personality and Social Psychology, 69,* 825–838.

Pittman, T. S. (1998). Motivation. In D. T. Gilbert, S. T. Fiske, & G. Lindzey (Eds.), *Handbook of social psychology* (4th ed., Vol. 1, pp. 549–590). New York: McGraw-Hill.

Prentice, D. (1990). Familiarity and differences in self- and other-representation. *Journal of Personality and Social Psychology, 59,* 369–383.

Prothro, E. T. (1955). The effect of strong negative affect on the placement of items in a Thurstone scale. *Journal of Social Psychology, 41,* 11–17.

Roese, N., & Olson, J. (1995). *What might have been: The social psychology of counterfactual thinking.* Hillsdale, NJ: Lawrence Erlbaum.

Rogers, C. P. (1951). *Client-centered therapy.* Boston: Houghton-Mifflin.

Romer, D. (1983). Effects of own attitude on polarization of judgment. *Journal of Personality and Social Psychology, 44,* 273–284.

Ross, L., Greene, D., & House, P. (1977). The "false consensus effect": An egocentric bias in social perception and attribution processes. *Journal of Experimental Social Psychology, 13,* 279–301.

Sherif, M., & Hovland, C. I. (1961). *Social judgment: Assimilation and contrast effects in communication and attitude change.* New Haven, CT: Yale University Press.

Sherif, M., & Jackman, N. (1966). Judgments of truth in collective controversy. *Public Opinion Quarterly, 30,* 173–186.

Smith, R. H., Hilton, D. J., Kim, S. H., & Garonzik, R. (1992). Knowledge-based causal inference: Norms and the usefulness of distinctiveness. *British Journal of Social Psychology, 31*, 239–248.

Sullivan, H. S. (1947). *Conceptions of modern psychiatry.* Washington, DC: William Alanson White Psychiatry Foundation.

Suls, J., & Wills, T. A. (1991). *Social comparison: Contemporary theory and research.* Hillsdale, NJ: Lawrence Erlbaum.

Taylor, S. E., Neter, E., & Wayment, H. A. (1995). Self-evaluation processes. *Personality and Social Psychology Bulletin, 21*, 1278–1287.

Tesser, A. (1988). Toward a self-evaluation maintenance model of social behavior. In L. Berkowitz (Ed.), *Advances in experimental social psychology* (Vol. 21, pp. 181–227). New York: Academic Press.

Tesser, A., & Campbell, J. (1983). Self-definition and self-evaluation maintenance. In J. Suls & A. Greenwald (Eds.), *Social psychological perspectives on the self* (Vol. 2, pp. 1–31). Hillsdale, NJ: Lawrence Erlbaum.

Upshaw, H. S. (1975). The effect of variable perspectives on judgments of opinion statements for Thurstone scales. *Journal of Personality and Social Psychology, 2*, 60–69.

Vallone, R. P., Griffin, D. W., Lin, S., & Ross, L. (1990). Overconfident prediction of future actions and outcomes by self and others. *Journal of Personality and Social Psychology, 58*, 582–592.

Weinstein, N. D. (1980). Unrealistic optimism about future life events. *Journal of Personality and Social Psychology, 58*, 806–820.

Wells, G. L., & Harvey, J. H. (1977). Do people use consensus information in making causal attributions? *Journal of Personality and Social Psychology, 35*, 279–293.

Wheeler, L. (1966). Motivation as a determinant of upward comparison. *Journal of Experimental Social Psychology, 2* (Suppl. 1), 27–31.

Wheeler, L., Martin, R., & Suls, J. (1997). The proxy model of social comparison for self-assessment of ability. *Personality and Social Psychology Review, 1*, 54–61.

Wills, T. A. (1981). Downward comparison principles in social psychology. *Psychological Bulletin, 90*, 245–271.

Windschitl, P. D., & Wills, G. L. (1997). Behavioral consensus information affects people's inferences about population traits. *Personality and Social Psychology Bulletin, 23*, 148–156.

Wood, J. V. (1989). Theory and research concerning social comparison of personal attributes. *Psychological Bulletin, 106*, 231–248.

Wood, J. V. (1996). What is social comparison and how should we study it? *Personality and Social Psychology Bulletin, 22*, 520–537.

Zanna, M. P., Goethals, G. R., & Hill, J. F. (1975). Evaluating a sex-related ability: Social comparison with similar others and standard setters. *Journal of Experimental Social Psychology, 11*, 86–93.

18

Comparing Comparisons

An Integrative Perspective
on Social Comparison and Counterfactual Thinking

JAMES M. OLSON, OSWALD BUHRMANN,
AND NEAL J. ROESE

As this volume illustrates, social comparison theory has stimulated many productive lines of research. In everyday life, we are constantly surrounded by information about other people—their performances, possessions, appearances, and so on. Comparisons between our own characteristics or outcomes and other people's characteristics or outcomes are inevitable. These social comparisons play a key role in the development of our self-concepts, in that we define our strengths and weaknesses in large part by how we measure up to others.

Other people constitute only one of many possible standards with which we can compare ourselves, however. For example, we can compare our current characteristics with our own characteristics in the past. Such temporal comparisons inform us about how we have changed over time and can have significant affective and cognitive consequences (e.g., see Albert, 1977; Gurr, 1970; Strack, Schwarz, & Gschneidinger, 1985; Suls, 1986). We also can compare ourselves to idealized versions of ourselves (Higgins, 1987) or to possible future versions of ourselves (Markus & Nurius, 1986).

Yet another comparison process involving the self is the focus of the current chapter. Specifically, we discuss comparisons between the self and a hypothetical self—a self that might have occurred but did not. These comparisons can be labeled *counterfactual comparisons*, because they involve imagined outcomes or states of being that did not actually occur (i.e., that are counter to the facts). The imagined outcomes in counterfactual comparisons are often what was expected to happen and/or what "should" have happened (Miller & Turnbull, 1990; Roese, 1997). For example, individuals might compare their current situation with the one they had hoped to achieve by this point in time.

In this chapter, we consider some of the similarities and differences between social

JAMES M. OLSON AND OSWALD BUHRMANN • Department of Psychology, University of Western Ontario, London, Ontario, Canada N6A 5C2.   NEAL J. ROESE • Department of Psychology, Simon Fraser University, Burnaby, British Columbia, Canada V5A 1S6.

Handbook of Social Comparison: Theory and Research, edited by Suls and Wheeler. Kluwer Academic/Plenum Publishers, New York, 2000.

comparisons and counterfactual comparisons—two processes that have generated largely independent literatures. We begin with a brief review of research on thoughts about "what might have been." We use the terms "counterfactual thoughts" and "counterfactual comparisons" interchangeably, because self-focused counterfactual thoughts (as opposed to counterfactual thoughts about alternative realities that do not involve the self)[1] implicitly evoke comparisons between the imagined and actual outcomes for the self. We then discuss several ways that social and counterfactual comparisons are conceptually related. These connections between social and counterfactual comparisons suggest some novel directions for research in each literature. Because the topic of the present volume is social comparison, we explicitly address in a final section some implications of research on counterfactual thinking for understanding social comparison processes.

COUNTERFACTUAL THINKING

Thoughts about how past events might have turned out differently are extremely common, ranging from pleasant, fanciful daydreams to painful, "if only" thoughts about traumatic experiences. From a child's imaginings in the classroom about what she would be doing right now if she were at the beach to a parent's ruminative thoughts about how his daughter would not have been injured in a car crash had he only driven more carefully, thoughts about alternative realities are ubiquitous. As in these examples, counterfactual thoughts typically mutate one or more elements prior to an event (e.g., going to the beach instead of to school, or driving more carefully) and then project how outcomes would have been different as a consequence (e.g., one would be swimming instead of sitting in class, or one's daughter would be healthy rather than injured).

Stimulated largely by Kahneman and Miller's (1986) norm theory, social and cognitive psychologists have increasingly turned their attention toward counterfactual thoughts (for a recent review, see Roese, 1997). Researchers have examined the triggers of counterfactual thoughts (the conditions under which such thoughts occur), the contents of counterfactual thoughts (what such thoughts typically consist of), and the consequences of counterfactual thoughts (the impact of such thoughts on cognition, affect, and behavior). We give a couple of examples of research on each of these topics in the following paragraphs.

Activation

With regard to the activation of counterfactual thinking, we (Roese & Olson, 1995a, 1997) have argued that the primary trigger is negative affect resulting from a negative outcome. That is, individuals are more likely to generate counterfactual thoughts spontaneously after a negative rather than a positive experience. For example, Roese and Olson (1997) asked participants to list the sorts of thoughts that might run through a student's mind after performing either well or poorly on an exam. Participants generated approximately three times as many counterfactual thoughts in the negative as in the positive condition (see also Sanna &

---

[1]In this chapter, we limit our consideration to self-focused counterfactual thoughts, that is, to thoughts about how one's own outcomes or characteristics might have been different. It is possible, of course, to generate counterfactual thoughts that have nothing to do with the self (e.g., "What might have happened if John Kennedy had not been assassinated?"). But just as the meaning of social comparison in this volume is limited to self–other comparisons (as opposed, for example, to other–other comparisons), we limit counterfactual comparisons in this chapter to those between the self and a hypothetical self.

Turley, 1996). Other studies have shown that negative affect, as opposed to shifts in expectancies or perceptions of controllability, mediates the activating effect of negative outcomes on counterfactual thinking.

Another trigger of counterfactual thinking is a "near miss" (or a "close outcome"). When an event almost happens, thoughts about that near event are likely to occur. For example, if a football team experiences a last-second defensive collapse that snatches defeat from the jaws of victory, thoughts about the counterfactual outcome of winning are likely to come unbidden into the players' minds. Similarly, when an automobile accident is barely avoided, thoughts about how one could have been killed or injured are likely to occur. This variable has been labeled "outcome closeness" by counterfactual theorists (Kahneman, 1995; Roese, 1997).

Content

One variable that influences the content of counterfactual thoughts is the normality of the antecedents to the event. Specifically, individuals often focus on unusual antecedents to an outcome when generating counterfactual thoughts. That is, in considering how things might have turned out differently, perceivers are likely to alter exceptional or unusual things that led to the outcome (with the alterations making the antecedents more normal) rather than routine or typical aspects of the situation. For example, Kahneman and Tversky (1982) had participants read about a man who was killed while driving home from work. When asked how the accident could have been avoided, participants who believed that the man left work early tended to say, "If only he had left at his usual time." In contrast, participants who believed that the man took an unusual route home tended to say, "If only he had taken his usual route home." Of course, either mutation was theoretically possible in both conditions.

A second feature of antecedent events that increases their likelihood of being included in counterfactual thoughts is controllability. Perceivers typically mutate controllable, rather than uncontrollable, aspects of the situation that led to an outcome (Girotto, Legrenzi, & Rizzo, 1991; Roese, 1997). For example, Markman, Gavanski, Sherman, and McMullen (1995) had participants generate counterfactual thoughts while they played a computerized game of chance, which included procedural aspects that were manipulated across subjects to vary in controllability. Participants' counterfactual thoughts focused on the controllable aspects of the game rather than the uncontrollable aspects.

Consequences

The most-researched consequence of counterfactual thinking has been affect. In their emotional amplification hypothesis, Kahneman and Miller (1986) proposed that events have greater emotional impact to the extent that they spontaneously activate thoughts about alternative outcomes. In other words, counterfactual thinking amplifies whatever emotional response would ordinarily be triggered by a particular outcome. Presumably, the emotional effects of counterfactual thinking result from contrast effects, whereby the actual outcomes seem better or worse based on the relative favorability of the counterfactual comparison outcomes (see Roese & Olson, 1995a, 1997). For example, if an individual does poorly on a test and can easily imagine how she might have done better, then her poor performance is contrasted against the counterfactual comparison of better performance, which will make her feel even worse about the actual outcome.

In an experimental test of the affective consequences of counterfactual comparisons,

Roese (1994) asked participants to think about an unpleasant life event. He then induced participants to list thoughts about either how the event could have been better (upward counterfactual thoughts) or how it could have been worse (downward counterfactual thoughts). On a subsequent mood measure, those participants who were induced to generate upward counterfactual comparisons reported more negative affect about the event than did those who were induced to generate downward counterfactual comparisons (see also Davis & Lehman, 1995; Markman, Gavanski, Sherman, & McMullen, 1993).

Counterfactual thoughts also can have cognitive consequences, such as influencing causal beliefs (Lipe, 1991). If the mental alteration of an antecedent to an event changes the imagined outcome of the event, then the antecedent is implicated as a cause of the outcome. For example, Wells and Gavanski (1989) had participants read about a woman who suffered a fatal reaction to an ingredient in her meal, which was chosen by her lunch companion. Some participants learned that the companion chose between two dishes that both contained the critical ingredient, whereas others learned that the companion chose between one dish that contained the ingredient and one that did not. The latter participants attributed the woman's death to her companion's choice more than did the former, presumably because the most salient counterfactual alteration of the choice (namely, imagining that the companion chose the other dish that had been considered) led to a different outcome in the latter but not in the former condition.

CONCEPTUAL SIMILARITIES BETWEEN SOCIAL COMPARISON AND COUNTERFACTUAL THINKING

There are numerous conceptual parallels between social comparison and counterfactual thinking. In this section, we identify four relatively fundamental similarities and consider their implications for our understanding of the two processes. The four similarities that we will discuss are listed in Table 1.

Comparative Judgments

Perhaps the most basic similarity between social comparison and counterfactual thinking is that they are both comparative judgments. That is, they both involve the comparison of a subject to a referent. Further, the subjects in both cases (at least in the kinds of social and counterfactual comparisons on which we focus in this chapter) are individuals' own actual characteristics or outcomes. Social comparisons involve comparing one's own characteristics or outcomes with other people's characteristics or outcomes. Counterfactual comparisons involve comparing one's own characteristics or outcomes with hypothetical characteristics or

Table 1. Conceptual Similarities between Social Comparison and Counterfactual Thinking

Both processes are comparative judgments
Both processes can occur automatically or in a controlled fashion
Both processes can have significant affective consequences
Both processes fulfill important psychological functions

outcomes for the self. In each case, there is an implicit—or even explicit—judgment about the relative favorability of one's actual outcomes or experiences.

The fact that both social comparison and counterfactual thinking are comparative judgments has a number of implications. For one thing, the two processes have been classified in similar ways based on their comparative structures. For example, both social comparison and counterfactual researchers have distinguished between "upward" and "downward" comparisons, or between comparisons that result in unfavorable versus favorable judgments about the subject of the comparison, namely one's own characteristics (e.g., Brickman & Bulman, 1977; Collins, 1996; Markman et al., 1993; Roese, 1994; Taylor & Schneider, 1989; Wills, 1981). An upward comparison involves comparing one's outcomes with a more favorable standard (either another person who did better or an imagined better outcome for the self), whereas a downward comparison involves comparing one's outcomes with a less favorable standard (either another person who did worse or an imagined worse outcome for the self). As we will elaborate shortly, upward and downward comparisons have been postulated to fulfill different functions and to produce different consequences in both the social and counterfactual comparison literatures.

Another implication of the shared comparative structure of social and counterfactual comparisons is that both processes should exhibit other characteristics that are true of comparative judgments generally (see Kruglanski & Mayseless, 1990). For example, selection of a comparison referent, whether social or counterfactual, may depend on motivational states (e.g., the importance of a correct decision) (see Kruglanski & Mayseless, 1987) and relevance considerations (e.g., the nature of the judgment, such as whether it is objective or subjective) (see Olson, Ellis, & Zanna, 1983).

One interesting effect in the domain of comparative judgments that has received some attention in the social comparison and counterfactual literatures is the subject–referent framing effect, deduced from Tversky's (1977) contrast model of similarity judgments. According to the contrast model, perceivers assess the similarity of two objects by comparing their features; if the objects share many features, they are judged to be similar, whereas if they possess many unique features, they are judged to be dissimilar. An interesting twist on this process uncovered by Tversky is that perceivers give more weight to the unique features of the subject in the comparison than to the unique features of the referent in the comparison. For example, if someone asks "How similar is A to B," then the unique features of A (the subject) will be weighted most heavily. If A is a familiar object about which the perceiver has much information (relative to B), then the A to B comparison will produce many unique features of A and a perception of dissimilarity between the objects. The B to A comparison, in contrast, will not produce many unique features of B (about which the perceiver knows relatively little), with a resulting perception of similarity between the objects.

How might the subject–referent framing effect influence social or counterfactual comparisons? Assuming that we have more information about ourselves than we do about others (and about hypothetical outcomes), if the self serves as the subject of the social (or counterfactual) comparison, greater dissimilarity will tend to be perceived than if the other (or hypothetical self) serves as the subject. That is, the framing of the comparison (self to other vs. other to self) may influence the perceived similarity between the self and the other (or between the self and the hypothetical self), which can have important implications. For example, perceived similarity might influence liking, attributions, or perceptions of the impact of decisions and events (see Holyoak & Gordon, 1983, for an example with social comparison, and Dunning & Madey, 1995, for an example with counterfactual comparison).

Automatic versus Controlled Comparisons

A second conceptual similarity between social comparison and counterfactual thinking is that both can occur either automatically or in a controlled fashion. Sometimes, individuals engage in social comparison or counterfactual thinking without intention, effort, or planning; the comparisons occur automatically (Bargh, 1996). At other times, the comparison process—whether social or counterfactual—is deliberate, effortful, and controlled. Theorists have suggested that these different types of comparisons occur under different conditions.

In the domain of social comparison, the automatic–controlled distinction often has paralleled researchers' substantive interests. Some researchers have investigated individuals' selections of comparison targets: the types of people chosen for comparison purposes (e.g., whether individuals prefer upward or downward comparisons: Gibbons, Benbow, & Gerrard, 1994; Sun & Croyle, 1995; Van der Zee, Oldersma, Buunk, & Bos, 1998; Wheeler & Miyake, 1992; Ybema & Buunk, 1993). In these studies, social comparison typically has been conceptualized as a deliberate, controlled process (but see Wheeler & Miyake, 1992, who postulated that affective states unconsciously prime cognitions, which in turn elicit either upward or downward social comparisons). Other researchers have investigated the consequences of exposure to particular kinds of comparison targets (e.g., to upward or downward comparisons: Alicke, LoSchiavo, Zerbst, & Zhang, 1997; Lockwood & Kunda, 1997; McFarland & Miller, 1994). In these studies, social comparison typically has been viewed as inescapable or involuntary, though not necessarily automatic. In an interesting integration of these ideas, Gilbert, Giesler, and Morris (1995) suggested that there are both automatic and controlled elements of social comparison. These researchers argued that perceivers make social comparisons spontaneously and unintentionally, even when comparison targets are logically "irrelevant" or "nondiagnostic" (e.g., even when a comparison target is dissimilar on related attributes); however, perceivers deliberately *undo* nondiagnostic comparisons subsequently. That is, social comparisons are initially made automatically (and effortlessly) but are then deliberately (and effortfully) corrected if the perceiver recognizes that the comparison is inappropriate (see also Wegener & Petty, 1997).

In the domain of counterfactual thinking, Kahneman (1995) has similarly distinguished between "automatic" and "elaborative" counterfactual thoughts. Automatic counterfactual thoughts are those that occur involuntarily, such as when an event almost occurs (a close outcome): "The 'fact' that a particular event almost occurred can sometimes be registered with all the immediacy of a percept" (p. 376). On the other hand, elaborative counterfactual thoughts occur when individuals deliberately and effortfully engage in mental reconstructions of past events, such as when a student carefully considers how she could have done better after a poor performance. These thoughts often are highly creative and can serve specific motivational goals such as mood enhancement or preparation for future tasks.

Affective Consequences

A third conceptual similarity between social and counterfactual comparisons is that both processes are postulated to have significant affective consequences. In our brief review of the literature on counterfactual thinking, we described some of the emotional consequences of counterfactual thoughts that have been documented, such as improved mood following downward counterfactuals and worsened mood following upward counterfactuals (e.g., Roese, 1994). Indeed, one of the primary reasons counterfactual thinking has caught the attention of psychologists is its apparent relevance to understanding negative emotions like regret, shame, frustration, and anger (e.g., Davis, Lehman, Wortman, Silver, & Thompson, 1995; Gilovich & Medvec, 1995; Landman, 1993; Miller, Turnbull, & McFarland, 1990; Niedenthal, Tangney, & Gavanski, 1994).

In a similar fashion, social comparison researchers also have documented affective consequences of this comparative judgment. Again, the direction distinction (between upward and downward comparisons) has been central in research on this issue. For example, Wills' (1981) well-known statement of downward comparison principles was predicated on the assumption that such comparisons would result in more positive mood. Also, comparisons with others who are better off than oneself can sometimes produce resentment and depression (see Collins, 1996; Crosby, 1976; Wheeler & Miyake, 1992).

As noted earlier, these mirror-image affective consequences of comparisons (with downward comparisons sweetening mood and upward comparisons souring mood) often are reducible to perceptual contrast effects, such that one's own positive (or negative) outcomes and characteristics seem even better (or worse) when contrasted with the referent outcomes or characteristics (Roese, 1997). Contrast effects require little cognitive processing and occur early in the information processing sequence (even before information has been integrated in impression formation) (see Wedell, 1994). Thus, in terms of the automatic versus controlled distinction discussed in the preceding section, the affective consequences of social and counterfactual comparisons usually may be automatic. Of course, comparisons also can be made deliberately to fulfill specific goals, including affective enhancement, as when individuals seek out downward-comparison persons to raise their own spirits (e.g., Pyszczynski, Greenberg, & LaPrelle, 1985; Taylor & Lobel, 1989) or when people try to comfort a grieving friend by generating downward counterfactual alternatives (a tactic that may often fail) (see Lehman & Hemphill, 1990). In research on both social and counterfactual comparisons, the most commonly discussed and observed affective consequences have been contrast effects.

More recently, theorists have noted that assimilation as well as contrast effects may result from the comparison process. For example, Taylor and Lobel (1989) argued that assimilation may result from contact with upward social comparison targets. In this case, the resulting affect centers on hopefulness and inspiration, because individuals may see the possibility of themselves eventually becoming like the upward target (see also Aspinwall & Taylor, 1993; Buunk, 1995; Buunk, Collins, Taylor, Dakof, & Van Yperen, 1990; Van der Zee et al., 1998). McMullen (1997) recently discussed assimilation effects in counterfactual thinking, as in the case where a narrowly avoided accident evokes not relief but rather anxiety and discomfort at just how close one came to tragedy.

What determines whether a comparison, either social or counterfactual, produces assimilation versus contrast? One variable is the type of processing goal currently active. For example, the goals of evaluation and assessment may lead more to contrast, whereas the goals of seeking out new information or making personal contacts might be more likely to evoke assimilation (McMullen, 1997; Pelham & Wachsmuth, 1995; Taylor & Lobel, 1989). Tesser's (1988) self-evaluation maintenance theory specifies another possible moderator variable: relevance to the self-concept (see also Alicke et al., 1997; Lockwood & Kunda, 1997; Major, Testa, & Bylsma, 1991). To the extent that a close other has succeeded along some dimension (e.g., athletic ability, academic achievement) that is highly relevant to the self, a "comparison process" is invoked, which results in affective contrast (i.e., negative affect). On the other hand, if the other person has succeeded on some dimension that is less relevant to the self, a reflection process emerges, in which one might bask in the reflected glory of the comparison target's achievements (an assimilation effect). The self-evaluation maintenance model centers mainly on social judgments in the context of close relationships, so it is probably not applicable to a wide range of social comparison instances, nor is it clear how the theory would apply to counterfactual thinking.

More generally, however, the determining variables identified in other areas of psychology presumably should apply to social and counterfactual comparisons. Thus, for example, assimilation should be more likely when the perceiver is unaware of or has no theories regarding the judgmental role of the comparison anchor than when the perceiver has clear expectations about the anchor (Lombardi, Higgins, & Bargh, 1987; Petty & Wegener, 1993). Clear expectations are a prerequisite for expectancy violation, which tends to induce a contrast effect. Similarly, assimilation is more likely when the anchor is moderate rather than extreme (Herr, 1986; Sherif & Hovland, 1961), because extreme anchors are more likely to deviate significantly from the stimulus, which will tend to induce contrast. Finally, assimilation is more likely when the judgmental domain is subjective rather than objective (Biernat & Manis, 1997), because objective judgments allow more confident perceptions of discrepancies between the anchor and the stimulus, which will tend to induce contrast.

A Functional Perspective

The final conceptual similarity between social and counterfactual comparisons that we will discuss is the most important one, because it reflects the profound overlap between the two processes and identifies some important directions for future research. This similarity has to do with the adaptiveness of the processes, namely, that both social comparison and counterfactual thinking are amenable to (or even require) a functional analysis.

Why do people engage in social and counterfactual comparison? Festinger (1954) originally suggested that self-assessment (making accurate judgments about one's abilities and opinions) was the primary motive for social comparison (see also Buunk, 1995; Wheeler, Martin, & Suls, 1997). Since then, other theorists (e.g., Fazio, 1979; Helgeson & Mickelson, 1995; Mandel & Lehman, 1996; Markman et al., 1993; Roese & Olson, 1995b, 1997; Sedikides & Strube, 1997; Taylor, Wayment, & Carrillo, 1996; Wood, 1989) have identified additional motives that might lead to social or counterfactual comparisons, with two proposed motives predominating: self-enhancement and self-improvement. Self-enhancement follows from the findings in the preceding section that comparisons have affective consequences; thus, downward comparisons can be generated strategically to elevate mood (Roese, 1994; Wills, 1981). Self-improvement reflects the central motivation of all organisms to maximize positive outcomes; this motive presumably underlies most information-seeking behavior, including the pursuit of comparison information. From this perspective, individuals seek out others who are better off than themselves (upward comparison persons) or think about how their own outcomes could have been better (upward counterfactual thoughts) because such persons and thoughts provide valuable information about how to obtain positive outcomes. The information gleaned from upward comparison targets, be they other people or counterfactual versions of oneself, can provide useful ideas, elicit optimism, and motivate behavior change (Collins, 1996; Johnson & Sherman, 1990).

If upward comparisons provide information useful for self-improvement and downward comparisons evoke more positive emotions, and hence may be marshaled for self-enhancement, then a key question is under what conditions are these respective comparison directions likely to be followed? One important variable may be the controllability of the outcome in question (Wills, 1981). To the extent that an event is controllable, individuals may take advantage of upward comparisons to obtain knowledge that may be more effectively deployed in similarly controllable future situations (Buunk et al., 1990; Testa & Major, 1990). When an outcome appears to fall outside the individual's personal control, however, upward comparisons are less useful and may be less likely to occur. For example, Roese and Olson (1995c) showed that subjects generated more upward counterfactuals for an outcome they perceived to be controllable, but more downward counterfactuals for an uncontrollable outcome. Similarly, Ybema and Buunk (1993) found that subjects preferred upward comparison information to downward comparison information when they believed that they could control relevant future performance.

A variable conceptually related to controllability is whether an outcome is likely to repeat (Markman et al., 1993). When a given situation is likely to occur again, individuals have much to gain by generating upward counterfactuals, which can provide information useful for maximizing performance the next time the same situation occurs. But when a situation is unlikely to recur, individuals have little to gain in terms of self-improvement, and hence, may turn to the self-enhancing benefits of downward counterfactual thoughts. Other moderator variables may similarly influence the relative activation of upward versus downward comparisons to the extent that they alter the availability, applicability, or usefulness of information derivable from the comparison process. From this perspective, upward comparisons should be the default, automated response in situations involving performance and achievement, which are usually controllable and repetitive; research employing free-response measures of counterfactual thinking has supported this prediction (e.g., Markman et al., 1993; see Roese & Olson, 1997).

We (Roese, 1994; 1997; Roese & Olson, 1995b, 1997) have proposed a sequence of psychological mechanisms between upward counterfactual thoughts and self-improvement. Specifically, we have suggested that upward counterfactual thoughts influence causal judgments about good performance (i.e., beliefs about the causes of good performance). In turn, these causal attributions lead to intentions to perform particular behaviors that are facilitative of success. Finally, these intentions will usually translate into actual behavior, thereby improving performance. For example, when students perform poorly on an exam, they may think about how they could have done better (e.g., by studying more). This analysis will lead them to conclude that studying hard causes good performance, which will lead them to intend to study more for the next test. In turn, this intention will probably lead to more intensive studying for the next test, which should result in actual improvements in performance. Thus, the inclination to engage in upward counterfactual thoughts following poor outcomes can be seen to have adaptive value for self-improvement.[2]

Thus, affective (self-enhancement) and preparative (self-improvement) functions have been identified in both the social comparison and the counterfactual thinking literatures. Further, the directions of comparisons hypothesized to serve each function best have been the same in both literatures—downward comparisons for self-enhancement and upward comparisons for self-improvement. Markman et al. (1993) noted that these competing functions served by upward and downward counterfactual thoughts produce a tradeoff between the negative affective and positive preparative effects of upward thoughts (or between the positive affective but limited preparative benefits of downward thoughts). Roese (1997) argued further that a tendency toward upward comparisons is nevertheless a bargain for the individual, in that relatively short-lived negative affect is more than compensated for by relatively long-lived

[2]These arguments about the benefits of upward counterfactual thoughts (and upward social comparisons, for that matter) rely on the assumption that the thoughts will yield accurate causal information (i.e., that they will point to actual determinants of the outcomes). This assumption may not always be true (e.g., see Sherman & McConnell, 1995), but we suspect that it is more often true than false.

inferential benefits; that is, the contrast-induced affective drawbacks of upward counterfactual thoughts dissipate over time, or the upward thoughts may even be inhibited by the individual, as is common for many cognitive and perceptual processes (Bodenhausen & Macrae, 1998; Taylor, 1991). The causal inferences that also derive from counterfactual comparisons, however, may be elaborated into more complex inferences, stored separately in memory or embedded within the frameworks of related concepts, thus continuing to exert their preparative benefits over time. Importantly, then, a key component of this functional argument is that upward comparisons predominate over downward comparisons following negative outcomes.

In this light, it is interesting to note that theorists interested in social comparison have emphasized different consequences of threat from those emphasized by counterfactual researchers. Specifically, some social comparison research has indicated that threat (e.g., resulting from failure on a task or some other personally relevant negative outcome) leads to downward comparisons: the individual repairs his or her ego by comparing with people who are worse off (e.g., Pyszczynski et al., 1985; Wills, 1981; Wood, Taylor, & Lichtman, 1985). In contrast, several experiments on counterfactual thinking have shown the reverse, that is, that threat leads primarily to upward rather than downward counterfactuals (Markman et al., 1993; Roese & Hur, 1997; Roese & Olson, 1995c, 1997; Sanna & Turley, 1996).

This discrepancy might be accounted for in several ways. First, much social comparison research has centered on threatening outcomes that are (relatively) uncontrollable, such as breast cancer and other illnesses, whereas counterfactual research has centered more on controllable outcomes, such as academic achievement. As noted previously, upward comparisons may be more likely to the extent that outcomes are perceived to be controllable (Roese & Olson, 1995c; Ybema & Buunk, 1993). On the other hand, the role of controllability is not unequivocal. Failure on controllable tasks sometimes has been shown to induce downward social comparisons (e.g., Pyszczynski et al., 1985), and some researchers have documented that patients with uncontrollable illnesses (e.g., cancer) prefer upward social comparisons, presumably because such comparisons evoke hope and inspiration, whereas downward comparisons are anxiety provoking about one's own potential future. For example, Van der Zee et al. (1998) designed a computer program that allowed cancer patients to examine the files of other patients. Participants selected more files and spent more time examining each file of patients who were doing well than of patients who were doing poorly.

Another explanation for the discrepant perceptions of the impact of threat centers on the time course of postevent cognitions and the possibility that measures taken at different points in time yield different results. Wood et al. (1985) found that downward social comparisons were more likely soon after rather than long after surgery for breast cancer, but this effect was weak ($r = .20$). Aspinwall and Taylor (1993) found that downward social comparisons unleashed more positive affect soon rather than long after an academic setback. However, in none of these cases were comparisons measured *immediately* after the target event. By contrast, studies of regret under the rubric of dissonance theory indicated that an immediate sense of regret (akin to an upward counterfactual) appeared instantly, but was then suppressed via dissonance reduction processes (e.g., Festinger & Walster, 1964). And in social comparison studies (e.g., Wheeler & Miyake, 1992; Ybema & Buunk, 1993) and counterfactual studies (Markman et al., 1993; Roese & Hur, 1997; Roese & Olson, 1993a, b, 1995c; Sanna & Turley, 1996) in which the dependent measure was completed immediately after the focal outcome, a preponderance of upward rather than downward comparison emerged.

Although untested, it may be that upward comparisons are an automatic, default response to threatening outcomes, whereas downward comparisons are more deliberative and effortful.

This would mean that nonreactive dependent measures may detect upward social and counterfactual comparisons very soon after failure. Because of their automaticity, such effects likely would be immune to depletions of cognitive resources. Subsequently, nonreactive measures may detect downward social and counterfactual comparisons, deployed strategically in the service of mood repair (cf. Sanna, Turley-Ames, & Meier, 1999). Due to their effortful nature, however, such effects may be relatively sensitive to depletions of cognitive resources (see Sanna, Meier, & Turley-Ames, 1998, for conceptually similar findings). A failure to invoke mood repair strategies, and hence to focus for long periods of time on affectively unpleasant upward comparisons, may be predictive of poor coping and depression (Davis et al., 1995; Roese & Olson, 1997). Thus, we suggest that upward comparisons appear immediately and automatically after threatening events, but more effortful attempts at mood repair and dissonance reduction, possibly but not necessarily involving downward comparisons, appear later on.

SOME IMPLICATIONS OF RESEARCH ON COUNTERFACTUAL THINKING FOR RESEARCH ON SOCIAL COMPARISON

The various conceptual similarities between social comparison and counterfactual thinking articulated in the preceding section underscore the links, both theoretical and empirical, between these two comparative processes. We touched only briefly, however, on a few ideas for research that derive from an integrative perspective as we discussed the similarities.

In this section, we consider in more detail some specific implications of research on counterfactual thinking for our understanding of social comparison. Given that the focus of this book is social comparison, we thought it was particularly important to identify some benefits that might accrue for this area of research from familiarity with work on counterfactual thinking.

We will address two general issues in this section: the determinants of counterfactual thinking (activation and content), and the psychological mechanisms that mediate the effects of counterfactual comparisons on emotions and behavior. Though conceptually distinct, these issues encompass many of the same empirical studies on counterfactual thinking. In each case, we think that the findings for counterfactual thinking might well be applicable to social comparison processes.

Determinants of Counterfactual Thinking

Counterfactual researchers have investigated the factors that influence the occurrence (activation) and content of counterfactual thoughts. With regard to activation, we have proposed that negative outcomes (or associated negative affect) constitute the primary trigger of counterfactual thinking. Another trigger of counterfactual activation that we have mentioned is outcome closeness: when an outcome almost occurred, counterfactual thoughts are evoked, which tend to center on the alternative outcome (Kahneman & Varey, 1990).

A third possible trigger of counterfactual activation is unexpected outcomes (Olson, Roese, & Zanna, 1996). By virtue of their unexpectedness, surprising events arouse a need to understand why they occurred—a motive that can be served by counterfactual thinking. A difficulty in testing this prediction is that the expectedness and valence of outcomes tend to be related (negative outcomes are usually unexpected). Empirical tests that have disentangled expectancy and valence consistently have shown that negative outcomes trigger counterfactual thinking, but have yielded more inconsistent results concerning the expectancy factor (see Roese & Olson, 1997). Nevertheless, we suspect that unexpected outcomes do constitute a trigger of counterfactual thinking, though a less powerful one than negative outcomes.

In terms of the determinants of the content of counterfactual thoughts, normality and controllability are two critical variables, as noted in our brief review of counterfactual research at the beginning of the chapter. Thus, abnormal antecedent events tend to be mutated in the direction of normality in counterfactual thoughts. Similarly, the particular antecedent events that are mutated within counterfactual thoughts tend more often to be controllable than uncontrollable. We also noted in the preceding section that controllability may influence whether the direction of comparison is upward or downward; thus, controllability affects counterfactual content in more than one manner.

Each of these five determinants of counterfactual thinking, whether relating to activation or content, can be construed as reflecting the extent to which knowledge about the likely causes of an event will be important or useful:

1. It is probably especially important to understand the causes of negative events, because they can have immediate implications for survival (see Taylor, 1991).
2. Similarly, the effect of outcome closeness seems functional in terms of self-improvement. It is sensible to focus on near misses rather than far misses, because such thinking throws a spotlight on an especially efficient arena for future improvement. Efforts that failed by just a hair probably require only minor fine-tuning to become effective in the future, whereas efforts that failed by a wide margin likely require a more extensive overhaul. If a basketball team loses by one point, they really did almost win; if someone misses a train by 1 minute, they really did almost catch it. Even very modest changes to the antecedent actions would have changed the outcome, so the counterfactual thought is not only compelling but also especially useful. Put another way, outcomes that almost occurred are probably more likely to occur in the future than are outcomes that did not come close to occurring. Given that it is more important to understand probable than improbable events, it seems sensible to selectively invest effort toward understanding the causes of "close" (rather than far) counterfactual outcomes.
3. Devoting attention to unexpected outcomes also makes sense, because such events disconfirmed predictions and therefore clearly require further analysis so that understanding and prediction can be improved in the future (Olson et al., 1996).
4. When something negative occurs, it makes sense to focus on any unusual or abnormal elements that preceded the outcome. If we assume that negative outcomes are relatively uncommon, then it follows that the most plausible causal variables that account for the outcomes are also rare. That is, unusual antecedents are more logically plausible than normally occurring features as causal candidates for unusual outcomes (Roese & Olson, 1997). Thus, there is good logic to searching for abnormal antecedents to negative events.
5. Similarly, it seems prudent to focus attention on those causes of performance that are controllable (Markman et al., 1995). After all, controllable elements of a situation are the ones that can presumably be improved by planning and behavior change.

Why, then, does counterfactual thinking occur under these conditions or in these ways? We propose that counterfactual thinking (1) is easy to perform and (2) is justifiably believed to provide useful information about the causes of outcomes (recall our discussion of the cognitive consequences of counterfactual thinking). The determinants of counterfactual comparisons reflect the extent to which causal information about the event is important or useful; once activated, counterfactuals provide causal insights that may then be enlisted in the service of ongoing social behavior.

But, of course, counterfactual thinking is not the only way (nor, perhaps, even the best way) to attain causal understanding. And this brings us to social comparisons. The preceding reasoning implies that *any* kind of cognitive activity or information seeking that increases causal understanding may be more likely to occur under these conditions. Indeed, such arguments have been explicitly proposed for at least one of the triggers of counterfactual thinking: Taylor (1991) described a range of cognitive activities that are provoked by negative outcomes, including heightened attention, systematic information processing, and attributional reasoning.

Social comparisons also can provide causal insights: the variation in outcomes between the self and some other person may be explained by differences between the two in personality, behavior, situations, and so on. The underlying logic is the principle of covariation, explicated by Kelley (1973), Jones and Davis (1965), and other attribution theorists. Like counterfactual thinking, social comparison can serve a self-improvement function by elucidating causal inferences (Buunk, 1995; Taylor & Lobel, 1989; Wood, 1989), and thus we might expect it to be activated under precisely the same conditions that activate counterfactual thinking. That is, people may be more interested in social comparison information following negative than positive events, near misses than far misses, and unexpected than expected outcomes. The presence of abnormal antecedents and controllable antecedents also might increase interest in social comparison information, with the goal of understanding the causal role of these antecedents.

Yet, relatively few researchers have investigated spontaneous interest in social comparison information (for exceptions, see Buunk, 1995; Foddy & Crundall, 1993; Roney & Sorrentino, 1995; Van der Zee et al., 1998), instead either forcing participants to choose between different kinds of social comparison information or exposing participants to a particular kind of social comparison information and then measuring their reactions (see Wood, 1996). The paucity of research on volitional social comparison probably reflects, at least in part, that social comparison information is frequently unavoidable. Therefore, although theorists have discussed general motives underlying social comparison (e.g., self-enhancement, self-improvement), they frequently have not translated these motives into specific eliciting conditions, or triggers.

Among those researchers who have studied volitional social comparison, the most common question probably has been the impact of outcome valence (one of the possible determinants of comparison mentioned above). For example, Levine and Green (1984) gave children around the age of 9 positive or negative performance feedback over 10 trials on a perceptual task. After each trial, participants had the opportunity to look at the performance of other children, who were consistently characterized as doing either better or worse than the participant. Children who received negative performance feedback engaged in more social comparison when others were allegedly doing poorly than when others were allegedly doing well; children who received positive feedback were equally interested in social comparison information irrespective of the alleged performance of the other children (the main effect for outcome valence was not significant). Similarly, Pyszczynski et al. (1985) gave participants bogus success–failure feedback on a social sensitivity test and led them to expect that most other students performed either well or poorly. Participants were then able to inspect up to 50 scored answer sheets from other participants. Participants who received success feedback evidenced little interest in social comparison information, whereas participants who received failure feedback showed considerable interest in social comparison information when they believed other participants did poorly, but not when they believed other participants did well.

Swallow and Kuiper (1990) asked mildly depressed and nondepressed university students to imagine that they had either failed, passed, or done extremely well on an exam and then to indicate how interested they would be in learning about other students' scores. Performance level did not affect interest in social comparison information, but mildly depressed students who also possessed "dysfunctional attitudes" (which involve considering oneself unworthy if one fails) were more interested in social comparison information than other participants, irrespective of level of performance. In another study, Swallow and Kuiper (1992) provided mildly depressed and nondepressed university students with false feedback on a number sequence task and then gave them the opportunity to look at the scores of other participants. Mildly depressed students were more interested in social comparison information after failure than after success, whereas nondepressed students showed the opposite pattern (neither the main effect for success–failure nor the main effect for depression was significant).

In a more naturalistic study of volitional social comparison, Wheeler and Miyake (1992) had participants keep records of their social comparisons over a period of 2 weeks, including information about their precomparison and postcomparison moods. Results suggested that upward comparisons decreased subjective well-being, whereas downward comparisons increased it. More relevant to the current issue, data presented in a table suggested that a positive precomparison mood was more common than a negative precomparison mood (though there was no measure of moods in the absence of comparisons to provide a baseline). Gibbons et al. (1994) found in two studies that students who thought they had performed poorly reported engaging in less social comparison than did students who thought they had performed well. Students who thought they performed poorly also reported shifting whatever social comparisons they did make in a downward direction, relative to students who thought they performed well.

Sun and Croyle (1995) had participants rate their interest in different kinds of social comparison information after learning about a health threat. No differences were obtained in overall interest in social comparison information as a function of either the negativity or controllability of the threat (although more negative threats diminished interest in one specific kind of social comparison information, namely, upward information about people in better health).

Thus, the data concerning the effect of outcome valence on social comparison have been mixed (paradoxically, perhaps, Taylor did not specifically mention social comparison information in her 1991 paper on the impact of negative outcomes, despite her prominence as a social comparison researcher). Based on counterfactuals research, we would predict that negative outcomes, relative to positive ones, should increase individuals' interest in social comparison information. As described in the preceding paragraphs, however, the experimental evidence does not provide consistent support for this prediction. Although negative outcomes may sometimes increase interest in social comparison information, especially downward information (e.g., Pyszczynski et al., 1985), negative outcomes also appear capable of lowering interest in social comparison information, especially upward information (e.g., Levine & Green, 1984; Sun & Croyle, 1995). Other studies have found interactions between outcome valence and characteristics like depression status (e.g., Swallow & Kuiper, 1990, 1992). We think that these mixed findings reflect that social comparison information has complex consequences, which influence both mood and cognition, and these consequences are sometimes differentially served by upward versus downward comparisons. We hope that outcome valence will receive more attention from social comparison researchers in the future.

The triggers other than negative outcomes identified in the counterfactual thinking literature have received virtually no attention from social comparison researchers. We predict that individuals will be more interested in social comparison information following near misses than far misses, unexpected outcomes than expected outcomes, and when antecedents are abnormal or controllable than when antecedents are normal or uncontrollable. These predictions are based on the rationale that social comparison information (or, for that matter, any information that can yield causal inferences) is more important or useful under the critical conditions.

Mediating Mechanisms

It is important for theorists in the areas of social and counterfactual comparisons to identify the psychological mechanisms through which comparisons affect emotions and behavior. A few mediating variables have been briefly mentioned in this chapter, such as assimilation effects, contrast effects, and causal inferences. In this final section, we suggest a unique relation between counterfactuals and social comparisons.

With regard to the contrast-induced affective impact of social comparisons, we propose that counterfactual thoughts constitute the critical, underlying mechanism. That is, we propose that the typical emotional effect of an upward social comparison—negative affect—is mediated by a counterfactual construction in which the self is transplanted into the shoes of the comparison target: "That could have been me!" Simply acknowledging the existence of a better-off other is itself insufficient to evoke distress; there must be the additional step of imagining that the fruits enjoyed by that upward target could or should have extended to the perceiver. Similarly, a downward comparison is affectively pleasant only to the extent that a counterfactual along the lines of "Lucky that wasn't me" is directly activated by the social comparison. It is for this reason that variables such as psychological closeness (Tesser, 1988) influence the magnitude of the emotional consequences of social comparisons: the more similar the perceiver is to the target, the fewer the mental changes to reality that will be required to construct the counterfactual in which the perceiver takes the place of the target. Thus, learning about other people's outcomes can make us happy or sad because such information alters our thoughts about "what might have been" for us.

This reasoning follows from our own and other people's work on the topic of *relative deprivation*: the feeling that one has been treated unfairly (Olson & Hafer, 1996). Social comparison usually has been postulated as a prerequisite for relative deprivation (e.g., Crosby, 1976; Olson & Hazlewood, 1986), such that individuals must perceive that other persons possess a desired object or state before they will feel resentful about not possessing it personally. Folger (1986), however, proposed in his *referent cognitions theory* that relative deprivation requires not social comparison but rather counterfactual thoughts about how one's own outcomes could have been better. Individuals will feel resentful when it is easy for them to imagine how their outcomes could have been better and when the antecedents that could have produced the improved outcomes are fairer than the antecedents that actually occurred. Thus, unfavorable counterfactual comparisons were proposed as the necessary factor, not unfavorable social comparisons (except insofar as social comparisons can alter counterfactual comparisons). Consistent with this reasoning, we have collected some data showing that variables that increase upward counterfactual thinking also intensify resentment in unfair situations (Olson & Roese, in press). For example, in one study, participants were asked to think of a negative event they had experienced in the past year that was either unfair (e.g., a poor test performance where they had been misled about the content or form of the exam) or fair (e.g., a poor test performance where they did not prepare adequately). Some participants were then asked to generate upward counterfactual thoughts about how the event might have turned out better, whereas other participants were asked to generate downward counterfactual thoughts about how the event could have been even worse. When asked to rate their resentment about the negative event, participants who thought about an unfair event reported more resentment than did participants who thought about a fair event. More importantly, this difference between unfair and fair events in reported resentment was much greater when participants generated upward counterfactual thoughts than when they generated downward counterfactual thoughts. Thus, upward counterfactual thoughts magnified resentment about an unfair negative outcome.

Our hypothesis that counterfactual thoughts underlie the contrast-induced impact of social comparison on affect implies that if counterfactual thoughts are measured directly, they should statistically mediate the effects of manipulations of social comparison information on emotions. We are currently testing this hypothesis. Another possibility is that individual differences in the ability to take another person's perspective (e.g., empathy) or in the tendency to use others as a guide for behavior (e.g., self-monitoring) might moderate the impact of social comparison manipulations on emotions by influencing the extent to which individuals imagine different outcomes for themselves based on other people's outcomes.

On the other hand, we think that when social comparisons produce assimilation effects on emotions, future-oriented thoughts rather than counterfactual thoughts are the critical mediators. For example, when upward social comparisons evoke positive affect, it is usually because hope and optimism about the future are aroused (e.g., when cancer patient encounters a long-term survivor). When downward social comparisons evoke negative affect, it is usually because anxiety and worry about the future are generated (e.g., when a cancer patient encounters dying patients). Counterfactual thoughts about how one's outcomes could have been different in the past seem largely irrelevant to these reactions.

Counterfactual thoughts also seem unlikely to be the mechanism underlying the impact of social comparison information on behavioral intentions and behavior. Rather, we expect that both social comparison and counterfactual thoughts can independently influence causal attributions, which will then affect intentions and behavior. Comparing one's own outcomes either with other people's outcomes or with personal outcomes that might have occurred can provide insight into the causes of the outcomes. For example, if a student who performed poorly on a test compares himself to another student who performed well and learns that the other student studied longer, then studying is implicated as a cause of good performance. Similarly, if a student who performed poorly thinks about how he could have done better and concludes that more studying would have helped, again, studying is implicated as a cause of good performance. We suspect that these causal attributions (resulting from either social comparison or counterfactual thinking) will lead to intentions to study harder for the next test, which will lead to more actual studying for the next test. Moreover, we think that social comparisons and counterfactual thinking potentially can affect attributions independently. For example, we predict that separate social and counterfactual comparisons that imply similar causes can combine additively to produce even more confident causal attributions.

CONCLUSIONS

These speculations illustrate some of the potential heuristic benefits of an integrative perspective on social comparison and counterfactual thinking. Given the conceptual similarities between these two kinds of comparative judgments, we think that an integrative approach is both theoretically plausible and likely to increase our understanding of the two processes. We hope that this chapter moves us in the direction of a broad framework that encompasses both social comparison and counterfactual thinking.

ACKNOWLEDGMENTS

The writing of this chapter was supported by a grant to James Olson from the Social Sciences and Humanities Research Council of Canada and by National Institute of Mental Health FIRST grant MH55578 to Neal Roese.

REFERENCES

Albert, S. (1977). Temporal comparison theory. *Psychological Review, 84,* 485–503.
Alicke, M. D., LoSchiavo, F. M., Zerbst, J., & Zhang, S. (1997). The person who outperforms me is a genius: Maintaining perceived competence in upward social comparison. *Journal of Personality and Social Psychology, 73,* 781–789.
Aspinwall, L. G., & Taylor, S. E. (1993). Effects of social comparison direction, threat, and self-esteem on affect, self-evaluation, and expected success. *Journal of Personality and Social Psychology, 64,* 708–722.
Bargh, J. A. (1996). Automaticity in social psychology. In E. T. Higgins & A. W. Kruglanski (Eds.), *Social psychology: Handbook of basic principles* (pp. 169–183). New York: Guilford.
Biernat, M., & Manis, M. (1997). Simultaneous assimilation and contrast effects in judgments of self and others. *Journal of Personality and Social Psychology, 73,* 254–269.
Bodenhausen, G. V., & Macrae, C. N. (1998). Stereotype activation and inhibition. In R. S. Wyer, Jr. (Ed.), *Advances in social cognition* (Vol. 11, pp. 1–52). Mahwah, NJ: Lawrence Erlbaum.
Brickman, P., & Bulman, R. J. (1977). Pleasure and pain in social comparison. In J. M. Suls & R. L. Miller (Eds.), *Social comparison processes: Theoretical and empirical perspectives* (pp. 149–186). Washington, DC: Hemisphere.
Buunk, B. P. (1995). Comparison direction and comparison dimension among disabled individuals: Toward a refined conceptualization of social comparison under stress. *Personality and Social Psychology Bulletin, 21,* 316–330.
Buunk, B. P., Collins, R. L., Taylor, S. E., Dakof, G., & Van Yperen, N. (1990). The affective consequences of social comparison: Either direction has its ups and downs. *Journal of Personality and Social Psychology, 59,* 1238–1249.
Collins, R. L. (1996). For better or worse: The impact of upward social comparison on self-evaluations. *Psychological Bulletin, 119,* 51–69.
Crosby, F. (1976). A model of egoistical relative deprivation. *Psychological Review, 83,* 85–113.
Davis, C. G., & Lehman, D. R. (1995). Counterfactual thinking and coping with traumatic life events. In N. J. Roese & J. M. Olson (Eds.), *What might have been: The social psychology of counterfactual thinking* (pp. 353–374). Mahwah, NJ: Lawrence Erlbaum.
Davis, C. G., Lehman, D. R., Wortman, C. B., Silver, R. C., & Thompson, S. C. (1995). The undoing of traumatic life events. *Personality and Social Psychology Bulletin, 21,* 109–124.
Dunning, D., & Madey, S. F. (1995). Comparison processes in counterfactual thought. In N. J. Roese & J. M. Olson (Eds.), *What might have been: The social psychology of counterfactual thinking* (pp. 103–131). Mahwah, NJ: Lawrence Erlbaum.
Fazio, R. H. (1979). Motives for social comparison: The construction–validation distinction. *Journal of Personality and Social Psychology, 37,* 1683–1698.
Festinger, L. (1954). A theory of social comparison. *Human Relations, 7,* 117–140.
Festinger, L., & Walster, E. (1964). Post-decision regret and decision reversal. In L. Festinger (Ed.), *Conflict, decision, and dissonance* (pp. 112–127). Stanford, CA: Stanford University Press.
Foddy, M., & Crundall, I. (1993). A field study of social comparison processes in ability evaluation. *British Journal of Social Psychology, 32,* 287–305.
Folger, R. G. (1986). A referent cognitions theory of relative deprivation. In J. M. Olson, C. P. Herman, & M. P. Zanna (Eds.), *Relative deprivation and social comparison: The Ontario symposium* (Vol. 4, pp. 33–55). Hillsdale, NJ: Lawrence Erlbaum.

Gibbons, F. X., Benbow, C. P., & Gerrard, M. (1994). From top dog to bottom half: Social comparison strategies in response to poor performance. *Journal of Personality and Social Psychology, 67*, 638–652.

Gilbert, D. T., Giesler, R. B., & Morris, K. A. (1995). When comparisons arise. *Journal of Personality and Social Psychology, 69*, 227–236.

Gilovich, T., & Medvec, V. H. (1995). The experience of regret: What, when, and why. *Psychological Review, 102*, 379–395.

Girotto, V., Legrenzi, P., & Rizzo, A. (1991). Event controllability in counterfactual thinking. *Acta Psychologica, 78*, 111–133.

Gurr, T. R. (1970). *Why men rebel.* Princeton, NJ: Princeton University Press.

Helgeson, V. S., & Mickelson, K. D. (1995). Motives for social comparison. *Personality and Social Psychology Bulletin, 21*, 1200–1209.

Herr, P. M. (1986). Consequences of priming: Judgment and behavior. *Journal of Personality and Social Psychology, 51*, 1106–1115.

Higgins, E. T. (1987). Self-discrepancy theory: A theory relating self and affect. *Psychological Review, 94*, 319–340.

Holyoak, K. J., & Gordon, P. C. (1983). Social reference points. *Journal of Personality and Social Psychology, 44*, 881–887.

Johnson, M. K., & Sherman, S. J. (1990). Constructing and reconstructing the past and the future in the present. In E. T. Higgins & R. M. Sorrentino (Eds.), *Handbook of motivation and cognition: Foundations of social behavior* (Vol. 2, pp. 482–526). New York: Guilford.

Jones, E. E., & Davis, K. E. (1965). From acts to dispositions: The attribution process in person perception. In L. Berkowitz (Ed.), *Advances in experimental social psychology* (Vol. 2, pp. 219–266). New York: Academic Press.

Kahneman, D. (1995). Varieties of counterfactual thinking. In N. J. Roese & J. M. Olson (Eds.), *What might have been: The social psychology of counterfactual thinking* (pp. 375–396). Mahwah, NJ: Lawrence Erlbaum.

Kahneman, D., & Miller, D. T. (1986). Norm theory: Comparing reality to its alternatives. *Psychological Review, 93*, 136–153.

Kahneman, D., & Tversky, A. (1982). The simulation heuristic. In D. Kahneman, P. Slovic, & A. Tversky (Eds.), *Judgment under uncertainty: Heuristics and biases* (pp. 201–208). New York: Cambridge University Press.

Kahneman, D., & Varey, C. A. (1990). Propensities and counterfactuals: The loser that almost won. *Journal of Personality and Social Psychology, 59*, 1101–1110.

Kelley, H. H. (1973). The process of causal attributions. *American Psychologist, 28*, 107–128.

Kruglanski, A. W., & Mayseless, O. (1987). Motivational effects in the social comparison of opinions. *Journal of Personality and Social Psychology, 53*, 834–853.

Kruglanski, A. W., & Mayseless, O. (1990). Classic and current social comparison research: Expanding the perspective. *Psychological Bulletin, 108*, 195–208.

Landman, J. (1993). *Regret: The persistence of the possible.* New York: Oxford University Press.

Lehman, D. R., & Hemphill, K. J. (1990). Recipients' perceptions of support attempts and attributions for support attempts that fail. *Journal of Social and Personal Relationships, 7*, 563–574.

Levine, J. M., & Green, S. M. (1984). Acquisition of relative performance information: The roles of intrapersonal and interpersonal comparison. *Personality and Social Psychology Bulletin, 10*, 385–393.

Lipe, M. G. (1991). Counterfactual reasoning as a framework for attribution theories. *Psychological Bulletin, 109*, 456–471.

Lockwood, P., & Kunda, Z. (1997). Superstars and me: Predicting the impact of role models on the self. *Journal of Personality and Social Psychology, 73*, 91–103.

Lombardi, W. J., Higgins, E. T., & Bargh, J. A. (1987). The role of consciousness in priming effects on categorization: Assimilation versus contrast as a function of awareness of the priming task. *Personality and Social Psychology Bulletin, 13*, 411–429.

Major, B., Testa, M., & Bylsma, W. H. (1991). Responses to upward and downward social comparisons: The impact of esteem-relevance and perceived control. In J. Suls & T. A. Wills (Eds.), *Social comparison: Contemporary theory and research* (pp. 237–257). Hillsdale, NJ: Lawrence Erlbaum.

Mandel, D. R., & Lehman, D. R. (1996). Counterfactual thinking and ascriptions of cause and preventability. *Journal of Personality and Social Psychology, 71*, 450–463.

Markman, K. D., Gavanski, I., Sherman, S. J., & McMullen, M. N. (1993). The simulation of better and worse possible worlds. *Journal of Experimental Social Psychology, 29*, 87–109.

Markman, K. D., Gavanski, I., Sherman, S. J., & McMullen, M. N. (1995). The impact of perceived control on the imagination of better and worse possible worlds. *Personality and Social Psychology Bulletin, 21*, 588–595.

Markus, H. J., & Nurius, P. (1986). Possible selves. *American Psychologist, 41*, 954–969.

McFarland, C., & Miller, D. T. (1994). The framing of relative performance feedback: Seeing the glass as half empty or half full. *Journal of Personality and Social Psychology, 66*, 1061–1073.

McMullen, M. N. (1997). Affective contrast and assimilation in counterfactual thinking. *Journal of Experimental Social Psychology, 33,* 77–100.

Miller, D. T., & Turnbull, W. (1990). The counterfactual fallacy: Confusing what might have been with what ought to have been. *Social Justice Research, 4,* 1–19.

Miller, D. T., Turnbull, W., & McFarland, C. (1990). Counterfactual thinking and social perception: Thinking about what might have been. In M. P. Zanna (Ed.), *Advances in experimental social psychology* (Vol. 23, pp. 305–331). New York: Academic Press.

Niedenthal, P. M., Tangney, J. P., & Gavanski, I. (1994). "If only I weren't" versus "If only I hadn't": Distinguishing shame and guilt in counterfactual thinking. *Journal of Personality and Social Psychology, 67,* 585–595.

Olson, J. M., Ellis, R. J., & Zanna, M. P. (1983). Validating objective versus subjective judgments: Interest in social comparison and consistency information. *Personality and Social Psychology Bulletin, 9,* 427–436.

Olson, J. M., & Hafer, C. L. (1996). Affect, motivation, and cognition in relative deprivation research. In R. M. Sorrentino & E. T. Higgins (Eds.), *Handbook of motivation and cognition: The interpersonal context* (Vol. 3, pp. 85–117). New York: Guilford.

Olson, J. M., & Hazlewood, J. D. (1986). Relative deprivation and social comparison: An integrative perspective. In J. M. Olson, C. P. Herman, & M. P. Zanna (Eds.), *Relative deprivation and social comparison: The Ontario symposium* (Vol. 4, pp. 1–15). Hillsdale, NJ: Lawrence Erlbaum.

Olson, J. M., & Roese, N. J. (In press). Relative deprivation and counterfactual thinking. In I. Walker & H. Smith (Eds.), *Relative deprivation: Specification, development, and integration.* Cambridge, England: Cambridge University Press.

Olson, J. M., Roese, N. J., & Zanna, M. P. (1996). Expectancies. In E. T. Higgins & A. W. Kruglanski (Eds.), *Social psychology: Handbook of basic principles* (pp. 211–238). New York: Guilford.

Pelham, B. W., & Wachsmuth, J. O. (1995). The waxing and waning of the social self: Assimilation and contrast in social comparison. *Journal of Personality and Social Psychology, 69,* 825–838.

Petty, R. E., & Wegener, D. T. (1993). Flexible correction processes in social judgment: Correcting for context-induced contrast. *Journal of Experimental Social Psychology, 29,* 137–165.

Pyszczynski, T., Greenburg, J., & LaPrelle, J. (1985). Social comparison after success and failure: Biased search for information consistent with a self-serving conclusion. *Journal of Experimental Social Psychology, 21,* 195–211.

Roese, N. J. (1994). The functional basis of counterfactual thinking. *Journal of Personality and Social Psychology, 66,* 805–818.

Roese, N. J. (1997). Counterfactual thinking. *Psychological Bulletin, 121,* 133–148.

Roese, N. J., & Hur, T. (1997). Affective determinants of counterfactual thinking. *Social Cognition, 15,* 274–290.

Roese, N. J., & Olson, J. M. (1993a). Self-esteem and counterfactual thinking. *Journal of Personality and Social Psychology, 65,* 199–206.

Roese, N. J., & Olson, J. M. (1993b). The structure of counterfactual thought. *Personality and Social Psychology Bulletin, 19,* 312–319.

Roese, N. J., & Olson, J. M. (1995a). Counterfactual thinking: A critical overview. In N. J. Roese & J. M. Olson (Eds.), *What might have been: The social psychology of counterfactual thinking* (pp. 1–55). Mahwah, NJ: Lawrence Erlbaum.

Roese, N. J., & Olson, J. M. (1995b). Functions of counterfactual thinking. In N. J. Roese & J. M. Olson (Eds.), *What might have been: The social psychology of counterfactual thinking* (pp. 169–197). Mahwah, NJ: Lawrence Erlbaum.

Roese, N. J., & Olson, J. M. (1995c). Outcome controllability and counterfactual thinking. *Personality and Social Psychology Bulletin, 21,* 620–628.

Roese, N. J., & Olson, J. M. (1997). Counterfactual thinking: The intersection of affect and function. In M. P. Zanna (Ed.), *Advances in experimental social psychology* (Vol. 29, pp. 1–59). San Diego, CA: Academic Press.

Roney, C. R., & Sorrentino, R. M. (1995). Uncertainty orientation, the self, and others: Individual differences in values and social comparison. *Canadian Journal of Behavioural Science, 27,* 157–170.

Sanna, L. J., Meier, S., & Turley-Ames, K. J. (1998). Mood, self-esteem, and counterfactuals: Externally attributed moods limit self-enhancement strategies. *Social Cognition, 16,* 267–286.

Sanna, L. J., & Turley, K. J. (1996). Antecedents to spontaneous counterfactual thinking: Effects of expectancy violation and outcome valence. *Personality and Social Psychology Bulletin, 22,* 906–919.

Sanna, L. J., Turley-Ames, K. J., & Meier, S. (1999). Mood, self-esteem, and simulated alternatives: Thought-provoking affective influences on counterfactual direction. *Journal of Personality and Social Psychology, 76,* 543–558.

Sedikides, C., & Strube, M. J. (1997). Self-evaluation: To thine own self be good, to thine own self be sure, to thine own self be true, and to thine own self be better. In M. P. Zanna (Ed.), *Advances in experimental social psychology* (Vol. 29, pp. 209–269). New York: Academic Press.

Sherif, M., & Hovland, C. I. (1961). *Social judgment: Assimilation and contrast effects in communication and attitude change*. New Haven, CT: Yale University Press.

Sherman, S. J., & McConnell, A. R. (1995). Dysfunctional implications of counterfactual thinking: When alternatives to reality fail us. In N. J. Roese & J. M. Olson (Eds.), *What might have been: The social psychology of counterfactual thinking* (pp. 199–231). Mahwah, NJ: Lawrence Erlbaum.

Strack, F., Schwarz, N., & Gschneidinger, E. (1985). Happiness and reminiscing: The role of time perspective, affect, and mode of thinking. *Journal of Personality and Social Psychology, 49*, 1460–1469.

Suls, J. (1986). Comparison processes in relative deprivation: A life-span analysis. In J. M. Olson, C. P. Herman, & M. P. Zanna (Eds.), *Relative deprivation and social comparison: The Ontario symposium* (Vol. 4, pp. 95–116). Hillsdale, NJ: Erlbaum.

Sun, Y.-C., & Croyle, R. T. (1995). Level of health threat as a moderator of social comparison preferences. *Journal of Applied Social Psychology, 25*, 1937–1952.

Swallow, S. R., & Kuiper, N. A. (1990). Mild depression, dysfunctional cognitions, and interest in social comparison information. *Journal of Social and Clinical Psychology, 9*, 287–300.

Swallow, S. R., & Kuiper, N. A. (1992). Mild depression and frequency of social comparison behavior. *Journal of Social and Clinical Psychology, 11*, 167–180.

Taylor, S. E. (1991). Asymmetrical effects of positive and negative events: The mobilization-minimization hypothesis. *Psychological Bulletin, 110*, 67–85.

Taylor, S. E., & Lobel, M. (1989). Social comparison activity under threat: Downward evaluation and upward contact. *Psychological Review, 96*, 569–575.

Taylor, S. E., & Schneider, S. K. (1989). Coping and the simulation of events. *Social Cognition, 7*, 174–194.

Taylor, S. E., Wayment, H. A., & Carrillo, M. (1996). Social comparison, self-regulation, and motivation. In R. M. Sorrentino & E. T. Higgins (Eds.), *Handbook of motivation and cognition: The interpersonal context* (Vol. 3, pp. 3–27). New York: Guilford.

Tesser, A. (1988). Toward a self-evaluation maintenance model of social behavior. In L. Berkowitz (Ed.), *Advances in experimental social psychology* (Vol. 21, pp. 181–227). New York: Academic Press.

Testa, M., & Major, B. (1990). The impact of social comparisons after failure: The moderating effects of perceived control. *Basic and Applied Social Psychology, 11*, 205–218.

Tversky, A. (1977). Features of similarity. *Psychological Review, 84*, 327–352.

Van der Zee, K., Oldersma, F., Buunk, B. P., & Bos, D. (1998). Social comparison preferences among cancer patients as related to neuroticism and social comparison orientation. *Journal of Personality and Social Psychology, 75*, 801–810.

Wedell, D. H. (1994). Contextual contrast in evaluative judgments: A test of pre- versus postintegration models of contrast. *Journal of Personality and Social Psychology, 66*, 1007–1019.

Wegener, D. T., & Petty, R. E. (1997). The flexible correction model: The role of naive theories in bias correction. In M. P. Zanna (Ed.), *Advances in experimental social psychology* (Vol. 29, pp. 141–208). San Diego, CA: Academic Press.

Wells, G. L., & Gavanski, I. (1989). Mental simulation of causality. *Journal of Personality and Social Psychology, 56*, 161–169.

Wheeler, L., Martin, R., & Suls, J. (1997). The proxy model of social comparison for self-assessment of ability. *Personality and Social Psychology Review, 1*, 54–61.

Wheeler, L., & Miyake, K. (1992). Social comparison in everyday life. *Journal of Personality and Social Psychology, 62*, 760–773.

Wills, T. A. (1981). Downward comparison principles in social psychology. *Psychological Bulletin, 90*, 245–271.

Wood, J. V. (1989). Theory and research concerning social comparisons of personal attributes. *Psychological Bulletin, 106*, 231–248.

Wood, J. V. (1996). What is social comparison and how should we study it? *Personality and Social Psychology Bulletin, 22*, 520–527.

Wood, J. V., Taylor, S. E., & Lichtman, R. R. (1985). Social comparison in adjustment to breast cancer. *Journal of Personality and Social Psychology, 49*, 1169–1183.

Ybema, J. F., & Buunk, B. P. (1993). Aiming at the top? Upward social comparison of abilities after failure. *European Journal of Social Psychology, 23*, 627–645.

IV

Applications

19

Social Identity and Social Comparison

MICHAEL A. HOGG

Social comparison is a pervasive and fundamental feature of group life. People compare themselves with fellow group members, they compare themselves with people in other groups, and they compare their own group with other groups. From these comparisons emerge group norms, group structure, and intergroup relations, which in turn provide the framework for group-based social comparisons. Any theory of the social group therefore would be a strange theory indeed if it did not deal with social comparison processes. In this chapter, I discuss social identity theory; a theory of the social group that originated in Europe in the very early 1970s, and that now has a significant and still burgeoning profile in contemporary social psychology.

Social identity theory is a theory that rests on people making social comparisons between in-group and out-group, or between self as in-grouper and other as out-grouper, in order to construct a sense of who they are and how they are evaluated. The outcome of such comparisons is status differentials and the entire edifice of intergroup behavior. The theory, particularly its more recent emphasis on self-categorization processes, also deals with intragroup comparisons; group-membership-based comparisons among people who belong to the same group.

In this chapter, I describe historically how social identity theory has incorporated social comparison notions and how it has modified such notions. I describe some of the basic social identity findings relating to group membership based social comparison, largely intergroup comparisons. I also describe the role of social comparison in self-categorization theory, and from there present some new ideas on the motivational underpinnings of social identity processes and social comparison in group contexts. I then try to tie some of these strands together to provide an integrative social identity model of social comparison processes in group contexts. Let us begin with a very short overview of social comparison theory.

MICHAEL A. HOGG • School of Psychology, University of Queensland, Brisbane, Queensland 4072, Australia.

Handbook of Social Comparison: Theory and Research, edited by Suls and Wheeler. Kluwer Academic/Plenum Publishers, New York, 2000.

A BRIEF OVERVIEW OF SOCIAL COMPARISON THEORY

Early Origins

Festinger's (1954a,b) theory of social comparison processes rests on the assumption that there is a "... motivation to know that one's opinions are correct and to know precisely what one is and is not capable of doing" (Festinger, 1954b, p. 217). Although the motivation itself is "... certainly non-social in character" (Festinger, 1954b, p. 217), its satisfaction becomes social when people are unable to evaluate opinions and abilities by testing them directly against physical reality. Under these circumstances, people evaluate their opinions and abilities by comparing themselves with people who are similar to them on relevant dimensions. They make social comparisons. Social comparison processes lead to pressures toward uniformity among people. However, Festinger believed that there is a "unidirectional drive upward" in which people make ability comparisons, in particular, with similar others who are marginally better than themselves.

In contrast to his earlier theory of informal social communication (Festinger, 1950), which focused on the power of the group, the theory of social comparison processes focused on interpersonal processes. In comparing the two theories, Wheeler (1991) concludes:

> comparison theory was more individually oriented. That is, the communication theory stressed the power of the group over the individual, whereas the comparison theory emphasized individuals using others to fulfill their own need to know.... The shift ... was clearly toward an individualistic focus. (p. 3)

Initially, social comparison theory never really "took off." Festinger quickly moved on to other things, and Schachter (1959) applied the general idea to emotions in order to explain how fear may lead to affiliation among similar people because people seek out similar others in order to evaluate their feelings (see Cottrell & Epley, 1977). In addition, Festinger's original formulation was criticized for being ambiguous about specifics (e.g., Arrowood, 1986). For a brief history of social comparison theory, see Wheeler (1991).

Upward Comparisons, Downward Comparisons, and Self-Enhancement

However, one far-reaching development was a distinction between upward and downward comparisons, introduced by Thornton and Arrowood (1966) but modified and developed by Wills (1981, 1991). People are motivated both by self-evaluation and self-enhancement needs. Self-evaluation is satisfied by making comparisons with people who are generally similar but slightly better than oneself (upward comparisons; predicated on the notion, described above, of a unidirectional drive upward) and self-enhancement by comparisons with people who are worse than oneself (downward comparisons). The notion that self-enhancement may motivate social comparisons was a new development on Festinger's original self-evaluation motivational base; it introduced the idea that people may make comparisons to feel better than others rather than to feel confident about the veracity of opinions. It also recognized that people may make comparisons with dissimilar others. Some circumstances when this may occur are (1) when people are simply trying to establish the range of abilities within which they fall, or (2) when the primary motive is self-enhancement. In the latter case, extreme upward comparisons do not harm self-esteem because the comparison other is so much better than self as to fall effectively in a different and incomparable category and extreme downward comparison really makes one feel good.

Of particular relevance to the present chapter's focus on intergroup relations, Wills (1981) suggests that prejudice and discrimination may reflect a downward comparison process where people with relatively low state or trait self-esteem compare themselves with people who are less well off than themselves because derogation of others may restore their self-esteem (cf. Luhtanen & Crocker, 1991). Downward intergroup comparisons may perpetuate derogatory out-group perceptions (Gibbons & Gerrard, 1991), and unfavorable upward intergroup comparisons may encourage compensatory downward interpersonal comparisons (e.g., Nagata & Crosby, 1991).

In their commentary on developments to 1991, Wills and Suls (1991) concluded that "similarity" also may take different forms that have different social comparison effects:

1. In order to make a comparison on a particular dimension, people may first look for similarity on a broad range of related attributes.
2. People may be willing to make transitory comparisons with people who like themselves have unfavorable personalities, but will avoid making more enduring comparisons with such people. People avoid enduring comparisons because such comparisons tend to accumulate discouraging information about the possibility that one might be able to improve one's own personality.
3. Similarity based on close interpersonal bonds encourages social comparison. However, it carries with it potentially enhanced negative consequences for self-esteem because it can be very difficult to avoid making enduring upward comparisons without severing the close relationship.
4. Similarity favors social comparison when the goal is self-evaluation but not when the goal is self-enhancement.

Research also shows that people may shift from upward or lateral comparisons to downward comparisons when they feel a threat to self-esteem. This threat can come, for example, from close interpersonal bonds (esteem-damaging lateral comparisons with close friends may be balanced by downward comparisons with strangers) or from health problems, or from being in a competitive relationship (for example an intergroup relation), or from having low trait self-esteem. According to Wills and Suls (1991), contemporary social comparison research places more emphasis on self-enhancement than self-evaluative functions of social comparison. One reason for this, is that people are generally fairly sure of their opinions and abilities and so they make comparisons largely in order to know that their position is a good one.

Historical Background to Social Identity Theory and Self-Categorization Theory

Social identity theory has its roots in Tajfel's perceptual overestimation and judgmental accentuation research of the late 1950s and early 1960s (e.g., Tajfel, 1959) and his analyses of stereotyping during the 1960s, culminating in his classic 1969 paper on cognitive aspects of prejudice (Tajfel, 1969). From the very end of the 1960s through to his death in 1982, Tajfel, in collaboration with Turner who joined him as a graduate student in the early 1970s, integrated his social categorization, ethnocentrism, and intergroup relations research around the concept of social identity (e.g., Tajfel, 1972, 1974, 1978; Tajfel & Turner, 1979, Turner, 1982; see Hogg & Abrams, 1988).

From the very end of the 1970s and during the first half of the 1980s Turner and his students refocused attention on the categorization process. These ideas were formalized as self-categorization theory (Turner, 1985; Turner, Hogg, Oakes, Reicher, & Wetherell, 1987), which can be considered the cognitive component of the wider social identity perspective (e.g., Hogg, 1996a; Hogg & Abrams, 1988, 1999; Hogg & McGarty, 1990; also see Farr, 1996).

Since the late 1980s there has been an explosion in publication on social identity and self-categorization processes (e.g., Abrams & Hogg, 1990, 1999; Hogg, 1992; Hogg & Abrams, 1988; Robinson, 1996; Turner, et al., 1987; Worchel, Morales, Páez, & Deschamps, 1998), and this research tradition has been a major influence on the recent and continuing revival of social psychological research on group processes (e.g., Abrams & Hogg, 1998; Hogg & Abrams, 1999; Moreland, Hogg, & Hains, 1994). For historical commentaries on aspects of the development of social identity theory see Hogg (1996a), Turner (1996) and Hogg and Abrams (1999).

Social Comparison Processes in Social Identity Theory

Tajfel's Incorporation and (Re)-Interpretation of Social Comparison Processes   Social comparison is of course central to social identity theory, because social identity processes hinge on self-definition as a group member within an intergroup social comparative context. It was not until 1972 that Tajfel introduced the term social identity. He did this in order to move from his earlier consideration of social, largely intergroup, perceptions (i.e., stereotyping and prejudice) to consideration of how self is conceptualized in intergroup contexts; how a system of social categorizations "… creates and defines an individual's *own* place in society" (Tajfel, 1972, p. 293). He defined social identity as "… the individual's knowledge that he belongs to certain social groups together with some emotional and value significance to him of this group membership" (Tajfel, 1972, p. 292). At exactly the same time (less than a page later) as he introduced the notion of social identity (drawing to some extent on work by Berger, 1966), Tajfel also for the first time discussed social comparison theory, citing only Festinger (1954a). He listed four consequences for group membership that follow from his conceptualization of social identity. The fourth consequence was that since "… all groups in society live in the midst of other groups" (Tajfel, 1972, pp. 293–294), the positive aspects of social identity (those aspects from which "some satisfaction" is derived), and the social value of a specific group membership (e.g., its social status and the social valence of its attributes) "… only acquire meaning in relation to, or in comparison with, other groups" (Tajfel, 1972, p. 294). Tajfel (1972) claimed that it is "… this comparative perspective that links social categorization with social identity" (p. 294). Thus, social comparison theory was necessary to develop social identity theory out of earlier social categorization ideas (also see Tajfel, 1974, 1978; Turner, 1975).

However, Tajfel (1972) extended Festinger's (1954a) theory in important ways; see Turner's (1975) careful summary. Although Tajfel agreed that there exists in the human organism a drive to evaluate opinions and abilities, he believed that almost all nontrivial evaluations rest on social comparisons. The scope of nonsocial means of acquiring knowledge is tiny. Even the most apparently nonsocial physical judgments acquire meaning, and therefore validity, socially. For example, we can confirm that an object is a bed by looking at it; but knowing that it is a bed rests on a wide consensus that things that look like beds are beds and that they are for sleeping on. If someone told you it was a table, you would be surprised; but if enough people told you continually from birth that it was a table, then it would be a table to you, and you would probably sit at it to eat. Tajfel's point is that what we take unquestioningly to be physical reality is to a large extent grounded in enduring and widespread social consensus (also see Garfinkel, 1967; Moscovici, 1976; Turner, 1991). Social comparison

processes may be much more widespread than Festinger (1954a) supposed; they may under-
pin virtually all evaluations of opinions and abilities.

Tajfel (1972) correctly recognized that Festinger was mainly concerned with individuals
comparing themselves with other individuals in order to evaluate their own personal characteristics, and therefore that Festinger's notion of similarity, both as a precursor and an outcome
of comparison, was interpersonal similarity (see Wheeler, 1991). Tajfel felt that Festinger
focused on within-group effects of social comparison, and thus pressures toward uniformity
among individuals within groups, and that comparisons between groups might have an entirely
different dynamic. Tajfel argued that groups, and thus social identity, acquire meaning because
in-groups are different from out-groups; logically it cannot be otherwise because it is differentiation that delineates categories. Thus intergroup comparisons seek to evaluate or confirm
differences, not similarities: "social comparisons between groups are focused on the establishment of distinctiveness between one's own and other groups" (Tajfel, 1972, p. 296). Furthermore, because social identity is self-evaluative and derives its evaluation from the evaluative
properties of one's own group relative to other groups, the intergroup social comparison
process strives to accentuate differences that evaluatively favor the in-group; that is, it strives
to achieve evaluatively positive intergroup differentiation.

Intergroup Comparisons and Intergroup Relations

It is quite clear from Tajfel's analysis that although self-evaluation is a motive for
intergroup comparisons (rendering in-group distinct from out-group and thus validating social
identity), self-enhancement, through evaluatively positive social identity, is also a very,
perhaps more, important motive. Turner (1975) clarifies this:

> An individual's need for positively valued identity requires that where an intergroup comparison can
> be made in terms of a dimension whose poles have a clear value differential, then his own group must
> differentiate itself relative to other groups on that dimension towards the positively valued pole. (p. 8)

Reflecting back on social comparison theory, Turner (1975) notes that

> the important comparative dimensions for social identity parallel those of abilities rather than opinions,
> i.e., they are value laden.... (T)he individual's need to evaluate himself in society is more correctly
> expressed as a need to make a favourable or positive evaluation of himself in society. (p. 9)

Intergroup social comparisons, as defined by Tajfel (1972), lie at the core of social
identity theory's explication of intergroup relations. Turner (1975) explains that intergroup
relations are characterized by "a process of competition for positive identity" (p. 10), and
Tajfel (1974) explains in detail how groups and their members may pursue different strategies
to protect or enhance positive distinctiveness and positive social identity. The choice of
strategy is determined by people's subjective understanding of the nature of relations between
groups (called subjective belief structures) in terms of (1) the relative status of groups, (2) the
stability of the status relations, (3) the legitimacy of the status relations, and (4) the permeability of intergroup boundaries, and thus the possibility of psychologically leaving one
group and becoming a member of the other group. This intergroup relations aspect of social
identity theory was slightly elaborated and published in Tajfel and Turner's (1979) landmark
chapter (but also see Tajfel, 1975, 1976), and has had an enormous impact on social psychology
(see Ellemers, 1993; Hogg & Abrams, 1988).

It is important to note that although the social identity theory conceptualization of
intergroup comparisons implicates downward comparison processes, the emphasis is on
intergroup comparisons and on the role of subjective belief structures in determining when

downward or upward comparisons are made. Social identity processes are associated with a self-enhancement motive that causes people to do whatever is contextually feasible to protect or enhance the valence of their social identity, and thus to protect or enhance their self-esteem. In intergroup contexts where intergroup permeability is perceived to be high (i.e., people believe they can successfully dis-identify from their in-group and pass psychologically into the out-group), the self-evaluative penalty of lower-status group membership is easily resolved by psychologically passing into the out-group, changing allegiance and identifying with the out-group. Social comparisons then reflect this change of allegiance; downward comparisons with the erstwhile in-group.

It is rare, however, for permeability really to be high and for passing to be genuinely possible. Intergroup boundaries are, in reality, usually hard and impermeable, despite ideologies to the contrary. In intergroup contexts where intergroup permeability is perceived to be low (i.e., people believe they cannot successfully dis-identify from their in-group and pass psychologically into the out-group), people generally try to compare themselves downward with relatively less favorable (i.e., lower status) out-groups. They also can try to reconstruct the in-group in a relatively more positive light by changing the dimensions of comparison or the valence of existing dimensions; in which case a limited form of upward comparisons may be possible. However, it is where subjective belief structures identify existing impermeable intergroup status relations as unstable and illegitimate that upward comparisons really occur, as part of a general competitive orientation toward the higher-status out-group. In contrast, Wills's (1981) later downward comparison, theory focuses only on interpersonal comparisons and therefore does not incorporate beliefs about the nature of intergroup relations as a moderating mechanism (see discussion by Luhtanen & Crocker 1991).

Self-Enhancement and Self-Esteem

The social comparison process in social identity theory also has been investigated in a more micro manner, which has largely moved the agenda within social identity theory away from social comparison processes and toward underlying motives for social identification and group behaviors (including, of course, self-enhancing intergroup comparisons).

As we have seen, the emphasis in social identity theory is very much on a self-enhancement motivation underlying intergroup comparisons. Turner (1975) in particular makes this quite clear, and Billig (1985) believes that this was a necessary theoretical development in order for social identity theory to be able to understand the dynamics of social change. In his subsequent research, Turner takes this idea one stage further by predicating a striving for favorable evaluation of self in society on a fundamental need for self-esteem. For example, Turner states that "those aspects of an individual's self-concept, and hence self-esteem, which are anchored in his social category memberships can be referred to as his perceived social identity" (Turner, 1978a, p. 105), and considers the "need for positive self-esteem" (Turner, 1982, p. 33) to be a fundamental human motivation that under conditions of heightened social identity salience is satisfied by relatively positive evaluation of one's own group (Turner, Brown, & Tajfel, 1979). Turner has stated: "I do assume that there is a need for positive self-esteem, not as an axiom, but on the basis of extensive research (into, for example, social comparison, cognitive dissonance, interpersonal attraction, self-presentation, defensive attribution, and so on)" (1981, p. 133).

Abrams and Hogg (1988) took this idea to its logical conclusion by postulating the existence of a self-esteem hypothesis in social identity theory. In intergroup contexts, (1) lowered self-esteem motivates people to identify with their group and thus to display intergroup behaviors, and (2) social identification elevates self-esteem. Reviews of research bearing on the self-esteem hypothesis reveal inconsistent and unreliable findings in which lowered self-esteem sometimes motivates identification and identification sometimes elevates self-esteem. The relationship between self-esteem and identification may be influenced by a number of factors such as the extremity of self-esteem, the degree to which people identify with the group, the extent to which groups and their members may feel under threat, and whether self-esteem is individual or group membership based (Abrams & Hogg, 1988; Hogg & Abrams, 1990, 1993; Hogg & Mullin, 1999; Long & Spears, 1997; Rubin & Hewstone, 1998). Crocker and colleagues, largely taking Wills's (1981) downward comparison theory as their departure point (e.g., Crocker, Thompson, McGraw, & Ingerman, 1987; Luhtanen & Crocker, 1991), have explored self-esteem processes in intergroup behavior extensively. They have developed a collective self-esteem scale that many researchers employ as a measure of social identity. In this work, social identity has largely become transformed into collective self-esteem (e.g., Crocker, Blaine, & Luhtanen, 1993; Crocker & Luhtanen, 1990; Luhtanen & Crocker, 1992).

Some Social Identity Research on Intergroup Social Comparisons

I have shown how social comparison theory, albeit only Festinger's early (1954a) version, was the critical ingredient for the development in the early 1970s of social identity theory from Tajfel's social categorization and prejudice research. We have seen how Tajfel viewed social comparison processes as much more widely applicable than did Festinger, and how he focused on intergroup comparisons that served a differentiation rather than assimilation function, and how this was associated with a greater emphasis on an underlying self-enhancement than self-evaluative motivation. We saw how this idea led in two directions: (1) macrosocial analyses of intergroup relations, and (2) the study of self-esteem as the critical motivation for social identity processes. Social identity theory largely has not kept up with developments in social comparison theory, and the notion of social comparison has become somewhat lost in analyses of motivation.

There is, however, a body of social identity research on intergroup social comparisons. This research tends to support the idea that in intergroup contexts social comparisons are governed by a striving for positive in-group distinctiveness; that is, for people to become more different rather than more similar. So, for example, Turner (1978b) found that people made more extreme in-group favoring comparisons when groups with stable status relations were similar than when they were dissimilar; Turner and Brown (1978) found that people made more extreme in-group–favoring comparisons when intergroup status relations were perceived to be unstable and illegitimate; and Turner et al. (1979) found more extreme in-group–favoring comparisons with more similar out-groups (also see Brown, 1978). These studies show that in intergroup contexts, increasing intergroup similarity motivates people to make comparisons that accentuate intergroup differences. Of course, there also are literally hundreds of minimal group studies that demonstrate the basic point that although people like to draw together through fairness and equality in interpersonal comparisons, this is significantly tempered by demonstration of distinctiveness and difference through in-group bias and favoritism in intergroup comparisons (e.g., Bourhis, Sachdev, & Gagnon, 1994; Diehl, 1990). Minimal group studies are laboratory experiments in which people are categorized into two groups on the basis of a random or trivial alleged criterion (e.g., over- or underestimation of numbers of dots). There is no face-to-face interaction, membership is anonymous, and the groups have no past or future; in short, the groups are mere categories that are only minimally defined. These studies show that when people are explicitly categorized in this way, such that an in-group–out-group relationship exists, they maximize intergroup difference in favor of the in-group on resource distribution tasks and in their evaluations of in-group and out-group.

In more naturalistic contexts there is substantial evidence that when social categories compare themselves with one another they generally draw attention to their differences, not their similarities (e.g., Brewer & Campbell, 1976; Sumner, 1906). Giles and colleagues report numerous social identity studies showing how ethnolinguistic groups can accentuate speech style (e.g., accent, language) differences in order to maintain distinctiveness and enhance the survival of their language and culture (see Giles & Johnson, 1987; Sachdev & Bourhis, 1993). Finally, Hornsey and Hogg (1999, 2000, in press) have conducted a series of studies that model multicultural national contexts to show that assimilationist strategies that try to obscure or submerge intercultural differences actually produce accentuated intergroup comparisons aimed at reasserting intercultural differentiation.

Since social comparison processes in intergroup contexts are predicated on the inevitable status differences that exist between groups, one of the critical research questions for social identity theory is what sorts of comparisons lower-status group members may make. Social identity theory answers this question by introducing the notion, which we discussed above, of subjective belief structures (e.g., Tajfel & Turner, 1979). If members of lower-status groups believe that intergroup relations are stable but permeable, they attempt to redefine themselves into the higher-status group (the strategy of individual mobility), and thus avoid esteem-damaging intergroup comparisons altogether. If they believe relations are stable and imperme-able, they make upward comparisons aimed at reevaluating in-group properties or aimed at selecting more favorable comparison dimensions (e.g., Hinkle, Taylor, Fox-Cardamone, & Ely, 1998), or they make downward comparisons with groups that are even further down the status hierarchy. If they believe that relations are impermeable but illegitimate and unstable, then they engage in highly competitive upward social comparisons aimed at changing real status relations. Hogg and Abrams (1988) describe how high-status groups make downward comparisons, but that these comparisons become accentuated when high-status groups per-ceive their status position to be under threat. Research, including the ethnolinguistic research mentioned above, provides reasonably good support for these processes (see Doosje & Ellemers, 1997; Ellemers, 1993; Ellemers & van Knippenberg, 1997; Hogg & Abrams, 1988; Jetten, Spears, Hogg, & Manstead, in press).

One finding that does not quite fit with this analysis is that low-status group members sometimes may identify strongly with their group and continue to make potentially self-esteem damaging upward comparisons. For instance Mlicki and Ellemers (1996) found that Polish students identified strongly as Poles and continued to make disadvantageous upward inter-group comparisons with Dutch students. This would clearly not serve the self-enhancement motive believed to sponsor intergroup comparisons. Mlicki and Ellemers suggest that inter-group distinctiveness itself may be a uniquely powerful motive in intergroup comparisons (also see Ellemers & van Knippenberg, 1997). This suggestion is consistent with the uncer-tainty reduction model of social identity processes discussed below.

SOCIAL COMPARISON PROCESSES IN SELF-CATEGORIZATION THEORY

Self-categorization theory (Turner, 1985; Turner, Hogg, Oakes, Reicher, & Wetherell, 1987) is an extension of social identity theory that refocuses attention on the categorization process. Social categorization transforms the basis of social perception, so that people are not perceived in terms of their unique properties, but in terms of in-group and out-group category attributes. Perception is "depersonalized" in terms of in-group or out-group prototypes that are formed according to the principle of metacontrast (i.e., maximization of the ratio of perceived intergroup differences to intragroup differences). Social categorization of self (i.e., self-categorization) likewise depersonalizes self-perception, but goes further in transforming self-conception and in assimilating all aspects of ones attitudes, feelings, and behaviors to the in-group prototype. Depersonalization is the "basic process underlying group phenomena" (Turner, 1985, p. 99). For self-categorization theory, prototypes are context-specific fuzzy sets that define and prescribe attitudes, feelings, and behaviors that characterize one group and distinguish it from other groups. Depersonalization refers simply to a change in self-conceptualization and the basis of perception of others; it does not have the negative connotations of terms such as "deindividuation" or "dehumanization" (cf., Reicher, Spears, & Postmes, 1995).

Although "... self-categorization theory is ... about the structure and functioning of the social self-concept (that based on social comparison and relevant to social interaction)" (Turner, 1985, pp. 93–94) with the aim "... to explain the social psychological basis of group phenomena, i.e., to identify the mechanisms by which individuals become unified into a psychological group" (Turner & Oakes, 1986, pp. 240–241), the motivational role of self-esteem in intergroup comparisons is no longer emphasized as it was in social identity theory. For example, Turner and Oakes (1986) believe that social identity theory "... seeks to explain intergroup discrimination in terms of the need for positive social identity/positive distinctiveness" (p. 241), and that the concomitant link of the "... individual need for self-esteem with the social regularities of intergroup behaviour" (Turner & Oakes, 1986, p. 240) was limited.

Self-categorization theory quite clearly grows out of Tajfel's and Turner's earlier ideas on social identity, and is thus a development of that theory, or perhaps more accurately is a part of a social identity perspective on the generative interrelationship of self-concept and social group (e.g., Abrams & Hogg, in press; Hogg, 1996a; Hogg, in press a; Hogg & McGarty, 1990; Hogg, Terry, & White, 1995). However, because of its different emphasis, some scholars draw attention to greater differences between self-categorization and social identity theory (e.g., Jetten, Spears, & Manstead, 1996; Oakes, Haslam, & Turner, 1994, p. 94).

Turner (1985) originally described self-categorization theory in terms of 12 assumptions and associated hypotheses. Social comparison enters into the theory primarily in so far as social categories are formed in contrast with other categories (i.e., similarities within and differences between categories) and intergroup comparisons are made between self and others. Turner states that "self-categorization and social comparison are mutually dependent and complementary processes in that neither can exist without the other" (1985, p. 96); by which he means that self-categorization requires social comparison, but social comparison itself occurs within the confines of comparability that are dictated by a higher-order self-categorization process. For example, for me to compare myself to a colleague on the basis of us being, respectively, social and cognitive psychologists requires a higher-order recognition that we are "comparable" because of a shared identity as psychologists. This idea has similarities to Goethals and Darley's (1977) "related attributes hypothesis," in which social comparisons occur only if there is a degree of background similarity on attributes related to the focal comparison dimension.

The self-enhancement aspect of social comparison is not represented in Turner's (1985) statement of self-categorization theory. Instead, the positive self-evaluative aspect of group membership is introduced as the idea that because in-groups are generally positively evaluated (they are represented by relatively favorable prototypes), evaluation of others as embodiments of such a prototype renders them prototypically attractive. Likewise, evaluation of self as an embodiment of such a prototype renders self prototypically attractive. This produces self-attraction or self-liking, and thus enhanced self-esteem. This idea is fully elaborated by Hogg in his theory of social attraction (e.g., Hogg, 1987, 1992, 1993; Hogg & Hains, 1996).

UNCERTAINTY REDUCTION AND SOCIAL IDENTIFICATION

From the previous section, we can see that social comparison theory does not really assume a role in self-categorization theory. However, by focusing on the categorization process, self-categorization theory may implicitly readmit Festinger's original belief that there is a "... motivation to know that one's opinions are correct and to know precisely what one is and is not capable of doing" (Festinger, 1954b, p. 217). In other words the motivation for self-evaluation rather than or in addition to self-enhancement may have a role in group-membership-based social comparisons. This idea recently has been conceptually developed and empirically tested as a new motivational model of social identity processes (Hogg, in press b; Hogg & Mullin, 1999; also see Hogg & Abrams, 1993; Hogg, 1996a).

Motivation to Reduce Uncertainty

People have a fundamental need to feel certain about their world and their place within it. Subjective certainty renders existence meaningful, and thus gives one confidence about how to behave and what to expect from the physical and social environment within which one finds oneself. Uncertainty about one's attitudes, beliefs, feelings, and perceptions, as well as about oneself and other people, is aversive (e.g., Fiske & Taylor, 1991; Lopes, 1987; Sorrentino & Roney, 1986) because it ultimately is associated with reduced control over one's life. Thus, uncertainty motivates behavior that reduces subjective uncertainty. The search for certainty is aimed at rendering the world subjectively meaningful (Bartlett, 1932). Although this may involve simplification of experience (James,1890), such simplification does not necessarily have to occur.

The motivation to minimize or reduce uncertainty may complement or even be more fundamental than the motivation for self-enhancement and maximization of self-esteem (for varying views on this issues see, Banaji & Prentice, 1994; Baumgardner, 1990; Crocker et al., 1993; Campbell, 1990; Sedikides & Strube, 1995; Stevens & Fiske, 1995; Swann & Schroeder, 1995). Although people may differ in their need for certainty (e.g., Adorno, Frenkel-Brunswik, Levinson, & Sanford, 1950; Rokeach, 1948, 1960; Sorrentino, Holmes, Hanna, & Sharp, 1995; Sorrentino & Short, 1986), these differences may be better understood as a function of enduring social contexts rather than personality differences. Uncertain times produce uncertain people. In keeping with social identity theory's emphasis on social contextual determination of behavior, the uncertainty reduction model described here focuses on uncertainty as a product of the social comparative context.

In his original formulation of social comparison theory, Festinger (1954a,b) believed that knowing one is correct (i.e., uncertainty reduction) is a critical human motivation that drives people to make social comparisons with individual others when nonsocial means are unavailable. The implication is that socially derived knowledge is less reliable and more superficial than physically derived knowledge, and it is less likely to be internalized because the information is peripherally (heuristically) rather than centrally (systematically) processed (following Eagly & Chaiken, 1993; Mackie, 1987; Mackie & Queller, 1999; Petty & Cacioppo,

1986). In contrast, as we saw above, social identity theory views social comparison as fundamental to all human knowledge (Tajfel, 1972; Turner, 1975; also see Moscovici, 1976; Turner, 1991), but as we saw above, social identity theory then quickly focused on the self-enhancement aspect of social comparison.

However, social identity theory does make some reference to motivations related to uncertainty reduction. Tajfel (1969) refers to the notion of a "search for coherence." Predicated on his belief that intergroup contexts are in a constant "flux of social change," he believed that people need to understand the causes of these changes. People satisfy this need for coherence through causal attribution processes that construct explanations that (1) equip people to deal with a changed situation, and (2) "preserve the integrity of the self image" (Tajfel, 1969, p. 92). "This need to preserve the integrity of the self-image is the only motivational assumption that we need to make in order to understand the direction that the search for coherence will take" (Tajfel, 1969, p. 92). As social identity theory developed, this motivational notion of a search for coherence fed into Tajfel's analysis of social functions of stereotypes (Tajfel, 1981). Stereotypes serve to explain and justify intergroup perceptions and behaviors. The idea that preservation of the integrity of self was a strong motive was not pursued. Instead, researchers mainly pursued the attributional (e.g., Hewstone, 1989) or social representational (e.g., Moscovici, 1983) dimensions.

Self-categorization theory, although more firmly grounded in the notion that correctness motivates social comparison, has tended to focus more on the social influence dimension. Uncertainty arises when we discover that we disagree in our beliefs, attitudes, feelings and behaviors with "similar" others, where similar others can be defined as people who we categorize as members of the same group as ourselves. Uncertainty is reduced when similar others agree with us, or when we can agree with similar others (e.g., Abrams, 1996; Abrams, Wetherell, Cochrane, Hogg, & Turner, 1990; Turner, 1985, 1991). Social agreements and disagreements map out the contours of social groups, and thus socially derived certainty resides in group membership within intergroup contexts, not interindividual comparisons with similar others. For example, regarding political attitudes, a Republican expects to agree with fellow Republicans and expects to disagree with Democrats, and so experiences no uncertainty if this is what occurs. Our Republican would experience uncertainty, however, if she found she disagreed with fellow Republicans but agreed with Democrats. In contrast, agreement or disagreement with interpersonal friends or acquaintances regarding political attitudes would not necessarily have implications for subjective uncertainty concerning political attitudes and political self-definition and identity.

Self-Categorization, Social Identification, and Uncertainty Reduction

The uncertainty reduction hypothesis proposed by Hogg (e.g., Hogg, 1996a, in press b; Hogg & Abrams, 1993; Hogg & Mullin, 1999) goes a step further. The process itself of self-categorization that is responsible for social identification and group-membership-based behaviors reduces subjective uncertainty. The social categorization process constructs contextually relevant in-group and out-group prototypes on the basis of the metacontrast principle. Such prototypes capture contextually meaningful similarities within and differences between groups, and the categorization process further accentuates prototypical similarities within groups and differences between groups. The perceptual field is rendered more clear and meaningful and less complex and perplexing. Social categorization of self (self-categorization) depersonalizes self by assimilating self to the in-group prototype. Self is contextually transformed so that self-conceptualization, attitudes, feelings, and behaviors are governed by the in-group prototype. This process also provides an in-group social comparative context containing similar others who all appear to validate one's self-concept and associated cognitions and behaviors. Thus, uncertainty about self-conceptualization, attitudes, feelings, perceptions, and so forth is reduced. The process of self-categorization reduces uncertainty, and in a more enduring sense people may join (identify with) groups because they reduce uncertainty.

Not all subjective uncertainty motivates self-categorization. For uncertainty to have motivational force, it needs to be subjectively important; it needs to matter that one is uncertain in that context. It is quite probable that contextually important uncertainties are those that reflect on self-conception, in so far as they represent uncertainty about things that define self and therefore about one's cognitions and actions. However, something that matters in one context may not matter in another context. For instance, people who are uncertain about their environmental attitudes may simply not care; it is an unimportant dimension that has little relevance to self-conceptualization. Subjective uncertainty has no motivational force. For other people this uncertainty may matter a great deal because the immediate context may demand attitude-based action, and/or contextual or more global self-definition requires certainty on this issue. Subjective uncertainty motivates uncertainty reduction.

The mechanism of uncertainty reduction is assimilation of self to the in-group prototype. Self-categorization is more effective in reducing uncertainty if people have a concentrated, clearly focused, and relatively unambiguous prototype. Indeed, if people cannot form a prototype at all then self-categorization does not reduce uncertainty. The prototype also should be relevant to the dimension of uncertainty; it should embrace dimensions that address the specific dimension of uncertainty or should be broadly relevant enough to the self-concept to inform the dimension of uncertainty. Typically, clearly focused prototypes are best furnished by homogeneous, consensual groups that are high in entitativity (e.g., Sherman, Hamilton, & Lewis, 1999) and are located in a crystallized intergroup context where intergroup relations are stable and clearly delineated. Indeed, in seeking uncertainty reduction people probably pay as much attention to in-group prototype clarity as to clarity of social structural differentiation among groups (the metacontrast principle actually ties these two aspects together in the dynamic of prototype formation). One implication of the analysis so far is that extreme, and possibly chronic, uncertainty about subjectively critical matters, for example, the self-concept itself, may motivate people to join extreme groups that are highly orthodox (very clear prototypes) and very distinct from other groups. The psychology of extremism may hinge on uncertainty reduction through self-categorization.

Because reduction of uncertainty is adaptive, people will feel good about themselves, and thus experience elevated self-esteem. Self-enhancement is a plausible consequence of uncertainty reduction. However, this is a generalized social self-enhancement that extends to embrace the group, its prototype, and its members, because self and group are psychologically integrated and because the group and its members validate one's cognitions and behaviors. In this way, the satisfaction achieved by group-membership-based uncertainty reduction generates not only positive self-attitudes but positive attitudes toward fellow group members (depersonalized social attraction) and positive attitudes towards in-group relative to out-group as a whole (ethnocentrism). Paradoxically, the certainty furnished by stable social structural relations among groups may sometimes generate satisfaction (and thus social attraction and ethnocentrism) even if one's own group has relatively lower status (see Jost & Banaji's, 1994, notion of system justification; also see Jost, 1995).

The uncertainty reduction model of social identity processes has substantial indirect support from a range of social psychological literatures (reviewed by Hogg & Mullin, 1999). Direct support comes from a continuing program of empirical research, such as Grieve and

Hogg (1999), Hogg and Grieve (1999), Hogg and Mullin (1998), Hogg and Reid (1998), Hogg and Schuit (1998), Jetten, Hogg, and Mullin (1998), Mullin and Hogg (1998, 1999), Sussman and Hogg (1998); see Hogg and Mullin's (1999) overview of many of these studies. Together, these studies show: (1) in minimal group contexts people who were explicitly categorized only self-categorized, and thus identified with the category, expressed group attitudes, and engaged in group behaviors when they were categorized under conditions of subjective uncertainty; (2) this effect was most pronounced when the dimension of subjective uncertainty was subjectively important and when the category was relevant to the dimension of uncertainty; (3) greater uncertainty, particularly self-conceptual uncertainty (uncertainty about who one is, in contrast to uncertainty about external attitude objects), was associated with identification with groups with clear and more distinctive prototypes; (4) support for extremist political groups was more evident among people who felt most uncertain; and (5) people categorized under uncertainty who were prevented from forming a group prototype (rather than being allowed to systematically/centrally process prototype relevant information, they were made to systematically/centrally process prototype irrelevant information) did not self-categorize.

AN EXTENDED SOCIAL IDENTITY MODEL
OF SOCIAL COMPARISON PROCESSES IN GROUP CONTEXTS

Social identity theory originally focused mainly on intergroup phenomena (e.g., Tajfel, 1972, 1974; Tajfel & Turner, 1979) and conceptualized social comparison as a pervasive and fundamental source of self-evaluation. It also focused on intergroup social comparisons that were considered to be primarily motivated by self-enhancement concerns: positive distinctiveness and ultimately self-esteem. This perspective on social comparison went well beyond Festinger's (1954a,b) more limited arena for social comparison processes, his interpersonal focus, and his emphasis on self-evaluation as opposed to self-enhancement. However, the self-enhancement emphasis was in keeping with independent developments in social comparison theory that explored upward and downward comparison processes (e.g., Wills, 1981, 1991). From a social identity perspective, intergroup relations are characterized by self-enhancement serving downward intergroup comparisons, unless lower-status groups are able to question the legitimacy and stability of the status quo, and thus make upward comparisons that do not damage positive distinctiveness.

Self-categorization theory specified how the process of social categorization of self (self-categorization) depersonalizes self-conception, by assimilating self to the in-group prototype, and generates group behaviors (Turner, 1985; Turner et al., 1987). Although, in its original form, self-categorization theory moved away from social comparison processes, particularly the self-enhancement emphasis of social identity theory, it tacitly reintroduced the notion that structural and epistemic motives may play a role in social identity and group contexts. This idea has been developed by Hogg in his model of subjective uncertainty reduction, just described (e.g., Hogg, in press b; Hogg & Mullin, 1999). People strive for subjective certainty, which can be achieved by self-categorization in terms of an in-group prototype that is constructed within the intergroup comparative context.

Another important aspect of self-categorization theory is that it has generated research on intragroup processes and perhaps most interestingly on intragroup differentiation. The main impetus for this has been the recognition that groups are internally structured with respect to prototypicality. Some people are more prototypical than others, and thus intragroup comparisons can be made that are *not* interpersonal but are genuinely based on common category membership. Initially, this idea was explored in the context of group cohesion and social attraction (Hogg, 1987, 1992, 1993), and group polarization (e.g., Abrams et al., 1990; McGarty, Turner, Hogg, David, & Wetherell, 1992; Turner, Wetherell, & Hogg, 1989), but it subsequently has produced other research on social-identity-based intragroup processes (Hogg, 1996a,b). For example, as group salience increases, (1) perceived leadership effectiveness becomes increasingly determined by prototypicality (e.g., Fielding & Hogg, 1997; Hains, Hogg & Duck, 1997; Hogg, 1996a; Hogg, Hains & Mason, 1998); (2) subgroups can become increasingly competitive unless subgroup membership is acknowledged (e.g., Hornsey & Hogg, 1999a–c, 2000, in press); and (2) marginal in-group members ("black sheep") become increasingly strongly rejected by the group (e.g., Marques & Páez, 1994; Marques, Páez, & Abrams, 1998).

The self-categorization perspective and associated uncertainty reduction model have implications for social comparison processes. Social comparison processes are governed by a desire to be sure about one's self-concept; in which case inter- and intragroup comparisons work in conjunction to construct a contextually relevant in-group prototype (via the meta-contrast principle). However, intragroup comparisons ultimately are likely to be more useful as they have more direct bearing on the extent to which self is group prototypical (intergroup comparisons require an additional inferential step), and thus on uncertainty reduction. Furthermore, such intragroup comparisons are probably likely to be upward comparisons rather than downward comparisons, because upward comparisons, albeit interpersonal ones, have been shown to satisfy self-improvement motives (e.g., Brickman & Bulman, 1977; Major, Testa, & Bylsma, 1991; Taylor, Neter, & Wayment, 1995). Within groups, people are likely to make group-membership-based comparisons with more prototypical members (i.e., upward comparisons). This is because these comparisons are more directly informative regarding the group prototype, and thus are more likely to render one's own behavior prototypical and result in more effective uncertainty reduction. Given that intragroup comparisons are made in the context of an intergroup comparative frame, self-enhancement is already being satisfied by downward intergroup comparisons.

Let us now try to tie all this together. People can relate to one another in one of three ways, reflecting three distinct social orientations: (1) as unique individuals (interpersonal), (2) as members of the same group, sharing a common social identity (intragroup), or (3) as members of contrasting or different groups, having a disjunctive social identity (intergroup). In reality, social orientations to some extent can co-occur, and their psychological salience is an interactive function of (1) individual motives (for self-enhancement or self-evaluation), (2) category accessibility in memory, and (3) how well the category accounts for others' behavior (normative fit) and relevant similarities and differences among people (structural/comparative fit). When social identity is salient (self-categorization and depersonalization processes are in operation), by definition people make intergroup comparisons with out-group members and intragroup comparisons with in-group members.

Intergroup comparisons are aimed at differentiating in-group from out-group on in-group–favoring dimensions. This serves an uncertainty reduction function in that it perceptually crystallizes structural relations among groups and produces a distinct in-group prototype, and it serves a self-enhancement function in that it evaluatively favors in-group (and thus self) over out-group. Social comparisons between groups are motivated by both uncertainty reduction (self-evaluation) and self-enhancement. Together, these are likely to produce generally downward comparisons. Intragroup comparisons are aimed at accurately establishing the in-group prototype and assimilating self to that prototype. Intragroup comparisons primarily serve an uncertainty reduction function in that they renders oneself more group prototypical.

Social comparisons within groups are motivated by uncertainty reduction (self-evaluation), and thus are likely to be upward comparisons with fellow members who are more prototypical than oneself.

Intragroup comparisons may sometimes become self-enhancing, particularly in the case of more highly prototypical in-group members. These people are to some extent constrained to make downward comparisons, because upward comparisons are difficult because there are few if any in-group members who are more prototypical than self. This may produce a motivational and social comparative framework that more closely resembles intergroup than intragroup comparisons, and may indeed be associated with a gradual reconfiguration of the group into higher- and lower-status subgroups. This process is consistent with Hogg's social identity theory of group leadership (e.g., Hogg, 1999; Hogg et al., 1998). One aspect of this analysis argues that leaders, who by definition are highly prototypical group members, gradually become distanced and separated from the group and develop an intergroup relationship with the rest of the group that produces typical intergroup behaviors including the exercise and sometimes abuse of power (Hogg & Reid, in press).

CONCLUDING COMMENTS

In this chapter I have traced the way in which social comparison theory has been incorporated and modified by social identity theory. Although the cornerstone of social identity theory is the comparative relations that exist between groups and the comparative nature of the social categorization process that underpins social identity phenomena, there is remarkably little systematic attention paid by social identity theorists to social comparison theory. Indeed, after Tajfel's (1972, 1974) and Turner's (1975) initial references to Festinger's early (1954a,b) theory there is very little attention to new developments and very little formal discussion of social comparison theory. Social identity theorists generally do not write about social comparison processes; Luhtanen and Crocker's (1991) chapter in Suls and Wills's social comparison book is about the nearest one gets.

The present chapter, then, is quite a new departure, and I have tried to be very explicit about the way in which social comparison processes may operate in social identity contexts. I have done this by means of an historical overview of social identity theory and self-categorization theory as they both relate to social comparison and motivational processes in social identity contexts and I have presented a model of the motivational role of subjective uncertainty reduction in group contexts. I closed by sketching out a new framework for social comparison and motivational processes that operate within and between groups; that is, when people relate psychologically to one another as members of the same group (common social identity) or members of different groups (disjunctive social identity).

From this wider social identity perspective, which incorporates the original intergroup emphasis (e.g., Tajfel & Turner, 1979), the later self-categorization development (e.g., Turner et al., 1987), and the recent subjective uncertainty framework (e.g., Hogg & Mullin, 1999), it was possible to draw some tentative conclusions about social comparison processes that operate in social identity contexts; that is, contexts in which people categorize and depersonalize themselves and others in terms of in-group or out-group–defining prototypes. Intergroup and intragroup social comparisons are interdependent. More precisely, intragroup comparisons are contextualized by the intergroup context. To the extent that the intergroup context is psychologically deemphasized, intragroup comparisons tend toward intergroup comparisons between subgroups or even simply interpersonal comparisons.

Social comparisons between groups satisfy an uncertainty reduction (cf. self-evaluative) motive because they crystallize and delineate structural relations among groups, and thus produce a clear and distinct in-group prototype. Intergroup comparisons also satisfy a self-enhancement motive because they secure evaluatively positive distinctiveness for the in-group, and thus favorable social identity and self-evaluation. Overall, intergroup relations are characterized by downward social comparisons. Social comparisons within groups primarily satisfy an uncertainty reduction motive because they clarify the in-group prototype and assimilate self to the prototype. Overall, intragroup behavior is characterized by upward social comparisons with more prototypical members. Downward comparisons with nonprototypical members do occur but are likely to be less directly useful for uncertainty reduction. Intragroup downward comparisons are more likely to occur when intragroup relations are decomposing into intersubgroup, thus intergroup relations in which satisfaction of the self-enhancement motive has been relocated from the original intergroup relationship to a new intergroup relationship within the erstwhile in-group.

REFERENCES

Abrams, D. (1996). Social identity, self as structure and self as process. In W. P. Robinson (Ed.), *Social groups and identities: Developing the legacy of Henri Tajfel* (pp. 143–167). Oxford, England: Butterworth-Heinemann.
Abrams, D., & Hogg, M. A. (1988). Comments on the motivational status of self-esteem in social identity and intergroup discrimination. *European Journal of Social Psychology, 18*, 317–34.
Abrams, D., & Hogg, M. A. (Eds.). (1990). *Social identity theory: Constructive and critical advances* (p. 7). Hemel Hempstead, England: Harvester Wheatsheaf, New York: Springer-Verlag.
Abrams, D., & Hogg, M. A. (1998). Prospects for research in group processes and intergroup relations. *Group Processes and Intergroup Relations, 1*, 7–20.
Abrams, D., & Hogg, M. A. (Eds.). (1999). *Social identity and social cognition.* Oxford, England: Blackwell.
Abrams, D., & Hogg, M. A. (In press). Collective identity: Group membership and self-conception. In M. A. Hogg & R. S. Tindale (Eds.), *Blackwell handbook in social psychology: Group processes.* Oxford, England: Blackwell.
Abrams, D., Wetherell, M. S., Cochrane, S., Hogg, M. A., & Turner, J. C. (1990). Knowing what to think by knowing who you are: Self-categorization and the nature of norm formation, conformity, and group polarization. *British Journal of Social Psychology, 29*, 97–119.
Adorno, T. W., Frenkel-Brunswick, E., Levinson, D. J., & Sanford, R. N. (1950). *The authoritarian personality.* New York: Harper.
Arrowood, A. J. (1986). Comments on "Social comparison theory: Psychology from the lost and found." *Personality and Social Psychology Bulletin, 12*, 279–281.
Banaji, M. R., & Prentice, D. J. (1994). The self in social contexts. *Annual Review of Psychology, 45*, 297–332.
Bartlett, F. C. (1932). *Remembering.* Cambridge, England: Cambridge University Press.
Baumgardner, A. H. (1990). To know oneself is to like oneself: Self-certainty and self-affect. *Journal of Personality and Social Psychology, 58*, 1062–1072.
Berger, P. L. (1966). Identity as a problem in the sociology of knowledge. *European Journal of Sociology, 7*, 105–115.
Billig, M. (1985). Prejudice, categorization and particularization: From a perceptual to a rhetorical approach. *European Journal of Social Psychology, 15*, 79–103.
Bourhis, R. Y., Sachdev, I., & Gagnon, A. (1994). Intergroup research with the Tajfel matrices: Methodological notes. In M. Zanna & J. Olson (Eds.), *The psychology of prejudice: The Ontario symposium* (Vol. 7, pp. 209–232). Hillsdale, NJ: Lawrence Erlbaum.
Brewer, M. B., & Campbell, D. T. (1976). *Ethnocentrism and intergroup attitudes: East African evidence.* New York: Sage.
Brickman, P., & Bulman, R. J. (1977). Pleasure and pain in social comparison. In J. M. Suls & R. L. Miller (Eds.), *Social comparison processes: Theoretical and empirical perspectives* (pp. 149–186). Washington, DC: Hemisphere.
Brown, R. J. (1978). Divided we fall: An analysis of relations between sections of a factory workforce. In H. Tajfel (Ed.), *Differentiation between social groups: Studies in the social psychology of intergroup relations* (pp. 395–429). London: Academic Press.

Campbell, J. D. (1990). Self-esteem and the clarity of the self-concept. *Journal of Personality and Social Psychology*, *59*, 538–549.

Cottrell, N. B., & Epley, S. W. (1977). Affiliation, social comparison, and socially mediated stress reduction. In J. M. Suls & R. L. Miller (Eds.), *Social comparison processes: Theoretical and empirical perspectives* (pp. 43–68). Washington, DC: Hemisphere.

Crocker, J., Blaine, B., & Luhtanen, R. (1993). Prejudice, intergroup behaviour and self-esteem: Enhancement and protection motives. In M. A. Hogg & D. Abrams (Eds.), *Group motivation: Social psychological perspectives* (pp. 52–67). Hemel Hempstead, England: Harvester Wheatsheaf.

Crocker, J., & Luhtanen, R. (1990). Collective self-esteem and ingroup bias. *Journal of Personality and Social Psychology*, *58*, 60–67.

Crocker, J., Thompson, L. J., McGraw, K. M., & Ingerman, C. (1987). Downward comparison, prejudice, and evaluations of others: Effects of self-esteem and threat. *Journal of Personality and Social Psychology*, *52*, 907–916.

Diehl, M. (1990). The minimal group paradigm: Theoretical explanations and empirical findings. *European Review of Social Psychology*, *1*, 263–292.

Doosje, B., & Ellemers, N. (1997). Stereotyping under threat: The role of group identification. In R. Spears, P. J. Oakes, N. Ellemers, & S. A. Haslam (Eds.), *The social psychology of stereotyping and group life* (pp. 257–272). Oxford, England: Blackwell.

Eagly, A. H., & Chaiken, S. (1993). *The psychology of attitudes*. San Diego, CA: Harcourt Brace Jovanovich.

Ellemers, N. (1993). The influence of socio-structural variables on identity enhancement strategies. *European Review of Social Psychology*, *4*, 27–57.

Ellemers, N., & van Knippenberg, A. (1997). Stereotyping in social context. In R. Spears, P. J. Oakes, N. Ellemers, & S. A. Haslam (Eds.), *The social psychology of stereotyping and group life* (pp. 208–235). Oxford, England: Blackwell.

Farr, R. M. (1996). *The roots of modern social psychology: 1872–1954*. Oxford, England: Blackwell.

Festinger, L. (1950). Informal social communication. *Psychological Review*, *57*, 271–282.

Festinger, L. (1954a). A theory of social comparison processes. *Human Relations*, *7*, 117–140.

Festinger, L. (1954b). Motivation leading to social behavior. In M.R. Jones (Ed.), *Nebraska symposium on motivation* (Vol. 2, pp. 121–218). Lincoln: University of Nebraska Press.

Fielding, K. S., & Hogg, M. A. (1997). Social identity, self-categorization, and leadership: A field study of small interactive groups. *Group Dynamics: Theory, Research, and Practice*, *1*, 39–51.

Fiske, S. T., & Taylor, S. E. (1991). *Social cognition* (2nd ed.). New York: McGraw-Hill.

Garfinkel, H. (1967). *Studies in ethnomethodology*. Englewood Cliffs, NJ: Prentice Hall.

Gibbons, F. X., & Gerrard, M. (1991). Downward comparison and coping with threat. In J. Suls & T. A. Wills (Eds.), *Social comparison: Contemporary theory and research* (pp. 317–345). Hillsdale, NJ: Lawrence Erlbaum.

Giles, H., & Johnson, P. (1987). Ethnolinguistic identity theory: A social psychological approach to language maintenance. *International Journal of the Sociology of Language*, *68*, 66–99.

Goethals, G. R., & Darley, J. M. (1977). Social comparison theory: An attributional approach. In J. M. Suls & R. M. Miller (Eds.), *Social comparison processes* (pp. 259–278). Washington, DC: Hemisphere.

Grieve, P., & Hogg, M. A. (1999). Subjective uncertainty and intergroup discrimination in the minimal group situation. *Personality and Social Psychology Bulletin*, *25*, 926–940.

Hains, S. C., Hogg, M. A., & Duck, J. M. (1997). Self-categorization and leadership: Effects of group prototypicality and leader stereotypicality. *Personality and Social Psychology Bulletin*, *23*, 1087–1100.

Hewstone, M. (1989). *Causal attribution: From cognitive processes to collective beliefs*. Oxford, England: Blackwell.

Hinkle, S., Taylor, L. A., Fox-Cardamone, L., & Ely, P. G. (1998). Social identity and aspects of social creativity: Shifting to new comparison dimensions of intergroup comparison. In S. Worchel, J. F. Morales, D. Páez, & J.-C. Deschamps (Eds.), *Social identity: International perspectives* (pp. 166–179). London: Sage.

Hogg, M. A. (1987). Social identity and group cohesiveness. In J.C. Turner, M. A. Hogg, P. J. Oakes, S. D. Reicher & M. S. Wetherell, *Rediscovering the social group: A self-categorization theory* (pp. 89–116). Oxford, England, New York: Blackwell.

Hogg, M.A. (1992). *The social psychology of group cohesiveness: From attraction to social identity*. Hemel Hempstead, England: Harvester Wheatsheaf, and New York: New York University Press.

Hogg, M. A. (1993). Group cohesiveness: A critical review and some new directions. *European Review of Social Psychology*, *4*, 85–111.

Hogg, M. A. (1996a). Intragroup processes, group structure and social identity. In W. P. Robinson (Ed.), *Social groups and identities: Developing the legacy of Henri Tajfel* (pp. 65–93). Oxford, England: Butterworth-Heinemann.

Hogg, M. A. (1996b). Social identity, self-categorization, and the small group. In E. H. Witte & J. H. Davis (Eds.),

Understanding group behavior (Vol. 2): *Small group processes and interpersonal relations* (pp. 227–253). Mahwah, NJ: Lawrence Erlbaum.

Hogg, M. A. (1999). *A social identity theory of leadership.* Manuscript submitted for publication, University of Queensland.

Hogg, M. A. (In press a). Social categorization, depersonalization and group behavior. In M. A. Hogg & R. S. Tindale (Eds.), *Blackwell handbook in social psychology: Group processes.* Oxford, England: Blackwell.

Hogg, M. A. (In press b). Subjective uncertainty reduction through self-categorization: A motivational theory of social identity processes. *European Review of Social Psychology.*

Hogg, M. A., & Abrams, D. (1988). *Social identifications: A social psychology of intergroup relations and group processes.* London: Routledge.

Hogg, M. A., & Abrams, D. (1990). Social motivation, self-esteem and social identity. In D. Abrams & M. A. Hogg (Eds.), *Social identity theory: Constructive and critical advances* (pp. 28–47). London: Harvester Wheatsheaf, New York: Springer-Verlag.

Hogg, M. A., & Abrams, D. (1993). Towards a single-process uncertainty-reduction model of social motivation in groups. In M. A. Hogg & D. Abrams (Eds.), *Group motivation: Social psychological perspectives* (pp. 173–190). London: Harvester-Wheatsheaf, New York: Prentice-Hall.

Hogg, M. A., & Abrams, D. (1999). Social identity and social cognition: Historical background and current trends. In D. Abrams & M. A. Hogg (Eds.), *Social identity and social cognition* (pp. 1–25). Oxford, England: Blackwell.

Hogg, M. A., & Grieve, P. (1999). Social identity theory and the crisis of confidence in social psychology: A commentary, and some research on uncertainty reduction. *Asian Journal of Social Psychology, 2,* 43–57.

Hogg, M. A., & Hains, S. C. (1996). Intergroup relations and group solidarity: Effects of group identification and social beliefs on depersonalized attraction. *Journal of Personality and Social Psychology, 70,* 295–309.

Hogg, M. A., Hains, S. C., & Mason, I. (1998). Identification and leadership in small groups: Salience, frame of reference, and leader stereotypicality effects on leader evaluations. *Journal of Personality and Social Psychology, 75,* 1248–1263.

Hogg, M. A., & McGarty, C. (1990). Self-categorization and social identity. In D. Abrams & M. A. Hogg (Eds.), *Social identity theory: Constructive and critical advances* (pp. 10–27). Hemel Hempstead, England: Harvester Wheatsheaf, New York: Springer-Verlag.

Hogg, M. A., & Mullin, B.-A. (1998). *Reducing subjective uncertainty by group identification: The role of group relevance.* Manuscript submitted for publication, University of Queensland.

Hogg, M. A., & Mullin, B.-A. (1999). Joining groups to reduce uncertainty: Subjective uncertainty reduction and group identification. In D. Abrams & M. A. Hogg (Eds.), *Social identity and social cognition* (pp. 249–279). Oxford, England: Blackwell.

Hogg, M. A., & Reid, S. (1998). *Uncertainty, social identification and extremism in Australia.* Unpublished manuscript, University of Queensland.

Hogg, M. A., & Reid, S. (In press). Social identity, leadership, and power. In A. Lee-Chai & J. Bargh (Eds.), *The use and abuse of power: Multiple perspectives on the causes of corruption.* Philadelphia, PA: Psychology Press.

Hogg, M. A., & Schuit, R. (1998). *The role of prototype construction in uncertainty reduction through self-categorization.* Unpublished manuscript, University of Queensland.

Hogg, M. A., Terry, D. J., & White, K. M. (1995). A tale of two theories: A critical comparison of identity theory with social identity theory. *Social Psychology Quarterly, 58,* 255-269.

Hornsey, M. J., & Hogg, M. A. (1999). Subgroup differentiation as a response to an overly inclusive group: A test of optimal distinctiveness theory. *European Journal of Social Psychology, 29,* 543–550.

Hornsey, M. J., & Hogg, M. A. (2000). Subgroup relations: A comparison of mutual intergroup differentiation and common ingroup identity models of prejudice reduction. *Personality and Social Psychology Bulletin, 26,* 242–256.

Hornsey, M. J., & Hogg, M. A. (In press). Intergroup similarity and subgroup relations: Some implications for assimilation. *Personality and Social Psychology Bulletin.*

James, W. (1890). *The principles of psychology.* New York: Holt, Rinehart, & Winston.

Jetten, J., Hogg, M. A., & Mullin, B.-A. (1998). Ingroup variability and motivation to reduce subjective uncertainty. *Group Dynamics: Theory, Research, and Practice.*

Jetten, J., Spears, R., Hogg, M. A., & Manstead, A. R. (In press). Discrimination constrained and justified: Variable effects of group variability and ingroup identification. *Journal of Experimental Social Psychology.*

Jetten, J., Spears, R., & Manstead, A. S. R. (1996). Intergroup norms and intergroup discrimination: Distinctive self-categorization and social identity effects. *Journal of Personality and Social Psychology, 71,* 1222-1233.

Jost, J. T. (1995). Negative illusions: Conceptual clarification and psychological evidence concerning false consciousness. *Political Psychology, 16,* 397–424.

Jost, J. T., & Banaji, M. R. (1994). The role of stereotyping in system-justification and the production of false consciousness. *British Journal of Social Psychology, 33*, 1–27.

Long, M. K., & Spears, R. (1997). The self-esteem hypothesis revisited: Differentiation and the disaffected. In R. Spears, P. J. Oakes, N. Ellemers, & S. A. Haslam (Eds.), *The social psychology of stereotyping and group life* (pp. 296–317). Oxford, England: Blackwell.

Lopes, L. L. (1987). Between hope and fear: The psychology of risk. *Advances in Experimental Psychology, 20*, 255–295.

Luhtanen, R., & Crocker, J. (1991). Self-esteem and intergroup comparisons: Toward a theory of collective self-esteem. In J. Suls & T. A. Wills (Eds.), *Social comparison: Contemporary theory and research* (pp. 211–234). Hillsdale, NJ: Lawrence Erlbaum.

Luhtanen, R., & Crocker, J. (1992). A collective self-esteem scale: Self-evaluation of one's social identity. *Personality and Social Psychology Bulletin, 18*, 302-318.

Mackie, D. (1987). Systematic and non systematic processing of majority and minority persuasive communications. *Journal of Personality and Social Psychology, 53*, 41–52.

Mackie, D., & Queller, S. (1999). The impact of group membership on persuasion: Revisiting "who says what to whom with what effect?" In D. J. Terry & M. A. Hogg (Eds.), *Attitudes, behavior, and social context: The role of norms and group membership* (pp. 135–156). Mahwah, NJ: Lawrence Erlbaum.

Major, B., Testa, M., & Bylsma, W. H. (1991). Responses to upward and downward social comparisons: The impact of esteem-relevance and perceived control. In J. Suls & T. A. Wills (Eds.), *Social comparison: Contemporary theory and research* (pp. 237–260). Hillsdale, NJ: Lawrence Erlbaum.

Marques, J. M., & Páez, D. (1994). The black sheep effect: Social categorization, rejection of in-group deviates, and perception of group variability. *European Review of Social Psychology, 5*, 37–68.

Marques, J. M., Páez, D., & Abrams, D. (1998). Social identity and intragroup differentiation as subjective social control. In S. Worchel, J. F. Morales, D. Páez, & J.-C. Deschamps (Eds.), *Social identity: International perspectives* (pp. 124–141). London: Sage.

McGarty, C, Turner, J. C., Hogg, M. A., David, B., & Wetherell, M. S. (1992). Group polarization as conformity to the prototypical group member. *British Journal of Social Psychology, 31*, 1–20.

Mlicki, P., & Ellemers, N. (1996). Being different or being better? National stereotypes and identifications of Polish and Dutch students. *European Journal of Social Psychology, 26*, 97–114.

Moreland, R. L., Hogg, M. A., & Hains, S. C. (1994). Back to the future: Social psychological research on groups. *Journal of Experimental Social Psychology, 30*(6), 527–555.

Moscovici, S. (1976). *Social influence and social change*. London: Academic Press.

Moscovici, S. (1983). The phenomenon of social representations. In R. M. Farr & S. Moscovici (Eds.), *Social representations* (pp. 3–69). Cambridge, England: Cambridge University Press.

Mullin, B.-A., & Hogg, M. A. (1998). Dimensions of subjective uncertainty in social identification and minimal intergroup discrimination. *British Journal of Social Psychology, 37*, 345–365.

Mullin, B.-A., & Hogg, M. A. (1999). Motivations for group membership: The role of subjective importance and uncertainty reduction. *Basic and Applied Social Psychology, 21*, 91–102.

Nagata, D., & Crosby, F. (1991). Comparisons, justice, and the internment of Japanese-Americans. In J. Suls & T. A. Wills (Eds.), *Social comparison: Contemporary theory and research* (pp. 347–368). Hillsdale, NJ: Lawrence Erlbaum.

Oakes, P. J., Haslam, S. A., & Turner, J. C. (1994). *Stereotyping and social reality*. Oxford, England: Blackwell.

Petty, R. E., & Cacioppo, J. T. (1986). The elaboration likelihood model of persuasion. In L. Berkowitz (Ed.), *Advances in experimental social psychology* (Vol. 19, pp. 123–205). New York: Academic Press.

Reicher, S. D., Spears, R., & Postmes, T. (1995). A social identity model of deindividuation phenomena. *European Review of Social Psychology, 6*, 161–198.

Robinson, W. P. (Ed.) (1996). *Social groups and identities: Developing the legacy of Henri Tajfel* (p. 7). Oxford, England: Butterworth-Heinemann.

Rokeach, M. (1948). Generalized mental rigidity as a factor in ethnocentrism. *Journal of Abnormal Social Psychology, 43*, 259–278.

Rokeach, M. (1960). *The open and closed mind*. New York: Basic Books.

Rubin, M., & Hewstone, M. (1998). Social identity theory's self-esteem hypothesis: A review and some suggestions for clarification. *Personality and Social Psychology Review, 2*, 40–62.

Sachdev, I., & Bourhis, R. Y. (1993). Ethnolinguistic vitality: Some motivational and cognitive considerations. In M. A. Hogg & D. Abrams (Eds.), *Group motivation: Social psychological perspectives* (pp. 33–51). Hemel Hempstead, England: Harvester Wheatsheaf.

Schachter, S. (1959). *The psychology of affiliation: Experimental studies of the sources of gregariousness*. Stanford, CA: Stanford University Press.

Sedikides, C., & Strube, M. J. (1995). The multiply motivated self. *Personality and Social Psychology Bulletin, 21*(12), 1330–1335.

Sherman, S. J., Hamilton, D. L., & Lewis, A. C. (1999). Perceived entitativity and the social identity value of group memberships. In D. Abrams & M. A. Hogg (Eds), *Social identity and social cognition* (pp. 80–110). Oxford, England: Blackwell.

Sorrentino, R. M., Holmes, J. G., Hanna, S. E., & Sharp, A. (1995). Uncertainty orientation and trust in close relationships: Individual differences in cognitive styles. *Journal of Personality and Social Psychology, 68*, 314–327.

Sorrentino, R. M., & Roney, C. J. R. (1986). Uncertainty orientation, achievement-related motivation and task diagnosticity as determinants of task performance. *Social Cognition, 4*, 420–436.

Sorrentino, R. M., & Short, J. C. (1986). Uncertainty, motivation and cognition. In R. M. Sorrentino & E. T. Higgins (Eds.), *The handbook of motivation and cognition: Foundations of social behavior* (Vol. 1, pp. 379–403). New York: Guilford.

Stevens, L. E., & Fiske, S. T. (1995). Motivation and cognition in social life: A social survival perspective. *Social Cognition, 13*(3), 189–214.

Sumner, W. G. (1906). *Folkways.* New York: Ginn.

Sussman, K., & Hogg, M. A. (1998). *Uncertainty, prototype clarity and group identification: A survey of campus groups.* Unpublished manuscript, Princeton University and the University of Queensland.

Swann, W. B., & Schroeder, D. G. (1995). The search for beauty and truth: A framework for understanding reactions to evaluations. *Personality and Social Psychology Bulletin, 21*, 1307–1318.

Tajfel, H. (1959). Quantitative judgement in social perception. *British Journal of Psychology, 50*, 16–29.

Tajfel, H. (1969). Cognitive aspects of prejudice. *Journal of Social Issues, 25*, 79–97.

Tajfel, H. (1972). Social categorization. English manuscript of "La catégorisation sociale." In S. Moscovici (Ed.), *Introduction à la psychologie sociale* (Vol. 1, pp. 272–302). Paris: Larousse.

Tajfel, H. (1974). *Intergroup behaviour, social comparison and social change.* Unpublished Katz-Newcomb lectures, University of Michigan, Ann Arbor.

Tajfel, H. (1975). The exit os social mobility and the voice of social change: Notes on the social psychology of intergroup relations. *Social Science Information, 14*, 101–118.

Tajfel, H. (1976). Exit, voice, and intergroup relations. In L. H. Strickland, F. E. Aboud, & K. J. Gergen (Eds.), *Social psychology in transition* (pp. 281–304). New York: Plenum Press.

Tajfel, H. (1978). Social categorization, social identity and social comparison. In H. Tajfel (Ed.), *Differentiation between social groups* (pp. 61–76). London: Academic Press.

Tajfel, H. (1981). Social stereotypes and social groups. In J. C. Turner & H. Giles (Eds.), *Intergroup behaviour* (pp. 144–167). Oxford, England: Blackwell.

Tajfel, H., & Turner, J. C. (1979). An integrative theory of intergroup conflict. In W. G. Austin & S. Worchel (Eds.), *The social psychology of intergroup relations* (pp. 33–47). Monterey, CA: Brooks/Cole.

Taylor, S. E., Neter, E., & Wayment, H. A. (1995). Self-evaluation processes. *Personality and Social Psychology Bulletin, 21*, 1278–1287.

Thornton, D., & Arrowood, A. J. (1966). Self-evaluation, self-enhancement, and the locus of social comparison. *Journal of Experimental Social Psychology, 2*(Suppl. 1), 40–48.

Turner, J. C. (1975). Social comparison and social identity: Some prospects for intergroup behaviour. *European Journal of Social Psychology, 5*, 5–34.

Turner, J. C. (1978a). Social categorization and social discrimination in the minimal group paradigm. In H. Tajfel (Ed.), *Differentiation between social groups: Studies in the social psychology of intergroup relations* (pp. 101–140). London: Academic Press.

Turner, J. C. (1978b). Social comparison, similarity and ingroup favouritism. In H. Tajfel (Ed.), *Differentiation between social groups: Studies in the social psychology of intergroup relations* (pp. 235–250). London: Academic Press.

Turner, J. C. (1981). Redefining the social group: A reply to the commentaries. *Cahiers de Psychologie Cognitive, 1*, 131–138.

Turner, J. C. (1982). Towards a cognitive redefinition of the social group. In H. Tajfel (Ed.), *Social identity and intergroup relations* (pp. 15–40). Cambridge, England: Cambridge University Press.

Turner, J. C. (1985). Social categorization and the self-concept: A social cognitive theory of group behavior. In E. J. Lawler (Ed.), *Advances in group processes: Theory and research* (Vol. 2, pp. 77–122). Greenwich, CT: JAI Press.

Turner, J. C. (1991). *Social influence.* Milton Keynes, England: Open University Press.

Turner, J. C. (1996). Henri Tajfel: An introduction. In W. P. Robinson (Ed.), *Social groups and identities: Developing the legacy of Henri Tajfel* (pp. 1–23). Oxford, England: Butterworth-Heinemann.

Turner, J. C., & Brown, R. J. (1978). Social status, cognitive alternatives and intergroup relations. In H. Tajfel (Ed.), *Differentiation between social groups: Studies in the social psychology of intergroup relations* (pp. 201–234). London: Academic Press.

Turner, J. C., Brown, R. J., & Tajfel, H. (1979). Social comparison and group interest in ingroup favouritism. *European Journal of Social Psychology, 9*, 187–204.

Turner, J. C., Hogg, M. A., Oakes, P. J., Reicher, S. D., & Wetherell, M. S. (1987). *Rediscovering the social group: A self-categorization theory*. Oxford, England: Blackwell.

Turner, J. C., & Oakes, P. J. (1986). The significance of the social identity concept for social psychology with reference to individualism, interactionism and social influence. *British Journal of Social Psychology, 25*, 237–252.

Turner, J. C., Wetherell, M. S., & Hogg, M. A. (1989). Referent informational influence and group polarization. *British Journal of Social Psychology, 28*, 135–147.

Wheeler, L. (1991). A brief history of social comparison theory. In J. Suls & T. A. Wills (Eds.), *Social comparison: Contemporary theory and research* (pp. 3–21). Hillsdale, NJ: Lawrence Erlbaum.

Wills, T. A. (1981). Downward comparison principles in social psychology. *Psychological Bulletin, 90*, 245–271.

Wills, T. A. (1991). Similarity and self-esteem in downward comparison. In J. Suls & T. A. Wills (Eds.), *Social comparison: Contemporary theory and research* (pp. 51–78). Hillsdale, NJ: Lawrence Erlbaum.

Wills, T. A., & Suls, J. (1991). Commentary: Neo-social comparison theory and beyond. In J. Suls & T. A. Wills (Eds.), *Social comparison: Contemporary theory and research* (pp. 395–411). Hillsdale, NJ: Lawrence Erlbaum.

Worchel, S., Morales, J. F., Páez, D., & Deschamps, J.-C. (Eds.) (1998). *Social identity: International perspectives* (p. 7). London: Sage.

20

Social Comparison and Fairness

A Counterfactual Simulations Perspective

ROBERT FOLGER AND EDWARD ELIYAHU KASS

People care about fairness. They care about the fairness of their outcomes (distributive justice) and the fairness of the procedures used to allocate outcomes (procedural justice). Fairness can have implications for current outcomes (e.g., "Did I get what I deserved?"), expected outcomes (e.g., "If nothing changes, what am I likely to get in the future?"), and plans about how to obtain outcomes (e.g., "What can I do to improve my expected future outcomes?").

In such ways, fairness judgments resemble those studied in the social comparison literature, which addresses how people come to understand themselves (Suls, 1977) and related questions (e.g., "Did I get what I deserved? Can I accomplish some future task? If I am unlikely to succeed at some future task, what can I do to improve my future task performance?"). Social comparison information can be highly diagnostic for such questions. In fact, sometimes answering questions about ourselves, such as about our relative attractiveness or intelligence, can only be known by comparing our thoughts, behaviors, and feelings with those of other people (Gilbert, Giesler, & Morris, 1995).

Social comparison and fairness judgments share many conceptual links. Revisions of social comparison theory have addressed various self-evaluative concerns relevant to obtained outcomes (e.g., Goethals & Darley, 1977). Some researchers have even explicitly noted that the outcomes to which one feels entitled (a form of fairness judgment) are important comparison standards (Kruglanski & Mayseless, 1990).

This chapter uses an integrated social comparison–counterfactual simulations approach as a lens through which to view the justice literature. Before saying more about social comparison and fairness judgments, however, we first briefly outline this orientation.

ROBERT FOLGER AND EDWARD ELIYAHU KASS • A. B. Freeman School of Business, Tulane University, New Orleans, Louisiana 70118-5669.

Handbook of Social Comparison: Theory and Research, edited by Suls and Wheeler. Kluwer Academic/Plenum Publishers, New York, 2000.

COMPARISONS AS COUNTERFACTUAL SIMULATIONS

Like the authors of Chapter 18, this volume, we treat comparison standards and judgments as subject to a counterfactual (counter-to-fact) and simulation (mental construction) process more generic than social comparison per se. Indeed, we view counterfactual simulations as the underlying process that Festinger (1954b) assumed people use in their "attempts to know what exists in the world ... and what [the] ... possibilities of action are in that world" (p. 193). Our counterfactual–simulation approach treats such attempts as "situations in which questions about events are answered by an operation that resembles the running of a simulation model" (Kahneman & Tversky, 1982). That is, in a manner similar to conducting simulation runs on computer models about hypothesized aspects of reality, humans conduct such simulation runs on their mental models about the world and its action possibilities.

The subjunctive tense also reflects this cognitive process of mentally modeled, counterfactual contrasts between one representation of reality and some not-yet realized or previously unrealized possibilities. The subjunctive deals with actual–counterfactual contrasts in denoting action possibilities or states of existence as conceived rather than as fact (e.g., "as if it were true that ..."). People use the subjunctive mood (e.g., present tense *be*, such as "if need be"; past tense, *were*) in describing something as contrary to fact (e.g., "I wish John *were* here") and in some idiomatic expressions ("If I *had* my way, fascism would vanish forever"). Because this tense's proper usage includes subjective or doubtful questions and statements (e.g., speculations, suppositions, hypotheses), it aptly fits the very conditions most germane to uncertainty reduction in Festinger's account of social comparison.

Consider again Festinger's language about "what exists" and "possibilities of action." People take some representation of what exists as "factual" or given. From information about reality that you take as given ("It's raining" or "It rained"), you can mentally construct one or more simulation models about various kinds of counterfactual possibilities (actual–counterfactual contrasts, for example, between the presence vs. absence of rain). People can mentally construct simulation models of actual events ("Did the fire start because those oily rags were too close to the candle?") and imagined alternatives to reality ("Would I have prevented the fire if I'd blown out the candle before going to bed?").

Explicitly or implicitly conducted simulation runs, for example, might use mental models involving social comparisons to generate alternative versions of the present ("It's raining. John has his umbrella and I don't. I wish I were him!") Other simulations reconstruct some aspect of the past ("I got wet—but I wouldn't have, if only I'd been carrying an umbrella"; "It's as if some demonic spirit had directed that rain cloud right over my head"). People also can simulate mental models concerning counterfactual contrasts about projected futures, using facts (e.g., existing storm clouds), others' opinions ("If my friends' opinions are correct, it's going to rain tomorrow; if the TV meteorologist's opinion is right, it's not going to rain"), or other information.

A mental simulation of counterfactual alternatives to actual realities occurs when people use comparison standards and make comparative judgments. Like social comparison theory, therefore, a simulated–counterfactual approach can address judgments such as self-assessment, self-improvement, and self-enhancement. Such judgments often involve comparisons between an object of judgment (e.g., an attribute such as ability; an outcome, such as pay) and a standard for evaluating that object; in other words, between some aspect of the object taken as given or "factual" and the comparative standard as its "counterfactual" contrast. When perceived unfairness involves an upward social comparison between yourself and someone with outcomes superior to yours, for example, that representation of events constitutes one of the "judgmental activities in which mental simulation appears to be involved ... [such as in] emotions that arise when reality is compared with a favored alternative" (Kahneman & Tversky, 1982, p. 202).

Social comparisons can be highly diagnostic for such judgments. Social comparison processes postulated by Festinger and subsequent theorists speak to that diagnosticity. Other relevant sources of information in addition to social comparisons, however, also might help people make inferences about "what exists" and "the possibilities of action" (Festinger, 1954b, p. 193). Research on mental simulation and counterfactual thought has generated many fruitful insights about information sources and inferences from them. We view social comparisons as encompassed within the more general processes of counterfactuals and simulation modeling.

Hence, as mentioned earlier, we use an integrated approach to social comparisons and counterfactual simulations as a lens through which to view the justice literature. Our literature review starts with links between equity and social comparison. Equity, a distributive justice (outcome fairness) norm, takes account of social comparisons such as different pay for different amounts of work or related "inputs" (e.g., expertise). Procedural justice shifted attention from fairness ends (*what* each person receives) to fairness means (*how* to conduct deliberations about the amounts that people will receive). The role of social comparison has diminished as inequity research has waned and procedural justice research has flowered. Despite the early association of inequity with social comparison theory, only some recent research (by Van den Bos, Lind, and their colleagues) again has addressed the role of social comparisons in fairness judgments. Much of the remaining justice research since the early work on inequity does not explicitly address that issue. We link the more recent work back to equity theory's association with social comparison theory by using a counterfactual–simulation approach, which provides a heuristically useful lens through which to interpret the justice literature. This perspective views fairness and social comparison as subject to the same underlying processes of information search, diagnosis, and interpretation. Even justice research that was not directly intended to address social comparison can be understood within our framework.

DISTRIBUTIVE JUSTICE: COMPARISONS AND INEQUITY

Distributive justice refers to outcome fairness. Distributive justice norms include equity, equality, and need (Deutsch, 1975), but we treat the Adams (1965) chapter on inequity as the classic reference. Shortly, we will return to issues of ambiguity, uncertainty, and the diagnosticity of social comparisons, and the direct bearing of such issues on fairness judgments viewed through the lens of a counterfactual–simulations approach. First, however, we present an account of the association between social comparison theory (Festinger, 1954b) and inequity theory (Adams, 1965). To preserve historical accuracy and conceptual specificity, our account focuses on how Adams himself described that association.

The Historical Association between Inequity and Social Comparison Theory

We begin our discussion of inequity with the following example. Imagine that you work as a diesel mechanic and report to one of several supervisors at DieselCo, each of whom supervises numerous diesel mechanics. All these DieselCo mechanics have the same tasks and an identical job title at the same level in the organizational hierarchy. They associate with one another and generally are comparable in all that Adams (1965) called a person's *outcomes* (designated by "O") from social exchanges such as the employment relation: "pay, rewards intrinsic to the job, satisfying supervision, seniority benefits, fringe benefits, job status and status symbols, and a variety of formally and informally sanctioned perquisites, such as the right of a higher-status person to park his [sic] car in a privileged location" (p. 278).

Adams used "inputs" (I) as a term for potential determinants of employee outcomes. Potential inputs include but are not limited to one's education, intelligence, training, seniority, or effort expended. Under special circumstances other attributes will be relevant. Whatever one perceives as his or her contributions to the exchange for which one expects a just return is an "input" (Adams, 1965). Note that because inputs refer to whatever one perceives as one's contributions, there is room for subjectivity and potential uncertainty. This increases the importance of social comparison information. One person might consider age a relevant input; another might consider it irrelevant. Like beauty, relevance and fairness are in the beholder's eye.

Adams portrayed inequity as any inequality between one outcome/input ratio (e.g., the ratio for you, mechanic *a* at DieselCo) and another O/I ratio (for *b*, such as some other mechanic). $Oa/Ia \neq Ob/Ib$, therefore, represents inequity between some *a* and some *b*. If you know your inputs and outcomes, social comparison information regarding others' inputs and outcomes might provide diagnostic information about your outcomes' fairness. Explicit citation of Festinger on social comparison theory occurs only twice, however, in the chapter that Adams (1965) wrote about inequity. The first citation does not appear until the following passage (14 pages into the chapter):

> While it is clearly important to be able to specify theoretically the appropriate reference person or group [i.e., constituting grounds for inequity perceptions], this will not be done here, as the task is beyond the scope of the paper and is discussed by others (e.g., Festinger, 1954[a] ...). For present purposes, it will be assumed that the reference person or group will be one comparable to the comparer on one or more attributes. This is usually a co-worker in industrial situations, ... but ... this generalization requires verification, as plausible as it may appear. (p. 280)

That passage obviously shows the relevance of social comparison theory to the Adams model of inequity, but it also shows that Adams himself did not focus much attention on that aspect of his model. Indeed, the only other explicit reference to social comparison theory comes in the next to the last paragraph of the chapter, where Adams referred to social comparison issues as one of two areas needing further work (the other being psychometric considerations):

> First, additional thought must be given to social comparison processes. The works of Festinger (1954[a]), Hyman (1942), Merton and Kitt (1950), Newcomb (1943), and Patchen (1961) are signal contributions but still do not allow sufficiently fine predictions to be made about whom Person will choose as a comparison Other when both are in an exchange relationship with a third party. (p. 297)

That passage refers to three parties in an exchange, which might surprise people who think of the Adams equation for inequity ($Oa/Ia \neq Ob/Ib$) as involving only two parties. The two-party inference seems logical, given that the theory's widely referenced formula for inequity involves an inequality between only two outcome-to-input ratios (those of *a* and *b*, commonly taken as referring to Person as *a* and Other as some other person, *b*). Adams, however, had a more generic view in mind. We describe that generic view for the sake of historical accuracy and because it fits with our subsequent account of fairness as subject to the generic process of simulation modeling. Moreover, the historically accurate account of what Adams wrote helps make two points sometimes overlooked about the term *Other* in the equity equation (which in turn has sometimes led to misconstruing equity as based solely on social comparison).

First, although "Other" tends to connote a person or group distinct from "Person,"

Adams did not insist that the comparison had to be social in a literal sense. That is, the comparison could either be interpersonal (a social comparison, between or across individuals) or intrapersonal (a within-individual comparison, perhaps over time), as the following passage clarifies:

> Other is usually a different individual, but may be Person in another job or in another social role. Thus, Other might be Person in a job he held previously, in which case he might compare his present and past outcomes and inputs and determine whether or not the exchange with his employer, present or past, was equitable. (Adams, 1965, p. 280)

Second, when referring to social comparisons that do involve some reference person or group as Other (the truly interpersonal case), theorists and researchers sometimes allude to Person and Other in relation to one another, as if the two were always and necessarily in direct exchange. Adams explicitly noted, however, that Other need not be in a direct exchange relationship with Person (e.g., Person and Other can both be in an exchange relationship with the same employer). The point is that just because Other is used for the comparative purpose of estimating the normative exchange rate (expectations about what's fair) does not mean that Person and Other are themselves in a direct exchange with one another. The same thing can be said of the Person-with-Other comparison when Other is Person at another point in time; clearly it makes no sense to describe Person as in direct exchange with himself or herself.

Thus, the Adams account of inequity included subtle nuances about Person, Other, temporal dynamics, the nature of the exchange or exchanges, the number of parties, and relations among them. We now address how the input-to-outcome relationship bears on the role of social comparisons, thereby summarizing the relation between inequity theory and social comparison theory. This relation also sets the stage for further integration of inequity, procedural justice, social comparison, and counterfactual simulations in subsequent sections of this chapter.

Adams (1965) indicated that the distinction between inputs and outcomes is useful conceptually but need not become a sticking point:

> In classifying some variables as inputs and others as outcomes, it is not implied that they are independent, except conceptually. Inputs and outcomes are, in fact, intercorrelated, but imperfectly so. Indeed, it is because they are imperfectly correlated that there need be concern with inequity. There exist normative expectations of what constitute "fair" correlations between inputs and outcomes. The expectations are formed—learned—during the process of socialization, at home, at school, at work. They are based by observation of the correlations obtaining for a reference person or group—a co-worker or a colleague, a relative or a neighbor, a group of co-workers, a craft group, an industry wide pattern. (p. 279)

The comment about "normative expectations" based on "a reference person or group" suggests that the perceived fairness of a social exchange is influenced by what someone considers to be a normatively appropriate rate of return for that type of exchange. That normative rate becomes the criterion used for judging the fairness of a person's outcome/input ratio from the exchange relationship. The normative rate is usually a matter for conjecture and interpretation rather than a matter that can be verified directly in some objective sense. That is, the "going rate" of fair return is not always identified so explicitly as in such statements as "This is a minimum wage job, which by law is [$x.xx] per hour." Instead, the normative rate is often inferred from other information. As indicated in the first of the two passages in which we showed Adams explicitly citing social comparison theory, he presumed that employees often use social comparison information about the return rate of a "reference person or group ... comparable to the comparer on one or more attributes" (1965, p. 280), but he left the question open empirically (reviews of empirical evidence relevant to that question include Goodman, 1977; Levine & Moreland, 1987; Kulik & Ambrose, 1992).

Having reviewed the historical association between inequity and social comparison theory, we turn now to a reframing of the same issues that brings ambiguity and the diagnosticity of various types of information back into the picture.

Equity, Ambiguity, Social Comparison, and Counterfactual Simulations

People can disagree about what constitutes a fair distribution of outcomes. They might have different standards of distributive justice (outcome fairness), for example, or different opinions about how to apply a given distributive standard, such as equity (equal outcome/input ratios, as defined above). Given this potential ambiguity, individuals might seek various types of information to assess the extent to which their outcomes are perceived as fair. These types of information can vary in diagnosticity and availability. Also, people contemplating fairness might consider links in causal chains capable of producing outcomes. Identifying possible causes of unfair outcomes can provide valuable information, such as information useful for action plans (e.g., for developing expectations and trying to improve future outcomes). In discussing the remaining topics related to inequity as outcome unfairness (distributive injustice), we consider in separate subsections each of several ways that people might seek diagnostic information to reduce uncertainty about the fairness of outcomes they have received.

Known Outcome/Input Ratios of Self and Others.   Suppose you take as "factual" certain information about your exchange relation with an employer. Your thoughts about its fairness or unfairness might begin with what you believe that you "know." In that sense, you might feel confident about the knowledge that you have about your own inputs to the exchange (e.g., your time and effort) and outcomes (e.g., rewards such as pay). You also might have certain social comparison information regarding others' inputs and outcomes or your own past inputs and outcomes. Such information can be highly diagnostic about the degree to which your current outcomes seem fair.

A simulation-modeling approach treats all such information as "counterfactual" in the sense of not describing your "actual" inputs and outcomes. As Olson et al. (Chapter 18, this volume) put it, these self-focused counterfactual thoughts involve implicit comparisons between the self's imagined and actual outcomes. Note that when people examine counterfactual information that they consider diagnostic of unfairness, they also might run simulations on one or more mental models of causal systems capable of correcting unfairness. Social comparisons and other types of outcome–input information relevant to fairness assessments, therefore, also can implicitly (or explicitly) evoke the cognitive activity of mental simulation. Such cognitive activity can model what exists (e.g., "What led to my outcomes?") and the action possibilities of virtual realities (e.g., "Under what circumstances might I have obtained the same outcomes as my more highly paid co-worker?").

Consistent with our overall characterization of actual–counterfactual contrasts as simulation-modeling activity, we can apply the same type of analysis to the outcome–input comparisons of inequity theory (Adams, 1965). Specifically, Adams argued that people need to compare their obtained outcomes with normatively expected outcomes in order to judge outcome fairness. Although he noted that normative expectations can come from a variety of sources, his discussion of social comparison information received the greatest amount of attention.

Let us start at this point, therefore, with a situation in which you compare the ratio of your inputs and outcomes to the corresponding ratio(s) of other people whom you consider diagnostic for the purpose of fairness assessments (in a social comparison sense; e.g., similar, relevant, possessing related attributes). If you perceive your outcome/input ratio as equal to those of relevant others, you perceive your outcomes as fair. Conversely, if your outcome/input ratio does not equal those of relevant comparison others, perceive an inequity—or at least initial grounds for assuming that an inequity might exist. To illustrate direct social comparisons about known outcome/input ratios, we consider two types of examples. The first parallels our earlier reference to you as a diesel mechanic. The second comes from recent research by Van den Bos, Lind, Vermunt, and Wilke (1997a).

Known Outcome/Input Ratios: A DieselCo Example.   As we mentioned earlier, you and the other diesel mechanics at DieselCo have the same tasks and an identical job title at the same level in the organizational hierarchy. You associate with one another and you perceive the other diesel mechanics as comparable to you in all respects relevantly diagnostic for assessing fairness via social comparisons. Under such circumstances, suppose you work 40 hours a week and receive $400 at the end of the week. The diesel mechanic working next to you, doing the same job, also works 40 hours a week and receives $400. Suppose both of you are also identical in terms of all the other types of work-related outcomes listed by Adams (e.g., salary and benefits, other types of rewards intrinsic to the job, satisfying supervision, and so on). Based on the Adams model, you should perceive that your pay conforms to your normative expectations about distributive justice, assuming that the outcome/input ratio of the mechanic next to you is your only (or best) diagnostic source of information for forming such normative expectations. You should perceive, therefore, that you received a fair outcome. Conversely, if the mechanic next to you (doing the same job, etc.) is paid $500 after working 40 hours, there is a good chance that you will feel unfairly underpaid. Although the Other described by Adams does not have to be some other person (e.g., you might know from the *Diesel Mechanics Newsletter* the going rate of pay for your position both locally and nationally), our example fits the pattern for typical illustrations of inequity. Such examples illustrate reduced fair outcome ambiguity through social comparison of known outcome/input ratios.

Known Outcome/Input Ratios: A Van den Bos et al. Example.   Van den Bos and colleagues (1997a) showed research participants information that manipulated inequity, or distributive injustice, by means of written scenarios (also obtaining, in a separate study, the same results from a laboratory experiment methodology). They asked participants to imagine that the experimenter was going to divide an allotment of lottery tickets between the participant and another participant (Other). Next, participants read that "The experimenter gives you 3 lottery tickets" (p. 1037). Then they read one of three things, which varied by an experimental manipulation that Van den Bos et al. called *outcome of other participant.* The text said "Other receives ..." That sentence ended with three tickets (Equal) or five tickets (Other's Outcome Better) in the conditions we describe here (the participants did not see either condition label shown in parentheses above).

Participants responded to this situation on 7-point scales; in particular, one questionnaire item asked them "how fair they considered the 3 lottery tickets that they received (1 = *very unfair*, 7 = *very fair*)" (1997, p. 1038). Ratings from the Outcome of Other Better condition (self = 3 tickets and Other = 5 tickets) differed significantly from ratings in the Equal condition (approximately 2.35 vs. 6.10, respectively). Of course, equity coincided with equality in this study, and the lack of input information presumably implied equality of inputs.

The two conditions of that Van den Bos et al. (1997a) study probably come as close as imaginable to situations in which people can evaluate fairness so conclusively by means of social comparison. Some everyday situations, however, will lack any objective criteria about fairness as checks on "physical reality" (cf. Festinger, 1954a,b) and also will lack such conclusively diagnostic information about social comparisons of known outcome/input ratios. We now turn to these less conclusive, more ambiguous cases and to another means of using social comparison information, namely, others' *opinions* about one's own outcomes and inputs.

Opinion-Based Comparisons.   Even in the absence of information about others' inputs and outcomes, one can still use social information to judge fairness. One can use knowledge of others' opinions about one's inputs or outcomes or the procedures to judge fairness. As Festinger's (1954a,b) theory of social comparison stipulates, such situations introduce some pressures toward opinion conformity and consistency. For example, you might know or might infer, based on various types of information, the opinions that other people have about your outcomes, your inputs, and your outcome/input ratio in an exchange relationship that you have with someone. In such a situation, others' opinions might provide diagnostic information about your exchange-related performance and the fairness of your outcomes from the exchange. Suppose you are a new employee and feel unsure about your level of performance. More experienced employees might provide you with information relevant to assessing your performance and also might indicate their opinions about it.

Furthermore, many times people have opinions about the fairness of other people's outcomes. Other employees might tell you to consider your pay unfair, for example, or they might imply (in various ways) that they consider your pay unfair. Others' opinions can serve as proxies for knowledge about your own "actual" inputs and outcomes, therefore, in a manner consistent with processes described by social comparison theory.

RESEARCH ON OPINION-BASED COMPARISONS
INFLUENCING PERCEIVED OUTCOME FAIRNESS

Greenberg and Folger (1983) discussed the use of others' opinions for assessments about one's own outcome fairness, and our discussion in this section follows their lead. In particular, they referred to others' opinions as potentially responsible for evoking comparisons between imagined and actual outcomes. Greenberg and Folger (1983) noted that evidence about others' opinions "can raise expectations," for example, and that "such expectations in turn, may subsequently be dashed" (p. 251). They cited dashed expectations as one way in which a sense of outcome unfairness "is experienced as the result of 'if only' thoughts (e.g., "If only the supervisor had seen things my way") that create an alternative frame of reference against which to compare existing reality (cf. Folger, Rosenfield, Rheaume, & Martin, 1983[a]; Folger, Rosenfield, & Robinson, 1983[b])" (Greenberg & Folger, 1983, p. 251).

Here again, then, we can integrate the social comparison and counterfactual–simulations approaches to perceived injustice. In fact, Greenberg and Folger (1983) also explicitly noted that with respect to effects on perceived outcome fairness such as those stemming from knowledge of others' opinions, a variety of findings "can be explained in terms of this susceptibility to influence via social comparison" (p. 245). Research on such effects that they reviewed includes a number of studies (e.g., Folger, 1977; Folger, Rosenfield, Grove, & Corkran, 1979; Thibaut, 1950; Thibaut, Friedland, & Walker, 1974).

A study by Folger et al. (1979), for example, created a salient norm of equitable distribution regarding a decision maker's allocation of rewards to two research participants as "workers." When asked to record privately their opinion about how much they should receive, all the workers endorsed that equity standard. Half the participants received no information about the other worker's outcome fairness opinion, however, whereas the remainder learned that it coincided with their own. In crosscutting *voice* conditions, each participant thought that he or she alone had been chosen randomly to provide his or her own fairness opinion to the allocator before the allocation decision was made. Participants in *mute* conditions, on the other hand, thought that neither they nor the other worker had such an opportunity. In all the conditions of this 2 × 2 design, the announced decision violated the equity standard for fair outcomes.

The results showed that when participants had no independent confirmation of the inequity (i.e., no information about the other worker's opinion), those in the *mute* conditions responded more unfavorably to the inequity than did those in the *voice* conditions. In the absence of social comparison information revealing a co-worker's opinion about the outcome, therefore, the fairness of a procedure with voice apparently tended to generalize to perceptions of the outcomes, a point to which we return in the next section. When participants knew that their co-worker's opinion indicated perceived outcome unfairness, however, the positive impact of voice disappeared. In other words, that social comparison information caused participants in both the mute and the voice conditions to display similar signs of dissatisfaction with the allocator and the decision (e.g., withholding money from that person when it was their turn to allocate). As Greenberg and Folger (1983) wrote about the implications of those findings, "expressions of dissatisfaction tend to be strengthened the more a person has reason to be convinced (via interpersonal validation) of an inequity" (p. 249). Interpersonal validation, of course, refers to social comparison information regarding another person's opinion about outcome fairness.

Allocation Procedures as a Source of Others' Opinions

If people lack information that directly addresses the fairness of outcomes, they may look to the procedures that yielded those outcomes as a source of distributive justice information. It makes sense to use fair procedures as a cue about the outcomes they produce. Hence, people tend to infer fair outcomes from fair procedures (cf. Lind, Kulik, Ambrose, & De Vera-Park, 1993; Lind & Tyler, 1988; Van den Bos, Lind, & Wilke, in press; Van den Bos, Lind, et al., 1997; Van den Bos, Vermunt & Wilke, 1997b; Van den Bos, Wilke, & Lind, 1998a; Van den Bos, Wilke, Lind, & Vermunt, 1998b), a finding known as the *fair process effect* (Folger et al., 1979).

Of course, it is certainly possible for fair procedures to produce unfair outcomes or for unfair procedures to yield fair ones. However, it is more likely that procedures will yield consonant outcomes. Research in other domains supports the notion that people use implicit theories (like mental-modeling simulations) to infer process information from outcome information (Staw, 1975) and to infer outcome information from process information (Guzzo, Wagner, Maguire, Herr, & Hawley, 1986).

In addition to implicit theories of processes and outcomes, procedural fairness information also might yield direct information for generating counterfactual outcomes. One of the most important elements of procedural justice perceptions is "voice" (Folger, 1977), the degree to which people are able to express their position as forcefully as they want to present it. If you are not allowed to voice your arguments to a judge and are found guilty, it is easy to imagine that if only the judge had listened to your arguments, the judge would have realized that you are innocent and judged the case more favorably. You do not know whether the (hopefully) cogent arguments you have developed (and would have presented to the judge, if only you'd been given a chance) are known to the judge. Now suppose instead that you voice your arguments to the judge and the judge appears to listen carefully to your arguments but still finds you guilty. Those circumstances might make it more difficult to generate upward close counterfactuals than if the judge did not listen to your arguments. This counterfactual referent has implications for both distributive justice and outcome satisfaction and acceptance.

Similarly, if you believe that you should get higher pay, you can discuss this with your supervisor. If the supervisor refuses to allow you to make your case or does not appear to listen to your arguments, you might be highly likely to imagine that if the supervisor had listened, she or he would have given you a raise. If your supervisor listens carefully to your arguments but still decides that you do not deserve a raise, however, it might be more difficult to imagine upward counterfactuals, thereby making you at least somewhat more accepting of and satisfied with the lack of a raise. In fact, if the supervisor maintains her or his belief that you do not deserve a raise even in the face of your arguments, you might infer that the supervisor must have some rather strong beliefs on her or his side to warrant her or his refusal.

That description of upward counterfactuals (thinking about how a better outcome might have been obtained) also relates to the augmentation effect (Kelley, 1972). *Augmentation* refers to the enhanced perception of a cause's being responsible for an effect when the causal factor produces the effect despite conditions that should inhibit it. For example, when a time of 10 seconds in a 100-yard dash is accomplished despite a 25-mile-per-hour wind blowing in the runner's face, greater athletic ability is attributed to the person who achieved that feat than to a person in another heat whose identical time was recorded when the wind was calm. Similarly, if a judge finds you guilty even after carefully hearing your arguments, you would be likely to infer that the judge must feel she or he has quite strong arguments in favor of a guilty verdict. In this fashion, the provision of voice can lead to greater acceptance of outcomes. The absence of a participatory process makes it easier to perceive an allocator's decision as having been made without much thought, whereas participation can contribute to the perception that it was a considered judgment.

When knowledge of similar others' outcomes is unavailable, you might instead use procedural justice information to infer the fairness of outcomes. It seems logical to assume that fair procedures tend to yield fair outcomes. In the absence of other information, people appear sensitive to procedural fairness information in their reactions to outcomes (Vermunt, Wit, van den Bos, & Lind, 1996). Specifically, people can compare the procedures used with counter-factual procedures, simulate what counterfactual outcomes would have obtained if only authorities had used the appropriate (counterfactual) procedure, and judge the actual procedure and actual outcome based on comparisons with those simulated procedures and outcomes. Logically, people can use social comparison information as a source of their expectations (Grienberger, Rutte, & van Kinppenberg, 1997). Alternatively, people might ask others for opinions about what procedure should have been used or rely on past experience (Vermunt et al., 1996).

PROCEDURAL JUSTICE AS AN OUTCOME

Individuals care about procedures as well as outcomes. A given procedure can be important not only as a source of information relevant for assessing outcomes, but also as a form of outcome in and of itself. There are a number of related reasons why people might value fair procedures. We describe some of the plausible reasons in separate subsections below. First, however, we present a general argument for treating procedures as outcomes on conceptual grounds (see also Cropanzano & Ambrose, in press). After the subsections on separate reasons for valuing procedures, we then use the procedure as outcome perspective to show how evaluating procedural justice conforms to the same generic comparison processes used for evaluating distributive justice (e.g., social comparison and simulated, counterfactual contrasts).

Why People Might Think of Procedures as Being Like Outcomes

Unquestionably, a conceptual distinction between procedures and outcomes has had great heuristic benefit for research on justice. Common experience also testifies to the usefulness of making this distinction, such as with respect to citizens' procedural rights (e.g., voting) versus the fairness of social benefits and burdens distributed on the basis of processes governed by applying those rights (e.g., taxes imposed by elected officials).

Consider also the importance of differentiating between procedural and distributive justice because norms for the two might conflict with one another. Suppose a court finds Sally guilty of a shoplifting crime that she did, in fact, commit. Despite conceptual grounds for rule violation as a case of retributive justice distinguishable from distributive justice (e.g., Hogan & Emler, 1981; Miller & Vidmar, 1981; Tyler, Boekmann, Smith, & Huo, 1997), let us suppose for the present purposes that you view "let the punishment fit the crime" as a matter of distributive justice. You apply the equity norm for assessing the fairness of the outcomes that Sally receives from the court (e.g., a guilty verdict; a $500 fine and 6 months' suspended jail sentence, no time served in prison). You consider these results as fully equitable. You have seen a video that indisputably shows her shoplifting. You think this criminal "input" warrants her punishment as an outcome. You also believe that the degree of punishment matches, in a correspondingly equitable manner, the degree of guilt or seriousness of the crime.

So far, everything in that example seems fair by the outcome-based standards of equity as a norm for distributive justice. But suppose you discover that the police, not knowing about the store videotape's existence, beat Sally brutally when first questioning her and thereby eventually obtained a confession from her. You learn that because of this violation of Sally's procedural rights, an appellate court has overturned her conviction (e.g., perhaps police presented the confession as evidence, without revealing the torture, but did not have the store videotape at the time of the trial). You then might feel that although her guilt warrants equitable punishment, the violation of her procedural rights constitutes a separate standard to use in assessing the fairness of the situation. Put simply, an unfair procedure might yield a fair outcome and vice versa.

Thus, there exist not only conceptual but also quite pragmatic (even profound) reasons for maintaining a careful distinction between procedural and distributive justice. Without any logical inconsistency, however, we also can conceptualize procedures as a special (or separate) type of outcome. Sally, for example, got several types of outcomes at various points during the episode we described. Nothing prevents us from treating her brutal beating as one of those outcomes, while simultaneously referring to it as a violation of her procedural rights as well.

Similarly, the use of a confession obtained by beating constitutes a procedural violation. Perhaps Sally's beating produced temporary amnesia. At the time of the trial, she did not recall that she had confessed only because the police had beaten her severely. If her memory returned after her conviction, she would then realize that she experienced a negative "outcome" during the trial, even prior to the verdict: the testimony itself. In short, because people can feel entitled to certain types of procedural rights for various reasons (e.g., constitutional guarantees), they also can feel unfairly deprived when they fail to receive such rights as their treatment.

Given such grounds for conceptualizing procedures as outcomes, we now turn to separate considerations about the various reasons why people might value procedures. Each subsection therefore presents a separate basis on which being deprived of a procedural right could constitute an experience similar to being deprived of a distributed benefit (i.e., an outcome). Each subsection pertains to a different type of psychological mechanism proposed to explain why people care about procedures.

Procedural Treatment as Evidence of Identity-Based Standing in a Group. Fair procedures might indicate your standing in a group that you consider important, one implication of explanations for procedural concerns according to the group-value model (Lind & Tyler, 1988) and the relational model of authority (Tyler & Lind, 1992). According to the Lind–Tyler identity-based group value–relational model (see also Tyler, 1997), to be treated unfairly and with disrespect indicates low social status or standing in the group. Such treatment by a group, or by its authorities as those who (ought to) embody its values, indicates that the group does not value you as a group member. This identity-based explanation of why people care about procedural justice hypothesizes a connection between people's concerns about their social identity and people's concerns about procedural legitimacy (and the perceived legitimacy of authorities who administer procedures). This hypothesis draws on social identity theory (e.g., Hogg & Abrams, 1988; Tajfel & Turner, 1986) and its assumption that your status in an important membership or reference group provides information from which to infer implications about your self-identity and self-worth.

Because feelings of self-worth thereby constitute one type of outcome from the group consistent with the Adams (1965) list of outcomes that included status, this proposal also conforms with our procedures as outcomes approach. In addition, the identity-based conception of self-worth also might relate to social comparison. For instance, you might compare your procedural treatment from the group (or authorities) with the procedural treatment received by other people. Presumably (an issue we consider empirically later) such comparisons might influence perceptions of your relative exploitation by the group, relative deprivation of procedural rights, or your sense of the extent to which you feel excluded from full-fledged membership in the group (being denied the full rights and privileges of membership).

Procedural Treatment and Expected Value Projections about Outcomes. Second, assessments of procedural fairness and the causes of fair or unfair outcomes might prove highly diagnostic for predicting (making projections of) the most likely future outcomes and the likely trends in outcomes over time. You might want such information to decide, for example, which organization to join. Based on preentry assessments about the fairness of various organizations' procedures, you might estimate for each organization a modal or expected value outcome (in a statistical sense) as a reasonable speculation about the outcomes you would receive from joining that organization and from continuing your membership in it over time (cf. Folger, 1986b).

Relatedly, suppose you believe that you have received unfair outcomes because your supervisor fails to assess your performance accurately. That situation also might affect your future plans. For instance, you might predict low future outcomes and develop a plan for improving your prospects (e.g., how to switch supervisors or to improve the measurement of your performance). You project future outcomes from your own actual experiences with a particular procedure in this supervisor example, whereas you infer projected future outcomes solely from characteristics of the procedures themselves in the example of your preentry selection among organizations.

Thibaut and Walker's Procedural Justice Theory as a Resource-Based or "Informed Self-Interest" Model.   The long-term or projected futures perspective that we just described also entered the procedural justice literature at its outset, when Thibaut and Walker (1975, 1978) introduced their pioneering analysis of procedures. Although we think that more than one possible interpretation might apply to their perspective, we describe it here in terms often used because of its characterization by Lind and Tyler (1988) as "the long-term self-interest perspective on procedural justice" (p. 225) or "an extended or informed self-interest model" (p. 223). Tyler (1997) also has called it a resource-based model.

Lind and Tyler (1988) argued that individuals recognize the need to subordinate some immediate desires for the sake of cooperation. Through cooperation with others, each individual is able to obtain greater outcomes in the long run. One such cooperative act is to accept outcomes and procedures based on fairness rather than based on their favorability to one's own interests. Procedural fairness acquires great significance as an "outcome" (membership-benefit) from belonging to a group therefore because procedural fairness increases the odds of long-term gains despite short-term losses.

Tyler and Lind (1992) also referred to the Thibaut–Walker model as an *instrumental* perspective on procedural justice. This term indicates that Thibaut and Walker saw procedural justice as the means for creating distributive justice, especially in the sense of equity as Adams (1965) had described it. The resource-based and self-interested labels apply because Thibaut and Walker focused on conflicts such as those resolved in the legal arena by judicial decision-making processes (e.g., trials in courtrooms) or in the more general public arena by political processes (e.g., voting). Such conflicts pit competing interests against one another for scarce resources. The merits of competing claims sometimes cannot be resolved by the disputing parties, which has led to institutionalized forums for dispute resolution such as civil courts.

Many institutionalized procedures grant a third-party decision maker absolute authority to impose outcomes. Such decision makers would tend not to be as familiar with the merits of competing claims as the claimants themselves, however, which led Thibaut and Walker to see such processes as problematic for equity in making inherently subjective determinations about the value of the parties' respective inputs to an exchange. (Note that this very ambiguity and uncertainty makes social comparison especially relevant.) Thibaut and Walker reasoned that the parties' self-interest would lead them to make the best possible equity-related case, which would then provide the decision maker both with all the relevant information and with offsetting forms of bias. Moreover, because disputants lose any direct control over outcomes that they might have had if they had continued bargaining, they should appreciate at least having this chance to augment their diminished role in resolving the conflict. That is, such a procedure gives them a "voice" in the process (Folger, 1977) as a form of indirect control (potential opportunities to influence the decision maker in their favor). Voting performs a similar function as a procedural right often guaranteed in the political arena.

Leventhal's Model: Procedural Features as Outcomes.   In speculating on why people care about procedures, Leventhal (Leventhal, 1980; Leventhal, Karuza, & Fry, 1980) suggested that several structural characteristics or features of procedures might seem desirable. Put another way, each might serve as a cue for assessing the fairness of a given procedure. Leventhal (1980) extended the Thibaut–Walker model beyond two- or three-party situations by subsuming voice as a special case of one type of procedural criterion, namely, representativeness (which applies to multiple parties, as implied above in reference to voting as a political process). His list of highlighted features of procedural fairness also included the following: consistency (applying standards uniformly over time and across persons), bias suppression (minimizing or offsetting personal self-interest and narrow preconceptions or prejudices), accuracy (relying on high-quality information and well-informed opinion), correctability (allowing decisions to be reviewed and revised or reversed), and ethicality (taking into account relevant standards of moral conduct).

As this list should suggest, these criteria tend to convey absolute standards of noncomparative justice (Feinberg, 1974) such as are embodied in conceptions of political rights, civil rights, and human rights. Perhaps that helps explain why social comparison considerations often have played only a small role in the procedural justice literature. Being beaten probably seems wrong, for example, no matter whether or not other people are beaten. Presumably you would need no social comparison with others' procedural treatment to know that yours was unfair, if yours includes being beaten.

Nonetheless, a procedures as outcomes perspective suggests that being denied the right to procedurally fair treatment can feel the same as an outcome deprivation in some sense. For that reason, surely relative deprivation effects might occur—such as those based on social comparison—in addition to those based on rights as absolutes. This highlights the relevance to our linkage of social comparison with counterfactual contrasts as simulated in mental models about what exists and what that implies about one's possibilities for action. We explore that linkage further in the following section.

A SOCIAL COMPARISON/COUNTERFACTUAL–SIMULATIONS APPROACH TO PROCEDURES AS OUTCOMES

Leventhal's consistency criterion can imply social comparison, namely, whether people under a decision-making authority all receive the same procedural treatment from that authority. This again implies procedural rights as procedural outcomes, subject to the same social comparison process as other types of outcomes. Consistency, however, can come in at least one of two forms: consistency across persons, as social comparison theory would emphasize, and consistency over time. The latter form of consistency implies that you might assess the fairness of your procedural treatment on comparative or relativistic (rather than absolute) grounds that do not necessarily involve social comparison. You might, for example, compare the procedural treatment you receive today with what you received yesterday. You might instead compare the procedural treatment you receive with an idealized conception, however, such as one derived from political philosophy or a theory of human rights. In that sense, a model of counterfactual contrasts applies even when dealing with what we referred to above as an absolute standard of noncomparative justice.

This section deals with these issues concerning forms of comparison and contrastive judgment applied to procedures as outcomes. Our counterfactual–simulation perspective borrows from the same source as the framework that Olson et al. (Chapter 18, this volume) used to link social comparison and counterfactuals, namely, Folger's referent cognitions theory (RCT). We apply this model only as it is relevant to procedural comparisons, and other sources should be consulted for discussions of RCT as originally developed (e.g., Folger, 1984, 1986a,c, 1987), as subsequently tested (e.g., Brockner & Wiesenfeld, 1986; Cropanzano & Folger, 1989; Folger & Martin, 1986; Folger et al., 1983a,b), and as expanded (e.g., Folger, 1993; Folger & Cropanzano, 1998; Folger & Skarlicki, 1998). Below we review empirical research on the topic of procedural comparisons largely inspired by RCT.

Consider, for example, a study conducted by Vermunt et al. (1996). As these authors noted, RCT assumes "that individuals evaluate the fairness of an actual event or state (e.g., outcome, procedure) by comparing it with a referent event (e.g., outcome, procedure; Folger, 1987)" (Vermunt et al., 1996, p. 117). Prior tests of RCT, however, had concentrated on reactions to unfair outcomes, although "the basic assumption of RCT also holds when the cognitive element is a procedure" (p. 117). Thus, what we have called actual–counterfactual contrasts refers to the same contrast that RCT called actual versus referent.

To test RCT implications for intrapersonal comparisons of procedures, Vermunt et al. (1996) had research participants first experience three rounds of an accurate (fair) scoring procedure, followed on a fourth round by a change either to a very inaccurate procedure (VIP condition) or a slightly inaccurate procedure (SIP condition). The study measured a running average of the participants' magnitude estimation performance on ten estimation tests during four rounds of testing. The participants believed that those scores would determine eligibility for a bonus awarded in a fifth round. Based on bogus feedback from ten tests for each of three rounds, all participants thought that their projected average made them approximately on target (or slightly borderline) for bonus eligibility. After the fourth round but before providing scores for that round, the experimenter announced a change in the scoring procedure. The change in the VIP condition meant calculating the adjustment to the running average based on a single test rather than on all ten from the fourth round. The SIP change, in contrast, meant an adjustment based on eight of those ten tests.

This announcement manipulated perceived accuracy without creating any between-conditions difference in expectations of winning the bonus. That is, participants in the VIP and SIP conditions did not differ in their expected outcomes. Despite the lack of difference in perceived outcomes, this VIP–SIP manipulation successfully induced differences in perceived procedural fairness of treatment from the experimenter. The results also showed that the more inaccurate (VIP) testing arrangement generated more negative affect (anger, irritation, and fury) and stronger protest intentions, with protest being mediated by negative affect about the procedural unfairness.

Grienberg et al. (1997) also tested the RCT predictions about the unfairness of an actual procedure relative to its counterfactual alternative. They used a social comparison manipulation (Other's procedure fair vs. nonfair) rather than the Vermunt et al. (1996) contrast of present procedures versus past procedures. Another Grienberg et al. manipulation involved whether the research participant's own procedure was fair or unfair, differentiated by varying the participant's perceived degree of control over a task assignment. High Own Control participants heard brief, deliberately vague descriptions of two tasks and then got to choose which one they would perform in trying to win a bonus. Low Own Control participants had no such choice. Both sets of participants heard that a personal decision by the experimenter (not random selection) had led to their being allowed or not being allowed to have that choice. The related procedural manipulation based on social comparison (High Other Control vs. Low Other Control) gave participants information regarding whether a co-participant did or did not have such a choice.

After learning that they did not receive the bonus, participants answered a questionnaire about their reactions to the study, which included a procedural justice item regarding how fairly the study had been conducted. Responses to that item produced a significant two-way interaction of Own Control and Other Control. In particular, the combination of Low Own Control with High Other Control produced ratings of more unfairness than from any of the other three conditions. That result demonstrates an effect on procedural fairness perceptions when people have unfavorable social comparison information about procedural differences between themselves and other people.

The Vermunt et al. (1996) and the Grienberger et al. (1997) studies thus provide evidence for an intrapersonal and an interpersonal type of effect involving procedural contrasts, respectively. By interpersonal effect, of course, we mean one involving social comparison. As Grienberger et al. put it, their results showed "that not only outcomes, but also procedures, are socially compared" (p. 919). Vermunt et al. (1996) reached a similar conclusion about procedures contrasted intrapersonally over time: "The perceived discrepancy between actual and past procedure led to feelings of unfairness, as would be predicted from RCT when the cognitive element of outcomes is replaced by that of procedures" (p. 117).

CONCLUSION

We have attempted to show that an integration of social comparison theory with social cognition theorizing about counterfactuals and mental simulations (Folger, 1984, 1986a,c, 1987; cf. Chapter 18, this volume) also helps provide an integrative perspective on the justice literature. Despite what appear to be promising prospects for this integration, the empirical base has only begun to expand in new directions. That is, as our last section showed, only recently have social comparisons of procedures yielded effects on perceived procedural fairness (although see Lind, Kray, & Thompson, 1998, for another exception).

Even the organization of our conceptual framework has just scratched the surface of potential for future integrative efforts. Indeed, we have only told "half the story." We have emphasized a one-sided approach to fairness that concentrates on effects experienced "as outcomes" (whether distributed as economic benefits, such as pay, or perceived more symbolically, such as when people feel entitled to procedural rights and respond to procedural deprivation in the same manner that they respond to outcome deprivation). The use of a moral term such as "fairness," however, makes little sense without also stressing issues such as blame, fault, intention, and moral accountability (see, e.g., Folger, 1993; Folger & Cropanzano, 1998).

Consider, for example, Leventhal's reference to consistency as a criterion for procedural fairness and why, too, Adams essentially treated equity as consistency (equivalent outcome/input ratios across persons or over time). Mere consistency need not demonstrate moral virtue; and, as Thoreau said, a foolish consistency is the hobgoblin of little minds. Look again at the equation for inequity, $Oa/Ia \neq Ob/Ib$, as a matter of consistency. This equation, as Bies (1987) pointed out, refers only to a mathematical imbalance. Why should that be morally offensive? Why have scholars since Aristotle's time insisted on similar treatment as a touchstone of fairness rather than as a mere preference for cognitive consistency?

A comprehensive answer to that question extends beyond this scope of this chapter, but we want to close by noting its significance for further work integrating simulated counterfactuals with social comparison and fairness. The short form of our answer is that fairness involves social treatment, not mere consistency. Put another way, the full story of fairness requires not only a focus on what happens to one or more persons who might or might not compare themselves and how they have been treated. Rather, it also requires a discussion of how such treatment—or perceived mistreatment—came about, and whether grounds exist for holding someone morally accountable for alleged (e.g., socially disparate) mistreatment.

We think social comparison and counterfactual simulation of mental models about social situations can address such questions. In fact, our analysis of ambiguity and the role of other people's opinions extends readily in that direction. Inferences about a person's intentions often prove to be determinants in assigning blame and in determining whether that person has treated others fairly (e.g., Cropanzano & Folger, 1989; Folger, 1993; Folger & Cropanzano,

1998; Folger & Skarlicki, 1998; Mikula, 1993; Robinson & Darley, 1995). Surely such inferences about intentionality and blame are at least as susceptible to conditions of ambiguity and uncertainty as are other situations in which social comparisons play a vital role. Just as assuredly, we argue, such situations should also prove susceptible to analysis from an integrative perspective on social comparisons and simulated counterfactuals. As math textbooks say, "the rest is left to the discerning reader as an exercise."

REFERENCES

Adams, J. S. (1965). Inequity in social exchange. *Advances in Experimental Social Psychology, 2,* 267–299.

Bies, R. J. (1987). The predicament of injustice: The management of moral outrage. *Research in Organizational Behavior, 9,* 289–319.

Brockner, J., & Wiesenfeld, B. M. (1996). An integrative framework for explaining reactions to decisions: The interactive effects of outcomes and procedures. *Psychological Bulletin, 120,* 189–208.

Cropanzano, R., & Folger, R. (1989). Referent cognitions and task decision autonomy: Beyond equity theory. *Journal of Applied Psychology, 74,* 293–299.

Cropanzano, R., & Ambrose, M. (In press). Do we need the distributive/procedural distinction? In J. Greenberg & R. Cropanzano (Eds.), *Advances in organizational justice.* Stanford, CA: Stanford University Press.

Deutsch, M. (1975). Equity, equality, and need: What determines which value will be used as the basis of distributive justice? *Journal of Social Issues, 31,* 137–150.

Feinberg, J. (1974). Noncomparative justice. *The Philosophical Review, 83,* 297–338.

Festinger, L. (1954a). A theory of social comparison processes. *Human Relations, 7,* 117–140.

Festinger, L. (1954b). Motivation leading to social behavior. In M. R. Jones (Ed.), *Nebraska symposium on motivation* (Vol. 2, pp. 191–218). Lincoln: University of Nebraska Press.

Folger, R. (1977). Distributive and procedural justice: Combined impact of "voice" and improvement on experienced inequity. *Journal of Personality and Social Psychology, 35,* 108–119.

Folger, R. (1984). Perceived injustice, referent cognitions, and the concept of comparison level. *Representative Research in Social Psychology, 14,* 88–108.

Folger, R. (1986a). A referent cognitions theory of relative deprivation. In J. M. Olson, C. P. Herman, & M. P. Zanna (Eds.), *Social comparison and relative deprivation: The Ontario symposium* (Vol. 4, pp. 33–55). Hillsdale, NJ: Lawrence Erlbaum.

Folger, R. (1986b). Mediation, arbitration, and the psychology of procedural justice. In R. J. Lewicki, B. H. Sheppard & M. H. Bazerman (Eds.), *Research on negotiation in organizations* (Vol. 1, pp. 57–79). Greenwich, CT: JAI Press.

Folger, R. (1986c). Rethinking equity theory: A referent cognitions model. In H. W. Bierhoff, R. C. Cohen, & J. Greenberg (Eds.), *Justice in social relations* (pp. 145–162). New York: Plenum Press.

Folger, R. (1987). Reformulating the preconditions of resentment: A referent cognitions model. In J. C. Masters & W. P. Smith (Eds.), *Social comparison, justice, and relative deprivation: Theoretical, empirical, and policy perspectives* (pp. 183–215). Hillsdale, NJ: Lawrence Erlbaum.

Folger, R. (1993). Reactions to mistreatment at work. In K. Murnighan (Ed.), *Social psychology in organizations: Advances in theory and research* (pp. 161–183) Englewood Cliffs, NJ: Prentice-Hall.

Folger, R., & Cropanzano, R. (1998). *Organizational justice and human resource management.* Thousand Oaks, CA: Sage.

Folger, R., & Martin, C. (1986). Relative deprivation and referent cognitions: Distributive and procedural justice effects. *Journal of Experimental Social Psychology, 22,* 532–546.

Folger, R., Rosenfield, D., Grove, J., & Corkran, L. (1979). Effects of "voice" and peer opinions on responses to inequity. *Journal of Personality and Social Psychology, 37,* 2243–2261.

Folger, R., Rosenfield, D., Rheaume, K., & Martin, C. (1983a). Relative deprivation and referent cognitions. *Journal of Experimental Social Psychology, 19,* 172–184.

Folger, R., Rosenfield, D., & Robinson, T. (1983b). Relative deprivation and procedural justifications. *Journal of Personality and Social Psychology, 45,* 268–273.

Folger, R., & Skarlicki, D. P. (1998). A popcorn metaphor for workplace violence. In R. W. Griffin, A. O'Leary-Kelly, & J. Collins (Eds.), *Dysfunctional behavior in organizations, Vol. 1: Violent behaviors in organizations* (pp. 43–81). Greenwich, CT: JAI Press.

Gilbert, D. T., Giesler, R. B., & Morris, D. A. (1995). When comparisons arise. *Journal of Personality and Social Psychology, 69*, 227–236.

Goethals, G. R., & Darley, J. M. (1977). Social comparison theory: An attributional approach. In J. Suls & R. L. Miller (Eds.), *Social comparison processes: Theoretical and empirical perspectives* (pp. 259–278). Washington, DC: Hemisphere.

Goodman, P. S. (1977). Social comparison processes in organizations. In B. M. Staw & G. R. Salancik (Eds.), *New directions in organizational behavior* (pp. 97–132). Chicago, IL: St. Clair Press.

Greenberg, J., & Folger, R. (1983). Procedural justice, participation, and the fair process effect in groups and organizations. In P. Paulus (Ed.), *Group process* (pp. 235–256). New York: Springer-Verlag.

Grienberg, I. V., Rutte, C. G., & van Knippenberg, A. F. M. (1997). Influence of social comparisons of outcomes and procedures on fairness judgments. *Journal of Applied Psychology, 82*, 913–919.

Guzzo, R. A., Wagner, D. B., Maguire, E., Herr, B., & Hawley, C. (1986). Implicit theories and the evaluation of group process and performance. *Organizational Behavior and Human Decision Processes, 37*, 278–285.

Hogan, R., & Emler, N. P. (1981). Retributive justice. In M. Lerner & S. C. Lerner (Eds.), *The justice motive in social behavior: Adapting to times of scarcity and change* (pp. 125–143). New York: Plenum.

Hogg, M. A., & Abrams, D. (1988). *Social identifications*. New York: Routledge.

Hyman, H. (1942). The psychology of status. *Archives of Psychology, 38*(269).

Kahneman, D., & Tversky, A. (1982). Availability and the simulation heuristic. In D. Kahneman, P. Slovic, & A. Tversky (Eds.), *Judgment under uncertainty: Heuristics and biases* (pp. 201–208). New York: Cambridge University Press.

Kelley, H. H. (1972). Causal schemata and the attribution process. In E. E. Jones, D. E. Kanouse, H. H. Kelley, R. E. Nisbett, S. Valins, & B. Weiner (Eds.), *Attribution: Perceiving the causes of behavior* (pp. 151–174). Morristown, NJ: General Learning Press.

Kruglanski, A. W., & Mayseless, O. (1990). Classical and current social comparison research: Expanding the perspective. *Psychological Bulletin, 108*, 195–208.

Kulik, C. T., & Ambrose, M. L. (1992). Personal and situational determinants of referent choice. *Academy of Management Review, 17*, 212–237.

Leventhal, G. S. (1980). What should be done with equity theory? In K. J. Gergen, M. S. Greenberg, & R. H. Willis (Eds.), *Social exchanges: Advances in theory and research* (pp. 27–55). New York: Plenum Press.

Leventhal, G. S., Karuza, J., & Fry, W. R. (1980). Beyond fairness: A theory of allocation preferences. In G. Mikula (Ed.). *Justice and social interaction* (pp. 167–218). New York: Springer-Verlag.

Levine, J. M., & Moreland, R. L. (1987). Social comparison and outcome evaluation in group contexts. In J. C. Masters & W. P. Smith (Eds.), *Social comparison, social justice and relative deprivation* (pp. 105–127). Hillsdale, NJ: Lawrence Erlbaum.

Lind, E. A., Kray, L., & Thompson, L. (1998). The social construction of justice: Fairness judgments in response to own and others' unfair treatment by authorities. *Organizational Behavior and Human Decision Processes, 75*, 1–22.

Lind, E. A., Kulik, C. T., Ambrose, M., & De Vera-Park, M. W. (1993). Individual and corporate dispute resolution: Using procedural fairness as a decision heuristic. *Administrative Science Quarterly, 38*, 224–251.

Lind, E. A., & Tyler, T. (1988). *The social psychology of procedural justice*. New York: Plenum Press.

Merton, R. K., & Kitt, A. S. (1950). Contributions to the theory of reference group behavior. In R. K. Merton & P. F. Lazarsfeld (Eds.), *Continuities in social research: Studies in the scope and method of "The American Soldier"* (pp. 40–105). Grencoe, IL: Free Press.

Mikula, G. (1993). On the experience of injustice. In W. Strobe & M. Hewston (Eds.), *European review of social psychology* (Vol. 4, pp. 223–244). New York: Wiley.

Miller, D. T., & Vidmar, N. (1981). The social psychology of punishment reactions. In M. Lerner & S. C. Lerner (Eds.), *The justice motive in social behavior: Adapting to times of scarcity and change* (pp. 125–143). New York: Plenum.

Newcomb, T. M. (1943). *Personality and social change: Attitude formation in a student community*. New York: Dryden.

Patchen, M. (1961). *The choice of wage comparisons*. Englewood Cliffs, NJ: Prentice-Hall.

Robinson, P. H., & Darley, J. M. (1995). *Justice, liability, and blame*. San Francisco: Westview Press.

Staw, B. M. (1975). Attribution of the "causes" of performance: A general alternative interpretation of cross-sectional research in organizations. *Organizational Behavior and Human Performance, 15*, 125–135.

Suls, J. M. (1977). Social comparison theory and research: An overview from 1954. In J. M. Suls & R. L. Miller (Eds.), *Social comparison processes: Theoretical and empirical perspectives* (pp. 1–19). Washington, DC: Hemisphere.

Tajfel, H. & Turner, J. C. (1986). The social identity theory of intergroup behavior. In S. Worchel & W. G. Austin (Eds.), *Psychology of intergroup relations* (pp. 7–24). Chicago: Nelson Hall.

Thibaut, J. (1950). An experimental study of the cohesiveness of underprivileged groups. *Human Relations, 3*, 251–278.

Thibaut, J., Friedland, N., & Walker, L. (1974). Compliance with rules: Some social determinants. *Journal of Personality and Social Psychology, 30*, 782–801.

Thibaut, J., & Walker, L. (1975). *Procedural justice: A psychological analysis*. Hillsdale, NJ: Lawrence Erlbaum.

Thibaut, J., & Walker, L. (1978). A theory of procedure. *California Law Review, 66*, 541–566.

Tyler, T. R. (1997). The psychology of legitimacy: A relational perspective on voluntary deference to authorities. *Personality and Social Psychology Review, 1*, 323–346.

Tyler, T. R., Boekmann, R. J., Smith, H. J., & Huo, Y. J. (1997). *Social justice in a diverse society*. Boulder, CO: Westview Press.

Tyler, T. R., & Lind, E. A. (1992). A relational model of authority in groups. In M. P. Zanna (Ed.), *Advances in experimental social psychology* (Vol. 25, pp. 115–191). San Diego, CA: Academic Press.

Van den Bos, K., Lind, E. A., Vermunt, R., & Wilke, H. A. M. (1997). How do I judge my outcome when I do not know the outcome of others? The psychology of the fair process effect. *Journal of Personality and Social Psychology, 72*, 1034–1046.

Van den Bos, K., Lind, E. A., & Wilke, H. A. M. (In press). The psychology of procedural and distributive justice viewed from the perspective of fairness heuristic theory. In R. Cropanzano (Ed.), *Justice in the workplace: Vol. 2. From theory to practice*. Mahwah, NJ: Lawrence Erlbaum.

Van den Bos, K., Vermunt, R., & Wilke, H. A. M. (1997). Procedural and distributive justice: What is fair depends more on what comes first than on what comes next. *Journal of Personality and Social Psychology, 72*, 95–104.

Van den Bos, K., Wilke, H. A. M., & Lind, E. A. (1998a). When do we need procedural fairness? The role of trust in authority. *Journal of Personality and Social Psychology, 75*, 1449–1458.

Van den Bos, K., Wilke, H. A. M., Lind, E.A. & Vermunt, R. (1998b). Evaluating outcomes by means of the fair process effect: Evidence for different processes in fairness and satisfaction judgments. *Journal of Personality and Social Psychology, 74*, 1493–1503.

Vermunt, R., Wit, A., van den Bos, K., & Lind, E. A. (1996). The effects of unfair process on negative affect and protest. *Social Justice Research, 9*, 109–119.

21

Social Comparison Processes in Health and Illness

HOWARD TENNEN, TARA EBERHARDT McKEE, AND GLENN AFFLECK

Social comparison processes play an increasingly pivotal role in psychological theories of how people interpret health threats, how they understand their own health risks, how and when they decide to seek care for physical symptoms, and how they adapt to serious illness and disability. Our goal in this chapter is to provide an overview of research in which social comparison principles have been applied to health-related situations. Medical problems or situations that create uncertainty about one's health are good arenas in which to study social comparison phenomena. People who are ill often have difficulty obtaining information about the course of their illness and its treatment, which may make it difficult for them to make objective self-evaluations. The emotional distress they experience may not always be alleviated by direct action. Individuals facing threatening medical encounters therefore may be compelled to search for comparisons as a way to counteract these and other negative consequences of their situation. As we hope to demonstrate, however, people who are not ill also turn to social comparisons to explain disconcerting symptoms and to make decisions about appropriate preventive behaviors.

As in most areas of psychological inquiry, several theoretical perspectives have been offered to explain how and why people facing threatening circumstances, including those facing health threats, engage in social comparison, and numerous methodological approaches have been employed to test these perspectives. Wood (1996) distinguished three methods commonly used to study social comparison processes: *selection* approaches, which examine the information that individuals seek in making social comparisons; *reaction* approaches,

HOWARD TENNEN AND GLENN AFFLECK • Department of Community Medicine, University of Connecticut Health Center, Farmington, Connecticut 06030. TARA EBERHARDT McKEE • Department of Psychology, University of Connecticut, Storrs, Connecticut 06269-1020.

Handbook of Social Comparison: Theory and Research, edited by Suls and Wheeler. Kluwer Academic/Plenum Publishers, New York, 2000.

which analyze how social comparison information influences people; and *narration* approaches, which study individuals' reports of the social comparisons they make in their everyday lives. Each method is represented in the review that follows. A common selection approach in the experimental studies we review involves manipulating a comparison dimension, such as level of threat, and then providing participants the chance to scrutinize social comparison information. The extent to which they take advantage of the opportunity to examine the information is then assessed. But as Wood (1996) notes, motives other than social comparison may influence the decision to examine available information. Reaction approaches include methods that present social comparison information and then measure its effects, as well as those that have participants rate themselves relative to another individual on a particular dimension. The narration approaches that are represented in our review include those that have participants report whether they compare themselves to others and with whom, as well the approach that examines the social comparison statements participants express spontaneously. Wood (1996) reminds us that these self-report indicators of social comparisons are subject to the same biases that limit any self-report measure, including the fact that people are not always aware that they are comparing themselves to others; the possibility that these reports are driven in part by social desirability motives; and the difficulty people may have recalling their comparisons to others. Because each method has its strengths and weaknesses, Wood (1996) suggested using a combination of methods.

To provide realistic boundaries for our review, we limited our search to articles published since 1990 that appeared in either PsychInfo (formerly known as PsychLit) or Medline, contained the words *social, downward, upward,* or *temporal comparison* in the title or abstract, and focused on health related issues based on our reading of the abstract. In addition to many empirical articles, our search yielded several review articles and chapters published since 1990, which included studies that were published prior to 1990. We also will summarize the findings of those investigations. We examined the reference lists of the articles produced by our search to determine whether other relevant studies had escaped our initial inspection, and we used Social Sciences Citation Index to ensure that we did not miss articles that cited the studies produced by our search. Studies in which social comparison was not a main focus of the research were excluded, as were studies that focused solely on social comparison and affiliation, which is the topic of Kulik and Mahler's chapter (Chapter 15, this volume).

Whereas our review includes all of the studies that emerged from our search of the literature since 1990, Table 1 lists only those studies that were not previously summarized in a review article or chapter on social comparison and health (e.g., Croyle, 1992; Klein & Weinstein, 1997; Suls, Martin, & Leventhal, 1997). One exception is the group of studies that appeared in Wood and Van der Zee's (1997) chapter on social comparison among cancer patients. Because these authors were examining specific findings from these studies, we decided to obtain the original sources, review the findings, and include those studies in Table 1. We divide our review into three sections: social comparison and serious medical problems, including disability; social comparison and health threats; and health-related comparison in everyday life, including the role of social comparisons in the maintenance of unrealistic optimism, in the development of health images, in risk reduction behavior, and in the decision to seek medical care. After reviewing the literature, we discuss remaining conceptual problems for this area of inquiry, including the notion of downward comparison as a coping strategy, whether such comparisons represent secondary control beliefs, and how social comparisons differ from other cognitive adaptations to health threats. We conclude by offering suggestions for expanding the methodological and conceptual scope of studies examining social comparison in health and illness.

SOCIAL COMPARISON AND SERIOUS MEDICAL PROBLEMS

Rheumatoid Arthritis

Rheumatoid arthritis (RA) is a common, chronic disease that includes such symptoms as severe joint pain, stiffness, and fatigue. Many individuals diagnosed with the disease face increasing disability. However, patients often experience fluctuating symptoms of disease activity with periods of remission as well as flares. Affleck and Tennen (1991) reviewed a program of research in which they found that patients made downward comparisons both in spontaneous descriptions of their illness and in ratings of its severity and their adjustment to the illness. Many of the spontaneous descriptions were downward temporal comparisons, with patients making comments such as "It was very painful at first ... now it's like it doesn't exist." Those patients who rated their own illness as less severe than that of the average patient with RA actually had less active disease than other participants, had been ill less long, and were rated by their care providers as adjusting better to their illness. To examine the accuracy of patients' comparisons, Affleck, Tennen, Pfeiffer, and Fifield (1988) examined the concordance between the comparisons and criterion measures of disease activity, functional status, and psychosocial adjustment as rated by care providers. Significant yet modest agreement with criterion measures was found for disease activity and disability comparisons but not for the adjustment comparison.

Research conducted at the University of North Carolina (Blalock, DeVellis, & DeVellis, 1989; DeVellis et al., 1990) found that RA patients compared themselves to other people with RA when they were encountering difficulties in tasks involving manual dexterity, whereas they compared themselves to healthy individuals when they were setting standards for desired functioning in this area. When given a choice to select information that could be used to make comparisons, participants preferred information about patients with more severe illness, but they also preferred information about patients who were coping and adjusting well to the illness. DeVellis and colleagues also constructed a measure of comparison by taking the difference between participants' ratings of themselves and their ratings of the typical RA patient on seven different dimensions (e.g., pain, stiffness, and trouble with housework and dressing). Although participants generally saw themselves as doing better than the typical patient, their comparisons were unrelated to indicators of well-being.

Blalock, Afifi, DeVellis, Holt, and DeVellis (1990) examined spontaneous social comparison statements made by individuals with RA during an interview. These statements were coded for direction of the comparison (upward, downward, or lateral), health status of the target (ill or healthy), and similarity of the participant to the target, that is, did the statement emphasize similarity or dissimilarity? They found that upward, downward, and lateral comparisons occurred with more or less equal frequency. Statements also were evenly divided between ill and healthy targets. Regardless of whether the target was ill or healthy, participants tended to emphasize their dissimilarities to the target. After controlling for physical functioning, Blalock et al. (1990) found that participants who compared themselves to healthy individuals and who emphasized the similarities between themselves and the target showed better psychological adjustment. This result is consistent with Blalock and co-workers' (1989) finding that RA patients compare themselves to healthy individuals when they set personal performance standards.

DeVellis et al. (1991) conducted an experimental study in which women with RA were randomly assigned to four groups in which they viewed a presentation of a woman with RA. The woman was depicted as either coping well or poorly with the illness and as having either

Table 1. Recent Studies of Social Comparison in Health and Illness

Authors	Participants/ sample size	Social comparison measure(s)[a]	Other measures	Accuracy examined?	Direction of comparison/results	Design	Method[b]
			Rheumatoid arthritis				
De Vellis et al. (1991)	72 women diagnosed with RA	Viewed slides and audiotape of woman either coping well or poorly with either severe or mild illness, then answered six items assessing coping and severity of target, self, and direct comparison of self to target	None	No	Rated good coper as better than self, poor coper as worse than self (indirectly), but when asked to compare directly, rated self as better than good coper	Experimental	Reaction
Blalock et al. (1990)	85 individuals diagnosed with RA	Semistructured interview with no questions directly soliciting SC info; content analysis of interview for spontaneous SC statements	Two composite scores: psychological functioning and physical functioning	No	Upward, downward, and lateral comparisons were all made equally	Cross-sectional	Narration
Giorgino et al. (1994)	235 individuals diagnosed with RA	Identified a person who they thought about when having performance difficulty in three domains, and when setting goals for those domains; rated difficulty experienced by chosen targets; identified times in own life they would think about when experiencing performance difficulties and establishing performance goals; rated amount of difficulty experienced at that time	Perceived ability in three domains, satisfaction with ability, importance of ability, control over ability, use of problem-solving and escape/avoidance coping strategies, arthritis disability, and symptom severity	No	Patients made more downward social comparison when setting goals in the pain management domain than in either the leisure or household activities domains. They made more temporal comparisons when experiencing performance difficulty and when setting goals in the pain management domain than in either the leisure or household activities domains.	Cross-sectional	Reaction/narration

Infertility

Stanton (1992)	52 couples trying to conceive for a minimum of 12 months	Structured interview designed to elicit same-sex and partner comparisons	Self-esteem, threat appraisal, SCL-90-R, infertility-specific distress, and coping	No	Men made more DC, women made more UC; lateral comparisons most frequent when target was partner; men and women who made more DC, less threatened by infertility	Cross-sectional	Reaction

Cancer

Buunk et al. (1990)	55 patients with cancer	Interview that asked how often patients felt (1) lucky or grateful and (2) fearful or anxious when exposed to worse-off others, and how often they felt (1) frustrated or depressed and (2) inspired or comforted when expose to better-off others	Personal control, control by external factors, self-esteem	No	Downward positive affect comparisons were the most common; positive affect comparisons, regardless of direction, were more common than negative affect comparisons; those high in self-esteem were less likely to feel badly when comparing both upward and downward than those low in self-esteem; those higher in personal control felt less negative affect when exposed to worse-off others	Cross-sectional	Reaction

(continued)

Table 1. (*Continued*)

Authors	Participants/ sample size	Social comparison measure(s)[a]	Other measures	Accuracy examined?	Direction of comparison/results	Design	Method[b]
Llewellyn-Thomas et al. (1992)	61 patients with cancer	Interviewed early in treatment regarding expected descriptions of health; after treatment, asked about current health and health state belived to be experienced by most others in community	POMS, subjective health evaluations	No	Social comparison was an inconsistent predictor of subjective health evaluations depending on the method employed	Cross-sectional	Reaction
Van der Zee et al. (1998a)	57 women diagnosed with breast cancer	Read a bogus interview fragment that contained either UC or DC information	Neuroticism, depression, affect checklist, 1 item asking if thinking of own situation while reading interview, and amount of identification with target	No	More positive affect after reading UC than DC; women higher in neuroticism had less positive and more negative affect after reading both UC and DC interviews and had less positive affect after reading only UC interviews (controlling for depression)	Experimental	Reaction

VanderZee, Buunk, et al. (1996)	475 patients with cancer and 225 healthy individuals (control group)	Questionnaire assessing need for comparison, frequency of downward comparison, and relative evaluation (how they were doing with respect to their health compared to others); targets for the cancer patients were other cancer patients while targets for the healthy individuals were general	Physical distress, psychological distress, and subjective well-being	No	Patients engaged in DC more often than healthy controls; patients more likely to rate themselves as better off than most other patients as compared to ratings made by healthy individuals; physical distress led to psychological distress, which led to comparison process (need, frequency, relative evaluation), which positively affected subjective well-being	Cross-sectional	Reaction
Taylor et al. (1993)	55 cancer patients	Asked patients about the stories they sought out and those that were told to them about the experiences of other cancer patients; asked about source of story, whether or not story helped, and how they compared to the target in the story	None	No	Few patients reported seeking out stories; of those who did, most compared themselves favorably to the target; many patients reported being told stories; positive stories were more helpful than negative stories; 85% of those who were told stories compared themselves favorably to the target in the story	Cross-sectional	Reaction

(continued)

Table 1. (*Continued*)

Authors	Participants/ sample size	Social comparison measure(s)[a]	Other measures	Accuracy examined?	Direction of comparison/results	Design	Method[b]
Van der Zee et al. (1998)	88 cancer patients	Computer program allowed patients to read interview fragments of fellow patients who were doing worse or better than the typical cancer patient; program recorded which interviews were read, number of times interviews were read, and total time spent reading; social comparison orientation measure also administered	Neuroticism, depression, general affect, recall task regarding interviews, interview-related affect measure, and identification with the patients in the interview	No	Patients selected more and spent more time reading upward interviews; those high in neuroticism and SC orientation selected more and spent more time reading interviews; reading upward interviews resulted in more positive affect and less negative affect; neuroticism and SC orientation were related to measures of general affect and interview-related affect	Cross-sectional	Selection, reaction
			Disabled individuals				
Ybema & Buuck (1995)	112 individuals receiving payments under the Disablement Insurance Act in the Netherlands	Read part of a hypothetical interview, which had UC or DC information about either the severity of disability or the coping of a target	Perceived control, adjective checklist, and identification with target	No	More positive affect after reading UC interview only when participants high in perceived control; more negative affect after reading DC interview regardless of level of control; participants high in control identified more with upward target, especially when coping was compared; effect of control on positive affect after reading UC interview was mediated by identification with target	Experimental	Reaction

Study	Sample	Method	Variables		Findings	Design	Reaction, selection / Other
Buunk (1995)	168 individuals receiving payments under the Disablement Insurance Act in the Netherlands	Questionnaire assessing need for affiliation and social comparison information, rating of own coping and severity, rating of coping and severity compared to others under the Act, preference for upward or downward information and affiliation	Uncertainty, frustration, subjective degree of health problems, threat to self-esteem, negative affect, and cognitive anxiety (worry)	No	Uncertainty, frustration, and worry related to need for SC; need for SC greater than need to affiliate with similar others; self-ratings were affected by health problems and by the perception of being worse off than others; participants more interested in obtaining information about others coping better than affiliating with such others.	Cross-sectional	Reaction, selection
Chronic pain							
Jensen & Karoly (1992)	118 patients who participated in an inpatient multidisciplinary pain program	Telephone interview assessing frequency with which patients engaged in four strategies when in pain: selective focus, hypothetical worse worlds, downward comparison, and normative standard	Depressive affect, intensity of pain, amount of control over pain, and social desirability	No	Pain duration and pain levels unrelated to frequency of comparison; greater control over pain related to greater use of self-evaluation; greater use of comparison associated with lower depression scores after controlling for demographics and pain-related variables; this relation was strongest for patients with a short duration of pain (< 5 years)	Cross-sectional	Other

(continued)

Table 1. (*Continued*)

Authors	Participants/ sample size	Social comparison measure(s)[a]	Other measures	Accuracy examined?	Direction of comparison/results	Design	Method[b]
Wilson et al. (1995)	334 college students	Manipulation of social comparisons between two trials of the cold pressor task	Pain intensity and pain tolerance (length of time hand stayed in the water)	No	Social comparison manipulation affected pain intensity ratings; those who were led to believe others had less pain during trial 1 reported lower trail 2 intensity ratings than would be predicted from their trial 1 ratings	Experimental	Reaction
			Other medical conditions				
Wilson et al. (1997)	47 African-American women with sickle-cell disease	Phone interview measuring self-evaluation style (5 UC items and 5 DC items); combined items for temporal comparison, comparing to worse/better worlds, and worse/better people	Depressive affect, pain intensity, perceived control over pain, coping, and an objective measure of disease severity	No	Overall self-evaluation style predicted depressive affect after controlling for demographics, disease, severity, and pain; more DC style related to less depression; more UC style related to greater depression	Cross-sectional	Narration

Study	Sample	Measures		Results	Design	
Helgeson & Taylor (1993)	60 individuals attending a cardiac rehabilitation program for less than 18 months	Questionnaire asking if patients ever compared; who they compared to; rate self and most patients on coping, severity, and resources; who patients preferred to interact with; who they actually interacted with; and what were the emotional and informational outcomes of comparison and affiliation	Self-esteem, psychological distress, two measures of physical health, nurse's rating of physical and emotional health	Yes: physical and emotional DC was related to measures of physical health and distress, but there was no relation between physical or emotional DC and nurse's ratings of physical or emotional health	40% of patients reported not comparing; only 20% made DC; patients rated themselves as better off than others on physical and emotional health, and resources: DC (based on ratings) was associated with lower psychological distress (controlling for physical health and disease severity); patients preferred to affiliate and actually affiliated in the upward direction	Cross-sectional	Narration, reaction, selection
Hemphill & Lehman (1991)	151 individuals diagnosed with multiple sclerosis	Questionnaire assessing upward and downward comparison, positive and negative feelings produced after comparison, and appropriateness of making comparisons	Dispositional optimism and beliefs of future course of illness	No	Most common to have positive affect following both UC and DC; DC was reated more to affect (both positive and negative) on the physical dimension than on the coping dimension; dispositional optimists had less negative affect following comparison; participants higher in appropriateness made more DC and also felt better after both DC and UC than those low in appropriateness	Cross-sectional	Reaction

(continued)

Table 1. (Continued)

Authors	Participants/ sample size	Social comparison measure(s)[a]	Other measures	Accuracy examined?	Direction of comparison/results	Design	Method[b]
			Health threats				
Suls et al. (1991)	91 people from a community sample over age 64	Interview assessing individual social comparison, group comparison, temporal comparison, and future or anticipated temporal comparison all with regard to health	Rating of present health, concern about health, and reported health problems	No	Lower health ratings related to mention of both kinds of temporal comparison; greater concern about health related to individual social comparison and both kinds of temporal comparison (controlling for number of illnesses); self-ratings higher among those who made DC	Cross-sectional	Reaction/ narration
Robinson-Whelen & Kiecolt-Glaser (1997)	91 middle-aged and older adults from a community sample	Asked how they were doing compared to others their age with regard to health and how they were doing compared to themselves 5 years ago	Self-rating of health, number of health conditions, and life satisfaction	No	Participants described their health as good and reported their health to be the same as 5 years ago and slightly better than their same-aged peers; social comparison ratings predicted self-rated health (controlling for number of health conditions)	Cross-sectional	Reaction
Dias & Lobel (1997)	147 pregnant women at risk for adverse birth outcomes	Questionnaire assessing comparison direction, frequency, and affiliation preferences (which one of six groups of women would the participants be most interested in meeting)	Vicarious control, personal control, pregnancy-related threat, self-esteem, and state anxiety (measured twice)	No	Less pregnancy-related threat and higher self-esteem were related to more DC; DC was related to less of an increase in anxiety; women most wanted to interact with other women who had babies, regardless of level of	Cross-sectional (only anxiety measured twice)	Narration, selection

Study	Sample	Manipulation/Measure	Dependent variable	Control	Design	Type	Results
Sun & Croyle (1995)	96 college students	Manipulated students' perceived cholesterol level (high-risk or borderline); half the students were told cholesterol level was controllable, half were told it was not; students rated their interest in reading the files of 4 types of people	Affective state (5 positive and 5 negative adjectives)	N/A	Experimental	Selection	personal control; younger, first-time pregnant women engaged in SC most often; Across all conditions, students preferred reading diet information from people with lower cholesterol levels than their own (UC); those in the low-threat condition were more interested in UC information, while those in the high-threat condition were equally interested in UC and DC information; though the control manipulation worked, level of control did not influence comparison preferences
Social comparisons in everyday life							
Van der Zee et al. (1995)	361 individuals from a random population sample	Questionnaire assessing relative evaluation (how one was doing with respect to health compared to others with comparable health problems), frequency of downward comparison, need for comparison	General subjective health evaluation, psychological distress, and health problems	No	Cross-sectional	Reaction	Results supported a mediational model in which psychological distress as a result of health problems led to a downward comparison process (need, frequency, relative evaluation) that had an impact on general health evaluation independent of the effects of health problems and psychological distress; the model fit better for women than men

(continued)

Table 1. (*Continued*)

Authors	Participants/ sample size	Social comparison measure(s)[a]	Other measures	Accuracy examined?	Direction of comparison/results	Design	Method[b]
			Changing AIDS risk behavior				
Tigges et al. (1998)	457 12th grade students (about half sexually active)	Compared their frequency of condom use to same-gender peers; asked if they preferred as a discussion group member someone who uses condoms more than, less than, or as frequently as they do; picked adjectives to describe teenagers who have AIDS (as an indicator of derogation)	Perceived threat of contracting AIDS, self-esteem, satisfaction with past condom use, and intended use of condoms	No	Whereas threat was unrelated to DC among high condom users, the more low users felt threatened by AIDS, the more they made downward comparisons; those who used condoms less showed a greater desire to affiliate upward; the more threatened subjects felt, the less they derogated other teenagers with AIDS; among low esteem subjects, the more satisfied they were with their past condom use, the stronger their DC	Cross-sectional	Reaction, selection, other

[a]Abbreviations: SC, social comparison; UC, upward comparison; DC, downward comparison; POMS, Profile of Mood States.
[b]Based on Wood's (1996) categorization.

mild or severe arthritis. Participants were then asked to rate both themselves and the woman in the presentation with regard to coping success and illness severity. These ratings provided an indirect indicator of social comparison. They were then asked to directly compare themselves to the woman in terms of how well they were coping and the severity of their illness. In the indirect comparisons, participants rated the stimulus woman who was coping well as managing better than themselves and rated the stimulus woman who was coping poorly as managing worse than themselves. However, when asked to directly compare themselves with the target, those who viewed the woman who was adapting well denied her superiority and rated themselves as coping somewhat better. DeVellis et al. (1991) speculated that their participants were faced with unavoidable social comparison information that was potentially threatening—a women coping better than they were. Since they could not refrain from making a comparison, they denied their own inferiority to the target in an effort to decrease the threat of the comparison.

Giorgino et al. (1994) asked individuals with RA to rate their perceived ability in household activities, leisure activities, and pain management; their satisfaction with and the importance of their ability in each domain; and how much control they experienced in each domain. Social comparison was measured by asking participants to identify a specific person they might think about when they were having difficulty in each area and who would come to mind if they were thinking about how easily they would like to be able to perform activities in each area. They then rated the amount of difficulty experienced by the person chosen for the comparison. Temporal comparison was measured by asking participants to describe other times in their own lives they would think about when they were experiencing performance difficulties and establishing performance goals. These RA patients reported having greater ability in the area of leisure activities than either household activities or pain management. Of those individuals who made comparisons, downward social comparisons in the goal-setting context and downward temporal comparisons in both the performance difficulty and goal-setting contexts were more common in relation to pain management than in relation to either leisure or household activities.

Infertility

Impaired fertility is a medical problem that can threaten one's self-esteem and create considerable uncertainty regarding the ultimate outcome. Thus it is an ideal context in which to examine the role of social comparison. Affleck and Tennen (1991) summarized their study of a group of infertile women. At the start of the study and 14 months later, these women were asked the extent to which they agreed with the downward comparison statement: "I think I'm fortunate compared to other people. I could have worse problems than infertility." They also rated their own coping success compared to other women with this problem. Both measures of social comparison were moderately stable over the 14-month period, with most women viewing themselves as coping better than other women. Explanations for why they thought they were coping better involved downward temporal comparisons such as "I've come a long way in being able to cope with this." In other words, these women were equating their own earlier adjustment difficulties with the current difficulties of other women with impaired fertility. They compared themselves favorably to others on several dimensions including social support, acceptance of the problem, infertility-related medical problems, the capacity to distract themselves from the problem, and the availability of other opportunities to have nurturing relationships with children. After 14 months of remaining infertile, women who agreed more with the downward comparison statement construed more benefits from their infertility and expressed greater acceptance of the prospect of not being able to bear a child. Favorable evaluations of comparative coping also were associated with more positive recent mood, fewer symptoms of distress, and less subjective stress.

Stanton (1992) interviewed 52 couples with impaired fertility to elicit same-sex and partner comparisons. Both women and men who believed they were coping better than same-sex others were less threatened by their infertility. Participants who made either downward or upward comparisons to same-sex others with regard to successful coping were asked to explain why they were coping either better or worse. Their explanations fell into three broad categories: personal characteristics (having a positive attitude, using a problem-solving approach), infertility-related characteristics, and the strength of their marriage. When asked to compare themselves to their partners, lateral comparisons emerged most frequently. Men were more likely than women to engage in downward comparison for both same-sex and spouse comparisons. No association emerged between downward comparisons and self-esteem. Stanton interpreted the prevalence of lateral comparisons with spouses as reflecting either intimacy with or greater knowledge of the target. As closeness and/or knowledge of the comparison target increases, downward comparisons may be viewed as less admirable. In a similar vein, acknowledging that one's spouse is worse off than oneself may be experienced as troublesome rather than self-enhancing.

Parents of Medically Fragile Infants

Parents of medically fragile infants are also faced with threats to self-esteem, uncertain outcomes, and difficulty obtaining unambiguous information about their child's problem. Affleck, Tennen, and Rowe (1991) examined the social comparisons of mothers whose infants were in a newborn intensive care unit (NICU). Social comparison was assessed by classifying spontaneous comparison statements as well as asking mothers to rate their child's medical condition relative to other infants in the unit and to rate their own comparative coping ability. Of those mothers who made spontaneous social comparison statements about their infant or compared themselves to other parents, all but one made downward comparisons. Twenty-five percent of mothers volunteered that their infant's outcome was better than it could have been. Other mothers compared their infant's survival to previous reproductive disappointments (e.g., miscarriages). These women perceived their child's medical condition to be less severe than that of the average NICU infant and their own coping to be better than that of the average parent in this situation.

Six months following NICU discharge, mothers continued to rate their own adjustment as better than the average parent caring for such an infant, and they rated their child's temperament more positively than that of other NICU graduates. Mothers who reported favorable comparison conclusions regarding their own adjustment reported more positive mood, less depression, and greater parental competence, even after controlling for baseline levels. Two thirds of the mothers continued to have memories of their child's condition while in the hospital. Many claimed that making downward temporal comparisons (i.e., recognizing that their child was worse then) helped to alleviate the distress of this recollection.

Most mothers wanted contact with similar others in order to reduce their feelings of isolation and to compare their situation (both themselves and their children) to that of other parents. Only one in five mothers desired no contact with other NICU parents. As a group, these mothers felt vulnerable for a recurrence of having an infant in NICU should they become pregnant again, rating their own risk (40%) as higher than the actual risk (approximately 25%) of recurrence. However, 40% of these women rated their current risk as equal to or less than that of the average mother about to have her *first* child. They judged the risk facing the average first-time mother (20%) as higher than the actual incidence (approximately 5%) of infants needing NICU. Perhaps by maintaining a stereotyped image of the average mother as someone who does not try to reduce her risk for this adverse outcome, these women were able to feel superior to the "average" mother. Further research has yet to be conducted in this area.

Cancer

Cancer is a particularly threatening illness that involves demanding treatment regimens, disruptions in work and home life, strains on family and friendships, and the uncertainty of recurrence. The nature and treatment of the illness make cancer an ongoing stressor, and as such a good context in which to examine social comparisons. In 1990, Buunk, Collins, Taylor, VanYperen, and Dakof found that among 55 people who had experienced different types of cancer, 82% stated that when they were exposed to worse-off cancer patients, they felt lucky or grateful. Fifty-nine percent felt fearful or anxious during such exposure. When exposed to better-off cancer patients, 78% of the participants reported feeling inspired or comforted, whereas 40% reported feeling frustrated or depressed. Comparisons resulting in positive affect were more common than comparisons resulting in negative affect, regardless of the direction, with patients most commonly comparing themselves to others with regard to prognosis.

Unlike Stanton's (1992) infertile couples, for whom self-esteem was unrelated to comparisons, cancer patients with high esteem were less likely than their low-esteem counterparts to feel bad when they made either upward or downward comparisons. Those who experienced more personal control over their daily symptoms and over the future course of their illness were less likely to feel bad when confronted with worse-off others, possibly because they were less threatened by such patients. This study advanced social comparison theory because it was among the first to demonstrate that both upward and downward comparisons can be construed as either positive or negative.

Llewellyn-Thomas, Thiel, and McGreal (1992) interviewed 61 patients with various forms of cancer at the beginning and end of their radiation therapy to determine the extent to which patients' subjective evaluations of their health were determined by how they compared themselves with others. Social comparison descriptions were inconsistently related to predictors of subjective health evaluations, depending on how both comparisons and health perceptions were measured. Anticipating Wood's (1996) call for the inclusion of multiple methods in studies of social comparison processes, Llewellyn-Thomas et al. (1992) stressed the importance of determining why findings in this area seem to be method dependent.

To evaluate the adaptational consequences of stories cancer patients heard about others dealing with cancer, Taylor, Aspinwall, Giuliano, Dakof, and Keardon (1993) asked 55 cancer patients about both the stories they sought out and the stories that others told them. Few patients (20%) reported seeking out stories about the experiences of other cancer patients. Participants who sought out stories reported that they typically felt better off than those they had heard or read about; 68% of them made downward comparisons to the patients described in these stories. On the other hand, many participants reported that they had been told unsolicited stories about other cancer patients, usually by friends or relatives. Two thirds of the stories told were about others who had died or had done poorly, and 63% of the participants reported that the stories they were told were not helpful to them. Eighty-five percent of these patients made downward comparisons to the targets in these stories. Positive stories were interpreted as being more helpful than stories with negative outcomes. Although patients typically made downward comparisons to the targets in the stories told to them, they questioned the motives of the storyteller. These findings suggest that stories told to a cancer patient by care providers, family, and friends about others who are less fortunate may not have the desired effect of making the person feel better. Taylor et al. (1993) speculate that reactions to these stories may differ depending on the time since diagnosis, with the need for social comparison being greater immediately following diagnosis and then decreasing over time.

Cancer patients in Van der Zee and co-workers' (1996) study reported levels of life satisfaction comparable to that of a healthy comparison group. These investigators found that these patients made comparisons with others who were worse off more frequently than did the healthy control group, and they were more likely to rate themselves as better off in comparison with others in the same situation than were the healthy participants. A path analysis of the data was consistent with Van der Zee and co-workers' (1996) model of social comparison and well-being, in which troubling physical symptoms lead to psychological distress, which in turn induces a stronger desire to compare oneself to others. Once made, these downward comparisons contribute positively to a sense of well-being. This model appears to capture comparison processes that are not specific to cancer patients.

In one of the few studies that hypothesized a specific personality moderator of comparisons among seriously ill individuals, Van der Zee, Buunk, and Sanderman (1998a) examined how neuroticism moderated affective reactions to social comparison information. Fifty-seven women with breast cancer read part of an interview with a hypothetical breast cancer patient that confronted them with either an upward comparison (i.e., a patient with few problems, who had a supportive social network and experienced a fast recovery) or a downward comparison (i.e., a patient with severe problems who had a slow recovery). These women experienced more positive affect after reading upward comparison information than after reading downward comparison information. More neurotic patients reported less positive and more negative affect after reading both the upward and downward comparison interviews. An interaction between direction of comparison and neuroticism revealed that for those patients who read upward comparison information, the higher an individual's neuroticism score, the less positive affect she reported, whereas neuroticism was unrelated to affective state for those reading the downward comparison information. The majority of participants in this study were no longer in active treatment, and Van der Zee et al. (1998a) acknowledged that time since diagnosis may well be an important factor in social comparison processes among chronically ill individuals. Nonetheless, longitudinal studies of health-related social comparison processes remain rare.

In a more recent investigation of the relation of neuroticism and social comparison orientation to social comparison processes in cancer patients, Van der Zee, Oldersma, Buunk, and Bos (1998b) created a computer program that allowed the 88 patients in their study to select and read interview fragments containing information about fellow patients who were either doing worse or doing better than the typical cancer patient. The computer program recorded the interviews that were read, the number of times each interview was read, and the total time that patients spent reading each interview. The patients in this study selected and spent more time reading upward than downward interviews, although high-neuroticism patients spent more time reading both upward and downward interviews than did their low-neuroticism counterparts. Those who scored higher on neuroticism and those who were more generally inclined to compare themselves to others (measured by an indicator of social comparison orientation) selected more interviews, regardless of direction. Among patients with a high social comparison orientation, those also higher on neuroticism experienced more negative affective reactions to social comparison information. Patients experienced more positive affect and less negative affect following interviews with upward information than following interviews with downward information. These findings are consistent with Taylor and Lobel's (1989) position that individuals facing threatening circumstances prefer upward comparisons regarding adjustment.

Disabled Individuals

Disabled individuals face many obstacles, including health problems, reduced income, and work loss. Buunk (1995) and Ybema and Buunk (1995) studied the social comparisons of individuals who were receiving payments under the Disablement Insurance Act in the Netherlands. At the time this research was conducted, proposals for changes in the benefits provided by the act were being considered, leaving those receiving payments uncertain about their future financial status. Buunk (1995) found that those who were more uncertain about their future disability status, who were more frustrated, and who were more worried reported a greater desire to affiliate with others under the Act and a stronger wish for information about such people. As a group, these disabled individuals preferred upward comparisons when they compared themselves to others with regard to how well they were coping, but less so when they compared themselves on the dimension of problem severity. Those who viewed themselves as doing worse than others on both the coping and severity dimensions had a preference for upward comparison information and affiliation. These findings, which are generally consistent with Taylor and Lobel's (1989) emphasis on upward comparison and self-improvement, led Buunk to conclude that the need for affiliation with and information about comparison others are two highly correlated processes affected by uncertainty, frustration, and worry.

These findings were extended by Ybema and Buunk (1995). They had another group of individuals who fell under the Disablement Insurance Act read part of a hypothetical interview, which contained one of four comparison targets: (1) a person with severe problems, in a wheelchair, with much pain, that is, a downward comparison regarding the severity of health problems; (2) a person with mild problems who could do most anything, that is, an upward comparison regarding the severity of these problems; (3) a person who had no problems adjusting to his or her situation, was optimistic, and had many hobbies, that is, an upward comparison about coping success; or (4) a person with many problems adjusting, who was depressed and frustrated about his or her situation, that is, a downward comparison about coping success. Those disabled persons who experienced greater personal control over their disability experienced more positive affect after reading upward as opposed to downward comparison information. The reading of downward comparison information generated more negative affect in participants than did upward comparison information, regardless of participants' level of perceived control. Those who experienced greater control identified more with the upward target, and the effect of perceived control on positive affect following upward comparison was mediated by this identification with the comparison target.

These findings suggest that by generating positive affect through identification with the target, upward comparison may be superior to downward comparison for those facing health threats. Although this pattern of findings appears to conflict with Wills' (1981) perspective on downward comparison as a way to improve subjective well-being, several of the studies described thus far (e.g., Affleck & Tennen, 1991; Affleck et al., 1991) and several to be reviewed (e.g., Jensen & Karoly, 1992; Wilson, Gil, & Raezer, 1997) have demonstrated the adaptational benefits of downward comparisons for individuals facing threatening health situations.

Chronic Pain

Individuals living with chronic pain are faced with unrelenting discomfort, functional limitations, uncertainty regarding the future, threats to self-esteem and self- efficacy, and emotional and physical exhaustion. The distress and uncertainty associated with chronic pain disorders make them an excellent context in which to explore social comparison processes. Jensen and Karoly (1992) studied the relationship between social comparison and depressive affect among patients who participated in an inpatient multidisciplinary pain program. Through a telephone interview, participants described depressive symptoms and rated the frequency with which they engaged in four different strategies when experiencing pain. The first strategy was termed *selective focus*, which involved focusing on positive attributes that others do not share. The second strategy involved *creating hypothetical worse worlds* by thinking that things could be worse. The third strategy was termed *downward comparison* and was phrased as the recognition that there are others worse off than oneself. The final strategy was called *creating a normative standard*, which involved rating one's own adjustment as better than that of the average pain patient. These four self-evaluation ratings were summed to create a composite score, with higher scores indicating a greater tendency to employ self-enhancing comparisons. Jensen and Karoly (1992) found that patients who experienced greater control over their pain made more self-enhancing comparisons. Controlling for demographic and pain-related variables, pain patients who reported using more self-enhancing comparisons also endorsed fewer depressive symptoms. This relationship was strongest for those patients who had been experiencing pain for less than 5 years, and was nonexistent for those patients who had experienced pain for greater than 11 years.

The influence of social, temporal, and hypothetical comparisons on the experience of pain was examined in a laboratory setting by Wilson, Chaplin, and Thorn (1995). Between two cold pressor trials, college students were exposed to social comparison manipulations. Participants in one condition recorded their pain intensity on a bogus list of other students' pain intensity ratings that ranged from 85 to 100. In a second condition, participants recorded their ratings on a bogus list of ratings that ranged from 35 to 60. Subjects in the neutral condition did not record their pain intensity. Participants exposed to information suggesting that others were experiencing more modest levels of pain reported less pain on trial 2 than would be predicted from their trial 1 ratings. Although acute and chronic pain are distinct phenomena, these findings suggest that having pain patients compare to others who are coping more successfully may motivate them to minimize pain behaviors, take less medication, and maximize functional gain.

Other Serious Medical Problems

Sickle-Cell Disease.   Wilson et al. (1997) studied what they called "self-evaluation style" among 47 African-American women with sickle-cell disease, an illness typically characterized by seizures, leg ulcers, renal complications, recurrent pain, and uncertainty regarding future health outcomes. Using a phone interview, the investigators assessed upward and downward comparison processes, including focusing on the positive or negative, comparing to hypothetical worse or better worlds, comparing to worse- or better-off people, and temporal comparison. Individuals who made greater use of downward comparisons reported less dysphoria, even after controlling for demographic factors, disease severity, and pain intensity. Individuals with an upward comparison style endorsed more negative thoughts.

Cardiac Rehabilitation.   Most individuals with coronary illness undergo extensive treatment protocols and are faced with uncertainty of recurrence. In a study of individuals attending a cardiac rehabilitation program for less than 18 months, Helgeson and Taylor (1993) found that 40% of these patients reported never comparing themselves with other patients.

Among those who did compare themselves to others, 20% reported making downward comparisons. Although the latter group did not actively compare themselves with other patients, they nonetheless viewed themselves as being in better physical and emotional health and as having more resources than other cardiac patients have. A downward evaluation composite score based on these ratings was associated with less psychological distress, even when controlling for time in the rehabilitation program, physical health indicators, and disease severity. More participants affiliated with others who they viewed as doing well. Although patients with higher self-esteem rated their physical health, emotional health, and resources higher than they rated that of others with cardiac problems, esteem was unrelated to their direct comparisons of other patients as being better off, worse off, or about the same as themselves. Upward affiliations in this cohort were associated with feelings of inspiration.

As one of only two studies in our review to examine the accuracy of downward evaluations, Helgeson and Taylor (1993) compared self-reports of comparisons to more objective indicators and to the judgments of independent sources. Individuals who rated themselves as being in better physical health than other cardiac patients indeed had positive indicators of physical health (e.g., exercising longer; working at a higher physical capacity). Participants who rated their own emotional health more positively than the emotional health of other cardiac patients reported lower psychological distress. However, there was no relationship between downward comparisons of physical and emotional health and primary nurses's corresponding ratings.

Multiple Sclerosis.   Another study of social comparison in response to a major medical problem examined individuals diagnosed with multiple sclerosis (MS), a disease associated with unpredictable symptom exacerbations and an uncertain and deteriorating course. Using a questionnaire, Hemphill and Lehman (1991) assessed the frequency with which MS patients made upward and downward comparisons regarding their level of disability, their ability to deal with their illness and its consequences, and the availability of supportive others. They also inquired about the frequency of positive and negative affective consequences following such comparisons.

These MS patients most commonly reported positive affect following both downward and upward comparisons. Downward comparisons led to more affect (both positive and negative) when respondents compared themselves to others on the physical condition dimension than on the coping dimension. Although participants' beliefs about the future course of their illness were not related to the affective consequences of their comparisons, dispositional optimists reported less negative affect as a result of comparing themselves to others. Those patients who believed that it was appropriate to engage in comparisons reported engaging more often in downward comparisons and felt better after making both downward and upward comparisons.

Summary

Our review indicates that social comparison is common among individuals facing a range of serious medical problems. Yet striking differences across studies in how comparisons were assessed make it difficult to draw firm conclusions regarding the adaptational benefits of any particular comparison process. Some areas of investigation, such as how comparisons are affected by perceived control over the illness, have yielded conflicting findings. These limitations not withstanding, the literature we reviewed indicates that downward comparisons are prominent and generally are associated with positive adjustment to serious medical threats.

Upward comparisons appear to inspire people facing these threats to seek self-improvement. We found few clues to help us unravel the dynamic whereby people compare themselves with less fortunate others while wishing to affiliate with those they view as adjusting well. We will return to some of these conceptual and methodological challenges later in this chapter, including the question of whether the accuracy of social comparisons influence their adaptive function.

SOCIAL COMPARISON AND HEALTH THREATS

Field Research

Health Perceptions among Older Adults. With increasing age, the threat of health problems also increases. Suls, Marco, and Tobin (1991) interviewed community dwellers over the age of 64, inquiring about their present health, health concerns, and current health problems. They also asked whether participants compared their present health to another individual, group of people, their own health in the past, or their future health. Those who endorsed individual or group comparisons were asked to describe and give an overall general health rating of the individual or group.

Most participants rated their own health as good and indicated that they were only mildly concerned about their health. Individuals who rated their health as less positive made downward temporal comparisons to their past health and future health. Those who reported greater health concerns made more individual social comparisons and more past- and future-oriented temporal comparisons. These associations remained after controlling for the number of illnesses reported. Among participants who made individual and group comparisons, self-ratings of health were higher when a person or group of worse health or a group of similar health was named as the target of comparison than when the target was a person or group of better health. Suls et al. (1991) posited that the elderly compare themselves with a cognitively constructed stereotype of a frail person rather than with a specific other person. Because few elderly actually fit this stereotype, individuals making such comparisons rate themselves as being in relatively good health.

Health was one of the domains in which Robinson-Whelen and Kiecolt-Glaser (1997) examined social comparisons among older adults. They asked community dwellers averaging 70 years of age how they were doing with regards to their health compared to others their age and compared to themselves 5 years ago. They also obtained a global self-rating of health. Participants generally described their health as good, about the same as it was 5 years ago, and slightly better than their same-aged peers. The more participants rated themselves as better off than their same-aged peers, the better they rated their own health. Social comparison predicted self-rated health after controlling for number of medical conditions. Temporal comparison was unrelated to self-rated health.

At-Risk Pregnancy. Pregnancy can be threatening for a woman at risk for adverse birth outcomes due to a medical condition such as diabetes, a previous miscarriage, or complications with the current pregnancy. Dias and Lobel (1997) studied 147 such women, who completed a questionnaire assessing the direction and frequency of their social comparisons, as well as their affiliation preferences. Younger women in their first pregnancy engaged in social comparison most often. Comparisons of physical states were more frequent than comparisons of emotions or interpersonal relationships. Women who experienced less pregnancy-related threat (i.e., fewer physical symptoms associated with the pregnancy; less worry about potential changes in the relationship with the baby's father) and those who reported greater self-esteem made more frequent downward comparisons. When self-esteem was controlled, threat no longer predicted comparison direction, although when threat was controlled, self-esteem continued to predict the direction of comparisons. Two other findings of this study are relevant to our review: (1) those who engaged in downward comparison experienced less of an increase in anxiety during the course of their pregnancy, and (2) women most wanted to interact with other women who had babies (an upward affiliation), regardless of their level of personal control over their pregnancy. These findings are consistent with the potential benefits of downward comparison *and* upward affiliation.

Experimentally Induced Health Threats

In 1992, Croyle reviewed a set of studies that examined social comparison processes using an experimental paradigm. In these studies, participants were tested for a fictitious enzyme deficiency (TAA), which ostensibly placed one at risk for the development of pancreatic problems. Studies employing this paradigm show that when people are told that they are one of four members of a group of five who test positive for the deficiency, they rate the disorder as a less serious health threat, and they are less likely to request information or a follow-up exam than those who are told they are the only member of a group of five who tested positive. Those who were told that they tested positive for the deficiency and who were with a confederate who tested negative reported stronger intentions to improve their health behavior than their counterparts who were tested with a confederate who also tested positive. This effect was mediated by participants' perception of the prevalence of the deficiency: When prevalence estimates were controlled, the test result of the confederate was no longer related to the intention to change health behavior.

Another experimental paradigm was used more recently to examine how level of health threat and perceived control over health outcomes influence social comparison processes (Sun & Croyle, 1995). In this study, subjects were led to believe that they had either a high-risk or borderline cholesterol level. Half the participants were told that cholesterol was controllable, whereas the other half were told that it was uncontrollable. These manipulations resulted in a 2 (cholesterol level) × 2 (controllability) design. Social comparison was measured with an indicator of participants' interest in reading the files of other participants.

Across all conditions, participants preferred upward comparison information over downward comparison information. A level of threat by direction of comparison interaction revealed that those in the high-threat condition (high-risk cholesterol level) showed similar preferences for upward and downward comparisons, whereas participants in the low-threat condition (borderline cholesterol level) had stronger preferences for upward comparison. The personal control manipulation did not influence comparison preferences. Sun and Croyle (1995) propose that the point in time when one measures social comparison (directly following the threat in the present study versus long after a medical diagnosis in field studies) can influence a study's findings. Individuals may be more interested in information seeking for self-evaluation and self-improvement directly following a threat, whereas self-improvement motives may be more prominent later on in the course of the threat.

HEALTH-RELATED SOCIAL COMPARISON IN EVERYDAY LIFE

To this point we have focused on social comparison processes among individuals facing a serious medical condition and those facing a potential health threat. We now turn our attention to the role of social comparison in how people manage health-related issues in everyday life. Van der Zee, Buunk, and Sanderman (1995) examined the role of social comparison in the general health perceptions of a community sample. They proposed a mediational model similar to the one examined among cancer patients by Van der Zee et al. (1996), in which psychological distress as the result of health problems induces a need for social comparison. This need then affects the frequency of downward comparison, which in turn influences perceptions of how well one is doing compared to others. Overall, the model was supported. Relative evaluations were positively biased, with 64% of the sample reporting that they were doing as well as others, 31% of the sample reporting they were doing better than others, and only 5% reporting that they were in worse health than others. Moreover, these relative evaluations influenced general health evaluations above and beyond the direct effects of self-reported health problems and psychological distress. The model fit better for women, who, more than their male counterparts, rated themselves as in better health than others.

Unrealistic Optimism

Most people believe that they are at less risk than their peers for experiencing negative life events, including health problems. Weinstein (1980) referred to this phenomenon as unrealistic optimism, and Klein and Weinstein (1997) reviewed what is known about how the social comparison process influences personal health risk judgments. People across all age groups are unrealistically optimistic regarding many potential health and safety problems, and they hold self-serving biases about specific health behaviors associated with problems (e.g., believe they eat less salt than others, sunbathe less often, etc.). Individuals show the strongest optimistic bias about events over which they experience some control and about events they have yet to experience.

Factors related to social comparison, such as the direction of the comparison, similarity to the target, and specificity of the target, also influence the extent to which people are unrealistically optimistic. Unrealistic optimism is reduced when the person making the comparison does *not* have a stereotyped conception of a victim (e.g., the typical accident victim as careless), when the target is a specific person rather than the average person, when the target is perceived as similar to the person making the comparison, and when the person making the comparison has personal contact with the target. Thus, the more specific, concrete, and nonstereotypical the target is, the less likely the person is to believe that his or her own risk is lower than that of the target. Unrealistic optimism appears to be greater when people fail to take the perspective of the comparison target or when the comparison target is at such high risk that people become convinced of their own invulnerability. These findings suggest that using similar, specific, and physically present others as comparison targets in health promotion campaigns may improve the effectiveness of such interventions.

Despite the tendency to overestimate the risk of the average person, people are occasionally confronted by accurate information about others. Klein and Weinstein (1997) reviewed studies (e.g., Rothman, Klein, & Weinstein, 1996; Klein & Kunda, 1993) in which participants were provided with either accurate information about others' risk or frequency of behavior, information that inflated the others' risk, or information that deflated the others' risk. Participants who received accurate and deflated risk information for others described their own risk as lower or reported engaging in the target risky behavior less frequently than participants who received information that inflated others' risk. This pattern of findings is consistent with Klein and Weinstein's (1997) hypothesis that actual and deflated risk information about others challenges people's tendency to view others as more vulnerable than they are themselves. Thus, they must distort their beliefs about themselves to maintain unrealistic optimism.

Klein and Weinstein (1997) also reviewed evidence of how people's affective, self-evaluative, and behavioral reactions to risk information are influenced by social comparisons related to risk status. Klein (1997), for example, found that being confronted with the absolute risk (chance of getting the disease) for a fictitious illness had no effect on how upset participants believed they would be if they tested positive for the illness, but relative risk (chance of getting the disease being either worse or better than average) did influence anticipated affective reactions. Similar findings from this study emerged when participants were told their absolute or relative risk of being involved in an automobile accident, and then reported their driving safety and willingness to change their driving behavior. Absolute risk had no effect on safety judgments or behavioral intentions. However, those who were led to believe that their relative risk of being in an accident was below average, even if that risk was 60%, believed they were safer drivers than those who were led to believe their risk was above average, even if that risk was 30%! Subjects who were led to believe that their risk was above average indicated that they would be more likely to drive at a safer speed, use seat belts more often, and utilize public transportation more frequently. These findings suggest that prevention campaigns that focus on increasing risk awareness might benefit from greater attention to social comparison information.

Health Images

Most people maintain an image of a typical member of a particular category of individuals (e.g., the typical athlete or smoker). Gibbons and Gerrard (1997) examined how these images or prototypes influence health behavior through social comparison. People form images of desirable groups that are similar to themselves, whereas images of less desirable groups tend to highlight the differences between the self and the group. These images can serve as social comparison targets and consequently influence health related behavior.

Studies examining health-impairing behaviors have found that health images also may increase unhealthy behavior. As we mentioned with regard to unrealistic optimism, social comparison with negative images of the typical victim increases unrealistic beliefs, which could lead to a decrease in the motivation to engage in precautionary behavior or an increase risky behavior. Studies of adolescents (Chassin, Presson, Sherman, Corty, & Olshavsky, 1981; Chassin, Tetzloff, & Hershey, 1985) demonstrate that those who have more positive images of someone who smokes or drinks report greater interest in the behavior and engage in the activity more often than those who have less favorable images.

Gibbons and Gerrard's (1997) model of adolescent health risk behavior proposes that social risk images influence changes in risk behavior through a social comparison process. Specifically, an adolescent with a more favorable image of the typical teenager who engages in risky behavior (e.g., the typical teenager who drinks frequently), and whose image of the typical teen is similar to her or his self-image, will be more likely to start or increase the behavior associated with the image. Characteristics of the image are more predictive of increases in risk behavior for adolescents who more frequently compare themselves to others (Gibbons & Gerrard, 1995).

This line of inquiry has important implications for improving health interventions. Identifying the negative components of adolescents' social images and emphasizing them in interventions that begin at an early age can help reduce the risk behaviors associated with the images. Including information about other adolescents' frequency of and attitudes toward risky behaviors in such interventions might help reduce young people's misperceptions of their peers' risk behavior.

AIDS Risk Behavior Change

AIDS and HIV have become worldwide health threats. The risk of HIV can be reduced significantly by avoiding risky behaviors such as unprotected intercourse and by engaging in preventive behaviors such as using condoms. Nevertheless, behavioral change by individuals is slow and inconsistent, even in high-risk populations (see Misovich, Fisher, & Fisher, 1997). Misovich et al. (1997) discussed the relevance of social comparison processes to their Information–Motivation–Behavioral Skills (IMB) model of AIDS-risk behavior change (Fisher & Fisher, 1992; Fisher & Fisher, 1993). This model asserts that an individual's knowledge of prevention information concerning AIDS and his or her motivation to reduce AIDS risk will be expressed through the application of risk reduction behavioral skills. When specific behavioral skills are not needed, information and motivation may have a direct effect on preventive behavior. Fisher and associates assert that social comparison can influence all the variables in their model.

When an individual is uncertain about AIDS prevention knowledge (e.g., unsure whether condom use reduces the transmission of HIV), she or he can use social comparison to evaluate that information, either by imagining what others believe to be true (constructive comparison) or by comparing directly with the information of others (realistic comparison). People may be motivated to seek accurate information through social comparison or they may be motivated to seek information that is consistent with their own beliefs and practices, regardless of its accuracy. Misovich et al. (1997) suggest that having a diverse group of high-status community members advocate for AIDS prevention may be an effective way to increase the motivation to seek information from more accurate sources such as health care providers, because these sources may be viewed as more credible and similar to the individual.

A person's motivation to reduce risky behavior also can be influenced by the attitudes and behaviors of his or her referent group. The more one encounters others who have positive attitudes about preventive behavior and who engage in preventive practices, the more likely it is that one will perceive normative support for such practices and have positive attitudes toward them. Believing that one is less vulnerable to HIV than others (unrealistic optimism) and comparing oneself to the stereotypical person with HIV, typically viewed as dissimilar to oneself, also can decrease an individual's motivation to engage in risk reduction behavior. Exposure to an HIV-positive individual who is perceived as similar to oneself in terms of background and past AIDS risk behavior can increase a person's perceived vulnerability of contracting HIV (Misovich et al., 1997).

People's skill in preventive behaviors and their level of self-efficacy regarding the performance of these behaviors also can be influenced by social comparison processes. In the absence of information regarding normative levels of required skills, individuals tend to believe they are superior to others when it comes to comparing abilities (Alicke, 1985; Goethals, Messick, & Allison, 1991). When a person's AIDS prevention skills are challenged, she or he will either seek out lower-ability others with whom to compare in order to preserve a sense of superiority or decide that his or her skills need to be improved. Misovich et al. (1997) argue that individuals are more likely to conclude that they need to sharpen their skills if they possess both prevention information and the motivation to engage in the needed behavior. Increasing skills can be accomplished in turn through observation of and affiliation with social comparison others who possess such skills.

Most recently, Tigges, Wills, and Link (1998) used three methods to examine how social comparison is related to condom use among high school students. These students: (1) compared the frequency of their condom use to that of same-gender peers; (2) stated their preference for a discussion group member by selecting a student who used condoms more than, less than, or with the same frequency as they did themselves; and (3) described a teenager with AIDS on a series of adjectives, which served as an indicator of derogation. Several interesting findings emerged from this study. First, the less students had used condoms, the more they wished to affiliate with peers who used condoms more than they did. Second, the more threatened these students felt about contracting AIDS, the less they derogated other teens with AIDS. A third interesting finding was that among students with low self-esteem, those who believed that they used condoms more than their peers reported greater satisfaction with their use of condoms. Tiggs et al. (1998) also provide evidence consistent with Taylor and Lobel's (1989) hypothesis that although people tend to compare themselves favorably to others, they prefer to affiliate with others who they view as superior on the comparison dimension. Although these findings are consistent with the idea that downward comparison may hamper preventive behavior, we are just beginning to understand the ways in which social comparison processes influence perceived risk for AIDS and other socially transmitted diseases, how they influence preventive behavior, and how these processes can best be used to promote behavior change.

The Decision to Seek Medical Care

Nonprofessional sources of information, including friends and relatives, can provide a context for social comparison processes when deciding whether to seek medical attention for a particular problem. Building on Safer, Tharps, Jackson, and Leventhal's (1979) proposal that three stages unfold from the time a person first discovers a symptom to her or his entry into medical treatment, Suls et al. (1997) examined the role of social comparison and the "lay referral network" in people's decisions to visit a doctor. Safer and co-workers' (1979) first stage, *appraisal delay*, represents the time that passes before a person interprets a symptom as a sign of illness. The second stage, *illness delay*, is the time between the realization that one is ill and the decision to seek medical care. The third stage, *utilization delay*, begins when the person decides to go to the doctor and ends when he or she arrives for treatment. Suls et al. (1997) argue convincingly that social comparison processes are involved in each stage of the decision to seek medical attention.

Since people in one's social network may have the experience necessary to determine whether a symptom is indicative of an illness and, if it is an illness, its future course, their knowledge and opinions can influence whether someone interprets a symptom as a sign of illness. The lay referral network is more convenient and accessible than seeking expert opinions as soon as one has symptoms. Consulting the lay referral network first also may be more financially efficient and may reduce the possibility of being embarrassed by unnecessary health care visits. Suls et al. (1997) describe a study in which they demonstrated that college students prefer to talk to someone prior to consulting a medical professional for the purposes of gaining information and advice about the problem. Students tend to seek friends and family members, both of whom could be considered similar social comparison targets.

Investigations of social comparison in the illness delay stage include those that have assessed how knowing someone with a similar medical complaint influences the decision to seek care and others that have examined how advice from one's social network influences care seeking. Individuals who have a family history of an illness or know someone with a similar problem are more likely to seek medical attention for that problem (Turk, Litt, Salovey, & Walker, 1985). Parents who consult another person prior to taking their children to the emergency room have ER visits deemed more appropriate than those who did not seek outside advice (Oberlander, Pless, & Dougherty, 1993). And when objective test results are negative, or when there is no objective information, advice from friends influences people's decisions to go to the doctor (Sanders, 1981).

Overall, advice from relatives and friends regarding the interpretation of symptoms and the decision to seek medical attention may contribute to both overuse and underuse of health care resources. There is currently a dearth of theoretical and empirical information in the area of social comparison and lay referral.

CONCEPTUAL PROBLEMS, METHODOLOGICAL ISSUES, AND FUTURE DIRECTIONS

We have described the role of social comparison in dealing with serious medical problems and health threats, in the maintenance of unrealistic optimism, in the development of health images, in the reduction of risky behavior, and in the decision to seek medical care. Throughout our review, we have hinted at several conceptual and methodological problems in this literature. In the following section, we focus on what we believe to be some of the most important conceptual and methodological issues in the study of social comparison and health.

Is Downward Comparison a Coping Strategy?

In what appears to be an evolving shift in how social comparisons are conceptualized, investigators have come to assume that when individuals facing health threats acknowledge worse possible situations or others to whom their circumstance compares favorably, they are engaging in emotion-focused coping (e.g., Gibbons & Gerrard, 1991; Langston, 1994; Taylor, Wayment & Carrillo, 1996). Wills' (1981, 1987) theory of downward comparison processes forms the foundation of this now-prevailing view, reflected in many of the studies we reviewed. Wills argued that downward comparisons are not only adaptive but common among people facing threatening events, and he suggested that the goal of such comparisons was to help the threatened individual experience her or his own situation as less aversive. At the same time, Taylor, Wood, and Lichtman (1983) discovered that an unexpectedly high proportion of women with breast cancer were taking advantage of opportunities to compare themselves with less fortunate others, and that those who did not know another woman with a more serious affliction *imagined* others who were not adapting as well. Wills' persuasive arguments and Taylor and co-workers' provocative findings led Gibbons and Gerrard (1991) to explicitly describe downward comparison as an emotion-focused coping strategy.

Are the downward comparisons reported by individuals facing health threats best conceptualized as coping strategies? We (Tennen & Affleck, 1997) have argued that by assuming that such comparisons reflect coping processes, investigators have lost important opportunities to understand how social comparison, and particularly downward comparison, fits with other adaptive dynamics (but see Suls & David, 1996). As Lazarus and Folkman (1984) remind us, "... not all adaptive processes are coping. Coping is a subset of adaptational activities that *involves effort* and does not include everything that we do in relating to the environment" (p. 132, italics added). The effortful nature of coping is also captured in Haan's (1992) distinction between coping and defending.

This widely accepted definition of coping as effortful excludes both higher-order beliefs, which can be held without corroborating evidence, and well-learned behavior that requires neither concentration nor effort. Lazarus and Folkman (1984) offer as an example the complex behaviors required to drive in traffic. Only when these behaviors are purposeful and require deliberate effort, as when one is learning to drive, are they coping strategies. When they become automatic—as they are for the experienced driver who brakes, changes gears, and directs the vehicle to its destination while concentrating on the events of the day—they are no longer coping strategies.

Consider an individual with a recently diagnosed serious illness or threatening medical condition such as those reviewed in this chapter. According to current conceptions of coping, if she actively scans her environment for evidence of less-fortunate others, she is coping. If she takes the time to remind herself that her condition is less serious than it is for others, she is coping. If she eventually *concludes* that she is fortunate compared to others and reports this belief when provided the opportunity during an interview, she is no longer coping. That her conclusion may have been reached through selective evaluations or is biased by objective standards is irrelevant to its status as a coping strategy. Its adaptive function is equally irrelevant to whether it is a coping strategy. We continue to maintain that although downward comparisons typically benefit those who offer them, as evidenced by the studies we reviewed in this chapter, the literature provides scant evidence that these comparisons function as coping strategies.

We have suggested that if social comparison is a coping strategy, it should be measured so as to capture its effortful and strategic qualities (Tennen & Affleck, 1997). In other areas of coping research, investigators explicitly define and assess the effortful and strategic aspects of the coping dynamic. Lazarus' (1993) definition of coping as "cognitive and behavioral efforts to manage psychological stress" (p. 237) fits well with what we usually consider a "strategy," as does Stone and Neale's (1984) Daily Coping Inventory, which "… asks if anything was thought or done with the intention of accomplishing the function …" (Stone, Neale, & Shiffman, 1993, p. 9). These investigators appreciate the effortful nature of coping.

Although social comparisons can be effortful, they are *not* effortful as measured in most of the studies we have reviewed. Consider, for example, participants in the studies of cancer patients in Table 1. Individuals experiencing intense discomfort from a round of chemotherapy may try to think of less fortunate others as a way of making their discomfort more bearable. They may try to recall an earlier course of chemotherapy when the discomfort was worse or when they felt less well equipped to endure it. These efforts at social and temporal comparison capture the intentional, strategic quality of coping. Of the field studies summarized in Table 1, only Jensen and Karoly (1992) assessed downward comparisons so as to capture their effortful nature, by asking participants about their intentional use of each strategy. Although the studies we reviewed examined the need for comparison, its direction and frequency, the conclusion of how well one fares compared to others, and the emotional antecedents and consequences of comparison, they have not typically pursued effortful comparisons intended to alleviate distress, that is, comparison coping.

Readers who are more familiar with the social comparison literature than with the coping literature may be inclined to construe our distinction between comparison conclusions and comparison coping as academic hairsplitting. We have demonstrated, however, that theoretical and measurement distinctions among appraisals, beliefs, and coping are not trivial (Affleck, Urrows, Tennen, & Higgins, 1992; Affleck & Tennen, 1993). For example, we found that among individuals with rheumatoid arthritis, the prospectively measured daily use of a positive reappraisal strategy is bimodal: although most individuals rarely employed this tactic, a few relied on it almost every day as a way of contending with their daily pain. However, responses to a reliable indicator assessing positive reappraisal of chronic pain (a conclusion) did not differentiate those who used this strategy frequently from those who used it rarely. This finding underscores empirically our distinction between conclusions or beliefs, and coping strategies.

We also believe that the focus on social comparisons as efforts to regulate one's emotions has had a somewhat limiting effect on the investigations described in this chapter. Although people regularly make efforts to regulate their mood (Mayer, Salovey, Gomberg-Kaufman, & Blainey, 1991; Thayer, Newman, & McClain, 1994), and several of the studies in Table 1 provide evidence that is not inconsistent with a mood regulation model (e.g., Van der Zee et al., 1995), it is far from clear that people employ downward comparisons to achieve such self-regulation, or that such mood regulation attempts are successful. Lazarus (1991, 1993) has reserved the term "emotion-focused" coping for mood regulation strategies. Other strategies aimed at changing the meaning of a threatening situation he depicts as "cognitive coping." This shift is far more than a lexical nuance. It represents an acknowledgment that strategies implemented to change the significance of a threatening event are not simply mood regulation strategies. Rather, they lead to a restructuring of goals (Lazarus, 1991; Smith & Lazarus, 1993). If downward comparisons are, as the literature suggests, efforts to change the significance of a threatening event, they should do more than regulate emotions. Yet, in keeping with its conceptual status as an emotion-focused coping strategy, most of the nonlaboratory studies in Table 1 have limited their focus to the relation between downward comparisons and emotional well-being, subjective distress, and subjective health appraisals.

Aside from being effortful and predicting more than mood regulation, cognitive coping strategies typically change over time. Temporal change is inherent in Lazarus and Folkman's (1984) description of coping. Yet none of the field studies described in Table 1 addressed the issue of naturally occurring changes in social comparisons. With few exceptions (e.g., Gibbons & Gerrard, 1991) change in comparisons over time has been *assumed* because individuals who have been facing a stressor for a longer time report making fewer downward comparisons than those facing the stressor for a shorter time. Aside from our concerns about the reliability of retrospectively reported coping strategies (see Tennen & Affleck, 1997), we suspect that any genuine decline in the deployment of downward comparisons as a coping strategy may reflect an unmeasured change in the comparison target from others to *oneself*. Early in the course of an unfolding medical threat, particularly a chronic or recurring condition, an individual has no real opportunity to make temporal comparisons (Suls & Mullen, 1983), because she or he has not had sufficient experience with the stressor. Over time, however, the most reliable and informative comparisons can be made to one's previous experience rather than the experience of others.

Comparisons to prior and more difficult experiences, which may or may not be coping efforts, require time to emerge. When they do emerge, however, they reflect not only that things could have been worse, but that they *have been* worse. Such comparisons appear to have far greater "assurance potential" than comparisons to less fortunate others. Changes in comparison processes, including possible declines in downward social comparisons and increases in downward temporal comparisons, require prospective designs. As our review and Table 1 demonstrate, such studies have yet to reach the agenda of social comparison researchers.

Are Downward Comparisons Secondary Control Beliefs?

Even if social comparisons are not coping strategies, as derived *conclusions* they might still function as self-protective beliefs or defensive appraisals. Rothbaum, Weisz, and Snyder (1982) speculated that such appraisals are "secondary control" beliefs, which provide an alternative to feelings of helplessness in the face of threatening experiences. Rothbaum and co-workers' (1982) formulation is captured in more recent depictions of social comparisons as strategies that emerge when a threat cannot be overcome through instrumental action (Wills, 1987), when events are uncontrollable (Taylor et al., 1996), and when expectations are violated (Leventhal, Hudson, & Robitaille, 1997). If secondary control represents a "fallback" position after attempts to control a health threat have failed, it follows that secondary control, including downward comparisons, should increase as an individual's sense of direct personal control declines. This type of dynamic relation between perceived control or perceived mutability and downward comparisons has yet to be examined. Empirical tests of this dynamic would provide evidence for currently untested formulations. They also would clarify the place of social comparison among theoretically related secondary control constructs. Such clarification is sorely needed. Thus far, however, even cross-sectional associations between personal control and social comparison activity follow no clear pattern. Whereas Jensen and Karoly (1992) found that those higher in control made more self-enhancing comparisons, Ybema and Buunk (1995) reported that those higher in control identified more with an upward target and felt more positive affect after upward comparison. Sun and Croyle (1995), despite manipulation checks demonstrating that their control manipulation was successful, found no relation between control and their measure of social comparison. These mixed findings, which could be method dependent, provide another reason to heed Wood's (1996) call to employ multiple methods within studies.

In our 1997 review of the pain coping literature, we concluded that downward comparisons do not seem to adhere to expectations for coping strategies nor do they appear to behave like other secondary control beliefs (Tennen & Affleck, 1997). We reasoned that if something does not look like a coping strategy or secondary control belief and does not act like a coping strategy or secondary control belief, it may function as something other than a coping strategy or secondary control belief. Whereas arguments to the contrary (e.g., Leventhal et al., 1997) assert that coping can be automatic, and need not be deliberate, effortful, or conscious, recent distinctions between coping and defense mechanisms turn on conscious, intentional efforts versus unconscious, nonintentional processes (e.g., Cramer, 1998). We urge investigators to clarify when and how downward comparisons function as conscious, effortful strategies. Because current models of the coping process (Lazarus & Folkman, 1984; Moos & Schaefer, 1992) differentiate beliefs from coping efforts and predict a causal relation between the two (Bandura, 1986; Lazarus & Folkman, 1984), it is important to operationalize these constructs so as to maintain their theoretical distinctions.

Distinguishing Social Comparisons from Other Cognitive Adaptations to Health Threats

It should be clear that we urge investigators to more carefully question the conceptual status of social comparison as a coping strategy and as a secondary control belief. As they do so, we hope they also will examine how social comparisons distinguish themselves from other cognitive adaptations, particularly the tendency to find benefits in threatening medical events. A review of this literature unearths a wide array of medical problems for which the majority of informants cite benefits or gains from their adversity. This evidence comes from studies of heart attack survivors, women with breast cancer, survivors of spinal cord injuries, women with impaired fertility, patients with chronic rheumatic diseases, stroke victims and their caregivers, parents of infants hospitalized on newborn intensive care units, and mothers of children with insulin-dependent diabetes (see Affleck & Tennen, 1996; Tennen & Affleck, 1999, for a review).

Several categories of perceived benefits cut across these problems. One common theme is the strengthening of relationships with family and friends. Another is the perception of positive personality change, including greater patience, tolerance, empathy, and courage. Yet another common benefit appraisal is a valued change in life's priorities and personal goals. Other benefits appear relatively specific to health-related adversity. For example, many men who have had heart attacks believe that this event taught them a valued lesson about the importance of health behavior practices to living a long life (Affleck, Tennen, Croog, & Levine, 1987).

The conceptual similarities between construing benefits and making downward comparisons is captured by Buunk (1994), who convincingly classifies both as manifestations of "selective evaluation." The similarities are equally well depicted by Schulz and Decker (1985), who found that individuals disabled by spinal cord injury rated their situation in relatively favorable terms compared to those who were not disabled. These disabled persons supported their self-enhancing comparisons by citing intellectual accomplishments, positive social relationships, and sensitivity to others—benefits of their injury! Yet the unique adaptational advantages of social comparisons, that is, distinct from the advantages of finding benefits in threatening medical circumstances, has received scant theoretical and empirical attention. Such distinctions are important because benefit finding has been consistently linked to positive adaptational outcomes, including less negative affect in cancer patients, less depression and greater meaningfulness in life in stroke victims, less psychological distress in infertile women, superior psychological adjustment in women with breast cancer, and less mood disturbance and intrusive thoughts in mothers of acutely ill newborns (see Affleck & Tennen, 1996; Tennen & Affleck, 1999, for a review).

A(nother) Call for Longitudinal Research

Nearly a decade ago, we concluded a review of the literature on social comparison and adaptation to major medical problems by urging investigators to conduct longitudinal investigations (Affleck & Tennen, 1991). Although cross-sectional designs are common in studies of adaptation to negative events, nowhere in the literature could we find a comparable dearth of longitudinal or prospective findings as in the social comparison and health literature. As our review reveals, this situation remains essentially unchanged. The follow-up periods in the few studies that employed longitudinal designs seemed somewhat arbitrary and were not tied to anticipated times of increased uncertainty. We again call for longitudinal designs, not as an obligatory concession, but because both theory (Festinger, 1954) and cross-sectional findings (Wood, Taylor, & Lichtman, 1985) suggest that social comparisons may emerge more frequently and intensely during early phases of a medical threat, and that they may decline as the problem unfolds or as its meaning becomes more clear.

Aspinwall (1997) astutely has noted that social comparison processes may not only vary depending on where an individual is in the course of a temporally unfolding event, but also as a function of what she or he expects to happen in the future. She distinguishes *proactive* comparisons—those that occur prior to the stressful event—from *reactive* comparisons—those that emerge after the stressful event has occurred. The goals of a comparison may differ depending on its temporal context. If the stressful event has yet to occur but has implications for the person's well-being, the need for self-improvement and information to modify future outcomes may be greater, thus resulting in more upward comparisons. On the other hand, once a stressful or threatening event has occurred, the distress experienced by the individual may result in more downward comparisons for the purposes of self-enhancement and affect regulation.

Aspinwall (1997) also reminds us that individuals who experience little personal control or only a modest potential for change may respond negatively to a downward comparison target, since without control or anticipated change the comparison target may portend one's own fate. But perceived control and opportunities for change may themselves change over time. Aspinwall's formulation suggests that investigators should turn to designs that both examine comparisons prior to a focal stressful event and monitor the comparison process following the event. As we suggested in 1991 (Affleck & Tennen, 1991), an exceptionally attractive study design would examine the trajectory of comparison processes among individuals at risk for a medical problem, with social comparisons measured prior to diagnosis and continuing through the course of the illness. Repeated measurement of comparisons could be linked to periods at which increased ambiguity, change in personal control, or greater threats to the self are anticipated. Although difficult to conduct, such studies would provide unique insights into the natural course of comparison activities.

Do Social Comparisons Predict Health Outcomes?

Perhaps reflecting its conceptual status as an emotion-focused coping strategy, social comparisons have been linked almost exclusively to subjective indicators of distress and emotional or physical well-being (see Table 1). We view these associations as important in their own right because subclinical levels of depression have significant societal costs (Judd, Akiskal, & Paulus, 1997), and because emotional distress predicts subsequent health complaints and health care utilization (Johnson, Weissman, & Klerman, 1992). Although we view established links between social comparisons and self-reported distress as theoretically and clinically meaningful, we hope that investigators will follow the lead of several studies of another selective evaluation, finding benefits, to expand their outcome indicators to actual health outcomes.

In a longitudinal study of the predictive significance of benefit-finding, Affleck et al. (1991) asked mothers before their child's discharge from a newborn intensive care unit whether they had found any benefits from their child's hazardous delivery and prolonged hospitalization. Seventy-five percent of them cited at least one benefit, including improved relationships with family and friends, the importance of keeping life's problems in perspective, increased empathy, positive changes in their personality, and the conviction that their child was now more precious to them (all perceived features of the self that might trigger downward temporal or social comparisons). These mothers' ability to find benefits not only predicted their well-being but also their child's actual developmental test scores 18 months later. Benefit finding, in fact, predicted developmental outcome far better than did the severity of the child's medical problems prior to hospital discharge.

Another demonstration of the predictability of objective outcomes from earlier benefit-finding comes from a cohort of heart attack survivors who participated in an unusually long prospective study (Affleck et al., 1987). After 7 weeks of recovery from their initial heart attack, 58% of these men cited benefits, the most common being anticipated changes in lifestyle to increase enjoyment, valued lessons about the importance of health behavior, and positive changes in their philosophy of life and basic values. Eight years later, those who had construed benefits were in better cardiac health and were less likely to have suffered a subsequent attack. These predictive relations remained significant even after controlling for the severity of their initial attack. We had hoped that these predictive relations between benefit finding and later health would trigger comparable studies of other selective evaluations, including social comparisons. To this point there has been no response.

Exploring the Within-Person Ebb and Flow of Social Comparisons

Although current theoretical models of social comparison in medical settings describe causal relations among medical threats, comparisons, and well-being, the correlational findings of the field studies depicted in Table 1 are unable to test causal relations. The laboratory studies we have reviewed, which allow causal inference, are fairly far removed from the everyday lives of research participants. Jensen, Turner, Romano, and Karoly (1991) believe that within-person designs are uniquely suited to understanding processes such as social comparisons. We agree. Such designs remain true to "real-world" experience, and they are uniquely suited to capture the "constantly changing cognitive and behavioral efforts" that define coping processes (Lazarus & Folkman, 1984). We encourage investigators to test existing models of the antecedents, dynamics, and consequences of social comparisons in the context of within-person intensive idiographic designs. These designs, which we describe in greater detail elsewhere (Tennen & Affleck, 1996, 1997), are able to capture health threats closer to their actual occurrence, track change in rapidly fluctuating processes like social comparisons and mood, and minimize recall error. By preserving temporal sequences among threatening medical experiences, social comparisons, and adaptational outcomes, such "daily process" studies promise to strengthen our causal inferences.

It is common in studies of social comparison under threat to draw within-person inferences from between-person associations. For example, that individuals who report more downward comparisons also report less distress tells us nothing about the effect of such comparisons on distress, nor does it speak to affective states that prompt comparisons. Yet, investigators typically translate between-person data in the form: "individuals who engage in more downward comparisons are less distressed" as if it were within-person data in the form: "*when* individuals compare themselves favorably to others they are less distressed" or "individuals engage in downward comparisons *when* they are distressed, and the comparison process alleviates the distress." Only intensive within-person designs can reliably address temporal associations because they preserve temporal sequences.

The several studies that have applied intensive within-person assessments of social comparisons raise significant questions about current conceptual formulations. Langston (1994) followed a group of sorority members for 15 days. At the end of each day they described one negative and one positive event and described how they responded to the event. Social comparison responses were combined with other "emotion-focused" responses, so their incidence cannot be evaluated. Yet as a group, these responses occurred more frequently in response to positive events than to negative events, providing indirect support for our concern that comparisons may not be associated with threatening situations as predicted by theory. Just as we might seek social contact to help us savor a joyous experience, so may we compare ourselves to others when we feel fortunate. This may explain why Wheeler and Miyake (1992), who examined social comparisons *as they occurred* every day for 2 weeks, found that people made upward comparisons when their mood was more negative and they made downward comparisons when their mood was more positive. This pattern contradicts the motivational explanation for comparisons offered in downward comparison theory.

More recently, we followed 25 chronic pain patients every day for 30 days (see Tennen & Affleck, 1997). Two items on a nightly questionnaire measured the effortful use of downward social and temporal comparisons concerning that day's pain. We found that social comparison use and temporal comparison use were each more frequent on *less* painful days. Furthermore, pain, which was assessed three times a day via an electronic diary, became *less* intense during the course of a day in which temporal comparisons were more prominent. A day with more temporal comparisons tended to be characterized by decreasing sadness and increasing happiness, liveliness, and stimulation across the day. These findings add credibility to our speculation that after years of living with chronic pain, downward temporal comparisons become more adaptationally significant than do downward social comparisons. During the course of a day when they report more temporal comparisons, these individuals evidenced an abatement in pain and, independently, a brightening of their mood. Taken together, the three studies we summarized capture the unique contributions that within-person designs have to offer studies of social comparison and health. We urge investigators to turn to such designs as a way of addressing the inherently dynamic nature of social comparison theory.

Personality and Social Comparison

Several studies in our review examined the role of personality in the social comparison process. The personality dimensions considered by investigators as most relevant to social comparison and health have been (1) self-esteem, (2) personal control, (3) neuroticism, and (4) dispositional optimism and pessimism. These are, with the addition of dysphoria and trait anxiety, the same aspects of personality considered in the broader social comparison literature (Leventhal et al., 1997; Diener & Fujita, 1997). Although we encourage further study of personality and social comparison, four aspects of this line of inquiry concern us. Our first concern is that the findings that have emerged thus far have been quite inconsistent. With regard to self-esteem, for example, one study found that self-esteem was unrelated to social comparison (Stanton, 1992); another study found that those higher in self-esteem made more downward comparisons (Dias & Lobel, 1997); and yet a third study found that self-esteem was related to social comparison depending on how social comparison was measured (Helgeson & Taylor, 1993). Our second concern is the tendency to "round up the usual suspects" (Tennen & Affleck, 1998). Psychological investigators interested in how people adapt to threatening events have repeatedly taken the now well-worn path of rounding up the usual moderational suspects without a fully developed theory of the phenomenon itself. As a result, the very same personality factors that have been examined in relation to social comparison also have been marched out to explain individual differences in crisis-related growth (Tedeschi & Calhoun, 1995), thriving in the face of adversity (O'Leary & Ickovics, 1995), and other emerging areas of investigation related to health and well-being.

Our third concern with how personality has been studied in this literature is that personal characteristics already suspected of being dimensions of one another have been studied independently as relevant to social comparison and health. For example, neuroticism and trait anxiety, which have been considered separately in relation to comparison processes, are difficult to distinguish empirically. Similarly, dispositional pessimism and neuroticism may be so highly correlated as to risk being redundant in the prediction of health and emotional well-being (e.g., Marshall, Wortman, Kusulas, Hervig, & Vickers, 1992). Likewise, low self-esteem and dysphoria, at least as commonly measured, provide little unique predictive value (Tennen & Herzberger, 1987). If we are to continue to examine these individual differences in relation to social comparison and health, we should examine them concurrently to determine their unique adaptational correlates.

An important exception to the common practice of rounding up the usual and redundant suspects is Gibbons and Buunk's (1999) concept of *social comparison orientation*, which was employed in Van der Zee and co-workers' (1998b) study of comparison preferences among cancer patients. Social comparison orientation refers to "the personality disposition of individuals who are strongly oriented to social comparison, who are strongly interested in their own standing relative to others, and who are interested in information about others' thoughts and behaviors in similar circumstances" (Van der Zee et al., 1998b, p. 802). Gibbons and Buunk (1999) demonstrated that those high in comparison orientation are more strongly affected by downward comparisons, and Van der Zee et al. (1998b) reported that cancer patients with a stronger social comparison orientation experienced more negative reactions following downward comparisons.

Although we view the notion of social comparison orientation as a potentially productive line of research using a dispositional context, we are nonetheless concerned that in the study of social comparison and health, personality has been limited to its dispositional manifestations. McAdams (1993, 1994), drawing from the work of McClelland (1951), Hogan (1987), and Cantor (1990) distinguishes three levels of personality: *dispositional traits, personal concerns*, and *life narratives*. Personal concerns refer to what a person wants at a particular point in life, and how she or he plans to get what she or he wants. Buss and Cantor (1989) refer to this level of personality as "middle-level units," whereas McCrae and Costa (1996) and Costa and McCrae (1994) prefer the term "characteristic adaptations." These are not traits nor are they epiphenomena of a more "fundamental" aspect of personality. People are quite aware of this second level of their personalities, because personal concerns guide everyday activities. Personality at the level of personal concerns might guide not only the direction of social comparisons in response to health threats, but also dimensions on which people compare themselves to others.

Personality as life narratives concerns the individual's attempt to shape an identity by finding unity and purpose in life. This level of inquiry into personality processes has gained momentum among those who are interested in personality across the life cycle (McAdams, 1993), those studying affective experience (Landman, 1993), investigators whose focus is personal crisis (Harvey, Orbuch, Chwalisz, & Garwood, 1991), and theoreticians interested in trauma (Herman, 1992; Pearlman & Saakvitne, 1995), but has not gained force in the study of social comparison processes. Citing Taylor's (1989) concept of "positive illusions," McAdams (1994) describes how narrative explanations of serious illness and other forms of adversity shape and reshape personal identity. His formulation seems to provide a much needed opportunity to broaden how personality is studied in relation to social comparison, health threats, and serious illness.

The Accuracy of Social Comparisons in Health-Threatening Circumstances

Only two of the studies in our review (Affleck et al., 1988; Helgeson & Taylor; 1993) examined the accuracy of patients' comparison conclusions, and both studies found only modest (and inconsistent) concordance between participants' comparisons and independent indicators of their relative status on the dimension they used to compare themselves to others. These findings and the constructivist underpinnings of modern social comparison theory could easily lead investigators to conclude that comparison accuracy is irrelevant to its mechanisms or adaptive benefits.

Yet recent evidence from studies of stress-related growth (e.g., Park, Cohen, & Murch, 1996) are beginning to reveal that a surprising proportion of people seem to change in positive ways after experiencing a major negative event, illness, or trauma, and that these changes can be verified. Whereas social comparison theory interprets downward comparison as an effort to bolster a threatened sense of esteem, the stress-related growth literature offers another interpretation. Simply put, without ready access to the temporal trajectory of others in their situation, individuals who show positive changes in the face of adversity may have good reason to presume that they are relatively well off compared to others facing their circumstances. It also seems reasonable that these positive changes will be captured in our indicators of well-being. Although experimental studies demonstrate (and reason dictates) that some people may strategically compare themselves favorably in relation to others, it is premature to assume that such comparisons are typically motivated by self-enhancement motives, that they typically reflect a stereotyped image of others, or that the relation between such comparisons and well-being is an indicator of their adaptive benefits.

CONCLUSION

The past decade has seen a spate of experimental and field studies documenting how social comparison processes play a role in people's evaluations of their health risks, whether they engage in preventive behavior, how they interpret symptoms, when they make the decision to seek medical care, and how they adapt to illness and disability. This converging evidence has important public health implications, and ultimately could offer health care providers effective interventions. To fulfill the promise of this research, investigators will need to address some thorny conceptual and methodological issues. The conceptual issues include questions such as: Are social comparisons are best conceived as coping efforts? Are they distinct from other cognitive adaptations to health threats? The methodological issues include the need to demonstrate that existing findings are not method dependent; to show through longitudinal designs that real world social comparisons anticipate and not simply reflect positive adaptation to threatening medical events; and to determine whether comparison processes predict subsequent health outcomes. We believe that by tackling these formidable challenges, social comparison theory and research will add greatly to our understanding of how people remain healthy and how they respond when their efforts to do so fail.

REFERENCES

Affleck, G., & Tennen, H. (1991). Social comparison and coping with major medical problems. In J. Suls & T. A. Wills (Eds.), *Social comparison: Contemporary theory and research* (pp. 369–393). Hillsdale, NJ: Lawrence Erlbaum.

Affleck, G., & Tennen, H. (1993). Cognitive adaptation to adversity: Insights from parents of medically fragile infants. In A. P. Turnbull, J. M. Patterson, S. K. Behr, D. L. Murphy, J. G. Marquis, & M. J. Blue-Banning (Eds.), *Cognitive coping, families, and disability: Participatory research in action* (pp. 135–150). New York: Brooks Publishers.

Affleck, G., & Tennen, H. (1996). Construing benefits from adversity: Adaptational significance and dispositional underpinnings. *Journal of Personality, 64,* 899–922.

Affleck, G., Tennen, H., Croog, S., & Levine, S. (1987). Causal attribution, perceived benefits, and morbidity following a heart attack. *Journal of Consulting and Clinical Psychology, 55,* 29–35.

Affleck, G., Tennen, H., Pfeiffer, C., & Fifield, J. (1988). Social comparisons in rheumatoid arthritis: Accuracy and adaptational significance. *Journal of Social and Clinical Psychology, 6,* 219–234.

Affleck, G., Tennen, H., & Rowe, J. (1991). *Infants in crisis: How parents cope with newborn intensive care and its aftermath.* New York: Springer-Verlag.

Affleck, G., Urrows, S., Tennen, H., & Higgins, P. (1992). Daily coping with pain from rheumatoid arthritis: Patterns and correlates. *Pain, 51,* 221–229.

Alicke, M. D. (1985). Global self-evaluation as determined by the desirability and controllability of trait adjectives. *Journal of Personality and Social Psychology, 49,* 1621–1630.

Aspinwall, L. G. (1997). Future-oriented aspects of social comparisons: A framework for studying health-related comparison activity. In B. P. Buunk & F. X. Gibbons (Eds.), *Health, coping, and well-being: Perspectives from social comparison theory* (pp. 125–166). Mahwah, NJ: Lawrence Erlbaum.

Bandura, A. (1986). *Social foundations of thought and action: A social-cognitive theory.* Englewood Cliffs, NJ: Prentice Hall.

Blalock, S. J., Afifi, R. A., DeVellis, B. M., Holt, K., & DeVellis, R. F. (1990). Adjustment to rheumatoid arthritis: The role of social comparison processes. *Health Education Research, 5,* 361–370.

Blalock, S. J., DeVellis, B., & DeVellis, R. (1989). Social comparison among individuals with rheumatoid arthritis. *Journal of Applied Social Psychology, 19,* 665–680.

Buss, D. M., & Cantor, N. (1989). Introduction. In D. M. Buss & N. Cantor (Eds.), *Personality psychology: Recent trends and emerging directions* (pp. 1–12). New York: Springer-Verlag.

Buunk, B. P. (1994). Social comparison processes under stress: Towards an integration of classic and recent perspectives. In W. Stroebe & M. Hewstone (Eds.), *European review of social psychology* (Vol. 5, pp. 211–241). New York: John Wiley.

Buunk, B. P. (1995). Comparison direction and comparison dimension among disabled individuals: Toward a refined conceptualization of social comparison under stress. *Personality and Social Psychology Bulletin, 21,* 316–330.

Buunk, B. P., Collins, R. L., Taylor, S. E., VanYperen, N. W., & Dakof, G. A. (1990). The affective consequences of social comparison: Either direction has its ups and downs. *Journal of Personality and Social Psychology, 59,* 1238–1249.

Cantor, N. (1990). From thought to behavior: "Having" and "doing" in the study of personality and cognition. *American Psychologist, 45,* 735–750.

Chassin, L., Presson, C. C., Sherman, S. J., Corty, E., & Olshavsky, R. W. (1981). Self-images and cigarette smoking in adolescence. *Personality and Social Psychology Bulletin, 7,* 670–676.

Chassin, L., Tetzloff, C., & Hershey, M. (1985). Self-image and social-image factors in adolescent alcohol use. *Journal of Studies on Alcohol, 46,* 39–47.

Costa, P. T., Jr., & McCrae, R. R. (1994). Set like plaster? Evidence for the stability of adult personality. In Heatherton, T. F. & Weinberger, J. L. (Eds.) *Can personality change?* (pp. 21–40). Washington, DC: American Psychological Association.

Cramer, P. (1998). Coping and defense mechanisms. What's the difference? *Journal of Personality, 66,* 919–946.

Croyle, R. T. (1992). Appraisal of health threats: Cognition, motivation, and social comparison. *Cognitive Therapy and Research, 16,* 165–182.

DeVellis, R. F., Blalock, S. J., Holt, K., Renner, B. R., Blanchard, L. W., & Klotz, M. L. (1991). Arthritis patients' reactions to unavoidable social comparisons. *Personality and Social Psychology Bulletin, 17,* 392–399.

DeVellis, R., Holt, K., Renner, B., Blalock, S., Blanchard, L., Cook, H., Klotz, M., Mikow, V., & Harring, K., (1990). The relationship of social comparison to rheumatoid arthritis symptoms and affect. *Basic and Applied Social Psychology, 11,* 1–18.

Dias, L. & Lobel, M. (1997). Social comparison in medically high-risk pregnant women. *Journal of Applied Social Psychology, 27,* 1629–1649.

Diener, E., & Fujita, F. (1997). Social comparisons and subjective well-being. In B. P. Buunk & F. X. Gibbons (Eds.), *Health, coping, and well-being: Perspectives from social comparison theory* (pp. 329–358). Mahwah, NJ: Lawrence Erlbaum.

Festinger, L. A. (1954). A theory of social comparison processes. *Human Relations, 7,* 117–140.

Fisher, J. D., & Fisher, W. A. (1992). Changing AIDS risk behavior. *Psychological Bulletin, 111,* 455–474.

Fisher, W. A., & Fisher, J. D. (1993). A general social psychological model for changing AIDS risk behavior. In J. Pryor & G. Reeder (Eds.), *The social psychology of HIV infection* (pp. 127–153). Hillsdale, NJ: Lawrence Erlbaum.

Gibbons, F. X., & Buunk, B. P. (1999). Individual differences in social comparison: The development of a scale for social comparison orientation. *Journal of Personality and Social Psychology, 76,* 129–192.

Gibbons, F. X., & Gerrard, M. (1991). Downward comparison and coping with threat. In J. Suls & T. A. Wills (Eds.), *Social comparison: Contemporary theory and research* (pp. 317–346). Hillsdale, NJ: Lawrence Erlbaum.

Gibbons, F. X., & Gerrard, M. (1995). Predicting young adults' health risk behavior. *Journal of Personality and Social Psychology, 69,* 505–517.

Gibbons, F. X., & Gerrard, M. (1997). Health images and their effects on health behavior. In B. P. Buunk & F. X. Gibbons (Eds.), *Health, coping, and well-being: Perspectives from social comparison theory* (pp. 63–94). Mahwah, NJ: Lawrence Erlbaum.

Giorgino, K. B., Blalock, S. J., DeVellis, R. F., DeVellis, B. M., Keefe, F . J., & Jordan, J. M. (1994). Appraisal of and coping with arthritis-related problems in household activities, leisure activities, and pain management. *Arthritis Care and Research, 7,* 20–28.

Goethals, G. R., Messick, D. M., & Allison, S. T. (1991). The uniqueness bias: Studies of constructive social comparison. In J. Suls & T. A. Wills (Eds.) *Social comparison: Contemporary theory and research* (pp. 149–176). Hillsdale, NJ: Lawrence Erlbaum.

Haan, N. (1992). The assessment of coping, defense, and stress. In L. Goldberger & S. Breznitz (Eds.), *Handbook of stress: Theoretical and clinical aspects* (2nd ed., pp. 258–273). Toronto: Free Press.

Harvey, J. H., Orbuch, T. L., Chwalisz, K. D., & Garwood, G. (1991). Coping with sexual assault: The roles of account-making and confiding. *Journal of Traumatic Stress, 4*, 515–531.

Herman, J. L. (1992). *Trauma and recovery: The aftermath of violence from domestic abuse to political terror.* New York: Basic Books.

Helgeson, V. S. & Taylor, S. E. (1993). Social comparisons and adjustment among cardiac patients. *Journal of Applied Social Psychology, 23*, 1171–1195.

Hemphill, K. J. & Lehman, D. R. (1991). Social comparisons and their affective consequences: The importance of comparison dimension and individual difference variables. *Journal of Social and Clinical Psychology, 10*, 372–394.

Hogan, R. (1987). Personality psychology: Back to basics. In J. Aronoff, A. I. Rabin, & R. A. Zucker (Eds.), *The emergence of personality* (pp. 79–104). New York: Springer.

Jensen, M. P., & Karoly. P. (1992). Comparative self-evaluation and depressive affect among chronic pain patients: An examination of selective evaluation theory. *Cognitive Therapy and Research, 16*, 297–308.

Jensen, M. P., Turner, J. A., Romano, J. M., & Karoly, P. (1991). Coping with chronic pain: A critical review of the literature. *Pain, 47*, 249–283.

Johnson, J., Weissman, M., & Klerman, G. (1992). Service utilization and social morbidity associated with depressive symptoms in the community. *Journal of the American Medical Association, 267*, 1478–1483.

Judd, L. L., Akiskal, H. S., & Paulus, M. P. (1997). The role and clinical significance of subsyndromal depressive symptoms (SSD) in unipolar major depressive disorder. *Journal of Affective Disorders, 45*, 5–18.

Klein, W. M. (1997). Objective standards are not enough: Affective, self-evaluative, and behavioral responses to social comparison information. *Journal of Personality and Social Psychology, 72*, 763–774.

Klein, W. M., & Kunda, Z. (1993). Maintaining self-serving social comparisons: Biased reconstruction of one's past behaviors. *Personality and Social Psychology Bulletin, 19*, 732–739.

Klein, W. M. & Weinstein, N. D. (1997). Social comparison and unrealistic optimism about personal risk. In B. P. Buunk & F. X. Gibbons (Eds.), *Health, coping, and well-being: Perspectives from social comparison theory* (pp. 25–64). Mahwah, NJ: Lawrence Erlbaum.

Landman, J. (1993). *Regret: The persistence of the possible.* New York: Oxford University Press.

Langston, C. A. (1994). Capitalizing on and coping with daily life events: Expressive responses to positive events. *Journal of Personality and Social Psychology, 67*, 1112–1125.

Lazarus, R. S. (1991). *Emotion and adaptation.* New York: Oxford University Press.

Lazarus, R. S. (1993). Coping theory and research: Past, present and future. *Psychosomatic Medicine, 55*, 324–247.

Lazarus, R. S., & Folkman, S. (1984). *Stress, appraisal, and coping.* New York: Springer.

Leventhal, H., Hudson, S., & Robitaille, C. (1997). Social comparison and health: A process model. In B. P. Buunk & F. X. Gibbons (Eds.), *Health, coping, and well-being: Perspectives from social comparison theory* (pp. 411–432). Mahwah, NJ: Lawrence Erlbaum.

Llewellyn-Thomas, H. A., Thiel, E. C., & McGreal, M. J. (1992). Cancer patients' evaluations of their current health states: The influences of expectations, comparisons, actual health status, and mood. *Medical Decision Making, 12*, 115–122.

McAdams, D. P. (1993). *The stories we live by: Personal myths and the making of the self.* New York: William Morrow.

McAdams, D. P. (1994). Can personality change? Levels of stability and growth in personality across the life span. In T. F. Heatherton & J. J. Weinberger (Eds.) *Can personality change?* (pp. 299–313). Washington, DC: American Psychological Association.

McClelland, D. (1951). *Personality.* New York: Holt, Rinehart, & Winston.

McCrae, R. R., & Costa, P. T., Jr. (1996). Toward a new generation of personality theories: Theoretical contexts for the five-factor model. In J. S. Wiggins (Ed.), *The five-factor model of personality: Theoretical perspectives* (pp. 51–87). New York: Guilford Press.

Marshall, G., Wortman, C., Kusulas, J., Hervig, L., & Vickers, R. (1992). Distinguishing optimism from pessimism: Relations to fundamental dimensions of mood and personality. *Journal of Personality and Social Psychology, 62*, 1067–1074.

Mayer, J. D., Salovey, P., Gomberg-Kaufman, S., & Blainey, K. (1991). A broader conception of mood experience. *Journal of Personality and Social Psychology, 60*, 100–111.

Misovich, S. J., Fisher, J. D., & Fisher, W. A. (1997). Social comparison processes and AIDS risk and AIDS preventive behavior. In B. P. Buunk & F. X. Gibbons (Eds.), *Health, coping, and well-being: Perspectives from social comparison theory* (pp. 95–124). Mahwah, NJ: Lawrence Erlbaum.

Moos, R. H., & Schaeffer, J. A. (1992). Coping resources and processes: Current concepts and measures. In L.

Goldberger & S. Breznitz (Eds.), *Handbook of stress: Theoretical and clinical aspects* (2nd ed., pp. 234–257). Toronto: The Free Press.

Oberlander, T. F., Pless, I. B., & Dougherty, G. E. (1993). Advice seeking and appropriate use of a pediatric emergency department. *American Journal of Developmental Care, 147*, 863–867.

O'Leary, V. E., & Ickovics, J. R. (1995). Resilience and thriving in response to challenge: An opportunity for a paradigm shift in women's health. *Women's Health: Research on Gender, Behavior, and Policy, 1*, 121–142.

Park, C., Cohen, L., & Murch, R. (1996). Assessment and prediction of stress-related growth. *Journal of Personality, 64*, 71–105.

Pearlman, L. A. & Saakvitne, K. W. (1995). *Trauma and the therapist: Countertransference and vicarious traumatization in psychotherapy with incest survivors.* New York: Norton.

Robinson-Whelen, S., & Kiecolt-Glaser, J. (1997). The importance of social versus temporal comparison appraisals among older adults. *Journal of Applied Social Psychology, 27*, 959–966.

Rothbaum, F., Weisz, J., & Snyder, S. (1982). Changing the world and changing the self: A two-process model of perceived control. *Journal of Personality and Social Psychology, 42*, 5–37.

Rothman, A. J., Klein, W. M., & Weinstein, N. D. (1996). Absolute and relative biases in estimations of personal risk. *Journal of Applied Social Psychology, 26*, 1213–1236.

Safer, M. A., Tharps, Q. I., Jackson, T., & Leventhal, H. (1979). Determinants of three stages of delay in seeking care at a medical clinic. *Medical Care, 17*, 11–29.

Sanders, G. S. (1981). The interactive effect of social comparison and objective information on the decision to see a doctor. *Journal of Applied Social Psychology, 11*, 390–400.

Schulz, R., & Decker, S. (1985). Long-term adjustment to physical disability: The role of social support, perceived control, and self-blame. *Journal of Personality and Social Psychology, 48*, 1162–1172.

Smith, C. A., & Lazarus, R. S. (1993). Appraisal components, core relational themes, and the emotions. *Cognition and Emotion, 7*, 233–269.

Stanton, A. L. (1992). Downward comparison in infertile couples. *Basic and Applied Social Psychology, 13*, 389–403.

Stone, A. A., & Neale, J. M. (1984). A new measure of daily coping: Development and preliminary results. *Journal of Personality and Social Psychology, 46*, 892–906.

Stone, A. A., Neale, J. M., & Shiffman, S. (1993). Daily assessments of stress and coping and their association with mood. *Annals of Behavioral Medicine, 15*, 8–16.

Suls, J., & David, J. (1996). Coping and personality: Third time's the charm? *Journal of Personality, 64*, 993–1005.

Suls, J., Marco, C. A., & Tobin, S. (1991). The role of temporal comparison, social comparison, and direct appraisal in the elderly's self-evaluations of health. *Journal of Applied Social Psychology, 21*, 1125–1144.

Suls, J., Martin, R., & Leventhal, H. (1997). Social comparison, lay referral, and the decision to seek medical care. In B. P. Buunk & F. X. Gibbons (Eds.), *Health, coping, and well-being: Perspectives from social comparison theory* (pp. 195–226). Mahwah, NJ: Lawrence Erlbaum.

Suls, J., & Mullen, B. (1983). From the cradle to the grave: Comparison and self-evaluation across the life span. In J. Suls (Ed.), *Psychological perspectives on the self* (Vol. 1, pp. 97–125). Hillsdale, NJ: Lawrence Erlbaum.

Sun, Y. & Croyle, R. T. (1995). Level of health threat as a moderator of social comparison preferences. *Journal of Applied Social Psychology, 25*, 1937–1952.

Taylor, S. E. (1989). *Positive illusions: Creative self-deception and the healthy mind.* New York: Basic Books.

Taylor, S. E., Aspinwall, L. G., Giuliano, T. A., Dakof, G. A., & Reardon, K. K. (1993). Storytelling and coping with stressful events. *Journal of Applied Social Psychology, 23*, 703–733.

Taylor, S., & Lobel, M. (1989). Social comparison activity under threat: Downward evaluation and upward contacts. *Psychological Review, 96*, 569–575.

Taylor, S. E., Wayment, H. A., & Carrillo, M. (1996). Social comparison, self-regulation, and motivation. In R. M. Sorrentino & E. T. Higgins (Eds.), *Handbook of motivation and cognition* (Vol. 3, pp. 3–27). New York: Guilford Press.

Taylor, S. E., Wood, J. V., & Lichtman, R. R. (1983). It could be worse: Selective evaluation as a response to victimization. *Journal of Social Issues, 39*, 19–40.

Tedeschi, R. G., & Calhoun, L. G. (1995). *Trauma and transformation.* Thousand Oaks, CA: Sage.

Tennen, H., & Affleck, G. (1996). Daily processes in coping with chronic pain: Methods and analytic strategies. In M. Zeidner & N. S. Endler (Eds.), *Handbook of coping* (pp. 151–180). New York: John Wiley.

Tennen, H., & Affleck, G. (1997). Social comparison as a coping process: A critical review and application to chronic pain disorders. In B. P. Buunk & F. X. Gibbons (Eds.), *Health, coping, and well-being: Perspectives from social comparison theory* (pp. 263–298). Mahwah, NJ: Lawrence Erlbaum.

Tennen, H., & Affleck, G. (1998). Personality and transformation in the face of adversity. In R. G. Tedeschi, C. L. Park, & L. G. Calhoun (Eds.) *Posttraumatic growth: Positive changes in the aftermath of crisis* (pp. 65–98). Mahwah, NJ: Lawrence Erlbaum.

Tennen, H., & Affleck, G. (1999). Finding benefits in adversity. In C. R. Snyder (Ed.), *Coping: The psychology of what works* (pp. 279–304). New York: Oxford University Press.

Tennen, H., & Herzberger, S. (1987). Depression, self-esteem, and the absence of self-protective attributional biases. *Journal of Personality and Social Psychology, 52*, 72–80.

Thayer, R. E., Newman, R., & McClain, T. M. (1994). Self-regulation of mood: Strategies for changing a bad mood, raising energy, and reducing tension. *Journal of Personality and Social Psychology, 67*, 910–925.

Tigges, B. B., Wills, T. A., & Link, B. G. (1998). Social comparison, the threat of AIDS, and adolescent condom use. *Journal of Applied Social Psychology, 28*, 861–887.

Turk, D. C., Litt, M. D., Salovey, P., & Walker, J. (1985). Seeking urgent pediatric treatment: Factors contribution to frequency, delay, and appropriateness. *Health Psychology, 4*, 43–59.

Van der Zee, K. I., Buunk, B. P., DeRuiter, J. H., Tempelaar, R., VanSonderen, E., & Sanderman, R. (1996). Social comparison and the subjective well-being of cancer patients. *Basic and Applied Social Psychology, 18*, 453–468.

Van der Zee, K. I., Buunk, B. P., & Sanderman, R. (1995). Social comparison as a mediator between health problems and subjective health evaluations. *British Journal of Social Psychology, 34*, 53–65.

Van der Zee, K. I., Buunk, B. P., & Sanderman, R. (1998a). Neuroticism and reactions to social comparison information among cancer patients. *Journal of Personality, 66*, 175–194.

Van der Zee, K., Oldersma, F., Buunk, B. P., & Bos, D. (1998b). Social comparison preferences among cancer patients as related to neuroticism and social comparison orientation. *Journal of Personality and Social Psychology, 75*, 801–810.

Weinstein, N. D. (1980). Unrealistic optimism about future life events. *Journal of Personality and Social Psychology, 39*, 806–820.

Wheeler, L., & Miyake, K. (1992). Social comparison in everyday life. *Journal of Personality and Social Psychology, 62*, 760–773.

Wills, T. A. (1981). Downward comparison principles in social psychology. *Psychological Bulletin, 90*, 245–271.

Wills, T. A. (1987). Downward comparison as a coping mechanism. In C. R. Synder & C. Ford (Eds.), *Coping with negative life events: Clinical and social-psychological perspectives* (pp. 243–268). New York: Plenum Press.

Wilson, J. J., Chaplin, W. F., & Thorn, B. E. (1995). The influence of different standards on the evaluation of pain: Implications for assessment and treatment. *Behavior Therapy, 26*, 217–239.

Wilson, J. J., Gil, K. M., & Raezer, L. (1997). Self-evaluation, coping, and depressive affect in African American adults with sickle-cell disease. *Cognitive Therapy and Research, 21*, 443–457.

Wood, J. V. (1996). What is social comparison and how should we study it? *Personality and Social Psychology Bulletin, 22*, 520–537.

Wood, J. V., Taylor, S. E., & Lichtman, R. R. (1985). Social comparison in adjustment to breast cancer. *Journal of Personality and Social Psychology, 49*, 1169–1183.

Wood, J. V. & Van der Zee, K. (1997) Social comparisons among cancer patients: Under what conditions are comparisons upward and downward? In B. P. Buunk & F. X. Gibbons (Eds.), *Health, coping, and well-being: Perspectives from social comparison theory* (pp. 299–328). Mahwah, NJ: Lawrence Erlbaum.

Ybema, J. F. & Buunk, B. P. (1995). Affective responses to social comparison: A study among disabled individuals. *British Journal of Social Psychology, 34*, 279–292.

V

Commentary

22

Toward an Enlightenment in Social Comparison Theory

Moving beyond Classic and Renaissance Approaches

BRAM P. BUUNK AND FREDERICK X. GIBBONS

Social comparison—how we use others to make sense of ourselves and the world—is a focal human concern. Indeed, scholars have long recognized the importance of social comparison for human adaptation and survival. As Suls and Wheeler (Chapter 1, this volume) note, theorizing and research on social comparison can be traced to some of the classical contributions to Western philosophy and to pivotal work in social psychology and sociology, including work on the self, adaptation level, reference groups, and social influence. Nevertheless, it was not until Festinger's (1954) classic paper that the term *social comparison* was proposed. The present volume clearly testifies that in the 45 years of its existence, social comparison theory has undergone numerous transitions and reformulations, and in the process, has developed from being a focused theoretical statement on the use of others for self-evaluation into a very complex area of research encompassing many different paradigms, approaches, and applications (e.g., Suls & Wills, 1991; Buunk & Gibbons, 1997). In the present chapter, we will discuss some trends that we see in the evolution of the theory in the past decades as apparent from the chapters in the present volume. We also will discuss some developments that are currently occurring and suggest an "enlightenment" that might help illuminate some of the unresolved issues and inconsistent findings manifest in current theorizing and research in the area.

CLASSIC SOCIAL COMPARISON THEORY

The present volume contains a number of chapters that are directly concerned with Festinger's (1954) original theory. Although these chapters provide important conceptual clarifications and some interesting data, they also illustrate the paucity of research on some of

BRAM P. BUUNK • Department of Psychology, University of Groningen, NL-9712 TS, Groningen, The Netherlands.   **FREDERICK X. GIBBONS** • Department of Psychology, Iowa State University, Ames, Iowa 50011-3180.

Handbook of Social Comparison: Theory and Research, edited by Suls and Wheeler. Kluwer Academic/Plenum Publishers, New York, 2000.

the more basic and central issues in classic social comparison theory. For example, as noted by Suls (Chapter 6, this volume), it is remarkable that while opinion comparison played such an important role in the formulation of social comparison theory, very little research has actually been done on this topic. This is evident in the chapter by Goethals and Klein (Chapter 2, this volume), and also in Suls's chapter in which most references are from the period before 1980. Suls notes various conceptual problems with earlier formulations, and in his triadic theory, provides an interesting expansion of Festinger's work. He suggests there are three types of opinion comparison that can be conceptualized in terms of three basic questions: (1) preference assessment (do I like X?), (2) belief assessment (is X true), and (3) preference prediction (will I like X?). The first and third questions may not always be easy to distinguish. However, it is interesting that Suls not only goes back to the original notion that similar others are the most important for opinion comparisons, but also emphasizes the role of dissimilar others in this respect. As Suls notes, there are many important implications of theorizing and research on opinion formation that have yet to be explored, a primary example being the ways in which new ideas and practices spread within a population. This topic should receive considerable attention in the future.

It is not just the central issue of opinion comparison that has been neglected, however; the other cornerstone of Festinger's original paper—comparison of abilities—also has received relatively little empirical attention. In Chapter 1 (this volume), Suls and Wheeler suggest that in the beginning of the 1980s, it seemed to be taken for granted that previous research had focused extensively on the comparison of abilities and on self-evaluation as a central motive for this kind of comparison. An important reason for the lack of recent research, as Smith and Arnkelsson (Chapter 3, this volume) suggest, was that Festinger was vague with regard to the concept of ability. He also was silent on the topic of the referent of ability appraisal and did not address explicitly how people infer ability from social comparison information. Chapter 3, by Smith and Arnkelsson, addresses these issues and in the process provides a useful clarification of the construct that should guide future research in this area: ability, they suggest, is the typical level of motivated performance.

A similar notion is offered by Martin (Chapter 4, this volume) in her *proxy model*, which concerns the impact of comparison on perceptions of one's ability to perform different tasks. According to the model, when trying to predict performance on a novel and important task that they are contemplating, people often will rely on performance information from another person—a proxy. That proxy will be most informative when two conditions are met: First, she or he must have performed similarly to them on a previous task, and second, that person must either have put out maximum effort on that earlier task or else be similar on related attributes (e.g., age, physical condition). Martin points out that "ideal" proxies such as this are rare in the real world, but she suggests that using comparison information to estimate one's own performance is certainly a common occurrence, which suggests that the proxy model will stimulate considerable research on ability comparisons in the future.

Whereas the factors affecting comparison choice were the major focus of early research that grew out of Festinger's (1954) original theory, this topic lost some of its prominence in contemporary social comparison research. Nevertheless, there is some recent work indicating that comparison choice can have significant effects on performance in important, real-world settings. In one such study, Blanton, Buunk, Gibbons, and Kuyper (1999) found that high school students who compared academically with students who were doing well in school—as indicated by the actual grade point averages (GPAs) of their preferred targets—had the highest grades at the end of the semester, controlling for their grades at the earlier assessment. Similar results were reported by Gibbons, Blanton, Gerrard, Buunk, and Eggleston (2000) also with regard to academic performance and by Reis-Bergan and Gibbons (2000) with regard to success at quitting smoking. This focus on the impact of target choice on behavior and performance may serve to revitalize interest in this central topic.

Despite the conceptual and paradigmatic progress that is attributable to Festinger's (1954) original theory, we also would suggest that Festinger's work was somewhat limited in scope, and may have actually inhibited social psychologists from asking a number of other important questions concerning social comparison processes. This is illustrated, for example, by Festinger's emphasis on the question "Can I do X?" as the question people would be most interested in when evaluating their abilities. Although certainly very relevant, the "Can I do X" question is a pragmatic one that concerns the self-evaluation of an ability mainly for instrumental purposes and not for the purpose of evaluating, for example, how competent one is, how one should feel about oneself, or what one's status in the groups is—issues that seem at least as basic human concerns. In a similar vein, even though Suls' model (Chapter 6, this volume) constitutes an important expansion of Festinger's work, there are various other types of questions concerning opinions that individuals may try to answer through social comparison, for example "Am I the only one who doesn't like this?" "What should I think about this?" or "Is this really bad, or am I mistaken?" In short, there are a number of important self-evaluative issues that individuals may address through social comparison besides those proposed by Festinger, which suggests that this will be a growth area for the theory in the future.

RENAISSANCE SOCIAL COMPARISON THEORY

In part the limitations of Festinger's theory were due to the fact that the theory arose to an important extent from his work on social influence in groups. In fact, it was not until the early 1980s, more than 25 years after the publication of the theory, that researchers began to explore comparison issues that were outside of the theory's original focus on group processes. The background and development of what Wheeler (1991) labeled "neo-social comparison theory" is outlined in an excellent manner by Suls and Wheeler (Chapter 1, this volume), and we will not reiterate that here. Instead, we will refer to the paradigm shift that occurred about two decades ago as a "renaissance" of social comparison theory. This new perspective was foreshadowed in the pioneering study by Morse and Gergen (1970), which focused attention on the potential negative consequences of upward comparison, and it was visible in the influential Suls and Miller (1977) book several years later. It was not solidified theoretically, however, until Wills' (1981) discussion of downward comparison as an active, motivated process aimed at self-enhancement. Eventually, the importance of *upward* comparisons for the purpose of mood improvement and coping was also acknowledged in the "renaissance," and so the question of what determines reactions to upward and downward comparison opportunities became a central issue in theorizing and research (Buunk, Collins, Taylor, Van Yperen, & Dakoff, 1990; Taylor & Lobel, 1989). In many respects, it remains an active topic in the area even today.

Evolution of Theory: Integration and (Especially) Expansion

There are several reasons why we prefer to talk about a "renaissance" of social comparison theory rather than about "neo-social comparison theory." First, social comparison theory underwent a vital "rebirth" in which much broader, not just different, perspectives on social comparison developed. These new perspectives considered basic comparison motives other than self-evaluation, namely, self-enhancement and self-improvement, and included a variety of ways of engaging in social comparison, perhaps the most noteworthy being the social construction of comparison targets (e.g., Goethals, Messick, & Allison, 1991). This approach used very different methods and paradigms, including interviewing people about their comparison habits and preferences and confronting individuals with vivid social comparison information. Most importantly, it took the theory out of the laboratory and looked at social comparison in populations—cancer patients and individuals in smoking cessation clinics, for example— that no researcher would have considered before this. One might argue that such approaches constituted a "revolution" rather than "classic" revival, and in some ways that is certainly the case. The reason to employ the term "renaissance," however, is that by asking different questions, such as (what are) the *effects* of social comparison on mood and self-evaluation, conceptual links were reestablished with classic approaches that previously had not been considered as being in the realm of social comparison theory but that were essentially concerned with social comparison in its broadest sense. Indeed, a number of these approaches were already cited in Festinger's original work. For example, work in this renaissance period revived interest in the classic paper of Hyman (1942) in which it was shown that the assessment of one's own status on such dimensions as financial position, intellectual capabilities, and physical attractiveness is dependent on the group with whom one compares oneself. Downward comparison theory (Wills, 1981), so influential in the renaissance, dealt with a similar issue that had actually been addressed much earlier in the American Soldier study (Stouffer, Suchman, DeVinney, Star, & Williams, 1949). In that study, black soldiers from Northern states reported less satisfaction with their situations than did black soldiers from the South, supposedly because both groups compared themselves with blacks outside the army, a reference group that at the time was considerably worse off in the South (e.g., Singer, 1980).

Equity theory also can be viewed as a "classic" social comparison approach that was, in part, based on Festinger's original social comparison theory (Adams, 1965) and on reference group theory (Singer, 1980). Typical of this renaissance period is the fact that equity theory is now thought to concern social comparisons (cf. Geurts, Buunk, & Schaufeli, 1994), but from a different perspective, one that generates new and quite different questions. A prime example of this is Chapter 20, by Folger and Kass (this volume), which discusses the importance of social comparisons for fairness evaluations. They suggest that, whereas social comparisons have traditionally been related to distributive justice concerns, the social comparisons of *procedures* also can affect justice evaluations: when the procedure for a comparison other is thought to be fairer than the procedure for oneself, perceptions of inequity are likely to be particularly acute.

Another theory that, like reference group and equity theories, shares a social comparison perspective, and was in fact based in part on Festinger's (1954) theory, is *social identity theory*, as developed by Tajfel and Turner (1986). This theory was absent in the Suls and Miller (1977) volume, but now seems to be moving toward a well-deserved place in the center of social comparison theory. This interesting development began with the research outlined by Luhtanen and Crocker (1991), and culminated in its prominent place in the present volume through the excellent chapter by Hogg (Chapter 19). Social identity theory rests on the assumption that groups compare their situation with that of other groups; in many ways, it reads as a group version of recent formulations in social comparison theory. In fact, social identity theory gave self-enhancement—or rather group enhancement—a central place long before Wills's (1981) seminal paper on downward comparison theory. Moreover, recent developments in social comparison theory have highlighted other important parallels with social identity theory. For example, the emphasis on permeability of group boundaries in fostering upward comparisons is conceptually similar to the emphasis on the role of control in recent versions of social comparison theory (e.g., Major, Testa, & Bylsma, 1991; Lockwood & Kunda, 1997). Also, the improvement of social comparisons in shaping one's identity is recognized in social identity theory, an emphasis that developed in social comparison theory only decades after the original formulation (e.g., Tesser, 1988). Moreover, the role Hogg ascribed to social comparison processes in reducing uncertainty is in line with recent work described by Buunk (1994) among populations under stress, which follows on Schachter's (1959) pioneering work.

The renaissance seemed to revitalize the theory in many ways. It brought a "rebirth" of classical theoretical ideas, innovations in approaches, and a very fruitful focus on the effects of social comparison on mood and the self-evaluation of the comparer. The renaissance also linked the theory to classic approaches in other areas of psychology as well. For example, recent work has emphasized the fact that social comparison might induce not only contrast with the comparison target but also assimilation (e.g., Brown, Novick, & Kelley, 1992; Buunk et al., 1990; Collins, 1996). In other words, there often is a bias in social comparison toward perceptions of similarity between the self and the target (virtually any target), a theme that appears in several chapters in this volume (see Chapters 2, 6, 13, 16, and 17; cf. Chapter 9). It would seem a logical step, then, to link work on the effects of social comparison on self-evaluation to classic work on social judgment, that is, how individuals judge and evaluate social stimuli in general (Buunk, 1998). Surprisingly, however, it was not until the present volume that the promising connection between social comparison and social judgment was given significant attention. We see this as one of the more significant contributions of this volume and the research described in it.

The increasing variety of perspectives in social comparison, which is typical of the renaissance, has resulted in a very liberal perspective as to what constitutes social comparison. It would appear that social comparison is now thought to be any process in which individuals relate their own characteristics to those of others. For example, anxiety reduction, which Schachter (1959) viewed as an alternative explanation to social comparison, from this perspective would be considered another type of comparison. In other words, individuals compare their levels of anxiety with that of similar others, perceive others to be less anxious than they are, and conclude that they are not anxious. Chapter 5 (this volume) by Forsyth is probably one of the most liberal in this respect in that a wide range of classic social psychological phenomena—most referring to some type of social influence—are considered as social comparison phenomena. The work on social projection and false consensus in which assumptions are made about the characteristics of others on the basis of one's own characteristics (Chapter 16, this volume) also suggests a liberal view of what social comparison is and what it is not. Once again, these are cognitive processes that have not typically been thought to fall within the realm of social comparison.

Equally liberal or inclusive are some of the notions in Chapter 10 (this volume). The conceptual scheme developed by Smith, which makes a distinction between assimilation and contrast and between self-focus and other-focus when confronted with upward and downward comparisons, is an important step toward understanding how individuals respond to the fate of others. Smith's scheme was long overdue, and may be viewed as typical for renaissance social comparison theory, as it builds clearly on the conceptual analysis of Fritz Heider, one of the founders of contemporary social psychology. According to Heider (1956, p. 277), when confronted with the fate of others, individuals may experience a variety of emotions, including happiness or antagonism, when they see others who are doing worse (malicious joy), and envy or sadness, when they see others who are doing better. He also suggests, however, that individuals may experience sympathetic identification when their individual feelings are concordant with the lot of the other, in which case downward comparison would generate negative affect (compassion) and upward comparison would lead to positive affect (sympathetic enjoyment). It is surprising that no systematic research has been done to test directly Smith's taxonomy.

One may question whether all responses discussed by Smith, such as admiration and pity really do involve social comparison, that is, relating one's own responses to those of others (Wood, 1996). Nevertheless, one of the novel contributions, and therefore strengths, of Smith's chapter and this volume is its recognition that social comparison has a dual focus—self and other—and that perceptions of both "targets" may be significantly altered by comparisons between them (see also Chapters 2, 14, and 16). Of course, if one assumes that impression formation (or person perception) necessarily involves social comparison (cf. Chapter 17), then the purview of the theory expands considerably. In general, we support this more liberal view; it is one reason why interest in comparison processes has continued to increase. At the same time, we share some of Festinger's concerns, as echoed by Suls and Wheeler (Chapter 1, this volume), that social comparison would no longer mean anything scientifically if it could be applied to everything. In light of this significant expansion, "focusing" the theory may be one of the primary (and most interesting) challenges facing social comparison researchers in the next decade.

Upward and Downward Comparison

As in Chapter 10 by Smith, a central issue in many of the chapters in the present volume is the direction of comparison: upward versus downward. Whereas Smith elaborated on the various affective responses that upward and downward comparison may generate, in other chapters the concern is more with the differential responses to upward versus downward comparison as related to threat, subjective well-being (e.g., depression), and individual difference variables (i.e., self-esteem; see Chapters 8–10 and 21, this volume). This issue has been a central one for renaissance comparison theory, and the present volume supports the conclusion that findings in this area are inconsistent (Buunk & Ybema, 1997). In fact, in their comprehensive review of 23 studies examining social comparison among populations facing a threat, such as those with rheumatoid arthritis, cancer, and chronic pain, Tennen et al. (Chapter 21, this volume) conclude that downward comparisons are prominent in populations with serious medical problems and generally are associated with positive adjustment. Tennen and co-workers' conclusion is in line with what we suggested in our volume on social comparison as related to health and well-being; that is, that individuals are likely to receive some emotional benefit from such comparisons when they engage in a form of counterfactual thinking vis-à-vis the target (Buunk, Gibbons, & Reis-Bergan, 1997; see also Buunk & Ybema, 1995; Van der Zee et al., 1996).

The significance of counterfactual thinking as a mediator in determining reactions to social comparisons in general, but especially downward comparisons, also is discussed in two of the chapters in this volume (Chapters 18 and 20). Basically, the idea is that comparisons with others who are thought to be worse off are likely to be tolerable, perhaps even encouraging, if the comparer believes the target's fate *could* happen to the self (which requires some perception of similarity) but will not (which requires some sense of control or perceived immunity). One implication of this is that individuals who believe their own situation will decline (such as those who are terminally ill, or depressed) are not likely to benefit from downward comparison.

Nevertheless, Tennen et al. point out that the findings on the role of personality variables, like self-esteem, in moderating the effects of social comparison are inconsistent. They also suggest that there are striking differences across studies in how comparisons are assessed, making it difficult to draw unequivocal conclusions regarding the adaptational benefits of a particular comparison process. Moreover, Tennen et al. argue that upward comparisons *can* inspire people facing health threats to seek self-improvement. In a similar vein, Wheeler (Chapter 8, this volume) points to many inconsistencies in the literature on the effects of social comparison as related to threat, subjective well-being, and personality variables. Wheeler concludes that low self-esteem (or depressed) individuals tend to respond with more positive affect to downward comparison, a pattern that was interpreted as support for one aspect of downward comparison theory (Wills, 1981). However, according to Wheeler, findings on the role of threat in moderating responses to social comparison are unclear, and the evidence for the preferred direction after failure among high- versus low-self-esteem individuals is inconsistent. Furthermore, several survey studies provide evidence for an upward social comparison preference, in some instances, especially among individuals facing threat (e.g., Buunk, Collins, Taylor, Van Yperen, & Dakoff, 1990; Buunk, Schaufeli, & Ybema, 1994).

As the social comparison literature has been plagued by seemingly discrepant findings on this issue of direction of comparison, a number of authors have tried to provide models reconciling the contradictions. They have done this in a variety of ways: by pointing to the different *measures* that have been used and the different *modes* of comparison that have been studied (e.g., evaluation versus affiliation) (Taylor & Loebl, 1989), for example, or by illuminating the different *motives* that social comparisons may serve (Wood, 1989), by underlining the role of *control* and *attainability* (Aspinwall, 1997; Lockwood & Kunda, 1997; Major et al., 1991), and by emphasizing the extent to which features of the comparison situation (such as the comparison dimension) promote *identification* and expected *similarity* to the target (Buunk & Ybema, 1997; Collins, 1996; Chapter 9, this volume).

We will not review these various models, but we would like to stress one point that has often been overlooked in this literature, which may help clarify this issue somewhat. That is a distinction between "true" downward comparison, defined as comparison with others who are or are thought to be worse off than the self, and "downward shift," which is simply a lowering of one's preferred comparison level (Gibbons, Benbow, & Gerrard, 1994). We have suggested elsewhere (Gibbons et al., 2000) that downward shifts may actually be much more common than true downward comparison. There are a number of reasons for this, including discomfort with the downward comparison process [which may be seen as gloating (cf. Wills, 1981), or what Smith (Chapter 10, this volume) calls *schadenfreude*], and the fact that the general performance level of a particular target is more likely to be known that his or her specific standing vis-à-vis the self. Moreover, availability of upward and downward targets on a particular dimension is often confounded with one's own standing on that dimension (cf. Wood & Giordano, 1998); if you are at the 90th percentile, then nine out of ten of your potential comparison targets are actually downward comparisons. Thus, what may appear to be a tendency for persons experiencing threat to report upward comparison preferences and for those who have succeeded to report engaging in downward comparisons (see Chapter 8, this volume) may in part be a reflection of the fact that for someone who has failed or is facing a difficult situation, most comparisons are in fact upward. By the same token, someone with low self-esteem is likely to believe that most others with whom they have compared are doing better. Focusing on absolute preferred level (e.g., a high performer vs. a mediocre performer) rather than target level vis-à-vis the self will avoid many of these confounds and ambiguities. For this reason, we suggest that researchers interested in comparison level use absolute measures (of comparison level) rather than, or in addition to, comparison relative to the self.

TOWARD AN ENLIGHTENMENT IN SOCIAL COMPARISON THEORY

We would like to suggest that there are now a number of emerging lines of research, many of them apparent in the present volume, that seem to indicate that after the "renaissance," an "enlightenment" in social comparison theory is in progress. By no means do we want to suggest that previous work was unenlightened. What we do mean is that efforts to link work on social comparison processes to more fundamental work on cognition, evolution, and personality may shed more "light" in the next decade or two on many little-understood phenomena and inconsistent findings in this field. As we see it, the impending enlightenment deals with three basic issues confronting research and theorizing on social comparison.

1. Relative to the two most recent volumes in this area (Suls & Wills, 1991; Buunk & Gibbons, 1997), the chapters in this volume devote more attention to the cognitive processes that mediate the relation between social comparison and its attendant outcomes—affective, cognitive, and behavioral [Chapters 2, 13, and 16–18; in addition, Kulik and Mahler (Chapter 15) write about the impact that comparison can have on "cognitive clarity" in threatening situations]. This focus is refreshing given that this central issue has received relatively little attention from preenlightenment comparison researchers. An important recent development in this area worth mentioning is the interesting work on "cognitive busyness" by Gilbert, Giesler, and Morris (1995). They have suggested that, after comparing, individuals may engage in a process of "decomparing," in which, for example, they "undo" the unpleasant effects of upward comparisons. As Gilbert et al. show in their research, such a process requires cognitive effort and does not occur when information processing capacity is blocked. If these results prove to be robust, varying cognitive load would provide a means for studying cognitive processes in comparison.

There is an obvious need for research examining the cognitive processes underlying social comparison, and the present volume contains a number of chapters that provide relevant paradigms to study such processes. For example, in their selective accessibility model, Mussweiler and Strack (Chapter 13) argue that social comparison involves a selective search for evidence indicating that one is similar to the comparison other. Using a lexical decision task, they showed that engaging in a comparison enhances the accessibility of words associated with the particular comparison target, but only after a self-related prime (see also Dijksterhuis et al., 1998). In a related vein, Dunning (Chapter 17) also reports data that are directly relevant for understanding the cognitive processes involved in social comparison. For instance, his research demonstrates that individuals give quicker responses about their own characteristics after judging others on these characteristics. He suggests this is because judging others on certain dimensions makes the same characteristics in oneself salient and cognitively accessible, that is, induces social comparison. It seems intuitive that, after moving from comparison choice to the effects of comparison, social comparison research may be further "enlightened" by employing techniques and models developed in the social cognition literature. Although social comparison theory has been influenced in various ways by work on social cognition [e.g., prototypes, false consensus, attribution (cf. Buunk et al., 1997; Gibbons & Gerrard, 1997; Goethals & Darley, 1977)], it is surprising that until recently, most methods of social cognition research had not found their way into social comparison laboratories. We expect that work on the "interface" between social comparison and social cognition will continue to evolve into an exciting area of research in the next decade.

2. Most theoretical perspectives on social comparison, as well as explanations for the various conflicting findings in the area have an ad hoc character, without a metatheory specifying why social comparison would be important, or what the ultimate motivations that

drive social comparison activity are. We believe that an evolutionary perspective has the potential to provide such a unifying and overarching focus. From this perspective, assessing one's status in the group would be the core goal of social comparison activity. In fact, Gilbert and colleagues have written extensively on this topic (Gilbert, 1990; Gilbert, Price, & Allan, 1995), suggesting that social comparison can serve several adaptive functions. Specifically, it assists individuals in (1) determining their rank in the group, (2) assessing what others find attractive in them, and (3) most importantly, providing information on how they should change their behavior to obtain favorable outcomes. An evolutionary perspective may help in reconciling some of the seemingly contradictory findings on social comparison. For instance, according to the theory of involuntary subordinate strategies (Price, Sloman, Gardner, Gilbert, & Rhode, 1994; Sloman, Price, Gilbert, & Gardner, 1994); there are in most social animals evolved mechanisms signaling submission that become manifest when an individual realizes he has lost a fight and is facing a lower rank. By behaving submissively, one signals to those higher in rank that one is no longer a threat, thus preventing further aggression from and restoring the relationship with these higher status others (Allan & Gilbert, 1997). From this perspective, depression results when individuals are facing a state of involuntary subordination, which puts them into a "giving up" state of mind. According to Buunk and Brenninkmeyer (1999), many findings regarding the comparison activity of depressed individuals can be interpreted from this perspective. For example, depression is characterized by thoughts that are deprecatory and pessimistic with regard to the self (Weary & Edwards, 1994); depressed individuals perceive themselves in general as incompetent, worthless, and critical of their own characteristics, thus indicating that they consider their own status as low (Hammen, 1997); and depressed individuals tend to feel that others are better off than they are, thus confirming their loss in rank and low status (e.g., Albright & Henderson, 1995). Although it is seldom viewed as such, poor health implies, almost by definition, some loss of status, which might offer a new perspective on social comparison strategies among individuals with threatening health problems.

Whereas Smith (Chapter 10, this volume) discusses briefly the relevance of an evolutionary perspective for understanding social emotions experienced in responses to better-off and worse-off others, the only elaborate evolutionary interpretation of social comparison in the present volume is indirect (Beach & Tesser, Chapter 7, this volume). In their interesting and thought-provoking evolutionary analysis of the self-evaluation model (SEM), they suggest that the mechanisms outlined in the SEM developed as elaborated mechanisms to prevent competition in groups on the same dimensions and to enhance cohesion because too much specialization could lead to downfall for the group. Beach and Tesser suggest that the tendency to "bask in reflected glory" might have evolved to ensure that the self is drawn to others who are producing valuable products and resources. As a result, individuals would be in a better position to engage in social exchange that will enhance personal survival and reproduction. Although an evolutionary perspective certainly has its limitations in directly guiding empirical work, in future research, hypotheses based on an evolutionary perspective on the way in which individuals use social comparison to assess and maintain their status in groups might be tested directly.

3. One problem that has both puzzled and intrigued social comparison researchers is that people often are reluctant to admit that they compare themselves with others. This reticence most likely results from a variety of factors. It may be partly cognitive—a lack of awareness or problems in selectivity, recall, and aggregation, for example (cf. Wood, 1996). It also may be partly self-presentational, because as outlined by Wood (1996; Chapter 11, this volume) and others, social comparison in general, and downward comparison in particular, is viewed as

socially undesirable (e.g., Brickman & Bulman, 1977; Wills, 1981). Finally, this reluctance is probably also partly dispositional: Some individuals may deny that they compare themselves with others, because they truly lack an interest in comparative information, and therefore engage in social comparison relatively infrequently. In fact, it has become increasingly clear, as Wheeler (Chapter 8, this volume) suggests that there are important individual differences in the extent to which people compare with others and in the way that comparison information is interpreted. In this regard (and as discussed by Wheeler, Chapter 8, this volume), recently we (Gibbons & Buunk, 1999) proposed the concept of social comparison orientation to refer to the personality disposition of individuals who are prone to comparison, and we developed a scale assessing such differences. In general, people who are high on this scale have a tendency to relate what happens to others to themselves and to be interested in information about others' thoughts and behaviors in similar circumstances. Social comparison orientation is positively related to other dispositions, such as self-consciousness, neuroticism, and an anxious avoidant attachment style, and negatively related to self-esteem. Evidence for the external validity of the scale comes from laboratory experiments and from research among cancer patients (e.g., Van der Zee, Oldersma, Buunk, & Bos, 1998). Theoretically, there is reason to believe that high and low comparers focus on and interpret comparison information differently. In general, then, it would seem important to include individual difference variables when examining the cognitive processes involved in social comparison, as well as reactions to it.

FINAL COMMENTS

Methodology and Focus

The present volume demonstrates convincingly that social comparison is becoming a central area of research in social psychology with expanding ties to many other topics in the area, social cognition being the primary example, but also group process, social exchange, justice, and health. It also is increasingly being linked to areas outside social psychology, such as organizational, clinical, and personality psychology. Presumably, the pathways of influence from social comparison to other areas and theories are "nonrecursive," and so we would expect that researchers working in these other areas will become much more interested in social comparison as a result of the publication of this volume. A similar type of expansion can be seen in the types of designs used by social comparison researchers. In this respect, it is worth noting that the ratio of field-to-laboratory studies within the empirically based chapters in this volume is noticeably lower than that in Buunk and Gibbons (1997). This appears to be largely a function of the more applied nature of the latter volume, however, and so we doubt it signals a significant change in methodology. Instead, we see it as another very healthy expansion of focus, characteristic or diagnostic of a theory that is flourishing. With this in mind, we would encourage the use, where feasible, of both types of research settings. We also would echo once again the call (see Chapter 21, this volume) for longitudinal designs that allow for assessment of change in both process and outcome over time. As many have suggested, the best way to understand a process or phenomenon is to watch it change.

Conclusion

One cannot help but wonder how Festinger would react if he could see how his firstborn but (perhaps) second-favorite theoretical child has matured into middle age. Given the modest circumstances surrounding its birth and childhood, we doubt that he or any of his students or colleagues would have thought this theory would ever demonstrate the longevity, or vitality, or especially the heuristic value that it has. In this respect, it appears to have surpassed its more famous younger sibling (dissonance theory) in terms of empirical attention, at least as documented by PsychLit searches of relevant social psychology journals in the past decade or so. What this volume reaffirms is that this popularity is largely a function of the significance and the ubiquity of the process itself. As a result of this popularity, there are now many more unanswered questions to be addressed than at any time since the theory was published; an exciting prospect, to be sure. For this reason, we remain optimistic that an enlightenment of the many unresolved issues will be forthcoming. In any case, we see an active and most likely continued controversial future ahead for the theory and its adherents. Although we are certainly not unbiased, in many respects, we see social comparison as the quintessential social psychological process. As such, it has that one characteristic that virtually all members of its 1950s cohort—baby boomers—crave: It never grows old!

REFERENCES

Adams, J. S. (1965). Inequity in social exchange. *Advances in Experimental Social Psychology, 2,* 267–299.

Albright, J. S., & Henderson, M. C. (1995). How real is depressive realism? A question of scales and standards. *Cognitive Therapy and Research, 19,* 589–609.

Allan, S., & Gilbert, P. (1995). A social comparison scale: Psychometric properties and relationship to pathology. *Personality and Individual Differences, 19*(3), 293–299.

Aspinwall, L. G. (1997). Future-oriented aspects of social comparisons: A framework for studying health-related comparison activity. In B.P. Buunk & F.X. Gibbons (Eds.), *Health, coping, and well-being: Perspectives from social comparison theory* (pp. 125–166). Mahwah, NJ: Lawrence Erlbaum.

Blanton, H., Buunk, B. P., Gibbons, F. X., & Kuyper, H. (1999). When better-than-others compares upward: The independent effects of comparison choice and comparative evaluation on academic performance. *Journal of Personality and Social Psychology, 76,* 420–430.

Brickman, P., & Bulman, R. J. (1977). Pleasure and pain in social comparison. In J. Suls & R. L. Miller (Eds.), *Social comparison processes: Theoretical and empirical perspectives* (pp. 149–186). Washington, DC: Hemisphere.

Brown, J. D., Novick, N. J., & Kelley, A. (1992). When Gulliver travels: Social context psychological closeness, and self-appraisals. *Journal of Personality and Social Psychology, 62,* 717–727.

Buunk, B. P. (1994). Social comparison processes under stress: Towards an integration of classic and recent perspectives. In W. Stroebe & M. Hewstone (Eds.), *European review of social psychology* (Vol. 5, pp. 211–241). Chichester, England: John Wiley & Sons.

Buunk, B. P. (1998). Social comparison and optimism about one's relational future: Order effects in social judgment. *European Journal of Social Psychology, 28,* 777–786.

Buunk, B. P., & Brenninkmeyer, V. (1999). Social comparison processes among depressed individuals: Evidence for an evolutionary perspective on involuntary subordinate strategies? In L. Sloman & P. Gilbert (Eds.), *Subordination and defeat: An evolutionary approach to mood disorders and their therapy* (pp. 147–161). Mahwah, NJ: Lawrence Erlbaum.

Buunk, B. P., Collins, R. L., Taylor, S. E., Van Yperen, N. W., & Dakoff, G. A. (1990). The affective consequences of social comparison: Either direction has its ups and downs. *Journal of Personality and Social Psychology, 59,* 1238–1249.

Buunk, B. P., & Gibbons, F. X. (1997). *Health, coping and well-being: Perspectives from social comparison theory.* Mahwah, NJ: Lawrence Erlbaum.

Buunk, B. P., Gibbons, F. X., & Reis-Bergan, M. (1997). Social comparison in health and illness. In B. Buunk & F. X. Gibbons (Eds.), *Health, coping and well-being: Perspectives from social comparison theory* (pp. 1–23). Mahwah, NJ: Lawrence Erlbaum.

Buunk, B. P., Schaufeli, W. B., & Ybema, J. F. (1994). Burnout, uncertainty, and the desire for social comparison among nurses. *Journal of Applied Social Psychology, 24,* 1701–1718.

Buunk, B. P., Van Yperen, N. W., Taylor, S. E., & Collins, R. L. (1991). Social comparison and the drive upward revisited: Affiliation as a response to marital stress. *European Journal of Social Psychology, 21,* 529–546.

Buunk, B. P., & Ybema, J. F. (1995). Selective evaluation and coping with stress: Making one's situation cognitively more livable. *Journal of Applied Social Psychology, 25,* 1499–1517.

Buunk, B. P., & Ybema, J. F. (1997). Social comparisons and occupational stress: The identification–contrast model. In B. Buunk & F. X. Gibbons (Eds.), *Health, coping and well-being: Perspectives from social comparison theory* (pp. 359–388). Mahwah, NJ: Lawrence Erlbaum.

Collins, R. L. (1996). For better or worse: The impact of upward social comparison on self-evaluations. *Psychological Bulletin, 119,* 51–69.

Dijksterhuis, A., Spears, R., Postmes, T., Stapel, D. A., van Knippenberg, A., & Scheepers, D. (1998). Seeing one thing and doing another: Contrast effects in automatic behavior. *Journal of Personality and Social Psychology, 75,* 862–871.

Festinger, L. (1954). A theory of social comparison processes. *Human Relations, 7,* 117–140.

Geurts, S. A., Buunk, B. P., & Schaufeli, W. B. (1994). Social comparisons and absenteeism: A structural modeling approach. *Journal of Applied Social Psychology, 24,* 1871–1890.

Gibbons, F. X., Benbow, C. P., & Gerrard, M. (1994). From top dog to bottom half: Social comparison strategies in response to poor performance. *Journal of Personality and Social Psychology, 67,* 638–652.

Gibbons, F. X., Blanton, H., Gerrard, M., Buunk, B. P., & Eggleston, T. J. (2000). Does social comparison make a difference? Optimism as a moderator of the impact of comparison level on outcome. *Personality and Social Psychology Bulletin, 26,* 637–648.

Gibbons, F. X., & Buunk, B. P. (1999). Individual differences in social comparison: The development of a scale for social comparison orientation. *Journal of Personality and Social Psychology, 76,* 129–142.

Gibbons, F. X., & Gerrard, M. (1997). Health images and their effects on health behavior. In B. P. Buunk & F. X. Gibbons (Eds.), *Health, coping, and well-being: Perspectives from social comparison theory* (pp. 63–94). Mahwah, NJ: Lawrence Erlbaum.

Gilbert, D. T., Giesler, R. B., & Morris, K. A. (1995). When comparisons arise. *Journal of Personality and Social Psychology, 69,* 227–236.

Gilbert, P. (1990). Changes: Rank, status and mood. In S. Fisher & C. L. Cooper (Eds.), *On the move: The psychology of change and transition* (pp. 33–52). Chichester, England: Wiley.

Gilbert, P., Price, J., & Allan, S. (1995). Social comparison, social attractiveness and evolution: How might they be related? *New Ideas in Psychology, 13,* 149–165.

Goethals, G. R., & Darley, J. M. (1977). Social comparison theory: An attributional approach. In J. M. Suls & R. L. Miller (Eds.), *Social comparison processes: Theoretical and empirical perspectives* (pp. 259–278). Washington, DC: Hemisphere.

Goethals, G. R., Messick, D. M., & Allison, S. T. (1991). The uniqueness bias: Studies of constructive social comparison. In J. Suls & T. A. Wills (Eds.) *Social comparison: Contemporary theory and research* (pp. 317–345). Hillsdale, NJ: Lawrence Erlbaum.

Hammen, C. (1997). *Depression.* Hove, England: Psychology Press.

Heider, F. (1958). *The psychology of interpersonal relation.* New York: John Wiley.

Hyman, H. (1942). The psychology of subjective status. *Psychological Bulletin, 39,* 473–474.

Lockwood, P., & Kunda, Z. (1997). Superstars and me: Predicting the impact of role models on the self. *Journal of Personality and Social Psychology, 73,* 91–103.

Luhtanen, R., & Crocker, J. (1991). Self-esteem and intergroup comparison: Toward a theory of collective self-esteem. In J. Suls & T. A. Wills (Eds.), *Social comparison: Contemporary theory and research.* Hillsdale, NJ: Lawrence Erlbaum.

Major, B., Testa, M., & Bylsma, W. H. (1991). Responses to upward and downward social comparisons: The impact of esteem-relevance and perceived control. In J. M. Suls & T. A. Wills (Eds.) *Social comparison: Contemporary theory and research* (pp. 237–260). Hillsdale, NJ: Lawrence Erlbaum.

Morse, S., & Gergen, K. J. (1970). Social comparison, self-consistency, and the concept of the self. *Journal of Personality and Social Psychology, 36,* 148–156.

Price, J., Sloman, L., Gardener, R., & Gilbert, P. (1994). The social competition hypothesis of depression. *British Journal of Psychiatry, 164,* 309–315.

Reis-Bergan, M., & Gibbons, F. X. (2000). The "typical smoker" as an aid to smoking cessation: Impact of comparison level on smoking cessation and maintenance of abstinence. Manuscript in preparation.

Schachter, S. (1959). *The psychology of affiliation.* Palo Alto, CA: Stanford University Press.

Singer, E. (1980). Reference groups and social evaluations. In M. Rosenberg & R. H. Turner (Eds.), *Social psychology: Sociological perspectives* (pp. 66–93). New York: Basic Books.

Sloman, L., Price, J., Gilbert, P., & Gardener, R. (1994). Adaptive function of depression: Psychotherapeutic implications. *American Journal of Psychotherapy, 48*(3), 401–416.

Stouffer, S. A., Suchman, E. A., De Vinney, L. C., Star, S. A., & Williams, R. M., Jr. (1949). *The American soldier: Adjustment during army life* (Vol. 1). Princeton, NJ: Princeton University Press.

Suls, J., & Miller, R. (1977). *Social comparison processes*. Washington, DC: Hemisphere.

Suls, J., & Wills, T. A. (Eds.) (1991). *Social comparison: Contemporary theory and research*. Hillsdale, NJ: Lawrence Erlbaum.

Tajfel, H., & Turner, J. C. (1986). The social identity theory of intergroup behavior. In S. Worchel & W. G. Austing (Eds.), *Psychology of intergroup relations* (2nd ed., pp. 7–24). Chicago: Nelson-Hall.

Taylor, S. E., & Lobel, M. (1989). Social comparison activity under threat: Downward evaluation and upward contacts. *Psychological Review, 96*, 569–575.

Tesser, A. (1988). Toward a self-evaluation maintenance model of social behavior. In L. Berkowitz (Ed.), *Advances in experimental social psychology* (Vol. 21, pp. 181–227). San Diego, CA: Academic Press.

Van der Zee, K. I., Buunk, B. P., DeRuiter, J. H., Tempelaar, R., VanSonderen, E., & Sanderman, R. (1996). Social comparison and the subjective well-being of cancer patients. *Basic and Applied Social Psychology, 18*, 453–468.

Van der Zee, K., Oldersma, F., Buunk, B. P., & Bos, D. (1998). Social comparison preferences among cancer patients as related to neuroticism and social comparison orientation. *Journal of Personality and Social Psychology, 75*, 801–810.

Weary, G., & Edwards, J. A. (1994). Social cognition and clinical psychology. Anxiety depression, and the processing of social information. In R. S. Wyer, Jr., & T. K. Shell (Eds.), *Handbook of social cognition*, Vol. II, *Applications* (2nd ed., pp. 289–338). Hillsdale, NJ: Lawrence Erlbaum.

Wheeler, L. (1991). A brief history of social comparison theory. In J. Suls & T. A. Wills (Eds.), *Social comparison: Contemporary theory and research* (pp. 3–21). Hillsdale, NJ: Lawrence Erlbaum.

Wills, T. A. (1981). Downward comparison principles in social psychology. *Psychological Bulletin, 90*, 245–271.

Wood, J. V. (1989). Theory and research concerning social comparisons of personal attributes. *Psychological Bulletin, 106*, 231–248.

Wood, J.V. (1996). What is social comparison and how should we study it? *Personality and Social Psychology Bulletin, 22*, 520–537.

Index

ISBN 0-306-46341-5

90000

9 780306 463419